Dickens the Novelist

Dickens
the Novelist

By Sylvère Monod

WITH AN INTRODUCTION BY
EDWARD WAGENKNECHT

UNIVERSITY OF OKLAHOMA PRESS
NORMAN

By Sylvère Monod

Dickens Romancier (Paris, 1953)
Charles Dickens (Paris, 1959)
Dickens Criticism, A Symposium (in collaboration with G. H. Ford,
Edgar Johnson, and J. H. Miller, Boston, 1962)
Dickens the Novelist (Norman, 1967)

Translations

Contes de Noël (2 volumes, Paris, 1946–47)
David Copperfield (Paris, 1952)
Oliver Twist (Paris, 1957)
Henry V (Paris, 1958)
"Pickwick" (Paris, 1958)
Les Grandes Espérances (Paris, 1960)
Barnabé Rudge (Paris, 1963)
Hurlemont (*Wuthering Heights*, Paris, 1963)
Jane Eyre (Paris, 1966)

Frontispiece: Dickens Writing at Gad's Hill Place

Library of Congress Catalog Card Number: 67–15589

Copyright 1968 by the University of Oklahoma Press, Publishing Division of
the University. Composed and printed at Norman, Oklahoma, U.S.A., by the
University of Oklahoma Press. First edition.

To James T. Nardin

INTRODUCTION

WHEN the famous English contralto, Clara Butt, asked Bernard Shaw to furnish an introduction to her autobiography, that generally not over-modest man replied that he wouldn't dare. Clara Butt, he declared, was a much bigger person than he was, and if he were to honor her request and presume to "introduce" her to the British public, he would only make himself ridiculous by posturing in her shadow.

When Sylvère Monod first did me the honor of asking me to write an introduction to this book, I was tempted to make a similar reply. And I think I should have done so had it not been for two circumstances.

In the first place, I could not but remember that I was, in a sense, the "onlie begetter" of the volume. Almost ever since Hachette published the French edition (*Dickens Romancier*) in 1953, I have been distressed that so important a work should not have been made available to English readers. Finally, knowing that Professor Monod was bilingual, I asked him whether he would not consider making a translation him-self, provided an American publisher should stand ready to bring it out, and at the same time I asked my own friend and publisher Savoie Lottinville whether he would not like to publish it. Now it happens that both Mr. Lottinville and M. Monod are very agreeable men. The publisher at once replied that he would be delighted to have an English version of *Dickens Romancier* on his list, and the author told me that he would welcome the opportunity not only to translate his book but to revise it. In a way, then, the wheel has now come full circle, and, for the time being at least, the updated version of M. Monod's distinguished work exists only in English.

This was the first reason which fortified me to be, for the moment, less modest than Bernard Shaw. The other was the reflection that all

vii

I had been asked to do was to introduce M. Monod to his new *American* readers That task I fancied I might be able to perform without blushing, while to introduce him to the world of Dickensian scholarship in general would have been preposterous.

When Sylvère Monod remarks in his "Conclusion" that "no attempt has been made in this book to evaluate Dickens' personality or even his stature as a novelist," the reader will do well to take this as an expression of *his* characteristic modesty. There is not much in either of these areas that he is not thoroughly familiar with. On the other hand, we may take at face value what he says about having tried to write "the history of his [Dickens'] art, a study of its evolution." This he has done more definitively, I think, than it has ever been done elsewhere.

The reader will also discover, very shortly, that Professor Monod belongs to no "school." He does not adhere to the neo- or post-Wilsonian orthodoxy in Dickens criticism; neither is he an old-line "Dickensian." Recent writers have so glorified the so-called "dark" novels in contrast to the rest of Dickens' output that it is almost a shock to find M. Monod underrating them as much as he does. I am sure that he will shock some readers also by finding *Dombey and Son* "the least felicitous" of the early novels. For him the unquestioned masterpiece is *David Copperfield*, to which he devotes well over a hundred manuscript pages, and neither its history nor its art has ever before been studied in such intelligent detail. It would be something of an exaggeration to say that M. Monod sees all Dickens' earlier work as a preparation for *David Copperfield* and all his later work as a falling-away from it, but he comes pretty close to this.

Does all this mean, then, that I see eye to eye with the writer on every point? I am sure he would be the last man to expect me ever to say anything so silly. I am not trying to write a variant version of his book, and there could be no point in considering our agreements and disagreements in detail. A few items, however, may be of interest. I think I relish the theatrical, even the melodramatic element in Dickens' art more than M. Monod does. I enjoy a number of characters to whom he takes exception. It troubles him that Dickens should have changed his mind in midstream about Edith Dombey's relations with Carker. Once upon a time it troubled me even more. But, though there is no denying the shift, it now seems to me that, even though the suggestion came from the outside, Edith would have been not more but less incredible than she is now if the original plan had been adhered to. Again, I would not deny that both David Copperfield and his creator had their self-centered aspects, but I question whether David's leaving Dora when she was ill to attend the unmasking of Heep by Micawber really illustrates this. The story requires David's presence at this scene—who could wish to deprive him of it?—and he would still have had to be there had he been the most unselfish man on the planet. As my old professor of Elizabethan drama used to say, when you come to such things, you simply have to "close your character eye and open your plot eye." And there is a great deal in the Victorian novel that descends quite legitimately from the unpsychological Elizabethan drama.

Yet there is only one novel which, it seems to me, M. Monod seriously underestimates (his grading down of *Hard Times* is a very useful corrective to the absurd overestimates of that minor work which have recently been made by Leavis & Co., Inc.), and that, oddly enough, is Dickens' only French novel, *A Tale of Two Cities*! Professor Monod being himself a Frenchman, I confess this amuses me, and I cannot quite explain it. I can well understand why a Frenchman might be aware of superficialities in that book which an Englishman or an American might pass by, and I would certainly yield to him on every such point. But he does not stop with these aspects. Indeed he does not even seem to feel that Jerry Cruncher is funny.

None of Dickens' detractors of recent years have been more frank than Professor Monod in indicating his faults as a man and his shortcomings as an artist; the difference between him and them is that he has spoken the truth in love. The constant underlying assumption of this book is that Dickens was so great a writer that no pains we can take to understand him can be too great and that no scrutiny to which his works can be subjected too intense; and if any reader doubts how M. Monod feels about the man himself, I must content myself by referring him to what is said in these pages about the novelist's death. The old-time, uncritical "Dickensian" swallowed Dickens, as Oliver Cromwell might say, "warts and all." He overlooked the warts whenever he could, and when they were forced upon his attention he insisted upon calling them beauty spots. The denigrators, on the other hand, made every wart a wen. Professor Monod fathoms the secrets that unveil themselves to love alone, but he knows, too, that the love which is based upon idealization is only infatuation. His is that deeper love which grows out of an understanding as complete as human beings are capable of achieving and which flowers into a perfect acceptance.

EDWARD WAGENKNECHT

West Newton, Mass.
November 20, 1966

PREFACE

THE PRESENT BOOK originates in my French *thèse de doctorat*, which was written between 1948 and 1951, sustained at the Sorbonne in 1952, and published in a shortened and slightly modified form in 1953. It already owed much to many persons living and deceased. Several scholars to whose help I had been deeply indebted have died since: Louis Cazamian, Floris Delattre, John Butt, and my father-in-law, Aurélien Digeon. Others are happily still living, and it is a great pleasure for me to renew the expression of my gratitude to Louis Landré, K. J. Fielding, and my father, Maximilien Vox, as well as to the trustees of the Forster Collection at the Victoria and Albert Museum and to Mr. Henry C. Dickens, without whose generous permission to consult and quote from Dickens' original manuscripts my book could not have been written.

The present American version has been undertaken at the suggestion of my dear and eminent friend Edward Wagenknecht, whom I heartily thank for his initiative and encouragement. Another very dear American friend to whom this book owes a great deal is James T. Nardin, of Louisiana State University, who has helped me with detailed advice and patient criticism and to whom therefore my book is affectionately inscribed.

The main problem facing me at the outset was that between 1952 and 1966 an immense amount of Dickensian criticism and other scholarly work had seen the light of print. If I may take the example best known to me, I must plead guilty of having published another book on Dickens, a number of articles in English and in French, taken part in a Symposium on Dickens criticism, co-edited one novel in the United States and brought out French editions of five other novels, thus altogether adding to the 520 pages of my early *Dickens Romancier* almost

xi

as many pages of comment and criticism and some 3,500 pages of Dickensian translation. In the course of these labors I have repeatedly contradicted statements and opinions contained in the French version of the present work. If I deplore the incomplete information that caused some of my later retractions, I see no reason to feel ashamed of having changed my mind at other points where opinions, not facts, were involved. For I should be sorry to think that anyone's reactions to Dickens should have become immutable in his early thirties. My own endeavors have of course been no more than a thin trickle in the steadily increasing stream of Dickensian studies.

It has by now become hopeless to provide even a succinct bibliographical note as a mere appendix to a book of the present kind. I must therefore content myself with referring the reader to Ada B. Nisbet's impressive survey in *Victorian Fiction: A Guide to Research* (Lionel Stevenson, ed., Harvard University Press, 1964). This most serviceable work lists and assesses all the significant Dickensiana down to the year 1962. Since then there have been several major contributions. Most of the works I have made use of are identified in footnotes. But I should like to mention the recent publications I have found most inspiring. They have been, in my own field (the study of Dickens' craftsmanship), John Butt and Kathleen Tillotson's *Dickens at Work* (London, Methuen, 1957); in biography: Edgar Johnson's *Charles Dickens: His Tragedy and Triumph* (New York, Simon and Schuster; London, Victor Gollancz, 1953); *The Speeches of Charles Dickens* (edited by K. J. Fielding, Oxford, Clarendon Press, 1960); Arthur A. Adrian's *Georgina Hogarth and the Dickens Circle* (Oxford University Press, 1957); *The Letters of Charles Dickens*, I (edited by Madeline House and Graham Storey, Pilgrim Edition, Oxford, Clarendon Press, 1965); in the field of critical history: George H. Ford's *Dickens and His Readers* (Princeton University Press, 1955); in criticism: Kathleen Tillotson's *Novels of the Eighteen-Forties* (Oxford University Press, 1954); K. J. Fielding's *Charles Dickens: A Critical Introduction* (London, Longmans, 1958; revised edition, Houghton Mifflin, 1965); J. Hillis Miller's *Charles Dickens, The World of His Novels* (Harvard University Press, 1958); *Dickens and the Twentieth Century* (edited by John Gross and Gabriel Pearson, London, Routledge and Kegan Paul, 1962); Philip Collins'

Dickens and Crime and *Dickens and Education* (London, Macmillan, 1962 and 1963); the new and revised edition of Edward Wagenknecht's *The Man Charles Dickens* (University of Oklahoma Press, 1966).

Beyond this brief list of unquestionably major works it would be rash to venture, for the books and articles I have read with interest and admiration or which I have found stimulating, are truly innumerable. The years that have elapsed since the first publication of my own book have been considerably more fruitful than any earlier period and have contributed more to our understanding and knowledge of Charles Dickens and his writings. It is significant that there are now two periodicals devoted solely to Dickens.

Some of the criticisms that could be made about writers on Dickens in 1952 are no longer valid, such as the frequent narrowness and arbitrariness of their point of view, their tendency merely to list their personal preferences and opinions, the undue interest often attached to minor problems like the identification of persons and places appearing in the novels, the presence or absence of real gentlemen in Dickens' fiction, solutions to the Drood mystery, or again comparisons with Thackeray established in order to determine which was the greater of the two. These have been largely abandoned by the recent Dickens scholars. One deficiency of the earlier Dickens studies, however, has been only partly remedied by John Butt's and Kathleen Tillotson's efforts. I am referring to the unaccountable lack of interest in the Forster Collection. Too many critics have written or go on writing about Dickens as though his manuscripts, working notes, and corrected proofs did not exist. Such documents were the most potent inspiration, and their systematic exploitation was the most novel aspect, of my *Dickens Romancier* in 1953.

My main purpose in 1952 was to study the way in which Dickens' fifteen novels—not his shorter stories, which, however intrinsically interesting, seemed to me to belong to another literary genre and to deserve a separate study—had been conceived, constructed, and written. My thesis was on the whole a protest against the often-expressed view that Dickens was a negligible craftsman. A reaction was needed against statements like the following by Richard H. Horne: "It may be said that Mr. Dickens is an *instinctive* writer. His best things are suddenly revealed to him; he does not search for them in his mind—they come to him; they break suddenly upon him or drop out of his pen. He does not tax his brain: he transcribes what he finds writing itself there."[1] Others echo this sentiment with, "He seems to be one of the least artistic of writers . . . there is an absence of composition in his work. . . . His books cannot be said to be composed, they are improvised,"[2] and, "The immediate impulse of a modern critic is to dismiss [Dickens' novels] as mere disorderly scrap-books with very brilliant scraps."[3] In 1933, one critic called Dickens "one of the anomalies of literature who would seem to have produced great results by defective means."[4] And as late as 1945, Una Pope-Hennessy still regarded Dickens as "a purely instinctive writer."[5] Neither the documents in the Forster Collection nor Dickens' prefaces nor his correspondence support such views.

Thanks to the general progress of Dickensian studies, a protest against such views has become less urgently necessary. Yet a detailed description of the evolution of Dickens' art as novelist may still be of some use and draw more attention to the documents available, which are by no means exhausted in this book. Owing to the recent publications listed above and also, I hope, to my own maturer approach, the present book, while it adheres to my original plan and preserves the same purpose and spirit, is in some ways a new work.

SYLVÈRE MONOD

Paris
May 15, 1967

[1] *A New Spirit of the Age* (London, 1844), I, 1–76.
[2] Walter S. Lilly, *Four English Humourists* (1895), 14–15.
[3] G. K. Chesterton, *Appreciations and Criticisms of the Works of Charles Dickens* (1911), 62.
[4] Pelham Edgar, *The Art of the Novel* (1933), 117.
[5] *Charles Dickens, 1812–1870,* (London, 1945), x.

Contents

1

PREPARATION

Abbreviations and References

The abbreviations used in the notes referring to Dickens' works are as follows:

AN: American Notes (1842)
BH: Bleak House (1852–53)
BR: Barnaby Rudge (1841)
CB: Christmas Books (1843–49)
CHE: A Child's History of England (1852)
CS: Christmas Stories (1850–66)
DC: David Copperfield (1849–50)
D&S: Dombey and Son (1846–48)
ED: Edwin Drood (1870)
GE: Great Expectations (1860–61)
HT: Hard Times (1854)
LD: Little Dorrit (1855–57)
MC: Martin Chuzzlewit (1843–44)

MHC: Master Humphrey's Clock (1840–41)
NN: Nicholas Nickleby (1838–39)
OCS: The Old Curiosity Shop (1840)
OMF: Our Mutual Friend (1864–65)
OT: Oliver Twist (1837–39)
PFI: Pictures from Italy (1846)
PP: Pickwick Papers (1836–38)
RP: Reprinted Pieces (various dates)
SB: Sketches by Boz (1836)
T2C: A Tale of Two Cities (1859)
UT: The Uncommercial Traveller (1860–68)

Abbreviated titles are used for a few tales and articles; e.g., *C.B., Carol* stands for *A Christmas Carol; R.P. Silverman* for *George Silverman's Explanation;* and *C.S., Marigold* for *Dr. Marigold's Prescriptions.*

Since there is so far no standard edition of Dickens' works, and individual readers may be using any of a wide variety of available editions, which are all, or almost all, equally reliable—or unreliable—it would be useless to give page numbers for the Dickens quotations; chapter numbers alone, therefore, are mentioned in the notes.

I: Preliminary Remarks

THE PURPOSE of this preliminary section is to indicate these circumstances and events in Dickens' life previous to his becoming a professional writer of fiction that had a formative influence on the later development of his art. No full-scale biography of Dickens is needed here. Nor can any be profitably attempted in any case after Edgar Johnson's monumental achievement[1] or K. J. Fielding's miniature masterpiece.[2] Such books are easily accessible and provide all the relevant information. But a brief summary of the first twenty-four years of Dickens' life still seems required at the outset.

The following chapters will deal successively with Dickens' parents and the way they brought him up, with the shock it was for him to work as a boy in a blacking factory, and the subsequent warping of his idea of childhood, with his formative years in legal and political circles, and with his experience of journalism. Finally, the more literary aspects of that early period must also be studied, i.e. his reading, his discovery of his vocation, and his first major experience as a writer in *Sketches by Boz*. In each case I propose to describe the after-effects of those early episodes and to determine how far or how well they equipped Dickens for the novelist's craft, his practice of which forms the subject of the later sections of this book.

Charles Dickens was born on the seventh of February, 1812, at Portsea; he was the son of John Dickens and Elizabeth Barrow. John Dickens was a clerk in the navy pay office. In 1814, the Dickenses moved to London. In 1817, John was transferred to Chatham, where Charles attended a school run by William Giles. In 1822, John Dickens was once more appointed in London; Charles joined his parents there only in the spring of 1823, and was not sent to any school. The year 1823 was a period of increasing poverty for the Dickens family. On February 7, 1824, in compliance with a suggestion made by a young relative of Mrs. Dickens, Charles began to work in a blacking factory; on the twentieth of the same month, John Dickens was arrested for debt and imprisoned in the Marshalsea; he was joined there, on March 25, by

[1] *Ch. D.: Tragedy & Triumph* (2 vols., N.Y. and London, 1953).
[2] *Ch. Dickens* (London, 1958; revised edition, 1965).

3

his wife and children (with the exception of Charles, who, because he was working in the factory, could only snatch time for an occasional meal in the prison). Shortly afterwards, John's mother died and left him a substantial legacy which enabled him to obtain his release from prison; the family settled down in the shabby district of Camden Town. In June, Charles left the factory; he soon began to attend a school called, somewhat pompously, *Wellington House Classical and Commercial Academy,* run by one Mr. William Jones.

In December, 1824, John Dickens was invited to retire from the navy pay office, but was granted a pension of £145 a year; in January, 1825, he became a Parliamentary reporter for *The British Press.* In May, 1827, Charles was regarded as having completed his education and became an office boy in the firm of Ellis and Blackmore, solicitors. In November, 1828, he obtained employment as a shorthand writer at Doctors' Commons. In 1829, he met and fell in love with Maria Beadnell; he was soon secretly engaged to her, but the engagement was finally broken four years later. On February 8, 1830, Charles Dickens applied for a reader's ticket at the British Museum Library and henceforth spent there as many of his leisure hours as he could.

On March 5, 1832, he became a Parliamentary reporter, first for *The True Sun,* and later (November, 1832) for *The Mirror of Parliament.* In December, 1833, he made his *début* as an author by publishing in the *Monthly Magazine* an anonymous, unpaid-for tale called "A Dinner in Poplar Walk." In August, 1834, he joined, still as shorthand reporter, the staff of *The Morning Chronicle;* about the same time, he began to sign with a pen name, Boz, the increasingly numerous short pieces he was writing for various periodicals. In September, 1834, he published in the *Morning Chronicle* the first of a series of "Street Sketches." At the end of the same year, he left his parents' home and settled on his own at No. 13, Furnivall's Inn. In January, 1835, he published several "London Sketches" in the *Evening Chronicle* (a newspaper edited by his future father-in-law, George Hogarth). On the seventh of February, 1836, the appearance of *Sketches by Boz* (two volumes of tales and sketches) turned him into a professional writer; he went on fulfilling at irregular intervals his duties as a reporter, until June 22, 1836 (the famous Norton *v.* Melbourne trial), i.e., after the launching of *Pickwick.*

II: DICKENS' PARENTS

THE PERSONALITIES of John Dickens and his wife, Elizabeth Barrow, are indistinctly known to us. There are few descriptions of them in the contemporary memoirs, probably because neither of them was a prominent person. Besides, the few writers who could mention them from personal acquaintance (in particular John Forster) have been embarrassed by the existence of some half-portraits sketched by Dickens in his novels. It was fairly widely known that Dickens had depicted his own father in *Copperfield*'s Mr. Micawber, and again as William Dorrit; it was similarly known that his mother had inspired him with the figures of Mrs. Nickleby and Mrs. Micawber. But such resemblances, inevitably resulting as they did in a number of inaccuracies, since Dickens' characters, like those created by other writers, were never mere portraits of living originals, have rather obscured our vision of his parents.

It will therefore be advisable to mention only a few unquestionable facts. John Dickens was the son of William Dickens, who had been footman and later steward in the employment of John Crewe, M.P. William Dickens died in 1785, the year of John's birth; his widow remained as housekeeper at Crewe Hall until 1820, when she came to live in London. Charles may thus have seen a good deal of his paternal grandmother in 1823 and until she died in the spring of 1824. John Dickens was of low birth, yet the support of the Crewes enabled him to obtain a junior post in the navy pay office in 1805. This circumstance determined his whole life, for he remained with the navy pay office (at Portsea, London, Chatham, and again in London) for nineteen years and married the sister of his colleague Thomas Barrow. Charles Barrow, John's father-in-law, was a higher official—his post was that of "Chief Conductor of Moneys in Town"—of the same service, but his career came to an end in 1810 when it was learned that he had embezzled nearly six thousand pounds of the navy's money. John Dickens' marriage raised him socially and was later to provide him (and his son Charles) with a substitute position in life, as his brother-in-law John Henry Barrow was a shorthand reporter for *The Times*.

John Dickens' character seems to have been in the main that of a jovial man, fond of the good things of life, improvident and not over-scrupulous. He was twice arrested for debt, in 1824 and 1834; on the second occasion, he was sued by a wine merchant. When his son was away, he cavalierly borrowed from Charles' publishers; he once sent Chapman and Hall the following characteristic note:

> Will you do me the favour to deduct the £4 I owe you from the enclosed bill for £20 due April 7, with 3s. 4d. the amount of the interest, and let me have the balance, £15 15s.?[1]

Like Micawber, John Dickens seems to have regarded his own signature appended to a bill as worth its weight in gold. Yet he was not an impressive personality. S. C. Hall describes him as "a gentleman of no great intellectual capacities."[2]

If John Dickens did exert some influence over his son Charles, it was mostly through a process of reaction; having observed at close quarters his father's constant pecuniary difficulties, he must have very early made the decision of securing before anything else a regular, ample source of income. Apart from this indirect influence, it is clear that they were profoundly unlike each other.

As to Elizabeth Dickens, it has been seen that she belonged to a circle of civil servants who stood fairly high up in the middle class; one would like to believe that Dickens thought of her when he wrote of King Alfred, "He had—as most men who grow up to be great and good are generally found to have had—an excellent mother."[3] Unfortunately, however, there is nothing in Dickens' fiction or correspondence to support such a view. Mrs. John Dickens was certainly not able to supply the energy and practical sense that were lacking in her husband, and her attitude toward Charles in the blacking factory episode[4] shows little maternal sensitivity. She never ceased to be a source of difficulty for her son. In July, 1839, for example, after having made minute arrangements for his parents to settle down in a house he was renting

---

[1] Quoted by Percy Fitzgerald, *The Life of Dickens as Revealed in his Writings* (London, 1905), I, 113. About the same time, John Dickens was also borrowing £20 from Macready, who lent the sum in spite of Forster's advice that he let John D. have only half of what he asked for (W. C. Macready, *Diaries* [London, 1912], II, 153).

[2] Samuel Carter Hall, *Retrospect of a Long Life* (London, 1883), I, 111. Hall was not particularly benevolent.

[3] *CHE*, chap. iii.

[4] See chap. ii below.

for them, Charles wrote to Forster: "Read my mother's letter, and my reply (from which I have struck out sundry "sneezing" passages) . . . I do swear that I am sick at heart with both her and father too, and think this *is* too much."[5]

No doubt, we should be chary of ascribing to Mrs. Dickens, while we know so little about her, all of Mrs. Nickleby's otiose loquaciousness or Mrs. Micawber's grandiloquent incompetence; but neither can we lay to her credit all of Mrs. Copperfield's tenderness and charm. In the latter character, it is probable that Dickens put some of his own mother's better features, while putting something of her worse side in the others, but in all three it will be seen later that he also introduced many different elements.

Such a brief examination of the circle from which Dickens issued can result only in a negative conclusion: his family origin casts but little light on our understanding of his personality. According to the testimony of Lord Houghton, the most gifted person among the novelist's progenitors would seem to have been his paternal grandmother:

> When Lady Houghton [*née* Annabel Crewe] was a girl at Crewe, the person who filled the responsible office of housekeeper at Crewe Hall was a Mrs. Dickens, the grandmother of Charles. Lady Houghton used to tell that, when she was a child, the greatest treat that could be given to herself and her brother and sister, was an afternoon in the housekeeper's room at Crewe; for Mrs. Dickens was an inimitable story-teller, and she loved to have the children round her, and to beguile them, not only with fairy tales, but with reminiscences of her own, and stories from the page of history.[6]

Yet one cannot rely unreservedly on a description so vague, so conventionally worded, and published at such a late date.

In any case, Dickens' family origin may illuminate at least one aspect of his fiction. In his intelligence and strength of character, Charles was immeasurably his parents' superior. The family atmosphere that surrounded him in his youth explains why nowhere in his novels is to be

---

[5] *The Letters of Charles Dickens*, (London, 1965), I, 560.
[6] T. Wemyss Reid, *The Life, Letters and Friendships of Richard Monckton Milnes, First Lord Houghton* (London, 1890), 227.

heard the echo of any profound filial love or of any vivid thankfulness of children toward their parents. The insolence of Nicholas Nickleby to his mother, with the author's approval,[7] the way in which Kate sermonizes the same lady,[8] or Edith Granger-Dombey's contemptuous coldness to Mrs. Skewton,[9] are representative examples of the tone in which children habitually address their parents in Dickens' books, and may be taken to convey the more or less conscious attitude of the author toward Mr. and Mrs. John Dickens. True, the parents of Dickensian heroes, whenever such parents happen to be alive, are not deserving of better treatment. As a breed, Mrs. Nickleby and Mrs. Skewton are both sorry mothers indeed. Very little can be alleged in the defence of parents such as Mrs. Clennam and William Dorrit in *Little Dorrit*. Nor can one justify Mrs. Wilfer (*Our Mutual Friend*), or Anthony Chuzzlewit, or either of the Gradgrinds (*Hard Times*)[10] or many others. The delightful Mrs. Copperfield herself, with all her charm, is weak and frivolous, quite incapable of providing her son with a suitable education, nor does Dickens entrust her with the task. In short, Dickens does not glorify the parental relationship. When parents appear, they are likely to be inefficient.

Often, indeed, he does not even give his major figures parents; Oliver Twist, David Copperfield, Nell (*The Old Curiosity Shop*), or Pip (*Great Expectations*), are all orphans. It would take up too much space to draw a list of complete orphans in Dickens' works—it will be enough to show, while dealing with *Copperfield*, how strikingly that novel illustrates the tendency. Dickens gives the impression of having believed himself better qualified to explore the psychology of orphans than of children who lived with and knew their parents. He even seems to have believed that in the persons of his mother and father nature had endowed him with no higher privileges or more efficient help than are granted to orphans. Even if the thought probably never became quite explicit in his mind, the whole trend of his fiction suggests it.

The only true parents presented to us by Dickens, the only ones

[7] See, e.g., *NN*, chap. lxiii.

[8] *Ibid.*, chap. xlii.

[9] See, e.g., *D&S*, chap. xxvii.

[10] In Mr. Gradgrind, indeed, there is a last-minute conversion and awakening of the paternal feeling.

worthy of their children's respect and love, are always adopted parents, such as uncles, aunts, or friends, Mr. Peggotty or Betsey Trotwood (*Copperfield*), John Jarndyce (*Bleak House*), Mr. Brownlow and Mrs. Maylie (*Twist*), all of whom are either unmarried or widowed. This fact again confirms the existence of a theory, which may have been either conscious or unconscious in his mind, according to which mere blood ties do not imply gratitude and filial love: these sentiments demand more positive virtues, such as the self-denial, patience, and generosity of Mr. Peggotty, or, better still perhaps, the amiable and morally constructive eccentricity of Miss Betsey.

Dickens once remarked that his organ of veneration must have been imperfectly developed. At any rate, it is clear that he venerated neither the position nor the name of father or mother, but revered only filial feeling. Father and Mother, names held sacred by most of his contemporaries, were both ridiculed by him: William Dorrit is far more ready to declare himself "Father of the Marshalsea," father of all insolvent debtors and providers of drink, than to claim that he is the father of his unfortunate daughter Amy. As for Mrs. Crupp, the sinister landlady of David Copperfield, she accounts for all her weaknesses, all her departures from discretion and honesty, by means of the same paradoxical but significant argument: "I'm a mother myself!"[11]

Dickens has gained the reputation of being *the* novelist of happy family life. The above remarks do not tend to wrest this title from him, yet there is in his fiction a transfer of all paternal, maternal, and filial feelings to more distant relatives than fathers and mothers, and for this transfer the deficiencies of John and Elizabeth Dickens must be held responsible.

III: THE EPISODE OF THE BLACKING FACTORY

THE EARLIEST definite event that had a perceptible influence on Charles Dickens' development and left an indelible stamp on his personality and art took place on the seventh of February, 1824, his twelfth birthday. In the brutal shock he underwent on that day and in the tragic events

---

[11] ". . . that statement of universal application, which fitted every occurrence of her life, namely, that she was a mother herself" (*DC*, chap. xxxiv).

of the following weeks, the novelist was to find a constant element of his inspiration.

The mere facts are familiar to all; they have been reported by all Dickens' biographers since Forster and are described besides under a very thin disguise in *Copperfield*. Charles became a laborer in a blacking factory at the age of twelve, a few days before his father was arrested for debt and placed in the Marshalsea Prison. What is less well known, or has been insufficiently emphasized, is the very short duration of the episode, a fact that can be easily established by examining the chronological sequence of the events. It occupied no more than the spring of 1824. Of course, four months of acute suffering held a whole world of experience for a sensitive child. When Dickens was writing to Forster, in 1847, "I have no idea how long it lasted: whether for a year, or much more, or much less,"[1] he may well have been sincere. But the impression made upon a reader of *David Copperfield* who has a vague idea of the autobiographical nature of the episode without knowing the historical dates is of a considerably longer period.

Nevertheless, Dickens had a sharp experience of the sufferings involved in poverty and hunger. The remembrance remained with him forever and may account for his permanent interest in descriptions of food as well as for the minuteness of his references to the sums of money handled by his characters.[2] Such details are mentioned with the expert assurance of a man who had known what was the lowest salary on which life could be supported and how it had to be spent in order to avoid starvation. His knowledge of the value of money was acquired throughout his childhood and adolescence: his parents had a limited, but regular and normal income, but their inability to run a budget caused them to be in constant difficulties. Certainly the time when

---

[1] Forster, *Life of Dickens* (Everyman edition), I, 32. David Copperfield says similarly, "I have never had the courage even to examine how long I was doomed to lead" that life (*DC*, chap. xiv).

[2] The reader is not kept in ignorance of the cost of a meal given by John Westlock to Tom Pinch (*MC*, chap. xii), or the amount of the money given by Florence Dombey to a poor man, by Louisa Gradgrind to Stephen Blackpool, by the Cheeryble brothers to Tim Linkinwater (*D&S*, chap. xxiv; *HT*, Book II, chap vi; *NN*, chap. xxxviii); in Dickens' travel notes, he gives every detail concerning the financial arrangements in a charitable institution for the blind in Boston (*AN*, chap. iii). And we know just how many pence David Copperfield has at his disposal when he walks from London to Dover, and what use he makes of each.

Charles had to support himself almost entirely on a weekly wage of six or seven shillings, while his family was in prison, furnished a harsh and precise initiation into the material difficulties of life. Thus one often finds in his novels a brooding atmosphere of poverty, convincingly conveyed, of wants not satisfied. All the incidents which habitually come as a consequence of financial difficulties, such as executions, sales of furniture, visits to the pawnbroker's shop, are frequently described in his fiction, because his early experience enabled him to endow them with the vividness of personal observation.[3]

It is rather improbable, on the other hand, that Charles suffered from hunger while he lived with his parents. His father was not likely to allow the family to lack food and drink simply because he lacked money; like Dick Swiveller (*The Old Curiosity Shop*) or Harold Skimpole (*Bleak House*), he would have preferred running into debt. It has been seen that his second arrest, in 1834, was for his wine merchant's bill. While he was working at the factory, however, Charles, like David, must have known hunger; his salary, which in any case he was too young and ill-trained to manage adequately, could not possibly have provided the food he needed, and whenever he yielded to the temptation of buying anything special, he had to go without the humblest necessities. Dickens seems never to have forgotten this aspect of his apprenticeship to life. In one sense, the experience was a help to him for some passages of his novels; in another, it became a drawback, because he was at times obsessed by food. In his *Christmas Carol,* for instance, and also in his *Child's History of England,* he evinces the strangest enthusiasm when he refers to huge quantities of food. And he can seldom mention a meal without describing the menu in detail, even when the menu has no part to play in the plot.

It was in the spring of 1824 also that young Dickens first became intimately acquainted with a kind of place that was to keep a powerful hold over his mind through life. When John Dickens was imprisoned in the Marshalsea, the whole family soon joined him there, with two exceptions: Fanny, the eldest daughter, was a boarder at the Royal Academy of Music, and Charles was working at the factory. His work

---

[3] Besides David's adventures as Micawber's lodger, see *SB,* "The Pawnbroker's Shop" (*Scenes,* chap. xxiii; *Scenes,* chap. iii; *MC,* chap. xiii).

never allowed him to reside in the prison permanently, but he would spend his Sundays there, and when a room had been found for him close to the prison, he visited it twice daily to have his morning and evening meals with the rest of the children. Thus, Forster, when relating that period of the novelist's childhood, makes use of the picturesque phrase: "he used to breakfast 'at home,' in other words, in the Marshalsea,"[4] and the brief moments spent "at home," in a sordid room in the prison, had to serve as his only relief from the dull days at the factory.

"I hope I may not be misunderstood on this subject," Dickens wrote in his *American Notes,* on coming to the description of several prisons he had visited in the States, "for it is one in which I take a strong and deep interest."[5] This clear statement was superfluous; there is not a single major work by Dickens in which prisons do not play a conspicuous part. Of course, he was not the first novelist to mention them. Prisons are inevitably a constant feature of the picaresque novel; Fielding has many prison scenes in *Joseph Andrews, Tom Jones, Jonathan Wild,* and of course *Amelia.* Yet both Fielding and Dickens had an emotional involvement and a serious interest in the subject that went far beyond their regard for literary tradition.

The spring of 1824 proved a fruitful period, since it also resulted in another characteristic tendency of his work. The long solitary walks the small boy had to take at that time to go from the factory to the prison and from the prison to his poor lodging aroused in him a keen curiosity about various aspects of the city he was thus crossing and recrossing. He indulged in other daily rambles, at the hour of his midday meal, in a spirit of more systematic exploration and discovery. The sixty minutes he then had at his disposal were too short to procure a real rest between two long periods of work,[6] but they were far too long to be fully occupied by his scanty meal, and thus tempted him to improve his acquaintance with several districts and manifold features

[4] *Life of Dickens,* I, 26.
[5] Chap. iii.
[6] Neither in *DC* nor in the autobiographical fragment quoted by Forster, does one find any precise information as to the hours of work at the blacking factory. Yet it is easy enough to gather an impression on this point, and it can be asserted that Dickens must have worked at least ten hours a day. (See A. Hayward, *The Days of Dickens* [London, 1925]; esp. the chapter called "A Chapter of Horrors," in which are described the conditions of work imposed on children in British industry in the nineteenth century.)

of the English capital. Thus was born within him a sense that he was to share with writers like Charles Lamb and Dante Gabriel Rossetti, the sense of a kinship between the city and himself, the need of being ever surrounded by its atmosphere of intense life and by its crowds at once familiar and mysterious, a liking for the streets and for street scenes. Thus was developed the germ of the centripetal tendency of the Dickensian novel, which was always to take London as its central point. Whether the hero had come from Devonshire like Nicholas Nickleby, from Suffolk like David Copperfield, from some anonymous provincial town like Oliver Twist or Pip, the main part of his fictional career would invariably take place in London. Even the itinerant novels, like *Pickwick* or *The Old Curiosity Shop*, have their essential scenes, or at least those that give coherence to the plot, in London. In such provincial novels as *Bleak House* or *Drood*, characters and author go to London from time to time, in order, it would seem, to imbibe its atmosphere and gather new life from it. It would be difficult to imagine a Dickensian novel with no scene in London.[7] *Oliver Twist, Great Expectations,* and *A Tale of Two Cities* present striking cases; in the last-named book, dealing in the main with the French Revolution, the novelist felt the need of creating strong links between the plot and the city he knew best and loved most; as for the anonymity of the provincial places in which are located many of the scenes of *Great Expectations* and *Oliver Twist*, it may be regarded as revealing the lack of precision or even the lack of interest with which Dickens considered cities other than his own.

Of course, he had known a few aspects of London before his father's arrest; yet he had never wandered about in such complete independence. Other objects had held his curiosity and his affection, of which his home until then had formed the center. One would like to hope that if young Charles felt a single comfort through that dark period it must have been the thought he later gave to Oliver: "London!—that great large place! . . . it was the very place for a homeless boy!"[8]

From 1824 to 1870, Charles Dickens continued ceaselessly to love

[7] *HT* is the only Dickens novel none of whose important incidents take place in London. Few readers and critics regard *HT* as representatively Dickensian; its background is artificial—or stylized—and unconvincing.

[8] Chap. viii.

and explore London. His works offer a varied and almost complete picture of the city (only the very rich and distinguished districts are omitted from it), yet the picture was somewhat transformed, for Dickens described the London he remembered rather than the London he saw at the moment,[9] and whenever he remembered the London streets, he also and chiefly remembered the unhappy little boy he had been in the spring of 1824. "When I tread the old ground," David Copperfield writes, "I do not wonder that I seem to see and pity, going on before me, an innocent, romantic boy, making his imaginative world out of such strange experiences and sordid things."[10]

The presence of the innocent, romantic child lends a peculiar color to the world described by Dickens in his fiction. It is almost impossible to exaggerate the importance of the blacking factory episode in the formation of his character or in the development of his literary creation. One can only wonder at the artistic use made by the writer of such suffering, or at the enrichment his inspiration derived from a period of extreme poverty.

IV: CHILDHOOD MADE PERENNIAL

My thoughts are drawn back, by a fascination which
I do not care to resist, to my own childhood.[1]

IN THE PRECEDING CHAPTER we have seen the most tangible marks left in Dickens' work by his labors in James Lamert's blacking factory. The way in which that event wrought havoc in his psychological evolution remains to be described. One major consequence of the upheaval was his attitude toward childhood, an attitude adopted, it would seem, once and for all at that early time.

It has often been stated that Dickens' attitude toward childhood was essentially sentimental, that the remembrance of childhood was to him an obvious obsession, that he always preserved several childlike char-

---

[9] "In nearly all of his books one has a curious feeling that one is living in the first quarter of the nineteenth century, and in fact he does tend to return to that period" (G. Orwell, "Charles Dickens," *Critical Essays* [London, 1946], 39).

[10] Chap. xi.

[1] *CS*, "A Christmas Tree."

acteristics (e.g., his keen sensitiveness and his faculty of wonder), and that he took pleasure in depicting children of all ages, from Little Paul Dombey to Mr. Dick in *Copperfield*, who can be regarded as a white-haired child.

Such facts can be easily understood by turning back once more to the events that occurred in Dickens' life early in 1824 and to the effect they could produce on a child's heart and soul. On becoming his cousin's "hind" at the age of twelve, he simply felt that his childhood was over, and that life, hateful adult life, had begun for him. "My rescue from this kind of existence," he was to write later,[2] "I considered quite hopeless, and abandoned as such altogether."

Thus, at the age of twelve, he regarded his whole childhood as a thing of the past and began to look back in tenderness on the first years of his life, still so close to him. The brutal change in his position and way of life urged him to cultivate in self-defense, as a protection against the numbing of his mind and the debasing of his morals, the memories of his childhood; his melancholy brooding over his past had begun prematurely and was to endure to the end of his days. Dickens was of course unable to understand how valuable for his literary career the rough apprenticeship he was submitted to would eventually turn out to be; on the other hand, he realized to the full the damage done to his emotional health; therefore, he idealized all that part of his childhood which had preceded the events of 1824. He was aware of having been defrauded of several years of normal, happy childhood, and when he left the factory, he could not resume its broken thread. In his parents' home, in June 1824, life had become less wholesome, less easy going than it had been in the Chatham days; besides, the boy could not simply forget the sights that had so powerfully upset him. Grieved by the loss of his child's soul, he experienced the nostalgia of childhood at a time of life when most boys tend to be more or less ashamed of their immaturity. Dickens thus missed going through the normal reactions of adolescence; he failed to live through that middle period when young people deliberately turn their backs on their childhood and avoid, as far as possible, its remembrance, in order to look upon themselves as real men. He enjoyed the privilege of preserving in its pure freshness

2 Thus in Dickens' autobiographical fragment; see Forster, *Life of Dickens*, I, 26.

his vision and his knowledge of the child's soul and the child's universe. All the sensations, emotions, and thought processes of children remained familiar to him, and he depicted them with unique and striking truthfulness.[3] Of course, there are in his fiction many scenes of unhappy childhood, but of his own early years he doubtless cherished a happy memory, enhanced by his projecting into the past his passionate longings and keen regrets.

For Dickens, as for Nicholas Nickleby, the slightest incident of childhood was unforgettable: "nothing in itself . . . yet more strongly and distinctly marked, and better remembered, than the hardest trial or the severest sorrows of a year ago,"[4] and the scenes of his youth are decked with the fairylike poetry of memory: "Magic scenes indeed; for the fairy thoughts of infancy dressed them in colours brighter than the rainbow, and almost as fleeting."[5]

The whole of childhood assumes the aspect of a happy dream; such is the impression he wishes men to preserve of their early years, "those lightsome hours which make our childhood a time to be remembered like a happy dream through all after life";[6] for him the memories of childhood and the dreams in which some of its scenes reappear are mingled together. When he writes, "It is pretty certain . . . that we have all dreamed much more of our youth than of our later lives,"[7] his attempt at making the remark general does but thinly disguise its very personal significance.

According to him—as according to Horace—memories need not be gay in order to be comforting. Dickens evinces and advocates equal fondness for images of past joy and of past sadness; Little Dorrit has become rich and looks at the water of a river, hoping to see once more in it "the prison again, and herself, and the old room, and the old inmates, and the old visitors: all lasting realities that had never changed."[8]

---

[3] See the early chapters of DC and GE, and, among the shorter pieces, "The Schoolboy's Story," the four tales of "Holiday Romance," and the chapter called "Boots" in The Holly Tree Inn (CS).

[4] NN, chap. lviii.

[5] SB, "Scenes," chap. xx; in later editions "the fairy thoughts of infancy" is replaced by "the fancies of childhood."

[6] NN, chap. lx.

[7] RP, "Lying Awake."

[8] LD, Book II, chap. iii.

Her father's voice, when he reasonably advises her to give up such un-wholesome worship of the past,[9] is by no means an echo of the author's; in Dickens' opinion, it is better to remain attached to the past one can remember, whatever it is; for he believes childhood, the thought of childhood, and the imitation of childhood to possess a moral value independent of any notion of happiness: "It is good to be children sometimes."[10]

V: APPRENTICESHIP AMONG THE LAWYERS

ON LEAVING Wellington House Academy, Charles Dickens was to spend five years in legal circles, first as errand boy to the firm of Ellis and Blackmore, solicitors (May, 1827, through November, 1828), and later as shorthand writer at the Court of Doctors' Commons (November, 1828, through March, 1832). He thus began his working life for good and all at the age of fifteen, but he never protested against that fact; he regarded the end of his school-days as normal, and the career offered to him as an honorable one. His five legal years yielded many elements for use in his future works. The large place held by lawyers and legal action in the novels is well known. Already in the *Sketches,* for example, there are chapters concerning the Criminal Courts (*Scenes,* chap. xxv) and Doctors' Commons (*Scenes,* chap. viii). The latter institution is again mentioned in *Copperfield,* and criticized in digressive passages which owe more to Dickens' private interest in the theme than to the needs of the plot.[1] In *Pickwick,* in *Bleak House,* in *Drood,* lawyers are among the leading characters. And others appear in every novel.

The legal period also—inevitably—influenced Dickens' style. He did not remain unscathed after many weary months of copying or writing legal documents. And though he seldom makes use of a word or phrase belonging incontestably to the legal vocabulary,[2] a number of metaphors were probably suggested to him by the remembrance of that experience. Of Mrs. Harris, in *Chuzzlewit,* he says: "she was a phantom

---

[9] *Ibid.,* chap. v.
[10] *CB, Carol,* chap. iii.
[1] Chaps. xxii, xxvi, xxxiii, xxxix.
[2] The most frequent of these is the form "aid and abet" or "aider and abettor." See *NN,* chap. viii; *PP,* chaps. xviii and xx; *DC,* chap. lx.

of Mrs. Gamp's brain, as Messrs. Doe and Roe are fictions of the law,"[3] and he advertises his knowledge of a few technical works, the titles of which at least were familiar to him (such as the *Commentaries* of Blackstone, and Tidd's *Practice*).[4] Yet one should not overemphasize Dickens' expertness in that field or forget that he never became a lawyer himself, that he did not study law—or not until a much later period of his life, and not very seriously then; on the contrary, he learned shorthand in order to escape as soon as possible from legal circles. In short, among the lawyers, he was fascinated by human types rather than by law. So the main benefit he derived from that phase of his apprenticeship was a splendid gallery of picturesque or dramatic, amiable or grotesque figures, who form a literally inexhaustible group, since there are lawyers in *Pickwick* (Perker, Dodson, and Fogg, etc.), and he still had fresh ones to put into *Drood*, where the character of Grewgious is particularly interesting.

The gallery of Dickens' lawyers is colorful and varied, but on the whole it is easy to see that he did not think highly of the profession. His caricature is not always so harsh and contemptuous as his presentation of magistrates in *Mudfog Papers*,[5] but he makes it abundantly clear everywhere that he has but little confidence in the administration of justice.[6] In his eyes, the jailer who puts Kit in prison is fairly representative of the current attitude of legal circles toward ideal justice when he declares to his prisoner's mother, "I won't contradict you. It's all one, now, whether he did it or not."[7] And in *Bleak House* is to be found the most sweeping indictment of the whole legal system of Great Britain, expressed this time in the author's own name:

> The one great principle of the English law is, to make business for itself. There is no other principle distinctly, certainly, and consistently maintained through all its narrow turnings. Viewed by

---

[3] Chap. xxv; a similar allusion is to be found in *OCS*, chap. xxxiii.

[4] *Commentaries on the Laws of England* (*1763–1769*), by Sir William Blackstone, mentioned by Mr. Micawber (*DC*, chap. xxxvi) and *Practice of the Court of King's Bench* *1790–1794*), by William Tidd, Uriah Heep's constant companion (*DC,* chap. xvi). In *OCS*, Quilp announces that to Swiveller Sally Brass will be "his Blackstone, his Coke upon Littleton, his Young Lawyer's Best Companion" (chap. xxxiii).

[5] *RP.*

[6] See Philip Collins, *Dickens and Crime* (London, 1962).

[7] *OCS,* chap. lxiii.

this light, it becomes a coherent scheme, and not the monstrous maze the laity are apt to think it. Let them but once clearly perceive that its grand principle is to make business for itself at their expense, and surely they will cease to grumble.[8]

Urged by such a ruthless theory, which had been born in a solicitor's office and an obsolete ecclesiastical court, the novelist yielded more than once to the temptation of turning his fiction into a weapon of attack against the law and the legal system of his country.

VI: Political Apprenticeship

From March 5, 1832, through June 22, 1836, Dickens went on with his training, now as a parliamentary shorthand reporter. On his escape from the legal world he disliked, he was hoping to find in Parliament men and ideas of greater value than those he had been in touch with at Ellis and Blackmore's or Doctors' Commons. His disappointment was immediate, complete, and decisive. When he came out of the House of Commons for the last time, after nine years of varied professional training, his view of the world and his political ideas had taken shape. And, however unsatisfactory and even incoherent they were, they never changed much from that time on. As they are of considerable importance for his literary creation, it seems best to consider them now, while dealing with the period of their origin.

Though he achieved remarkable success in that field and was very proud of it through life, there are few allusions in Dickens' work to the technical aspects of the shorthand writer's craft. Apart from the episode in *Copperfield* in which David describes his difficulties while learning the trade,[1] there is only one brief, rather insignificant passage in *Pictures from Italy;*[2] elsewhere, stenography is not even mentioned. On the other hand, the politicians whose speeches and debates Dickens had written down through four years are referred to, described, criticized, laughed at with supreme contempt. Out of scores of references to Parliament in Dickens' novels, not one is favorable. The only noncontemptuous

8 Chap. xxxix.
1 Chap. xxviii.
2 "To Rome."

expressions ever used by him about it occur in a letter to G. Lovejoy, who had written suggesting that the novelist stand for Parliament in the constituency of Reading: "I am much obliged and flattered. . . . My principles and inclinations would lead me to aspire to the distinction you invite me to seek . . . and I hope I should do no discredit to such an honour if I won and wore it."[3] Everywhere else, contempt is irresistibly called forth, and Dickens even goes out of his way more than once to express it.

In the *Sketches*, we read the following description: "that singularly awkward and ungainly-looking man . . . apparently deluding himself into the belief that he is thinking about something, is a splendid sample of a Member of the House of Commons concentrating in his own person the wisdom of a constituency,"[4] the rest of that particular sketch is devoted to showing that Parliament is made up of cranks and crooks. Still in the same early book, Dickens offers a striking summary of what a political career means to him: "Horses and dogs—play and wine— grooms, actresses and cigars—the stable, the green-room, the saloon, and the tavern; and the legislative assembly at last."[5] In *Nickleby* a man is mentioned who "has a tolerable command of sentences with no meaning in them, and, in short, every requisite for a very good member indeed."[6] At about the same time, Dr. Losberne says to Harry Maylie: "they will get you into Parliament at the election before Christmas, and these sudden shiftings and changings are no bad preparation for political life."[7] Tony Weller's unfortunate resurrection in *Master Humphrey* enables him to define parliamentary courtesy as "that 'ere pleasant and uniwersal fiction,"[8] while it is in his own name that Dickens writes in *American Notes:* "I do not remember having ever fainted away . . . at sight of any legislative body. I have borne the House of Commons

---

[3] May 31, 1844, *Letters* (M. Dickens–G. Hogarth edition, subsequently referred to as MDGH), I, 44. The strength of the position developed here is diminished by the fact that this is a letter; in Dickens' correspondence, he almost always writes courteously and with an obvious desire of adapting himself to his correspondent's mood, unless he wishes to be insulting, in which case he brilliantly achieves his purpose.

[4] "Scenes," chap. xviii.

[5] "Tales," chap. viii.

[6] Chap. xvi.

[7] *OT*, chap. xxxvi.

[8] Chap. v.

like a man, and have yielded to no weakness, but slumber, in the House of Lords."[9] A few months later, he launches a fresh attack: "lovers . . . can . . . give utterance to more language . . . in any given short space of time, than all the six hundred and fifty-eight members in the Commons . . . who are strong lovers, no doubt, but of their country only, which makes all the difference, for in a passion of that kind (which is not always returned) it is the custom to use as many words as possible and express nothing whatever."[10]

David Copperfield's voice is used time and again to convey Dickens' own attitude very directly; having turned his hero into what he had himself been, a parliamentary stenographer, he describes the miniature Parliament meeting at David's to help him with his training, and adds: "the inconsistency and recklessness of Traddles were not to be exceeded by any real politician."[11] Later, when David has taken up his duties, he says: "Britannia, that unfortunate female, is always before me, like a trussed fowl; skewered through and through with office-pens, and bound hand and foot with red tape. I am sufficiently behind the scenes to know the worth of political life. I am quite an Infidel about it, and shall never be converted."[12] Later, David will speak once more of "the music of the parliamentary bagpipes . . . the old drone . . . without any substantial variation."[13] In *Hard Times*, Parliament is called a "little noisy and rather dirty machinery" or a "national cinder-heap."[14] In *Great Expectations*, Pip is referring to Mrs. Gargery's feeble cries after her accident and says: "I doubt if they had more meaning in them than an election cry, and I cannot suggest a darker picture of her state of mind."[15] In the Christmas story for 1865, a hawker shows that his calling offers more than one analogy with that of political hucksters: "Except that we are Cheap Jacks and they are Dear Jacks, I don't see any difference but what's in our favour."[16]

Thus it is clear that Dickens throughout his career, lost no oppor-

[9] Chap. viii.
[10] *MC*, chap. xliii.
[11] Chap. xxxviii.
[12] Chap. xliii.
[13] Chap. xlviii.
[14] Book I, chap. xiv and Book II, chap. xi.
[15] Chap. xviii.
[16] *Marigold*, chap. i.

tunity to depict politicians as foolish, vain, idle, verbose, unreliable, tedious men, as insignificant and thoroughly despicable persons. But to him Parliament is not merely farcical, it is also harmful. "I am not at all prepared to say . . . that if Caleb had been . . . a Member of Parliament . . . he would have dealt in toys one whit less whimsical. . . . I have a great doubt whether they would have been as harmless."[17]

The childish games of Members of Parliament do not amuse Dickens like those of other grown-up children in his fiction, like Mr. Dick's kite, for instance, in *Copperfield*; they seem to him too dangerous for the English nation. He expresses unequivocal approval of Cromwell's dismissal of the House of Commons, almost an ideal solution in his eyes: "Parliament does so little and talks so much that the most interesting ceremony I know of in connection with it was performed (with very little state indeed) by one man, who just cleared it out, locked up the place, and put the key in his pocket."[18] And to his friend John Forster, a warm supporter of Parliamentary institutions, he writes that he is "so sick of the shortcomings of representative government as to have no interest in it."[19]

Moreover, the ridicule and inefficiency with which Dickens reproaches the House of Commons also characterize in his view every other assembly of human beings: the Pickwick Club,[20] the committee of the "United Metropolitan Improved Hot Muffin and Crumpet Baking and Punctual Delivery Company,"[21] a vestry,[22] the trade-unions[23] and even juries.[24] He saw them as grotesque and unpractical, and that is the way he presented them.

Yet the House of Commons is composed of representatives elected by the nation, by the good people of England in whom Dickens has implicit trust; how is it then that they are so ill chosen? The reason is that any man, as soon as he becomes a voter, loses in Dickens' opinion all his noble qualities. The novelist does not think more highly of the

---

[17] *CB, Cricket*, chap. ii.
[18] Letter to Mr. Rawlinson, Jan. 25, 1854; quoted in Kitton, *Dickensiana*, 486.
[19] May 2, 1860; MS, Forster Collection.
[20] *PP*, chap. i.
[21] *NN*, chap. ii.
[22] *RP, Our Vestry* (1852).
[23] *HT*, Book II, chap. iv.
[24] *CS, A Trial for Murder*.

elector than of the elected. "Beastly as the electors usually are . . . ,"[25] he wrote, after reporting a partial election at Kettering; while in *Chuzzlewit* he shows an innkeeper whose political ignorance he seems to regard as fairly representative of the general situation:

> ". . . our member in the House of Commons, who is returned upon the Gentlemanly Interest."
> "Which Interest is that?" asked Martin. . . .
> It was quite clear the landlord didn't know. They always told him at election time that it was the gentlemanly side, and he immediately put on his top-boots, and voted for it."[26]

The pronoun "they" in "they told him" is revealing. In order to preserve his theoretical belief in the value of popular judgment, Dickens would like to ascribe the responsibility for the unsatisfactory government of the nation to a group of evil-minded individuals; but "they," of course, remains indefinite.

So many attacks against Parliament may surprise the reader, since they come from a writer who regarded himself as democratic in spirit. They cannot mean that at bottom Dickens would have preferred the yoke of another Cromwell, or that he was prepared to trust monarchy, for the kings of England he regarded with a mixture of suspicion and contempt at least equal to anything he felt towards parliamentary assemblies.[27]

He did not side with the supporters of monarchy or with the aristocracy he was constantly—and not very competently—belittling and laughing at. It was on the side of the people that Dickens wished to place himself; it was the people's cause that he always warmly advocated; with the people he felt completely at one. Like his defense of children, like his criticism of prisons and magistrates, like his caricature of Parliament, monarchy, and aristocracy, his defense of the poor and of the people is an ever-present purpose of his work. In 1842, he inquires: "Are we quite sure that we . . . have not formed our idea of the 'station' of working people, from accustoming ourselves to the con-

25 Letter to Miss C. Hogarth, Dec. 1, 1835, *Letters*, I, 100.
26 Chap. xxxv.
27 See *CHE*.

templation of that class as they are, and not as they might be?"[28] And in 1854 he says: "I entertain a weak idea that the English people are as hard-worked as any people upon whom the sun shines."[29] Humble labor occupies a high place in his esteem, and he expresses unequivocal preference for the poor: "if ever household affections and loves are graceful things, they are graceful in the poor."[30]

The notion that Dickens was a democrat is supported mainly by a few statements of that kind. He was at least a friend of the people. But he seems to have perceived no correlation between the sublime qualities he ascribed to the people and the worthlessness of the government emanating from them. The paradoxical contrast did not shock him. He could never resign himself to the conclusion that democratic government fails because it is democratic; he did not clearly wish to see it become more democratic; the thought of a revolution appalled him, and he believed he had seen proof that legislative reforms are deceptive; hence he came to the idea that the chief fault of government is that it exists as a government. Such is, indeed, the impression to be derived from a passage in *Bleak House* (1852): "England has been some weeks in the dismal strait of having no pilot . . . to weather the storm: and the marvellous part of the matter is that England has not appeared to care very much about it, but has gone on eating and drinking."[31]

Insofar as Dickens' political thinking can be defined and has any unity or coherence, his basic views will be found in the idea that men are good, but that politics is a bad thing because it corrupts natural goodness and tends to stimulate the selfish quest for personal satisfaction and the disregard of the common good for the sake of private interests. In other words, politics is in itself obnoxious. From a political speech heard in the United States, Dickens would remember but "two sentiments, one of which was, Somebody for ever! and the other, Blast everybody else! which is by no means a bad abstract of the general creed in these matters."[32] But even such a broad summary is not enough to

[28] *AN*, chap. vi.
[29] *HT*, Book I, chap. x.
[30] *OCS*, chap. xxxviii.
[31] Chap. xl.
[32] *AN*, chap. xiii.

resolve the contradictions of Dickens' political attitudes, for it remains difficult to see how a country can be democratically governed without having political life, representative assemblies and popular elections. The discrepancy would not appear so important to us if it had not influenced the general vision of the world presented by Dickens in his novels. It has been somewhat too glibly asserted by G. K. Chesterton[33] that Dickens was an optimistic writer. No doubt, on the whole, his novels do end well, if not always happily. Evil is never triumphant, even where misfortune prevails. The bad—Quilp and Ralph—are invariably punished, even where the good, the excellent—Nell and Smike[34]— perish. But an attempt to formulate Dickens' philosophy (a thing he wisely refrained from doing himself, except for desultory maxims) in- dicates that he had four major tenets in his system: 1) theoretically, man, especially isolated, natural man, is good; 2) Dickens has clearly asserted in some of his occasional writings[35] that he believed neither in the Noble Savage, nor in the virtues of solitude; 3) man is exposed to all kinds of pernicious influences (and these will be all the more pernicious as the individual's environment is more highly civilized and more socially refined); 4) man is reduced to impotence as soon as he belongs to a group.

There *are* in Dickens' work a few resolutely optimistic statements:

The world is, in all great essentials, better, gentler, more for- bearing, and more hopeful, as it rolls![36]

The vigorous tenacity of love, always so much stronger than hate[37]

Treachery don't come natural to beaming youth, but trust and pity, love and constancy—they do, thank God![38]

[33] *Appreciations*, 39.
[34] In *OCS* and *NN*.
[35] *RP, The Noble Savage:* "I beg to say that I have not the least belief in the Noble Savage. . . . His calling rum fire-water, and me a pale face, wholly fails to reconcile me to him. I don't care what he calls me. I call him a savage." "Tom Tiddler's Ground" (*CS*, 1861) contains a somewhat ill-tempered apologue directed against hermits and other sup- porters of the ivory tower. In order to analyze Dickens' political thought, one has to draw on works remote in time from the formative period, for the novelist never summed up his opinions himself in one specific work.
[36] *PFI, Diorama.*
[37] *T2C,* Book III, chap. xiv.
[38] *CS, Lirriper's Legacy.*

But Dickens' distrust of society is just as unequivocally expressed:

However fresh from the country a young lady (by nature) may be . . . she will have quite as strong an innate sense of the decencies and proprieties of life as if she had run the gauntlet of a dozen London seasons—possibly a stronger one, for such senses have been known to blunt a little in this improving process.[39]

As regards social groups, what happens is that Dickens, who instinctively rebels against every form of oppression, will not even bow to the majority, who in his opinion are almost always insufficiently enlightened and therefore likely to oppress the minority. *Barnaby Rudge* is particularly illuminating in this respect.[40]

It remains difficult to understand how, by adding up deserving individuals, one inevitably produces a grotesque and inefficient sum. Dickens nowhere explains how it happens. But what can account for his attitude is the shock he underwent when he entered the House of Commons. His instinctive bent, before he began to serve as a parliamentary reporter, lay in the direction of a warm democratic optimism. His generous temper, and his genuine emotion at the sight of the sufferings of the people always prevented him from wholly giving up that position, while his experience of the parliamentary system of government annihilated his trust in a great many human institutions without providing him with any precise positive ideal instead. From that moment on, his political and human ideal was to be nothing better than a half-conscious, unformulated belief in some dim, utopian aristocracy of the heart and the mind.

Such facts are of considerable importance in their effect on his craftsmanship as a novelist, for it is clear that in the construction of his plots and the design of his characters, Dickens was to be guided by several conflicting principles: the upheaval of his thinking, never again to become organized and coherent, accounts for more than one illogicality in the course of his narratives and in the psychology of his characters.

---

[39] *NN*, chap. xix.

[40] A close study of *BR* shows that Dickens' siding with the underdog occasionally resulted in his assuming an anarchist's positions (see S. Monod, "Rebel with a Cause: Hugh of the Maypole," *Dickens Studies*, Vol. I, No. 1 [Jan., 1965], 4–26).

VII: JOURNALISTIC APPRENTICESHIP

DURING THE FOUR YEARS he spent in the service of *The True Sun, The Mirror of Parliament,* and *The Morning Chronicle,* Charles Dickens fulfilled mainly, but not exclusively, the duties of a parliamentary shorthand reporter. Even before he left the office of Ellis and Blackmore, he had, if S. C. Hall's testimony can be trusted, performed for *The British Press* (then employing John Dickens) a humbler function, more in keeping with what is traditionally referred to as journalism: "Now and then there came to the office a smart, intelligent, active lad, who brought what was then called, and is still, I believe, named 'penny-a-line stuff'; that is to say, notices of accidents, fires, police reports, such as escaped the more regular reporters, for which a penny a printed line was paid. The lad to whom I refer was Charles Dickens."[1]

No other contemporary witness confirms S. C. Hall's statement, which seems to have been disregarded by most biographers of Dickens.[2] His book was written in 1883, nearly sixty years after the time in question, and under those circumstances he may have been tempted to embellish his earliest remembrance of a famous man, who had himself been dead for thirteen years. Yet the fact he mentions is by no means improbable. In December, 1835, Dickens is known to have done the reporting of a fire in Hatfield.[3] He probably began to climb the literary ladder from the lowest rung at a very early age.

It is in any case certain that the newspapers that later employed Dickens as shorthand writer did not limit his task to merely reporting parliamentary debates. For the *Morning Chronicle* in particular, from which he drew for the first time a regular monthly salary, even during parliamentary recesses, he was called upon to report speeches delivered in other assemblies, in various places. Owing to this wide experience, he could write in 1836: "of all entertainments of this description . . . we think the annual dinner of some public charity is the most amusing."[4] To this particular form of amusement, Dickens was to contribute a large share before the end of his life.

---

[1] Hall, *Retrospect,* I, 111.
[2] Only Johnson, *Ch. D.: Tragedy & Triumph,* mentions it (I, 53).
[3] See Pope-Hennessy, *Ch. Dickens,* 50.
[4] *SB,* "Scenes," chap. xix.

But the most natural way of giving employment to shorthand writers while the House was not sitting was of course to send them out of London, wherever prominent politicians might happen to be speechifying. Thus Dickens went on many trips to provincial cities, far and near, and he was to preserve through life a somewhat nostalgic remembrance of such outings, whether by mail coach or in a post-chaise or even on horseback. His whole work is influenced by this remembrance; journeys play an important part in his fiction, and his accounts of them clearly reflect his own first-hand knowledge of the road. The technical use Dickens was to make of traveling, the groupings and migrations of his characters, the place held by these incidents in his plots will be dealt with later on. For the time being it will be enough to note that Dickens, always preferring to draw from the fund of his personal experience as much as possible of the substance of his fictional episodes, often returned in spirit to the memories of a young stenographer along the roads of England. The journalist's greater liking for remote trips cannot be called in doubt: they were to him infinitely more attractive than the dull or exasperating sittings of the Commons.

When he toured the provinces, Dickens also enjoyed the pleasure of writing something other than political speeches and of seeing his own prose in print thereafter. For he would sometimes be asked to describe the atmosphere of a place where a by-election was to take place, to report an official dinner, or to depict the decoration of a banquet or a lecture hall. Such papers had more or less to be written in the style used by his colleagues, the style appreciated and demanded by the public, even though it had but little literary value and made use of conventional mannerisms. Topical references, for example, were indispensable. It is unfortunate that Dickens should for a few years have adhered to this practice, now through half-conscious caricature, and again in the form of passing allusions which have long ceased to be comical and can now only obscure the passages in which they are to be found.

When he writes of "the fat oyster in the American story . . . [which] takes a good many men to swallow it whole,"[5] the outline at least of the American story in question can be guessed at easily enough, but who will

[5] CS, *Seven Poor Travellers*, chap. i.

28

nowadays remember, on reading "we are as great friends to horses . . . as Mr. Martin, of costermonger notoriety,"[6] that Richard Martin (1754–1834) had been one of the chief founders of the Society for the Prevention of Cruelty to Animals? And who is likely to be amused by any of the following allusions: "requested to find out particular houses, in particular streets, which it would have been a task of some difficulty for Mr. Horner . . . (of Colosseum notoriety) to discover";[7] "he ventured to make a joke which . . . was almost equal to one of Mr. Hobler's";[8] "the infant Lambert,"[9] or " 'The Prince Regent was proud of his legs, and so was Daniel Lambert . . . so was Miss Biffin; she was —no,' added Mrs. Nickleby, correcting herself, 'I think she had only toes, but the principle is the same.' ";[10] or again, "There's a lot of feet in Shakespeare's verse, but there arn't any legs . . . they're all Miss Biffins to the audience";[11] "guarding his head on a principle invented by Mr. Thomas Cribb,"[12] and "furnished, as Mr. Robins would say, in a style of more than Eastern splendour"?[13]

These jokes can be enjoyed only by the reader who happens to know (or is told in a footnote, if footnotes have ever procured enjoyment), that George Robins, an auctioneer, wrote catalogues of sales in poetical style, that Thomas Cribb had been a boxing champion from 1809 to 1838, that Sarah Biffin, who had been born without arms or legs, painted miniatures with the help of a brush held between her teeth, that Daniel Lambert's sole claim to fame was his colossal weight, that Francis Hobler was a lawyer and a great cracker of jokes, and that Mr. Horner, the founder of the Colosseum, had painted for it an extremely detailed panorama of London. Nor can we be sure that even to one armed with so much knowledge the passages quoted above possess much value; the two references to Miss Biffin are in shockingly bad taste, considering that the unfortunate woman was still alive in the days of *Nickleby* and

[6] *SB,* "Scenes," chap. vii.
[7] *Ibid.,* chap. xii.
[8] *SB,* "Parish," chap. i; see also "Scenes," chap. xvii.
[9] It is Joe, Mr. Wardle's "fat boy," who is thus described (*PP,* chap. vii).
[10] *NN,* chap. xxxvii.
[11] *MC,* chap. xxviii.
[12] *Ibid.,* chap. ix.
[13] *AN,* chap. i; see also *SB,* "Tales."

Chuzzlewit,[14] a fact of which Dickens may not have been aware; but even the other allusions are no more than samples of a vulgarly knowing tone, of a cheap and facile pseudo-elegance which it would be more pleasant not to find in Dickens' writings; their presence there, at the outset of his literary career, is explained by his recent experience in the least refined form of journalism.

VIII: Dickens' Culture

Dickens describes himself as "a great reader of fiction at an unusually early age,"[1] as one who frequently reread the books he had read in childhood[2] and who remembered "everything I read then as perfectly as I forget everything I read now,"[3] thus clearly asserting that, as far as he knew, the only books that had an influence on him were those he had read in the early period of his life.

There are two possible methods for determining which books had been read by Dickens: one can examine the contents of his library and find out, from his correspondence and the memoirs of his friends, what books were mentioned in his letters or in conversations; or one can gather from his published works the largest possible collection of quotations from and allusions to other writers. The first method yields disappointing results, for Dickens' conversation with his friends seldom concerned literary matters, while his library seems to have been largely haphazard and conventional. The second was systematically applied by James S. Stevens, whose *Quotations and References in Charles Dickens* was published in Boston in 1929. The book comprises 845 items, classed as follows: the Bible, 365; classical writers, 71; Shakespeare (mostly *Macbeth, Hamlet,* and *The Merchant of Venice*), 69; proverbs, 66; songs, 37; modern authors, 103; sundry, 55; *Robinson Crusoe,* 14; legends (mostly Oriental), 30; nursery rhymes, 35.[4] This arrangement is not ideal. Terms like "classical" writers and "modern authors" are vague; and what is one to make of the group of "sundry" sources? Some

---

[14] Sarah Biffin died in 1850. Dickens mentions her again in *LD* (Book II, chap. xvii). Thackeray, who remained a journalist longer than Dickens, also mentions her in an article (*Fraser's Magazine,* Vol. XXXV, No. CCV [Jan. 1847], 126).

[1] *UT*, chap. xxxiii.

[2] *Ibid.*, chap. xv.

[3] *RP, Lying Awake.*

[4] Pp. 9–11.

of Stevens' figures, besides, are questionable (especially as Dickens' allusions are not always clear). Yet the book still provides a general impression of Dickens' culture. In the following paragraphs, I shall in my turn glance at Dickens' works in order to find out what they have to tell about the books he had read; the order will be based on chronology, and I shall begin with such works as he may have come across in his very earliest childhood, and in the first place, with the Bible.

The high number of Biblical quotations and references should occasion no surprise, since Dickens was a sincere believer—to the point of composing for the use of his own children a *Life of our Lord*—even though he was not very religious minded. The majority of his allusions are to the New Testament, with which he appears to have remained familiar through life. The references vary from the purely verbal to the faintly, not irreverently humorous, but they seldom have any moral connotation.

My second category for Dickens' readings is the literature of his early childhood. Dickens' memory is quite exceptionally accurate where the first narratives that struck his imagination are concerned. More than once, he alludes to the "nursery tales" he had heard: "My first impressions of an Inn dated from the nursery";[5] "At odd dull times, nursery tales come up into the memory";[6] and a whole paper of *The Uncommercial Traveller* is devoted to them.[7] Familiar phrases and short fragments out of nursery rhymes have also stayed with him and crop up under his pen; they are easily recognized, and there is no need for him to refer to their source, which belongs to the common store of his British public. A good example of this attitude is provided by his adroit adaptation of a well-known tongue-twister in "I . . . came to the conclusion, that if patriotic Peckham picked a peck of pickled poetry, this was the peck of pickled poetry which patriotic Peckham picked."[8] There are also two references to the same episode in the career of Humpty Dumpty: "Not all the king's horses nor all the king's men could have set Mr. Pecksniff up again"[9] and "fall to work with the power of all the queen's horses and all the queen's men or it will come

[5] *CS*, "Holly-Tree Inn."
[6] *DC*, chap. xxii.
[7] Chap. xv ("Nurses' Stories").
[8] *UT*, chap. xxxv.
[9] *MC*, chap. xxxi.

31

rushing down and bury us all alive."[10] In this class special mention must be made of Jack Horner, who comes in for frequent allusion through all kinds of verbal mechanisms.[11] Yet Jack Horner does not hold the field alone. Pip "felt rather like Mother Hubbard's dog whose outfit required the services of so many trades," then felt inclined to take Drummle in his "arms (as the robber in the storybook is said to have taken the old lady) and seat him on the fire," and, in the same novel, a man is seen "pulling a lock of hair in the middle of his forehead like the bull in Cock-Robin pulling at the bell-rope."[12]

Pickwick mentions "the ferocious giant Blunderbore," *Chuzzlewit* "Peter the Wild Boy," and *Copperfield*, among many others, "the Dragon of Wantley" and "the man in the south."

Among the more substantial, more literary narratives, no longer belonging to the almost purely oral tradition of the nursery, the most common are the *Arabian Nights* and other Oriental Tales, like *The Tales of the Genii*, constantly quoted by Dickens, who remained sentimentally attached to them: "the good Caliph Haroun Alraschid (let me have the corrupted name again for once, it is so scented with sweet memories!)";[13] it is obvious here that Dickens' melting mood is due to the remembrance of his own childhood.

The technical usefulness of such allusions (allusions are always much more frequent in Dickens' works than formal quotations, probably because they do not break the thread of the narrative or require that an author's name should be mentioned) is twofold: at one time, as in the case of Jack Horner or Mother Hubbard's dog, for instance, the effect aimed at is comical, and it is achieved through the mock-solemn commentary of the most primitive forms of literature; at another, more significantly, while attempting to evoke some real sensation or some real object, Dickens illustrates it through analogy with another object or another sensation drawn from fairy tales or other fanciful literature. This is a significant tendency, showing that for Dickens, thanks to the

---

[10] *OMF*, Book III, chap. viii.
[11] See, e.g., *SB*, chap. xii; *PP*, chap. xviii; and *CS*, "Seven Poor Travellers."
[12] *GE*, chaps. xix, xliii, and xx.
[13] *CS*, "Haunted House," II; see also, e.g., *MC*, chaps. v, vi, and xxxvi; *AN*, chap. ix; *DC*, chaps. iii and lix; and Jane W. Stedman, "Good Spirits: Dickens's Childhood Reading," *Dickensian*, Vol. LXI, No. 3 (Sept., 1965), 150–54.

permanence of his juvenile reading, the imaginary and the fairylike are in some ways more familiar than daily reality.

On emerging from infancy, particularly in William Giles's school at Chatham, Dickens became acquainted with loftier literary works. The poems he learned at that stage can be traced through his own works; they are few, and generally very well-known ones. He seems to have quoted no poems of earlier date than those of Isaac Watts; the eighteenth century is represented by two ironical references to Pope,[14] one mention of Crabbe ("I could not but think . . . of Crabbe's musings over the Parish Register"),[15] one of Collins,[16] and two humorous adaptations of the celebrated line by James Thomson: "To teach the young idea how to shoot." These are fairly characteristic of the way in which Dickens makes purely verbal use of a few words taken from a universally known passage; the reader's amusement results from mixed sensations of familiarity and incongruity: "a disciple of that school of trainers of the young idea which holds that childhood . . . must be shaken and rattled"[17] (here the allusion consists merely in the words "the young idea" being used as an equivalent of "children"); "Mrs. Pocket taught the young idea how to shoot by shooting it into bed whenever it attracted her notice."[18]

Of the Romantics, Dickens seems to have known a few poems only; he alludes once (again, humorously) to a line by Wordsworth,[19] and three times to the *Ancient Mariner*. Two of these allusions are to be found in the same novel and concern the same line, the last but one and one of the most famous in that famous poem: "Becoming a sadder and a wiser man he mused and held his peace," and later, ". . . resumes Cousin Feenix in a graver tone, as if he had suddenly become a sadder and a wiser man";[20] the third is almost a unique case in Dickens' work and a curious phenomenon, for Dickens paraphrases Coleridge's text, not in order to ridicule it, but on the contrary to make it still more poetical: "a solitude which has no parallel but in the thirst of the shipwrecked

14 *MC*, chap. xxxvii; *RP, The Noble Savage.*
15 *AN*, chap. ix.
16 *GE*, chap. vii.
17 *D&S*, chap. iii.
18 *GE*, chap. xxxiv.
19 *CB, Carol*, chap. ii.
20 *D&S*, chaps. iv and xxxi.

mariner, who, tossed to and fro upon the billows of a mighty ocean, his red eyes blinded by looking on the water which hems him in on every side, has not a drop to cool his burning tongue."[21] The end of the sentence is a perfect iambic pentameter ("has not a drop to cool his burning tongue"), but few will think it superior to the poet's simple line "Nor any drop to drink."

In fact, Dickens realizes that deliberate poetical quotations, such as are used by essayists and other writers of the careful, or even ornate, style, would be out of place in his own works. His attitude is clearly illustrated by the case of three characters: Dick Swiveller in *The Old Curiosity Shop*, Silas Wegg in *Our Mutual Friend*, and Mr. Micawber in *David Copperfield*. Quotations as well as bombastic circumlocutions and turgid metaphors are constantly being used by these characters in conversation, and, by the last named, in letter-writing. It is thus obvious that Dickens has intended to ridicule the use made by them of such borrowed riches and to show through their example how easy it is to adorn one's style with these spurious decorations, even out of the thinnest fund of knowledge. Mr. Micawber's quotations, ever pompously introduced into his letters and speeches, are always of the tritest. He will quote Gray's *Elegy* or Goldsmith's *Traveller*, but most of his references are taken from *Auld Lang Syne*, the work, as he says, of "the Immortal Exciseman nurtured beyond the Tweed,"[22] yet this work, for him as well as for Dickens, belongs to the field of popular songs much rather than to that of literature.

The eighteenth-century novel of course has its place in Dickens' reading. Students of Dickens' reading generally support their conclusions chiefly by means of a famous passage in *Copperfield*,[23] the strictly autobiographical value of which is confirmed by Forster,[24] and where the books read by David-Dickens in childhood are enumerated. The list comprises *Roderick Random, Peregrine Pickle, Humphrey Clinker, Tom Jones, The Vicar of Wakefield, Don Quixote, Gil Blas,* and *Robinson Crusoe.* It is completed, later, by mentions of *The Arabian Nights* and *The Tales of the Genii.* The very order in which the list is drawn

21 *OCS*, chap. xliv.
22 *DC*, chap. xlix.
23 Chap. iv.
24 *Life of Dickens,* I, 7.

up has significance: three of Smollett's novels come first, and Defoe's masterpiece is placed at the end; the authors mentioned between the two great figures all occupy a slightly inferior position. The allusions contained in other novels, and a few unquestionable marks of the influence of Dickens' predecessors in his own field confirm the impression left by *Copperfield*.

There is an additional reference to *Don Quixote* in the Preface to *Nickleby*, and Le Sage is mentioned in *American Notes*.[25] To Goldsmith, Dickens was indirectly indebted for his pen-name, Boz, and *The Vicar of Wakefield* is also mentioned in another chapter of *American Notes*.[26]

Sterne, to whom the origin of the Dickensian pathos has been ascribed,[27] must have been less familiar to Dickens, or less keenly enjoyed by him, than the other writers of the same period. Yet, before going to work on *The Uncommercial Traveller*, the general purpose and title of which irresistibly recall Sterne's *Sentimental Journey*, Dickens may have reread the book, for he mentions it twice. But at that stage, his childhood reading is no longer necessarily a factor. Richardson's name is quoted in the *Sketches* when we find a character who "looked something like a vignette to one of Richardson's novels, and had a clean-cravatish formality of manner, and kitchen-pokerness of carriage, which Sir Charles Grandison himself might have envied!"[28] Swift is represented in Dickens' work by one comparison which may have been due to reminiscence,[29] and by one direct allusion which contains some interesting aspects. In *American Notes* (chap. ix), he writes, "That travelled creation of the great satirist's brain, who fresh from living among horses, peered from a high casement down upon his own kind with trembling horror." Without pausing to comment on the conventional triteness of expressions like "the great satirist" for "Swift," or "creation of the brain" for "character," or the pretentious tone of the epithet "travelled,"

---

25 Chap. xii.

26 Chap. vii; *Boz* was a corruption, through childish pronunciation, of *Moses*.

27 "Of his pathos, so far as it has a literary source, Sterne is the father," W. L. Cross, *The Development of the English Novel* (N.Y. 1899), 186.

28 *SB*, "Tales," chap. x; such a purely external allusion does not even prove that Dickens had read the book.

29 See *GE*, chap. xl, in which one sentence is strongly reminiscent of Swift's *Meditation upon a Broomstick*.

35

it is useful to turn to Swift's own text, which runs as follows: "I ventured to look out of the back window. By degrees, I was brought into another room, whence I peeped into the street, but drew my head back in a fright."[30] Dickens' memory thus appears to have strangely altered the passage; he replaces "peep" by the more lugubrious "peer"; he turns an ordinary "back window" into a more refined and impressive "high casement"; and he considerably intensifies the mild expression "in a fright," which becomes in his text "with trembling horror." All of these transformations, especially when they are taken in connection with his similar treatment of Coleridge, are significant.

Walter Scott is mentioned, and a commonplace tribute is paid to him by Dickens, who calls him "the great writer,"[31] but his influence has not been very notable, except perhaps in the case of *Rudge*.

Dickens' admiration for *Robinson Crusoe* is more genuine, more striking, more often asserted, partly perhaps because this was undoubtedly one of the books Dickens had thoroughly enjoyed as a child, so that his fond recollection of Crusoe was at the same time a fond recollection of the child he had himself been.[32] A long passage in *The Uncommercial Traveller* is devoted to *Crusoe*. Many of Dickens' references to *Crusoe* could have been made by a writer who, without having read it, knew only the outline of the story: "My aunt, like a female Robinson Crusoe," or "more solitary than Robinson Crusoe, who had nobody to look at him."[33] Rather more convincing is the description of an "airy rustic dwelling, that brought De Foe's description of such places strongly to my recollection,"[34] while other allusions tend to show that Dickens mainly remembered minor facts likely to have struck the imagination of a child or a simple-minded person: "the sort of impromptu arrangements that might have suggested themselves to Robinson Crusoe,"[35] "a kind o' Robinson Crusoe set o' steps, as he could let down when he got out,"[36] an image to be

[30] *Gulliver's Travels*, chap. xi.

[31] *CHE*, chap. xxxi.

[32] An identical phenomenon is admirably analyzed by François Mauriac, *Nouveaux Mémoires Intérieurs* (Paris, 1965).

[33] *DC*, chaps. xxxiv and v; the fact that there are four allusions to *Crusoe* in *DC* alone seems to show that Dickens had reread the book, or perhaps seen it in his children's hands, about 1849.

[34] *AN*, chap. ix.

[35] *MC*, chap. xxxvi.

[36] *PP*, chap. xliv.

found again in *Copperfield:* "to feel, when I shut my outer door, like Robinson Crusoe, when he had got into his fortification, and pulled his ladder up after him."[37] The passage containing the most precise allusion (to one of the best known incidents in Defoe's book) is the description of Miss Slowboy and her legs: she "never effected the smallest ascent or descent, without recording the circumstance upon them, with a notch, as Robinson Crusoe marked the days upon his wooden calendar."[38] It is on the whole striking to find from this example that, out of a book he knew well and quoted often, Dickens did not draw any important materials, but mere familiar allusions and easily recognizable analogies.

It has been seen that at the beginning of *Copperfield* he had given to Smollett a higher place than to any other of the writers he had read in childhood. Other passages of his works confirm the part played by Smollett and Fielding in Dickens' literary formation. There are few direct allusions (far fewer than in the case of *Crusoe,* for instance), but they are much warmer and more intimately associated with the author's emotional life; for example, "when I was a not very robust child, sitting in by-places, near Rochester Castle, with my head full of Partridge, Straps, Tom Pipes and Sancho Panza."[39] Among Smollett's novels, *Roderick Random* seems to have been Dickens' favorite: it is mentioned twice in *Copperfield* and a more detailed reference will be found in *The Uncommercial Traveller:* "Through many changes and much work, I had preserved a tenderness for the memory of Joe, forasmuch as we had made the acquaintance of Roderick Random together, and had believed him to be no ruffian, but an ingenuous and engaging hero."[40] Dickens' preference for Smollett is asserted by J. T. Fields: "He preferred Smollett to Fielding, putting 'Peregrine Pickle' above 'Tom Jones' "[41] and this sentimental attachment corresponds to a clearly marked literary influence, mostly in Dickens' early writings. It was from Fielding, however, that he borrowed the epigraph of *Oliver Twist,* his first real novel, and it was Fielding's, not Smollett's, name that he gave his most gifted son, Henry Fielding Dickens. His indebtedness to Fielding and Smollett

---

[37] Chap. xxiv.
[38] *CB, Cricket,* chap. ii.
[39] *NN,* Preface.
[40] Chap. xii.
[41] James T. Fields, *Yesterdays with Authors* (Boston, 1872), 239.

is considerable, and insofar as he has been any other writer's disciple, he has been theirs, more or less collectively: in the same way as his own contemporaries tended to associate Thackeray's fame with his, or even to get them mixed up, as in the anecdote of the man who spoke of "Thackens and Dickery," or "Thickens and Dackeray," Dickens' grati- tude went to "Smolling and Fieldett." Yet, unlike his avowed indebt- edness to Henry Mackenzie,[42] he did not so much choose to follow their example as become imbued with their fiction as a very youthful reader.

Popular literature (legends and songs) provides a fifth category. Among the works quoted by Dickens which must be examined here, however briefly, because they played some part in his formation, many stand at a very inferior level, far below *Roderick Random* or *Robinson Crusoe*. He was acquainted with all the most popular forms of liter- ature. Among his fellow laborers at the blacking factory, or even among the errand boys at the solicitors' office, Smollett may not have been too familiar. On the other hand, Dickens had learned singing at an early age, and the popular songs contemporary with his youth also provide his novels with many ready allusions.

Joe Miller's Jests, or the Wits' Vade-Mecum,[43] a small collection of a few hundred witticisms, some of them extremely coarse, must have been relished by Dickens, who, until 1842, frequently refers to it: "the wandering Jew of Joe Millerism," "an Astley-Cooperish Joe Miller," "like Mr. Joe Miller's Frenchman," or "your talented and witty coun- tryman, Mr. Miller."[44]

Mention is made in addition of "the sixpenny history (with highly- coloured folding frontispiece) of Mr. Daniel Dancer," and of "certain interminable novels . . . over some of which I remember to have shed innumerable tears before I had served my apprenticeship to life"; these show that Dickens had really absorbed every kind of literary or sub- literary fodder.

The songs and ballads quoted by him are numerous. His references are sometimes to the lyrics: "When we say a shed, we do not mean the

[42] See the *NN* chapter in this book.
[43] John Mottley (London, 1739).
[44] *MC*, chap. xxii. Amy Richards, in "The Honourable Mr. Miller" (*The Dickensian,* Vol. LXI, No. 1 [Jan., 1965], 27–29) has attempted, with more ingenuity than success, to demonstrate that this particular reference must have been to *Hugh* Miller, a geologist.

conservatory sort of building, which, according to the old song, Love tenanted when he was a young man";[45] "Tamaroo . . . a word from an old English ballad";[46] "there's a song that says 'I'd crowns resign, to call her mine!' I hope to do it, one of these days!"[47] Sometimes, too, they are visual, as when the song mentioned is one of which Dickens has had the printed text in his hands: "The compound figure of Death and the Lady at the top of the old ballad was not divided with a greater nicety . . . than the two profiles of Zephaniah Scadder."[48] They are much more rarely auditive: "a novel air, compounded of 'Bay of Biscay' and 'A Frog he would.' "[49]

When he refers to songs, ballads, or legends that are better known his allusions are both more precise and more concise: "this Gilpinian triumvirate,"[50] he will write; or, concerning Dick Whittington, who, like Jack Horner or Robinson Crusoe, is a great favorite of his: "since the time of noble Whittington, fair flower of merchants"; "you remind me of Whittington, afterwards thrice Mayor of London"; "he was a perfect Whittington, without his cat, or the remotest chance of being made Lord Mayor"; "the case of his being reserved, like Whittington, to become Lord Mayor of London."[51]

The popular literature of the stage was also known to Dickens. His friend Percy Fitzgerald refers to one interesting example: "he knew all the familiar ones [songs] . . . as in the case of 'When the wind blows,' at the opening of 'The Miller and his Men.' "[52] *The Miller and his Men* is a two-act play performed in 1822, and the case demonstrates the close link that existed for Dickens between songs and the drama. A tireless reader of novels, a tireless lover of songs, he was also, whenever he could afford it, a tireless spectator of popular theatrical performances and maintained a lifelong, manifold, passionate interest in the theater.

45 *SB*, "Scenes," chap. xx.
46 *MC*, chap. xxxii.
47 *DC*, chap. xxv.
48 *MC*, chap. xxi; also *PFI*, "Genoa."
49 *PP*, chap. xxxii.
50 *UT*, chap. xxxv.
51 *BR*, chap. xxxi; *MC*, chap. vii; *DC*, chap. xlviii; and *BH*, chap. xxxi.
52 Percy Fitzgerald, *The Life of Dickens as Revealed in His Writings* (London, 1905), 219. Fitzgerald also relates how disappointed Dickens was, shortly before the end of his life, by a revival of the old play: "It was not absurd, it was simply tedious—there was nothing to laugh at." *Recreations of a Literary Man* (London, 1882), II, 141.

The stage occupies in his life and work a position which is the exact opposite of that held by Parliament. Of Parliament as of the theater, and of the popular theater in particular, Dickens had an early and intimate knowledge, but whereas Parliament inspired him with immediate, incurable disgust, the stage exerted over him a constant fascination, to which he yielded willingly and often, and which ruled the final years of his life. This fascination he analyzes while recalling the end of a performance he had witnessed as a child: "Now too, I perceive my first experience of the dreary sensation—often to return in after-life—of being unable, next day, to get back to the dull, settled world; of wanting to live forever in the bright atmosphere I have quitted."[53]

The stage almost invariably finds in him an indulgent appraiser. He alludes to plays of every description, like *Raymond and Agnes, or the Bleeding Nun*, a drama performed in 1825; *Monsieur Tonson*, a farce by W. T. Moncrieff (1821); *The Dog of Montargis*; Kotzebue's *The Stranger; Jack's Delight is his Lovely Nan*. Yet, once more, Dickens has one favorite play: it is George Lillo's *The London Merchant, or the History of George Barnwell* (1731), which he must have seen as a child and from which he quotes many times, usually with ironical comments on the personality of the chief character: "that interesting, though somewhat rash young gentleman, George Barnwell."[54] "Never mind George Barnwell," Sam Weller says, and adds, ". . . the young 'oman deserved scragging a precious sight more than he did";[55] and for Sim Tappertit, the ambitious apprentice, "a stigma had been cast upon the body by the execution of George Barnwell."[56] Other allusions are also to be found in *Chuzzlewit*, in "A Christmas Tree," while in *Great Expectations*, the reading of the *London Merchant* by Mr. Wopsle is a choice episode.[57]

It is not only on account of such brief descriptions and allusions that the drama plays an important part in Dickens' work. It will be seen that it exerted an influence also on his style, on his psychological outlook, and on his plots. From that point of view, the dramatic elements should

[53] *CS, Christmas Tree.*
[54] *SB,* "Tales," chap. v.
[55] *PP,* chap. x.
[56] *BR,* chap. iv.
[57] *GE,* chap. xv.

not be forgotten if one wishes to understand the Dickensian technique. Recent criticism by both Robert Garis and Edward Wagenknecht[58] has emphasized this fact. The influence has by no means been always felicitous; for the plays most familiar to the young Dickens had most often been mediocre and vulgar. The actors he had seen made great use of pantomimic gesticulation, for which the novelist ever felt keen admiration and which he liked to describe in some of his characters: "the young gentleman, having expressed the bitterness of his contrition by affecting to wipe away scalding tears with his apron, and afterwards feigning to wring a vast amount of water from that garment . . . ."[59] The plots were often strained and melodramatic; it is only fair to ascribe something of the same defect, when we meet it in the Dickensian novel, to the influence of that popular drama. Fortunately, in one direction at least, the memory of many mediocre performances was to supply the novels and stories with equally numerous passages of a high order, for the clear-sighted yet benevolent description of such performances, the friendly denunciation of the conventional artificiality, stressing the contrast between purpose and achievement, is often irresistibly funny, as in the following example: "Many wondrous secrets of nature had I come to the knowledge of in that sanctuary: of which not the least terrific were, that the witches in Macbeth bore an awful resemblance to the Thanes and other proper inhabitants of Scotland; and that the good King Duncan couldn't rest in his grave, but was constantly coming out of it, and calling himself somebody else."[60] The conclusion of the passage is characteristic: "To the theatre, therefore, I repaired for consolation."

In any examination of Dickens' sources, Shakespeare has to be placed in a category by himself because of his particular importance, but he has to be placed fairly close to the popular theater, because Dickens became acquainted with his works in the same way he came to know the lower forms of drama—on the stage. Such is the conclusion one is inevitably

[58] See Robert Garis, *The Dickens Theatre: A Reassessment of the Novels* (Oxford, 1965), and Edward Wagenknecht, "Dickens and Katherine Mansfield," *Dickens and the Scandalmongers* (Norman, 1965).
[59] *MC*, chap. xi.
[60] *UT*, chap. xii.

led to by studying the Shakespearean quotations and references in his works.

This does not mean that Dickens never *read* Shakespeare, especially after he had become a literary figure himself; he reports that, in Verona, he read *Romeo and Juliet* in his hotel room (and adds, ironically, "of course no Englishman had ever read it there before");[61] yet, when Thomas Wright called him "an ardent Shakespearian,"[62] the phrase was conspicuously misleading. Dickens was a Shakespearean only in the sense that he never tired of attending new performances of the great plays; but he was not one of those who know Shakespeare's works inside out; he despised scholarly research devoted to the playwright's biography,[63] and it can be shown that he did not feel the true Shakespearean reverence.[64]

His Shakespearean knowledge is not strikingly wide; he evinces knowledge of several plays: *Othello, Julius Caesar, Coriolanus;* but the majority of his references are to two plays that have always been among the most popular in the canon, *Hamlet* and *Macbeth*. To these two his allusions are frequent.

With the exception of one interesting quotation, they are of two kinds only, words and visual images.[65] The interesting exception is the quotation from *Macbeth* made by Steerforth in *Copperfield*, with its accompanying commentary. It is perfectly apposite and gives evidence of some literary refinement. Besides, it is typographically detached from the rest of his speech, and thus placed in relief. Finally, it is not entirely

---

[61] *PFI,* "To Verona."

[62] *The Life of Charles Dickens* (London, 1935), 242.

[63] See the titles chosen by Dickens for the dummy book backs hiding a door in his library at Gadshill: *"Was Shakespeare's Mother Fair?* (4 vols.); *Had Shakespeare's Uncle a Singing Face?* (5 vols.); *Was Shakespeare's Father Merry?* (6 vols.),"* R. Langton, *The Childhood and Youth of Dickens* (London, 1912), 126.

[64] See in *NN,* chap. xxvii, Mrs. Wittiterly's exclamation: "Shakespeare is such a delicious creature!" and in *MC,* chap. xxviii, a Dickensian. aristocrat's comment: "Shakespeare's an infernal humbug . . . . There's a lot of feet in Shakespeare's verse, but there arn't any legs worth mentioning." Admittedly the two passages are unequivocal caricatures, yet wouldn't an "ardent Shakespearian" have regarded such attitudes as unworthy even of being caricatured?

[65] No allusion will be found in Dickens similar to Thackeray's in *Vanity Fair* (chap. iii): "If you had told Sycorax that her son Caliban was as handsome as Apollo . . ." Sycorax has no existence for Dickens as a character in *The Tempest*, since she does not appear on the stage.

commonplace.[66] Steerforth is almost the only Dickens character who goes to a university; he stands as the representative of the upper middle class, with the highest possible amount of culture. It is as though the author had wished to hint that he was capable, if necessary, of quoting Shakespeare in the same way as more learned writers did and that if he did not do so it was because he thought it preferable, and in better taste, not to do it.

The verbal allusions are usually introduced for a humorous purpose, and in that case they concern the most celebrated passages. What does Dickens draw from Hamlet's soliloquy, for instance? On one hand the poetical conclusion of the first chapter in *Copperfield*: "the light upon the window of our room shone out upon the earthly bourne of all such travellers." Here the allusion consists of a mere alliance between the words "bourne" and "traveller," without any reference to the Shakespearean idea. On the other hand, he uses the idea when he plays with that same soliloquy in making two jokes: "Conscience made cowards of us both,[67] [David says when Mr. Waterbrook's valet and himself pretend not to know each other]," or "if I am gone to that what's-his-name from which no thingumbob comes back."[68]

Similarly, in the case of *Macbeth*, Dickens has Mr. Squeers exclaim: "What's come of my milk of human kindness? It turns into curds and whey when I look at him."[69] Mr. Crisparkle "would go out, as confident in the sweetening powers of Cloisterham Weir and a wholesome mind, as Lady Macbeth was hopeless of those of all the seas that roll,"[70] and Mr. Micawber declares: "Then it was that I began, if I may so Shakespearianly express myself, to dwindle, peak and pine."[71] In none of these examples does Dickens borrow from Shakespeare the shade of a single

---

66 " 'So much for that!' he said, making as if he tossed something light into the air, with his hand.

> Why, being gone, I am a man again,

like Macbeth. And now for the dinner! If I have not (Macbeth-like) broken up the feast with most admired disorder, Daisy,' " (*DC*, chap. xxii). Even here, the quotation may well have been suggested to Dickens' mind by the gesture he describes, which may have called up a vision of an actor's play in this scene.

67 *DC*, chap. xxv.

68 *MC*, chap. iv.

69 *NN*, chap. xxxviii; see also *MC*, chap. iii.

70 *ED*, chap. x.

71 *DC*, chap. lii.

idea: he takes from the plays only words and images, some of which owe more to the actor (and more especially to the poor actor) than to the dramatist. Nothing but superficial familiarity with performance rather than with text is evinced, for instance, by the following allusions: " 'With a marriage!' gasped Hicks, compared with whose expression of countenance Hamlet's when he sees his father's ghost is pleasing and composed";[72] "the most domestic and confidential garments of coachmen and their wives usually hung, like Macbeth's banners, on the outward wall";[73] Jasper's housekeeper's face "looked to me as if it were all disturbed by fiery air, like the faces I had seen rise out of the Witches' caldron";[74] a valet's leg is "always lingering after he and the tray had disappeared, like Macbeth's leg when accompanying him off the stage with reluctance to the assassination of Duncan."[75]

The exact extent and limitations of Dickens' general culture are revealed to us not only by the works and the facts he quotes or shows his knowledge of, but also by his attitude toward the various branches of human learning. His biographers tell us that his mother (unlike Mrs. Micawber in that respect, since the latter confused "Experientia docet" with "Experientia does it") had taught him a little Latin,[76] and that in Jones' school in London he had studied mostly mathematics, history; Latin and dancing.[77] Those studies, which, apart from the last-named one, obviously contributed to the fashioning of his mind, have left but little trace in his work. Dickens is much readier to quote the favorite figures mentioned in the preceding sections (Jack Horner, Robinson, Joe Miller, Hamlet's father's ghost or George Barnwell) than the heroes and deities of Greece and Rome. In the *Sketches* will be found one reference to Jupiter's daughter,[78] and a real vulgarization (in the least laudatory sense of the term) of the story of Damon and Pythias. The tone of the paragraph concerning them will occasion no regret over Dickens' almost complete abandonment of this kind of allusion in his

[72] *SB*, "Tales," chap. i.
[73] *D&S*, chap. vii.
[74] *GE*, chap. xxvi.
[75] *ED*, chap. xi; see also *OMF*, Book III, chaps. x and xvi. The allusion to "Hamlet's aunt" in *DC*, chap. xxv, is, however, slightly more refined.
[76] Forster, *Life of Dickens*, I, 6.
[77] Edgar Johnson, *Ch. D.: Tragedy & Triumph*, 48–49.
[78] "Jane, the Hebe of Bellamy's," *SB*, "Scenes," chap. xviii.

later works,[79] since it begins as follows: Damon and Pythias were undoubtedly very good fellows in their way: the former for his extreme readiness to put in special bail for a friend, and the latter for a certain trump-like punctuality in turning up just in the very nick of time."[80] A passing remark in *Bleak House* (1852) is illuminating of the deliberate nature of the later attitude: "How Alexander wept when he had no more worlds to conquer, everybody knows—or has some reason to know by this time, the matter having been rather frequently mentioned."[81] For Dickens, therefore, illustrations taken from ancient literature are no more than contemptible commonplaces, evincing more poverty of imagination than wealth of culture.

With regard to the whole historical past, he feels a lack of respect amounting at times to contempt, but his position in this respect is reminiscent rather of the self-satisfied ignoramus than of the disillusioned dilettante. When Mr. Dick asks David: " 'I suppose history never lies, does it?' . . . 'Oh, dear, no, sir!' I replied, most decisively. I was ingenuous and young, and I thought so."[82] What is suggested here is fairly obvious: since only young and ingenuous people can believe that history never lies, and since in fact historians do often lie, one need not take the trouble of reading their works. Besides, they can teach us nothing. For Dickens, the wisdom of our ancestors was composed of seven parts only: "I. Ignorance.—II. Superstition.—III. The Block.—IV. The Stake.—V. The Rack.—VI. Dirt.—VII. Disease."[83] In the face of history and the past an infirmity of Dickens is manifested most glaringly: what he himself called "some imperfect development of my organ of veneration."[84] Yet it would be unfair not to mention in this place his conscientious research into the history of the Gordon Riots before writing *Barnaby Rudge*, and of the French Revolution before

---

[79] There are two allusions to Marius on the ruins of Carthage (*D&S*, chap. ix; and *UT*, chap. xiv: "like that lumbering Marius on the ruins of Carthage, who has sat heavy on a thousand million of similes"), one to Laocoon (*CB*, *Christmas Carol*, chap. v) and one to Prometheus (*UT*, chap. xiv).

[80] *SB*, "Characters," chap. xi.

[81] Chap. ii.

[82] *DC*, chap. xvii.

[83] Dummy book backs at Gadshill; the series was called "The Wisdom of our Ancestors"; see Langton, *Childhood & Youth of Ch. D.*, 126.

[84] *AN*, chap. viii.

writing *A Tale of Two Cities,* together with his keen enjoyment of Carlyle's *French Revolution.*

Dickens must have learned some French at school; yet he soon gave up the habit of using French words as ornaments of his English prose, another of those journalist's mannerisms practiced by so many of his contemporaries, including Thackeray. He certainly read in English translations the few French writers mentioned in his fiction: Le Sage, Madame Roland, Voltaire, Buffon, and perhaps La Fontaine. In later life, he was to give proof of a creditable ability to learn foreign languages (to the point of speaking some Italian and of chattering in French with tolerable fluency and writing letters in decent French), but he wisely refrained from letting this freshly-acquired knowledge interfere with his writing of English prose.

Dickens' artistic culture seems to have been also very limited. Only two painters are mentioned in his novels: Adrian Van Ostade, and Hogarth, for whom he often expressed admiration and with whose work he was quite familiar. He was to form friendships with several of the leading English painters of his own time, but he never pretended that he could understand or judge their work, and about painting in general he expressed his views, such as they were, with engaging frankness: "I am not mechanically acquainted with the art of painting, and have no other means of judging of a picture than as I see it resembling and refining upon nature, and presenting graceful combinations of forms and colours."[85] John Forster's opinion of Dickens' attitude as a visitor to the Italian galleries and museums could be applied to the many other large departments of culture of which the novelist had only the most superficial and rudimentary kind of knowledge: "He saw everything for himself. And from mistakes in judging for himself which not all the learning and study in the world will save common men, the intuition of genius almost always saved him."[86]

The intuition of genius certainly went a long way. Yet, it was only "almost always" that it could save Dickens from self-betrayal when he ventured outside his favorite fields. These, fortunately, were extensive; but they did not comprise very much of what is generally known as culture.

85 *PFI,* "To Verona." 86 *Life of Dickens,* I, 348.

IX: The Awakening of the Writer's Vocation

Perhaps the most consistent criticism of Dickens both by his contemporaries and by later commentators concerns his lack of intellectual background in his formative years and his continued indifference to acquiring such a background. A sampling of the comments by his contemporaries illustrates how early this criticism occurs:

> Thought is strangely absent from his works. I do not suppose a single thoughtful remark on life or character could be found throughout the twenty volumes.[1]

> He is utterly deficient in the faculty of reasoning. . . . He is often troubled with the idea that he must reflect, and his reflections are, perhaps, the worst reading in the world.[2]

> Les idées chez Dickens sont rares et faibles.[3]

> Perhaps, properly speaking, he had no *ideas* on any subject.[4]

Other writers, mostly of later date, have stressed his lack of interest in a wide variety of subjects, and his lack, in short, of curiosity, or at any rate of intellectual curiosity:

> For a professional man of letters, he was unusually little the student or even reader. . . . his rather complacent ignorance of more than mere literature.[5]

> He had no capacity for meditation, none for mere reasoning; he had no longing to deepen or extend his mental powers by varied culture, either by means of study or conversation.[6]

> [about his correspondence] We doubt if as many letters of the men worthy to be ranked as his compeers could be collected which would

---

[1] G. H. Lewes in *Fortnightly Review*, Feb., 1872, quoted by Kitton in *Dickensiana*, 417.

[2] W. Bagehot, "Charles Dickens," *National Review*, Oct., 1858, p. 465.

[3] E. Hennequin, *Ecrivains Francisés*, Paris, 1889, p. 49. "Ideas in Dickens are few and feeble."

[4] George Santayana, *Soliloquies in England* (London, 1922), 59.

[5] Walter C. Phillips, *Dickens, Reade and Collins: Sensation Novelists* (New York, 1919), 153.

[6] *Fraser's Magazine*, Jan., 1872, 113.

show such a limited concern for the world in which he personally played no part.[7]

But many critics understood that it was idle to separate so completely the man from his works, and that the existence of the novels, admirable, or at least admired, as they were, compelled one either to deny them high literary value, or to admit that the author's lack of culture and intellectual curiosity had paradoxically played a formative part. The former attitude is Frederic Harrison's: "no doubt, this utter severance from books, which we feel in his tales, will ultimately tell against their immortality."[8] It is also, to a lesser extent, Gissing's: "that his lack of education . . . shows from time to time as a disadvantage in his books there is no denying."[9] The latter attitude came to be more and more frequently, more and more openly adopted; it is to be found in W. S. Lilly's comments: "His ignorance of the great literary traditions of the western world threw him back upon himself, upon his own observation, his own experience, his own creative gift";[10] in Andrew Lang's: "as he owed all to native genius and hard work, he owed almost nothing to literature, and that little we regret";[11] and in George Orwell's: "Dickens had had little or no formal education, but he lost nothing by missing it, and on the whole he seems to have been aware of this."[12]

The problem raised here—of Dickens' opinion about his own education—is an interesting one. I tend to believe that he did not ask himself the question, that he accepted the training he had in part received and in part given himself as a fact, happy or the reverse, but in any case both accidental and definitive, and he did not feel called upon to try to modify it deliberately. I am convinced that for him the problem was not one of education or even of abilities, but of vocation. When he became a writer, Dickens thus did not ask himself whether he had sufficient culture and sufficient maturity to write well and usefully; he

[7] W. C. Brownell, *The Nation*, Dec. 4, 1879, p. 389.

[8] *Dickens's Place in Literature* (London, n.d.), 19.

[9] *Charles Dickens, a Critical Study* (London, 1898), 18–19.

[10] *Four English Humourists*, 17. G. Stott (quoted by Kitton, *Dickensiana*, 133) had already written in *The Contemporary*, 1864: "It is no more than natural that he should show no signs of having imitated or been influenced by writers whom he had never read."

[11] *Essays in Little* (London, 1912), 131.

[12] "Ch. Dickens," *Critical Essays*, 20.

was obeying an irresistible inner call. If there is in *David Copperfield* one passage whose tone of lucid, eager sincerity proves its autobiographical nature, it is David's analysis of the motivations which led him to turn himself into a novelist or, as one might almost put it, to let himself be turned into one:

> Having some foundation for believing, by this time, that nature and accident had made me an author, I pursued my vocation with confidence. Without such assurance I should certainly have left it alone, and bestowed my energy on some other endeavour. I should have tried to find out what nature and accident had made me, and to be that—and nothing else.[13]

Because he felt that nature and circumstance had made him a writer, Dickens irrevocably determined to be a writer and to be nothing else, without contemplating the possible need for completing his culture or submitting himself to the schooling of other authors. In fact, it has been judged by some that he was already "splendidly equipped"[14] to enter the literary life, and it is striking to find how adequately George Eliot's definition of those she regards as "the most fortunate Britons" fits Dickens' case:

> I have always thought that the most fortunate Britons are those whose experience has given them a practical share in many aspects of the national lot, who have lived long among the mixed commonalty, roughing it with them under difficulties, knowing how their food tastes to them, and getting acquainted with their notions and motives not by inference from traditional types in literature or from philosophical theories, but from daily fellowship and observation.[15]

Certainly, most of the views quoted in the above paragraphs, such as that Dickens did not and could not think, will appear immensely outdated now that he has finally come into his own as one of the truly great writers of England. Yet, even if he were still to be taken at the

---

[13] Chap. xlviii.
[14] A. Maurois, *Un Essai sur Dickens* (Paris, 1927), 25.
[15] G. Eliot, *The Impressions of Theophrastus Such,* chap. ii.

lowest possible intellectual valuation, no one ought to question the right he had, or sincerely thought he had, to become an author. Such was his vocation.

X: Literary Apprenticeship: *Sketches by Boz*

The question may well be asked on what grounds *Sketches by Boz*, which of course is not a novel, should be discussed in a study of the Dickensian novel. But this uneven, imperfect collection holds a privileged place in Dickens' career. Though they lack artistic unity and maturity to the point of still forming part of the period of apprenticeship, the *Sketches* represent an important stage in Dickens' life: they are on the threshold, nay, they are themselves the threshold of his literary career. That is why it is useful to examine them here. And this dress rehearsal before the real "opening night" of the Dickensian work will enable us to complete the history of the formative years and to catch a brief glimpse of the human as well as literary personality of the man who was going to become the author of *Pickwick Papers.*

The first of the *Sketches* appeared in 1833 in the *Monthly Magazine*, unsigned, and Dickens received no pay for it. It was followed by several more, on the same terms. The name Boz was not used until August, 1834. More *Sketches* were published in the *Morning Chronicle*,[1] the daily newspaper then employing Dickens as shorthand reporter, and later in the *Evening Chronicle*, where they were received on the recommendation of George Hogarth, the father of the future Mrs. Charles Dickens and her sisters. These early pieces attracted attention from a few well-known critics like Albany Fonblanque, S. C. Hall, and William Jerdan and from writers like W. H. Ainsworth, who invited young Boz to meet the publisher Macrone. By January, 1835, on the strength of the sketches published during the last twelve months, Dickens had already gained enough reputation for Macrone to prevail on N. P. Willis, the American journalist, to include Boz among his interviews of the celebrities of the day. A few months later, it was again Macrone who suggested that Dickens collect the pick of the articles and stories he had so far published separately and undertake to print them. A selec-

[1] Including the series of *Street Sketches* (Sept., 1834).

tion was made, fresh sketches were composed specifically to increase the bulk of the forthcoming work, the help of a well-known artist, George Cruikshank, was secured, and *Sketches by Boz* appeared on the seventh of February, 1836, Dickens' twenty-fourth birthday and only a few weeks before the first issue of *Pickwick* and the author's marriage with Catherine Hogarth.

The book, which in later editions was to undergo only minor alterations, was composed of four parts. "Our Parish" had seven chapters, which together made up approximately one-tenth of the whole. "Scenes" consisted of twenty-five sketches, three-tenths of the book. "Characters" had twelve chapters, a bit more than one-tenth. Twelve "Tales," of uneven length, made up about one half of the work. The division into four parts is formal rather than justified by the reality of their contents. In "Our Parish" there are portraits and short tales. The "Characters" also tend to develop into brief tales, and their separate titles often show how artificial is the general designation of this category: "Thoughts about People," "The New Year," "The Dancing Academy," etc. The "Scenes" are on the whole more in keeping with what they claim to be, although, as will be seen, Dickens often subordinates observation to imagination, and the title of Chapter VI, "Meditations in Monmouth Street," suggests how far he could stray from mere observation. As to the "Tales," their web is often very thin.

Still more striking is the absence, in the fifty-six sketches as a whole, of any unity of tone and inspiration. Most of them, admittedly, deal with London life, particularly among the lower middle class and the poorer, if not quite working-class, sections of the community. The complete title of the book in fact refers to this aspect: *Sketches by Boz: Illustrative of Everyday Life and Everyday People*. No one will think of resenting the youthful author's choice, as the theme of his first book, of the kind of life he was best acquainted with. What he failed to do was to choose one attitude and adhere to it. He did not quite know what he wished us to think of his figures. Should we laugh at them, despise them, pity them, admire them sometimes? As yet Dickens has clearly not made up his own mind.

Such as they were, the *Sketches* achieved great success. Later readers cannot easily account for it. There are undoubtedly in the book many passages that one still reads and rereads with pleasure, and if a list had to be drawn up of the best in *Sketches by Boz*, it would probably comprise the charming story of "The Four Sisters," the little London adventures described in three of the "Scenes" (chaps. xv, xvi, xvii), the moving pages devoted to a prison ("Scenes," chap. xxv) and a hospital ("Characters," chap. vi), and three or four other amusing stories ("Characters," chaps. vii and viii; "Tales," chaps. ii and iv). The rest is not uniformly disappointing, yet there are but few gems in it.

One frequent stumbling block to anyone who reads or rereads the *Sketches* immediately after one of Dickens' greater works is the poverty of the style. The incorrect use of words and phrases, so rare in his later books, is fairly frequent here. He writes, for instance: "a man who is particular anxious to adjust the difference" or "young men who smelled very strong of tobacco-smoke"; in his use of the strong verbs about whose use there was still some hesitation at the time, his instinct is less sure than in some of his contemporaries: "a deadly feud sprung up," "he has drank," "we rung our bell." He writes "infantine" in the sense of "parental," "marvellous" in the sense of "remarkable," "commemoration" for "celebration" (of an event still to come); he mistakes in one paragraph the meaning of both "dilemma" and "alternative."

All the episodes of his formative years that may have influenced his style do so more heavily here than elsewhere. To his legal experiences can be ascribed forms like "for the use and behoof of" and chiefly the frequent recurrence of compounds like "thereon" and "thereof" ("with the address indented thereon," or "with the owners thereof"). Yet it is from his journalistic training, his many years of work for and with newspapers, that his style gains its most characteristic coloring. Topical allusions are more numerous in the *Sketches* than in the rest of Dickens' work; they concern, for instance, "Dando, the oyster-swallower"[2] and "the late Mr. Simpson." And the prose of Boz is still encumbered with a great many spurious refinements, much valued by his colleagues of the popular press, and which he shed not long after this trial period of the *Sketches*. The refinements are of vocabulary as well as syntax. The maturer Dickens unlike Boz was not taken with terms like "sylvan luxury," "aver," "in tempting array," "hapless," "sapient," or "evanish-

---

[2] In addition to the characters already mentioned in chap. vi, above.

ment," nor did he give the impression that he saw something funny in every long or learned word, like "demolition," "ebullition," "concatenation," "serio-pantomimic fascination." Neither did he share Boz's habit of replacing as often as possible, again with humorous intent, "some" or "several" by "divers" or "sundry." There are in the *Sketches* twelve such uses of "divers" and five of "sundry" and two additional passages in which Boz used both epithets.

The use of foreign words, to be explicitly proscribed from Dickens' later writings, is another form of the journalistic quest for spurious distinction and display. Two Latin terms—*quondam* and *unâ voce*—and twelve French words or expressions—*bonbons, protégés, beau idéal* (twice), *gourmand, élite, liqueurs, chevaux de frise, début, corps dramatique* (twice), and *en passant*—appear in *Sketches by Boz.*

Literary and classical allusions are also more frequent in this book than in its successors. And their comparative plethora seems due to the same desire for borrowed plumes. Superficial and irreverent references to personages as diverse as Pope, Sterne, Ixion, Atlas, Napoleon, Cincinnatus, Sheridan, Mrs. Radcliffe, Byron, Nebuchadnezzar, Mercury, Richardson, Paul and Virginia make the text gaudy rather than brilliant and evince facile elegance rather than mature culture. It is interesting to note in this respect that out of four Shakespearean references in the *Sketches* two concern ghosts, and one, not the person, but only the voice of Desdemona, "with the pillow over her mouth." As to the allusion to Bernardin de Saint-Pierre's hero—"Paul, not the saint, but he of Virginia notoriety"—it might sound more impressive if it were not illuminated, four pages later, by another reference, to "a duet from the opera of 'Paul and Virginia.'" In short, the *Sketches*, in spite of the many visits to the British Museum mentioned in the tenth chapter of "Characters," confirm that their author's culture had been acquired not so much in the reading room as in the playhouse. It is understandable that, in later days, he should have been more chary of displaying such fragile and unconvincing knowledge.

Finally, one must admit that journalism exercised one further detrimental influence on Dickens' style, a tendency to use phrases which supposedly conveyed an impression of easy elegance but which were merely vulgarly pretentious. Such are expressions like "do the misanthropical," "do the amiable," "do the ornamental," "did the luxurious," and self-conscious circumlocutions like "organ of vision" for "eye," "specimen of the species" for "man," "anti-temperance fluid" for "gin." Indulging himself in original hyphenated compounds, Dickens slips into the spurious juvenile cleverness of clumsy expressions, like "an I-wish-you-may-get-it sort of expression," "circulating-library-subscribing daughters," "snuff-shop-looking figure," "amateur-pickpocket-sort-of-manner," "mourning-coach-looking-steed" [i.e., black horse], "some of the amateur-painted and never-to-be-sufficiently-admired scenery." No doubt, the author of the *Sketches* was thus treating himself to the illusion that he was handling the English language cleverly. But he cannot compel us to share that illusion; the truth is plain enough: he had the makings of a style, but no real style as yet, and lived largely on borrowings and tricks. The models within his reach were often of an undistinguished kind, and vulgarity of tone is one of the most perceptible characteristics of *Sketches by Boz*. It is glaringly present in the complacent description of low pantomimes,[3] vile toadyism,[4] or disgusting meals and table-manners,[5] as well as in the coarseness of a few jokes.[6]

On second thought, however, there is nothing surprising in any of this. Taking into account the training Dickens had received and the circles he had frequented before 1836, the unquestionable and often painful vulgarity of the *Sketches* is quite understandable and even normal. One might more profitably wonder at the sharp contrast between the occasional poverty of the style used in the *Sketches* and the original and attractive language to be found already in the best pages of *Pickwick*. Dickens' style became finer and finer, until, in the days of *Copperfield*, it developed into an incomparable artistic medium of expression.[7] Nearly all of the defects mentioned in the preceding para-

---

3 "Parish," chap. iv.
4 "Scenes," chap. xi.
5 "Scenes," chap. xviii.
6 See "Tales," chap. i. "I sent to you, to know whether you'd oblige me by acting as father."

"I should have been most happy, I assure you . . . but, you see, I shall be acting as bridegroom. One character is frequently a consequence of the other; but it is not usual to act in both at the same time . . . ."

7 A study of Dickens' style at its nadir will be found in Part Three, chap. xxi, below.

graphs disappeared within a few months. But in the *Sketches*, Dickens was still groping his way, had not quite found himself.

Additional evidence of this uncertainty and hesitancy is provided by the characters in the *Sketches*. Although Dickens' later writing shows him to be—among other things and perhaps above everything else—a creator of unforgettable figures, he is here unable to give life to a single character worthy of the name, to a single complete, human, touching, or even convincing person. There are no characters, properly speaking, in the *Sketches*. There are only grinning and grotesque puppets or hateful and sketchy caricatures. Of course, the narrow bounds of a scene or brief tale do not lend themselves to the creation of a gallery of figures comparable to what is found in the great Dickensian novels; the *Sketches*, in particular, are ill-adapted to the use of the cumulative method of characterization to be practiced later by Dickens. Yet the beings depicted in this early work lack not merely breadth and variety, but also depth and vitality. The reason is that to nearly all of them[8] Dickens has denied his sympathy; without the slightest spark of such vivifying tenderness, all the characters here are, rather than merely ridiculous, hateful or contemptible. With the pitiless pertinacity of extreme youth, the author labors hard to destroy any illusion we might temporarily harbor about them. One characteristic example will sufficiently illustrate this attitude. While describing a member of the London middle class, Dickens tells us: "He was hospitable from ostentation, illiberal from ignorance, and prejudiced from conceit. Egotism and the love of display induced him to keep an excellent table."[9] Thus, in such a depressing catalogue, everything is bad, everything is vile: the most surface defects appear but as the consequences of other, more serious defects, while even the virtues are at best superficial, their presence being accounted for by the existence of additional deficiencies. Instead of attempting to attach himself to his characters so as to endear them to us, Dickens aims at appearing superior to them. This is again a youthful attitude, and further illustration of the self-satisfied exhibition of ease that the author of the *Sketches* obviously regards as the infallible

---

8 The few exceptions will be found in the early chapters of "The Parish."
9 "Tales," chap. v.

key to literary success. Of course, there is in it an admixture of mere gusto and animal spirits, which are much more pleasant to behold; but they are not, for the time being, sufficiently under control.

Certainly, the contempt and hatred so richly deserved by the characters of the book, the disheartening picture of mankind presented in it, do not mean that the author is more often inclined to cry than to laugh. Pathos of the most melodramatic order and occasional touches of genuine emotion are not absent from *Sketches by Boz*; yet laughter carries the day, in the form of whole-hearted mirth. The comic elements in that book are neither refined nor strikingly original. They are often ponderous; they lay great store by heavy irony and mock-heroic procedures;[10] they tirelessly exploit the laboriously stressed real age and involuntary celibacy of ugly, coquettish, old maids;[11] they will never run the risk of being misunderstood, even though this involves the most awkwardly explicit statements.[12] There are puns and other forms of wordplay in the *Sketches*, in great abundance.[13] A sample of one type will show sufficiently the tediousness of many of his verbal tricks. He frequently introduces, by means of one verb or one preposition, two disparate complements: "we enter at once into the building and upon our subject"; "in a hackney-coach and a state of insensibility." When this crops up for the first time, the reader is only moderately amused; repetition soon palls whatever sense of amusement might have been felt.

Yet, however ponderous or trite the comic often is in the *Sketches*, it has at any rate the virtue of existing, obviously and even forcibly. Whatever else they may lack, their comic force, drollery, and gusto do impose themselves upon the reader's attention, and here we do catch a glimpse of the future development of Dickens' genius. Nor is the comedy invariably of the lowest order. A few pages, or *obiter dicta*, about the beadle's dignified ways, cheap theaters or London transport,[14] others caricaturing the popular or the middle-class style,[15] show vigorous

---

[10] See "Parish," almost *in toto,* and also, e.g., "Scenes," chap. xviii, and "Characters," chap. xii.

[11] See, *inter alia*, "Parish," chap. iii, and "Tales," chap. viii.

[12] See "Tales," chap. x.

[13] Long series will be found in "Scenes," chap. vii, and "Tales," chap. x.

[14] "Parish," chap. i, and "Scenes," chaps. xii and xvii.

[15] See "Scenes," chap. xii, and "Tales," chap. ii.

inspiration. The short letter of a youthful father to his baby's future godfather is a miniature masterpiece, and a perfect specimen of the best Dickensian humor.[16]

The most valuable quality in the young writer revealed by such pages is his extraordinary vitality. *Sketches by Boz* is emphatically not a refined work of art; it evinces no effort at psychological penetration; but intense life is felt to be swarming through its pages. That is probably why the book was received by the contemporary critics with a degree of favor that can still surprise us nowadays. They recognized in Boz, with a clear-sightedness we cannot but admire, a talented author, a writer with a future. They recognized the vital impulse of which the *Sketches* were but an early, shapeless manifestation, but which was to assert itself through the whole Dickensian work. In *Chambers's Edinburgh Journal,* for instance, was published on the ninth of April, 1836, the following prophecy: "he can scarcely fail to become a successful and popular author."[17] Nor was this particular critic's insight by any means unique.

When we attempt to find out in the *Sketches* the signs that held promise of a brilliant future, we feel envious of the chance enjoyed by contemporary readers. They opened the book with unprejudiced minds, and their opinions were based on pure, genuine first impressions that we can no longer recapture nowadays. The reader and admirer of *Copperfield, Great Expectations* or *Our Mutual Friend* cannot avoid, in front of Boz's sketches, a feeling or disappointment and frustration; he cannot help noticing chiefly what is wanting in the book and what it would have been better to omit. Under such circumstances, patient analysis and a systematic attempt to forget the rest of Dickens' work, to judge the *Sketches* by other standards than those of *Copperfield*, could alone enable one to discover the source of their success. Even thus, the prophetic enthusiasm of many contemporary reviewers is only imperfectly explained. Perhaps on the whole, the *Sketches* tell us more about the man than about the artist, about the author's character than about his art. They reveal several important trends of his personality and enable us to draw a brief first portrait of Dickens, to be completed and confirmed in later chapters.

[16] "Tales," chap. x.   [17] Kitton, *Dickensiana,* 205.

57

In the *Sketches* one can already perceive the existence in Dickens of two interesting conflicts between opposing sets of tendencies: on the one hand, the gifts of observation and imagination vying for predominance in him; on the other, the assertion of an original genius struggling against his regard for conventional forms and procedures. In the second case, the struggle was short-lived, because Dickens' strong originality soon eliminated all borrowed or merely traditional elements; the first conflict, on the other hand, remained a permanent feature and an essential source of his artistic inspiration.

The ponderous use, in a work intended to be as light handed and as light spirited as the *Sketches*, of the cumbersome editorial "we" weighs constantly over them and helps give many a passage a conventional atmosphere. So does the display of purely formal modesty in phrases like "the time for closing the office had arrived; and thus deprived us of a pleasure, and spared our readers an infliction" or "looking forward as anxiously to the termination of our journey as we fear our readers will have done, long since, to the conclusion of our paper."

The style and occasionally the sentiments expressed betray a similar absence of genuine personal inspiration. When Boz claims that he would like to withdraw "in some quiet nook with people of whom we shall never tire," or when he refers to "the deep forests, or the thundering waters, or the richest landscapes that bounteous nature ever spread,"[18] one hardly recognizes in him the more convincingly passionate observer of London life to be found in most pages of the *Sketches*.

Side by side with such evidences of his submission to the tyranny of custom, one notices the first signs of his vigorous rebellion. One felicitous paragraph parodies certain conventional procedures. Boz has remained alone in a pub, and he tells us: "If we had followed the established precedent in all such instances, we should have fallen into a fit of musing without delay." And several disdainful references to the habits of novelists reinforce our impression of his already incipient revolt and desire to adopt a personal position: "Then, as standard novelists expressively inform us, 'all was a blank'!" "We are not about to adopt the license of novel-writers, and to let 'years roll on.'" "We will

18 Bill Sikes's use of the word "thundering" in *OT* is considerably more picturesque and convincing.

draw a veil, as novel-writers say, over the scene that ensued." The man who could thus laugh at his fellow authors was not likely to content himself very long with aping them.

He did not need their help in order to produce a valuable literary work, and the *Sketches* already show the existence, even when they were poorly used, of the essential gifts that so wonderfully equipped him for his future creative work.

The efficiency of his observant eye is many times proved. The author of the *Sketches* has seen much and well. His memory is as retentive as his sight is keen, and almost on every page concrete details—and even, though more rarely, psychological notations—create an impression of familiar life and truthfulness. This awareness of the real is supported and nourished by inexhaustible curiosity, a quality that Boz admits he possesses and sometimes even flaunts. Curiosity is frequently mentioned in the *Sketches:* "the first object of our curiosity was the Court," "curiosity has occasionally led us into both the Courts at the Old Bailey," or "we felt an irrepressible curiosity to witness this interview." His attempt at making us believe that curiosity is a universal attitude is at best half-hearted; when he asks us, "What London pedestrian is there who has not . . . cast a hurried glance through the wicket . . . and surveyed the few objects he could discern with an indescribable feeling of curiosity?" He does not succeed in glossing over the fact that his own curiosity is quite exceptionally acute. Let us be more specific: it is clear enough that Dickens had, at the beginning as at the end of his career, but little intellectual curiosity; a closer examination, in a few precise cases, of the manifestations of his curiosity, shows it to have been essentially that of a London saunterer, more eager to see than to know things. He goes to Vauxhall Gardens and lets himself be carried along by the moving crowd toward some new sight, without knowing what it is: "We, from the mere force of habit, found ourselves running among the very first, as if for very life." Again he passes a prison when the gate opens: "We turned round as a matter of course, and saw two persons descending the steps. We could not help stopping and observing them." In a third passage, he says simply, "Somehow we can never resist joining a crowd." What does it matter, in any case, that Dickens' instinctive preference should not have led him to the most inspiring sights; whether we call it curiosity or merely a taste for sauntering, this tendency circulates through his works like a nutritious sap, and has established his works as one of the greatest popular contributions to English literature.

Observation by itself, even systematically exploited, could not account for the creation of the Dickensian novel, if we did not find already from many passages in the *Sketches* how imagination works now in collaboration with, now in opposition to, observation. For it often happens that Dickens' imagination interferes with the vision of reality he is presenting to us, by defining and deforming at the same time its contours. Two brief extracts from the same story will sufficiently illustrate this tendency: "a lock . . . which, taken in conjunction with the iron nails with which the panels were studded, gave the door the appearance of being subject to warts" and "a large flat stone bottle, which looked like a half-gallon jar that had been successfully tapped for the dropsy." Thus does Boz, in a way familiar to the readers of his later works, provide inanimate objects with, if not a soul, at least a living human body; they are lit up in the process, but with a quaint light, since the author's own brand of imagination leads him toward grotesque, excessive, even morbid forms.

On the other hand, the efficient alliance between the two faculties of observation and imagination is to be seen at work in almost every page of *Sketches by Boz*. The method used is invariably the same. Dickens starts from concrete observation and then lets loose his power of imaginative inference and amplification: "We are very fond of speculating, as we walk through a street, on the character and pursuits of the people who inhabit it," and "one of our principal amusements is to watch the gradual progress—the rise and fall—of particular shops." He describes walking among second-hand clothes dealers' shops: "We love to walk among these extensive groves of the illustrious dead, and to indulge in the speculations to which they give rise." And, "hurrying to the numerous houses where an annual festival is held in honour of the occasion we can fancy one of these parties, we think, as well as if we were duly dress-coated and pumped, and had just been announced at the drawing-room door." The alliance is a close one, and the benefit mutual, since imagination is quite obviously nourished and set going by observation, to which it gives in return manifold extensions. The phrase that shows the working of this alliance in the clearest light is again to be found in the chapter devoted to the clothes dealers of "Monmouth Street"; Dickens reconstructs the supposed career of some imaginary being from the aspect of his wardrobe as seen in a shop-window, and declares, ". . . we felt as much sorrow when we saw, or fancied we saw—it makes no difference which—the change that began to take place now." At such a level of creative and persuasive power, indeed, "it makes no difference which."

Apart from the few preceding remarks, the *Sketches* do not give much forecast of what was to be the development of Dickens' writings. One can, if one is interested in so doing, give oneself the facile advantages of *ex post facto* prophecy, and discern the origin of a few Pickwickian episodes, names, and characters. One can see, in the arrangement of some of the sketches, a prefigurement of the later Dickensian plots, yet such inferences remain thin, blurred, uncertain. Dickens is not totally present in the *Sketches*, where the part played by artifice and effort is still considerable, more considerable, perhaps, than the place of inspiration and talent.

Fortunately, there is no need to search for an adequate phrase in order to censure this beginner's work. Dickens himself did it once and for all, when he wrote in his thoughtful preface to the reissuement of 1847:

"The whole of these sketches were written and published, one by one, when I was a very young man; they were collected and republished while I was still a very young man; and sent into the world with all their imperfections (a good many) on their heads. . . . I am conscious of their being extremely crude and ill-considered, and bearing obvious marks of haste and inexperience." No later critic will wish to be more Bozolatrous than Boz. No one, that is, except John Forster, who believes that Dickens has "decidedly underrated"[19] his own *Sketches*; the majority of critics,[20] however, have ratified the author's more clear-sighted

---

[19] *Life of Dickens*, I, 60.

[20] See, e.g., A. Lang, introduction to the Gadshill edition of *SB*, and Chesterton, *Appreciations*. E. Johnson finds in *SB* evidence of "brilliant reporting talent" (I, 110) and "outstanding triumph of [the] descriptive faculty" (I, 111), but also a style "often crude and clumsy" (I, 112) and "the flaws and shortcomings that disclose it to be the work of an apprentice" (I, 114). And K. J. Fielding concludes his shrewd analysis of the real value of *SB* by saying, "To-day, their interest is chiefly in the way in which they foreshadow the works to come" (*Ch. Dickens*, 11).

verdict. The book was not yet illumined by the spark of inspiration or the flame of genius.

Yet, without giving evidence of Dickens' genius, the *Sketches* at least supplied final proof of his vocation. One section is especially significant in that respect. He had called it "Characters" because, as we have seen, he intended to present in it characters, types, psychological portraits, but the best parts of this section (chaps. vi, vii, viii, ix and xi) do not adhere to the author's purpose. As far as characters are concerned, these chapters are disappointing, but they are satisfactory enough as short narratives. Dickens was not able to stick to one character, still less to one type. Hardly had he begun to deal with one when a crowd of other varied figures sprang up irresistibly and organized themselves into a coherent, continued, narrative. He had nothing in common with a La Bruyère, and his unsuccessful attempt to create "characters" at least showed that his vocation lay in another direction: he was above all a born story-teller. But of course it was still necessary, before his real career began, for him to make one more decision—whether his narratives were to be short or full-length; in other terms, whether he was going to become a novelist or remain a teller of tales.

The appearance of *Pickwick* solved this problem decisively.

2

GOING UP

XI: Dickens' Working Method (Preliminary Remarks)

Dickens was a professional novelist. Whereas Walter Scott and Anthony Trollope, for instance, were high officials as well as writers of novels, Dickens' single profession for thirty-four years was the composition of fiction. Under such circumstances, it is important to find out his views about the calling he had chosen and the way in which he practiced it. Of course, a novelist's professional duties are considerably less definite than a civil servant's, a physician's, or a lawyer's. Provided that success enables him to do so (admittedly a proviso of some magnitude), the novelist can organize his life to his liking; his every action therefore reveals the conception he entertains of his art. Though Dickens never admitted, as did Trollope,[1] that literary labors were for him a means of livelihood or an ordinary profession, he could not help treating them as such in practice.

In fact, the first thing to be perceived is that he did regard his profession as demanding serious work, steady and patient endeavor; he says ironically of some of his Christmas stories that "they occupied a much longer time in the getting together than they will in the perusal. And this is probably the case with most reading matter, except when it is of that highly beneficial kind (for Posterity) which is 'thrown off in a few moments of leisure' by the superior poetic geniuses who scorn to take prose pains."[2]

In the second place, he regarded his profession as an art, as an occupation that differs from most others in that it fascinates a man who gives himself to it, and in the end absorbs his whole life, becomes for him "pursuits that have insensibly grown to be a part of [his] nature."[3] His eldest daughter described the way in which material life vanished for him when imaginative creation took hold of his mind:[4] "Often, after a hard morning's writing," she says, "when he was alone with his family . . . he has come in to luncheon and gone through the meal without uttering a word, and then has gone back to the work on

---

[1] See A. Trollope, *Autobiography*, I, 143; II, 168, 213.

[2] *CS*, "Mugby Junction," chap. ii.

[3] *AN*, chap. vi.

[4] David Copperfield, mentioning his third novel, makes use of a significant expression in this respect: "a new fancy which took strong possession of me" (chap. lviii).

which he was so completely absorbed."[5] Such a phenomenon shows the difference between Dickens' artistic conception of the novel and the attitude of a Trollope, who treated it as a mere handicraft. Of the two types of novelist, the handicraftsman is the man who, on the one hand, preserves complete control over his work and a certain amount of detachment from it, and, on the other, never allows it to impinge on his private life (or on his other professional life, if he happens to be something else besides a novelist), while the artist is the man who is clutched, swayed, possessed by his creation, and who, in moments of inspiration, ceases to be a man, a husband, a friend, or a father, and becomes a novelist exclusively. Two additional facts tend to show that Dickens ascribed to his novels greater importance and value than to the rest of his work. While he liked to co-operate with other writers on his Christmas stories and a few short tales,[6] he never sought or accepted any external help for his major works.[7] Moreover, he always refrained from dictating a single page of his novels, every line of which was written with his own hand, whereas his *Child's History* was dictated to Georgina Hogarth, and most of the articles and short tales published in *All the Year Round*, to a professional secretary.[8] It is perfectly clear, therefore, that he regarded the novelist's profession as superior to that of the journalist or occasional writer, and, indeed, considered it an art.

He regarded it also as involving both moral and social responsibilities. He hoped his work might destroy a number of social abuses and injustices. One sentence from the preface to *Nickleby* points to the curiously exalted idea he had formed of his role in that respect: "When [this story] was begun . . . there were . . . a good many cheap Yorkshire schools in existence. There are very few now."[9] And he hoped his novels might exert a beneficial moral influence on his readers,

[5] "Ch. Dickens at Home, by his Eldest Daughter," *The Cornhill Magazine* (Jan., 1885), 32–51; quoted in *Dickensiana*, 80.

[6] He wrote "The Lazy Tour" (1857) and "No Thoroughfare" (1867) in collaboration with Wilkie Collins.

[7] It will, however, appear that John Forster, insofar as the single available testimony—his own—can be trusted, deserves, owing to the nature and extent of his suggestions and corrections, to be called a collaborator in Dickens' writing of fiction, over which he exerted unquestionable influence.

[8] See "Tit-Bits" article quoted in *Dickensiana*, 482.

[9] Dickens' ideal and the influence he hoped to exert in that field are defined in the final paragraph of the preface to *Pickwick*.

as he makes especially clear by this statement at the end of *Hard Times:* "Dear reader! It rests with you and me, whether, in our two fields of action, similar things shall be or not. Let them be! We shall sit with lighter bosoms on the hearth, to see the ashes of our fires turn gray and cold."[10] Similarly, in a letter to a clergyman, he asserts his constant moral purpose: "While you teach in your walk of life the lessons of tenderness you have learnt in sorrow, trust me that in mine, I will pursue cruelty and oppression, the enemies of all God's creatures, of all codes and creeds, so long as I have the energy of thought and the power of giving it utterance."[11]

Perhaps, however, in that direction, the novelist's statements should not be accepted without some reservations, for they may have contained an element of literary pose. Though he had relatively little in common with the conventional figure of the "man of letters," parading a noble attitude not often supported by his private life, and eager to discover after the event decorous purposes, he was still exposed to the same temptations as his colleagues. The assertions contained in his prefaces are particularly to be distrusted, because they were always written, as will appear later, after the novels concerned had been completed. Yet, whether perfectly sincere or not, Dickens' repeated, explicit proclamation of his moral intentions at any rate discloses the impression he wished to create; and it is very difficult, and somewhat artificial, when discussing a writer's systematic attitude, to distinguish between the elements of sincerity and of pose it may contain.

Still more than by the various features mentioned above, the Dickensian conception of the novel is characterized by what might be called its conversational aspect, for Dickens says, "it is desirable that a story-teller and a story-reader should establish a mutual understanding as soon as possible."[12] He is no aggressive author; he has no wish to shock, to wound, to irritate his public; success based on scandal has no appeal to him. What attracts him on the contrary is a kind of sentimental exchange with the reader, out of which the author claims he receives as much as he is giving. This is a striking notion, and it is echoed in the

---

[10] *HT*, Bk. III, chap. ix.
[11] Letter to Rev. Thomas Robinson, April 8, 1841, *Letters* (MDGH), III, 17.
[12] *CB, Chimes*, chap. i.

last words of Esther Summerson, when she opens the final chapter of *Bleak House* in autobiographical form: "The few words that I have to add to what I have written are soon penned; then I, and the unknown friend to whom I write, will part for ever. Not without much dear remembrance on my side. Not without some, I hope, on his or hers."[13]

How strange and Sternelike is the notion of this "unknown friend" for whom and to whom one is writing, and of whom, in spite of his silent anonymity, one preserves precious memories. Yet no one can question the reality, in Dickens' mind, of his contacts with this friend, or of his desire to make such contacts ever closer and more regular. When in *Master Humphrey's Clock* he adopts a division of his novels into weekly fragments, instead of adhering to the monthly numbers of *Pickwick, Twist,* and *Nickleby,* he explains that he does so mainly "hoping that to shorten the intervals of communication between himself and his readers would be to knit more closely the pleasant relations they had held for forty months."[14] Such phrases involve a certain amount of voluntary ambiguity. For Dickens, communication with the reader is an exchange; the novelist's work is a dialogue rather than a soliloquy.

What, then, does he claim to be receiving from the public to whom he is giving his novels? This can be understood by calling up the image of a good actor, or even of a lecturer or teacher, who is aware of the reactions of his audience, feels warmed up and cheered by contact with the house, follows the taste of the spectators and adapts himself to it, becomes conscious of any decrease in attention and modifies his acting in consequence, and is encouraged by applause to renewed endeavor and even induced thereby to surpass himself. Dickens needs to be supported by the warm approval of his readers; he cannot speak in a vacuum; his novel is not a structure raised toward the sky but is directed entirely toward the reader. Certainly, Dickens digresses into apostrophizing the reader less often than writers like Thackeray or George Eliot, but the whole of his narrative *is* familiarly addressed to the reader.

The analogy between his own attitude and the actor's was perceived

[13] Chap. lxvii.
[14] *MHC,* Preface.

by Dickens himself, who wrote, in *Pictures from Italy* that, "bent on correcting a brief mistake I made, not long ago, in disturbing the old relations between myself and my readers, and departing for a moment from my old pursuits, I am about to resume them joyfully, in Switzerland: where . . . I can . . . while I keep my English audience within speaking distance, extend my knowledge of a noble country . . . ."[15] The phrase "my English audience within speaking distance" was written more than twelve years before the first public readings, at a time when he had not yet conceived the idea of making his contacts with the public closer and more lively in that way; it is thus made all the more striking and significant by its date.

The instinctive need of a dialogue with the public accounts for Dickens' choice of the periodical form of publication. Instead of giving completed works to the public and thus being informed only of their overall impressions, too late for altering them if they are unfavorable, Dickens had determined on giving out his books piecemeal. Not one of his novels was ever written out before publication; the majority appeared in monthly numbers, a few in weekly fragments.[16] Hence the impression of conducting a dialogue was not purely imaginary; the public did make their opinion known to him. His friends' comments, echoes of reactions reported to the author from various quarters, and letters, many letters from unknown correspondents, were the constituents of the popular response that alone could make Dickens' inspiration flourish. In still another, more accurately measurable form, the figures of sales hinted at the state of public opinion, and as will be seen, Dickens knew how to interpret and exploit information of that kind.[17]

It might seem at first sight as if the form of publication adopted by Dickens, which is tempting to ascribe only to its conformity with his temperament and his notion of the novelist's art, had been in fact imposed upon him by the mere force of circumstance. The *Sketches* had appeared as separate articles in various periodicals long before Macrone thought of collecting them into two volumes, which turned out to be Dickens' first book, and thus created a precedent. Dickens'

[15] *PFI*. The "brief mistake" referred to here was the launching of the *Daily News*.
[16] *OCS* and *BR* in *MHC*; *HT* in *Household Words*; *T2C* and *GE* in *All the Year Round*.
[17] See chap. xvi (about *MC*) below.

first book was made up of a series of fragments already known to the public. And again in the case of *Pickwick*, Dickens' influence on the choice of the form of publication was very slight. As will be seen in the next chapter, the firm of Chapman & Hall asked young Boz to supply them with copy to "illustrate" the etchings by Robert Seymour, an artist whose forte lay in sporting caricatures. There were to be each month four etchings and twenty-four pages of print (though from the third number on, there were only two etchings and thirty-two pages of text). Such were the terms Dickens was offered by the publishers.

The idea was not entirely original; there had already been some novels published in monthly parts;[18] on the other hand, no one could think at the time that *Pickwick* would ever come to be regarded as a novel, and collections of sketches—sketches were what Chapman, Seymour and Dickens had in mind when they launched *Pickwick*—were normally published in monthly issues.[19] Dickens is therefore guilty of a slight inaccuracy when he asserts that he "revived" that form of publication "in the Pickwick Papers after long disuse."[20] Yet it is undeniable that he cheerfully agreed to base his literary career on the monthly parts, that he gave them hitherto-unheard-of glamor—to the point of making them for a time the inevitable form of publication for the English novel, and imposing them on Thackeray—and that, once he had let himself be compelled by circumstance to adopt them, he remained faithful to them, of his own free will, to the end of his life. After the publication of *Pickwick,* his success had been such that he might have demanded anything from his publishers. He was known at one time to draw from them a monthly salary without committing himself to writing anything; with all the greater ease he could have made arrangements enabling him to write a complete novel that he might have published in its entirety at the end of a period of retirement. Or, if he feared such a massive contact with his public, he might at least have written the complete novel, to be published later in installments, while preserving the chance of modifying it if need were. This he never did, because he had no

---

[18] E.g., *Tom Cringle's Log*, by Michael Scott, and various works by Theodore Hook; see also *PP*, Preface, "certain interminable novels in that form . . . carried about the country by pedlars."

[19] Like the works of Surtees, and some of Pierce Egan's publications.

[20] *OMF*, Postscript.

desire to do it. Certainly, without perceiving the weaknesses and defects of his procedure as clearly as Trollope did,[21] Dickens was not unaware of them—he spoke twice of "desultory" publication[22]—yet, such as it was, he preferred it above any other form, and it became dear to him: "I hold the advantages of the mode of publication to outweigh its disadvantages."[23]

His mode of periodical publication imposed on him certain methods of work, which were to determine the material aspect of Dickens' technique to the end. Dickens had to supply the printer each month with matter for one number, each number to contain thirty-two octavo pages, of fifty lines each, in small type. Thirty-two pages of print were equivalent to a varying number of Dickens' manuscript pages for several reasons. He wrote a looser hand when he was young, or whenever he neared the completion of a novel. He wrote a closer hand whenever he used a new pen and when he used the fluid blue ink predominant in his later years instead of the thicker black ink of his early years.[24] So, because he had reason to distrust the accuracy of the result, the novelist would always try to write somewhat more than was needed to fill thirty-two printed pages. Practically, he would fill three or four pages of his manuscript in one normal day's work (which tended to be in fact one morning's work only); he must thus devote something between ten and fifteen days each month to the writing of his monthly installment. The manuscript sheets are very carefully corrected: words are blotted out, and new fragments inserted between the lines, or wherever space is left. But Dickens' manuscripts must have been the compositor's nightmare, as they have now become that of Dickensian scholars because they are excruciatingly difficult to read. Though he was a conscientious artist, he never took the trouble to copy a page he had written, to make it cleaner;[25] the manuscript was sent to the printer

21 "It was my theory . . . to see the end of my own work before the public should see the commencement" (Anthony Trollope, *Thackeray*, [London, 1880], 51); "I was aware that an artist should keep in his hand the power of fitting the beginning of his work to the end," Trollope, *Autobiography*, I, 185.

22 In the prefaces to *PP* and *LD*.

23 *OMF*, Postscript.

24 See Kitton, *Dickens, His Life, Writings, and Personality* (London, 1902), 454.

25 See, in *Dickensian*, Nov., 1912, p. 296, the postscript of a letter in which Dickens was sending (July 19, 1840) one page of the MS of *OT* to C. E. Lester: "I should tell you,

as it came out of the writer's hands. The proofs he received, or at any rate the proofs that have been preserved, were in general not galley proofs, but page proofs. Compelling, though undefined, motives seem to have demanded that the monthly number contain neither more nor less than thirty-two pages. The utmost possible concession would be a blank of two or three lines (but never more than one-fifth of a page) at the bottom of the thirty-second page. No overflow could be admitted onto the nonexistent thirty-third page; the composition was so close already that it was out of the question to squeeze any additional matter into it.[26] How was this situation handled? There were two distinct possibilities. When, as occurred now and again, the number was too short, Dickens would introduce the few missing lines, usually toward the end;[27] it would most often be a bit of dialogue or description adding nothing to the action, so as not to impinge on the next number, which would already be in course of being written or at least thought out while the proofs were being corrected. If, as more frequently happened, the installment was too long, the lines in excess would be printed on one or more unnumbered additional sheets, placed after the thirty-second, and sometimes headed "Overmatter"; the overmatter had to be taken out. This Dickens did by first counting the lines (the marks of his calculations, penciled at the back of some batches of proofs, are still visible) and cancelling a corresponding number of lines in the text of the issue; he would cancel here a half line, there a whole paragraph. Once more, conversations and descriptions were particularly threatened in the process, which was inevitably somewhat hasty; thus did many fragments disappear from Dickens' novels, which are, as will be seen, neither

---

perhaps, as a kind of certificate of the Oliver scrap, that it is a portion of the original and only draught. I never copy."

[26] This is to be inferred from the corrected proofs preserved in the Forster Collection. Such significant details were unrecognized by Dickens' critics until the work of John Butt and Kathleen Tillotson was published in the 1950's. Gissing, for one, wrote (*Ch. Dickens, Critical Study,* 56) that the novelist rarely found his calculations wrong even by a line." Of course, he was in this merely following Forster, who thought fit, though he knew better, to propagate that kind of misleading statement, even though the corrected proofs show that Dickens' calculations were always tentative, and that the margin of error sometimes rose to two printed pages.

[27] Trollope saw in this obligation one of the worst disadvantages of periodical publication and constrained himself to write precisely 250 words to the page (see *Autobiography,* II, 199).

better than the rest, nor inferior to it, and have long remained, technically, unpublished. The calculation was made more complex by the fact that the novelist often inserted a few fresh lines while reading the proofs of an installment already too long, and thus increased the bulk of the overmatter that would have to be cancelled. The job was most often done, however, with admirable precision, and it seldom occurred that the second set of proofs—also preserved in a few cases— failed to have been trimmed to size. It must be added that the two sets of proofs would go through Forster's hands before publication and that he was more than once entrusted with the task of making the necessary cancellations! This was a fine proof of Dickens' trustful friendship, perhaps, but not an instance of his artistic scruples.

The thirty-two pages were then published as one monthly part. It should be observed that the successive parts had consecutive page numbers; Part II went from page 33 to page 64, Part III from 65 to 96, etc., to the end of Part XVIII. The nineteenth number, termed "Numbers XIX & XX," was somewhat thicker than the others, but not twice as thick. Unlike the others, it was limited at one end only: it had to begin at page 577 of the future book, but the author was free to close his novel as he pleased, and in accordance with purely literary—or moral— impulses. The nineteen parts (such is by far the most frequent number) could then be bound into a single volume to make up the first popular edition in volume form, brought out at the same time as the final installment. It has sometimes been thought surprising that the first edition should contain no significant corrections, that Dickens should not have effaced from it the evidence of his mistakes and oversights or shown that he had taken advantage of the most intelligent and incontestable criticisms. Gissing, among others, through his ignorance of the documents in the Forster Collection, was led to mistake Dickens' attitude on this point;[28] in the case of *Hard Times*, whose installments appeared in *Household Words*, the first edition in volume form (though it followed close upon the end of the periodical publication) does show evidence of an attempt at improvement;[29] but for the monthly novels, as the first edition had been for commercial reasons printed in advance,

[28] *Ch. Dickens, Critical Study*, 43.
[29] See *HT*, ed. G. H. Ford and S. Monod (Norton Critical Library, N.Y., 1966).

no last-minute corrections could be made. Yet what is true of the first no longer holds good for the next editions: Dickens might have (many will think that he ought to have) emended the text of later editions of his novels, and perhaps worked on a definitive edition; he did, in 1867–68, do some slight revision of the earlier novels for what was called the "Charles Dickens Edition," but the revision was very slight indeed; it failed to correct a number of mistakes, and even became the occasion of introducing fresh ones and conferring a kind of authority on a very imperfect text. So the definitive text of Dickens, which he did not give us himself, is not yet in existence; it would be of considerable interest to have such an edition, or even a reliable critical text, based on careful collation of manuscript, corrected proofs, and all the editions revised, however slightly, by the author; many passages cancelled at proof stage, for instance, for reasons which often had little to do with the writer's artistic purpose, unquestionably belong to the history of the text, if not to the real text of the novels.[30] To a certain extent, it looks as though Dickens impatiently felt that he would be more profitably employed if he wrote new works than if he polished the old ones, or that elaborate revision might weaken his creative urge; also, perhaps, that he was sentimentally committed to his earliest readers, in the sense that what had been good enough for them, what had entertained them and gained their approval, could be in need of little further improvement.[31]

Dickens, therefore, did his writer's work in curiously cramping conditions which imposed upon the development of his art certain limitations, certain external characteristics common to all his novels. One is thus enabled to perceive the general outline of a typical Dickensian novel.

Unlike many writers, Dickens chose the title of his book before he had written a single line of it. Instead of composing his novel first and only then trying to find a title that might describe, define, summarize

[30] K. Tillotson has edited *OT* in accordance with such principles for the Clarendon Press; her edition has not yet appeared at the time (Dec., 1965) of writing this note; it will almost certainly be followed by similar editions of the other Dickens novels.

[31] *PP* contains a famous example of this refusal to alter what he had written. Jingle has anachronically alluded to the Revolution of July in Paris. Instead of cancelling or modifying the passage, Dickens contents himself with adding an ironical note (*PP*, chap. ii): "A remarkable instance of the prophetic force of Mr. Jingle's imagination; this dialogue occurred in the year 1827: and the Revolution in 1830."

or symbolize it, Dickens worked, and worked hard, on the title in the very first place. Indeed, when he set to work, especially at the beginning of his career, it may be asserted that Dickens had chosen nothing but the title and one or two hazy ideas about the nature of the narrative and the main characters in it. This peculiar procedure often resulted in anomalies, all the more so as, for many years, he indulged his preference for quaint, detailed, interminable titles;[32] there might be at the outset no intimate harmony between the title of a book and its contents. What part does the old curiosity shop play in the novel of that name? Can it be claimed that Martin Chuzzlewit *Senior* is the hero of the novel supposedly devoted to him? The art of selecting an adequate title was one that Dickens mastered slowly and arduously, and all the useless frippery with which he saw fit to clothe the core of his titles has been discarded by posterity. What remains of all the elaborate titles coined by him? Leaving aside *The Old Curiosity Shop*, a wholly accidental choice, we find four symbolical phrases: *Hard Times, A Tale of Two Cities, Great Expectations,* and *Our Mutual Friend,* all belonging to the later phase of his career; one place name: *Bleak House*;[33] but mostly nine names of unforgettable characters: *Pickwick, Twist, Nickleby, Rudge, Chuzzlewit, Dombey, Copperfield, Dorrit,* and *Drood,* placed simply at the head of the books relating their adventures, according to the traditional practice of Fielding and Smollett. In short, after much endeavor, much misguided inventiveness, Dickens hit on the simplest of all methods for the titles of his novels; the title is neither more nor less than the name of the central figure; of course, simple as it is, the method is none the less effective, because the personality of these characters *is* the life and soul of the novels.

Once the novel was provided with a title, one other preliminary decision still had to be made before the first chapter could be written—how the book was to be divided. Into chapters only, or into books and chapters? Dickens' decision had to be made at the very beginning, be-

[32] See, e.g., the title originally chosen for *MC*: "The Life and Adventures of Martin Chuzzlewig, his Family, Friends and Enemies. Comprising All his Wills and his Ways. With an Historical Record of what he did, and what he didn't. The whole forming a Complete Key to the House of Chuzzlewig." (Forster, *Life of Dickens*, I, 273). The final title was even longer.

[33] Which can be regarded also as symbolic of the legal system of England, and particularly of the Court of Chancery.

cause, if he wished, for instance, to adopt division into books, the first words to be published, immediately after the title, would have to be "Book the First"; after the first monthly part had appeared, it would already be too late. This is true also of chapter headings; if these were present in the first installment, it would be impossible not to have them in the second, and conversely. In fact, Dickens contented himself with division into chapters at the outset of his career. Only four of his novels are divided into books, and all four belong to the final period,[34] which corresponds to his overall evolution toward a reinforced structure for his novels as well as toward a greater predominance of the symbolical or allegorical elements. The chapter headings tend to undergo a transformation parallel with that of the general titles. From *Pickwick* to *Dombey*, they are long and detailed, usually comprising one or more complete sentences, except in the more dramatic moments, when they become shorter and more condensed.[35] In the early days, they are in accordance with contemporary usage (*The Life of an Actor*, a brief novel by Pierce Egan, published in 1825, was composed of six chapters whose headings took up a half page each). Clear and neat in *Copperfield*, they become more and more symbolical and terse from *Bleak House* to *Edwin Drood*. Three works only have chapters without any headings: *The Old Curiosity Shop, Barnaby Rudge*, and *Great Expectations*, all of which were published in weekly fragments instead of the usual monthly numbers.[36]

Dickens' chapters are of fairly even length. There are usually three, and sometimes four, to each monthly part; they are often shorter and more numerous in the final number. *Nickleby, Chuzzlewit, Dombey, Copperfield, Bleak House, Dorrit*, and *Our Mutual Friend*, which are approximately each 1,000 pages long, have 65, 54, 62, 64, 66, 70 and 67 chapters respectively (they average fifteen pages per chapter). The novels published in weekly periodicals have shorter chapters; *The Old Curiosity Shop* has 73 for about 650 pages, *Rudge* 82 for some 750

---

[34] HT, LD, T2C, and OMF. But the division of HT into three books with allegorical titles did not appear before the first edition in volume form (1854).

[35] See in OT the chapters called simply "The Expedition" and "The Burglary" (chap. xxi and xxii).

[36] The chapters of HT had no headings in *Household Words*; the headings were adopted at the same time as the division into books.

pages, *Hard Times* 37 for only 300 pages, *A Tale of Two Cities* 45 for
400 pages, and *Great Expectations* 59 for 500 pages—a little less than
ten pages to the chapter in every case. As for *Oliver Twist* (53 chapters
for 500 pages), it is different from the other novels in that it combines
features of the monthly system with aspects characteristic of the weekly
arrangements.

Since the novels published in weekly fragments do not follow the
same rules as the monthly parts, there are in Dickens' work two distinct material techniques. The alternate practice and interaction of the
two techniques[37] makes it more difficult to determine the general evolution of Dickens' art as a novelist.

Once the first decisions had been made, about the title and the main
divisions of the novel, Dickens would launch into the narrative proper.
His openings are as a rule fairly straightforward. *Twist, Dombey* and
Copperfield each begin with a birth. The most striking ones are that
of *Hard Times:* "Now, what I want is, Facts!" and that of *Edwin Drood:*
"An ancient English Cathedral Tower?" followed by a paragraph describing Jasper's blurred vision under the effect of opium. But *Hard
Times* is in some respects a pamphlet as much as a novel, and its careful,
systematic structure shows an effort unique in the author's work, while
Drood has many features in common with the tense form of the detective novel. In no other case does the beginning of a Dickens novel
evince any attempt at originality;[38] most of them are simple, and, so
to speak, normal. Some early scenes of exposition, particularly in *Our
Mutual Friend*[39] and *Dorrit*,[40] are written in theatrical style: as on the
stage, two characters inform each other of circumstances familiar to
both, and this is only one of the many examples of the influence exerted
on the Dickensian novel by dramatic techniques.[41] Generally, however,
the novelist prefers to the use of such artifices a neat, straightforward

---

[37] See Part IV, chap. xxv, below.

[38] One cannot regard as original the rather laborious machinery with which are introduced the stories of *PP* (the meeting of the Club), *OCS* (the anonymous observer's stroll),
and *MC* (the Chuzzlewit genealogy). They are merely complicated, and slow down the
action at the outset.

[39] Book I, chap. iv.

[40] Book II, chap. xxiv.

[41] There are also, in the novels, soliloquies (*HT*, Book II, chap. xi), symmetrical conversations (*OMF*, Book I, chap. iii), and even an aside (*BR*, chap. xlv).

paragraph summing up the events with which the reader must be made conversant.

Once it has thus been launched, how does the novel progress? The very general description that can alone be given at this stage must consider two main components—narrative and dialogue;[42] there are few digressions. The narrative is almost always written by an impersonal narrator: *Copperfield,* part of *Bleak House,* and *Great Expectations* alone make use of the autobiographical method. The narrator's point of view is external to the characters; unlike George Eliot, Dickens does not analyze their thoughts: he describes their appearance, gestures, and actions, and transcribes their speech; he makes them live before us rather than think and feel. In order to convey their psychological attitudes, he often uses words like "looked," "appeared," "seemed," and still more often the form "as if,"[43] all of which point to this external point of view; the author is, in common with the reader, a spectator; he observes the movements of his heroes and seldom seems to share their inner life; he does not arrogate to himself the right to enter their souls. A comparison with the stage is once more enlightening: Dickens' narrative resembles the description of scenes taking place in the theater of his imagination. Even in *Copperfield,* in spite of its autobiographical form, the narrator sometimes gives us the impression that he is a spectator: "Let me stand aside to see the phantoms of those days go by me, accompanying the shadow of myself, in dim procession."[44]

Whether the novelist's point of view is internal to the characters, like George Eliot's,[45] or external like Dickens', the progress of the

[42] According to Walter C. Phillips, the proportion of dialogue in the Dickensian novel amounts to more than one-third of the text (the calculation has been made from *GE*), i.e., it is somewhat higher than in George Eliot (*Felix Holt* and *The Mill on the Floss* contain rather less than one-third of dialogue) and a good deal higher than in Trollope (*The Warden* has only one-fifth). See *Dickens, Reade and Collins,* 204.

[43] In a single chapter of *DC* (chap. lvii), for instance, we find the following phrases: "Mr. Micawber . . . appeared to be quite at home . . . talked as if he were going to the farthest limits of the earth . . . flourished off the contents as if he had made the voyage . . . seemed to think . . . folded his arms as if he were then stationed on the figure-head."

[44] *DC,* chap. xliii.

[45] The end of *The Mill on the Floss* is characteristic of the difference between the two writers. George Eliot claims that she knows the feelings of two characters as they are being drowned (Book V, chap. vii). Dickens would only have seen a few bubbles on the surface. At the end of *OMF,* there is a similar incident, which illustrates his own method (Book IV, chap. xv).

story from episode to episode, or from incident to incident, depends on his conception of time. Now, Dickens' notion of the novel seems to be spatial rather than temporal. He regards each of his novels as a journey, as a road to be traveled over,[46] and his transposition of time into visible distances is revealing; it commands his treatment of the novel. Time is a psychological phenomenon which can be indefinitely divided, and whose fragments can be contemplated in any order whatsoever.[47] A road, however, has to be traveled over from beginning to end; in order to see again a point one has already passed, one has to go back along the distance already covered. Thus the progress of the novel for Dickens bears the mark of psychological continuity: "If I am to tell a story, I must begin at the beginning."[48]

There are in his work a few brilliant exceptions to this rule: in *Copperfield* the chronological development of the narrative is made more flexible thanks to the brief "Retrospect" chapters,[49] and the tempo less uniform and more subtle through the frequent recall of past events and the discreet foreshadowing of future ones. Each significant episode thus casts its shadow both backward and forward, not only by means of its material causes and consequences, but also through the interplay of premonitions and psychological aftereffects. But this is not usual in Dickens. In *Bleak House* and *A Tale of Two Cities,* the novelist takes the reader farther and farther back into the past, not merely in order to extricate himself in the final chapters from a mesh of complex relationships—as he must do in *Twist, Nickleby*, and again later in *Expectations* —but also in order gradually to cast more light on the previous events. As a result, the progress of the novel becomes twofold: it proceeds forward, while at the same time is explores more and more remote layers of the past. Such subtlety remains rare, however, and on the whole the outline of a Dickensian novel is chronologically continuous.

---

[46] "I look along the road before me, where the distance already shortens and the journey's end is growing visible" (*BH*, chap. xxxvii); similarly, in *DC*: "I resume the journey of my story" (chap. xlii).

[47] See *Tristam Shandy* and the *Nouveau Roman* in France, or Rayner Heppenstall and William Golding in England.

[48] *CB, Cricket,* chap. i.

[49] In *SB*, as has been seen, Dickens was parodying the conventional procedure: "We are not about to adopt the licence of novel-writers, and let 'years roll on'." ("Tales," I, chap. i); in the "Retrospects" of *DC*, he rises above it.

In order to render its progress easier and to hurry on the normal course of events, Dickens allows himself considerable license—to be studied later in more detail. He employs coincidences and chance encounters (which diminish the demands made on the writer's inventive energy) and presentiments and prophecies—mostly as dreams—which have the advantage of throwing out feelers into the future. Since no strict plan has been determined in advance, the progress of the novel can be altered when an unexpected difficulty crops up.[50]

Through these various devices Dickens would take his novel to the point where the required length was achieved. For his great novels in monthly parts, this was almost unalterable. Since the publishers demanded eighteen installments of 32 pages, plus one of variable length, the total made up a little less than 650 octavo pages of close type (or approximately 300,000 words). Such was the amount that enabled them both to provide the public each month with a sizable fragment of the work in progress and to issue later several editions, one of which would be an expensive edition in three volumes—the inevitable Victorian "three-decker" which cost some thirty shillings. In the current modern editions, those novels will usually comprise about one thousand pages; only *Bleak House* significantly exceeds this figure. As for the novels published in weekly installments, it has been seen already that Dickens seemed to have been out of breath sooner in their case. *Edwin Drood* is different from the other monthly novels. At the time of Dickens' death, six numbers, approximately 300 pages in a modern edition, had been written; his working notes show that he had made up his mind to limit himself to twelve numbers instead of the usual twenty. Whether this was because of weariness or owing to a change in his approach to the novel, it is impossible to tell. But, if completed, the book would have been about 600 pages long.

When the end came in sight, Dickens would use characteristic procedures to wind up his novel. "A story is nothing without the sequel,"[51] Boz had written; and Charles Dickens adhered to the principle rigidly; he gives us the conclusion of every incident in the novel, and the end often assumes the form of a large scene which partakes of

---

[50] It would be easy to show that Walter Scott, Thackeray, and Trollope, among others, are not more scrupulous than Dickens on that point.

[51] "Scenes," chap. xvii.

prize-giving and Last Judgment. Especially in the early novels, the final chapters are the occasion of a very artificially staged gathering of all the secondary characters. The most sensational scenes are to be found at the end of *Twist, Nickleby,* and especially *Chuzzlewit,* where Mrs. Gamp, then Young Bailey, appear one after the other, for no earthly reason, to do nothing but totter in and out. The ending is always happy,[52] or else pathetic and edifying—for it cannot be contended that the ending of *The Old Curiosity Shop* is at all happy, or that of *A Tale of Two Cities* unmitigatedly so. The principle of the method is explained in the following statement: "A parting glance at such of the actors in this little history as it has not, in the course of its events, dismissed, will bring it to an end."[53] The actors, then, have to be dismissed, or, to speak more courteously, taken leave of; in Dickens' eyes the novel would not be complete if the reader were not made acquainted with the fate of even the most insignificant characters.[54]

After the last chapter, Dickens would finally write the preface for the first edition in volume form. This text has a peculiar character; it is at once a polemical and a sentimental gesture; it has the twofold purpose of replying, not to possible or foreseeable criticisms, but to recent and real onslaughts, while saying a few words of farewell to the reader. Nowadays, Dickens' prefaces give such a disappointing or disconcerting impression that many modern editions rightly omit them altogether or place them in an appendix. They are more a rejoinder to ephemeral detractors than an introduction to his work. He felt this so clearly himself that he did for *Our Mutual Friend* what he might have done for his other novels; he placed the preface at the end of the book and called it "Postscript in Lieu of Preface."

Now that the main stages in the genesis and development of a Dickens novel have been defined, this chapter can be brought to a close with a few lines about a notion which appears curiously modern and which it is important to keep in mind in order to understand the element of

---

[52] Percy Fitzgerald, admittedly a foolish writer, claims that in Dickens' letters to him "will be found admirable counsels to the novelist—one special one—avoid painful and disagreeable endings." *Recreations,* I, 40.

[53] *BR,* "Chapter the Last."

[54] Dickens even wrote a letter to Forster, from Paris, because he had inadvertently omitted from the final chapter of *D&S* no less a character than the dog Diogenes.

artistic thought at the back of Dickens' apparently artificial plots. He believed that all human beings are bound together by manifold links out of "the mighty store of wonderful chains that are for ever forging, day and night, in the vast iron-works of time and circumstance."[55] He had observed that men, things, and places find themselves constantly connected with one another in all sorts of unexpected ways: "There are so few persons in the world that they continually cross and recross."[56] He had already shown Nicholas Nickleby "ruminating upon the strange manner in which the register-office seemed to start up and stare him in the face every now and then, and when he least expected it."[57] So, for each human being, there seems to be forming a fabric of life or destiny, woven with all those links, and the bonds uniting men are so numerous that the web of every individual life is almost inevitably mingled with the webs of all other lives: "Mr. Jarndyce . . . and Allan Woodcourt . . . both, thinking, much, how strangely Fate has entangled this rough outcast in the web of very different lives."[58] Dickens has a dim notion of a secret, preordained destiny that organizes the complex weaving and crossing of the threads and webs of all individuals: "In our course through life we shall meet the people who are coming to meet *us*, from many strange places, and by many strange roads . . . and what it is set to us to do to them, and what it is set to them to do to us, will all be done."[59]

To a man who has been able, if not to work out these notions clearly and turn them into the basis of a conscious, coherent theory—this Dickens never did—at least to glimpse them and see how profoundly interesting they could be, the novelist's function must be to cast some light on one fragment of the universal web of human destinies, and to follow a few of the threads in their many crossings and recrossings; this Dickens has done,[60] and, by so doing, has worked in the same direction as one of his greatest successors. It was to be Marcel Proust's glory to place the theory at the very core of his work and give it more complete expres-

[55] *ED*, chap. xiii.

[56] *RP, No Thoroughfare.*

[57] *NN*, chap. xliii.

[58] *BH*, chap. xlvii; see also *LD*, Book I, chap. ix, "the destined interweaving of their stories."

[59] *LD*, Book I, chap. ii.

[60] David calls the Peggotty episode "one thread in the web I have spun" (*DC*, chap. lxiii).

sion: "Certainly, if our hearts alone are concerned, the poet[61] was right
who spoke of the mysterious threads broken by life. Yet it is still truer
to say that life ceaselessly weaves fresh threads between human beings,
between events, that life crosses these threads, doubles them to make
the web thicker, so that between the least point in our past and all
the other points, an immense network of memories leaves us free to
choose."[62] Marcel Proust boldly made a wide use of the idea; Dickens
more guardedly molded his work according to it. Yet when one takes
a bird's-eye view of the Dickensian novel, one realizes that the web
of Fate is not unimportant to an understanding of his literary creation.

XII: *Pickwick*, OR TRIUMPHANT IMPORTATION

DICKENS' CAREER as a novelist falls easily into three main periods: before
Copperfield (1836–49), *David Copperfield* (1849–50), and after *Copperfield* (1851–70). That novel, indeed, is both the center and the summit
of his work; it is the result of a slow progress pursued from 1836 to 1849;
it is a masterpiece; it is a turning point in the history of Dickens' technique, whose further evolution it launched into new directions.

From 1836 to 1849, Dickens' predominant literary purpose was
comedy. Insofar as he had achieved a clear consciousness of his calling,
he wished to be, above everything else, an entertainer and a humorist.
The beginning of the period coincided with his marriage, which was
not to be in every respect a happy one, but which enabled him to live
a few years of peaceful comfortable family life. Up to this point, the
overflow of his energy was absorbed by his ceaseless creative activity;
he was supported and strengthened by success; he was young and out-
going. This was the comparatively happy portion of his life.

One influence, moral as well as literary, was at that time exerted on
him: John Forster's devoted, clear-sighted friendship was valuable and
helpful to him as a man, even if Forster's literary interference was more
open to question.

In November, 1835, Robert Seymour, an artist who had just been illustrating for Chapman and Hall their *Squib Annual,* proposed to them

---

[61] The poet is Victor Hugo, but in his verse it is not Life, but Nature (*"Nature au
front serein"*) that breaks the threads.
[62] *Le Temps Retrouvé,* II, 230.

a new and more ambitious publication, to be made up of a series of "Cockney-sporting plates." The publishers had been satisfied with the success of the previous work and felt sure that Seymour's reputation would make the new venture profitable; they closed with his offer at once, merely stipulating that the plates would have to be accompanied by a text of some kind, so as to form a monthly publication, to be sold for one shilling.[1] This was the origin of *The Pickwick Papers*.

Chapman and Hall then looked about them for an author who might agree to write the accompanying texts. They applied in the first place to William Clarke (1800–38), the then popular author of *Three Courses and a Dessert,* but he rejected their proposal, perhaps because he did not like to submit himself to the illustrator's authority. The publishers next made an offer to Charles Whitehead, the author of the *Autobiography of Jack Ketch* (1834), who turned it down for the same reason. But this was a step in the right direction, since Whitehead did Chapman and Hall a good turn by recommending to them another possible writer, young Boz, who was supplying sketches to *Bell's Life* (a magazine edited by Whitehead). Boz was less popular than either Clarke or Whitehead, yet he was not completely unknown; his *Sketches* were being well received, and he was warmly recommended by Whitehead. Hall therefore called on Boz and offered him £14 a month to write twenty-four pages of printed text "illustrating" Seymour's Cockney-sporting plates. Dickens had every reason to pounce on the offer: he was short of money; he was engaged to be married; and he yearned to become a professional author in order to escape from parliamentary journalism. In any case, in those days Dickens never turned down an offer of any kind made by any kind of publisher. But he made one or two stipulations in his turn: the themes for his narratives might not all be sporting, and Seymour must consent to illustrate the various adventures, to be selected and narrated by the writer before the plates were made. These demands acceded to, he undertook the task. On the

---

[1] This mode of publication was suggested to Chapman and Hall by the great success, fifteen years back, of Pierce Egan's *Life in London, or the Adventures of Tom and Jerry* (1821). "In a stage version it was played simultaneously in ten theatres. The author declared that sixty-five different publications had been derived from his Sketches . . ." Phillips, *Dickens, Reade and Collins,* 42–43.

tenth of February, 1836, he broke the news to his fiancée, Miss Catherine Hogarth, with the memorable comment: "The Work will be
no joke, but the emolument is too tempting to resist."[2]

"My views being deferred to," Dickens wrote in 1847, while summing up in a new preface the circumstances that had preceded the
publication of *Pickwick Papers*, "I thought of Mr. Pickwick, and wrote
the first number."[3] Nothing could be more tantalizing than such a
phrase to the critic who had hoped to find in Dickens' preface some
illumination of *Pickwick*'s genesis. "I thought of Mr. Pickwick, and
wrote the first number." The mystery of literary creation is untouched.
Other evidence has to be looked for.

The title originally chosen ran as follows: "The Posthumous Papers
of the Pickwick Club, Containing a Faithful Record of the Perambula-
tions, Perils, Adventures, and Sporting Transactions of the Corresponding Members." Under this title the first part was published, on the
thirty-first of March, 1836. It contained four etchings and twenty-four
pages of print; the matter is divided between two chapters, the first
describing the meeting of the Club and the determination to let a limited
group of four members go on a succession of journeys, and the second
dealing with Mr. Pickwick's departure with his friends, their quarrel
with a cabman, their encounter with Jingle and their conversation
during the coach-journey from London to Rochester, the travelers'
arrival in Rochester and their experiences at their hotel, the ball in the
evening, with Jingle's and Tupman's adventures, followed by Dr. Slammer's challenge to Winkle, and the failure of the duel. There is nothing
strikingly original so far; the author of *The Pickwick Papers* is emulating the example of Pierce Egan and Theodore Hook as another of
the humorous story-tellers who would relate droll incidents without

---

[2] *Letters*, I, 129. The financial argument thus put forward contradicts more than one
formal statement made by Dickens himself later on as to his own disinterestedness; this is only
a myth, complacently propagated by Forster ("No man could care essentially less for mere
money than he did . . .," *Life of Dickens*, II, 355, at the beginning of a chapter devoted
to the "Last Readings"). Without candidly admitting it like Scott, Thackeray, Trollope, or
George Eliot, Dickens was always careful of his material interests; he never ceased to be
scrupulously honest, and was often very generous, yet he also conducted himself as a keen,
wide-awake businessman.

[3] Preface.

aiming at the continuity demanded by a real novel. He is also, as it were, emulating himself, since his own *Sketches* had already described a duel that failed to materialize.[4]

Dickens was later to explain, in his somewhat plodding preface to *Pickwick,* that what these papers are "they were designed to be";[5] but his statement, which is part of his effort at self-justification after the event, does not alter the facts, expounded more candidly by Forster: "At its beginning, where or how he was to end was as little known to himself as to any of its readers."[6] Dickens' uncertainty about the progress of his narrative is manifest in several ways. His early design, for instance, must have been to write all his chapters in the style of the first, that is, to give them the form of reports of meetings of the club, or documents addressed to the club by the travelers; yet, as soon as he came to the end of the first chapter, he must have realized that such a procedure would make the book so monotonous and lifeless that he gave up the original plan to adopt instead a continuous narrative method: "We have no official statement of the facts which the reader will find recorded in the next chapter, but they have been carefully collated from letters and other manuscript authorities, so unquestionably genuine as to justify their narration in a connected form."[7]

Thus is the first chapter of the *Posthumous Papers of the Pickwick Club* the only one (out of fifty-seven) to fulfill the promises contained in the title. Henceforth, there will be no further mentions of "Papers,"[8] but only of adventures and dialogues, any more than the Pickwick Club properly speaking will appear, since this cumbrous body will have finally receded into the background, leaving in the limelight the more limited group of its four traveling members. Apart from one allusion to Mr. Blotton, Mr. Pickwick's inveterate opponent, on the occasion of the antiquarian discovery at Cobham, and the perfunctory dissolution effected when all the readers have long since dismissed it from their

[4] "Tales," "The Great Winglebury Duel" (the name is remarkably close to both Jingle and Winkle).

[5] Preface.

[6] *Life of Dickens,* I, 70.

[7] In chapters devoted, like the present, to a single work by Dickens, the chapter numbers will be given, not in notes, but in the text itself, immediately after each quotation, whenever no additional information or comment can justify a note.

[8] In chap. ii, however, Mr. P., on his arrival in Rochester, sets about jotting down his impressions.

thoughts,[9] the book, from Chapter II on, might just as well have been called: "The Travels and Adventures of Mr. Pickwick and his Three Friends."

The second chapter was itself modified while it was being written. An undated letter to Catherine Hogarth, probably sent on February 21, 1836,[10] indeed explains: "I have at this moment got Pickwick and his friends on the Rochester coach, and they are going on swimmingly, in company with a different character from any I have yet described, who I flatter myself will make a decided hit. I want to get them from the ball to the inn before I go to bed; and I think that will take me until one or two o'clock at the earliest. The publishers will be here in the morning." This has the interest of disclosing Dickens' original plan: he had intended to take *all* the Pickwickians to a ball *before* bringing them to their hotel in Rochester; in the text he finally wrote, Tupman and Jingle alone repair to the ball, which takes place in the hotel itself, while Pickwick, Snodgrass and Winkle are asleep in their rooms. On the other hand, the letter also shows under what remarkable pressure Dickens was working. Chapman and Hall must have requested to see a sample chapter at short notice in order to enable Seymour to get to work. Since the first issue of *Pickwick* did appear, as arranged, on March 31, 1836, the sample must have been deemed satisfactory.

Two days later, the novelist married Catherine Hogarth. The link between the two events is not purely fortuitous: Dickens had had to wait until his literary undertakings could be counted on for earnings sufficient for a young couple. Chapman and Hall had guaranteed a regular salary of £14 a month,[11] and an advance payment of two numbers together enabled him to be married immediately after the publication of the first. The early days of April were taken up by the honeymoon trip—an unpretentious one, indeed, since it took the newlyweds only to the Rochester area, i.e., to the vicinity of the Pickwickians' first feats, but it was further enlivened by Dickens' writing of a farce.

---

9 The Club, of course, had to be dissolved, since the original title made mention of "Posthumous" Papers.

10 This is the date given in *Letters*, I, 133.

11 Forster says fifteen guineas. From Number VIII on, Dickens received £25 per month. In all, taking into account the additional payments made by Chapman and Hall, he got about £2,500 for *Pickwick* in 1836–37.

Back in London, the author, who still did occasional duty as a parliamentary reporter, just managed to complete in hot haste Number II of *Pickwick,* to be published on April 30. But by that time, the first tragic incident connected with the composition of *Pickwick* had taken place: on April 20, Seymour had committed suicide, after completing only three of the illustrations to Number II, which thus appeared in the imperfect form of having only three etchings to its twenty-four pages of printed text. In full agreement with his publishers, Dickens then determined to grant fuller predominance to the text over the plates. All the following numbers contain thirty-two pages of text and two illustrations only. The second installment comprised three chapters. Therein the author first had recourse to a makeshift meant to render his task easier and whose use is particularly understandable in such a hectic period of his private life: he introduced into Chapter III a detachable tale, the first of nine "inserted" tales in *Pickwick,* the "Dismal Man's Tale," relating the death of the clown.

The composition of that brief narrative calls for no comment here; all nine "inserted tales" illustrate Dickens' technique as a story-teller but have no relation to his art as a novelist. It will be enough to observe that several motives may have urged Dickens to place them in his book. Before beginning to write *Pickwick,* he had published nothing but tales and sketches; the success of the *Sketches by Boz* encouraged him to think he had achieved both competence and recognition in that field while his ability to produce full-length narratives was still problematical. Since it supplied prospective buyers with known and valued wares instead of with new, untried matter, the insertion of tales could act only as a stimulus to the sales of *Pickwick.* Furthermore, Dickens must have had in his desk several tales, already written and meant for publication in some periodical or other. If pressed for time or short of inspiration, it was easy enough to write a paragraph of transition and inflate his number by means of such a narrative. He found the method so convenient that he used it in five consecutive numbers: there are inserted tales in Parts II, III, IV, V, and VI of *Pickwick.* Finally, it must be admitted that Dickens had a sincere liking for the concentric form of composition, for what Sam Weller calls "veels vithin veels";[12] in

[12] The reference is to Ezek. I : 16, "as it were a wheel in the middle of a wheel,"

this he saw an artistic effect which can be connected with the tradition of the *Canterbury Tales,* or more directly with the example of Cervantes and the picaresque writers, followed by all the great eighteenth-century novelists. There had already been an "inserted tale" in the *Sketches.*[13] After *Pickwick, Nickleby* was to contain some more; *Master Humphrey's Clock* was to be invented specifically in order to make the proliferation of narratives easier,[14] and every Christmas Number of *Household Words* and *All the Year Round* was to be composed according to the same principle: a sheaf of independent narratives bound together by the meagre link of a central plot, however sketchy. In *Pickwick* the inserted tales are obviously by no means essential, but they are, in the author's own view, rather more than the cheap, though convenient, makeshift we tend to see in them nowadays; to him they are an additional ornament.

Besides the stroller's tale, the second installment of *Pickwick* contained a visit paid to Mr. Pickwick by some Rochester officers (chap. iii), the great day of the military demonstration, leading to the encounter with Mr. Wardle, who invites all the Pickwickians to Dingley Dell (chap. iv), and their journey from Rochester to the latter place (chap. v). In all three episodes (the last of which was directly inspired by Robert Surtees, the author of *Jorrocks' Jaunts and Jollities,* who had specialized in scenes of grotesque hunting and horsemanship), the hero is made ridiculous.

Nothing so far is powerfully original; there is little enough to account for pronounced success. But success, without being very marked, was yet sufficient to give the impression that Boz's new enterprise was a promising one. After Seymour's death, many artists showed themselves desirous of associating their fate with Pickwick's and applied to Chapman and Hall and Dickens; among these both Thackeray and John Leech were turned down, and Robert Buss illustrated the third number;

adapted by Blake (*Jerusalem*, 15, 20) as "Those in Eden which wheel within wheel in freedom revolve . . . ."

13 "Mr. Bung's Narrative," inserted in "The Parish," chap. v.

14 *MHC* contains Dickens' most sensational feat in that field: There is a story related by Giant Magog to his comrade Gog, in a collection (*The Giant Chronicles*) presented by the deaf old companion of Master Humphrey, the latter having first introduced him to the reader. *"Parturiunt montes,"* wrote a contemporary critic of the sorry result of this gigantic threefold machinery, *"nascetur ridiculus mus"* (*Monthly Review* [May, 1840], art. IV, 41).

but the technique was new to him, and his conscientious study of it over a short period of time did not enable him to master it, and he failed to give satisfaction. The vacancy was again opened one month later, and from the fourth number, Hablôt K. Browne—"Phiz"—did all the remaining plates. A further sign of *Pickwick*'s early success, at least in the trade, i.e. in the circles where its commercial value could best be appraised, can be found in the many offers made to Dickens by Macrone (the publisher of *Sketches by Boz*) in June, 1836, and by Richard Bentley in August. Dickens accepted every single offer that was made: in June he committed himself to giving Macrone, six months later, a completed novel for £200, wrote a pamphlet called *Sunday under Three Heads,* which he signed Timothy Sparks, and gave up for good and all his reporter's duties; in July he wrote an operetta; on August 22, before the sixth number of *Pickwick* came out and showed that success was assuming stupendous proportions, he signed a contract with Bentley: he would become editor of a new magazine in January, 1837, and draw a salary of £20 a month, publish installments of a new novel in this magazine for two additional monthly pounds, and write at some undetermined date still another novel for £500.

While imprudently piling up such flattering commitments for the future, Dickens went on writing his monthly thirty-two pages of *Pickwick*: Parts III (May 31, 1836, chaps. vi, vii, and viii), IV (June 30, chaps. ix, x, and xi) and V (July 31, chaps. xii, xiii, and xiv) were duly written and published amidst this overflow of achievements and schemes. The three numbers did little except proceed with the slow, intermittent launching of the action. Number III opens with a disparate chapter containing a poem, a tale ("The Convict's Return"), and a small static portion of the central narrative (chap. vi); it goes on with Winkle's misfortunes as a sportsman and the description of a cricket match (chap. vii); Jingle, chance-met, is invited to Dingley Dell and robs Tupman of Rachael Wardle's attachment (chap viii). Number IV begins in livelier style: Jingle has eloped with Rachael and is pursued by Pickwick and Wardle (chap. ix); overtaken in London, in an inn where the waiter is one Sam Weller, Jingle gets Wardle and the lawyer Perker to bribe him into giving up Rachael and vanishing (chap. x); a letter written by Tupman from Cobham causes Mr. Pickwick to join him there and read "A Madman's Manuscript," the most singular of the "inserted tales" (chap. xi).[15] After Number IV had come out, the author must have heard of flattering reactions to the first appearance of Sam Weller and decided, as a consequence, to put this new character in a prominent place in the story. At any rate, Number V begins with Mr. Pickwick's engaging Sam as his personal servant, which occasions a deplorable misunderstanding: Mrs. Bardell, Mr. Pickwick's landlady, mistakes the cautious announcement of the event for a marriage-proposal and faints in his arms (chap. xii). Yet hardly has the main plot begun in earnest, when it is interrupted: the Pickwickians go to Eatanswill in order to attend an election (chap. xiii) and listen in addition to "The Bagman's Tale" (chap. xiv).

From that moment on, *Pickwick*'s success became phenomenal. This should be borne in mind whenever one is tempted to pass severe judgments on the author. Why should he have shown himself more artistically ambitious, more rigorously exacting toward himself, than were tens of thousands of enthusiastic readers? Supported by success, by popular approval, he was justified in feeling that he had reached his goal at one blow, that he had found the most perfect form for his art; it is only normal that he should have had no desire to chance any departure from this form, so that the next installments evinced no noticeable tightening of his grasp over the story.

At the end of the year, Dickens was energetically helping prepare the performance of both his farce and his operetta, while he also worked on the imminent launching of *Bentley's Miscellany*,[16] whose first editor he was so soon to be, wrote the beginning of *Oliver Twist* for serialization in the *Magazine*, and probably did something about *Barnaby Rudge*, the other novel promised to Bentley. He was at long last realizing that he had perhaps too many irons in the fire; and the expectation of child-birth in his home did not particularly mend matters.

Pickwick, however, went on appearing at regular intervals. On the thirty-first of August, 1836, it was Number VI (chaps. xv, xvi, and xvii):

15 Its most interesting aspect is a resemblance with Tennyson's *Maud*. *Maud* appeared in 1855, and for many years Tennyson had been Dickens' friend and his favorite contemporary poet.

16 "Why go to the other extreme?" asked Barham on being told that this would be substituted for the original choice of "The Wits' Miscellany."

the Pickwickians go to a fancy-dress party at Mrs. Leo Hunter's, where they meet with Jingle once again (chap. xv); Pickwick decides to follow him to Bury St. Edmunds, there to be duped by him (chap. xvi) and console himself by writing the story of Nathaniel Pipkin (chap. xvii). Number VII (chaps. xviii, xix, and xx), published at the end of September, does little for the progress of the plot: after a hunting-scene in the course of which both Pickwick and Winkle are ridiculed—an obvious legacy of the late Robert Seymour—Pickwick goes back to London, summoned by Mrs. Bardell's solicitors, Dodson and Fogg, and tries to get in touch with Mr. Perker's clerk (chap. xx). The bright feature of the installment is the first appearance of Tony Weller, Sam's father, an admirable illustration of the way in which Dickens knows how to exploit and repeat his success. Parts VIII and IX (October and November, chaps. xxi–xxiii and xxiv–xxvi) form a single whole, the Ipswich episode; the Pickwickians repair to that place on the suggestion of Tony Weller, still in pursuit of Jingle, after hearing in a tavern the tale of the "Queer Customer" (chap. xxi); they triumph over Jingle (chap. xxv), after a number of ludicrous mishaps; they then return to London (chap. xxvi). Number X, at the close of 1836, is a veritable Christmas number, in which, after Sam's visit to his stepmother (chap. xxvii), are to be found a digressive meditation about Christmas, a Christmas party at old Wardle's, a Christmas poem (called *A Christmas Carol,* chap. xxviii) and a Christmas story (the abduction of Gabriel Grub the sexton, which clearly foreshadows the future *Christmas Carol in Prose,* chap. xxix).

At the end of Number X, the author of *Pickwick* inserted an announcement to his readers: "it is his intention to adhere to his original pledge of confining this work to twenty numbers . . . he is most anxious that when the *Posthumous Papers of the Pickwick Club* form a complete work, the book may not have to contend against the heavy disadvantage of being prolonged beyond his original plan."[17] This sentence reflects Dickens' fairly constant attitude, which makes nearly all his comments about his own art so disappointing; his eagerness to justify himself, his knack of discovering precise purposes after the

---

[17] From the facsimile in Arthur Waugh, *A Hundred Years of Publishing* (London, 1930), 36.

event (he makes mention here of his "original plan," while it has been seen that there had been no such thing) preclude his giving us useful information as to the actual development of his works.

The year began for Dickens in febrile agitation: on January 2 the first number of *Bentley's Miscellany* appeared, the first sixteen pages of *Oliver Twist* being, however, reserved for the February issue. From that moment, in addition to the installment of *Pickwick,* Dickens had to write each month a fragment of his new novel and fulfill his editorial duties, select and correct the articles, poems, and stories of the whole number, make sure that it was the required size (about a hundred pages), and often himself supply one or two articles besides his *Twist* chapters.[18] On January 6 his first son was born, an event which compelled him to move from his flat and leave the three rooms in the sole possession of the child, its mother and two grandmothers. This circumstance made his work so much more painful and difficult that he determined at once to look for more spacious accommodations. Also in January, realizing at last that he had undoubtedly committed himself to far too much, he negotiated with his publishers. He persuaded Macrone, in exchange for the whole copyright of *Sketches by Boz,* to give up the novel promised in June, 1836, not a single line of which had as yet been written. In March, 1837, Dickens wrote and helped stage his second operetta, *Is She His Wife? or Something Singular.* In early April, with wife and child, his own brother Frederick, and, reportedly, his wife's younger sister Mary, Dickens moved to 48 Doughty Street, the pleasant little house which is still nowadays "The Dickens House."

From the point of view of his craftsmanship, the most important of all those changes, is of course the fact that Dickens was now writing two books at the same time, for the monthly number of *Pickwick* and the monthly sixteen-page fragment of *Oliver Twist* made enormous demands on his imaginative powers. Perhaps the inferiority of four numbers of *Pickwick* (parts xi to xiv) is the result of Dickens' overwork and divided energy at this particular time. With the exception of Part XII (the February number, chaps. xxxiii and xxxiv), which contains the

18 When his idea of an editor's duties had undergone a change, however, and his relations with Bentley had deteriorated, he wrote to Lady Holland (Sept., 1838) that he had "little to do with the business part of the publication."

entirely admirable description of the *Bardell v. Pickwick* trial, there are no signs of improving composition. Number XI lacks unity: it begins at Wardle's—with the skating-party of Chapter XXX, which is the last item in the inheritance from Seymour—and then returns to London (chap. xxxi), where the Pickwickians are ridiculed after spending an evening with two medical students, Bob Sawyer and Ben Allen (chap. xxxii). Number XIII is spectacularly empty: after the trial, it is discovered that two months must elapse before proceedings against Pickwick can actually begin. The plot is thus broken, and Dickens seems to be at a loss how to make it move on again. Pickwick asks the question, "Where shall we go next?" (chap. xxxv) and decides in favor of Bath for a feeble reason: "None of us have ever been there." But perhaps the real motive for such a choice lies in its obviousness, since Bath is a traditional meeting-place for fictional or theatrical characters; when Pickwick goes to Bath, he is following in the footsteps of Smollett, Sheridan, and Jane Austen. But the Bath episode of *Pickwick* by no means outshines *Humphry Clinker* or *The Rivals* or *Northanger Abbey*. At Bath, nothing important happens: eccentric Dowler is introduced to the reader (chap. xxxv), Mr. Pickwick reads, by chance, the story of Prince Bladud (chap. xxxvi), and Sam goes to a "swarry" with the footmen of Bath (chap. xxxvii). Number XIV is livelier: owing to a ridiculous misunderstanding, Winkle flies to Bristol (chap. xxxviii), where he finds, by chance, the two medical students, then Dowler; Pickwick joins Winkle, and Sam enables the latter, thanks to two coincidences of the first magnitude, to have an interview with the girl he loves (he had met her lately at Wardle's, but there were artificial obstacles to his courtship of her, in chap. xxxix).

The issue of *Pickwick* narrating the above-mentioned incidents appeared on April 30, 1837. At the end of May no installment was published. In the meantime had occurred the most tragic event of Dickens' life, the event that had the most pervasive, most lasting influence on his emotional health as well as on his literary work, the event that transformed the end of *Pickwick*: the death of Mary Hogarth.

Shortly after their marriage, the Charles Dickenses had invited Kate's younger sister, Mary—then aged sixteen—to stay with them. All the contemporary evidence agrees in granting the girl exceptional charm. Her company was to the novelist a source of vivid joy. She understood, admired, appreciated him, and her presence was a help to him; he did not disguise his own feelings, least of all from his wife. One need not perhaps attempt to probe the nature of Dickens' love for his young sister-in-law; it is enough to see that he was passionately attached to her and that her sudden death, on May 7, 1837, in his arms, a few hours after they had come back together from some theatrical performance, and she had seemed to be at the height of health, enjoyment, and mirth, was to him a most severe blow, as is shown by the following fragments written by him in the ensuing months: (October 26, 1837) "I have never had her ring off my finger, by day or night, except for an instant at a time, to wash my hands, since she died. I have never had her sweetness and excellence absent from my mind so long. I can solemnly say that, waking or sleeping, I have never lost the recollection of our hard trial and sorrow, and I feel that I never shall . . . the gentlest and purest creature that ever shed a light on earth"; (January 1, 1838) "sympathising with all my thoughts and feelings more than anyone I knew ever will or did."[19] Again, in the original preface to *Pickwick*, Dickens calls his sister-in-law's death "the saddest and most severe affliction of his life."[20] Stunned by the blow, he had to desist from his literary labors for a while; neither *Pickwick* nor *Twist* appeared in late May or early June; he spent a few weeks in the country, then went on a short trip to Belgium.

At the end of May another important event had occurred; John Forster had called on Dickens in the days when the latter was at his most impressionable, and their friendship had developed almost at once; it was to be a lifelong attachment on both sides. From that moment, to the end of Dickens' life, Forster was to be associated with Dickens' work in many ways, and after his friend's death, he was to write a *Life of Dickens,* his own greatest book.

When *Pickwick* reappeared at last, on June 30, 1837, exuberant mirth no longer was its dominant characteristic. The very heading of the first chapter in Number XV sounded like an echo of the author's grief: "Chapter Forty. Introduces Mr. Pickwick to a new, and not uninteresting

---

[19] *Letters*, I, 323; and Dickens' Diary, quoted in *Letters* (MDGH), III, 8.
[20] From the MS in the Forster Collection.

scene, in the great drama of life." Mary Hogarth's death had undoubtedly been to Dickens just that—an introduction to the great drama of life.

During the summer of 1837, spent by the Dickens household at Broadstairs—where, according to one contemporary witness,[21] the author of *Pickwick* had fully recovered his spirits—fresh uneasiness and fresh difficulties arose in the novelist's relations with his publishers. Macrone had expressed his intention of bringing out a new edition of *Sketches by Boz* in monthly parts; this was a way of making capital out of the copyright he had acquired a few months earlier and at the same time trading on the success of *Pickwick* in rival hands. But Dickens saw that such republication would severely damage his reputation, as the public would not know he was not getting anything out of the new edition and would merely therefore suppose him to be exploiting *Pickwick*'s triumph for all it was worth, if not more. Dickens prevailed on Chapman and Hall to purchase the copyright of *Sketches by Boz* from Macrone for £2,000. On the other hand, by June, 1837, Dickens was realizing more clearly than ever that his commitments to Bentley were crushing, and, in view of *Pickwick*'s triumph, unreasonable; they had been entered into before the writer had risen to his present market-value. New negotiations were opened, and they proved so tense that the publication of *Twist* was again interrupted in September, before a compromise was achieved: Bentley gave up the third novel promised by Dickens, who now undertook to supply the whole of *Barnaby Rudge* (or, as it was called at that stage, *Michael Varden or the Locksmith of London*) in November, 1838. The novelist's position was but slightly improved by this agreement, for he still faced three herculean tasks within thirteen months: to complete *Oliver Twist* (only one third of which had appeared as yet); to write the whole of *Barnaby Rudge*; and, for Chapman and Hall, to finish *Pickwick* and no doubt begin another monthly narrative almost immediately afterwards. Those were superhuman labors, yet Dickens cheerfully accepted them, as he also undertook about the same time to revise and edit, with his father's help, the memoirs of the famous clown Grimaldi,[22] to be published by Bentley.

[21] See Pope-Hennessy, *Ch. Dickens*, 70–73. This isolated testimony is also, it must be admitted, obviously malicious.

[22] *PP* has one allusion to Grimaldi which reflects the author's contemporary preoccupations: Bob Sawyer "made a face after the portraits of the late Mr. Grimaldi, as clown," chap. l.

It was in an atmosphere of hard labor that Dickens, between June and October of 1837, continued and finished the composition of *Pickwick*. Number XV (June 1837) is wholly devoted to the Fleet Prison, where Mr. Pickwick is taken as an insolvent debtor, because he refuses to pay the cost of the trial he has unjustly lost (chap. xl); the tone is at times almost tragic. Jingle is again found in new surroundings (chap. xlii). Number XVI (July 1837) betrays further uncertainty and fails to ensure the progress of the plot; this number is again located in the prison, where Sam has himself incarcerated, voluntarily, so as not to desert his master (chap. xliii), who is visited by his friends, while a poor prisoner dies in the Fleet (chap. xliv); Tony Weller and his wife call on Sam (chap. xlv); and the number ends with a break of the continuous narrative rhythm preserved so far: "Mr. Pickwick steadfastly adhered to this determination. For three long months he remained shut up," (chap. xlv).

Three months, then, have elapsed when Number XVII (August 1837) begins; it forms, together with Number XVIII (September), a single unit: Mrs. Bardell has been arrested at the request of her lawyers, Dodson and Fogg (chap. xlvi); thus will Sam and Perker be enabled to persuade Mr. Pickwick that he must pay the costs, all the more so as Winkle, who has become a married man, in secrecy—one wonders why— needs his old friend's help to reconcile both families to the fact (chap. xlvii), which Pickwick duly does, first in Bristol (chap. xlviii), then in Birmingham (chap. l), after having listened to the last of the "inserted tales," the story of the bagman's uncle (chap. xlix); Number XVIII closes with a farcical scene at an inn (chap. li). Finally, on the thirty-first of October, 1837, was published the double final issue (Numbers XIX and XX) in which everything is pleasantly wound up: Tony Weller's cantankerous wife dies (chap. lii); Jingle becomes an emigrant with Pickwick's help (chap. liii); Snodgrass is about to marry Wardle's daughter (chap. liv); Sam refuses to leave his master (chap. lvi) but becomes a married man in his turn (chap. lvii) after the Pickwick Club has been dissolved.

With that final number there appeared a preface which was cancelled —and replaced by another—in later editions. It asserted that because of the mode of publication "it was necessary—or it appeared so to the author—that every number should be, to a certain extent, complete in itself, and yet that the whole twenty numbers should form one tolerably harmonious whole, each leading to the other by a gentle and not unnatural progress of adventure. It is obvious that in a work published with a view to such considerations, no artfully interwoven or ingeniously complicated plot can with reason be expected." The final assertion is sufficiently belied by Dickens' later works and need not be commented on here. As to the opening statements, an examination of the plot of *Pickwick*—as described in the foregoing paragraphs—shows them to be far from accurate.

It can hardly be seriously contended, for instance, that each installment is "complete in itself"; it has just been seen on the contrary that most numbers are noticeably disparate and that Parts VIII and IX, and Parts XVII and XVIII form wholes only when coupled together. As to the description of *Pickwick* as "one tolerably harmonious whole, each [number] leading to the other by a gentle and not unnatural progress of adventure," this corresponds only to the ideal work that Dickens' belated scruples caused him to think he ought to have written.

Without having to side completely with the many critics who deny the existence in *Pickwick* of any kind of plot and see in it only a disconnected series of independent episodes, one is nevertheless led to the conclusion that the book does not possess one firmly designed, self-evident, plot, but is composed of four plots—three of which are secondary—interwoven, and broken by many interludes. The main plot, main at least in the sense that it has greater importance than any other for the narrative as a whole and covers the largest number of chapters, is the misunderstanding between Mrs. Bardell and Mr. Pickwick, with all its consequences. An excellent "digest" of *Pickwick* could be produced by printing a version that would begin with that story in Chapter XII, with Sam's engagement, and take it as far as its winding-up in Chapter XLVIII; thus could be presented a "Bardell *v.* Pickwick Trial," which would of course have to omit many delightful passages, but nothing essential; the result would be a poorer book, but a better novel, than *Pickwick* is.

The novel obviously contains several elements scarcely connected with the main plot: (a) a group of episodes whose center is old Wardle (repeated invitations and visits, sporting scenes, Winkle's and Snodgrass' love affairs); (b) the pursuit of Jingle, his tricks, his punishment, pardon, and final conversion; (c) the Weller Saga, with the family relationships of the Wellers and their contacts with the Temperance Society and the "Reverend" Mr. Stiggins. The third subplot, in accordance with the tradition of the French classical theater and the eighteenth century English drama, reproduces at an inferior level, among the servants, their masters' adventures.[23]

In addition to these four plots, *Pickwick* contains a number of episodes artificially and loosely connected with one or other of them which interrupt the progress of the general story. The chief episodes—without counting the nine "inserted tales"—are the quarrel with the cabman and Mr. Winkle's abortive duel with Slammer; the antiquarian discovery; the Eatanswill election (it is Tupman's friendship with Wardle that takes the Pickwickians to Dingley Dell; it is Wardle's friendship with Perker, then Perker's with Pott, that takes them to Eatanswill; it is Pott's with Mrs. Leo Hunter that takes them to the fancy-dress party—through this primitive principle of association, it was easy enough to go on, apparently forever); the second hunting-party; the meeting with Peter Magnus and his fiancée; the whole of the Christmas number; the evening at Bob Sawyer's; the parties at Bath (masters and servants); the interview between Pott and Slurk.

Four plots, nine inserted tales, and ten interludes. One may agree with Dickens that such elements form "a tolerably harmonious whole." But then, again, one may beg to differ. Much will depend on the meaning attached by individual readers and critics to the word *tolerably*.

Can it be more seriously claimed that there is in *Pickwick* "a gentle and not unnatural progress of adventure"? The word progress invites us, if only because of its etymology, to examine the Pickwickians', or at least Pickwick's, itinerary from beginning to end of the book—leaving aside Sam's and Winkle's separate movements—in order to find out just how continuous is the line followed. The result is a little disconcerting: the book begins in London (chap. i), then moves to Rochester (chaps. ii–iv), Dingley Dell (chap. v–viii), back to London (chap. ix–x), out again

---

[23] When Dickens saw fit to resurrect *Pickwick* in *MHC*, he resurrected the Wellers at the same time, and created a symmetrical club in the basement, called "Mr. Weller's Watch."

to Cobham (chap. xi); then come London (chap. xii), Eatanswill (chap. xiii–xv), Bury (chap. xvi–xix), London (chap. xx–xxi), Ipswich (chap. xxii–xxv), London (chap. xxvi–xxvii), Dingley Dell (chap. xxviii–xxx), London (chap. xxxi–xxxiv, at the time of the trial), Bath (chap. xxxv–xxxviii), Bristol (chap. xxxix), London (chap. xl–xlvii, in prison), Bristol (chap. xlviii–xlix), Birmingham (chap. l) and London (to the end). The movement resembles a star of irregular shape (since a few places, like Dingley Dell and Bristol, are visited more than once) rather than a continuous line. On the other hand, the various journeys often result from feeble and arbitrary motives, such as invitations (Wardle's to Dingley Dell, chaps. iv and xxvii, Tupman's to Cobham, chap. ix, Dodson and Fogg's summons, which is an invitation of a kind, chap. xviii), mere curiosity (in the case of Rochester, chap. ii, and Bath, chap. xxv), or chance encounters (Jingle, chap. xv and xxiii, Bob Sawyer and Dowler, chap. xxxviii). Chance encounters and coincidences of every description are in fact the youthful novelist's supreme resource to extricate himself and his characters out of every difficult situation; chance is the omnipotent *deus ex machina* of his plots; it is by chance that Jingle overhears the conversation between Wardle's mother and the fat boy (in the course of which the latter reports what he himself has by chance overheard going on between Tupman and Rachael); it is by chance that Sam Weller finds in Bristol the maidservant of Ipswich, and by chance that her neighbor is the future Mrs. Winkle.

Thus, in spite of the author's later comments, the absence of a well thought-out plan and the lack of internal unity are striking; a true novel would be based on a coherent sequence of events, instead of making use, as *Pickwick* does, of the same kind of incident over and over again, in slightly modified forms; since poverty of invention is out of the question here, hectic haste alone can account for the many redundancies of that kind: Mr. Pickwick's compromising positions with Mrs. Bardell in London, then in the girls' school at Bury, and again at Ipswich with Peter Magnus' *fiancée,* as well as Winkle's similar complications with Mrs. Pott at Eatanswill and in Bath with Mrs. Dowler, are but one and the same adventure, the ever-entertaining, but hardly novel adventure of the placid man placed by circumstances in the position of an apparent seducer. The cowardice of Winkle (at Rochester, then at Bath and

Bristol) and that of Pott and Slurk (at Towcester) supply three very similar episodes. Winkle's ignorance of every form of physical exercise is worn threadbare: his riding, hunting (twice), and skating all evince the same ignorance and the same pretensions. Further illustrations could be adduced; the above examples are enough to show how repetitive the composition of the book is, when two or three comic situations provide large collections of episodes thinly related to the main plot.

There is so little systematic organization in *Pickwick* that Dickens more than once comes to forget some of his own fleeting intentions. Chapter LIII led the reader to expect further legal action of Dodson and Fogg against Pickwick,[24] but the idea is given up. The strolling actor of Rochester had promised a manuscript in Chapter V;[25] no more is heard about it for some fifty chapters; then the author suddenly remembers it, and his belated scruples, at the moment of general dismissal, make him turn the Stroller, in defiance of verisimilitude, into Job Trotter's brother and a merry soul—in spite of the lugubrious and sentimental nature of his first tale—whom he compels retrospectively to emigrate to America (chap. liii).

So many repetitions, so much remissness, such a jerky progress preclude our bestowing upon the author of *Pickwick* the last compliment he is ready to pay himself; it is impossible conscientiously to recognize in his work the "gentle and not unnatural progress of adventure" he invites us to see in it. Why could he not content himself, like Scott, with saying: "I write for general amusement" and, again like Scott, invoke the example of Smollett and Le Sage: "These great masters have been satisfied if they amused the reader upon the road; though the conclusion only arrived because the tale must have an end—just as the traveller arrives at the inn, because it is evening"?[26] All the imperfections analyzed so far were a normal consequence of the author's youthful lack of experience. When he began to write *Pickwick*, he was barely twenty-four years old; he had never written novels as yet, and had not read a very large number. No wonder then, under such circumstances, and although he was already providing unquestionable evidence of his genius as narrator, char-

24 "If there's law in England, sir . . . you shall smart for this."
25 The stroller says very clearly of this "leaf from the romance of real life": "You shall have it."
26 "Introductory Epistle," *Fortunes of Nigel*.

acter-painter, and humorist, that his book should strike us as the work of a prentice hand in the field of novel-writing.

As far as structure was concerned, the author's youthfulness was betrayed by a comparative lack of ingenuity. The same youthfulness is just as apparent in other directions, where it involves the opposite defect, excessive ingenuity, a lavish extravagance, a squandering away on insignificant details of his creative energy.

Thus do the chapter-headings display an amount of elaboration that can only be deplored. In order to vie with his most popular contemporaries, Dickens is much more concerned to coin a fresh joke for each chapter than to inform the reader concerning the chapter's contents. Often the chapter-headings are analytical and enumerative, and the attempt at deriving comic effects from the heterogeneous items of the list calls attention to the lack of unity in the chapter—as in the case of Chapter III: "A new acquaintance—The Stroller's Tale—A disagreeable interruption, and an unpleasant encounter." But the method sometimes results in headings of such length—as in Chapter VII: "How Mr. Winkle, instead of . . . , etc.," which goes on for six lines and yet closes with a summary: " . . . other interesting and instructive matters"—that the author appears to become discouraged in the end. The heading of Chapter XVI reads like a mere confession of impotence: "Too full of adventure to be briefly described." Other chapters are headed by a kind of descriptive advertisement; the author will, for instance, promise "an affecting interview . . . showing also . . . what a capital chapter the next one will be" or "Mr. Pickwick's extraordinary and startling announcement" or merely "matter of thrilling interest herein set down." Of course, this is not unamusing, and the author's perceptible high spirits are in some instances communicative, especially at the beginning; but even if this style of chapter-headings can be regarded in some respects as a good thing, it is definitely the kind of good thing of which there can be, and soon is, too much.

The chapter is clearly for Dickens in those days no more than a measure of length. The thirty-two pages of the installment have to comprise three chapters, or at least two if he has let himself be carried away and make them longer than usual; so he will just pile up incidents until his chapter is the required length. The manuscript of *Pickwick* has unfortunately not been preserved; but it is highly probable that it would have shown headings written or at any rate completed after the chapters had been finished. The text of the book proves, through the awkwardness of more than one transition, that such had been the author's practice; if the chapters had possessed real organic unity, there would have been no need to write, at the end of some installments, phrases like these: " . . . for reasons of sufficient importance in this eventful history to be narrated in another chapter"; "any reference to that most important undertaking demands a separate chapter"; "As this chapter has been a long one, and as the old man was a remarkable personage, it will be more respectful to him, and more convenient to us, to let him speak in a fresh one"; " 'All in good time, sir', replied Sam. Whether it was done in good time or not, will be seen hereafter." Once more, inexperience goes side by side with this display of ingenuity; the jocularity stresses the artificiality of the transitions; the mechanism of the novel does not as yet run smoothly.

A similar impression is produced by the names chosen by Dickens for his episodic characters. No fewer than 360 characters have been numbered in *Pickwick*.[27] The major ones have felicitous names. Pickwick (which was the name of the owner of some stage-coaches plying between London and Bath), Snodgrass, Tupman, Winkle, are agreeably natural and familiar names. They already reveal Dickens' special preference for certain letters and combinations of letters in proper names: the vowel "i" (often repeated twice in the same name), the consonants "p," "k," and "w," the "le" ending, all have great attractions for him. Names like Pickwick and Winkle come near to representing his ideal in that respect. Many other "le" endings are to be found in the same book: Truckle, Wardle, Trundle, Raddle, Pruffle, Jingle, Sniggle, and, last but not least, the variant in Bardell; and the following names contain the double "i": Skimpin, Pipkin, Wilkins, Mivins, Stiggins; while combinations of "p," "k," and "w," appear in Perker, Tomkins, Blink, Wicks, Jinks, Boldwig, Weller, Walker, and Wugsby.[28] The risk of confusion being avoided because the characters with similar names are present in separate sections

27 Pope-Hennessy, *Ch. Dickens*, 131. The list of main characters in the Everyman's Library edition has ninety-six names.

28 In *OT* are to be found a few names belonging to the same family: Twist, Chitling, Limbkins, Grimwig, Bedwin, Chickweed, Crackit.

of the book, the result in the end is only an impression of familiarity, of a certain sonorous uniformity of the Pickwickian universe, which is by no means unpleasant. On the contrary, the names given to yet humbler figures follow the example of Ben Jonson and the novelists and dramatists of the eighteenth century and assume a precise significance which sometimes makes them farcical: Prosee, the eminent counsel, the Dowager Lady Snuphanuph, Young Lord Mutanhed (for the aristocracy comes in for a larger share of such ridiculous names than other classes of society), Dr. Nockermorf, Sidney Porkenham, Count Smorltork, or a place-name like Eatanswill . . . it is needless to go on. To the modern taste, the richer the invention, if it is exerted in that direction, the poorer the impression achieved.

Dickens' reasons for coining such mediocre names for his secondary characters will be more clearly understood if the manner in which he designates anonymous characters is now examined; this is another problem, and to him, particularly in the first twenty chapters of *Pickwick*, before he has acquired any experience, a frequent source of difficulty. The characters who are not, or have not yet been, given a name, are usually identified by means of some physical detail: "he of the green coat," "the tall man . . . the long gamekeeper . . . the long man"; a conversation between four anonymous persons is the occasion of using, in succession, the following phrases: "the black-eyed man . . . the one-eyed man . . . the dirty-faced man . . . a very red-faced man . . . the placid gentleman . . . the placid one . . . the placid man . . . he of the dirty countenance . . . the bagman with the lonely eye . . . the bagman . . . the man with the roguish eye . . . the traveller." This procedure Dickens had already employed in his *Sketches*.[29] Even some more familiarly known characters are sometimes just as laboriously labeled: Jingle is called "the Spanish traveller"[30] because he has incidentally mentioned, some twenty pages back, that he had visited Spain; Sam becomes "that eccentric functionary," and, instead of "Mrs. Pott," Dickens once goes to the length of writing "the feminine Pott."

[29] "He of the slippers" ("Tales," I, chap. ii); "the pelisse-wearer" ("Tales," I, chap. ii); "he of the dirty face" ("Tales," I, chap. i); see also in "Characters," chap. iv, a characteristic scene.

[30] Chap. iii; already in *SB* ("Tales," Book I, chap. i) a character was called "the Byron quoter" and "the Don Juan reader."

All those marks of the youthful author's inexperience are in fact closely linked: he created incidents and persons too lavishly, he could hardly coin enough names to give them all, and, when he did not give them names, he did not know what to call them. In other words, while Dickens' talent was already widely developed, he still lacked the art of husbanding it. In the matter of names, he had not yet achieved mastery and flexibility. Perhaps it is not too far fetched to read a confession of this inadequacy in the scene in which Peter Magnus, called at first "the newcomer," then "the red-haired man," asks for Pickwick's name and declares: "I like to know a man's name, it saves so much trouble. That's my card, sir. Magnus, you will perceive, sir—Magnus is my name," (chap. xxii). In fact, from that moment, Dickens' difficulties in that field are perceived to diminish. That is one of the minor technical points where, within *Pickwick* itself, his craftsmanship undergoes a change and achieves progress.

It is only one point in the whole that can be called the composition of *Pickwick*. As has been seen, the composition of *Pickwick* is unsatisfactory, partly on account of the circumstances that imposed on the book the aspect of a series of improvisations and partly because of the author's comparative lack of experience, perceptible mostly at the beginning. The book does not achieve unity, harmony, coherence; the devices used are uncertain and sometimes clumsy. Does this mean that the success is incomprehensible? Of course not, and the early readers' judgment has been a thousand times ratified by posterity. Yet it can be asserted that, had *Pickwick* been better composed, its success might have been wider still, and posterity's appreciation still more warmly unanimous. Dickens' successive prefaces all amount to an effort to justify precisely the least defensible aspects, so that his *a posteriori* apology—which concerns mainly the composition of *Pickwick*—does not appear acceptable. Moreover, Dickens had no need to justify himself for being the author of *Pickwick*, whose popularity was due to qualities already superbly shown in its pages: primarily his comic genius.

One at least of the criticisms traditionally proffered against his works is not deserved by *Pickwick*: sentimentality and the quest for pathetic effects are practically absent from the book; there are indeed a few sentimental and even mawkish phrases in some of the inserted tales and in the final portion of the work, written after Mary Hogarth's death; and there are a few scenes of genuine emotion—particularly those in which is manifested Sam's attachment to his master (chaps. xlv and lvi). Yet on the whole *Pickwick* is pre-eminently and resolutely a comical book. The ironical statement at the close of the first paragraph in Chapter XIX— "But we grow affecting; let us proceed"—is significant evidence of the author's determination not to let sentimentality interfere with his work; it could hardly be transplanted into *The Old Curiosity Shop*. Comedy secured *Pickwick*'s triumph.

Certainly, the comic in *Pickwick*, as well as in the *Sketches*, is not invariably of the highest order; it comprises scenes of sheer farcical caricature, as in the passage following the wound accidentally inflicted upon Tupman by Winkle in Chapter VII, or Count Smorltork's conversation with "Peek Weeks" in Chapter XV; it sometimes exploits threadbare themes, such as conjugal unhappiness—" 'Married!' exclaimed Pott . . . 'It serves him right!' "; it lays great store by pseudo-scientific vocabulary and pedantic periphrases ("a strange specimen of the human race,"; "the stream of life which issued from his nose,"; "from one auricular organ to the other,"; "the lethargic youth,"; "the narcotic bedstead,"; "the incipient chemist,"; "a little hydraulic shower"), a form of humor which can never be very exhilarating, but which is more tolerable when practiced by such cultured novelists as Thackeray or George Eliot than in an almost self-taught writer like Dickens;[31] and finally, it overwhelms the reader under a veritable deluge of puns and other forms of wordplay; to that end, Dickens will employ the names of his own characters— which a writer should refrain from doing who does not wish to be charged with having coined them on purpose—and have pairs like "Cluppins/muffins," "Phunky/monkey," "Job Trotter/Job, trot," "Pott/ pot-valiant in a double sense," as well as other kinds of *double entendre*; from Chapter I ("Mr. Pickwick would not put up to be put down by clamour") to Chapter LIV (" 'Have you been seeing any spirits?' inquired the old gentleman. 'Or taking any?' added Ben Allen"), it is a

[31] The *Eclectic Review* critic, in March, 1837, already charged the author of *PP* with this fault, in appropriate terms: "We observe also . . . the frequent use of those hackneyed, threadbare and silly phrases 'organs of vision' for eyes; 'auricular organs' for ears, &c., where plain, simple language would be in far truer taste and have a far greater effect," (reproduced in *Dickensian*, Aug., 1907, p. 212).

continuous flow, although it is noticeably more plentiful in the earlier than in the later part of the novel. And I think puns are to be objected to on other grounds than their being the translator's nightmare.

Dickens also has recourse to the time-honored device of the malapropism ("wash-up/worship"; "boa-constructer"; "referee/reverie.") A further device used in *Pickwick* is akin to malapropism and may have contributed—together with *Humphry Clinker* and other early models— in suggesting to Thackeray the idiom of James Yellowplush. This device consists in the use of words which, when deformed by popular mispronunciation or misspelling, become comical in themselves without closely resembling other existing words; such are, in *Pickwick:* "sapparised" (surprised), "wenchure" (venture), "irrepairabel" (irreparable), "harmcheer" (armchair), "appleplexy" (apoplexy), "eggzekiter" (executor), "cabriolily" (cabriolet); such will be, in the *Yellowplush Papers*, "omlibuster" (omnibus), "suckmstancies" (circumstances), "ajew" (adieu), and hundreds of other admirable coinages which show Thackeray's greater inventiveness and gusto in that particular field, and make up a considerable part of the charm and originality of his book.[32]

The last inferior, somewhat mechanical aspect of the comic in *Pickwick* is the massive use made of irony in order to stress certain intentions; at the beginning of the book the device—then applied mostly to Pickwick and the Pickwickians—is almost constant: "the gigantic brain of Pickwick," who "displayed the perfect coolness and self-possession, which are the indispensable accompaniments of a great mind"; "the enchanting Rachael" (Mr. Wardle's abundantly mature sister); "the interesting pair" (Rachael and Tupman); "the youth" (plump, elderly Tupman); "in common with many other great men ... like all truly great men"; "his lovely burden" (Mrs. Bardell); "the promptness and energy which characterized, not only the public proceedings, but all the private actions of this extraordinary man"; "Snodgrass ... as modest as all great geniuses usual-

---

[32] The publication of *PP* was completed on Oct. 31, 1837; the very next day there appeared in *Fraser's Magazine* the first chapter of *Yellowplush*; one passage of a later chapter shows that Thackeray was quite familiar with *PP*: "On [the Fleet] I'm rather shy of writing, partly because the Admiral Boz has, in the history of Mr. Pickwick, made such a dixcripshun of a prizn that mine wooden read very amyousingly afterwidd." And the presentation of "Dr. Dioclesian Larner" is strongly reminiscent of Mrs. Cluppins' entrance at the trial. As for James Yellowplush's language, even if he owed the germ of it to Dickens, or both of them owed it to Smollett, Thackeray considerably enriched the idea.

ly are." The use of this crude form of irony becomes less frequent in the later portion of the book, yet it never completely vanishes from *Pickwick*; in fact, till the days of *Chuzzlewit*, it remained a prominent feature of Dickens' art and comedy; after *Chuzzlewit*, it had but a minor place. In the end of *Pickwick*, irony is mostly employed at the expense of the two Wellers; nearly all their speeches are followed by ironical descriptions: "this infallible maxim . . . this notable resolution . . . these indications of a musing spirit."

Fortunately, the comic in *Pickwick* does not stay at such a primitive level, and the enduring glory of the book rests on its superior forms, and more particularly on the depth and wealth of the original psychological perceptions it conveys. The Dickensian comic, when of the highest order, derives its effects from the truthfulness with which certain fleeting observations, caught with unique insight, have been arrested and given permanence—much to the reader's delight. Every individual reader may find in a few simple scenes (the flight of the hat blown along by the wind, chap. iv, Phunky's attitude when the gaze of the crowd makes him blush, chap xxxiv, Sam's elaborate penmanship when he writes a letter, chap. xxxiii), reflections of feelings experienced or visions glimpsed by himself in real life, whose comicality had however escaped him; recognition, the alliance of impressions of familiarity and novelty, are the sources of his delight in such cases.

Yet it is mostly in the creation of his major characters that Dickens has concentrated his psychological observations, at first with purely comical purpose and effect, in the end with graver intent. No aspect of his art, perhaps, has been more harshly criticized than his characterization,[33] but, in *Pickwick* already, it is precisely through his characterization, especially his comic characterization, that Dickens achieves unexampled success.

The characters in *Pickwick*, as has been said, are very numerous; some of them can be regarded as having a literary source: the Sam Weller–Pickwick pair, for instance, has always been associated with the Sancho Panza–Quixote tandem; Pickwick's pursuit of Jingle is chivalrous in exactly the style of Cervantes' hero. *Don Quixote* was one of the tales

[33] Bagehot, for instance, grants him no more than that "in one or two instances, Mr. Dickens has been so fortunate as to hit on characteristics, which, by his system of idealisation and continual repetition, might really be brought to look like a character," (*National Review*, Oct., 1858, p. 475).

read by Dickens in childhood, and it is a reasonable inference that he may at that point have undergone some influence from his predecessor. Yet the resemblance is limited. By dint of scrutinizing it too carefully, one would run the risk of losing sight of the essentials in Pickwick's character, and a close comparison of him with the Spanish knight might impoverish rather than enlighten our conception of the Dickensian figure. Jingle's case is different, since his character is less studied than Pickwick's: his most striking feature—apart from his unscrupulous ingenuity—is a staccato style of speech, whose source can be traced: the ultimate literary origin of it seems to be one Goldfinch, a character in *The Road to Ruin* (a highly popular drama, by Thomas Holcroft, performed in 1792).[34] It cannot be totally denied, however, that Dickens contributed elements from his own observation of life and his own creative imagination to the portrait.

When Dickens' characterization is adversely criticized, it is on two mutually contradictory counts: his characters are charged, now with immutability, now with inconsistency. There is a grain of truth in either reproach, but as far as *Pickwick* is concerned, both cannot be applied to the same portion of the book. At the beginning, most of the characters are indeed immovable, to the point of being mechanical; if the successive episodes offer such close resemblances, it is because the characters always have the same attitudes and the same reactions; Dickens' psychology at that stage is amusing, but static; he describes a group of colorful persons, not their evolution: Winkle is a pseudo-sportsman, Snodgrass a pseudo-poet, Tupman a pseudo-amorist, Pickwick a pseudo-knight. The only genuine thing in any of them is their absurdity. In the second part, on the contrary (and particularly in the portion written after Mary Hogarth's death), when amusing the reader has ceased to be the writer's sole purpose and a didactic ambition has crept into the book, they are changed beyond recognition; Tupman is wiped out: his part as a ridiculous lover can no longer be sustained without becoming hateful by the side of his two young friends Winkle and Snodgrass who have been transmuted into genuine romantic lovers, with even a faint admixture of

---

[34] Before Holcroft was brought into the consideration, a correspondence published in the *Times Literary Supplement,* London, called attention to a likeness between Jingle and a character in Surtees' *Jorrocks's Jaunts and Jollities* (1831–34), then between both and a figure in Theodore Hook's *Maxwell* (1830).

heroism into their attitudes, since they are ready, in the service of true love, to face the opposition, however ephemeral, factitious, unconvinced, and unconvincing, of their brides' respective families. As for Pickwick, his conventional quixotism is metamorphosed into a sincere and efficient devotion to the cause of virtue and the defense of oppressed people: he will no longer get drunk; in order not to countenance a swindle, he will spend months in prison; in order not to keep Mrs. Bardell in prison, though she has been the source of all his difficulties, he will consent to an unjust sacrifice; instead of hunting Jingle down, he will overwhelm him with kindness. In short the comedy of usurped reputations, which had been the major theme of the first part, vanishes, and the characters, when they have grown sincere, come to life. Dickens was to give later the following explanation of the metamorphosis: "I do not think this change will appear forced or unnatural to my readers, if they will reflect that in real life the peculiarities and oddities of a man who has anything whimsical about him generally impress us first, and that it is not until we are better acquainted with him that we usually begin to look below these superficial traits, and to know the better part of him."[35] The explanation is more ingenious than satisfactory: it is not because we grow more intimate with a man that he ceases to become drunk, that he ceases to be conceited, that he ceases to have grotesque experiences, that he begins to throw his money about, in short, that he stops being "the man who had traced to their source the mighty ponds of Hampstead," to become "an angel in tights and gaiters." The change has occurred in Dickens, as the result of a normal evolution in his conception of the novelist's art, when the growing number of his readers enhanced his feeling of moral responsibility and his hope of exerting a beneficial influence, and the evolution had been hastened by Mary Hogarth's death.

A revealing phrase will be found in the preface to the *Christmas Books*: "I could not attempt great elaboration of detail in the working out of character within such limits."[36] Dickens believed that no one can be psychologically profound when painting on a small canvas: his method consists in illustrating one trait at a time in every scene, in spreading out his portrait over a large number of episodes. Compared to the method of

[35] *PP*, Preface.
[36] In later editions, "I could not attempt" becomes "I never attempted."

Thackeray or George Eliot, who aimed at being just as searching and truthful in one page as in a hundred, the Dickensian procedure would seem to belong to an inferior order of fictional art. His characters, nevertheless, possess a quality that has made them immortal and is seldom to be found in George Eliot's: they have charm, and they are universally appealing; even the critic who does not approve of the creative process which has given us Pickwick and Sam Weller cannot fail to love them and be entertained by them. The secret of their charm may well be the secret of Pickwick's immediate and enduring success.

The example of Sam Weller will enable us, if not to dispel the mystery, at any rate to cast some light on it. The creation of that character is Dickens' greatest triumph in *Pickwick*. He has been universally enjoyed. His entrance into the book sent the sales skyrocketing, and he has occupied a place ever since in the first rank of the great Dickens characters. His first originality is that he is a twofold person; he can hardly be separated from his father, Tony Weller, when one comes to examine the elements of his charm and the sources of his comic power.

The literary origin, if there is one, of the Wellers, may lie in the character of Simon Spatterdash, in *The Boarding-House, or Five Hours at Brighton*, by Samuel Beazley, a play performed for the first time at the Lyceum on August 27, 1811, and very popular through several years. The part of Spatterdash was long acted by one Sam Vale, who made it a habit to scatter in his speeches fanciful comparisons in which one may see the source of the famous Wellerian comparisons.[37] Yet the truest origin of Sam Weller is Dickens' observation of a certain type of Londoner. Even before the first appearance of Sam, there had been minor characters in his works whose speeches irresistibly call to mind Pickwick's future servant: thus, the shoeblack in the *Sketches* who declared: "I shall alter the expression of your countenance so completely, that the next time you look in the glass you'll ask vether you're gone out of town, and ven you're likely to come back again";[38] or, again, the groom who, commending a hired horse to Pickwick (before the reader has heard of Sam) reassures his customer in these words: "Shy, sir?—he wouldn't shy if he was to meet a vagin-load of monkeys with their tails burned off." And just as Sam has an existence previous to his birth in the pages of *Pickwick*, he

---

[37] See *Notes and Queries* (July–Aug., 1878), "Sam Vale and Sam Weller."
[38] *SB*, "Tales," chap. viii.

also has a later life. In *Master Humphrey's Clock*, the resurrection of the two Wellers is rather a sorry sight,[39] and they are reduced to a few mechanical tricks, but in several novels of later date than *Pickwick* will be found Wellerisms or characters possessed of the same ingenious verve as Sam.[40]

The Wellers' value and charm for the reader derive largely from their never being at a loss: whatever the situation, whatever the surroundings, the Wellers are always perfectly at ease. Though the comparison may appear almost impious, one is tempted to associate the pleasure afforded by the Wellers and that offered by hypocritical Pecksniff in *Chuzzlewit*. Both have the same nature: it is a delight to see difficulties piling up around them, because it is known in advance that their *aplomb* and ingenuity will pull them through. Yet there is certainly more to Sam and his father than just that: they delight the reader equally by their authority and dogmatism. On no subject are they unprepared to pronounce themselves vigorously and categorically; when Tony Weller states that " 'circumscribed' . . . ain't as good a word as 'circumwented' " or that poetry is "unnatural," or when Sam asserts that "there's another thing that no man never see, and that's a dead donkey," such phrases give one a comfortable sense of solidity; it is felt that no reasoning can shake conviction not founded on reasoning; it has the supreme appeal of arbitrary and gratuitous things. The attitude of happy human beings who have never learned doubt certainly belongs to the cockney; but not to him alone; it is just as characteristic of the *gavroche* or *titi* of Paris; belongs, in fact, to every time and country, and its presence bestows universal value upon the Wellers.

Among the external traits of the Wellers, the most striking is that of the baroque simile. Curiously enough, Dickens has made that a family failing; it is difficult to tell whether he did it on purpose, because he believed that such a pronounced turn of mind could but be congenital and hereditary—like the Heeps' humbleness and the Murdstones' hardness later in *Copperfield*—or through remissness, if he occasionally forgot that the father, not the son, was speaking. In any case, Tony Weller makes use of four Wellerian similes and his son of some forty, a few of which, in

[39] Chap. iii.
[40] Particularly Mark Tapley in *MC*.

fact, are rather underdeveloped.[41] The device is adopted as early as Chapter V, on the occasion of Sam's first appearance; there are three comparisons in Chapter V and three in Chapter XLIV; in every other Wellerian chapter, there are one or two only.

Dickens has been reproached with having based many of the Wellers' comparisons on allusions "utterly irreconcilable with their habits and station . . . images borrowed from sources wholly inaccessible to them."[42] In fact, the criticism can be applied only in the case of three or four of Sam's similes, and even here its validity is doubtful: "He wants you partickler; and no one else'll do, as the devil's private secretary said ven he fetched avay Doctor Faustus," or, "Business first, pleasure arterward, as King Richard the Third said w'en he stabbed the t'other King in the Tower, afore he smothered the babbies," or, "Sorry to do anythin' as may cause an interruption to such werry pleasant proceedin's, as the King said wen he dissolved the parliament." Certainly there are here two references to literature—or at least to two very well-known plays—and one to a familiar historical circumstance, but there is nothing in the least learned, nothing exceeding the elementary level of knowledge that a young Londoner might be supposed to have acquired.

A far more constant feature of the Wellerian similes is their macabre tendency; the most felicitous and amusing often concern sudden death or the circumstances that led to it: "If you wally my precious life, don't upset me, as the gen'l'man said to the driver, when they was a carryin' him to Tyburn"; "now we look compact and comfortable, as the father said, ven he cut his little boy's head off, to cure him o' squinting"; "It's over, and can't be helped, and that's one consolation, as they always says in Turkey, ven they cut the wrong man's head off"; "I only assisted nature, ma'am, as the doctor said to the boy's mother, after he'd bled him to death." The macabre is indeed a predominant feature of the Wellers' vision of the universe; it is found also in the few anecdotes related by Sam, in which the course of events is always stupendously brutal: such are the story of Tony Weller's marriage, the story of the pie-vendor, that

---

[41] "What the devil do you want with me, as the man said, when he see the ghost?" (chap. x); "dumb as a drum with a hole in it" (chap. xxv). Beazley and Vale's "valerisms" had been of a similar order: "Come on, as the man said to his tight boot," "I'm down upon you, as the extinguisher said to the rush-light."

[42] *Quarterly Review* (Oct., 1837), 484–518.

of the sausage-manufacturer who fell into his own machine, and that of the crumpet-eater. The Wellers' world would thus be lugubrious, since death occurs again and again in it, unforeseeably, if it were not at the same time fairylike, since death is so brutal as to be painless, so unexpected as to be incongruous and even comic; in which it resembles the other incidents of this fortunate universe in which everything is possible and easy. The Weller spirit, imbuing every circumstance of life, whether commonplace and vulgar, or dramatic, or again coarsely comical, bestows on all and on *Pickwick* as a whole a kind of poetical aura. Sam is one of the undying figures of literature; the wish expressed by Dickens in *Sketches by Boz* can be confidently applied to Sam: "There he is, at his old post every night, just as we have described him; and, as characters are scarce, and faithful servants scarcer, long may he be there say we."[43]

Whatever the weaknesses of its composition and other technical deficiencies may have been, a book need not contain many figures of the calibre of the Wellers and Pickwick in order to achieve success. That of *Pickwick* was and is glorious. It influenced Dickens' whole career by persuading him that he had indeed chosen the right road for him and that he was already assured of immortality.

Yet success, though the only criterion by which to judge a work—since fiction has no unquestioned canons—is an ambiguous touchstone; *Pickwick*'s success meant that Dickens had procured keen pleasure to his readers, but it did not mean that he had become an accomplished novelist and that he had no more to learn.

After the completion of *Pickwick*, Dickens himself did not in fact feel too sure of his literary status, and did not unhesitatingly regard himself as a novelist. In the manuscript version of the first preface written in October 1837 for *Pickwick*, there occurs the following sentence: "If it be objected to the Pickwick Papers that they are a mere series of adventures, in which the scenes are ever changing . . . [the author] can content himself with the reflection . . . that the same objection has been made to the works of some of the greatest novelists in the English language." When he read the proofs of this preface, Dickens changed the word *novelists to writers*;[44] his correction is meaningful. He claims to be a

---

[43] "Scenes," chap. xviii.

[44] Forster Collection. However the continental editions of 1838 (Baudry, Galignani, etc.) print "novelists."

writer, not a novelist. He is right, insofar as *Pickwick* is not a true novel in the sense commonly given nowadays to the word. Had he written nothing but *Pickwick*, whatever has been said of his instinctive, spontaneous technique, of his uncertain progress, of his constant hesitations, would be true; and what has been said on this point was said because of *Pickwick*; in that sense, the book's triumph has done a disservice to its author's reputation.

At the close of Number X, Dickens, characteristically calling himself "Mr. Pickwick's Stage-Manager," announced to his readers: "Ladies and gentlemen, for these marks of your favour we beg to return our sincere thanks; and allow us to inform you, that we shall keep perpetually going on beginning again, regularly, until the end of the fair."[45]

The following chapters must show whether he adhered to the resolve expressed here, whether he was content until the end of the fair in 1870, to "keep perpetually going on beginning again," or, on the contrary, endeavored to become, year after year, a greater master of his art.

XIII: A Novel Tailored to the Time: *Oliver Twist* (1837–39)

WHEN ENUMERATING Dickens' works chronologically, one is led to place *Oliver Twist* between *Pickwick* and *Nickleby*. It is easy to perceive, however, that the evolution of his art as a novelist does not follow a continuous line from *Pickwick* to *Oliver Twist,* and then on to *Nickleby*. The continuous line goes straight from *Pickwick* to *Nickleby*, and *Oliver* is on a side track. In fact, the evolution of Dickens' craftsmanship through this early phase, which might be termed that of his masterly apprenticeship, is not simple. It has been seen that there had been evolution within *Pickwick* itself; this happened again in the next few books, whose publication again spread over a considerable period of time. On the other hand, the composition of *Oliver Twist* did not follow that of *Pickwick* any more than it preceded that of *Nickleby*; it coincided with the close of the former (January through October, 1837) and the opening of the latter (from March, 1838, on). Finally, *Oliver Twist*, unlike both *Pickwick* and *Nickleby*, was not published in monthly installments of thirty-two pages. Its fragments were monthly, but they were only half as long (sixteen

---

[45] From the facsimile in Waugh, *A Hundred Years of Publishing*, 36.

pages), and they were not sold as separate units. *Oliver Twist* appeared at first in *Bentley's Miscellany,* together with more than eighty pages of other material. For a long time *Oliver* was the *Miscellany*'s single continuous narrative and its chief attraction; the rest of the magazine stood or fell, sold or did not sell, according to the value of Dickens' Twistian contribution.

The publication of *Oliver* was attended by further peculiarities. Whereas Dickens' main novels appeared through nineteen months and mounted to something like a thousand pages, *Oliver,* which was only five hundred, was published from February, 1837, to April, 1839—a period of twenty-seven months. Admittedly there were several interruptions—first at the time of Mary's death, in May, 1837, second when the author's differences with his publisher became painfully acute, especially in September, 1837. Finally, the last third of the novel was written in great haste and in one uninterrupted effort, through the summer of 1838, in order to allow for publication in book form as early as October, 1838, while there yet remained six monthly installments for publication in the *Miscellany.* The effort involved, a unique one in Dickens' career, is not easily accounted for. He states, in a letter to T. N. Talfourd (July 15, 1838) : "It is indispensably necessary that Oliver Twist should be published in three volumes in September next. I have only just begun the last one."[1] The phrase "indispensably necessary" is characteristic of Dickens' temperament. The decision had been made, in part for financial motives, or to avoid the inconvenience of piratical publications,[2] but chiefly, no doubt, because the author was becoming impatient. It had been accepted by Bentley, who did not find it disastrous, now that the serialization of W. H. Ainsworth's *Jack Sheppard* in the *Miscellany* could sustain the sales. These two stages passed, it had become for Dickens a supreme law, whose imperative urgency neither the word "indispensable" nor the word "necessary" could, if unsupported by the other, sufficiently convey.

Thus, the real dates of the composition of *Oliver* are from January, 1837, to September, 1838. The story, when reduced to its outline, does not

---

[1] *Letters,* I, 415.
[2] Both an *Oliver Twiss,* by "Bos," and an *Oliver Twiss* by "Poz" were coming out regularly.

appear exaggeratedly complex or disconnected: a boy, who has been born in the workhouse of a small nameless town, becomes the apprentice of a coffin-maker, escapes from the latter's house and flees to London, where he is received and employed—innocently on his part—by a gang of robbers; in spite of his innocence, he is soon arrested, but sheltered by his accuser; he is then recaptured by the robbers, compelled to take part in a burglary, and again sheltered by the intended victims of his evil-doing patrons; the malevolent action of the boy's half-brother results in the ruin of the criminal band and the disclosure of kinship between the two half-brothers and the two groups of benefactors.

It cannot be contended that the story is what Forster calls it—"simply but well constructed."[3] The story is by no means simple, at least to the modern taste; but it does have real unity, and its parts are firmly held together, with excess, indeed, rather than lack of firmness, since, at the end of the book, the reader can hardly see anything else than the threads connecting the episodes. It seems almost as if, when writing *Oliver Twist*, Dickens had wanted to prove that he could write a true novel, construct a really impressive plot.

And yet his demonstration is not conclusive. It cannot be conclusive because the story has not been completely thought out in advance, and because the absence of a precise anticipation of the course of events is even more damaging in the case of a coherent plot than it could be in that of a series of independent episodes, like *Pickwick*. As evidence that Dickens had not really set out to write a "well-made" novel, we have a letter in which he told Yates, the actor, who proposed to adapt *Oliver* to the stage: "I am quite satisfied that no one can have heard what I mean to do with the different characters in the end, inasmuch as, at present, I don't quite know myself."[4]

Besides the uncertainties of his preliminary planning, the circum- stances of publication imposed upon the author many hesitations. He

[3] *Life of Dickens*, I, 83. On his copy of the biography Wilkie Collins wrote, more judiciously, in the margin: "Nonsense! The one defect of that wonderful book is the helplessly bad construction of the story." (See in *Pall Mall Gazette* [Jan. 20, 1890], the article called "Wilkie Collins about Charles Dickens").

[4] *Edmund Yates, His Recollections and Experiences* (London, 1884), I, 18. The letter is undated, but seems to have been written in 1838, when the story was sufficiently ad- vanced to lend itself to theatrical adaptation; the editors of the *Letters* (I, 388) tentatively give the date as "mid-March, 1838."

found it difficult to cut out his chapters so that two or three of them would accurately fill up sixteen pages of the magazine. In April, 1837, for instance, with his third installment, Dickens, who had to pause in the middle of an episode—Oliver's quarrel with Noah Claypole, the undertaker's other apprentice—devoted another chapter to the close of the same episode. The title of the new chapter emphasizes the artificiality of the division: "Oliver continues refractory."[5] In Chapter XII the reverse happens: Dickens is relating Oliver's recovery in the house of his first benefactor, Mr. Brownlow; on the manuscript the chapter comes to an end at the moment when Oliver faints on hearing him notice the likeness between a young woman's portrait on the wall and the little invalid's face: "he fainted away. A weakness on his part, which affords the author an opportunity of relieving the reader from suspense, in behalf of the two young pupils of the Merry Old Gentleman," after which Chapter XIII begins with the words "When the Dodger, and his accomplished friend Master Bates . . . ," the whole chapter being devoted to the two young thieves' return to Fagin's and the ensuing scenes. But Chapter XII proved too short to complete the issue of the *Miscellany*; two pages were wanting, not enough for a separate chapter; Dickens was pressed for time and comparatively uninspired—this must have been some time in June, 1837, shortly after Mary Hogarth's death—so he could not think of extemporizing two additional pages in order to inflate Chapter XII. Hence he coolly detached the first two pages of Chapter XIII, and gave to the two fragments the monstrous aspect they have preserved till now. After ". . . the Merry Old Gentleman," he added "and of recording . . ."; before the first word of Chapter XIII, he interpolated "that";[6] Chapter XII goes on to, "The door was slowly opened; and the Dodger and Charley Bates entered, closing it behind them." Chapter XIII consequently began with the phrase: " 'Where's Oliver?' asked the furious Jew."[7]

In the last installments of the *Miscellany* containing fragments of

[5] For similar reasons, Dickens is led to promise in the title of chap. ix, "further particulars concerning" Fagin.

[6] Probably on the corrected proofs, for there is no trace of such a change on the MS itself.

[7] Chaps. xii and xiii. The heterogeneity of chap. xii is further stressed by the transfer into its heading of one section from that of chap. xiii: "And in which the narrative reverts to the Merry Old Gentleman and his youthful friends."

Oliver, the method underwent a change, because Dickens had by then already written and published all the end of his novel, and could no longer modify the numbering of his chapters: the monthly portions then became variable in size and one chapter could even come to be divided between two successive numbers of the periodical.[8] It would be pleasant to believe that artistic scruple caused this change of method, or the feeling that posterity's aesthetic satisfaction was of more moment than the convenience of an ephemeral magazine; but nothing shows that to have been the case.

And many incoherencies have been left: the novel had been at first published in three books comprising twenty-two, seventeen, and fifteen chapters; but the division into books corresponds to no internal necessity. The separation between Books II and III is even particularly awkward: it occurs, on the manuscript, immediately after the first interview of Monks—Oliver's half brother—and Bumble the Beadle, and before their second encounter; the present Chapter XXXVIII was to have been called "Book the Second. Chapter the Eighteenth"; the words "Second" and "Eighteenth" were crossed out by the writer and replaced by "Third" and "First." This unsatisfactory division disappeared for good and all in the first edition in volume form (Bentley, October, 1838); yet, instead of the fifty-four chapters to be found in the magazine, there were now only fifty-one in the three volumes; later editions have fifty-three,[9] because they restore, for mysterious reasons, two accidental anomalies of the original division. This is a characteristic incident: Dickens not only did not avail himself of the opportunity afforded by the publication of his novel in book form to restore to it the aspect that serial publication had deprived it of; he even allowed the few improvements he had made to disappear from the text. In fact, he may not himself have looked very closely into this chapter-count, which was enough to exasperate many a writer more patient than he.[10] Few of Dickens' novels are nowadays

---

[8] See *Bentley's Miscellany,* Vol. 5 (1839).

[9] Chaps. xxx and xxxi, and chaps. xliv and xlv, are merged in the Bentley edition, and later editions until 1847.

[10] In addition, the original heading of chap. xxxvii comprised the following sentence, "The reader, if he or she resort to the fifth chapter of this second book, will perceive . . ." This reference was preserved in the Bentley edition of 1838, but made no sense there, since the novel was no longer divided into books; in later editions (1839, etc.), the heading is altered to "if he or she resort to the twenty-third chapter," which is understandable, but

commonly offered to the public in a form so imperfect and so remote from the author's real purpose as *Oliver Twist*.

The chapter-headings suffer from the uncertainties of this division; as he is not sure he will not have to curtail or spread out his chapters according to the needs of the magazine, Dickens does not venture to give them precise headings; quite often the title of a chapter becomes a kind of fraud and could be summed up as "continuation of the preceding chapter"; such are the titles of Chapters XVI, XXVI, XXXVI, and XL: "Relates what became of Oliver Twist after he had been claimed by Nancy"; "In which . . . many things, inseparable from this history, are done and performed"; ". . . should be read . . . as a sequel to the last, and a key to one that will follow when its time arrives"; "A strange interview, which is a sequel to the last chapter."

Thus does *Oliver Twist* in the first place strike us as a novel composed and published in small fragments over many months and subjected to many vicissitudes and accidents. No one should be surprised at finding weak points in its structure. Dickens makes a larger use than in his other works of digressions. However poorly constructed *Pickwick* had been, it had contained no digressions; true, one can digress only from a straight line, while the outline of *Pickwick* had been so broken and zigzagging that there was no knowing when the author went away from it. In *Oliver Twist*, whose story is more consecutive and closely knit, many digressive passages stand out: Oliver's conversation with Mr. Brownlow about books and the writer's profession (chap. xiv) is as superfluous as it is improbable; yet its conclusion, as Mr. Brownlow tells Oliver—"We won't make an author of you, while there's an honest trade to be learnt, or brick-making to turn to,"—shows it to have been but a fresh example of the author's youthfulness; dazzled at finding himself in the position of a professional and prosperous novelist at the age of twenty-five, he relishes such ironical and conventional allusions to his craft. And there are in *Oliver Twist* other digressions as well as other kinds of unnecessary elements: a long and commonplace description—as commonplace as most of Dickens' general remarks are at the time—of rustic pleasures (chap. xxxii); a too detailed presentation of a huckster whose part is at

still unsatisfactory, since chap. xxiii is not the same as chap. v of Book II. From 1847 on, the reference is omitted altogether.

best episodic, during Sikes' flight (chap. xlviii); or again, the unduly developed description of "Jacob's Island" (chap. l). Some of those fragments may possibly have been added or expanded at proof stage in order to fill up deficient installments. Yet their more obvious purpose generally appears to be an attempt at smoothing the passage from one chapter or one scene to another. Dickens, as a youthful novelist, has not yet mastered the art of securing an easy transition between two incidents, or the greater art of linking incident to incident solidly enough to be able to dispense with a transition altogether. Transitions in *Oliver Twist* are often ponderous and artificial. Here, as in *Pickwick*, a great display of ingenuity betrays the author's uncertain hand; thus, when Dickens declares, at the end of Chapter XXVII, "With these words, the beadle strode . . . from the undertaker's premises. And now that we have accompanied him so far on his road home . . . let us set on foot a few enquiries after young Oliver, and ascertain whether he be still lying in the ditch where Toby Crackit left him" (chap. xxvii), his hesitation might have been less glaring if he had contented himself with closing the chapter after the first of the above-quoted sentences, and beginning the next chapter without a preamble. A similar feeling is elicited by several passages of the book; two additional examples may be given: "Talking all the way, he followed Mr. Giles up stairs; and while he is going up stairs, the reader may be informed, that Mr. Losberne, a surgeon in the neighborhood . . . " (chap. xxix); "Upon the very same night when Nancy . . . hurried on her self-imposed mission . . . there advanced towards London . . . two persons, upon whom it is expedient that this history should bestow some attention" (chap. xlii). Such phrases, involving active interference of author, reader, or more or less personified "history," are the hallmark of immature technique, of a narrative method still in need of external aids to insure its progress.

Side by side with those unquestionable weaknesses can however be observed in *Oliver* evidence of the author's earliest conscious artistic attempt; its result will be better understood when its purpose and other peculiarities have been defined. *Oliver Twist* is no isolated production; the book belongs to what Thackeray called "The Newgate School of Fiction," a series, very popular in the eighteen-thirties, of novels whose heroes are great criminals. This kind of literature, whose origins are very remote,[11] had been very fashionable in the eighteenth century, with the works of Defoe (*Moll Flanders*)[12] and Fielding (*Jonathan Wild*) among others; yet the criminal ideal had again flourished more recently thanks to Byron, whose *Lara* appeared in 1814. Bulwer Lytton, ever ready and eager to adapt himself to the passing taste, wrote two "Newgate Novels" (*Paul Clifford* in 1830 and *Eugene Aram* in 1832), W. H. Ainsworth two also (*Rookwood* in 1834, and *Jack Sheppard,* which succeeded *Oliver* in *Bentley's Miscellany* in 1839); Charles Whitehead, the writer who had recommended Boz to Chapman and Hall, published *The Autobiography of Jack Ketch* in 1834. In that field, then, Dickens was by no means a pioneer, and was in fact rather fighting a rearguard action, since *Oliver Twist* came out shortly before the reaction set in against the "Newgate Novels"; the reaction was led mainly by Thackeray, who wrote no fewer than three parodies of the genre: *Catherine* in 1839–40, *Barry Lyndon* in 1844, and *George de Barnwell* in 1847. At the end of *Catherine*, when he was about to introduce the most violent and sanguinary scene, the author exclaimed: "We are now prepared, O candid and discerning reader, who are sick of the hideous scenes of brutal bloodshed which have of late come forth from the pens of certain eminent wits, to give to the world a scene infinitely more brutal and bloody than even the murder of Miss Nancy ... if you turn away disgusted from the book, remember that this passage has not been written for you, who have taste to know and hate the style in which it has been composed; but for the public, which has no such taste .... Stretch your throats, sweet ones—for our god, the public, is thirsty, and must have blood."[13]

"And there was the body—mere flesh and blood, no more—but such flesh, and so much blood!" Dickens had been writing in *Oliver Twist* (chap. xlviii). If the public was as bloodthirsty as Thackeray believed it to be, Dickens was ready to slake its thirst. He was ready to cater to its taste for every kind of sensation[14]—for violence, mystery, emotion and

[11] See F. W. Chandler, *The Literature of Roguery* (Boston, 1907). Chandler traces the literature of roguery back to Chaucer (I, 47–48).

[12] The composition of *Oliver Twist* has been interestingly connected with the influence of another work by Defoe. See Marie Hamilton Law, "The Indebtedness of *Oliver Twist* to Defoe's *History of the Devil*," *PMLA*, XL (Dec. 1925), 892–97.

[13] Thackeray, *Catherine*, chap. xiii.

[14] See Phillips, *Dickens, Reade, and Collins*. The only weak point of this work, which offers a mine of valuable information on many subjects, is its somewhat artificial attempt to

horror: the death of Old Sally, just as she seemed about to reveal the identity of Oliver's mother (chap. xxiv); the mysterious apparitions, in various places, and the hideous disease and general aspect of Monks (chap. xxxvii); the harmony between the storm, the surroundings, and the broken speech of the characters during his interview with the Bumbles (chap. xxxviii); the secret kinships suddenly disclosed and other sensational identifications (chaps. xl, xlvi, xlix); the past events revealed in theatrical style, as ". . . in the West Indies—whither, as you well know, you retired upon your mother's death" (chap. xlix); the fantastic form in which had been couched a will which has been destroyed but remains compelling (chap. li); and the no less fantastic entanglement of secret relationships—such that, in the final scene, "a father, sister, and mother, were gained, and lost, in that one moment" (chap. li)—all those incidents which, nowadays, do little, if anything, for the success of the book, were introduced by Dickens for the purpose of pleasing the contemporary popular taste, and can be looked upon as so many effects of his careful and complex, though slightly mistaken, technical labor.

The quest for sensational effects is favored by the alternation of comical with tragical scenes. The procedure is first criticized in the digressive introduction to Chapter XVII, in a style characteristic of Dickens' imagery: "It is the custom on the stage, in all good murderous melodramas, to present the tragic and comic scenes, in as regular alternation, as the layers of red and white in a side of streaky bacon." If the novelist's terms are correct, then *Oliver Twist* undoubtedly is "a good murderous melodrama," for the tendency to a change of atmosphere after the more dramatic passages is clearly marked, as if to relieve the tension. In general, Dickens relinquishes his London characters and takes us to see some incident in Bumble's life. He does so in Chapter XVII, after the great quarrel in the thieves' den following Oliver's return there; in Chapter XXIV, while Oliver lies, wounded, in a ditch; in Chapter XXVII, after the mysterious interview between Monks and Fagin has come to a close; in Chapter XXXVII, after the separation between the quaint lovers, Harry and Rose Maylie. All of these changes do not merely modify and relax the atmosphere of the narrative; they also

make up a sensational "school" by associating Collins and Reade, whose significant fiction was published after 1855, with Dickens, whose "sensational" works are *BR* (1841) and *OT*.

result in a change of scene. Thus the composition of *Oliver* is more complex than that of *Pickwick*, which had been founded on a mobile group of characters, ever escorted by the narrator; in *Oliver*, on the contrary, two, then three groups of characters evolve in separate areas, but find themselves linked together by increasingly manifold bonds. In spite of the ironical tone of the statements on the subject also to be found at the beginning of Chapter XVII ("sudden shiftings of the scene and rapid changes of time and place, are not only sanctioned in books by long usage, but are by many considered as the great art of authorship"), it is clear that Dickens is obeying the impulse to display his technical skill. The result is on the whole creditable: some of the shiftings from one scene to another are either too abrupt or too labored, but the sequence of incidents is controlled with a certain cleverness and appears methodically organized. This is mostly the case from the moment Oliver has been admitted into the home of the Maylies—his second benefactors. There are then three series of scenes providing information about Oliver's progress and the Maylies family life, about the uncertainties and anxieties of the Fagin gang, and about the evolution of affairs in the Bumbles' small anonymous town. The scenes are superficially independent, but the reader is made to feel their increasing unity. Oliver himself is a permanent link: he had been born in an unknown town, and it is the mystery of his birth that is looked for there; among the thieves, it is his disappearance that causes alarm, and a good deal of plotting against him is constantly going on; Monks, Oliver's half-brother, is first seen in connection with Fagin's gang (chap. xxvi); then Oliver himself catches sight of him (chaps. xxxiii–xxxiv); finally he shows himself to Bumble (chap. xxxvii). A fresh link is created and the triangle becomes complete when Nancy, the thieves' accomplice, has an interview with Rose Maylie.

Through the firmness of its plot, then, *Oliver Twist* is a work superior, not only to *Pickwick*, but also to *Nickleby*, and indeed to all the other novels of Dickens' first period; it has better construction; indeed, it has *more* construction than the others. Traces of inexperience can still be discerned in it, however, for, while the outline of the narrative is coherent, the machinery is still somewhat artificial. There was not enough organization in *Pickwick*, but there is rather too much of it in *Oliver*, and the result is the same in both cases: the passage from one incident to the next is jerky, and occasionally forced; the use of coincidence is just as lavish as in the preceding book, and the whole plot rests on a twofold monumental coincidence; Oliver is twice made to work for the thieves: the first time, he is present when the victim of a robbery happens to be Mr. Brownlow, his father's oldest friend, and the second time, the boy is constrained to take part in the burglarizing of a house where his aunt happens to be living. The fact that the first link was no afterthought with Dickens is proved by the existence in Mr. Brownlow's house of a portrait of Oliver's mother, to which the reader's attention is drawn as early as Chapter XII, and even earlier, when Mr. Brownlow finds something familiar to him in Oliver's countenance.

Several minor coincidences could be listed; those above mentioned will suffice to show what an important part that convenient procedure is called upon to play in the book. Its value is indeed openly proclaimed, both by virtuous characters who see in it the action of divine providence, like Mr. Brownlow, when he says to Monks: "Your brother . . . was cast on my way by a stronger hand than chance" (chap. xlix), and by evildoers, who see in it Satan's influence, like Monks, when he says to Bumble, with theatrical cynicism: "I came down to this place to-day, to find you out; and, by one of those chances which the devil throws in the way of his friends sometimes, you walked into the very room I was sitting in."[15]

Through its accidental encounters, *Oliver Twist,* in spite of its uniqueness among Dickens' works, has something in common with most of them. The ending of the novel is equally characteristic of the usual Dickensian manner. Like all Dickens' early novels, *Oliver Twist* is crowned by what Forster calls "the quiet closing chapter,"[16] in which, within four pages, the reader is informed of the fate of some twelve characters.

"And now the hand that traces these words falters, as it approaches the conclusion of its task; and would weave, for a little longer space, the thread of these adventures"—thus Dickens wrote in his concluding chapter. Forster has fortunately described the mirthful evening in the course of which those melancholy lines were penned, when the owner of the

---

[15] "In my way," says Brownlow; "On my way," says Monks. The principle is the same, and the method allowing the novelist to find on his way, by chance and without any more justification, the character he needs to find, is a facile method.

[16] *Life of Dickens,* I, 87.

faltering hand did not conceal his joy at having done with Oliver for good and all.

Our perception of the differences and resemblances between the composition of *Pickwick* and that of *Oliver Twist* should not be taken to mean that there has been an evolution from one to the other of two works which were in great part contemporaneous, but rather that two distinct efforts coexisted in the early experimental phase of Dickens' career, from 1836 to 1839; he was only gradually finding himself, through trial and error as well as through trial and triumph. As far as style is concerned, his search is less hesitant already. As a considerable portion of the manuscript of *Oliver*[17] has been preserved, it is possible to form an idea of his purpose by looking at the way in which he corrected himself.

In the first place, the vocabulary employed by Dickens in *Oliver Twist* shows a greater tendency to archaism—not without a touch of pedantry —than is often believed. As in the *Sketches*, "sundry" and "divers" are often used where "some" or "several" would have done just as well, and Dickens introduces dubious refinements, such as calling Fagin's abject gang "that respectable coterie"—or unusual grammatical forms: "nor stopped they once to breathe." But, side by side with such poorly written passages, there are others in *Oliver Twist* of higher quality. Dickens, at some apparently inspired moments, seems to rise almost to a kind of poetry; for instance, in three paragraphs of Chapter X (each beginning with the cry, "Stop thief!"), through the incantatory iteration of those two words, as well as through cumulative, intensifying, and quickening effects, the style of the passage becomes exalted. This again occurs in the tragic episode of the murder; it would seem that Dickens, while writing that portion of his narrative, had been obsessed by the remembrance of Shakespeare, and particularly of *Macbeth,* in which are also to be found the preparation of a crime and the hauntings of remorse; the words in which Fagin greets Sikes emulate Shakespearean syntax through the omission of the relative pronoun, and might, *mutatis mutandis,* have been used by Lady Macbeth to salute her husband: "I've got that to tell you, Bill, will make you worse than me" (chap. xxxvii). Likewise, the admirable chapter describing the criminal's flight (chap. xlviii), begins

[17] The MS fragment in the Forster Collection comprises chaps. xii–xiii, the whole of Book II (chaps. xxiii–xxxviii) and chaps. i–vi of Book III (chaps. xxxix–xliii).

in solemn, quasi-inspired style: "Of all bad deeds, that under cover of the darkness . . . that was the worst," in which the very use of the word "deed" to mean "murder" is once more reminiscent of *Macbeth*—"I have done the deed"—as is, throughout the passage, the obsessive presence of blood-stains; "There were spots that would not be removed. How those stains were dispersed about the room!"

Apart from the most mediocre and the most felicitously written passages that have just been mentioned, Dickens' use of language in *Oliver Twist* already illustrates some of his more permanent characteristics, such as the sentimental coloring that has often been noticed in his works. One word that was to play a great part in Dickens' style, the adjective "old," already appears here with its most idiosyncratic connotation: to a novelist who is deeply attached to whatever in the past is personal, anything that belongs to former days, anything familiar, tends to be treated as touching and moving. Such is the value assumed by "old" in phrases like "faces that the grave had changed and closed upon, but which the mind . . . still dressed in their old freshness and beauty . . .";[18] the association of "old" with "freshness" is at first sight paradoxical; it is less so, of course, when one thinks of the adverbial form "of old"; and in any case, it is the direct outcome of Dickens' sentimental vision of the past, so that his use of "old" is always one of the most easily identifiable leitmotivs of his work. Sentimentality is frequently allied with intensity of expression; Dickens constantly reinforces his assertions by means of such adverbs as "quite" and "indeed," such forceful adjectives as "great," and any number of superlatives; in one page of *Oliver* will be found the following expressions: "the most eager desire . . . the greatest caution and most circumspect behavior . . . great politeness . . . great benevolence . . . great crash . . . the most unmitigated wonder"; whenever Dickens is powerfully taken by his theme, and participates in the emotions he is describing, such expressions inevitably crop up in his writing.

An examination of the manuscript reveals that *Oliver Twist* was written with uneven ease; the number of corrections varies greatly from page to page. The general aspect of the manuscript, if compared to those of later works, affords an impression of more flowing inspiration or less careful labor. The handwriting is broad and swift; the cancelled words

18 Chap. xi; similar examples will be found in *Copperfield*.

are at first crossed with one horizontal line that leaves them comparatively legible; then, half way through Chapter XIII, the straight line is given up in favor of a series of close loops which are thereafter Dickens' single system of self-correction and make his other manuscripts much harder to interpret. On the whole, there are few corrections in *Oliver Twist*; occasionally, two whole paragraphs occur in succession without a single change being made;[19] and when there are extensive changes, the cause is easy enough to guess. As often as not, it is due to some peculiar difficulty experienced by the author. When composing some pseudo-philosophical digression on a general theme, Dickens was less sure of his ground than in narrative or dialogue; in Chapter XII, for instance (called Chapter XIII on the manuscript), he canceled, after much hesitation, a whole sentence: "In proof of which proposition I need hardly [refer][20] appeal to everybody's experience of every day and every school," which may, understandably, have struck him on second or third thoughts, as rather too commonplace and vague. In the same chapter one gesture was added—perhaps as he reread his page—in order to increase the shock of Sikes's brutality; after " 'She's a honour to her sex,' said Mr. Sikes, filling his glass," he inserted, above the line, "and striking the table with his enormous fist." That is on the occasion of Sikes's first appearance, and Sikes is one of the book's most sensational figures; the writer cannot spare his most vivid colors. Similarly, the first time we see—or rather hear—Rose Maylie, (chap. xxviii) a girl of ideal sweetness, the manuscript discloses a great deal of effort and hesitation between such words as "light," "soft," "gentle," "musical," and "tripping," before Dickens could satisfy himself that he had conveyed the right impression. The description of a dilapidated house which he wished to render impressive—for it is there that the momentous interview between Monks and the Bumbles will take place—apparently occasioned him the same kind of problem (chap. xxxviii).

In the final section of the book, Dickens apparently sought to tone down, rather than enhance, the impressions of brutality and coarseness. That, at least, appears to be the cause of corrections of the following

---

[19] E.g., in chap. xiii; no change is made in the two paragraphs beginning with "This was a vagrant of sixty-five . . . ."

[20] In every quotation from Dickens' MSS, the words in square brackets are those he had himself crossed out.

kind: "Let me get off this [thundering] [cursed bed] thundering bed anyhow." A little later, after "Sikes struck her" (Nancy), the author cancels "in the face." Sikes shouts to Nancy: "bustle about, or I'll beat it out of you" ("it" being "your foolery"), but the end of the sentence is turned into the much tamer "and don't come over me with your woman's nonsense." Fagin, who had been called at first "false-hearted old swine," is reduced to being termed merely a "false-hearted wagabond." A few chapters earlier there had already occurred the following extenuation, whose involuntary humor need not be pointed out: Fagin asks Nancy, " 'And where should you think Bill was now, my dear, eh?' ['In Hell, for anything I know," the girl replied without raising her face.] The girl moaned out [that she could] some scarcely intelligible reply."[21]

But, however interesting a study of Dickens' manuscript, apart from the general impression that the writer did his job seriously and conscientiously enough, it is difficult to gain from his corrections any clear idea of his stylistic principles.

Any survey of style in *Oliver Twist* would be grievously incomplete if it did not refer to the way in which Dickens handles one word which must have been originally meant to belong to the book's main theme. The complete title of the novel is *Oliver Twist, or the Parish Boy's Progress.* The word "progress" immediately calls to mind Hogarth—who is incidentally mentioned by Dickens in the preface, as an artist whose unique realism he wishes to emulate—and his famous *Rake's Progress*, while the alliteration in *Parish . . . Progress* is yet more markedly reminiscent of Bunyan's *Pilgrim's Progress.* The title thus stresses the fact that Oliver is a parish-boy, a boy raised, that is, since there is little or no ecclesiastical connotation attaching to the word "parish," as a pauper, at the expense of the community. It will be observed that the word "parish," together with its derivatives "parishioner," "parochial," and Bumble's delightful variant of the latter, "porochial," are used some thirty times in the course of the first four chapters, and keep recurring to the end of the book. With two other terms—"workhouse" and "pauper"—equally evocative of the idea of administrative, impersonal, inhuman charity, the word "parish" is thus closely linked with the purpose of the narrative, as an attack

21 Chap. xxxvi; all the above quotations are previously unpublished extracts from the original MS of *Oliver Twist* in the Forster Collection.

launched against the New Poor Law of 1834 and its rigid parochial organization of spurious official philanthropy. The method—perhaps only half consciously adopted in *Oliver*—which consists in bestowing permanent prominence on one idea through the constant iteration of the same word or words, was used again and systematically enlarged in later novels.

Thus we find more unity in the style and composition of *Oliver Twist* than in those of *Pickwick*. This is all the more surprising since Dickens' second continuous narrative was written, not only in shorter installments and over a longer period of time than the first, but also amidst a great turmoil of actions, labors, and events.

In December, 1837, Dickens' son was baptized. In February, 1838, appeared *Sketches of Young Gentlemen*, a short work written anonymously by Dickens for Chapman and Hall. On January 16, he had written, in a letter to Forster, "I am as badly off as you. I have not done the Young Gentleman, nor written the preface to *Grimaldi*, nor thought of *Oliver Twist* or even suggested a subject for the plate,"[22] and on the twenty-fifth, to Ainsworth, "my month's work has been dreadful, Grimaldi, the anonymous book for Chapman and Hall, Oliver and the Miscellany. They are all done, thank God."[23] Early in February, he was off to Yorkshire, and on his return began to write the first number of *Nickleby,* to be published on April 1. The extraordinary success of this book was to sustain the writer's work on the completion of *Oliver*; but the inception of *Nickleby* also meant that Dickens had once more—after a brief and very incomplete respite of three or four months—two major works in process at the same time. On March 6 his second child, a daughter, was born. Through the spring of 1838 he went on working at *Oliver* with cheerful pertinacity and devoted his evenings to the effort, a thing he never did again for any of his later novels. He had decided, as we have seen, that he must have done with it by the end of the summer, and he occasionally wrote as many as sixteen manuscript pages in a single day, or three or four times as much as his normal practice allowed. A letter of August, 1838, casts some light on the atmosphere in which this strenuous

---

[22] See *Letters*, I, 355, and, for a slightly different version of the same letter, a footnote in the early editions of Forster's *Life of Dickens*. Forster altered *suggested* to *supplied*; the footnote is not reprinted in the Everyman's Library edition.

[23] *Letters*, I, 359.

labor was conducted: "I worked pretty well last night—very well, indeed, —but although I did eleven close slips before half past twelve I have yet four to write to complete the chapter; and as I foolishly left them 'till this morning have the steam to get up afresh."[24] The final image is significant: Dickens worked under high pressure; it took him some time to get under way, but once he was fairly launched, he could write on happily enough.

It was in the years 1837 and 1838 that Dickens gained access to more wealthy and distinguished circles. At that time, he made the acquaintance, not only of the poet Samuel Rogers, but also of a few genuine, if somewhat marginal, members of the aristocracy, since he began to be a regular visitor, both at Lady Blessington's and at Lady Holland's; he was elected to the Athenaeum Club. It is curious to observe that the period when he became familiar with the higher classes of London society is also the period when, in *Oliver Twist*, he was depicting its lower strata. The enlargement of his experience was to be of some literary use to him later, but for the time being he had no occasion to let it penetrate into his work.

The end of 1838 was marked by more traveling—Dickens visited, among other places, Manchester—and no one ought to be surprised at finding that his health began to be affected at that time, as is shown by his correspondence: "My side had been very bad since I left home," he wrote to his wife on November 1, 1838, and went on in his usual hyperbolic style, "I suffered such an ecstacy of pain all night at Stratford that I was half dead yesterday."[25] His disagreements and misunderstandings with the publisher Bentley had developed almost uninterruptedly through 1838, and it had become more and more painful to work for him. Early in 1839, he made arrangements with Chapman and Hall to be released from all further obligations to Bentley: on receiving a down payment of £2,250, Bentley gave up the copyright of *Oliver Twist* and the contract for *Barnaby Rudge*, and Dickens ceased to edit the *Miscellany*.

Of all the events in Dickens' private life that coincided with the composition of *Oliver*, the most significant, as in the case of *Pickwick*, was the

24 *Ibid.*, 425; the letter is tentatively dated as of August 8; Forster (*Life of Dickens*, I, 87) gives the impossible date of "May."
25 *Letters*, I, 448.

death of Mary Hogarth. The marks left on the book by that tragedy are even deeper than on the preceding novel, and they affect the creation of Rose Maylie very particularly.

There are clearly three distinct categories of characters in *Oliver Twist:* the comic figures who are fully alive, the melodramatic villains, and the angels. The comic figures are the most characteristically Dickensian creations. There are many, especially in the small anonymous city of Oliver's birth; they are true photographic reproductions of living beings, treated in unquestionably realistic style; such are Mrs. Mann, Mrs. Corney—though she tends to join the second category once she has degenerated into Mrs. Bumble—the two Sowerberrys, and the immortal Bumble.

The melodramatic villains also reappear in Dickens' later works. "I fear there are in the world some insensible and callous natures, that do become, at last, utterly and irredeemably bad," the novelist wrote in his preface to *Oliver.* Such malevolent beings, who do evil for evil's sake, are a great resource of Dickensian plots; they create any number of difficulties and obstacles to the happiness of the heroes and heroines, and the annihilation of these evil-doers tends to become the ultimate purpose of the plot. These dark figures never completely disappear from Dickens' work, but their psychology becomes increasingly complex and flexible.[26] There are plenty of characters of this class among the thieves, and they are not all contemptible creations; if Monks may be thought too purely spectacular, too inhuman, with his hideous disease and almost gratuitous malevolence, Sikes on the contrary is a well-drawn figure of a brute, and his flight and remorse are convincingly described. As for Fagin, he is vigorously depicted and comes to life with his perpetual greed, but also with his disquieting mirth and scathing irony; he can even be regarded as one of Dickens' few truly great villains.

Finally, there are in *Oliver Twist* a number of angelic figures meant to arouse our admiration and touch our hearts; yet they are drawn in a way that is not likely to convince the modern reader. To that group belong chiefly Oliver himself, Rose Maylie, and Nancy from the time of

---

[26] It is a far cry from Sikes (*OT*) to Jasper (*ED*). And in between these two are to be found Quilp (*OCS*), Rudge Sr., Carker (*D&S*), Heep (*DC*), Rigaud-Lagnier-Blandois (*LD*), Orlick (*GE*) and a few more.

her conversion. Oliver totally lacks the naturalness that gives such appeal to other Dickensian children, like David Copperfield or Pip. He is too uniformly pure and pious. It may seem unpleasant to criticize a literary creation inspired by such a noble ideal; yet Oliver is an almost perfect illustration of André Gide's dictum that bad literature is produced by worthy feelings; the noblest ideal cannot become art without a modicum of truth and life, and this is conspicuously lacking in the portrait of Oliver. Several critics have rightly protested against the purity of both language and feeling which Oliver simply could not have acquired in the workhouse, where religion and morals were not taught, and where the only kind of language spoken was that of Bumble, superbly picturesque and entertaining, but fundamentally ungrammatical and corrupted. Yet the young hero, under the most stupendous circumstances, will more than once preach and pray in impeccable English. "For the love of all the bright angels that rest in Heaven!" he tells the two robbers who are taking him along on their expedition, "have mercy upon me!" (chap. xxii); and in Fagin's condemned cell, Oliver is not yet twelve when he holds forth thus: "Let me say a prayer. Do! Let me say one prayer. Say only one, upon your knees, with me, and we will talk till morning" (chap. lii). Such an attempt ought perhaps to be touching; but it could hardly be more glaringly unreal; and the Merry Old Gentleman would lose much of his convincing force if he could comply with such an edifying invitation; however, in addition to not being a Christian, he has other views of the least intolerable way of spending one's last few hours on earth.

In the character of Nancy is to be seen another new and interesting effort on Dickens' part. She is not all of a piece, being neither uniformly good like Oliver or Rose, nor uniformly bad like Sikes or Fagin. Dickens was thoroughly convinced of her being true to life, and in fact she has many real traits. The appearance in the midst of the dishonest gang of a child who wishes to keep himself pure awakens in her some feelings of motherly tenderness. Such an evolution can be justified. What is less defensible is the kind of language she uses once she has been redeemed. Admittedly Dickens was hampered by the Grundyism of his time. He could not say outright that Nancy was a prostitute. He had to content himself with referring to "that particular species of humanity to which

Nancy belonged" (chap. xvi); the word "prostitute" was to appear only three years later, in the 1841 preface.[27] Therefore, when she becomes repentant, she is unable to let the reader know, except in the form of the vaguest allusions, what faults she is repenting. This modesty after the event makes her language sound extremely artificial and unconvincing. Thackeray's comment concerning prostitutes seems appropriate: "as no writer can or dare tell the *whole* truth concerning them, and faithfully explain their vices, there is no need to give *ex parte* statements of their virtue."[28] Dickens' acceptance of the rigid rules of Victorian discretion did make it impossible for him to produce any satisfactory and balanced portraiture in this field.[29]

Rose Maylie's case is different. The history of that character is closely linked with the remembrance Dickens preserved and cherished of his young sister-in-law's death. Her psychological or aesthetic interest is practically nonexistent. Her significance for an understanding of Dickens' art is immense.

It is curious to find how Rose Maylie, meant to embody purity, innocence, beauty, and joy, is constantly associated with the theme of death. Even before the terrible occurrence of May 7, 1837, the theme of youth and death had already inspired the author of *Oliver Twist* with at least one passage whose pathos will nowadays sound very thin and unreal; Dick, the consumptive orphan boy, is speaking: "I heard the doctor tell them I was dying. . . . I know the doctor must be right, Oliver, because I dream so much of Heaven, and Angels, and kind faces I never see when I am awake." (chap. vii). After Mary's death, Dickens' allusions to the same theme become more frequent and sound more sincere and moving; in Chapter XII, written immediately after May, 1837, Oliver is speaking of his mother, who had died in childbirth, and says: "If she had seen me hurt, it would have made her sorrowful; and her face has always looked sweet and happy, when I have dreamed of her."[30] At the beginning of Chapter XXIV, there is a description of human faces in death, which

27 "The girl is a prostitute," Preface.
28 *Catherine,* "Another Last Chapter."
29 Wilkie Collins (*Pall Mall Gazette,* Jan. 20, 1890) felt unqualified admiration for Nancy and called her "the finest thing [Dickens] ever did."
30 The sentence echoes the author's experience accurately. Dickens claimed that he had dreamed every night, for several years, of Mary in happiness.

opens with the words, "It is a common thing for the countenances of the dead . . ."; in spite of the generalization, this deserves to be read with some respect, for it is doubtless a description of Mary's countenance, "so calm, so peaceful." When Rose Maylie plays her part, and especially, of course, when she is dangerously ill, there are recognizable allusions in increasing number: "The memories which peaceful country scenes call up, are not of this world," (chap. xxxii); "I have seen enough . . . to know that it is not always the youngest and best who are spared to those that love them"; "Oh! the suspense, the fearful, acute suspense, of standing idly by while the life of one we dearly love is trembling in the balance!"; "We need be careful with those about us, when every death carries to some small circle of survivors, thoughts of so much omitted, and so little done!" (chap. xxxiii).

Still more significant and moving than the preceding allusions are those which Dickens canceled before publication and which remained unreproduced for more than a century. While describing Oliver's return to consciousness at Mr. Brownlow's after his fever, Dickens had first thought of evoking the remembrance of his sister-in-law's recent, fatal illness, and saying that, after a troubled dream, the boy "awoke with an effort so strong and painful that it seemed as if death would have been easier and sweeter than life," but he crossed out this sentence on rereading Chapter XII. And on the occasion of Rose's first appearance, he had intended to use the sadly personal exclamation: "Oh! where are the hearts [that] which, following some halting description of youth and beauty, do not recall a loved original that [Death] Time has sadly changed, or Death resolved to Dust."[31]

Vivid personal emotion cannot produce felicitous artistic results with such a sentimental novelist as Dickens was in those days, and Rose Maylie is not a success. She can touch us only through the evocation of Dickens' sincere grief, not through her own intrinsic merits as a characterization. There is no more to be said of her: she is perfect, and perfectly

31 The sentence is at the back of p. 39 of the MS (Book II, chap. vii; which is the present chap. xxix); but the MS page thus begun is numbered twenty-nine, which enables us to know where the cancelled fragment was intended to come in. The complete page numbered twenty-nine in the MS begins in fact with the words "She was not past seventeen . . . ," in chap. xxix. The unpublished fragment must thus have been meant to precede this paragraph.

vague, as must inevitably be the idealized remembrance of some dear departed being. Besides, she is called upon to play in the novel an awkward part. The author needed a pair of lovers; they are supplied by Rose and her pseudo cousin Harry Maylie. In other words, he needed a love story, some obstacle to be surmounted before marriage became possible. The obstacle is but a shadow: it consists of Rose's ill-defined scruples. Thus the love scenes in which the heroine takes part, and in which she ought to display her full charm, like Dora later, and to a lesser extent Agnes also, in *Copperfield*, are slow, solemn, turgid, and grandiloquent. The reader cannot be overjoyed when the happy ending looms in sight, since it has been both too laboriously delayed, and too easily foreseeable. Harry Maylie evinces some clear-sightedness only when he defines the victory he has gained: "to level all fancied barriers between you and me."

The final happiness, rustic, frugal, seraphic, of the whole large family of characters in the novel is of the kind which Dickens himself criticized later, when referring to some edifying pictures: "Have [the authors] considered the awful consequences likely to flow from their representations of virtue? . . . When they were leaning against a post," he says of the characters thus represented, "drunk and reckless, with surpassingly bad hats on . . . they were rather picturesque, and looked as if they might be agreeable men. . . . But, when they had got over their bad propensities, and when, as a consequence . . . their hair had got so curly that it lifted their blown-out cheeks up . . . and their eyes were so wide open that they never could do any sleep, they presented a spectacle calculated to plunge a timid nature into the depths of infamy."[32]

Colored by the author's obsessive grief and somewhat weakened by a multiplicity of social and moral purposes, *Oliver Twist* is not, like *Pickwick*, an essentially comic book. The young hero, Oliver, does not make the reader laugh even once. An examination of the comic elements in this book can be conducted rapidly. There is Jack Dawkins, the "Artful Dodger," a near relation of Sam Weller through his gusto, aplomb, and popular gift of gab. There are a few eccentrics, like Grimwig, ceaselessly offering to eat his own head, and Brittles the footman, who is still being treated as a small boy though he is over thirty. The case of these two is significant in that it illustrates a mistake made by Dickens. Although as

[32] *UT*, chap. xii.

a rule he had a remarkably accurate perception of public taste, he would occasionally make a serious mistake. The most monumental was to be the creation of *Master Humphrey*. Among the minor errors are a number of eccentrics characterized by a single trait, often very unnatural—such as Grimwig's baroque threat or the confusion as to Brittles' age. Because that trait seemed to him irresistibly droll, Dickens fancied, not only that the reader could not fail to share in his amusement, but also that he would never tire of seeing it reiterated. Thus does Grimwig tirelessly repeat his offer. Thus is Brittles' name constantly followed by the word "boy," until in the final chapter (liii) "the last-named boy" is said to be "quite grey."

Yet the most important comic figure is Bumble, who embodies the parochial theme of the novel, and thus possesses a far richer kind of comic force. He thinks only of the parish, lives but for and by the parish, speaks of nothing else. He is a sincere believer in his own supreme importance and dignity. Of the parish, in fact, he embodies every fault: its cruel hardness and spurious amiability, its affectation of paternal kindness, and its fundamental indifference to the sufferings of the poor.

At the beginning of the novel, an attempt is made to exploit the themes of macabre humor, almost always present in Dickens' fiction and embodied here by Mr. Sowerberry, the undertaker, with his coffin-shaped snuff-box, who is "rather given to professional jocosity." It is only natural that, after Mary's death, after his painful contact with the realities of the Sowerberrys' trade, Dickens should have momentarily refrained from deriving comic effects from it.

In *Oliver* once more, as in the *Sketches* and *Pickwick*, there is a considerable display of ironical epithets, with a more aggressive intent than formerly; Mrs. Mann, the superintendent of the country branch of the workhouse, is described as Oliver's "benevolent protectress"; Mr. Brownlow is introduced "into the imposing presence of the renowned Mr. Fang"; Dawkins has a smile "on his intellectual countenance"; mature, hard-boiled Mrs. Corney is "the bashful beauty," and so on.

In spite of all this, however, the reader can hardly forget the central interest of the book, the cruelty of the parochial system and the shadow of the gallows in which the malefactors live. *Oliver Twist* is an admirable rendering of an atmosphere, and the atmosphere is not a mirthful one.

Dickens' earliest preface for *Oliver* was written as late as 1841. As usual, it was devoted to a justification of the work against certain criticisms that had been made on its publication. Against those who reproached him with excessive realism and the choice of low types, he invoked in succession the authority and example of Fielding, Hogarth, Cervantes, Defoe, Goldsmith, Smollett, Richardson, and Mackenzie. Thus the preface to *Oliver* is the most literary preface ever written by Dickens. To those who thought the character of Nancy improbable, he replied: "It is useless to discuss whether the conduct and character of the girl seem natural or unnatural, probable or improbable, right or wrong. IT IS TRUE." Among the charges that had been made one was not mentioned by the author. The preface does not refer to the construction of the novel; yet the reviewer of the *Dublin University Magazine* had written: "It is a jumble of striking scenes ... carelessly thrown together, and obviously framed with little regard to mutual dependence or sequence, one upon the other,"[33] and the critic of the *Monthly Review*: "It is a mere string of sketches that might be carried to any length, or if cut short at any part, a chapter might wind up the indefinite thread."[34] Such strictures would have been fair enough, if applied to *Pickwick*, and they can only be accounted for by a superficial examination of *Oliver*, under the vague impression that it must resemble its immediate predecessor. Dickens could easily have shown that such an impression was unfounded.[35] But it has been seen already that he ignored all undeserved reproaches and put up a defense only when confronted by justified attacks. His attitude was not ignoble; whenever the work was sufficiently demonstrative, he would let it take care of itself; on the other hand, he was thus led to defend only the indefensible. He might have gloried in the characters and in the comedy of *Pickwick* instead of justifying its plot. He might have drawn attention to the plot of *Oliver* instead of endeavoring to demonstrate the genuineness of its psychology.

In fact, through its comparatively elaborate composition, *Oliver Twist* occupies a unique place in Dickens' work. No other novel, at least in the first period, again achieved comparable precision and solidity of struc-

---

[33] Dec., 1838, quoted in *Dickensiana*, 220.
[34] Jan., 1839, reproduced in *The Dickensian*, Feb., 1905, p. 32.
[35] As I hope I have shown above, pp. 122–25.

ture. But what makes the original strength of this first novel also makes its weakness, for technical ingenuity and the quest for the sensational are pursued at the expense of naturalness, spontaneity, verve—at the expense, in short, of the kind of pleasure normally expected from a book by Dickens. The composition of *Oliver Twist* is as isolated in the history of Dickens' technique as Chapter III is in Oliver's story. Just as the boy narrowly escaped being taken into the service of Gamfield the chimney-sweep, Dickens narrowly escaped joining the sensational school of novelists. This chapter might have been entitled, in a slightly modified form of the heading to Chapter III in the novel itself: "Relates how Charles was very near getting a technique, which would not have been a sinecure." Fortunately, in both cases, the danger is avoided, the paren-thesis is closed, and the hero's career is more happily launched in the very next chapter.

XIV: TOWARDS THE DICKENSIAN NOVEL: *Nicholas Nickleby*

ON NOVEMBER 19, 1837, Dickens signed a contract with Chapman and Hall, committing himself to write "a new work, whereof the title shall be determined by him, of a similar character and of the same extent as the Posthumous Papers of the Pickwick Club."[1] Such a description of the future novel was significant. Neither the subject nor the title had yet been determined, yet the length and character were, and in both respects it was intended to recall *Pickwick*. The first installment was to be published on March 15, 1838, and the author was to receive £150 per month, or ten times as much as for his first work, a figure which suf-ficiently expresses the progress he had already made in his brief literary career. Finally, the copyright of the new novel was to become his own property after five years.

Dickens, as has been seen, was snowed under with work through the end of 1837, and so he did not do much about his fresh contract before the beginning of February, 1838. By then he had conceived the idea of launching in his new book an attack against the "Yorkshire schools," which were cheap boarding schools for children in whom their parents did not take much interest, so that they were cruelly ill treated

---

[1] Forster, *Life of Dickens*, I, 82.

by incompetent masters. Dickens went to Yorkshire to collect information and took his illustrator, Browne, with him. He had procured a recommendation from a London solicitor to a solicitor in Yorkshire, under the pretense of looking for a school in which to place the children of a widowed friend of his. The stratagem enabled him to visit the notorious Bowes Academy, an institution managed by a man named Shaw, who had already been sentenced by a tribunal for not giving sufficient food and care to his pupils.

As soon as he was back in London, Dickens set to work. The first chapter was begun on February 6 and completed on February 9. The other chapters of the first number—II, III, and IV—were more slowly composed and the installment was not published till April 1 instead of the proposed March 15. During the publication of *Nickleby*, from April, 1838, through October, 1839, the author never was a single number in advance of the printer.

Forster says that fifty thousand readers bought the first number of *Nickleby* on April 1, 1838. The complete title, preserved in the later editions of 1839 and 1840, was *The Life and Adventures of Nicholas Nickleby, Containing a Faithful Account of the Fortunes, Misfortunes, Uprisings, Downfallings, and Complete Career of the Nickleby Family.* Of course, that cumbersome title had to be discarded later, especially as it did not describe the contents. The novel does not relate Nicholas' life and even less "the complete career of the Nickleby family." It is concerned only with the adventures of the hero, and his sister, mother, and uncle, through two or three years at most. Perhaps, when he coined the original title, Dickens mistrusted his own powers and did not feel assured that he could write a thousand pages about the adventures of Nicholas himself, so that he thought it safer to preserve a possibility of enlarging his theme almost *ad infinitum*, if inspiration should fail him in the narrower field.

The real title of the new work—the title to which, already on the cover of the first number, typographical prominence was given—was the hero's name, *Nicholas Nickleby*. In the choice of that name, Dickens seems to have been influenced by the example of Smollett's *Roderick Random* and *Peregrine Pickle*. Certainly, alliterative titles were not Smollett's monopoly, and there had been many other illustrious examples in English literature, from *The Pilgrim's Progress*[2] to Jane Austen (*Pride and Prejudice, Sense and Sensibility*). Closer to Dickens' days had appeared the works of Peacock (*Headlong Hall, Maid Marian, Crotchet Castle, Gryll Grange*), of Theodore Hook (*Gibert Gurney*, 1836) and of Surtees (*Jorrocks's Jaunts and Jollities*). Dickens' own alliterative titles, i.e. *Pickwick*—which has internal alliteration and assonance in the very name of Pickwick, together with alliterative association with both *Posthumous* and *Papers*—and *Nickleby*, belong to a period when such titles, always appealing, were particularly fashionable. The fashion was to be continued after him, with Samuel Lover's *Handy Andy* and *Treasure Trove* (1842–44) and later Charles Reade's *Griffith Gaunt* (1865). Yet it is highly probable that Dickens was directly influenced by Smollett, while the invention of Nicholas Nickleby's name also reflected his instinctive fondness for verbal harmonies and his preference for sounds like "i," "k," and "le."[3]

When Forster asserts that fifty thousand readers bought *Nickleby* on April 1, 1838, it is absurd to infer from the figure, as he does, that the merits of the new book were appreciated by a wide public. Purchasing *Nickleby* on that day was an act of faith in the author of *Pickwick*. The number of copies sold of the first installment of *Nickleby* was the supreme and striking confirmation of *Pickwick*'s triumph. The purchasers' attitude resulted from the same spirit of confident expectation which had also produced the liberal terms of the above-quoted contract. But *Nickleby* still had to show that expectation was justified and to make its own way with its own public.

The readers of Number I were probably not disappointed. It launched the plot vigorously and directed it at once toward the goal Dickens had chosen, the Yorkshire Schools. After a summary of the Nicklebys' family history for three generations and an account of the circumstances under which Mrs. Nickleby had been left a widow with her two children, Nicholas and Kate (chap. i), the author introduced the children's uncle, Ralph the usurer, and his clerk, Newman Noggs,[4] then took the reader

[2] This may have influenced the invention of *Peregrine Pickle*, "peregrine" being a doublet of "pilgrim."

[3] See above, p. 103. Dickens' pronounced liking for the syllable "ick" (*Pickwick*, *Nich*olas, *Nick*leby) may have been due, unconsciously, to its presence in his own surname.

[4] Another alliterative name in "n," in the same novel!

to a meeting of the "United Metropolitan Improved Hot Muffin and Crumpet Baking and Punctual Delivery Company," in which a parliamentary assembly was parodied (chap. ii); Mrs. Nickleby left Devonshire and arrived in London with her children, so that the hero could now be introduced to the reader in the course of an interview with his uncle, who suggested that he become usher in a Yorkshire school (chap. iii); finally, the headmaster of that school, one-eyed Squeers, made his appearance, welcomed new pupils, and agreed to take Nicholas into his employment.

The contents of the number were thus different from *Pickwick*, yet varied, lively, and promising. The following installments were written at a time when Dickens was working hard to complete *Oliver Twist*, and he found it somewhat difficult to fill them up. In May there occurred a form of failure the author had never experienced in the days of *Pickwick*: "Could not write a line till three o'clock," he told Forster—and the confession sounds rather dire when it is borne in mind that Dickens was the father of two children and that his pen was the sole support of the family; after two years' fantastic fecundity, he was already struggling against a temporary drying-up of the source of his inspiration—"and have yet five slips to finish, and don't know what to put in them, for I have reached the point I meant to leave off with."[5] The number eventually reached the required length, but it is sparsely supplied with incident: it contains no more than the narrative of Nicholas' journey from London to the school of Dotheboys Hall (chap. v), interrupted by a breakdown which provides opportunity for two *inserted tales* ("The Seven Sisters of York" and "The Baron of Grogzwig," both in Chapter VI, which, therefore, is more packed with irrelevant matter than any chapter of *Pickwick*), and his arrival at the Squeerses'. Together with the two following numbers (III in June and IV in July, 1838), the May issue contains the gist of Dickens' criticism of the cheap schools; in it one becomes acquainted with the whole Squeers family—husband, wife, and two children, Wackford and Fanny. One attends a period of tuition and a meal in the school. Young Smike, one of the unhappiest pupils, arouses Nicholas' compassion, so that, when the boy is taken back after his attempted escape and is about to be beaten, Nicholas rises in his

[5] Forster, *Life of Dickens*, I, 99.

defense, thrashes Squeers, and leaves Dotheboys Hall. The narrative of this episode is interrupted by that of incidents occurring in London at the same time (chap. x at the close of Number III and chap. xi at the beginning of Number IV), where Kate Nickleby obtains employment in the Mantalinis' dressmaking concern.

By bringing Nicholas back to London as early as the end of the fourth number—before one-fifth of the novel had been completed—Dickens seemed to give up his plan of making the Yorkshire schools theme central to the whole work. Yet the attack he had launched against them preserved its strength and value. Although the existence and the scandalous nature of those places were notorious, no man of letters had as yet dealt with them. Dickens' attempt, socially speaking at least, was new and needful. It proved quite efficient besides. Disgraced through the popularity of the book, the Yorkshire schools disappeared, and the novelist could write with understandable pride in the revised preface of 1847 of the part he had played in eliminating the many cheap Yorkshire schools. The literary value of his attempt remains to be discussed. One is tempted nowadays to charge Dickens with exaggeration in his description of the Yorkshire schools.

Of Squeers the schoolmaster he makes a veritable monster, monstrously ignorant, as is shown by his every attempt at teaching anything (e.g., chap. lvii), monstrously cruel and insensitive, since his chief delight is to make young children suffer (chap. xxxviii), and monstrously cynical also.[6] Mrs. Squeers is just as monstrous as her husband. Her avarice is unfathomable and her sadism revolting: "having called up a little boy with a curly head, and wiped her hands upon it," when she has treacle on her hands; limp hair is not good enough for her to wipe them on: she must have a curly-headed boy! The Squeers children, Fanny and Wackford, are at all points the worthy offspring of such parents. The boy has all the defects usually not apparent in the children in a Dickens novel, and follows in his father's footsteps, as the latter—in spite of his avarice—gives him money to reward and encourage him whenever he has been particularly selfish and brutal. Fanny is very much like the London girls in the *Sketches*, giggling and blushing in their perpetual caricature of the externals of courtship. Against all the Squeerses,

---

[6] As is especially shown in the course of his conversation with Snawley (chap. iv).

who are more hateful than ridiculous, the novelist lets himself loose unreservedly. He seems to believe he is repaying cruelty with cruelty when he refers with insistent irony to their physical imperfections: "Mrs. Squeers . . . with her own fair hands," "Mr. Squeers, regarding the spectators with a malevolent eye—literally *a* malevolent eye." And when Fanny's maid declares "The reason's plain," the author takes the trouble of adding, parenthetically "(if Miss Squeers was the reason, it was very plain)."[7] Yet some of the most shocking details among those used by Dickens to convey the cruelty of the Yorkshire schools are precisely those he drew from reality. The letters sent home by Dotheboys Hall pupils have been adapted from genuine samples.[8] And Squeers' hideous description of his wife in her capacity as nurse— "one of our boys . . . got a abscess on him last week. To see how she operated upon him with a pen-knife!" (chap. xxxiv)—is but an echo of the early experience, related in the preface, which is the primary impulse of Dickens' whole attack. The echo is even somewhat toned down. And the charge of exaggeration has been repudiated in advance by the author of *Nickleby* writing in his preface that "Mr. Squeers and his school are faint and feeble pictures of an existing reality, purposely subdued and kept down, lest they should be deemed impossible." Perhaps the effort made to "subdue and keep down" the truth was not very vigorous, for Dickens did not tend to believe that any artistic claims were superior to a regard for truth. He thought more highly of liveliness than of verisimilitude. Of liveliness there is great abundance in the Squeers episode.

The three numbers containing this episode served another purpose by making the reader better acquainted with the titular hero, Nicholas, and his character, which was disclosed in Number IV in a curious, not wholly pleasing light. Nicholas Nickleby's merits are taken for granted, for the very reason that he is young and handsome and the novel's hero, but they are neither defined nor shown in any very convincing manner. He assumes an insolent attitude to his uncle during their first interview, when there is as yet no ground for it. He then behaves with

---

[7] Chaps. vii, xii, xlii. The attitude involved in the top-heavy wordplay on "plain" is again observable when Dickens deals with Miss Knag, Mrs. Mantalini's forewoman (chap. xviii).

[8] Cf. chap. viii, and *Letters*, I, 365.

extreme indelicacy and imprudence during the tea party to which Fanny Squeers treats him. Fanny is in love with him, but her love, like every other feeling—except cruelty—in her family, is purely ludicrous. The only other guests are Matilda Price and her fiancé John Browdie. The young people play cards and the conversation runs on as follows:

> [Miss Price speaking] "I should like to have you for a partner always."
> "I wish you had."
> "You'll have a bad wife, though, if you always win at cards," said Miss Price.
> "Not if your wish is gratified," replied Nicholas. "I am sure I shall have a very good one in that case."⁹

It should be borne in mind that this ponderous jocularity is carried on in the presence of the loutish fiancé, who can hardly be expected to relish it. Admittedly, the author explains later that there had been in Nicholas a "happy unconsciousness of making anybody uncomfortable." Yet his blind callousness does not make his attitude much more amiable. A lack of perception of other people's feelings is always a characteristic of even the most delicate among the Dickensian heroes, like David Copperfield, who remains for ten or fifteen years ignorant of Agnes' love and overwhelms her with cruel questions and confidences, or like Pip, who treats Biddy likewise. Nicholas gives further evidence of his blindness in the same novel. It is only in Chapter LVIII that we read, "Nicholas learned for the first time that the dying boy . . . loved his sister Kate." The dying boy is the unfortunate Smike, whose love has long been obvious to the reader. But Dickens regarded as artistic rather than otherwise the co-existence of obviousness to the reader and ignorance in the hero. Certainly, dramatic irony has never been thought inartistic. But the main point seems to be that, to Dickens, in a novel the hero may be blind, however unlikely such blindness is in real life. And his heroes are thus astonishingly blind.

The character of Nicholas is an interesting mixture of contradictory

⁹ Chap. ix; similarly, in order to explain to Fanny that he is not in love with her, he expresses himself with truly Dickensian, though superfluous and uncivil vehemence: "This is the grossest and wildest delusion, the completest and most signal mistake, that ever human being laboured under or committed" (chap. xiii).

aspects. At the beginning of his career at Dotheboys, his master's scandalous brutality does not elicit from him a single protest. We are merely informed that "Nicholas . . . ground his teeth at every repetition of the savage and cowardly attack." Yet there comes a time when no amount of teeth-grinding can any longer satisfy him. All of a sudden, he becomes indignant and rebellious. Curiously, at the moment when the change occurs in him, he uses the very same words as Nancy in *Oliver Twist* when she revolts against Fagin's ill treatment of Oliver: "I won't stand by and see is done!"[10] These words are Dickens' own outcry at the sight of cruelty to the weak, which he could not tolerate in silence. But Nicholas is not content with protests. He passes, without transition, from complete apathy—apart from grinding his teeth—to brutal action. He suddenly assumes the right of administering justice to Squeers, whom he thrashes violently enough to be afraid of having perhaps killed him. He will be seen later to treat Sir Mulberry Hawk similarly (chap. xxxii), thus placing himself—easily enough—in the first rank of Dickensian heroes for muscular energy and brutal force. The fact can be explained by remembering that Nicholas is the first fictional character in whom Dickens may have, more or less consciously, intended to picture himself. Of course, he gave him both the qualities he had or thought he had and the features he envied in other people and was humiliated at not possessing. It is fairly clear, for instance, that he was always anxious not to be regarded as having a somewhat feminine sensitivity and also that he did not feel sure of his social status, that he feared he was not genteel, not a *gentleman*. Now he insists on Nicholas' virility[11] and on the respect due to his genteel birth.[12] Thus, with the character of Nicholas, a young hero who conforms to the tradition of the novel, who is as quixotic as heart can desire, as impulsive as his creator, and who loves romantically, Dickens has for the first time written a book which resembles a traditional type. The central figures in his first two books, Pickwick, an old man, and Oliver, a mere boy,

---

[10] *OT*, chap. xvi and *NN*, chap. xiii. The only difference is that Nicholas says "will not" instead of "won't."

[11] "His figure was . . . manly" (chap. iii); "He acted . . . in a manly and spirited manner" (chap. xxxviii); "He bears it so manfully" (chap. lxi). His brutality is but an outward sign of his manliness.

[12] It is because he is "a gentleman's son" that Nicholas is welcomed by his three successive employers—Squeers, Crummles, and the Cheerybles.

had been far more unconventional figures. Neither Winkle and Snod-grass, belatedly turned into anxious lovers, nor Harry Maylie, whose appearances had been short and dull, could in any sense be regarded as the heroes of the novels in which they had played their parts. The period of Dickens' apprenticeship in the craft of fiction—to which *Nickleby* still belongs—is curiously marked by a decrease in originality at some important points. Nicholas is certainly a less original hero than either Pickwick or Oliver. He has at least one virtue in that he is not possessed of every possible virtue; he is not all of a piece, not entirely foreseeable like too many Dickensian characters. It is noticeable, though not surprising, that the author thought fit to defend himself against that kind of remark, presented by some critics as a reproach. In fact, he declares at the close of his preface: "If Nicholas be not always found to be blameless or agreeable, he is not always intended to appear so. He is a young man of an impetuous temper and of little or no experience; and I saw no reason why such a hero should be lifted out of nature." It might have been more candid to add that he had seen no reason either why such a hero should be lifted out of literature, or made too unlike Roderick Random or Tom Jones.

The Yorkshire episode had come to an end in the fourth number of *Nickleby*, published in July, 1838. For the ensuing summer, the Dick-enses rented a small house at Twickenham, where the novelist wrote the fifth and sixth numbers (chap. xv–xx) to be published in August and September. They comprise a variety of incidents. In order to create a link between the Yorkshire group and the events that had occurred in London during Nicholas' absence, Dickens makes the hero and Smike call on Newman Noggs upon their arrival. Newman is Ralph Nickleby's clerk, and Ralph has connections both with Kate and her mother and with Squeers. This creates the opportunity for describing an evening party at the home of Newman's neighbors, the Kenwigses. Nicholas looks for a job and is sent from the register office to Mr. Gregsbury, an M.P. The long scene at the latter's does not further the development of the plot, since Nicholas does not find employment there and is still looking for a job when he emerges from the house. He decides to teach French to the Kenwigs children. At the end of Number V, Dickens takes his readers back a few days in order to bring the narrative of

Kate's adventures to the point in time reached by Nicholas and thus prepare for their meeting. Several incidents have occurred during the early days of her career at the Mantalinis'. She has been asked to dine at her uncle's with several wealthy aristocrats who behave disrespectfully to her. On the day when Ralph, who has been informed of Nicholas' conduct by a gloriously funny letter from Fanny Squeers, is conveying the news to Mrs. Nickleby, the hero dramatically bursts into the room, only to withdraw after a brief and painful family quarrel. The division between the two installments occurred in the middle of Kate's adventures. The most striking feature of the group of episodes was the appearance of the noblemen. It has been seen that in 1838 Dickens had already begun to be received in more or less aristocratic circles. Yet what he gives us here is but a mediocre caricature, conventional in the extreme and showing no sign of personal observation. The aristocrats in *Nickleby* are faint and unconvincing figures. From the outset, their very names are disappointing: the two most prominent members of the circle are Sir Mulberry Hawk and Lord Frederick Verisopht.[13] The latter name is particularly embarrassing to the critic who believes that Dickens *is* a major artist. Besides, it provides fresh evidence of the author's lack of foresight. He could hardly have coined such a feeble and ridiculous name if he had thought he might later be led to make his character act in a tragic and solemn scene and conduct himself with true nobility. Certainly, when he decided on calling his young lord "Verisopht," Dickens did not foresee that he would one day write about him the following paragraph: "The sun came proudly up in all his majesty . . . and, amidst it all, and pressing down the grass whose every blade bore twenty tiny lives, lay the dead man, with his stark and rigid face turned upwards to the sky." In fact, all through the sixteen pages of the tragic chapter, the name Verisopht is used but twice, and the character is generally called "Lord Frederick" or "the young lord" instead. The scene itself is not deprived of tragic force in its exceptionally sober tone, but the misadventure of the nobleman's name shows

13 Such names are reminiscent of Peacock, or of Thackeray's *Book of Snobs*. The others are Pyke, Pluck, Mr. Snobb, and Colonel Chowser. Dickens seems to have had a special hatred of the innocent mulberry, always connected by him with unpleasant characters. Here it is Hawk's first name; in *PP* and *DC*, it is the color of Job Trotter's livery and Uriah Heep's coat.

that Dickens had not yet mastered his technique of periodical publication, had not even realized that he must practice at least a minimal form of planning ahead.

Neither, in the days of *Nickleby,* had he yet learned the art of husbanding his character-creation. In that novel no fewer than 117 of the characters speak,[14] and that, even in a thousand pages, is a lavish expenditure of creative energy. Thirty of the characters are anonymous: thus Dickens has coined—not to mention the inserted tales—eighty-seven names, in which recur the familiar sounds already mentioned in the *Pickwick* chapter, endings in "le" or "kins" (Crummles, Curdle, Muntle, Tomkins, Grimble, Cheeryble, Lukin, Jenkins, Chopkins, and a few others). One passage in the novel is enlightening regarding an important aspect of Dickens' sensitiveness to sounds and names. The persistence of some favorite vowels and consonants from novel to novel is to be accounted for by the fact that Dickens perceives a correspondence between names and characters, as is shown by the following fragment (when Nicholas has asked Newman Noggs to find out the name of his beloved):

"The name—the name, my dear fellow!"
"The name's Bobster," replied Newman.
"Bobster!" repeated Nicholas, indignantly.
"That's the name," said Newman. "I remember it by Lobster."
"Bobster!" repeated Nicholas more emphatically than before.
"That must be the servant's name" (chap. xl).

Strangely enough, Nicolas is almost right; Bobster is not the servant's name, but that of a ridiculous person who has nothing to do with his enchantress. The important word here is "indignantly." And Nicholas' indignation is shared by Dickens: it is unthinkable that a well-born hero should fall in love with a girl whose name is at all ridiculous. Therefore the dividing line is sharply drawn in the Dickensian world: there are on one side worthy and respectable people and on the other the comic characters. Among the former everything is normal, among the latter everything is burlesque: features, speech, feelings, clothing, and names.[15]

---

[14] Cf., Pope-Hennessy, *Ch. Dickens,* 144.
[15] Dickens' reaction is intensely idiosyncratic, for few people would have thought they were taking a stride in the direction of respectability by bartering the name of Bobster for that of Nickleby or Pickwick or Chuzzlewit.

Thus there is no mistaking the fairly large class in *Nickleby* of the characters with quaint or baroque names: Wittiterly, Belvawney, Glavormelly, Peltirogus. Or those who, like Verisopht, bear poorly and transparently jocular ones: Snewkes, Wrymug, Gallanbile, Snuffim. Many of these characters are unimportant and play no real part in the story, being only incidentally mentioned by name. Several of the above are pupils at Dotheboys Hall. Dickens' inventive effort is perhaps all the more to be deplored since it is superfluous as well as mediocre. There was no need for him to name, for instance, the Portsmouth pilot who becomes Mr. Crummles' landlord: "Mr. Crummles lived . . . at the house of one Bulph, a pilot." If we had to know where Mr. Crummles lived in Portsmouth, it would have been enough to tell us that he lived in the house of "a pilot." Yet it is only in the case of briefly glimpsed and very subordinate characters that the reader may resent the writer's ill-judged efforts at coining names. The chief characters, Squeers, Noggs, Nickleby, Crummles, seem to be aptly provided with picturesque or suggestive names in a way that has made part of their fame.

The source of such a plethora of characters lies in the picaresque form adopted in the early part of *Nickleby*. The procedure consisted in alternating Nicholas' and Kate's adventures. On the one hand, Dickens thus had to have two groups of characters in action at the same time. On the other, the jobs held by both brother and sister were always precarious, and caused them to move a great deal and to penetrate into new circles repeatedly.

In Number VII (October, 1838), two fresh groups of secondary characters were thus introduced into the novel. Kate loses her employment with the Mantalinis, owing to their bankruptcy. But Mrs. Nickleby has happily chanced to read an advertisement: a lady companion was wanted. Kate is given that position in Chapter XXI, which closes with: "She betook herself . . . to Mrs. Wittiterly's mansion, where for the present we will leave her." As in the previous numbers, Dickens had determined to divide his narrative between Kate and her brother, possibly with a view to gratifying both his female and his male readers in each installment. So, in Chapter XXII, Nicholas and Smike leave London for Portsmouth, in the hope of getting employment on board a ship. While they are on their way, they chance to meet Vincent Crummles, the manager of an itinerant theatre, who proves willing to take both of them into his company. The final chapter of the number (chap. xxiii) was devoted to an introduction of the other actors and actresses.

Among Dickens' novels, *Nickleby* is probably one of the most clearly theatrical both in theme and in technique. The Crummles episode plays its part in the story, and it is an important, though not an essential, one. As far as the plot is concerned, the episode allows for the removal of Nicholas from London at the time when Uncle Ralph's first machinations are begun. It fosters the intimacy between Nicholas and Smike. It provides the hero for the first time with employment which he likes and which supports him. Yet the chief reason for its presence here undoubtedly is the opportunity it affords of dealing with one of Dickens' favorite themes, from which he derives inexhaustible comical effects. The description of a poorly acted play is ever, from the *Sketches* to *Great Expectations*, one of his surest ways of making the reader laugh.[16] Dickens' evident expertness in the handling of the highly successful Crummles episode does not prove that he had belonged in his youth, as has sometimes been lightly asserted, to a similar traveling company. His passionate, permanent interest in every kind of theatrical activity has already been discussed. And detailed information could have been supplied by his actor friends, by his own experience of private theaters in London, and also by printed sources such as *Life of an Actor*, by his predecessor, Pierce Egan.[17]

But *Nickleby* is a theatrical novel in other respects than through the presence of Crummles. Dickens is amiably critical of the artifices resorted to by the cheap company. Nevertheless he seems to emulate many of those artifices himself in other parts of his novel. When he wrote *Nickleby*, he had possibly not yet outgrown the phase of his dramatic ambitions. He may have thought himself destined to write also, or even to write mainly, for the stage. It was the time of his operettas and farces, and the two styles and techniques occasionally interfered. In the title of a chapter, for instance, the novel would be compared to a stage.[18] In the dialogue, some attitudes and gestures would be described in the manner of stage

[16] See chaps. xxii, xxiii, and xlviii.

[17] London, 1824. The hero of that book, which is more of a documentary than a novel, owes something to Smollett's example since his name is Peregrine Proteus.

[18] E.g., "Positively his last appearance on this stage" (chap. xlviii).

directions: " 'Have *you* ever done anything, sir?' (turning to his nephew)." When Ralph has propounded to Mrs. Nickleby his own version of the happenings at Dotheboys Hall, he ends with a question: " '... Assault, riot, theft, what do you call these?' 'A lie!' cried a voice, as the door was dashed open, and Nicholas came into the room." The beginning of another chapter runs as follows: "The place was a handsome suit of private apartments ... the time was three o'clock in the afternoon ... the persons were ...."

More generally, the whole final section of the book is composed, as will appear later, in the manner of a melodrama. It is a succession of surprises, mysterious appearances, sudden arrivals, rooms plunged into darkness, etc. In short, Dickens, however alive he was to the ridiculousness of the plays performed by Crummles' company in Portsmouth, made use in his novel of procedures akin to theirs. Yet, one should not wonder overmuch at the apparent contradiction, for it can be perceived that the novelist takes a benevolent view of Crummles—as later of Sleary in *Hard Times*—and is grateful to him for attempting to please the popular public by the most proper means, without trying to train or educate their taste. It is hardly an exaggeration to say that such is, fundamentally, Dickens' own attitude. To write what will please the public is the guiding principle of all Dickens' conscious efforts, especially in his early days. No doubt Dickens' genius raised his achievement high above his purpose. At any rate, in the case of *Nickleby*, the purpose of entertaining the public was brilliantly fulfilled.

The unrestrained mirth which is the dominant characteristic of the theatrical scenes is easily accounted for when one bears in mind that the period beginning in October, 1838, was for Dickens the end of his hardest labors. Not only had he completed *Oliver Twist*, but for the first time in two years he had but one novel in course of publication. Even the uncertain health already alluded to could not darken his mood. He availed himself of his comparatively leisurely position to travel about a little. At the end of October, 1838, he visited Warwickshire, went to Kenilworth, then to North Wales, and later stayed in Manchester. He was thus enabled to visit some factories which aroused his interest in the fate of workers. He toyed fleetingly with the idea of describing them in *Nickleby*—another proof that his general plan was by no means determined.

On returning from Manchester, he wrote to Edward Marlborough Fitz-gerald: "I mean to strike the heaviest blow in my power for those un-fortunate creatures, but whether I shall do so in Nickleby or wait some other opportunity I have not yet determined."[19] Yet with the close of the year the first half of the book also came to an end. Numbers VIII, IX, and X appeared in November and December, 1838, and January, 1839.

Number VIII contains two chapters (xxiv and xxv) about Nicholas in Portsmouth—where he is accidentally seen by an uncle of Noggs's neighbor—and one London chapter (xxvi) about the efforts made by Ralph's aristocratic friends to get in touch with Kate once more. Number IX, written in November for publication in December, occasioned un-usual difficulties. On November 20, he had written only one of the three chapters that were required for the installment—Chapter XXVII, Kate's encounter with the noblemen at the theater. He confided to Forster, "I have just begun my second chapter . . . think there *will* be a Nickleby at the end of this month now (I doubted it before)."[20] The aforesaid second chapter (xxviii) relates the continuation of Kate's misadventures, when she is pursued by the noblemen at Mrs. Wittiterly's and arouses her employer's jealousy, as she had earlier aroused the jealousy of Mrs. Mantalini's forewoman, and as Nicholas had aroused Fanny Squeers'. The composition of the chapter was interrupted by the news that a man named Stirling, a professional adapter of novels to the stage, was having *Nickleby* performed with a winding-up of his own invention. Dickens went to a performance, with mixed feelings. Literary property being un-protected, he could derive no profit from such an undertaking. There was obvious dishonesty in the adapter's appropriation of an unfinished novel to his own use and advantage. Dickens' single act of retaliation was the introduction, later on in the novel, of a revengeful episode. He resurrected Crummles, who invited Nicholas to a farewell dinner, to-gether with an adapter of novels to whom the hero gave a piece of his mind. His lengthy speech—"You take the uncompleted books of living authors . . . "—is most improbable in the novel, since no one in real life will thus patiently listen to verbose insults, but it is in fact addressed to

---

[19] Dec. 29, 1838, *Letters*, I, 483–84. It was only in *HT* (1854) that Dickens found an opportunity for striking the blow in question.

[20] Forster, *Life of Dickens*, I, 100.

Stirling, and Dickens, not Nicholas, is speaking. The incident is revealing of his artistic ideal. If taken in conjunction with an earlier episode—in Nicholas' conversation with Gregsbury—in which the laws of verisimilitude are just as blithely violated in order to force in, under an ironical disguise, a professional grievance,[21] it supports the view that Dickens saw nothing objectionable in the use of the novel for the defense of his private interests or the expression of his ideas on a variety of subjects.

This has nothing to do with what is known as the *roman à thèse*. Nearly all Dickens' novels are to a certain extent *romans à thèse—Pickwick* is leveled at debtors' prisons, *Oliver* at officialized charity, *Nickleby* at the Yorkshire schools, and later *Dombey* at selfishness and *Chuzzlewit* at pride, etc. The thesis is often either conceived as an afterthought or quickly forgotten by the author, thus seldom interfering with the freshness of his inspiration. But, in addition, Dickens does not think he is infringing upon the rules of artistic conscientiousness when he turns aside from the course of his narrative in order to pursue some precise object of his own, wholly detached from pure literary creation. In that respect he differs from many other writers, like Trollope,[22] and the simple laws of ordinary verisimilitude show that he is mistaken. Certainly, the passages just alluded to are but slight blemishes in the bulk of the book, whose unquestionable greatness is hardly affected by them. Yet there they are, and even a minor aspect of that kind has to be taken into consideration if a complete picture of Dickens' artistic stature is to be given.

In spite of his wasted evening at the theater and the ensuing shock to his emotional equilibrium, he managed to complete the second chapter of Number IX in three days' time. On November 23, however, he was again writing to Forster, "Have not yet got the subject of my last chapter which *must* be finished to-night."[23] The chapter which had caused so much difficulty was eventually finished by the time it was due. It reverted, as if duty bound, to Nicholas, and concerned, for the fourth time in that novel, the theme of jealousy. It was now (chap. xxix) the actor

21 "If any preposterous bill were brought forward, for giving poor grubbing devils of authors a right to their own property . . ." (chap. xvi).

22 See his *Autobiography,* II, 56: ". . . in a novel. Every sentence, every word, through all those pages should tend to the telling of the story."

23 Forster, *Life of Dickens,* I, 100.

Lenville who envied Nicholas' professional success. Number X was composed on the same pattern as the preceding ones, but it resulted in an acceleration of the tempo of events. It dealt in the first place with Nicholas taking leave of the Crummles family—the hero is called to London by Noggs (chap. xxx)—then returns to the capital, where his arrival is expected (chap. xxxi). Nicholas meets Sir Mulberry Hawk by chance in an inn, and learns that the nobleman is pursuing Kate. A quarrel ensues, and on being struck, the hero knocks Hawk down (chap. xxxii). He then joins his mother and Kate, who has left Mrs. Wittiterly (chap. xxxiii).

Through the same months of late 1838, Dickens also wrote a farce—*The Lamplighter*—for his friend Macready, the manager of Covent Garden, who found he could do nothing with it. He contributed articles to *The Examiner*, a weekly whose most influential critic was Forster: Dickens reviewed a few books for it, including Lockhart's *Life of Walter Scott*. At the beginning of 1839, his prospects looked most brilliant. He was to have henceforth a single publisher, Chapman and Hall, he had already two highly successful books to his credit, the third was deservedly just as popular, and he was not yet twenty-seven. In January, he paid two more visits to Manchester, and from then on took more and more interest in social problems, and particularly in the condition of workers. As far as *Nickleby* is concerned, the single positive result was the appearance in the February number of the Cheeryble brothers, who had their originals in the Grant brothers, mill-owners of that city. In his preface, Dickens owned his debt: "There *are* two characters in the book which are drawn from life."

In Number XI, which is somewhat thin (it comprises two interludes—the Mantalinis' visit to Ralph, chap. xxxiv, and Nicholas' to Kenwigs, chap. xxxvi) the chief events are the arrival in London of Squeers (chap. xxxiv), who helps Ralph plot against Nicholas and Smike, and Nicholas' accidental encounter with the Cheeryble brothers, who take him into their employment (chap. xxxv). Those aged twins have a few pleasant features, in particular their delicate generosity, a feeling which Dickens is expert at conveying, yet they lack the variety which makes characters live. Through a curious misconception, Dickens believed he would make them more attractive and more interesting by making them entirely identical. Admittedly they are twin brothers, and there is no objection to a novelist's showing twins. It is rather less understandable that the few details which might have caused them to differ should be turned into reasons for increased resemblance: "Both had lost nearly the same teeth, which imparted the same peculiarity to their speech." Nor does the result in any way justify such treatment. After an introduction of that kind, frequent scenes of comic confusion and substitution are to be expected: they do not occur. The two brothers are identical, yet they are always effortlessly differentiated. Nobody mistakes one for the other, and even if one did make such a mistake, it would have no comic value, since the twins are in reality but one character in two identical persons. At no time is it of any importance that either, or both, should be involved in a scene; their reactions, attitudes and speeches, are in constant, perfect, and touching harmony. Should Nicholas mistake Charles Cheeryble for Ned Cheeryble, he would amuse us no more than by mistaking one fine candlestick for the other candlestick of the same pair.

The only kind of comedy Dickens aimed at in the creation of the Cheerybles was the comedy of symmetry and repetition, of the same order as the effect sought through another pair of characters, those of Pyke and Pluck, two of Sir Mulberry Hawk's companions. In their case also, identical speeches are made by the two members of the pair, each of whom merely echoes what the other says. Now, symmetry and repetition undoubtedly possess comic power. On the stage, as is abundantly evidenced by Molière's plays, they can and will arouse laughter. Yet it is clear that Dickens had overestimated the amount of entertainment they could provide in a novel, where the reader expects a modicum of truth or psychological verisimilitude. There are admirable *couples* in Dickens' fiction, such as the Sowerberrys and Bumbles in *Oliver* and the Squeerses in *Nickleby*. *Pickwick* had shown, with the Wellers—father and son— what *Copperfield* would confirm with the Heeps—mother and son—and the Murdstones—brother and sister—that pairs can be as entertaining as couples, through the subtle interplay of surface differences and essential likenesses. But, where there are *no* differences, there can be no dialogue, no life. Dullness is the inevitable result in the case of the Cheeryble twins, as even some of Dickens' contemporaries noted.[24]

___

[24] The monotony had already been resented by some contemporary critics. Bagehot (*National Review*, Oct., 1858, p. 466) wrote: "The Messrs. Cheeryble are among the

But the moment when Nicholas is engaged by the Cheeryble brothers is important for another reason bearing upon the construction of the novel. He is unemployed and moneyless: he has broken with Ralph, wrenched his sister from the Wittiterlys, deserted Squeers and Crummles in succession. He wonders, as we wonder, what he is going to do. He then utters a crucial phrase: " 'Egad!' said Nicholas, 'I'll try that register office again.' " This is significant apart from the outmoded ejaculation at the beginning: in the very middle of the novel, the hero is placed once more in his initial situation. Nicholas must look for a job, and will do so at the same office. The circumstance is reminiscent of the cyclical composition of *Pickwick*—of which we had already been reminded by the four cases in which the hero or heroine's livelihood had been endangered by jealousy. Some progress is, however, noticeable. In *Pickwick*, the characters' movements had been quite arbitrary, and the conclusion of each episode had taken them back to a situation unmodified by its incidents: besides, this situation did not usually involve in itself the need for an evolution toward the winding-up. Here there is still a good deal of resemblance between the episodes: yet, each time Nicholas or Kate is once more out of work, the general situation has taken one step forward in the direction of the winding-up. Ralph had procured both Kate's and Nicholas' first jobs. The quarrel at Dotheboys Hall has deprived Nicholas of his uncle's support: yet the latter continues to protect Kate and her mother. When Nicholas returns from Portsmouth and thrashes Hawk, the break between Ralph and the rest of the family is complete: war begins. Besides, the need to support three persons is more of a motivation than the Pickwickians' idle curiosity.

On March 1, 1839, Number XII of *Nickleby* appeared. It contained Chapters XXXVII (Nicholas' *début* in office work), XXXVIII (a glimpse of Hawk on his sickbed, an accidental encounter between Smike and Squeers, who captures him and locks him up at Snawley's), and XXXIX (the opportune arrival in London of John Browdie, now a married man, who sets Smike free in the course of a very vivid comic scene). Immediately after the publication of Number XII, Dickens went away once more, but this time not as a mere tourist. He wanted to ac-

---

stupidest of Dickens's characters. He forgot that breadth of platitude is rather different from breadth of sagacity."

complish a scheme he had cherished for some time and which appeared more and more urgently necessary to him. His present purpose was to find a house in the country for his parents. Mr. and Mrs. John Dickens' presence in London was embarrassing to him: his father made debts, borrowed money, and might create difficulties that would impede the novelist's career. Neither his father nor his mother could be introduced into the circles in which he wished to move henceforth. The visit to Exeter is connected with the work in progress by two circumstances, both related with the same episode, now not far distant. Smike, a deformed and ailing youth, has fallen in love with Kate. The unfortunate boy is not an acceptable match for her. She is meant for another, so that the end of the novel may offer the requisite number of satisfactory weddings. In the Dickensian view of novel endings, there is no place for a pitiable rival in love: no compensatory prize can be bestowed on a broken heart. The conclusion is obvious: Smike has become embarrassing and must therefore disappear. Just as Dickens had seen fit to get rid of Jingle and Mrs. Weller in *Pickwick* and of Monks in *Oliver Twist*, by means of emigration and death, so does Smike's love for Kate seal his doom. Now, the author of *Nickleby* wished to organize the life of his family on the same lines as that of the characters in his novels: like Smike, Mr. and Mrs. John Dickens had become nuisances, and like Smike they must clear the London scene. By placing them in a cottage at Alphington, near Exeter, their son hoped he was settling their fate forever, as though he had written in the last chapter of the novel of their life, "and they lived happily ever after in their cottage."[25] Dickens acted likewise later with one of his brothers, then with his own sons, whom he sent to distant colonies when they came of age or earlier. At that point, there is absolute coincidence between the novelist, Dickens, and the family man.

On the other hand, it was in Exeter, Devonshire, that Dickens had to spend a few days in preparation for his parents' exodus. It was to Devonshire also that he sent Smike to die and Nicholas to keep him company. It is clear that the landscapes described in *Nickleby* in the course of that

[25] The phrases used by Dickens to describe the cottage he has selected for his parents' use show that he is trying hard to convince himself that they will live a pleasant life there: "A splendid view . . . I don't think I ever saw so pleasant or cheerful a spot . . . . The place [is] clean as the utmost excess of snowy cleanliness can be" (*Letters*, I, 524).

episode are those that Dickens observed in March, 1839, in the vicinity of Exeter.

The problem of his parents' exile was settled with so much energy and promptness that Dickens was back in London at the end of one week, so that the composition of *Nickleby* was not affected by his absence. Numbers XIII, XIV, and XV appeared in April, May, and June, 1839. They comprised Chapters XL through XLVIII and gave the plot a more markedly melodramatic turn. A beautiful girl in distress, whom Nicholas had already met at the Register office, appears mysteriously at the Cheerybles' (chap. xl). The following chapter (xli) is a wonderful comic interlude and shows a love scene between Mrs. Nickleby and her neighbor, a madman. The scene is probably the climax in the career of Mrs. Nickleby, one of the most admirable characters in the book, in the convincingness with which her psychology is conveyed and in the entertainment she provides. The novelist's mother is traditionally regarded as having sat for this portrait. In fact, on one occasion at least, the author confessed that there was an original.[26] Yet it is hardly probable that Dickens portrayed his mother in Mrs. Nickleby at all points. He must have taken some features from Mrs. Dickens and completed the character from observations from other sources. But whatever its origins, the portrait of Mrs. Nickleby is a brilliant success, ranking with Sam Weller, Mrs. Gamp, and Micawber among Dickens' immortals. No scene in which she takes part is weak or disappointing. Her chief characteristics are the desultory zigzag of her speech, continually interrupted by the introduction of additional details unconnected with what she is trying to convey, her inaccuracy in every matter of importance, the elasticity of her moods, and her faculty of building, like the Micawbers, castles in the air. These are efficient, far-reaching sources of comedy, originating mostly in the lack of correspondence between her imagination, memory, and language and the facts of the case.

After the interlude of the madman's love, Nicholas calls on John Browdie at his hotel. They are joined by the Squeerses, and a rather coarse quarrel ensues, during which Squeers threatens Nicholas with disclosures concerning the identity of Smike's father (chap. xlii). The

[26] See Pope-Hennessy, *Ch. Dickens*, 143.

number comes to an end, abruptly, after the departure of the Squeerses. At the beginning of Number XIV, Nicholas is still at the hotel with the Browdies (chap. xliii), where a fantastic concatenation of coincidences is about to begin. Nicholas hears people violently quarreling in another room of the hotel; he interposes and learns the occasion of the dispute. One customer had alluded disrespectfully to a girl who was not present, and another customer who knew her had chastised the author of the insult. It will be observed that this episode exactly repeats the circumstances of Nicholas' quarrel with Hawk in Chapter XXXII, besides being founded on an accidental encounter of some magnitude in itself. But there is worse—or, as Dickens thought, better—to follow, for (a) the girl thus insulted and whose honor had been questioned and vindicated is the mysterious Madeline Bray, whom Nicholas loves; (b) her champion is Frank Cheeryble, the nephew of Nicholas' employers, who returns to England in the nick of time after spending several years in Germany; (c) the offender is a clerk in the Register Office attended by the hero. The last detail, which is of slight interest since the character will not be heard of again, only increases the improbability of the whole passage. In order to justify his abundant use and exploitation of chance, Dickens raises his trickery to the dignity of a principle which he has Tim Linkinwater— the Cheerybles' head clerk—express the next day: " 'That those two young men should have met last night is, I say, a coincidence—a remarkable coincidence. Why, I don't believe now,' added Tim . . . 'that there's such a place in all the world for coincidences as London is!' " (chap. xliii) If applied to Dickens' London, in which coincidences assume a supernatural and fairy-like aspect, Tim's phrase is unquestionably valid. Elsewhere in *Nickleby*, as in *Pickwick* and *Oliver*, will be found any number of coincidences and chance encounters, which need not be enumerated here: they are all the mainsprings of the plot.

The Cheerybles' nephew, after thus appearing out of the blue, will confirm Smike's doom by falling in love with Kate.

Chapter XLIV takes us back to Ralph and deeper into mystery. A former partner of his addresses him in threatening terms. Ralph plots with Squeers. Both of them, together with a third man who holds documents proving him to be Smike's father, burst into Nicholas' lodgings (chap. xlv). The hero refuses to give up his young friend to them. That is the end of the fourteenth installment. Number XV contains some of the most melodramatic incidents in the whole book. Nicholas is sent by the Cheerybles to the house of his mysterious beloved. Ralph receives a visitor, the hideous old man Gride, who plans to marry Madeline with the interested help of her father Bray and of Ralph (chap. xlvii). The number closes with the interlude mentioned earlier in which Dickens-Nickleby wreaks vengeance on the adapter Stirling (chap. xlviii).

Dickens and his family spent part of the summer of 1839 at Petersham and the rest at Broadstairs. In those two places the composition of *Nickleby* was finished, while new schemes were already being sketched out and even absorbing a certain amount of the novelist's attention and creative activity. Those schemes were to result in the publication of *Master Humphrey's Clock* in the following spring. The main fact revealed by the new plans was Dickens' essential preoccupation: he wanted above all to give up, at least temporarily, the writing of novels for monthly serialization, in which he had been indulging from March, 1836, through September, 1839, or for forty-three months on end. The work had been undertaken with cheerful enthusiasm and a feeling of inexhaustible energy. It had gradually turned to hard labor, and though the reader was unaware of the drudgery behind each installment, the writer's life was darkened. It has been seen already that Dickens had been more than once short of inspiration, while the increasing demands his technique imposed upon him and the growth of his desire to construct solid plots made it clear that the strain would become ever harder. What he now had in mind was a weekly publication, to which he would be the chief, not the sole, contributor, and in which he might bring out essays and sketches, as well as tales and short novels. As early as July, 1839, he opened negotiations with Chapman and Hall, who received his overtures favorably.

In the same month appeared Number XVI of *Nickleby*, in which Smike is grievously ill (chap. xlix). Then, after a duel, Lord Frederick Verisopht, who had nobly risen in defense of Nicholas and Kate, is killed by Hawk, who becomes a fugitive (chap. l). Finally, Noggs, and later Nicholas, learn the date chosen for Madeline's marriage to old Gride (chap. li). As the close of the story draws nearer, a few transformations of Dickens' methods become visible. Several chapters are provided with introductions on general themes, others with plain, sober, final paragraphs, nearly all with brief, natural, apposite titles.

Every mark of an evolution, toward the end of *Nickleby*, concurs in showing that, once he had completed *Oliver Twist*, Dickens resolved to devote himself more methodically to the practice, though not to the theoretical study, of his art. Nevermore would he attempt to write two novels at the same time. His dawning consciousness of the duties devolving upon a conscientious artist would preclude it. Unfortunately, his perceptible technical progress is not paralleled by a similar improvement in psychology. During the sixteenth number, Lord Frederick Verisopht is too suddenly transfigured. He had been both a simpleton and a rake: he no longer is either the one or the other. A number of other characters undergo similar changes. Miss La Creevy, the miniature painter, loses at one blow all her ridiculous conceit. John Browdie, the Yorkshire miller, sheds all his churlishness to become a jovial Quixote. Nor are such transformations preceded by any psychological evolution that might justify them. The only thing that evolves is the author's attitude to his characters: he becomes fonder of his creations. Dickens' sympathy with an increasing number of characters as the novel proceeds toward its close redounds to the credit of his sensibility and generosity, but it makes light of psychological verisimilitude.

In *Nickleby*, generally, characters are stiff and all of a piece. Psychological analysis is perfunctory. The case of Sir Mulberry Hawk and his companions is characteristic. They belong to a class that Dickens is unfamiliar with: he cannot therefore apply to them his usual method, which consists of making real beings live and talk in front of the reader, of recording the combined results of his observations. This method, whenever it is employed, as it is in the case of Mrs. Nickleby and a few others in the same novel, endows the tale with matchless life and truth. But nothing could be more labored than the author's explanations of Hawk's motives. It is most embarrassing to the reader to find Dickens stressing the fact that Hawk is preparing "to execute a plan of operations concerted by Sir Mulberry himself, avowedly to promote his friend's object, and really to obtain his own" (chap. xxvi). Nor could double-dealing be more crudely expressed than in " 'What a happiness this amiable creature must be to you,' said Sir Mulberry, throwing into his voice an indication of the warmest feeling" (chap. xxxvi). When he thus launches into psychological analysis, Dickens clearly gets out of his depth, and his explanations detract from the value of his observation. Hence the limitations of Dickensian psychology in the days of *Nickleby*. He is able to create a larger number of truthful and lively characters than almost any other writer, when he takes them from the social classes he knows well, from paupers to the middle middle class, but the aristocracy and the higher middle class are beyond his scope. And though he can convincingly reproduce gestures, speech, and attitudes, he cannot as yet explore souls. It takes him another ten years to become the equal of the truly great psychological novelists: this he does when his genius reaches full maturity in *David Copperfield*.

In the final numbers of *Nickleby*, psychology is almost out of the question. Event now follows event in quick succession, and the plot thickens tragically. Nicholas makes up his mind to see Madeline and prevent her from marrying Gride (chap. lii). He cannot persuade her, or Gride either (chap. liii). On the morning of the day appointed for the wedding, Madeline's father dies opportunely and Nicholas provides a home for the orphaned girl. He goes to Devonshire with Smike, who is alarmingly ill. Gride's housekeeper has disappeared and taken away some compromising documents, among others Madeline's grandfather's will, which Squeers must attempt to recover on behalf of Ralph (chap. lvi). The moment he is possessing himself of the paper, Noggs and Frank Cheeryble burst into the room (chap. lvii).

That is the end of the eighteenth and last but one number, published on September 1, 1839. Dickens devoted the month of September to the composition of the final installment, supposedly of double size—it is called *Nos. XIX & XX*—which must disentangle all the difficulties and ensure the happiness of the worthy and the punishment of the wicked. The task is not an easy one. The first chapter of that number is entitled: "In which one scene of this History is closed" (chap. lviii). This phrase adequately sums up the novelist's attitude from that time on. Hemmed in by the episodes and characters he has so lavishly created, he resorts to young Horace's strategy in Corneille's play, and endeavors to tackle each of them separately. "I am hard at it," he was writing to Forster, from Broadstairs, on September 9, 1839, "but these windings-up wind slowly, and I think I shall have done great things if I have entirely finished by the twentieth." On the eighteenth, he could confirm this date: "I shall not finish entirely before Friday, sending . . . the last twenty pages of ms by the night-coach. I have had pretty stiff work as you may suppose, and I have taken great pains. The discovery is made. Ralph is dead. The loves have come all right, Tim Linkinwater has proposed, and I have now only to break up Dotheboys Hall and the book together. I am very anxious that you should see this conclusion before it leaves my hands . . . and we will devote [Saturday] night to a careful reading."[27] His letter alludes to the last events in the narrative. Smike is dead (chap. lviii). The "discovery" is that of Smike's identity: he is Ralph's son (chap. lx). Ralph kills himself when he has lost every kind of hope (chap. lxii). The "loves" are Nicholas' for Madeline and Frank Cheeryble's for Kate, which result in a twofold wedding after overcoming imaginary obstacles, made up once again of unclear scruples. Tim—the Cheerybles' aged clerk—marries Miss La Creevy. Dotheboys Hall is dissolved after Squeers has been sentenced.

Almost simultaneously with the final number, the first edition in book form was published, preceded by the original preface. The bulk of the preface is devoted to the Yorkshire schools question and asserts that they are truthfully described in the book. Besides this, the author expresses his regret at leaving his beloved readers and the hope that they will experience regret also and regard Dickens' works "as the correspondence of one who wished their happiness and contributed to their amusement."[28] The volume was inscribed to the actor W.C. Macready, to whom Dickens also dedicated, a few weeks later, his second daughter, born in October. The actor standing godfather to her, she was christened Kate Macready Dickens. When he asked his friend to play that part, the prospective father described the forthcoming child as destined to be "the last and final branch of a genteel small family of three."[29] He was a little out in his calculations, however, since the genteel small family was to be adorned with seven additional branches in the next dozen years.

At the end of 1839, the Dickenses left their small house in Doughty

[27] Forster, *Life of Dickens*, I, 101–102.

[28] 1838 edition. The fragment—perhaps because it did not sound unduly modest—was omitted from the later versions of the preface.

[29] *Letters*, I, 571.

Street, in which half of *Pickwick* and nearly the whole of *Oliver Twist* and *Nickleby* had been composed, to occupy Devonshire Terrace, a glamorous house, close to Regent's Park and more in keeping with the income of a great popular novelist. For that is the title which his contemporaries were prepared to grant him after *Nickleby*. Perhaps the critics of today would be more reluctant to concede that he was a great novelist on the strength of his first three works of fiction alone.

He had certainly not completely mastered his art. The structure of his narratives had made slow progress, and he was still often carried away by inspiration or led astray by incidental circumstances and needs foreign to his central purpose. When he moved from one scene to another, when he turned back to an earlier period, the vagaries of his narrative were often ponderously stressed, rather than justified or excused by phrases like these:

> This narrative may embrace the opportunity of ascertaining the condition of Sir Mulberry Hawk (chap. xxxviii), this history may pursue the footsteps of Newman Noggs, thereby combining advantage with necessity ... (chap. li), [or what discloses yet more clearly the lack of a firm grasp of events on the author's part] the course which these adventures shape out for themselves, and imperiously call upon the historian to observe, now demands that they should return to the point they attained previous to the commencement of the last chapter (chap. lvi).

He still had much to learn. It has been seen that in the final section of his novel, he had made an attempt to write more artistically and thus given evidence at least of his desire to learn and progress.

Yet Dickens' chief purpose in *Nickleby*—apart from the permanent need of earning money—remained sentimental rather than artistic. He wished above all to be in sympathy with his readers and to be loved by them. When he sent Macready the first copy of the original edition, he defined *Nickleby* as "the book itself, my whole heart for twenty months."[30] He felt he must gain the affection of the people to whom he was thus surrendering his whole heart. The finest tribute he ever received must have been the most gratifying to him: it was paid by Thackeray, who said:

[30] *Ibid.*, 593.

All children ought to love him. I know two that do, and read his books ten times for once that they peruse the dismal preachings of their father. I know one who, when she is happy, reads "Nicholas Nickleby"; when she is unhappy, reads "Nicholas Nickleby"; when she is tired, reads "Nicholas Nickleby"; when she is in bed, reads "Nicholas Nickleby"; when she has nothing to do, reads "Nicholas Nickleby"; and when she has finished the book, reads "Nicholas Nickleby" over again. This candid young critic, at ten years of age, said, "I like Mr. Dickens's books much better than your books, papa," and frequently expressed her desire that the latter author should write a book like one of Mr. Dickens's books. Who can?[31]

Dickens was quite prepared to content himself with being an inimitable enchanter, even if, in point of technical mastery, he was not yet a great novelist. In fact, he did not himself lay claim to the latter title. On the contrary, in the preface to *Nickleby*, he represented himself, not as the successor of Fielding and Smollett or of Scott and Jane Austen, but as the emulator of Henry Mackenzie, the author of *The Man of Feeling* as well as of several magazines analogous to Addison's and Johnson's, made up of essays and miscellaneous articles.[32] At the close of a lengthy quotation from Mackenzie about the right enjoyed by the author "of a periodical performance" to be loved by his readers, he concluded with a description of himself—in spite of the recent development of his own technique in the direction of more solid and methodical construction—as "the periodical essayist, the author of these pages."

XV: Master Humphrey's Two Narratives:
The Old Curiosity Shop and Barnaby Rudge

1. Master Humphrey's Birth

Nickleby's UNQUESTIONABLE SUCCESS might have induced the author to believe he had found the right way, and that after the fresco-like mean-

---

[31] "Charity and Humour," *Miscellaneous Essays, The Works of Thackeray* (36 vols., Smith, 1885), XXV, 371. In her *Records of Tennyson* (London, 1892), 39, Lady Ritchie (Anne Thackeray) relates that in the poet's presence her little sister "looked up suddenly from the book in which she had been absorbed, saying . . . , 'Papa, why do you not write books like 'Nicholas Nickleby.' "

[32] *The Mirror* (1779–80); *The Lounger* (1784–85).

derings of *Pickwick* and the sensational structure of *Oliver Twist,* he need only in the future refrain from going to either of these extremes, as he had already done in his third fiction, by granting prominence, within a carefully constructed though unobtrusive frame, to those elements which had made the irresistible appeal of all three of his previous books, namely, the creation of lively characters presented in a succession of varied and diverting scenes.

But it has been seen that, while writing *Nickleby,* Dickens had undergone a feeling of weariness and intellectual drought. So, although his difficulties had not for one moment become perceptible to the average reader, the writer yearned above all henceforth to free himself from the necessity of ceaselessly producing long works of fiction. However, since he had no resource but the labor of his pen to support his family, he contemplated a different class of publication, whose outward characteristics would be the substitution of three-pence weekly numbers for the shilling monthly parts. In content, the new venture was to emulate Addison's *Spectator* and Goldsmith's *Bee*: such were the examples mentioned in the letter to Forster[1] outlining the scheme, but Dickens must also have had in mind Henry Mackenzie's *Mirror* and *Lounger,* which he had certainly read or reread recently, before he wrote the preface to *Nickleby.* It was Mackenzie who gave him the surprising idea of calling himself a "periodical essayist" on the strength of his most workmanlike novel so far, while he was only preparing himself to become a periodical essayist in his next work by preparing his readers to accept him as such. The periodical would thus resemble the early masters, but, at the same time, Dickens took care to point out, "it would be far more popular, both in the subjects . . . and its mode of treating them." It would comprise from the start a central group of characters, to whom others might be added later, such as Mr. Pickwick and Sam Weller. Dickens proposed to write "amusing essays on the various foibles of the day as they arise," and to introduce into his publication other essays, sketches, tales, and adventures, as well as letters from imaginary correspondents. His ideas, then, were neither very precise nor strikingly original, since they had already been exploited by the predecessors he mentioned. Likewise, when he planned to work into his new periodical "a series of satirical

[1] *Life of Dickens,* I, 112–13.

papers, purporting to be translated from some Savage Chronicles, and to describe the administration of justice in some country that never existed, and record the proceedings of its wise men," he felt he had to make his meaning clearer by explaining that the result would be "something between *Gulliver's Travels* and *The Citizen of the World*." About his few truly original inventions he held strange illusions, believing for instance that by showing Gog and Magog and making them bandy "stories and descriptions of London as it was many years ago, as it is now, and as it will be many years hence ... dividing them into portions like the Arabian Nights," he might create "an almost inexhaustible field of fun, raillery, and interest."

Whoever has examined, as has been done in the preceding chapters, the few technical weaknesses and uncertainties as well as the exceptional appeal of his first works of fiction must see that a project of that kind could only impair Dickens' originality by causing him to interrupt his progress in the new genre he was beginning to master, and look for success along lines that many another writer might have followed with greater ease than he.

When he had nevertheless obtained his publishers' acceptance of the general principle of the new publication, Dickens endeavored to define more precisely the physiognomy of the central figure. He turned him into Master Humphrey, who, despite the author's attempt to refer to him with casual light-handedness,[2] is, like the few companies around him, dull, sad, addicted to sermonizing, and drably humorless. Dickens seems to have fancied that by endowing him with profound sentimental attachment to an old clock—destined to serve, among other purposes, as a storage place for manuscripts—and making him date all his communications "from my clock-side," he had hit upon a splendid invention. In fact, he was at the time going through a crisis in his inspiration and appeared to lose his intuitive perception of the public's tastes. His new idea was vague, not easily to be imparted, not likely to yield many further developments. The enthusiastic admirers of *Pickwick* and *Nickleby,* of their tangible reality and broad comedy, would doubtless have been alarmed if they had known what was brewing: Boz was preparing to sell them a collection of tales and essays linked together

---

[2] Dickens calls him "this old file" (Forster, *Life of Dickens,* I, 115).

merely by the personality, colorless and ill defined, of one Humphrey, "mixing up his enjoyments with some notion of his clock."

Once Humphrey's name and the presence of the clock had been decided on, Dickens still balanced for some time between two possible titles: *Old Humphrey's Clock,* and *Master Humphrey's Clock.*[3] The words *Humphrey's Clock,* to be found in both titles, are supposed to have been suggested by the signboard of a clockmaker seen in York while looking about for information to be used in *Nickleby*: the clockmaker's name was Humphrey. Yet the sound of the two words is once more irresistibly reminiscent of Smollett and his *Humphrey Clinker.* As to the final choice of *Master* rather than *Old*—which might have been more pleasantly familiar—it is difficult to believe that it was uninfluenced, at a subconscious level at least, by the fact that *M*aster *H*umphrey's initials would coincide with *M*ary *H*ogarth's. If one takes into account the vivid emotion Dickens felt later when he discovered that he had involuntarily given David Copperfield his own initials reversed, there can be but little doubt on that point, especially as Humphrey's dull virtues embody at once the internal peace that the novelist would have dearly liked to possess and the haunting memory of Mary as it became more idealized, purer and purer, but also less and less clear and definite.

In order to carry out his intentions, Dickens demanded and obtained highly satisfactory financial terms. He was to get £50 a week, plus one-half of the profits from each number, separate accounts being settled every week. The undertaking was to last at least a year, and might go on for five years. One important item in the agreement, in Dickens' view, was the employment, after a few weeks, of contributors chosen and superintended by himself but remunerated by the publisher: this, he thought, would materially lighten his own task.

The first number of *Master Humphrey's Clock* appeared on April 1, 1840. It had been carefully prepared, since Dickens had undertaken no other considerable literary labor since the conclusion of *Nickleby* in September, 1839.[4] High expectations were shared by author and publishers alike. In order to exploit to the utmost the success they felt so sure

[3] *Ibid.,* 116.
[4] He had written, slowly and unenthusiastically, only a few pages of *BR* at the close of the year, 1839.

of, they had made arrangements for early proofs to be sent to American and German publishers.[5] Success did seem at first to be proportioned to their hopes. Seventy thousand copies of the first number were sold in April. But the disappointment of Dickens' customary public soon became evident. They had looked forward to reading a new *Pickwick* or a new *Nickleby*. They had never intended to pay the same price for the privilege of attending the meetings of Humphrey's fogyish friends or of hearing Gog and Magog's laborious interchange of confidences. Whereas the sales of the previous works had gone up continually, those of *Humphrey* fell fast and alarmingly. In order to save the publication from being the first failure in Dickens' career, what was needed was a continuous narrative by himself. His attempt at escape had proved impossible. He remained the prisoner of his fate, of the peculiar shape of his creative genius, and of the habits he had given his public. *Master Humphrey's Clock* began to soar again from the day when the tale called "Personal Adventures of Master Humphrey: The Old Curiosity Shop" made its appearance in its pages.

Dickens had made two mistakes. He had created a whole batch of un-Dickensian and tiresome characters and placed them at the focal point of his new publication. And he had constructed an intricate machinery to hold together disparate, and for most part unoriginal, elements. As for the former point, he admitted openly and repeatedly that he had been mistaken, and explained for instance that he had "insensibly fallen into the belief that [these gentle spirits] are present to his readers as they are to him, and has forgotten that like one whose vision is disordered he may be conjuring up bright figures where there is nothing but empty space."[6] But as for the advantages of the method employed, Dickens refused to believe that he had been in error. Yet the explanations he gave[7] in an attempt to make purely accidental developments appear deliberate and premeditated do not in the least account for the history of *Humphrey* and *The Old Curiosity Shop*; nor

[5] See *Letters* (MDGH), I, 28.

[6] Preface, *MHC*. Already at the end of Number I, Humphrey had been made to express similar fears—"lest . . . I should grow prolix . . . confounding the enthusiasm with which I regard this chief happiness of my life with that minor degree of interest which those to whom I address myself may be supposed to feel for it."

[7] See *MHC*, Preface (Sept., 1840), and the preface to Vol. II of the same (March, 1841).

do they justify the various changes in the parts assigned to Humphrey himself.

2. *Enters Nell*

It would be unfair to contend that the notion of writing *The Old Curiosity Shop* was suggested to Dickens or imposed upon him entirely by the failure of *Humphrey*. Already in February, 1840, in the course of a three-day visit to Walter Savage Landor, in Bath, in company with John Forster and the painter Daniel Maclise, the idea had occurred to him of telling the story of an orphan girl living with her grandfather in a curiosity shop. But such a tale was to comprise no more than a dozen chapters, and the author's purpose was to bring them out, one by one, in the *Clock,* together with other articles and on the same footing as several similar narratives. When the unexpected financial difficulties of the new venture supervened, Dickens was merely led, first, to publish the first chapter of the tale earlier than he had planned; second, to exclude from his magazine, little by little, every other kind of material; and third, to expand the story far beyond the bounds he had originally contemplated for it. So, although the invention of Nell and her grandfather preceded the crisis in the sales of *Master Humphrey*, Forster was justified when he wrote that Dickens had had in that case "less direct consciousness of design . . . than I can remember in any other instance of all his career."[8]

The invasion of the periodical and ousting of Master Humphrey by Nell and her circle were progressive. The first issue (Number IV) in which she appeared contained Chapter I only and was eked out by a letter from an imaginary correspondent. The three following numbers were devoted to the introduction of Mr. Pickwick into the Humphrey group—which tends to show that Dickens still hoped the group might survive, otherwise he would hardly have thought it worth his while to add to it. Then came Chapter II of *The Old Curiosity Shop,* together with a meditation by Humphrey; Chapters III and IV made up the whole of the next number; Chapter V shared a number with Sam and Tony Weller; then came Chapters VI and VII on their own; finally,

[8] *Life of Dickens,* I, 117.

after one issue in which Chapter VIII rubbed shoulders with a meeting of the Weller circle (Number XII), the rest of the novel was published without further interruption, at the rate of two chapters a week, through January, 1841.

Under these circumstances, as the design of the work had been gradually worked out while the early chapters were already being written and when perhaps the author had been suddenly engrossed in his novel and lost interest in the rest of the magazine, two facts remain astonishing as well as mutually contradictory. On the one hand, it must be admitted that the extraordinary conditions which caused Dickens to enlarge his canvas have left very few marks upon the novel and have not impaired the creative energy at work in it. Admirers of Quilp and —if any are left—of Nell might remain ignorant of the hesitations and accidents that attended the birth of the book. The impression produced by Dickens' early works is thus splendidly confirmed: the peculiar temper of Dickens' genius enabled him to build a monumental and enduring structure on the basis of a series of extemporizations. Extemporization is identified as such only through close critical scrutiny of the technical aspects. But on the other hand, there is one stupendous exception, one glaringly obvious mark left by the author's changing purposes; and it is astonishing that he should never have wished to get rid of it.

The earliest title of the novel had been, as we have shown above: "Personal Adventures of Master Humphrey. The Old Curiosity Shop." The relevance of the second part can certainly be questioned, since the shop is left forever at the end of the twelfth chapter. Dickens, however, and Forster after him, have concocted a kind of symbolic justification for that title by maintaining that not only the baroque furniture of the house in which Nell dies and the carvings of the church in which she is buried, but also such quaint and contorted figures as Codlin and Short the puppet-showmen, Mrs. Jarley with her waxwork, Quilp and the Brasses are real *curiosities* in their way, that Nell's whole life takes place within a strange and grotesque *décor*, which imparts profound unity to the outwardly disconnected scenes of the narrative. Such explanations have the usual *a posteriori* aspect that causes one to distrust them. Yet it might be admitted that, even if he had not at first formulated it to himself quite so clearly and consciously, such a thought had guided the artist's pen, as his poetical inspiration often went beyond the deliberate purposes of his work.

But for the first part of the original title, *Personal Adventures of Master Humphrey,* no such extenuating claims can be made. The first two chapters of the tale are narrated by Humphrey in the first person: he meets with Nell, takes her back to her grandfather, and pays them another visit a few days later. After the end of Chapter III, it has become impossible to make him a witness of every incident in the story. He then withdraws with the following mediocre comment—which does nothing to account for the way in which he may have become informed of what he reports, e.g., Quilp's interior monologues: "And now, that I have carried this history so far in my own character, and introduced these personages to the reader, I shall, for the convenience of the narrative, detach myself from its further course, and leave those who have prominent and necessary parts in it to speak and act for themselves" (chap. iii).

For the modern reader of *The Old Curiosity Shop,* no more is said on that point. It would have been easy for Dickens to improve the beginning of the book, by substituting for the first three chapters a more impersonal introduction. But Dickens is known to have been very reluctant to introduce major changes into his works after they had seen the light of print, after they had been, so to speak, consecrated by the public's affectionate approval. He therefore preserved, not only the original beginning of the novel—admittedly lost sight of by the reader as soon as by the author—but also another *a posteriori* account of the title *Personal Adventures,* reprinted with scrupulous care among the fragments gathered under the heading of *Master Humphrey's Clock* in every edition of his complete works. When he belatedly remembered that the novel was supposed to contain the narrative of Humphrey's personal adventures—and it should be borne in mind that the whole of *The Old Curiosity Shop* had appeared in a magazine called *Master Humphrey's Clock*—Dickens then looked about for some anonymous figure in the story whom he might identify with the narrator of its beginnings. What he needed was an old man who was a bachelor and had not died before the last chapter. There being very few eligible candidates, the author then decided that Humphrey was Nell's great-uncle. And as that disclosure made nonsense of the early chapters, in which chance alone had led Humphrey, at a time when the great-uncle was not in England, to the shop kept by the man who now became his brother, the character writes of the opening part: "You will . . . forgive me . . . if, for the greater convenience of the story, and for its better introduction, that adventure was fictitious. I had my share—no light or trivial one—in the pages we have read, but it was not the share I feigned to have at first. The younger brother, the single gentleman, the nameless actor in this little drama, stands before you now."[9] Thus did Dickens adopt three distinct attitudes successively toward the same character in the novel. No artistic scruple was strong enough to prevent him from letting the three versions of the same facts co-exist side by side in his complete works, in defiance of psychological verisimilitude, for Humphrey's personality does not in the least resemble that of the great-uncle. Had Master Humphrey been as vigorous, impetuous, and lively as Nell's great-uncle, his *Clock* would doubtless have been better received, and there might have been no need to create the *Curiosity Shop*.

Dickens himself did not regret the change in the long run. He had launched *Humphrey* in order to desist from writing long novels which were too much of a strain. When he referred to those circumstances in his preface to the *Curiosity Shop*, he tended to convey the opposite impression and suggested that the new form of publication had been imposed upon him by some mysterious external power, while he himself only yearned to resume his usual occupation as soon as possible: "I had already been made uneasy by the desultory character of [*Master Humphrey*] and . . . I believe, my readers had thoroughly participated in the feeling. The commencement of a story was a great satisfaction to me, and I had reason to believe that my readers participated in that feeling, too. Hence, being pledged to some interruptions and some pursuit of the original design, I cheerfully set about disentangling myself from those impediments as fast as I could." "Those impediments" were no other than the grandiose scheme whose chances of success had appeared to him, a few months before, "very great, very great in-

---

[9] In *MHC*, the appearance of Humphrey in this passage chiefly serves to manage the transition from *OCS* to *BR* still under the general title of *Master Humphrey's Clock*.

deed; almost beyond calculation."[10] But the scales had now fallen from his eyes and intimate contact had been restored between him and his readers.

3. *The Structure of* The Old Curiosity Shop

The novel which was thus "cheerfully" written and published, week after week, in *Humphrey's Clock,* is curiously constructed. It is composed of two clear-cut narratives, each staging the adventures of a distinct set of characters.

At the beginning of the book, Nell and her grandfather—who has gambled and lost borrowed money—are turned out of their home by Quilp the usurer. After a succession of travels and adventures, they eventually both die in a peaceful village. From time to time, the narrative of their tribulations is interrupted in order to show what becomes of the people who are looking for them: Quilp and his attendants, young Kit—a former assistant in the shop—and later a mysterious and wealthy eccentric who turns out to be the grandfather's brother. Many subplots are created which occasion encounters and clashes between the various pursuers. As in the other part of the novel, the central figure meets with a tragic fate: Quilp is drowned. Soon after Nell's death, and shortly before her grandfather's, the latter's brother and Kit have tracked them down, a general reunion has taken place, and the unity of the narrative has thus been restored.

This plan had been conceived so as to provide several sources of interest and movement. No doubt, the transitions from one group of characters to the other remain somewhat weak and reminiscent of similar passages in *Oliver* and *Nickleby*,[11] while in the Nell and Trent section, the development of the adventures is on rather Pickwickian lines, with constant fresh beginnings and furtive departures, and a purposeless journey. There are far fewer coincidences than in the previous novels. Yet, when Nell drops to the ground, exhausted by her long walks, she does so at the feet of a charitable schoolmaster she had already en-

---

[10] Forster, *Life of Dickens*, I, 114.

[11] See chap. xxxiii: "The historian takes the friendly reader by the hand . . ."; chap. xlii: "It behoves us to leave Kit for a while . . . ," etc.

countered a few months back (chap. xlvi), who is now traveling to join his new post. He takes Nell and her grandfather Trent with him. In the village where he is going to run the school lives the brother of Kit's new employer. But such artificialities and blemishes are few and unimportant. On the whole there is marked technical progress from the first novels to the *Curiosity Shop*. The greatest originality lies in the efforts made by one group of characters to evade the eager pursuit of the other group, and in the gradual success of the pursuit. As the two series of incidents are clearly distinguished, except at the very beginning and at the very end of the book, they will be more conveniently examined in separate sections here.

4. *Quilp, Brass, & Co.*

The evil genius of the novel is the dwarf, Quilp. Like his immediate predecessor in the villain's role, Ralph Nickleby, he occupies a somewhat shadowy, as well as wholly shady, position in society. Like Ralph also, he seems to make his living chiefly by usury, although he has an office, in which, however, more private plots are hatched than business transacted. Like Ralph once more, he has a grudge against mankind and hates everybody, with the single exception of Tom Scott, his youthful clerk and errand-boy, who never has any work to do and is privileged to insult and threaten his master to his heart's content (chap. v), just as Newman Noggs could indulge in some liberties with Ralph Nickleby. But as far as monstrosity is concerned, Quilp goes beyond Ralph. His deformity, ugliness, fiendish jocularity, cynical sadism, and brutality make him a much more colorful and livelier figure than Ralph. It is as though the systematic malice which in both cases becomes the mainspring of the plot had appeared a more acceptable and convincing moral characteristic to Dickens in an individual whose physique was symmetrically anomalous and repulsive.

Quilp is, in the first place, a cruel husband. He beats his wife, torments her in mean ways—such as pinching her arm in the dark—and compels her to play unpleasant parts. Unfortunate Mrs. Quilp, a pale embodiment of patient suffering, manages to feel distressed even when, in order to achieve the acme of persecution, her husband resolves to desert her. Quilp's animosity of course includes his mother-in-law as well as his wife, and the former is a much more diverting character in proportion as she is less patient than her daughter. It is harder to find out why Quilp should so persistently pursue Nell and old Trent. The motivation ascribed to him explicitly is greed. He thinks they are rich, partly because they have departed in secret, partly because they are also sought by other people. As self-interest is in Quilp's eyes the single cause of human action, he can form no other conjecture. Yet the mere desire to do evil, the intrinsic delight of inflicting pain, could sufficiently account, Dickens felt—and this is not the only sign that he understood sadism—for Quilp's strangest actions. Whatever its psychological origin, Quilp's hatred for Nell and Trent is extended to all their well-wishers, and particularly to their former assistant, young Kit. " 'He needs be careful,' " Quilp said of the latter in a passage cancelled by Dickens at proof stage, which went on to provide the following explanation of his attitude: "His dislike of Kit had indeed gradually mounted into the most intense and concentrated hatred, and as all his passions were violent and stopped at nothing when once roused, this sly threat had a deeper meaning in Quilp's mouth than it would have had in that of any other man."[12] The innocent boy is again the occasion for a disclosure of Quilp's reason for hating so many people, when the dwarf declares: "I hate your virtuous people! . . . ah, I hate 'em, every one!" (chap. xlviii). Yet, so all-embracing is his feeling toward mankind that he does not content himself with hating virtuous beings. He is just as hostile to the unscrupulous people, like Dick Swiveller, and to the infamous creatures, like Brass and his sister, who are made to serve his own ends: he makes Brass employ Swiveller and would have Swiveller marry Nell; he has Brass perjure himself in order to compromise Kit. Fortunately, Brass and his sister and Quilp are not pure embodiments of evil, but comic figures also, and all the scenes in which they take part with Swiveller contain passages of admirable comedy, among the most amusing in the book.

Sampson Brass—whom Dickens had first intended to call Septimus Brass[13]—is a dishonest attorney. Up to the time of his inevitable final collapse, he has the alluring effrontery and the entertaining verve which

---

[12] Unpublished (Forster Collection); meant to be part of Chap. xlviii.
[13] See Forster, *Life of Dickens*, I, 118–19.

characterize all legal swindlers in Dickens' work, from *Pickwick*'s Dodson and Fogg on.

As in the case of Sam Weller, Sampson's comic appeal is cleverly exploited and increased, thanks to the presence by his side of his sister, Sally Brass, fully as much a "man of law" as her brother. One may well deplore the excessive insistence with which the novelist stresses the virility of the termagant and the ensuing confusions about her sex. Yet, from her very first appearance and the masterly portrait then drawn of her (chap. xxxiii) to her final flight, Sally Brass is immensely diverting. The published text of *The Old Curiosity Shop* has unfortunately omitted several droll traits of that colorful figure. Among the canceled fragments is a scene in which Sally Brass approaches the pony of Mr. Garland, Kit's employer, "not with the timid and bashful advances or little fondlings and caresses with which the weaker portion of her sex are wont to coax dumb animals, but by boldly wrenching open his mouth to see how old he is, or seizing one of his legs, and requiring him, in a hoarse and manly voice, to exhibit his shoe."[14] And also a picturesque description of her by her brother: "A sister, the tenderest in her affections and the toughest in her knowledge of business that ever bloomed and blowed!" (chap. lix)

Among the cancelled and so far unpublished passages of *The Old Curiosity Shop,* one assumes still greater importance. The Brasses have in their employment the little girl nicknamed by Swiveller "The Marchioness," whom they ill-treat. All that the official text of the novel has to tell about the girl's identity will be found in the following few phrases of "Chapter The Last": [She] herself supposed she was an orphan; but Mr. Swiveller, putting various light circumstances together, often thought Miss Brass must know better than that; and . . . entertained . . . misgivings whether [Quilp] . . . might not also have been able to solve the riddle, had he chosen." There is here a discreet hint that the child was the offspring of Quilp's and Sally's guilty love, but the hint is so discreet that some critics have been able to shut their eyes to it.[15] Dickens' first intention had been to provide fuller explan-

---

14 Part of chap. lvii cancelled by Forster on the proofs.

15 *Times Lit. Sup.,* London, April 6, 1940: "The idea is not agreeable that [Dickens] may have imagined either Quilp, or Sally, or both of them, as being responsible for the existence of that enchanting elf."

ations, formally contradicting his own earlier statements regarding Sally's past—"That amiable virgin, having clung to the skirts of the Law from her earliest youth . . . had passed her life in a kind of legal childhood. . . . Miss Brass could know but little of the world, otherwise than in connection with the law. . . . Miss Sally's accomplishments were all of a masculine and legal kind. They began with the practice of an attorney, and they ended with it. She was in a state of lawful innocence, so to speak." (chap. xxxvi) Now, in the manuscript and on the proofs, the very same "amiable virgin" emerges from her "lawful innocence" to inform her brother unequivocally, though gradually: " 'No worse for the artful wretch to be the ruin of her own mother!' . . . 'Is it not worse, I ask you . . . for her to be my ruin than yours?' . . . 'I am her mother. She is my child.' "[16] The suppression of this passage may have been due in part to the feeling that it was too bold for the Victorian public, in part also to the unpleasant nature of the circumstances thus half-disclosed, as well as to the grossness of the contradiction involved. In fact, had the passage been preserved, it could hardly have increased the reader's enjoyment, and it would have reinforced the impression created by the end of the novel, that Dickens had all of a sudden begun to hate the Brasses, brother and sister. After they had contributed so much to the reader's delight through so many chapters, the final punishment inflicted on them may be thought too harsh, and the irony with which its details are described superfluous. Sampson and Sally, as two superb comic figures, deserved perhaps a better fate than to become two "cowering, shivering forms, looking into the roads and kennels as they went in search of refuse food or disregarded offal" (chapter the Last).

The clerk forced upon the Brasses by Quilp—for reasons as obscure as those that caused Ralph Nickleby to keep Newman Noggs with him or those that make Heep, in *Copperfield,* give employment to Micawber, with disastrous results in both cases—is himself one of the finest figures in the book. His name is twice revealing of Dickens' affection for him: *Dick* Swiveller.[17] He belongs to the class of half elfin creatures, whose soul is beyond the reach of the little mishaps of daily life. His language,

---

[16] Part of chap. lxvi, cancelled by Dickens on the proofs.
[17] Cf., S. Weller and Swiveller, Dick and Dickens.

made up of poetical quotations adapted to the circumstances of ordinary conversation, is original and charming. His constant use of quotations and allusions in the long run imparts a poetical character to his own thoughts. He is endowed with a high degree of the sense of humor which transfigures humble realities and enables him to be happy even in abject poverty. His psychological metamorphosis is certainly not very artfully contrived. He is at first a selfish, drunken, scatter-brained idler; he is in the end the chivalrous champion of widows—Mrs. Nubbles, Kit's mother—and orphans—The Marchioness. No evolution has been convincingly shown. Yet his intrinsic appeal makes the change less difficult to admit than in most similar cases.

In the plot of the novel, Dick has no definite part to play. But the very gratuitousness of his appearances lends him additional charm. He has the freshness of a child, ever indulging in games of make-believe. He plays at being brokenhearted by the desertion of his first fiancée, Sophy Wackles, he plays at humorously courting Sally Brass, he plays at being grownups with the Marchioness. And if he serves practically no function in the plot, he serves a considerable one in the improvement of Dickens' style. He seems to have been created, more or less consciously, as an outlet for the novelist's frequent urge to use poetic diction or some ornate and bombastic form of the mock heroic. The use of that kind of style—alternating with mock cockney—is fairly constant in Dickens' correspondence, in which, like Dick, he is always "yielding to his destiny, and saying whatever came uppermost" (chap. xxxv). The two attitudes result from a similar enjoyment of acting, or disguising himself, now as a man of the people, now as a conventional man of letters. In the *Sketches, Pickwick, Oliver,* and *Nickleby,* the frequency of the pseudo-poetical vocabulary, of words like *swain, sable, effusion,* was noticeable. In the *Shop,* they have almost disappeared from the passages of narrative, as they have been concentrated into the overflowing stream of Dick's speech, which thus purifies the author's own style. The same kind of thing happens once more in *Copperfield* with the Micawbers, much addicted to verbose phrases and poetical quotations. The result is both wholesome, for Dickens' style is improved by the loss of such garish ornaments, and diverting, for the characters concentrating them in their own persons assume a kind of gaudy bright-

ness. It is even amusing to find that in *The Old Curiosity Shop* the un-
sentimental Sampson Brass is eventually contaminated by his clerk's
example and pays him back in kind, so that in a few chapters they
bandy poetical quotations with bewildering effect.

The surest sign of Dickens' success in the creation of Swiveller is
the fact that this character, like Sam Weller, and Micawber, remains
delightfully entertaining once he has been converted to virtue and
become the champion of the oppressed. In the first group of characters
here, the oppressed are mostly Quilp's and the two Brasses' victims, and
more particularly young Kit, whom their plottings cause to be sentenced
for a theft of which he is innocent. In spite of his misfortunes and his
sometimes too edifying feelings and speeches, Kit is a well-drawn figure
of a boy, lifelike and real. He is, so to speak, redeemed by his little weaknesses, his impatient impulses, his naïve joys, his pride. It is about Kit
that Dickens reported to Forster a case of almost hallucinatory inspiration: "I have opened the second volume, with Kit; and I saw this
morning, looking out at the sea, as if a veil had been lifted up, an
affecting thing that I can do with him by and by. Nous verrons."[18] The
affecting thing was doubtless the struggle of Kit, torn between two loves,
his pure and etherealized passion for Nell, a hopeless worship, and his
growing fondness for Barbara, the pretty girl he would eventually
marry. That complex sentimental situation already foreshadowed David
Copperfield's attachment to both Dora and Agnes. One statement of
Kit's to Barbara, cancelled on the manuscript of the novel: ". . . I have
been used to think and talk'd about her as if she [Nell] was an angel . . .
dear Barbara . . . and if I hadn't felt like this for her, I don't believe
I should ever have got to be so truly fond of you."[19] calls to mind
David's strange refinement when he says to Agnes: "My love [for Dora]
would have been incomplete without your sympathy. I had it, and it
was perfected."[20]

Kit's affection for Nell is the closest material and sentimental link
between the two groups of characters in *The Old Curiosity Shop.*

[18] *Life of Dickens*, I, 120. The letter refers to chap. xxxviii of the novel.
[19] Unpublished quotation from MS of *OCS*, II (chap. lxix).
[20] *DC*, chap. lxii.

5. *Little Nell*

Passing from Quilp and his attendants to Nell and her grandfather and the few people around them involves a change of atmosphere as well as scenery. The variegated comedy and the unrestrained mirth that prevail in the first group in spite of Quilp's cruelty are left far behind, and the field of sentimentality has to be entered. The very name of Nell, the sound of which is suggestive of "knell," could not fail to call up for Dickens, whose keen sensitiveness to sounds has been many times recognized, notions of peaceful sorrow and melancholy harmonies.

The outline of Nell's and Trent's fates is sad: they travel from ruin to death. Their journey is not uniformly grim, for it goes through bright enough oases, yet the point of departure is the shop distrained by Quilp, a pitiless creditor, and the point of arrival is the village church where the grandfather dies on the child's grave. At the moment when they were setting out, Dickens hesitated between two possible terms, and his final choice, as well as his hesitation in itself, was significant. On the manuscript, he had written at first: "two poor pilgrims, wandering they [knew] not wither." "Pilgrims" was then replaced by "adventurers"—and "wither" by "whither" (chap. xii). Nell and Trent were thus thought unworthy of being called pilgrims. Their flight is unglorious and unambitious. The old man has no will-power, and Nell's proposal "Let us be beggars and be happy!" (chap. ix) though courageous enough, is not particularly noble and inspiring. They have no purpose; they do not go on a pilgrimage, but merely on their adventures.

Nell and her circle are an early example, and an illustrious one, of Dickens' growing tendency to pathos. The word "bathos" has even been used more than once in criticism of the *Shop*. *Pickwick* and *Nickleby* had been essentially and resolutely comic novels. *Twist* was dramatic or melodramatic rather than pathetic. In *The Old Curiosity Shop* pathos, or perhaps bathos, holds first place. No other words could describe the scene in which the pauper woman whose son is in prison asks the police inspector whether the son was not deaf and dumb: " 'You know he was not.' 'He was,' cried the woman. 'He was deaf, dumb and blind to all that was good from the cradle' " (chap. xlv). The horrible and unreal equivocation makes it clear that Dickens is shooting point-blank at the reader's sensibility. He does so many times, in the course of some conversations between Nell and other children, in the funereal village, or between Nell and the schoolmaster, on the subject of the death of the young and the survival of benevolent actions.[21] The influence of pathos modifies the characters' speech. A certain exaltation, at once moral and literary, of the style employed by socially and intellectually humble people, betrays the author's desire to move the reader at any cost. Kit's mother, on hearing that her son is charged with larceny, delivers a splendid oration: "*I* believe it! *I* that never knew you tell a lie, or do a bad action from your cradle—that have never had . . ." and on she goes, for some ten lines, to her classically worded conclusion ". . . and that I never laid down in anger with! *I* believe it of you, Kit!"[22]

Yet the passage that most urgently clamors for the reader's emotion is, of course, the description of Nell on her death bed. There has been much argument about whether it was bathetic or merely pathetic. The debate is to a large extent idle, as the question can be answered only according to one's individual taste. One man's pathos is another man's bathos. But it is probable that in most cases the Victorian man's pathos tends to become the present-day reader's bathos. One fact, however, is clear: Dickens' own emotion is abundantly proved to have been sincere. Before he wrote the description of Nell's death, he sent Forster the following lines: ". . . this part of the story is not to be galloped over . . . . I am the wretchedest of the wretched. It casts the most horrible shadow upon me, and it is as much as I can do to keep moving at all. I tremble to approach the place a great deal more than Kit. . . . I shan't recover it for a long time. Nobody will miss her like I shall. It is such a very painful thing to me that I really cannot express my sorrow."[23] Only at the close of the same letter does one perceive, not any lack of sincerity, but a methodical fostering of, and deliberate quest for, emotion: "I have refused several invitations for this week and next, determining to go nowhere till I had done. I am afraid of disturbing the state I have been trying to get into, and having to fetch it all back again." To George Cattermole, the artist who was illustrating the novel, he

---

[21] See chaps. liv, lv lxx.

[22] Chap. lxi. The use of "laid" for "lay" is not meant to bring down Mrs. Nubbles' speech to the level of her class. The same mistake is often committed by Dickens in his own right.

[23] *Life of Dickens,* I, 122–23.

gave precise directions and wrote, on January 14, 1841, after completing the most emotional part: "I am, for the time being, nearly dead with work and grief for the loss of my child."[24]

The vividness of the author's feelings is clearly apparent from the text of the narrative itself. He is carried away and exalted by his grief, and allows himself to interfere in the description in his own person, a thing he had seldom done before, except jocularly: "Waking she never wandered in her mind but once, and that was of beautiful music which she said was in the air. God knows. It may have been" (chap. lxxii).

Dickens' emotion proved infectious. Nell on her deathbed drew tears from the majority of contemporary readers, even among the greatest minds, such as Jeffrey, Carlyle, and many more.[25] Modern readers are not necessarily impressed in a favorable way by such precedents. Objective examination of the relevant passages, so far as it can be achieved, reveals that Nell's death is announced in simple language, contrasting very effectively with the grandiloquent speech delivered a moment before by Trent's brother. The contrast has not been deliberately sought by Dickens, whose purpose could not have been to make one character utter tirades of cheap bombast in order to set off and emphasize the emotion and beauty of the next scene. Yet such is the effect produced. The central paragraph is perfectly sober. The manuscript is in a somewhat chaotic state, owing to the author's extreme care and hesitation: "For [Nell] was dead. There, upon the [little] [lowly] little bed, she lay at rest. The solemn stillness was no marvel now. [That sleeping white form] [The presence of the very air within the room seemed hushed] [She was dead and the strong heart]" Of which the printed text preserves no more than three brief, crystal-clear sentences: "For she was dead. There, upon her little bed, she lay at rest. The solemn stillness was no marvel now."

Her death, however, is but the acme and the conclusion of a series of adventures often sinning against verisimilitude. It has been pointed out by some critics, for instance, that the distances covered by Nell and Trent in their walks, their ever impeccable cleanness while they travel

---

24 *Letters* (MDGH), I, 37.
25 Thackeray, however, was sounding a dissonant note (see "Jerome Paturot, with considerations on novels in general," Thackeray, *Works*, Vol. XXXV).

without luggage or money, are not accounted for. Dickens no doubt counted—and perhaps rightly—on the beauty and sadness of the final pages to make the reader overlook the few weaknesses of the book. With the author's emotion the remembrance of Mary Hogarth is mingled once more, more and more idealized and made more and more youthful with time. As long as Nell was alive, Dickens' obsessive grief had adorned her with supernatural perfections that precluded her becoming either convincing or attractive. At her death, the writer's mourning mood is again in agreement with his theme, and he seems to be writing with greater naturalness and sincerity. In the *Curiosity Shop*, as in the preceding books, more than one passage is revealing of Mary Hogarth's presence. Such is the case of the paragraph about Nell's death which begins: "It is hard to take to heart the lesson that such deaths will teach, but let no man reject it . . ." (chap. lxxii); such also the case of an unpublished sentence meant to have been spoken by the compassionate schoolmaster: "If it is ignorance of the world which makes me think that a friendship linked with the memory of those that are gone, though they be but children, should be of all others true and lasting, God keep me from its knowledge."[26] In fact, the letter to Forster had laid stress on the sentimental link between the two deaths in Dickens' mind, and the overwhelming force of his twofold grief; "Old wounds bleed afresh when I only think of the way of doing it. What the actual doing will be, God knows. I can't preach to myself the schoolmaster's consolation, though I try. Dear Mary died yesterday when I think of this sad story."[27]

Out of a novel composed of elements so diverse as those of the *Shop*, it is only natural that individual readers should select different aspects for praise. Edward Fitzgerald had copied out all the part of the novel devoted to Nell's adventures,[28] while Saintsbury held that Nell "could be cut out of the book with little loss except of space. . . . There would remain enough to make a book of the first class."[29] Of the book as a whole, Forster writes sensibly enough that Dickens' art in it is "such as all cannot fail to recognize who read the book in a right sympathy

[26] Cancelled by Dickens on the proofs of chap. xlvi.
[27] *Life of Dickens*, I, 122.
[28] See Pope-Hennessy, *Ch. Dickens*, 149.
[29] *Cam. Hist. of Eng. Lit.* (1916), XIII, 319.

with the conception that pervades it."[30] The attitude advocated by Forster does enable the reader to appreciate both Fitzgerald's and Saintsbury's private versions of *The Old Curiosity Shop*. As for the author himself, he had loved his characters and endeavored to give each of them something of his most valuable gifts, now the ability to arouse laughter, now the faculty of eliciting emotion. The letter he sent his friend after completing the book—it is quoted in the *Life of Dickens* and the original has been pasted onto the beginning of the manuscript of the novel—shows the creator's particular attachment to that group of characters: "After you left last night I took my desk upstairs, and writing until four o'clock this morning, finished the old story. It makes me very melancholy to think that all these people are lost to me for ever, and I feel as if I never could become attached to any new set of characters."

6. *Barnaby Rudge*

It was necessary, for two reasons at least, to create another set of characters without further delay. The contract concerning *Humphrey* demanded that Dickens continue his weekly publication for a whole year. It had been alive for nine months only when Little Nell departed this world. And it was out of the question to substitute for her a resumption of the original principle of short, disconnected stories: it was clear that this would have meant inevitable failure. A new novel was needed.

Dickens had been contemplating for several years a new work, which he had promised to Macrone in June, 1836, and which had later been transferred to Bentley. With the latter publisher it had been the occasion of no fewer than seven distinct agreements, the general purpose of which had always been to postpone its publication so as to enable the author to face his other commitments. In May, 1840, when Dickens realized he was going to have to write *The Old Curiosity Shop* in weekly installments, it grew more obvious than ever that he could not compose another novel at the same time. Forster was then entrusted with the task of completing the negotiations with the publishers, which he did from May 20 to July 2, 1840, with the result that the projected novel was finally transferred from Bentley to Chapman and Hall. At the

[30] *Life of Dickens*, I, 125.

beginning of the negotiation, two chapters of *Barnaby Rudge* were already in their hands, for Dickens had not been entirely idle in that direction during the preceding four years. It has been seen that in November, 1839, he had forced himself to write a few pages of the projected novel. The new contract stipulated that *Barnaby Rudge* must be in length the equivalent of ten numbers of *Pickwick* or *Nickleby* size—about five hundred pages. It was later decided that *Barnaby* would in fact succeed *The Old Curiosity Shop* in *Humphrey's Clock* instead of appearing in monthly numbers. In January, 1841, when the final chapter of Nell's adventures was published, Dickens thus had a little ready material, which enabled him to breathe for a few weeks.

Barnaby Rudge has sometimes been thought reminiscent of Walter Scott, chiefly, no doubt, because of its historical character. Yet there is no need to go so far back in order to find a possible source of inspiration. Admittedly the vogue of the historical novel had been encouraged by the spectacular success of Scott's works, but two at least of Dickens' friends and contemporaries had followed before him in Scott's footsteps. Bulwer-Lytton had written several novels in this vein, as he had written several under the influence of the Newgate school of fiction, ever ready to adapt his fertile pen to the public's passing tastes, and in the same manner as he wrote society novels to emulate Disraeli's success. And W. H. Ainsworth was becoming famous through his clever reconstruction of great scenes of the past, involving the crowds of London. After Dickens, many great novelists were to try their hand at the historical genre, with varying measures of success. *Esmond* ranked high in Thackeray's work, but Trollope's *La Vendée* fell flat and George Eliot's *Romola* never achieved popularity. In Dickens' career there were two attempts in that direction, *Barnaby Rudge* and *A Tale of Two Cities*, but they have little in common apart from treating the past and presenting violence.

The manuscript of *Barnaby Rudge* shows no sign of planning ahead. The author's letters to Forster describe the way in which, four years after conceiving the original idea and over a year after writing the early chapters, he set about finally organizing the plot of his novel. On January 29, 1841, when the first installments had already appeared, he wrote: "I didn't stir out yesterday, but sat and thought all day; not writing a line. . . . I imaged forth a good deal of Barnaby by keeping my mind steadily upon him."[31] His statement is interesting in several respects. It shows clearly that in those days at any rate Dickens did not write down the outline of his story. While thinking hard, he wrote nothing whatever, but merely "imaged forth" the sequence of events so as to stamp it on his mind only. On the other hand, the need he felt to devote a considerable length of time to meditation on the arrangement of the story was a new factor. He had taken no similar precautions for *Pickwick* and *Nickleby*. With *Barnaby Rudge,* which marks in this respect a turning-point or at least a transition, the method was becoming systematic. One month after the above-quoted letter, he was telling Forster: "The contents of one number usually require a day's thought at the very least, and often more."[32]

As each number comprised two brief chapters—amounting to seventeen or eighteen pages in all—which must have meant about three mornings' normal writing, *Barnaby* appears to have been composed much more slowly and carefully than the preceding novels. The comparative slowness is partly accounted for by the lack of enthusiasm and gusto with which the book was finally begun in earnest. For four years it had been a nightmarish incubus, and Dickens had failed in his repeated attempts to free himself completely from the necessity of writing it. In the early phase at least, for the first time in his career, Dickens wrote a novel with more care than enjoyment, with more professional conscientiousness than overflow of high spirits.

The novelist's care is particularly marked in his style, which is more exalted than in the previous novels and occasionally rises to a kind of poetical level. The poetical prose to be found in *Barnaby Rudge* is of many classes. Edward Chester's conventional speech (chap. xiv) will probably not be recognized as such in spite of the author's labored attempt. But there is beyond question a certain poetical force in some images (chap. ix–x), in some admirably light-handed paragraphs (chap. lxxi), in some conversations possessing the poetical and tragical quality of horror and once more reminiscent of Shakespeare and *Macbeth*. Duncan's murderer could have described himself as Rudge does in

[31] *Ibid.,* 137.
[32] *Ibid.,* 138 (Feb. 25, 1841).

Dickens' book, "fresh from the horrors my own hands had made" (chap. lxii). In *Barnaby* there also appear in increasing number the symbolical elements which are temporarily being relegated to the end of chapters,[33] but will later be more systematically employed by Dickens and become a major characteristic of his art.

The novelist's care is less apparent in the structure of his narrative. The lack of unity of *Barnaby Rudge* and the sudden shifting of its main center of interest have often been adversely criticized. Yet, though the book lacks regular and methodical organization, there is undeniable ingenuity in its construction. The opening paragraphs are indeed reminiscent of Walter Scott and convey in the very first words the author's intention to write a historical novel: "In the year 1775, there stood upon the borders of Epping Forest . . ." (chap. i).

Protracted description is followed by a dialogue used for the double purpose of introducing the characters and laying the foundations of a criminal mystery in the plot, which concerns events of twenty years before. Other chapters in the book are still introduced, as in *Nickleby* and the *Curiosity Shop*, by sententiously general phrases: "Chroniclers are privileged to enter where they list . . ." (chap. ix), "The thoughts of worldly men are for ever regulated by a moral law of gravitation . . ." (chap. xxix), "Misfortunes, saith the adage, never come singly . . ." (chap. xxxii), or by transitional sentences which make a somewhat awkward attempt to justify some shifting of the action by means of a pseudo-explanation: "It is necessary at this juncture to return to Hugh . . ." (chap. lxix), "The Golden Key lies in our way . . . so to the Golden Key this chapter goes" (chap. lxxix).

The title of the novel is accounted for as early as the third chapter, when Barnaby Rudge is first glimpsed. It can hardly be contended that Barnaby is the novel's *hero*. He has not a single heroic quality, being no more than an unfortunate idiot and playing no essential part. Yet the title stands to show that in the author's opinion the character was significant and that he wished to draw the reader's attention to him and the tragic circumstances of which his mental deficiency made him the living relic. His rather dramatic first appearance—he stands by the side of a traveler who has been assaulted by a bandit—results from an artistic

---

[33] See, e.g., the end of chaps. iv, v, xlii.

effort which Dickens had not thought of making in his other works so far. Pickwick, Oliver, Nicholas, and the Curiosity Shop had been presented to the reader in the very first chapter of the novels in which they played their respective parts, without any elaborate staging. Another novelty—not in the history of fiction, but in the work of Dickens, who had earlier criticized the artificiality of the procedure involved—is the five-year break between the first thirty-two chapters and the remaining fifty-one: "And the world went on turning round, as usual, for five years, concerning which this narrative is silent" (chap. xxxii). The longest such silent interval lasts but six months in *Pickwick* and three in *Oliver Twist.* As for *Nickleby* or *The Old Curiosity Shop,* the chronology of events in those books is too vague to enable us to form an idea of the time that elapses between two successive episodes.

The five-year break is cleverly exploited by Dickens. He does not present, at the beginning of the second part, a complete summary of the intermediate occurrences, nor does he inform the reader at one blow of all the changes in the characters' situations. He reveals, little by little, how new links have been created between people who were formerly independent of one another. The progressive disclosure of these bonds suggests the passing of time more efficiently than a general summary might have done. It is seen, in the first place, that the society of "Prentice Knights" to which Sim Tappertit—the apprentice of Varden the locksmith—belonged has now become affiliated with Lord George Gordon's Protestant Association (chap. xxxvi). It later appears that Hugh, the coarse ostler of a country inn, is in his turn engaged by Gordon, and also received in the house of another nobleman, Sir John Chester, whose natural son he turns out to be in the end of the novel—for hidden parentage must remain, almost to the last days of Dickens' career, a favorite resource of every sensational winding-up.[34] It is then revealed that Stagg, the blind man who used to shelter the apprentices in the cellar he was then inhabiting, has become the companion of Rudge, Senior, the murderer, and persecutes Mrs. Rudge, the supposed widow and Barnaby's tearful mother. Again, when, at the climax of the riots, the

---

[34] It has already been seen that, in *NN*, Smike was Ralph's illegitimate son, that, in *OT*, Oliver was Rose Maylie's nephew and Monks' half-brother, and that, in *OCS*, the little maid servant had nearly become Quilp's and Sally Brass's illegitimate offspring.

house of a vintner is threatened with destruction, he is found to be the very vintner whom Joe Willet, the son of the village innkeeper, had briefly visited in the first part of the novel. Finally, at the most critical moment, the same Joe, escorted by Edward Chester, who like him had not been heard of for five years, bursts into the house and saves both the Catholic vintner's life and the virtue of the two girls Edward and he will marry.

The last two circumstances on the above list stress the drawback of the method whose advantages have just been defined, in that it narrows down the universe to which all the characters belong. There can be in the whole of England but one blind man, one vintner, one handsome officer, one one-armed non-commissioned officer. Yet one valuable result is achieved: the two parts of the novel—the story of love and crime and that of the anti-Catholic riots—are firmly linked together. After the riots are over, the interest flags, and the final chapters are, like the first, too slow and too long. Although the characters are far fewer than in *Pickwick* or *Nickleby,* Dickens does not succeed in dismissing them rapidly. His prize-giving scene is spread over several chapters, and his scrupulous desire to forget no one and deal equal justice to all results in tiresome passages, as when he grants Hugh, Chester's natural son, who has been hanged, a kind of posthumous compensation in the form of a discreet burial and one or two indulgent phrases (chap. lxxix). The prolonged death throes of the story detract from the final impression left with the reader. Had the novel come to its end a score of chapters earlier, one would on the contrary remember a vivid narrative, devoted mainly to the "No Popery" riots of 1780 in London, known as the Gordon Riots.

In Chapman and Hall's advertisements for the book, when it came to be published in book form, the subtitle was given as "A Tale of the Riots of Eighty,"[35] which shows what had by then become, in the author's and publisher's view, the main attraction of the story. Such had not been, however, the original idea, since the novel had at first[36] been intended to be called "Gabriel Varden, or The Locksmith of London."

---

[35] See the lists of Chapman and Hall's new publications in magazines and at the end of books in 1842.

[36] At the time of the earliest contracts with Bentley (1837–38).

In *Rudge*, the locksmith certainly distinguishes himself during the riots, but in Dickens' early plan the riots must have played but a secondary part.

The reasons which caused Dickens to select the Gordon Riots as the theme of his first historical novel, whether the historical theme was to be essential or not, are worth inquiry. The riots organized in 1780 by Lord George Gordon and the Protestant Association were directed against Roman Catholics. Their immediate purpose was to make Parliament repeal some measures that had been passed a few weeks before in their favor.

A general view of Dickens' life and work affords plentiful evidence that he was himself anti-Catholic. He said as much in his preface to *Barnaby Rudge*: the riots, he claims there, "are impartially painted by one who has no sympathy with the Romish church." Yet he assumed an attitude of unequivocal hostility to the supporters of the riots. His defense of the Roman Catholics and their rights to equal civil status, proposed through the medium of Haredale, a Roman Catholic gentleman, even sounds passionate (chap. xliii). The writer does not thereby evince, however, any amount of pro-Catholic feelings. He merely rises in support of a cause he had ever held sacred, the cause of tolerance. His choice of the Gordon Riots as the subject of a historical novel is thus to be accounted for precisely by his desire to preach tolerance while showing what hateful disorder extremes of intolerance produce.

He seems to have taken his role as a historical novelist seriously enough and to have made use of documents he had been working on at the British Museum. From hints given in his preface and allusions made in the text of the novel to precise historical facts, it is clear that he had read widely and carefully about the riots, consulting the contemporary press, the *Annual Register*, the *Parliamentary Debates,* and the *State Trials,* as well as several historical works and memoirs of the time. The sources of many dates, figures, and similar details can be traced, and there is no reason to question the assertion made in the preface that "reference has been had to the best authorities of that time, such as they are; and . . . the account given in this Tale, of all the main features of the Riots, is substantially correct."

The description of the first riot with the division of the demonstrators into four parties may have been suggested by the *Parliamentary History of England*.[37] The attack against a distillery which was set on fire, with the ensuing scenes of drunkenness, is related by Sir Samuel Romilly.[38] The name of the governor of Newgate Prison, Akerman, is to be found in an autobiographical fragment by George Crabbe,[39] together with additional details about the attack and firing of the prison and the prisoners' escape.

At two points, however, Dickens' implicit conclusions can be called in doubt. The first is the personality of the principal agitator, Lord George Gordon. In the novel, he is shown as a sincere believer and a somewhat feeble-minded man. Forster protested against such an interpretation, for he regarded Gordon as having been stark mad.[40] A similar impression is indeed conveyed by most of the contemporary evidence. Romilly calls him "that madman" and "this frantic incendiary,"[41] while the chronicler of the Parliamentary debates speaks of "his usual strange and very singular way of speaking" and relates how he delivered a disorderly speech, many times interrupted and resumed, and how on another occasion Gordon got no other vote than his own in favor of a motion he had initiated, and a few days later withdrew another motion before a vote could be taken.[42] His later career, after the riots, betrays the same lack of balance. The ardent defender of the Protestants was converted to the Jewish faith in 1786, grew a beard, created fresh troubles, and finally died a prisoner in 1793, after having been sentenced for slander. Of course, Dickens has not been blamed merely for his indulgent view of Gordon. Others have been more favorably impressed than he. Crabbe had seen in Gordon mostly "a lively-looking young man in appearance,"[43] and the author of a book devoted to the Gordon Riots regards him as "a revolutionary of the first water."[44] The historical truth—if

[37] London, 1814; see XXI, 665.

[38] *Memoirs of His Life*, 1840, I, 126. This book is quoted by Dickens in another connection in the preface to *BR*.

[39] *Life of the Rev. George Crabbe, by his Son* (1838), 82. Crabbe called the prison attacked "the Old Bailey."

[40] *Life of Dickens*, I, 141–42.

[41] Romilly, *Memoirs*, 118–19.

[42] *Parliamentary History*, XXI, 149, 171, 534.

[43] Crabbe, *Life of Rev. George Crabbe*, 83.

[44] J. Paul de Castro, *The Gordon Riots* (London, 1926).

there is *one*—is not easily got at, and Dickens at any rate has not sinned against the duty that was his, as a novelist and not a professional historian: he has made his Gordon coherent and plausible.

On the contrary, his picture of the London City authorities, and particularly of the Lord-Mayor, is far too much of a caricature. Dickens makes the Lord-Mayor a grotesque and farcical figure, both cynical—he is constantly referring to his "good place"—and abjectly servile—he will not act because "there are great people at the bottom of these riots" (chap. lxi). The historical accounts also stress the inertia and cowardice of the London authorities, but they do not turn the chief magistrates into mere Dickensian automatons of the most deplorable type.

As to the essential element (essential, that is, from the point of view of the novel) in the description of the days and nights of rioting, of the mobs let loose, Dickens' success is complete. It has been seen that in the case of individuals, when he does not content himself with their lifelike externals, his psychological approach tends to be primitive. But there is one soul that he can admirably explore, for he knows it inside out and knows how to convey its slightest motions; that is the soul of a crowd, and more particularly of the London mob. Such a talent is an indispensable one for the historical novelist who wishes to tackle riots or revolutions, and Dickens here reveals for the first time that he possesses it supremely. Hence a series of scenes of epic magnitude. In that sense, if the purpose of the historical novel is to make the scenes of history come to life, *Barnaby Rudge* is a great historical novel.

Yet the purpose of the historical novelist is on the whole twofold. He does not merely aim at clothing history with the appeal of fiction. He wishes also, by associating fictitious persons and private emotions with the great upheavals and stimulating atmosphere of famous real events, to increase the impression of truthfulness thus produced and clothe the novel with the appeal and convincingness of history.

The case of Dennis the hangman in *Barnaby Rudge* shows how a trifling historical fact can be used as the starting point for a major novelistic achievement. The real element was of the thinnest. The authors of contemporary memoirs merely report that the hangman had been arrested, together with other rioters, while plundering a private house. Dickens made the hangman one of the leaders of the riots as well as an

impressive figure in his own right. The hangman had to him the appeal
of the macabre, to which it has already been seen that he would yield
delightedly and from which he would rejoice in deriving comic effects.
Through many chapters, Dennis' companions are kept in ignorance of
his calling, while he himself, who regards it rather as an art or even a
disinterested service to mankind than as a mere livelihood, refers to it
more than once in mysterious terms: "When I look at that hand," he
says, "and remember the helegant bits of work it has turned off, I feel
quite molloncholy to think it should ever grow old and feeble. But such
is life!" (chap. xxxix). In his technical speech to "work off" means to
execute, so that his esoteric expression establishes a secret understanding
between him and the reader, which is deftly exploited by Dickens.

Towards the end of the novel, when Dennis is arrested, then in his
turn sentenced to death, the author's tone changes. The case of a man
looking at his own certain impending death is one that haunted Dickens
throughout his career and is described many times by him. In his *Child's
History*, the way in which monarchs and statesmen faced death is always
examined with interest, and the place held by capital punishments in
that book may be thought surprising when one calls to mind that it was
intended for children. Dickens never denies the tribute of his admiration
even to those historical characters whom he detests if they show plain
courage in the hour of that supreme ordeal. He does not even deny his
sympathetic interest to ordinary criminals, to the most sordid murderers
when they must expiate their offenses. In *Sketches by Boz* is to be found
a striking passage about the last hours of such a prisoner in the condemned cell: "Conceive the situation of a man, spending his last night
on earth in this cell . . . ."[45] In *Oliver Twist* the next to last chapter is
devoted to relating the hideous wait of Fagin for the hangman. And in
Barnaby we are shown the total collapse of the abject Dennis. His transformation, from arrogance to servility, from exultation in other people's
death to terror, is not meant to be grotesque: the scene has a tragic
quality, and it has truth, of a deep kind. Dennis' disintegration when he
is deprived of his office shows the unreality and the purely incidental and
external nature of his pride in his profession, of "the insolence of office."
His is indeed a tragic version of what Bumble had so comically embodied.

45 *SB*, "Scenes," chap. xxv.

Yet before he is thus finally annihilated, Dennis has had ample time to leave other impressions in the reader's memory, as a superb figure of mixed horror and fun, as the cynical and cruel hangman, who believes in hanging but joins the Protestant Association because of the prospect of trouble and plunder, and consequent hanging, it affords, and is inspired to justify himself by the memorable outcry: "No Popery! I'm a religious man, by G——!" (chap. xxxvii). In him, therefore, history, colorfully Dickensianized, fruitfully supports creative imagination.

Dickens' invention, to satisfy some needs of his narrative, of a pseudo-historical figure, Gordon's secretary, Gashford, is less felicitous. Gashford belongs to the class of his melodramatic villains. False, servile, malevolent, urged by implacable and obscure animosities—held by Dickens to be indispensable to the progress of his plot—he is by no means convincing, and psychological analysis, where he is concerned, is once more of a crude order.[46]

Similar disappointment is unfortunately elicited by many other fictitious characters of Dickens' historical novel. The whole Rudge circle, in particular, labors under painful unreality coupled with dullness. The circle includes Barnaby himself, the idiot, Grip the raven—whose I.Q. makes him the only fit member of the cast for companionship with Barnaby[47]—and Mrs. Rudge, who passes for a widow while her criminal husband is still alive and dangerous, since the corpse mistaken for Rudge's twenty years before was in fact his victim's. Mrs. Rudge is an example of uninspired creation and, once more, of the worst Dickensian bathos. Her fate has assuredly been tragic and may account for her not smiling once throughout the novel. But she is not even endowed with one of those ridiculous foibles that could have provided innocent entertainment for the reader. When Dickens created a character bowed down by misfortune, his own generosity hampered him. Misfortune moved and intimidated him, and he did not dare to show any lack of respect to its victims. The result, in this case, was cold, dull perfection. As Mrs. Rudge herself puts it, in surprisingly fine language for one in her station:

[46] Particularly in chap. xxxvi, when he pretends to believe that Gordon is asleep and soliloquizes audibly in his master's praise.

[47] Smollett may have been responsible for the idea of associating a raven with an idiot. See *Roderick Random,* chap. xiii: "The old man was the landlord's father, who had been an idiot some years, and diverted himself with a tame raven."

"Every faculty of life seems dead within me" (chap. vi). At the close of one of her lengthy moralizing tirades, the reader can hardly help fleetingly sympathizing with the criminal husband who replies: "What is the meaning of young canting words . . . speak so that I may understand you!" (chap. lxxiii).

In the flight of Barnaby and his mother, attempting to elude the pursuit carried on by Rudge and his accomplice, the central theme of Nell's adventures in the *Curiosity Shop* is again presented. There are two furtive departures, and there is the same enjoyment of quiet happiness in the bosom of nature. But the new version is different in that, while Nell had been wisdom incarnate, Barnaby is mad. His madness, produced by his father's crime a few months before Barnaby was born, is meant to create pathos. Such is, at any rate, its function at the beginning of the book, though it is altered in the course of the narrative. In the early phase of his career, Barnaby speaks the conventional, supposedly poetical language of stage madmen: "He's a merry fellow that shadow, and keeps quite close to me, though I *am* silly" (chap. vi); "the bright moon . . . looking down upon the other moon that lives in the water" (chap. xlvi). The outward signs of his mentally deficient state are no more than a few speeches of that kind and a few impulsive acts. They have, however, been pronounced convincing by some experts, who have even defined Barnaby's illness in scientific terms as "a regression psychosis of the paraphrenic type."[48] To less knowledgeable readers, the presentation seems artificial and improbable. It is, besides, seriously lacking in interest. Only one side of Barnaby's idiocy provides the novelist with artistic effects. He endows him with a profound horror of blood, because of the circumstances of his birth. And the theme of blood, haunting all the Rudges, is a source of mystery and horror which has a large share in creating the atmosphere of the novel.[49]

As the story of *Barnaby Rudge* gets farther away from historical truth, its interest seems to flag more and more. There are few picturesque char-

[48] See *Dickensian*, (Winter, 1934–35), 24–25.
[49] Not every allusion is in the best possible taste. Mrs. Rudge refuses to drink wine—red, one presumes—in the house where her husband's crime had been committed many years before, and declares melodramatically: "Not for the world . . . it would have another taste . . ." (chap. xxv). What ghoulish experiences would have enabled her to identify the "other taste" is not made clear.

acters to match those in the earlier books. A characteristic sign of the strained conditions under which many parts of *Barnaby* were written can be found in the case of John Willet, the landlord of the Maypole Inn. His chief, almost his single, feature is slowness. An insistent description of slowness can hardly be made in lively style, and the scenes in which John Willet appears are extremely ponderous. Only one group of non-historical figures rises to the level of the greatest Dickensian creations. Most of Dickens' critics, when they mention *Barnaby Rudge* at all, are singularly unenthusiastic about it,[50] but they usually recognize the value of the Varden household. Little Dolly is one of the very few girls portrayed by Dickens in his early days whose physical presence is made memorable, thanks to inspired descriptions[51] and also to a number of weaknesses which make her human and credible. Gabriel Varden is convincingly drawn, as a kind, generous, courageous man, endowed with a true sense of humor. His apprentice, Sim Tappertit, is a picturesque figure in his conceit, jealousy, and malevolence. Mrs. Varden is almost as true to life as Mrs. Nickleby, and her servant Miggs plays by her side a part already sketched out in *Pickwick* for Mrs. Pott's maid,[52] while her splendidly realistic and droll speech foreshadows the immortal Mrs. Gamp. No reader of *Barnaby* can fail to recognize and remember pronouncements like the following: "I hope I know my own unworthiness and that I despise myself and all my fellow-creatures as every practical Christian should" (chap. xiii). Dickens had written to Forster, as early as February 25, 1841: "I build greatly on the Varden household."[53] He had not been mistaken. At one point he had achieved what we have defined as the second purpose of the historical novel, by placing in eventful circumstances a group of realistic and lively characters and thus producing a stronger sense of truthfulness. In the final analysis, however, *Barnaby Rudge*, as Dickens' first historical novel, had reached no conclusive results. Since the author had himself been deficient in enthusiasm while undertaking and carrying on his task, the novel had merely disclosed his ability to describe large scenes of popular historical

[50] Wilkie Collins, (see *Pall Mall Gazette*, Jan. 20, 1890), called it "the weakest book that Dickens ever wrote."
[51] See in chap. xli the paragraph beginning "How well she looked!"
[52] See *PP*, chap. xviii.
[53] *Life of Dickens*, I, 138.

events. His half-success in that field had been gained at the expense of his usual gusto and of his surest kind of originality, almost completely eclipsed here by the historical interest. It was only natural then that the next book should not pursue the same attempt, but revert to the form abandoned after *Nickleby*, of the great novels in monthly installments.

7. *Dickens—and Forster—at Work*

The circumstances of Dickens' private life during the publication of *Barnaby* can be very briefly summarized. At the beginning of the year 1841, he thought his health was failing and decided he must take more exercise. On February 8, his second son and fourth child was born. In April, to help widowed Mrs. Macrone, he wrote "The Lamplighter," a tale based on the farce he had lately offered to Macready. In June, 1841, he went to Edinburgh to receive the official freedom of that city. During the summer, he wrote several anonymous poems about political subjects. In October, he fell ill. During the summer fresh negotiations had taken place with Chapman and Hall, the purpose of which were to organize the next step in his career. They were conducted by Forster with brilliant success. It was determined that Dickens would take a year's rest from the labors of novel-writing. He was to be supported by a monthly allowance of £150, to be paid by the publishers through 1842 and later deducted from the royalties of the next novel, which would be launched in November, 1842. Meanwhile, he would visit the United States.

On account of the pauses between *Chuzzlewit* and the works that preceded and followed it, as well as of the circumstances which characterized the publication of both the *Curiosity Shop* and *Barnaby* and those two works alone, it seems appropriate to examine at this point Dickens' working methods in those days and the part taken by Forster in the composition of the books.

After the first few issues of *Humphrey's Clock*, which had contained disconnected fragments, the organization of Dickens' weekly labors had been adopted and adhered to with perfect regularity, as is shown by the surviving parts of both manuscripts and also by the volumes of the magazine. Dickens would write each week sixteen or seventeen manuscript pages—which he called "slips," and later "sides." The sixteen pages were divided into two chapters almost invariably. The two chapters always had to be short, as compared with those of *Chuzzlewit* and *Dombey*, for instance, which were to comprise from eleven to twenty-eight pages, but one of the two was always longer than the other, and, in compliance with a somewhat childish but understandable practice, Dickens would always write the longer chapter—of at least ten pages—first, and the shorter chapter—of no more than six or seven pages—last, so as to relax after, and not before, the greater effort. This division of creative labor may seem artificial and incompatible with the spontaneity of artistic inspiration, but it suited Dickens' own habits and preferences, for he enjoyed regularity and felt the need of such rigid outward restraints, which he found stimulating. Now and again, he would, however, complain of being compelled to move within too narrow a technical framework. His grievances were not clearly defined, but seemed to boil down to the idea that he lacked elbow room and could not fully develop and exploit some of his most cherished effects. Mentioning the *Curiosity Shop* in a letter to Forster, after only a few weeks of weekly labor, he said: "I was obliged to cramp most dreadfully what I thought a pretty idea in the last chapter. I hadn't room to turn."[54] Then, commenting on *Barnaby* this time, he wrote on August 5, 1841: "Oh! if I only had him, from this time to the end, in monthly numbers!" and moaned again on September 18: "I want elbow-room terribly."[55]

Lack of space is not in itself a satisfactory explanation of the difficulties experienced by the novelist. The phrases he uses—"no room to turn," "want of elbow-room,"—and his nostalgia for the accustomed form merely prove that if he had published *The Old Curiosity Shop* and *Barnaby Rudge* in monthly numbers, the two novels would have been longer, which does not mean that they would inevitably have been better than they are. If the only result of Dickens' being thus hampered was increased condensation, the harder way may even have been the more fruitful one. As Forster has it: "With so much in every portion to do, and so little space to do it in, the opportunities to a writer for mere self-indulgence were necessarily rare."[56] In other words, within a chapter of some twenty-five pages, itself forming part of one number with two

54 *Ibid.,* 119.
55 *Ibid.,* 142–43.
56 *Ibid.,* 125.

other chapters, the author could dilute a piece of narrative or dialogue to his heart's content. When he had to present within sixteen pages at least two distinct incidents and to make the plot take at least two steps forward, he must control himself more severely. It has been seen that when he launched *Master Humphrey*, his hope had been thus to free himself from the obligation of producing about forty-five pages of manuscript every month. Eventually, he found that he must now write over sixty, each of which demanded a more strenuous effort. Far from liberating Dickens, *Humphrey* had increased the rigor of his slavery. From April, 1840 through October, 1841—a period corresponding under normal circumstances to the writing of one novel, or one thousand pages, in nineteen installments—he had to produce two novels, or a total of fourteen hundred pages, without enjoying the opportunity of lightening his load by means of a single interlude or digression.

The manuscripts of both *The Old Curiosity Shop* and *Barnaby Rudge* have been preserved and bear the marks of the care with which the novelist now carried out his work. His corrections in one paragraph from each will sufficiently illustrate that point. In Chapter XVII of the *Shop*, the first paragraph assumes on the manuscript the following aspect:

Another bright day, [shining upon] [streaming] shining in through the small [window] *casement*, and [shining with the child's eyes, awoke her,] claiming fellowship with the [bright] *kindred* eyes of the child, awoke her ... in which she seemed to have [laid some] [fall] [gone to sleep] fallen *asleep*, last night ... conveyed. But [a moment's thought] [in a moment afterwards, she remembered all that had passed upon the previous day.] Another glance around called to her mind all that had *lately* passed [upon the previous day] and she [arose hoping and] [trustful] sprung from her bed hoping and trustful.[57]

The corresponding part of the printed text contains only the following words: "Another bright day, shining in through the small casement and claiming fellowship with the kindred eyes of the child awoke her ... another glance called to her mind all that had lately passed and she sprung from her bed hoping and trustful." It is thus seen that Dickens'

[57] Unpublished, from original MS of *OCS* (Forster Collection).

corrections are of two sorts. Some are made while the sentences are taking shape and interrupt their progress—these are the words between square brackets in the above text—while others are introduced when he is rereading a completed sentence, paragraph, page, or chapter and substitutes a word or phrase inserted above the original line for a part cancelled at that stage—the new terms are italicized in the above text. It will be seen also that most of his corrections are due to his desire to avoid repetition of words—"shining," "bright"—to make his style terser—"lately" instead of "upon the previous day"—or more vigorous—"sprung from her bed" for "arose."

A similar impression is conveyed by the manuscript of *Barnaby Rudge*. Let us take one unpublished paragraph from Chapter XLIII:

It happened [twice or more] *once or twice* that some late [houseless] *homeless* lounger, cheered perhaps by the light within, paced to and fro for a long time, and loitered near the [window] *house*. When this occurred, he groped his way in the dark to the upper window, and opening it without noise, [looked down on] [with such tiger fierceness in his eyes as though] [if he] [he would] *upon him as though if he had been* [the] *other than he was he would have leaped into the* street and sprung upon him. But [here was disappointment too,] it was [but] *only* a poor *shivering* wretch [shivering and cowering upon the stones such as haunting the streets of great cities] *great city muttering complaints* or curses in his cold, and to-morrow morning saw him, as the last had, leaving the place with slow and hesitating steps and [often] turning often to look back [up] on the [place] [lonely place] *deserted house roof* he had quitted.[58]

A close examination of the manuscripts reveals the author's occasional weariness. There are several mistakes in the numbering of chapters—Chapter XVII and Chapter XXV are both duplicated, and in the latter case John Forster made a note in the margin: "XXVI. It ought to be." In one sentence, quoted earlier in this chapter, Dickens had written "wandering they not wither" for "they knew not whither." Elsewhere we

[58] This paragraph from the MS should have been included in chap. xliii. As the corrected proofs for that chapter are not extant, it can only be supposed that the paragraph was deleted at that stage. But it will be seen that it had not been made coherent in the MS.

have "ringing" for "wringing" her hands (chap. xxv). At the beginning of Chapter XLII, one of the most laboriously corrected, is to be seen for the first and only time in all Dickens' manuscripts a small drawing, doubtless mechanically sketched by his pen in a moment of idle abstraction.[59] Chapter XLV is called the "Fourty-Fifth" and Dickens' handwriting becomes increasingly illegible. One characteristic of his manuscripts, however, does not change. His directions to the printer are always remarkably precise whenever he departs in the least from current typographical practice. After the passage relating the death of Nell's grandfather, he writes: "To the printer. Leave a small space between this, and the next paragraph on following folio, as in the last page of No. 35—The space should be a little wider—say by one line."

Yet there is in the manuscript of *The Old Curiosity Shop* one very important novelty. In it are to be found for the first time Dickens' "mems," the memoranda or working plans that were to assume later such a considerable place in the composition of his novels. The "mems" of the *Shop* are fragmentary, perhaps because they have not all been preserved, perhaps because the author only gradually saw the advantage of jotting down a few notes before he wrote a chapter or a number. Only the memoranda for the final numbers of *The Old Curiosity Shop* are extant. It was probably when the end was in sight that Dickens felt the urge to become more methodical and orderly, as he had then to extricate himself and his novel from an entanglement of characters and incidents. The technical improvement thus adopted was short-lived, and there are no similar working notes in the manuscript of *Barnaby Rudge*. Those of *The Old Curiosity Shop* comprise the following items:

(1) A summary of the explanations to be given by Nell's great-uncle (in chap. lxix) concerning his own identity and the past history of the whole family. The summary includes no detail differing from what is given in the narrative as published, yet it is interesting as showing in a glaring light the curiously regressive method of construction employed by Dickens. He had, without caring to account for them, without perhaps foreseeing that he might have one day to account for them, created two anomalous situations. Nell and her grandfather had been living on

[59] It is a small crown copied from the plain relief stamp on Dickens' notepaper.

their own at the beginning of the novel. The grandfather's uncle had suddenly appeared and begun to hunt them down. It was only at the end of the novel, and from those data, that Dickens set about rearranging the events of the past in such a way that the two anomalous situations might appear to result from them.

(2) A list of twenty-eight characters or groups of characters, a few of them preceded or followed by the word "Query" in the abbreviated form invariably used by Dickens when he was thus asking himself a question, "Qy." With the single exception of Miss Monflathers, for whom the "Qy" is answered in the negative, the names of all the characters are ticked off to show that their fate has been settled in the novel. Obviously, the list had been drawn up to make sure that no one would be overlooked in the winding-up.

(3) The "mems" proper for Numbers XLI through XLIV of *Humphrey,* i.e., Chapters LXV through LXXI of *The Old Curiosity Shop.* The "mems" are not subdivided into chapters, and consist of hints concerning incidents to be related—"Plot to make Brass confess. Kit released." etc.—of author's self-questionings regarding whether he should include certain incidents and information in the current number—for Number XLI, the text of the "mems" has: "Hints of Nell. Qy" and the margin: "Hints of Nell. No"—and of advice from the writer to himself about the way in which he should treat his materials—in the margin of the notes concerning Numbers XLII and XLIII, he wrote twice: "Keep the child in view." They are an early sketch of the complex system Dickens was later to adopt for all his great novels, and the sketch already contains the germ of every essential ingredient. The last section of the "mems" is very moving. In preparation for Number XLIV (chap. lxxi) Dickens had merely written down, with a tremulous hand, the single word "Dead."[60]

The manuscript would be sent to the printers in the state described above. As a substantial portion of the corrected proofs of *The Old Curiosity Shop* and a small fragment of those of *Barnaby* have been preserved, it is possible to find out what happened next.[61] In most cases, the novelist

[60] All the quotations in the preceding and following paragraphs were unpublished before the French edition of this book, in 1953, first made use of them.

[61] The Forster Collection has the corrected proofs of chap. xviii of *BR,* and chaps. xl–lxvi of *OCS.*

had prudently written rather too much copy. Penciled statements in the margin of the proof sheets stand as evidence of the fact: "thirty-two lines too many" in one place, "half a page too much" in another, "two pages over" in a third. Deletions were thus imperative. Two kinds are to be described separately, according to whether they were effected by Dickens himself or entrusted to Forster.

When Dickens had to cancel a sizable number of lines, he would most often take them out of a description or a paragraph on a general theme, such as a moral discussion. Occasionally he would come to grips with his dialogues, but they were less easy to reduce without extensive reworking. Now and then Dickens would also effect less bulky deletions as the result of a change in his attitude to his own text. For instance, in Chapter LII of the *Shop*, he cancelled a premature allusion to the Bachelor's identity—the Bachelor being an inhabitant of the village in which Nell has taken shelter: "This was a little old gentleman, in whom the reader would have recognised a strong resemblance to another little old gentleman already familiar to these pages; but of that in its place—who lived . . . ." Thus manuscript and proofs. The published text preserves only this: "This was a little old gentleman who lived . . . ." In the meantime Dickens must have convinced himself that "its place" was definitely elsewhere.

An interesting example of trite commonplaces being sacrificed is provided by Chapter LXI, in which Dickens, commenting on Kit's unjust imprisonment, had composed a long paragraph which began with the words: "There was—and may be now—a custom extant in England, of waving flags with certain honorable ceremonies above the graves of those who had been wrongfully put to death by the law, being believed to be guilty." The paragraph did not survive proof stage.

In a few cases, when the number was, on the contrary, too short, manuscript additions can be found on the proofs. In Chapter LI, for instance, several sizable fragments were thus inserted into the text. They are almost invariably pieces of dialogue, for dialogue, while it cannot always be curtailed, can be diluted more easily than the narrative of events. And when the need arises for a specific number of extemporized *lines*, the result can be achieved least strenuously by inserting a bit of brisk dialogue made up of very short lines.

The urgency of proofreading and the pressure of work were such that Dickens was often induced to entrust Forster with the task of choosing what would be deleted. In such cases, he repeatedly gave him a free hand. "Don't fail to erase anything that seems to you too strong," he wrote to him on April 5, 1841, during *Barnaby's* progress. And three weeks later, he was apologizing: "It was too bad of me to give you the trouble of cutting the number, but I knew so well you would do it in the right places."[62] Forster's influence was thus called upon to play a significant part in the genesis of Dickens' novels. That influence was usually exerted in the right direction. Forster did not possess a hundredth part of his friend's creative genius, but his views were a hundred times more reasonable than the novelist's, and their alliance was harmonious, as Forster restrained the occasionally extravagant impulses that Dickens was all too ready to succumb to.

Thus when, in *Barnaby Rudge*, the author toyed with the notion of having the riots led by a party of lunatics escaped from Bedlam, it was Forster who ruled out the idea. When Dickens wrote an advertisement to the readers of *Humphrey's Clock*, he intended to account for his return to the monthly form of publication as follows: "For (comparing great things with small), I cannot help thinking that the effect of a flash of lightning would be materially impaired if it came in sparks, and that your admiration of a great mass of iron would undergo a considerable diminution if it came to you in filings." But Forster, probably disliking both similes, because an author's likening himself to lightning was not exactly modest, whereas no one admires "a great mass of iron," wrote in the margin: "Qy? End this differently." His advice was taken, and the whole sentence deleted.

At the close of the same advertisement, Dickens was announcing his departure for the United States in language at once complacent and somewhat hypocritical. He was begging for pity, as though the trip had been cruelly imposed upon him, while in fact he—understandably—yearned to go, and had even had to display immense pertinacity in order to overcome such obstacles as his wife's reluctance, his friends' distaste for the scheme, and the discomfort of leaving four young children be-

[62] (April 29), *Life of Dickens*, I, 140, 141.

hind. Yet he had written: "And now I come to an announcement which gives me mingled pain and pleasure; pain, because it separates me, for a time, from many thousands of my countrymen who have given my writings, as they were myself, a corner in their hearts and homes, and a place among their household gods; pleasure, because it leads me to the gratification of a darling wish, and opens to me a scene of interest and wonder." When he read the proofs, Forster made away with the whole paragraph, and substituted for it a sentence of his own, cruder and drier, but more truthful: "The pleasure I anticipate from the realization of a wish I have long entertained, and long hoped to gratify, is subdued by the reflection that it must separate us for a longer time than other circumstances would have rendered necessary."[63] And Dickens was wise enough to submit to such sensible correction.

At least one important contribution was made by Forster to the development of the novels published in *Master Humphrey*: he was the first to suggest that Nell should die. Dickens' indebtedness to him in that respect is freely admitted by the novelist in a letter reproduced in the *Life of Dickens*, whose original has been preserved at the beginning of the manuscript of the *Shop*: "When I first began (on your valued suggestion) to keep my thoughts upon this ending of the tale, I resolved to try and do something which might be read by people about whom Death had been—with a softened feeling and with consolation." Yet Forster's most constant function, over and above that of literary and sentimental adviser, was the technical function of a proofreader. His corrections are usually easily identifiable, whenever they are not mere brief deletions. He wrote a more virile and less graceful hand than his friend, and he was not sparing of commentaries and recommendations addressed to the printer's men. Whoever has handled manuscripts of both writers is unlikely to mistake one for the other. The future biographer's share in the modifications, and even in the choice of passages to be deleted, can therefore be accurately determined. Forster would cancel whatever appeared to him immoral or cynical, as, for instance, a paragraph in which Dickens explained how "To have drunk too much, to have had a great holiday, and to have fallen in love, are one and the same thing in their

---

[63] Unpublished; from MS and proofs in Forster Collection.

next day's consequences" and spoke of "the common dust into which these three great things of the earth resolve themselves next day."[64] He would cancel, as he had been instructed by Dickens to do, whatever seemed too violent—for that was what Dickens must have meant by "too strong." Thus, in the course of a dramatic interview between Mrs. Rudge and her husband, he deleted the following phrases: " 'I am desperate, I warn you' "; "[her hands] held up at arms' length toward Heaven"; " 'By this right hand, whose history you know, and by this devil's seal stamped upon me . . . ' (He pulled his slouched hat from his brow, and pointing, as he spoke, to the gash upon his cheek . . .)"; "She . . . towered above him as though she could have crushed him in her passion."[65]

Forster's proofreading is sometimes amusingly revealing of some aspects of his own character. A marginal dialogue between him and the compositor thus discloses his boorish impatience. The compositor had written beside a passage that seemed obscure to him: "Qy? Compositor." Forster retorted: "Why, it's capital, you donkey reader."[66] His scrupulousness is also evinced, when he has done his best, but fears he may have been mistaken by a line or two in his calculations. In two successive numbers, he draws a line around a paragraph close to the end, and appeals to the printer: "I hope I have taken out enough, but if I have not, you must cancel this paragraph. Let it stand if possible. J.F." and "Let this stand—unless it is *necessary* that it shd come out. J.F."[67] In both cases, however, his calculations had been correct, and the two paragraphs in question were saved from destruction.

Forster's help, then, was valuable. On one occasion only did he make a mistake by taking out a paragraph that seemed rather gratuitously improbable when it occurred—it was a lengthy meditation of Quilp about the notion of causing his wife to be drowned and the delight it would be to him to hear her scream before she was swallowed up by the river (chap. lxii). Yet the fragment served a purpose, in view of the later developments, and Dickens then wrote to Forster: "The part you cut out . . . I had put in with a view to Quilp's last appearance on any stage, which is casting its shadow upon my mind; but it will come well enough

---

[64] Unpublished, *OCS*, chap. xl.
[65] Unpublished fragments of *BR*, chap. xviii.
[66] *OCS*, corrected proofs of chap. xlii.
[67] *OCS*, chaps. xlvii and xlviii.

without such preparation, so I made no change."[68] By letting Forster perform so generously and on the whole so competently a portion of his own task, Dickens was implicitly renouncing the right to be severe with him.

The reading and cutting of the proofs by Forster, or by Dickens, or in some cases by Forster and Dickens, constituted the final stage in the preparation of the text. The text we can read nowadays has not been further modified in any significant way. Not one of the cancelled passages has been restored to it. The artificial title of *Master Humphrey's Clock* has alone been jettisoned. The chapters composing *The Old Curiosity Shop* and *Barnaby Rudge* are just as they appeared in serial form.

Yet, before he put an end to the life of his periodical, Dickens informed his readers of the reasons for which he was giving up weekly publication. Though his explanation is once more disappointing and superficial, the gist of it may be extracted to show the kind of attitude he saw fit to assume when he decided that Master Humphrey's narratives were to have no followers, and that *Chuzzlewit* would revert to the pattern of *Nickleby*. What Dickens wrote to his readers[69] was this:

> I should not regard the anxiety, the close confinement, or the constant attention, inseparable from the weekly form of publication . . . if I had found it advantageous to the conduct of my stories, the elucidation of my meaning, or the gradual development of my characters. But I have not done so. I have often felt cramped and confined . . . by the petty space in which I have been constrained to move. I have wanted you to know more at once than I could tell you. . . . I have been sometimes strongly tempted . . . to hurry incidents on. . . . I have found this a most anxious, perplexing and difficult form. . . . Many passages, in a tale of any length, depend materially for their interest on the intimate relation they bear to what has gone before, or to what is to follow. . . . in the present form of publication, it is often . . . quite impossible to preserve [this needful connection] sufficiently through the current number . . . for [those] reasons, and on account of many other difficulties connected with the movement of a story by

[68] Dec. 16, 1840. See *Life of Dickens*, I, 122.
[69] *To the Readers of MHC*, Sept., 1841.

such little levers[70] with which it is unnecessary to weary you. . . . I have with especial reference to the next new tale I bear in mind . . . arrived at the conclusion that it will be better to abandon this scheme of publication, in favor of our old and well-tried plan, which has only twelve gaps in a year, instead of fifty-two.

XVI: AFTER THE AMERICAN HOLIDAY: *Martin Chuzzlewit*

FOURTEEN MONTHS ELAPSED between the completion of *Barnaby Rudge* and the appearance of the first number of *Martin Chuzzlewit* in January, 1843. Meanwhile, Dickens had visited the United States—January through June, 1842—where he had been warmly received, but had been cruelly disappointed in several respects. He had felt the disappointment of a theoretical democrat when confronted with democratic reality at close quarters. And he had been hurt by a glimpse of slavery, by the tone of the press, and by the indignant refusal of the Americans to contemplate the establishment of some form of international copyright. Shortly after his return to England, he had written his *American Notes,* a thin volume containing a narrative of his visit and a summary of his impressions. The book had been composed during the summer, by the seaside. In October, 1842, Dickens had published a serious article in the *Monthly Chronicle* in support of the working class. He had then gone to Cornwall on a prolonged tour with Forster and two painter friends, Daniel Maclise and Clarkson Stanfield. At the close of the year, he had written a prologue in verse for a play by Westland Marston that was being put on by Macready.

A significant event in Dickens' family life at the same time was the arrival in his home of Georgina Hogarth, a younger sister of his wife's, who, it turned out, had come to stay—she was still there in 1870— and who gradually replaced Mary in the novelist's affection. A letter from Dickens to his mother-in-law casts some light on the psychological phenomenon: "I trace in many respects a strong resemblance between [Mary's] mental features and Georgina's—so strange a one, that when she and Kate and I are sitting together, I seem to think that what has

---

[70] There is at least one reader—but he is one whom Dickens can hardly have had in mind—who would not have been "wearied" had the novelist been less sparing of details about his "little levers."

happened is a melancholy dream from which I am just awakening."[1] The value of such a novelty for Dickens' literary creation will be readily felt when one bears in mind the many embodiments in his heroines of the author's grief and tenderness. His grief was to a large extent healed; his tenderness had become once more happy and living. It was therefore in an atmosphere of joy that he began the writing of his new novel.

His first intention had been to locate its first scene either in the lantern of a lighthouse or on some desolate spot of the Cornish coast.[2] In fact, he tended to attach considerable importance to the initial setting of his tales, because it would set their tone as well as launch their plots. Fairly often, a broad outline of the narrative, combined with one precise idea for the initial scenery, was enough for him to plunge into the writing of a work of fiction. Yet, in the present case, the eccentric beginning was not finally adopted.

The title printed on the cover of the first number, and in the advance advertisements for it, was the longest, most cumbersome, and most jovial he had coined so far: "The Life and Adventures of Martin Chuzzlewit, His Relatives, Friends and Enemies. Comprising All his Wills and his Ways: With an Historical Record of what he did, and what he didn't: showing, moreover, Who inherited the Family Plate, Who came in for the Silver Spoons, and Who for the Wooden Ladles. The whole forming a complete Key to the House of Chuzzlewit." There were to be two Martin Chuzzlewits in the book, grandfather and grandson—as usual, no father. The original title shows that Dickens had first intended to give Martin Chuzzlewit, Sr., a central part in the story, and probably also, since he mentioned the inheritance, to have him die in the course of it. In fact, however, old Martin did not die, and his grandson turned out to be the hero of the novel. The title then dwindled to its opening words: "The Life and Adventures of Martin Chuzzlewit." Dickens was thus giving further proof of his love of variety in the choice of heroes. The hero or heroine had been an elderly man in *Pick-*

[1] May 8, 1843, *Letters* (MDGH), III, 51. The end of the letter shows how vivid the remembrance of Mary still remained: "The recollection of her is an essential part of my being, and is as inseparable from my existence as the beating of my heart is."

[2] See Forster, *Life of Dickens*, I, 258–59. "I have some notion of opening the new book in the lantern of a lighthouse" (July 18, 1842). "I think of opening my new book on the coast of Cornwall, in some terribly dreary, iron-bound spot" (Sept. 16, 1842).

wick, a child in *Oliver* and the *Curiosity Shop,* an idiot in *Barnaby.* Only *Nickleby* had had a young man for its central figure. *Martin Chuzzlewit,* after its uncertain beginnings, was, in that respect at least, clearly *Nickleby's* successor.

For the two Martins, grandfather and grandson, the chief moral theme is the same: both are illustrations of the vice that Dickens is out to denounce—selfishness—and both redeem themselves at the end of the book. On the other hand, neither of them is among the most interesting figures in the novel, because they are too selfish at the beginning, too angelically altruistic in the end,[3] to leave a striking impression in the reader's mind.

The first chapter of *Chuzzlewit,* in which Dickens describes with a great display of irony and a plethora of puns, the genealogical history of the Chuzzlewit family, would seem to have been inspired by Fielding.[4] But that chapter does not actually set the story going and serves rather as a kind of preamble. When the story does begin, the situation is as follows: Pecksniff, an architect who has no practice and therefore prefers to teach architecture, lives in the country, near Salisbury, with his two daughters, Charity and Mercy. He takes pupils into his home, such as Tom Pinch, a poor half-witted youth, and John Westlock, who is leaving him when the book begins (chap. ii), and whose place will be taken by Martin Chuzzlewit (chap. v). Martin is Pecksniff's cousin, an orphan, and has lately been turned out of doors by his grandfather for wishing to marry one Mary Graham, the old man's protégée. Old Martin is traveling about and puts up at an inn close to Pecksniff's house (chap. iii). He falls ill, and all his would-be heirs rush to his bedside, but he denies them admittance and vanishes (chap. iv). Pecksniff repairs to London (chaps. vi–viii), where he stays in Mrs. Todgers' boardinghouse (chap. ix) and meets old Martin, who decides to trust him (chap. x). Pecksniff then goes home (chap. xi) and turns young Martin out, to please the latter's grandfather (chap. xii).

The first twelve chapters made up the first five installments of the novel, published from January through May, 1843. While writing them,

---

[3] See the scene (chap. xliii) in which Martin tells his fiancée she must not desert the old man she is tending "though I could count the years we are to wear asunder."

[4] *Jonathan Wild,* chap. ii.

Dickens had been unevenly inspired, now carried away by a powerful impulse, now plodding along painfully.[5] A characteristic incident had occurred as early as the beginning of the third number: for the first time in his career, he had given up a substantial fragment that he had already written out. Chapter VI of the manuscript[6] is preceded by another version of its beginning. In the cancelled fragment, which is seven pages long, there are incidents not to be found in the published version. After Martin's arrival in the architect's house, there is a grand quarrel between his two daughters, followed by their reconciliation. The plot was making no progress through the seven pages. In the later text, there is no such quarrel; instead, Pecksniff blurts out the announcement of his intended visit to London.

The serious uncertainty about the progress of the tale went together with further difficulties. Although—as will appear later on—there was no link between the two circumstances, the comparatively low figures of *Chuzzlewit* sales—20,000 copies to *Pickwick*'s 40,000 and *Humphrey*'s 60,000 or 70,000—were a source of additional worry and caused Dickens to make fresh attempts in order to increase the popularity of his current novel. The first of these consisted in having young Martin, at the close of the fifth number (chap. xii), announce: "My mind is made up. . . . I'll go to America."[7] Well could Dickens hope that the announcement would have a favorable effect on the sales. Tony Weller had already advised Mr. Pickwick to write a book "about the Merrikins as 'll pay all his expenses and more if he blows 'em up enough."[8] Such was the advice that *Pickwick*'s creator was preparing to take. As far as he was concerned, circumstances were even more promising. The public was aware that he had visited the States, that he had not expressed himself unreservedly in his *American Notes*, and that the very hostile reception

[5] Forster, *Life of Dickens*, I, 275. "I have been hammering away, and at home all day" (Jan. 8, 1843). "I couldn't write a line yesterday; not a word, though I really tried hard" (Feb. 12, 1843).

[6] In the Forster Collection.

[7] Forster shows Dickens' determination to have been just as sudden as Martin's.

[8] *PP*, chap. xlv. Dickens was referring to the success of such books as Mrs. Trollope's (*Domestic Manners of the Americans*, 1832) and Harriet Martineau's (*Society in America*, 1837; *Retrospect of a Western Travel*, 1838) and perhaps also to the work—in six volumes —Frederick Marryat was known to be working on, *A Diary in America, with Remarks on its Institutions* (1839).

of that book beyond the Atlantic might induce him to throw his reticence to the winds.[9] A vigorous and diverting piece of satire was what could be anticipated. In that respect, expectation was not to be disappointed. The American episodes of *Chuzzlewit* did sharply criticize more than one aspect of the American way of life and the American character. They can enable the reader to form a clear idea of Dickens' grievances against the United States, as well as of the way in which he turned personal experiences to account while writing fiction.

His first criticism is unoriginal: it concerns the importance ascribed to money in America. Already in the *Notes*, he had called the United States "that vast countinghouse which lies beyond the Atlantic" (chap. iii). And in *Chuzzlewit* a journalist explains that the aristocracy of the country is made up "of intelligence and virtue. And of their necessary consequence in this republic—dollars, sir" (chap. xvi). Dickens charges the Americans with letting their fondness for wealth develop into dishonesty. Martin is imposed upon by speculators who sell him a piece of ground in a splendid city called Eden. When he gets there, the city is nonexistent, and there are only a few wooden huts in a very unwholesome area.[10] In a chapter containing more direct attacks, Dickens further declares: "All their cares, hopes, joys, affections, virtues and associations seemed to be melted down into dollars. . . . Make commerce one huge lie and mighty theft" (chap. xvi).

Another thing that shocked Dickens, in common with other British visitors, was the practice of slavery in a country that claimed to be the champion of freedom. Several sentences on that subject in *Chuzzlewit* are strikingly energetic, particularly the passage in which Mark Tapley, Martin's quixotic Sam Weller, describes a slave's fate and concludes: "And now he's a-saving up to treat himself, afore he dies, to one small purchase; it's nothing to speak of, only his own daughter—that's all! . . . Liberty for ever!" (chap. xvii).

Against the American press, Dickens lets himself loose with especial

[9] A controversy, in which Dickens himself did not take part, occupied the British and American presses throughout the year 1843. See *Foreign Quarterly Review,* Vol. XXXI. John Forster was its editor. In *Dickens From Pickwick to Dombey* (New York, 1965), the American critic Steven Marcus calls the American chapters of *MC* "brilliantly just satires," p. 219.

[10] According to Pope-Hennessy, *Ch. Dickens,* 173, Dickens had himself been a sufferer from a similar swindle. The story has been convincingly disproved.

violence, due both to his disappointment—he had hoped he might find it more enlightened and independent than its British counterpart—and to the treatment he had experienced at its hands. To the New York newspapers, he gives such vindictive titles as these: "The Sewer, the Stabber, the Family Spy, the Private Listener, the Reaper, the Plunderer, the Keyhole Reporter, the Rowdy Journal" (chap. xvi). He charges the press with being untruthful, and with throwing dirt on the private lives of its opponents, for base and selfish motives. His satire, however, is weakened, when he goes on to caricature the grandiloquence and conceit of American journalists, by their resemblance to the provincial journalists of England, as shown in *Pickwick*.[11] Yet the characteristic most constantly criticized by the novelist is indiscretion—unbridled curiosity —which is not a monopoly of the press. Of that universal curiosity, Dickens, who had visited the States as a famous writer and the guest of honor of the whole nation, had unquestionably been the victim. Thousands of men and women had everywhere insisted on seeing him, shaking his hand, entering his hotel rooms, touching his clothes, occasionally even cutting out a fragment of his coat as a precious relic. Their curiosity had certainly been annoying; yet it had also been to a certain extent normal, or at least understandable. In the case of Martin, poor and unknown as he is, it is far less so, and the author's utmost ingenuity cannot satisfactorily explain why the American population as a body invades the youthful architect's hotel room. At that point, then, the author's personal experience has been more of a hindrance than a help. In order not to leave out of the novel a trait that was among the most striking remembrances of his own American tour, he violates the laws of verisimilitude.

Other features criticized by Dickens were less specifically American. Self-complacency, dirtiness—of linen, of the streets crowded with pigs, of the habit of chewing tobacco and spitting, of table manners—have their counterparts in the English section of *Chuzzlewit*, particularly in the boardinghouse scenes.

In order to introduce his criticisms and grievances, Dickens resorts to various techniques. Most often, he simply has the attack launched

---

[11] Pott, the editor of the *Eatanswill Gazette,* has a great deal in common with Colonel Diver and Jefferson Brick.

by the Americans themselves, either by showing us schismatic Americans who pass judgment on their own country, like the gentleman who says to Martin-Dickens: "You are right. So very right that I believe no satirist could breathe this air;"[12] or another who delivers a long digressive tirade in a tone of spurious impartiality while he is in fact expounding the author's theories: "I do not find, and cannot believe, and therefore will not allow, that we are a model of wisdom" (chap. xvii); or else by presenting persons so cynical that their own words sit in judgment on them, like the editor who claims: " 'we have a hold upon our citizens, both in public and in private life, which is as much one of the ennobling institutions of our happy country as—' 'As nigger slavery iself,' suggested Mr. Brick. 'En-tirely so,' remarked the colonel" (chap. xvi). One emerges from the reading of *Chuzzlewit* with an impression that the United States is generally contemptible. The author's own over-all judgments are surpassingly severe; he calls the country "that republic, but yesterday let loose upon her noble course, and but to-day so maimed and lame, so full of sores and ulcers, foul to the eye and almost hopeless to the sense, that her best friends turn from the loathsome creature with disgust" (chap. xxii). In his preliminary statement to the *American Notes*, Dickens had indeed written: "To represent me as viewing America with ill-nature, coldness or animosity, is merely to do a very foolish thing, which is always a very easy one." There was certainly no coldness in his attitude to the United States as seen through *Chuzzlewit*. But though he was to form a more favorable opinion later, before and after his second visit, for the time being the only kind of warmth he was evincing was polemical heat. It had certainly not produced an impartial description or a balanced judgment, but it had resulted in a lively chain of episodes.

The first of these episodes had been written in June, 1843. Martin, on being turned out by Pecksniff goes to London, and Mark Tapley, a waiter in the inn close to Pecksniff's house, volunteers to become his

---

[12] Chap. xvi. The method employed here consists in having one's opponent plead guilty and say, "You are right." It makes the polemical writer's task easier, though it usually fails to make the opponent feel that he has not been misrepresented. Thus did the French President Edouard Daladier, in Sept. 1939, claim that the German soldiers in their trenches were thinking: *"Je ne me bats pas pour une cause juste."*

servant (chap. xiii). After an interview with Mary Graham (chap. xiv), Martin and Mark sail for New York (chap. xv). When they arrive there and their first adventures have been related (chaps. xvi–xvii) Dickens takes his narrative back to London, where old Martin's brother Anthony Chuzzlewit dies (chap. xviii). He is buried (chap. xix), and then his son Jonas calls on Pecksniff and asks for the hand of Mercy (chap. xx). The number containing these incidents—Number VIII, August, 1843—came to a close at the moment when old Martin is unexpectedly knocking at Pecksniff's door. The number, which had been written in a small cottage at Finchley, also ushered in a very important character, whose creation was Dickens' second attempt at increasing the success and enlarging the sales of his book. Mrs. Gamp, midwife and sick-nurse, was engaged by Jonas Chuzzlewit to take care of his father's old clerk Chuffey. Dickens soon realized that he had been felicitously inspired and that the new character was possessed of admirable resources. An examination of Mrs. Gamp ought to yield information about the progress made by Dickens in comic characterization.

According to Forster, who devotes two pages of first-rate criticism to Mrs. Gamp,[13] she was painted from life, and a sick-nurse employed by some wealthy friends of the novelist may have sat for the portrait. Mrs. Gamp's manifold professional activities give rise to valuable comedy. Some of the effects may appear to be barely—thanks to their allusiveness—on the safe side of the barrier between decency and boldness from a Victorian point of view. Mrs. Gamp was, however, readily accepted by the middle-class Victorian public, who were abundantly aware of the realities of the midwife's trade, but who may have chosen to ignore the connection between childbirth and any previous circumstance. In any case, there she is, in the novel, with some clothes hanging from her bedposts: "One gentleman, coming on the usual hasty errand, had said indeed that they looked like guardian angels 'watching of her in her sleep.' But that, as Mrs. Gamp said, 'was his first'; and he never repeated the sentiment, though he often repeated his visit" (chap. xlix).

[13] Chap. i, 297–98. *The Life of Dickens* is richer in biographical information than in valid criticism. The comments on Mrs. Gamp and her *doppelgänger*, Mrs. Harris, are the most brilliant, but not the only, exception. See "John Forster's *Life of Dickens* and Literary Criticism" in *English Studies To-Day*, 4th Series, Rome, 1966.

The cynicism with which, in common with her colleague Betsey Prig, she looks upon the invalids confided to her care—of far less consequence in her eyes than the victuals and spirits supplied for the nurse's sustenance—is splendidly rendered: "You needn't mind him," Gamp tells Betsey of the sick man by whose bedside the latter has come to relieve her, "But, Betsy Prig . . . try the cowcumbers, God bless you!" (chap. xxv). Some of the comic effects due to Mrs. Gamp are of the macabre kind. She is occasionally called upon to prepare bodies for burial, and thus, after contemplating an invalid's emaciated face, "stooping down, she pinned his wandering arms against his sides, to see how he would look if laid out as a dead man . . . her fingers itched to compose his limbs in that last marble attitude. 'Ah!' said Mrs. Gamp, walking away from the bed, 'he'd make a lovely corpse' " (chap. xxv).

Mrs. Gamp's character is simple enough—self-interest, greed, and a partiality for liquor being its main ingredients, with an admixture of conceit, a faint touch of tenderness for the young, and a keen desire to be thought respectable. The harder she drinks, the harder she strives to be believed sober; when ordering her favorite beverage, she makes a feint of having to protect herself against threatening offers that nobody has made, and says to the maidservant: "Whatever you do, young woman, don't bring me more than a shilling's worth of gin-and-water warm when I rings the bell a second time, for that is always my allowance, and I never takes a drop beyond" (chap. xxv).

One of Mrs. Gamp's supreme assets is her gloriously original speech. Her pronunciation and syntax already mark her off from the common run of human beings and impart peculiar flavor to her words. She says: "I will not denige that I am worrited and wexed this day, and with good reagion . . . the Anckworks package" (chap. xl), or "propojals, aperiently, mortial creetur, perfeejus wretch" (chap. xlix). She thus provides fresh evidence of her creator's ability to coin ever renewed forms of speech, each of which has its own idiosyncrasies, while all of them bear the stamp of the same inventive genius. Her manner of addressing in turn every member of the company, in the course of one and the same tirade, through a variety of artifices meant to secure each person's kind opinion, imparts to her language a kind of staccato rhythm which is highly entertaining (chap. xlvi). In addition, some of her anecdotes reveal a stupendous amount of imagination, not unlike Sam Weller's:

> The blessing of a daughter was deniged me; which, if we had had one, Gamp would certainly have drunk its little shoes right off its feet, as with our precious boy he did, and arterwards send the child a errand to sell his wooden leg for any money it would fetch as matches in the rough, and bring it home in liquor—which was truly done beyond his years, for ev'ry indiwigle penny that child lost at toss or buy for kidney ones; and come home afterwards quite bold, to break the news and offering to drown himself if sech would be a satisfaction to his parents (chap. xxv).

Finally, Mrs. Gamp sometimes makes use of phrases which are possessed of remarkable comic force, though their sources are not easily isolated. When she declares: "Whether I sicks or monthlies, ma'am, I hope I does my duty" (chap. xxv), perhaps we are chiefly taken aback by her stylistic audacity. When she says: "Gamp is my name, and Gamp my nater" (chap. xxvi), the sentence is irresistibly droll, though practically meaningless. And when she is angered by Sweedlepipe the barber, and protests: "You're always a-comin' in, I think, except when you're a-going out. I ha'n't no patience with that man!" (chap. xlix), laughter seems to be aroused by the very absurdity of her reproach, coupled with the palatable eccentricity of her speech.

Yet Dickens' most felicitous invention, as far as Mrs. Gamp is concerned, is the creation of Mrs. Harris, a purely mythical person whom the midwife is forever quoting as having held with her long and flattering conversations. Thus does every incident narrated by Mrs. Gamp assume the form of conversation on a quasi epic scale and the reader's mental image of Mrs. Harris becomes more and more precise, although she is not meant to appear on the stage of the novel. Mrs. Harris' main characteristic is her boundless affection and admiration for Sarah, whom she calls "Sairey," Gamp. "As a good friend of mine has frequent made remark to me, which her name, my love, is Harris—Mrs. Harris through the square and up the steps a-turnin' round by the tobacker shop—'O Sairey; Sairey, little do we know what lays afore us!' 'Mrs. Harris,

ma'am,' I says, 'not much, it's true, but more than you suppoge . . . .' "
(chap. xl). These conversations almost invariably end in a compliment
paid by Mrs. Harris to Mrs. Gamp: " 'Sairey,' she says, 'is it a public
wharf?' 'Mrs. Harris,' I makes answer, 'can you doubt it? You have
know'd me now, ma'am, eight-and-thirty year; and did you ever know
me go, or wish to go, where I was not made welcome? Say the words.'
'No, Sairey,' Mrs. Harris says, 'contrairy quite!' And well she knows
it too" (chap. xl). Such a twice fictitious creature is an invention of the
very first order. It is only to be deplored that the author should have
thought fit to lay bare her mechanism explicitly, instead of leaving
the reader to infer that she did not exist at all.[14]

More powerfully even than the American episode, Mrs. Gamp drew
fresh readers to *Chuzzlewit*, yet without making the book a real success,
comparable to *Nickleby* or the *Curiosity Shop* in point of popularity.
The last eleven installments took the story to its conclusion without any
other attempt being made at infusing fresh interest into it. In the States,
Martin buys a piece of ground at Eden, which turns out to be unin-
habitable (chaps. xxi–xxii). In England, old Martin comes to live in
Pecksniff's house, where preparations are being made for Mercy's wedding to Jonas (chap. xxiv). After the wedding, Mercy is unhappy (chap.
xxvi), and Jonas takes part in a large-scale swindle (chap. xxviii). Pecksniff thinks of marrying Mary Graham (chap. xxx) and turns out Tom
Pinch (chap. xxxi). Young Martin, cured of his selfishness by his trials,
returns to England (chaps. xxxiii–xxxv). Pinch finds employment in
London (chap. xxxix). Jonas, more and more involved in the swindle,
tries in vain to flee (chaps. xxxviii–xl). His partner wants him to em-
bezzle Pecksniff's money, and Jonas thinks he had better kill that partner (chap. xli). Old Martin, still living at Pecksniff's, refuses to forgive
his grandson (chap. xliii). Jonas kills his partner (chaps. xlii, xliv, xlvi,
xlvii). It then comes to light that Jonas has already poisoned his own
father (chap. xlviii), and that Old Martin is in fact acting a part with
Pecksniff, in order to deceive and punish him, and that he has been

14 See chap. xxv, the passage beginning with "a fearful mystery surrounded this lady
of the name of Harris . . . ," and "the prevalent opinion was that she was a phantom of Mrs.
Gamp's brain . . . created for the express purpose of holding visionary dialogues with
her . . . ."

favorable to young Martin throughout (chap. l) After Jonas' suicide (chap. li), the usual judiciary meeting takes place, the good are rewarded and the wicked are chastized.

Such a brief summary can give but a very imperfect notion of the variety of incidents and the wealth of characters. Yet it shows at least the outline of the narrative. In order to understand the relative and temporary failure of *Chuzzlewit*, one must look more closely at some aspects of its composition. In that respect, the readers had some grounds for dissatisfaction with Dickens. At first sight, however, one is mainly struck by the superior composition of *Chuzzlewit* in comparison with *Pickwick* and *Nickleby*, the only two earlier books that suggest themselves for such comparison because of their size and general characteristics. In *Chuzzlewit*, the outline of the narrative is coherent and intelligible. Every section of the story, every sequence of incidents is connected with every other, at least through the kinship between the various characters. The book truly relates the history of the Chuzzlewit family through a few months. Yet there are a few signs of remissness. In Chapter XIV, Martin is astonished to hear from Mary Graham that she is about to join the Pecksniff household, but a couple of pages later, he takes out of his pocket a letter he had written the night before, and in which he had had the foresight to impart the same news to Tom Pinch! In Chapter XXXI, to secure Mary's secrecy, Pecksniff threatens her with taking steps through which Martin would be "plunged in deeper ruin." But at that moment, Martin is on his sickbed at Eden. Nobody in England has his address. Pecksniff's threat is thus idle; yet it serves as one of the mainsprings of the action, for it effectively prevents Mary from confiding in old Martin, and thereby delays the annihilation of the hypocrite. In Chapter LI, Tigg, Jonas' partner, has been killed by him immediately after leaving Pecksniff on the conclusion of the agreement through which the latter's fortune was to be given up to him. Yet we hear on the next day that two other members of the dishonest gang have fled and taken Pecksniff's money with them. The way in which the money can have been conveyed to them is not accounted for.

There are, in *Chuzzlewit,* as in the preceding novels, extravagant coincidences, such as Pecksniff's silent entrance into a room at the precise moment when Jonas is exulting over his father's will (chap. xviii). Three episodes involve the participation of a medical man:[15] each time the same practitioner, Dr. Jobling, is called in. One wonders what kind of pleasure Dickens thought he could give his readers by means of such blatant unlikelihood. When Martin and Mark take possession of their pitiful residence at Eden, they find that their immediate neighbors are their former traveling companions (chap. xxxiii). When Jonas tries to steal away and go abroad, he is accidentally joined by Tom Pinch, and Mrs. Gamp is met by chance in the course of the same scene.

One peculiarity of the structure of *Chuzzlewit* is the alternation of English with American scenes through a considerable portion of the narrative. That circumstance—whose fortuitous occurrence has been seen above—caused some uneasiness to Dickens, who wrote to Forster: "I have been at work all day, and, it being against the grain with me to go back to America when my interest is so strong in other parts of the tale, have got on but slowly."[16] The difficulty was not eased by there being a further subdivision of the English scenes between the London incidents and the provincial incidents. The difficulty is not altogether a novelty. *Nickleby* had alternated Nicholas' adventures with Kate's, and *Oliver Twist* had had three centers of action, and generally there had been so many characters in Dickens' early novels that no narrative could be plainly continuous. In that respect, *Chuzzlewit* can even be said to show some progress over its predecessors, in that the divisions are skillfully placed and the proportions of the different ingredients harmoniously contrived. The transitions alone are still lacking in light-handedness. Nor is light-handedness, in any case, what Dickens would seem to be aiming at. To the natural, imperceptible transition, he still prefers a display of ingenuity which draws the reader's attention to the articifiality of his structural procedure: "Leaving [Martin and Mark] to blend and mingle in their sleep the shadows of objects afar off . . . be it the part of this slight chronicle—a dream within a dream—to change the scene, and cross the ocean to the English shore" (chap. xvii); or "But at that mo-

15 Lewsome's and Chuffey's illnesses, and the medical services required by the pseudo-insurance company.
16 Forster, *Life of Dickens*, I, 292 (July 26, 1843).

ment a loud knocking was heard at the hall door" [chap. xxi]. "The knocking at Mr. Pecksniff's door, though loud enough, bore no resemblance whatever to the noise of an American train at full speed . . ." (chaps. xx–xxi); or again, "From Mr. Moddle to Eden is an easy and natural transition, Mr. Moddle living in the atmosphere of Miss Pecksniff's love, dwelt (if he had but known it) in a terrestrial Paradise. The thriving city of Eden was also a terrestrial Paradise . . ." (chap. xxxiii). Lastly, the ending of *Chuzzlewit* is probably the most fantastic of all the prize-giving scenes staged by Dickens in his fiction. It is composed of two melodramatic processions of characters (chaps. li–lii). In the second of these no fewer than twelve figures take part, several of them being all too visibly forced in. The amiable Young Bailey, who was supposed to have died in the collapse of his master's carriage, revives in order to come in and dance about in front of the assembled company. Martin's unfortunate American neighbors also revive, in the very center of London, in order to show that Dickens overlooks no one, and that for kind hearts misfortune cannot be everlasting. There are, thank God and thank Dickens, miracles for the deserving.

In spite of such unquestionable weaknesses, there are many signs of the novelist's growing attention to the construction of his book, a capital aspect of his art. Twice in *Chuzzlewit*, the tempo of events is suddenly accelerated. Immediately before the murder, Dickens had been giving a consecutive relation of Jonas' doings. The last day alone is summed up with striking vividness: "The day passed on. Noon, afternoon, evening. Sunset" (chap. xlvii). In fact, all that touches on Jonas' crime is treated with extreme care and great skill. The tale of the murder itself is told in a few lines, but it casts its shadow over all the preceding and following chapters. Similarly, in the final chapter we are taken without transition from the farcical scene in which Charity Pecksniff fails to get married, to the evocation—with which the novel closes—of Tom Pinch playing the organ a few years later. This is a sober poetical picture, introduced by the question, "What sounds are these which fall so grandly on the ear?" preceded itself by a thin printed rule, a procedure practically never resorted to by Dickens elsewhere. The two cases show the new preoccupations of the author of *Chuzzlewit*. One paragraph in the original preface explains them:

I have endeavoured in the progress of this tale, to resist the temptation of the current monthly number, and to keep a steady eye upon the general purpose and design. With this object in view, I have put a strong constraint upon myself from time to time, in many places; and I hope the story is the better for it, now.[17]

Nothing could express more clearly the lack of spontaneity in Dickens' attempts to improve his technique, and also the resolution and energy with which he nevertheless pursued them.

The chapter headings, as usual, disclose the direction in which he is evolving. It is all the more interesting to examine them here as there had been none in the two preceding novels, published in *Master Humphrey's Clock*. At the beginning of *Chuzzlewit*, Dickens is carried away by his high spirits and indulges in the coining of long, elaborate, ironical, or humorous chapter headings, similar to those in *Pickwick*, or, for that matter, to those in Smollett's novels—for Smollett's chapter headings had been chiefly lists of incidents or episodes. One sample will suffice: "Chapter XVI. Martin Disembarks from that Noble and Fast-sailing Line-of-packet Ship, the 'Screw', at the Port of New York, in the United States of America. He Makes Some Acquaintances, and Dines at a Boardinghouse. The Particulars of those Transactions."[18] Dickens makes particularly frequent use of the old-fashioned method of treating the chapter as a person and making it the subject of a verb which then becomes the first word in the title: "Comprises . . . Important Matters" (chap. vi); "Does business . . ." (chap. xviii); "Treats of Todgers's Again (chap. xxxii); "Bears Tidings of Martin" (chap. xlviii); "Surprises Tom Pinch" (chap. l). The last chapter "Gives the Author Great Concern" chap. liv). In the latter part of the novel, however, some simplification occurs, and a new kind of effect is looked for. Several chapter headings, for instance, are symmetrically constructed: "Mr. Montague at Home. And Mr. Jonas Chuzzlewit at Home" (chap. xxviii); "In Which Miss Pecksniff Makes Love, Mr. Jonas Makes Wrath, Mrs. Gamp Makes Tea, and Mr. Chuffey Makes Business" (chap. xlvi).[19] In a few cases, the symmetry is reinforced by alliteration: "In Which Some People Are Pre-

[17] Written on June 25, 1844, and not reprinted in later editions.
[18] See also chaps. iv and xvii.
[19] See also chaps. xxxi, xxxiii, and lii.

cocious, Others Professional . . ." (chap. xxix); "An Unexpected Meeting and a Promising Prospect" (chap. xxvi). But the most representative title of what Dickens' later manner will be is the heading, brief and alliterative, of chapter ix: "Town and Todgers's."

The slight evolution of Dickens' technique, which we tend nowadays to regard as evidence of his progress, may have been partly responsible for the poor response of the contemporary public. Dickens' early readers were sentimental people and would resent every form of change which detracted from their pleasant familiarity with the author's world. They may have felt cheated. Their disappointment must also have had other causes. *Chuzzlewit*, when read from cover to cover, strikes us as being mainly, like *Pickwick* or *Nickleby*, an amusing novel, even though it is not mirthful in the sense that the reflections it suggests are not optimistic. But when its details are more closely examined, it is found to contain many explicit moral lessons. The impressions left by the passages of preaching must have been felt—and even resented—more strongly by the purchaser of the monthly parts, who would deplore that a portion, however small, of his thirty-two pages of entertainment should have been subtracted from the narrative proper to be devoted to moral teaching. It has been mentioned, at the beginning of the present work, that Dickens saw in his position as a novelist an opportunity for doing service to the community in things moral and social. This was a legitimate purpose, whenever the novelist did not go out of his way and contented himself with the implicit lesson of events without expounding moral principles at length.

Morality had held an important place in Dickens' thought ever since Mary Hogarth's death had shocked him into changing his outlook on life. Moral purpose seemed now to come to the forefront of his literary preoccupations. His teaching in *Chuzzlewit* is twofold. It concerns itself faintly with a positive lesson of the kind to be found in Wordsworth's theories about nature. The landscape about Tigg—Jonas' partner, who is about to be murdered by him—is very beautiful, but the man is going to die and his whole life will have been meaningless, for "He had never read the lessons which those things conveyed" (chap. xlvii). It concerns itself more energetically with a negative lesson: that selfishness is evil and must be avoided at all costs. The lesson is taught in every possible form throughout the novel[20]—implicitly when events and misfortunes cure young Martin of his self-centeredness; explicitly when one of the characters is inspired to deliver painstaking comments, like old Martin, who in the course of the closing scenes is almost transfigured when he draws the lesson of every individual person's adventures: "The trembling figure of the old man shook with the strong emotions that possessed him. But, with the same light in his eye, and with his arm outstretched, and with his grey hair stirring on his head, he seemed to grow in size and was like a man inspired" (chap. li). The author is explicit again when the lesson is conveyed by his own digressive ejaculations, for he will pounce on every opportunity of emphasizing the motivations and the general principles at work in his story: "O late-remembered, much-forgotten, mouthing braggart, duty, always owed and seldom paid in any other coin than punishment and wrath, when will mankind begin to know thee?" (chap. xxxi).

The over-all impression left by the moral atmosphere of *Chuzzlewit* is sad. In order to punish one of the chief villains, hypocritical Pecksniff, old Martin spends many months in the latter's home, watching him, pretending to love him and to defer to him. Old Martin himself says: "I have lived in his house . . . and had him fawning on me, days and weeks, and months. . . . I have suffered him to treat me like his tool and instrument. . . . I have had his base soul bare before me, day by day, and have not betrayed myself once" (chap. l). His words sound like a valid analysis of hypocrisy from the inside. One wonders whether hypocrisy really was the single weapon at old Martin's disposal against Pecksniff. Without even taking into account the grotesque unlikelihood of such a childish plot, childishly conceived and childishly carried out, it must be admitted that Pecksniff's protest remains unanswered—because it is unanswerable—when he says to old Martin: "Whether it was worthy of you to partake of my hospitality, and to act the part you did in my house, that, sir, is a question which I leave to your own conscience. And your conscience does not acquit you, no, sir, no!" (chap. lii).

It is tempting to infer that, as Forster suggests, hypocrisy was England's national vice, which Dickens was out to denounce. But the Ameri-

---

[20] To the bitter end in the closing scene, when old Martin proclaims: "The curse of our house has ever been the love of self" (chap. lii).

cans in *Chuzzlewit* are not a whit superior to the English in that respect, as is glaringly shown by their attitude toward liberty and slavery in theory and in practice. Likewise, another target of the novelist's satire is confused. If he had aimed at showing that the United States was the natural home of dishonest speculators, he should not have had another gang of dishonest speculators operating in England at the same moment. Besides, Mrs. Gamp, Betsey Prig, and Pecksniff himself are not morally superior to the worst American swindlers. In short, the moral inference to be drawn from *Chuzzlewit* is pessimistic, and that comic novel paints mankind in a dark light. The artificiality of the winding-up—for no one will feel that such miraculously fair prize-givings can occur in real life—only enhances the saddening aspect of the picture presented in the novel. *Chuzzlewit*, even more than any of the previous works, is in great part a *roman à thèse*, whose thesis—that selfishness is widespread and leads to evil consequences—is not encouraging. It may have been one of the things the contemporary public did not relish in this novel.

Finally, there was one more element that could displease them. Many scenes in the book are very vulgar. There had been no vulgarity in *Oliver Twist*, though that novel had concerned itself with the lowest classes of English society, for there had been no complacency on the author's part and no pretensions on the characters'. Here, at Kenwigs' in *Nickleby*, the atmosphere of the least felicitous sections of *Sketches by Boz* is revived, and it is the atmosphere of the circles Dickens had been familiar with in his youth, junior clerks, small shopkeepers, the very lowest fringe of the middle class, whose vulgarity is made all the more striking by their desire to be thought genteel. In *Chuzzlewit*, vulgarity is displayed mainly at Mrs. Todgers'. But another painful specimen is provided by the scene in which Charity Pecksniff stands in front of a furniture shop, and, "betraying a soft embarrassment," inquires of her fiancé about the cost of a "full-sized four-post bedstead" (chap. xlvi). It is somewhat strange and deplorable that Dickens should have thought the purchase of a bed by a prospective couple a fit subject for jocularity. Of course, this is only the less decorous form of his overflow of high spirits, perceptible throughout the book. In Dickens' correspondence is to be found plentiful evidence that the more cheerful he is, the more he delights in affecting vulgarity of style and feeling.

Whether its main cause lay in imperfect structure, or in explicit and pessimistic moralizing, or in vulgarity, the comparative failure of *Chuzzlewit* had serious consequences. The contract for that novel had granted sensational advantages to the author, but it had been stipulated that, should the sales fail to procure sufficient profits, a deduction of £50 might be made from his monthly fee. In June, 1843, Hall, Chapman's partner, referred to that stipulation in conversation with Dickens. Although Hall's words could by no means be interpreted as a statement of the publisher's actual intentions, and still less as a threat, Dickens was sorely hurt and irritated. He could not bear that anyone—least of all the people his labors were enriching—should appear to believe that his success was on the wane. He made up his mind at once to break with Chapman and Hall as soon as possible.

Nor was the psychological effect of the incident less damaging. In spite of his energetic assertions—"I feel my power more than I ever did. . . . I have a greater confidence in myself than I ever had. . . . I could sustain my place in the minds of thinking men though fifty writers started up to-morrow"[21]—or rather on account of these very assertions, one feels that his confidence in himself, in his genius and his success, had been shaken, and that he now thought of the way in which his resources might be imperiled by fresh competitors in his field. He had never before felt the urge to assert what was certain and obvious. He was weary;[22] he had run into debt to keep up a costly standard of living, and any sign of diminishing income was a cause for anxiety. He therefore decided to expatriate himself once more and go, with the whole family this time, to France and Italy where life was cheaper.

In November, 1843, he wrote the admirable *Christmas Carol* and had it printed at his own expense, in the hope of thus making the £1,000 he needed to balance his budget. In spite of the little book's colossal popularity, however, his profits amounted to but one-fourth of the expected sum. A fifth child was born in January, 1844. Furthermore, Georgina Hogarth had become a permanent member of the household, so that

---

[21] See Forster, *Life of Dickens*, I, 289 (November 2, 1843).

[22] *Ibid.* "It is impossible to go on working the brain to that extent for ever. The very spirit of the thing, in doing it, leaves a horrible despondency behind."

henceforth eight mouths had to be fed. In the spring of 1844, Dickens went to Manchester, to Liverpool, and to other provincial cities in order to attend the opening of various establishments meant to promote social progress and popular culture. He thus had to face considerable professional expense in addition to the cost of running the house for the family. Obviously he had to be more prudent. Finally, the poor reception of *Chuzzlewit* almost compelled the novelist to go away.

And yet the poor reception was a superficial and ephemeral reaction. By the end of Dickens' life, the book had gained the third place among Dickens' works—after *Pickwick* and *Copperfield*—in the order of popularity, as measured by the number of copies sold. Its final success is more easily accounted for than the coldness of its early reception.

When Dickens began to write *Chuzzlewit* in January, 1843, he was in excellent physical and moral condition. According to Forster, "Perhaps no story was ever begun by him with stronger heart or confidence."[23] After the period of six months devoted to *American Notes* and to settling down again into English surroundings, he had resumed his steady working habits. Before the completion of the book, he had been through a little sentimental episode which had pleasantly diversified his life. In the course of one of his provincial tours, at Liverpool, he had become acquainted with a young musician, Christiana Weller, whose charm had greatly impressed him as well as his friend T. J. Thompson. The latter, being a bachelor, had been able to marry the girl.[24] Yet the encounter had acted on Dickens' sensibility, and *Chuzzlewit* contains evidence of a more lively appreciation of feminine beauty, mostly perceptible through the portrait of graceful Ruth Pinch.

The manuscript of *Chuzzlewit* shows greater ease and gusto than the manuscripts of *Barnaby Rudge* or the *Curiosity Shop*. It is written in a larger and clearer hand. There are few corrections in the early chapters. In a letter to his American friend, Professor Felton, Dickens himself referred to his enjoyment in the writing of *Chuzzlewit*: "I am . . . powdering away at Chuzzlewit, with all manner of facetiousness rising up before me as I go on."[25]

23 Forster, *Life of Dickens*, I, 274.
24 See, for that episode, E. Johnson, *Ch. Dickens: Tragedy & Triumph*, I, 497–504.
25 March 2, 1843, *Letters* (MDGH), III, 46.

Dickens' easy inspiration is also apparent in the style, or rather styles, of *Chuzzlewit*, for there is considerable variety of tone in that book. The poetical elements in the author's prose are increasingly numerous. They are mostly of an impressionistic kind and can be divided into two distinct groups—the tragic and the graceful.

In the tragic category are to be found a number of chapter endings. Such is the passage referring to the churchyard where Anthony Chuzzlewit has been buried: "One new mound was there which had not been last night. Time, burrowing like a mole below the ground, had marked his track by throwing up another heap of earth. And that was all" (chap. xix). Such, also, the paragraph about an invalid's mental wanderings: "Oh, weary, weary hour! oh, haggard mind. . . . Oh, weary, weary hour! What were the wanderings of Cain to these" (chap. xxv). And again, the symbolical allusions to Nadgett's mysterious appointments with the man who never came (chaps. xxix, xl). Again, the preparation for the murder through equivocal phrases. " 'It will be a stormy night!' exclaimed the doctor, as they started" (chap. xli), and the harmony introduced between the elements and the feelings of the actors in the drama: "The thunder rolled, the lightning flashed; the rain poured down, like Heaven's wrath" (chap. xlii). Or, later: "It was now growing dark. As the gloom of evening deepened into night, came on, another dark shade emerging from within him seemed to overspread his face, and slowly change it . . ." (chap. xlvi). The careful preparation leads to the murder itself, related with great tragic force: "What had he left within the wood, that he sprang out of it as if it were a hell! The body of a murdered man" (chap. xlvii). As in the case of Sikes, the consequences of the murder, in the form of remorse and horror, are also powerfully and impressionistically rendered: "Hark! It came on, roaring like a sea. . . . The sounding street repeated Murder; barbarous and dreadful Murder; Murder, Murder, Murder. Rolling on from house to house, and echoing from stone to stone, until the voices died away into the distant hum, which seemed to mutter the same word!" (chap. li). The same power upholds Dickens to the end of the chapter and the murderer's own death: "They dragged him out into the dark street; but jury, judge and hangman, could have done no more, and could do nothing now. Dead, dead, dead!" (chap. li). Thus does Jonas' death round off the episode that had begun with his father's, and make Anthony and Jonas a kind of tragic dynasty.

The passages of graceful poetical prose contrast pleasingly with the preceding quotations. They refer mostly to Tom Pinch and his sister Ruth, and also to John Westlock's love for the latter. Tom Pinch is the occasion of two poetical descriptions of his travels, in which are blended the vividness of motion and the innocent happiness of an inexperienced man for whom every image is like a wonderful discovery. Pinch travels twice in the novel: once, on foot, to go to Salisbury and the second time by coach to go to London. In both cases, his journey is depicted in remarkable style. In the first (chap. xii), there is a kind of refrain: "Better than the gig!" and in the second a striking succession—impressionistic, once more—of swift, fleeting visions, ushered in by the exclamatory "Yoho, past hedges, gates and trees. . . . Yoho, among the gathering shades! . . . Yoho, down countless turnings! . . ." (chap. xxxvi), thus giving an almost physical sensation of speed.

Then come Tom's and Ruth's life in London, every detail of which is transfigured by their happiness. The purchase of a piece of meat by Tom is made genuinely poetical, thanks to the purchaser's enthusiasm (chap. liii). Similarly, for John, who is in love with Ruth, the most common messengers encountered in the street become "celestial" (chap. xxxix). Dickens supplies a description of Ruth's eyes, inspired perhaps by the recent remembrance of Christiana Weller's, and in any case, very different from the treatment bestowed on his earlier heroines, and making Pinch's sister a thousand times more lively and attractive than the heroine-in-chief of the novel, Mary Graham: "By-the-bye, how bright they were! Looking into them for but a moment, when you took her hand, you saw in each such a capital miniature of yourself, representing you as such a restless, flashing, eager, brilliant little fellow . . ." (chap. xxxix). The Ruth Pinch–John Westlock idyl is the occasion of more than one tender and delicate allusion or description. Dickens, for instance, exclaims: "Oh! foolish, panting, frightened little heart, why did she run away?" (chap. xlv). And in the Temple gardens occurs a charming scene, Ruth's discovery of her own feelings, played to the tune of the fountain, a subtly varied burden:

Merrily the tiny fountain played, and merrily the dimples sparkled
on its sunny face. . . . Merrily the fountain plashed and plashed, until
the dimples, merging into one another, swelled into a general smile
that covered the whole surface of the basin. . . . Merrily the fountain
leaped and danced, and merrily the smiling dimples twinkled and
expanded more and more, until they broke into a laugh against the
basin's rim, and vanished (chap. xlv).

Later, when John declares his love, the same musical theme is resumed,
still with the same delicacy: "Brilliantly the Temple Fountain sparkled
in the sun, and laughingly its liquid music played, and merrily the idle
drops of water danced and danced, and peeping out in sport among the
trees, plunged lightly down to hide themselves . . ." (chap. liii). Nothing
so pretty could have been found in *Oliver Twist* or *Nickleby*.

The pity is that, while he has achieved such progress in the art of
happily and beautifully suggesting emotion, Dickens should still be
unable to make the very words of love convincing and passionate. This
is a deficiency he has in common with many other novelists, no doubt,
and perhaps the language of love *is* dull enough in real life. But in any
case, after the symbolical suggestiveness of the Temple Fountain, John
Westlock's cold platitudes are a comedown: "Dear Ruth! sweet Ruth!
If I had loved you less, I could have told you that I loved you long ago.
I have loved you from the first. There never was a creature in the world
more truly loved than you, dear Ruth, by me!" (chap. liii).

The images in *Chuzzlewit* are another striking element of its style,
and they are many and picturesque. Some possess wonderful terseness.
Thus, the American woman of letters, Mrs. Hominy, "came slowly
up . . . in a procession of one" (chap. xxxix), and it would be hard to
use fewer words or to give a more precise idea of the character's attitude. An American general rises after a fall: "His uniform was so fear-
fully and wonderfully made that he came up stiff and without a bend
in him, like a dead clown."[26] Here the brevity of the words associates
two images which lend support to each other, by superimposing the
stiffness of the clown over the stiffness of the corpse. Charity Pecksniff's
voice is so shrill that "it might have belonged to a wind in its teens"

[26] Chap. xvii. That example provides a perfect illustration of Henri Bergson's famous
theory that laughter is produced by a hardening or stiffening of living reality.

(chap. ii). In an unpublished fragment of the manuscript appeared the following image: "Mr. Pecksniff uses his pocket-handkerchief as if he were not only in a figurative, but in a literal sense, melted, and were oozing out at his own eyes."[27] In every one of the above cases, rare verbal power is combined with no less rare perception of attitude.

There is, then, more definite progress in the style than in the composition of *Chuzzlewit*, which may account in part for the later appreciation of that novel. Another main source for this later appreciation undoubtedly lies in the successful characterization. Few of Dickens' novels contain quite so many great figures. The characters are once more rather too numerous. Such is, at any rate, one's impression on seeing the names invented by Dickens for some of them and partaking of farcical caricature rather than of realistic fiction. In the States, there are names like Brick, La Fayette Kettle, Choke, Chollop, and Hominy. In Britain, some names are also transparently significant: the undertaker is called Mould, and the dishonest doctor Jobling. Two men, Spottletoe and Sweedlepipe, whole names are comical without being precisely descriptive, have inherited parts of names originally intended for the two Martins. Dickens, whose attention to proper names never relented, had indeed contemplated seven different possibilities—Sweezleden, Sweezleback, Sweezlewag, Chuzzletoe, Chuzzleboy, Chubblewig, Chuzzlewig—before hitting on Chuzzlewit. It is worth noticing that all eight names, and Spottletoe, Sweedlepipe, and Nickleby as well, are similarly constructed with the syllable "le" in the middle.

First names are chosen with equal care. The Misses Pecksniff are called Charity and Mercy. It is a legitimate procedure to express the parent's attitude in his choice of his children's Christian names. The high spirits with which the book was written appear also in a few familiar nicknames. Mercy and Charity are habitually called Merry and Cherry by their father. The former is addressed by her fiancé under the name of "Other One,"[28] and for the latter, like Dickens himself in private life, Mr. Pecksniff extemporizes a brilliant variation, the "playful little name . . . my Cherrywerrychigo" (chap. xliv). It will be seen in the study of *Copperfield* that the adoption of distinct forms of address

[27] Cancelled beginning of chap. vi (Forster Collection).
[28] Chap. xi: "Other One, will you come here?"

for one and the same character by various members of his circle is a significant and original aspect of Dickens' approach.

As for the characters in themselves, a few call for additional comment. Mary Graham, whose first name is of course reminiscent of the dear departed[29] is not often seen or heard by the reader. Nor is this felt as a deprivation, for it is clear that she would always remain true to herself, a worthy member of the wearisome group of saints. But this is a class of characters whose place in the novels is fortunately doomed to decrease. In *Nickleby* both heroines were perfect. Now that Dolly Vardens and Ruth Pinches have put in an appearance in his novels and Christiana Wellers in his private life, the writer cannot fail to become less sensitive to the appeal of marble-like perfection. Mary Graham is a stiff, starched character, who never discloses her emotions or else overcomes them at once. When Martin tells her of his departure for the United States, he reproaches her: " 'See now. How you droop directly.' 'If I do, or I hope I may say if I did,' she answered, raising her face after a short silence, and looking once more into his face, 'it was for grief to think of what you are resolved to undergo for me' " (chap. xiv). To so much supernatural firmness, it is to be feared the average reader would weakly prefer some vivacity and life. When Martin describes Pinch to her, and, with characteristic selfishness, tells her: "You needn't mind laughing at him, for he'll not care about it. He'll rather like it indeed!" she replies, "I don't think I shall put that to the test, Martin!" And her lover's prediction: "I think you'll find him a little too much for your gravity" (chap. xiv) is not likely to be accomplished. Indeed it stresses all too accurately the weakness of Mary's portraiture. There is too much gravity in her for a girl of her age and for the modern reader's taste. Well may she preach tolerance to Martin: "If you would but sometimes . . . think of . . . anyone who ever wronged you . . ." (chap. xiv), but she is too infallibly right. Mary Graham's fate in the novel, subjected as she is to systematic trial by old Martin—"resolved . . . to prove the constancy and truth of Mary" (chap. lii)—makes her a kind of Griselda. But of a Victorian Griselda, the sufferings can hardly move us since her fortitude enables her to bear them almost too well.

[29] Unconsciously, no doubt, Dickens has also made her name a partial anagram of Mary Hogarth's, the letters "g," "r," "a" and "h" being found in both.

Pecksniff and his daughters are better inventions, and might even have been masterpieces in characterization had Dickens treated them a trifle less insistently. The Pecksniff girls are interesting. The elder, Charity, a simpering though cantankerous old maid, is a fine figure of fun, although pictured somewhat cruelly: "Quarrels, Miss Pecksniff said, were dreadful things in families; and though she never could forgive her dear papa, she was willing to receive her other relations" (chap. liv). Her sister Mercy is at first almost identical with her, the only difference being the younger girl's affected mirth and light-heartedness. But once she has married Jonas, poor Mercy, ill-treated by her brutal and dishonest drunkard of a husband, repents and is changed into a tragic figure. The atmosphere of her unhappy home is not unlike that in George Eliot's "Janet's Repentance."[30] Like most of Dickens' tragic figures, she becomes much less convincing in the course of her conversion and gains instead painful moral and sentimental complexities. Old Martin had tried to dissuade her from marrying Jonas. When the marriage has turned disastrous, she claims to forgive Martin for not checking her in time through even greater insistence. On the lips of a Dickensian character meant to be tragic, the words she then uses: "Tell him that I don't blame him . . . but . . . " (chap. xxxvii), are a clear and solemn condemnation.

Mercy's father is one of the best-known characters in English fiction. His reputation is equal to that of the French Tartuffe, to whom he owes a few traits. The illustration for the original edition which showed Pecksniff's final collapse included a table with a few books on it, and in the foreground could be distinctly seen a volume called: "Le Tartuffe. Molière."[31] Dickens' purpose is thus made clear. Pecksniff's early appearances are admirable, as are all his gestures and speeches. Even when joking, he preserves "a kind of saintly waggishness" (chap. ii). He is forever moralizing: " 'Even such a thing as this,' said Mr. Pecksniff, laying the fore-finger of his left hand upon the brown paper patch on the top of his head, 'slight casual baldness though it be, reminds us that we are but—' (he was going to say 'worms', but recollecting that worms were not remarkable for heads of hair, he substituted 'flesh and blood' " (chap. ii).

[30] *Scenes of Clerical Life*, III.
[31] The illustrations are known to have been designed according to the author's precise directions and under his control.

Graceful and incongruous metaphors are rife on Pecksniff's lips: "It will be a week before we again deposit our olive branches. . . . I mean our unpretending luggage" (chap. vi). Yet hypocrisy implies a series of artifices, and in the description of these artifices, Dickens does not avoid the repetition of identical effects, which tend in the end to appear mechanical. He writes: "He tried to drop a tear upon his patron's hand, but couldn't find one in his dry distillery" (chap. xxx). And again, a few chapters later: "Here Mr. Pecksniff, accidentally dropping the tear in question on a bald part of Mr. Chuzzlewit's head, wiped the place with his pocket-handkerchief, and begged pardon" (chap. xlii). This is both highly improbable and somewhat disgusting. Finally, still more unsatisfactory results are achieved when Dickens ploddingly shows Pecksniff in his true colors through marginal commentary, in order to emphasize the moral teaching of the book: "He squeezed his pocket-handkerchief against his eyes with both hands, as such men always do, especially when they are observed" (chap. xxx); "the more he was found out, the more hypocrisy he practised . . . it is in the nature of a knave to think . . . " (chap. xliv). What is obvious need not be exposed and Dickens has made Pecksniff's hypocrisy so abundantly, so unmistakably clear that the author's attacks against him are a ponderous waste of time. Apart from such fast-forgotten deficiencies, however, the portrait of Pecksniff is on the whole masterly.

Only one other figure in the novel calls for comment. If one could explain the appeal of Tom Pinch's character, an important step would be taken toward an understanding of Dickens' art. For Tom Pinch is a poor, simple creature, mentally underdeveloped. But such had already been the case with Barnaby, Smike, and, to a lesser extent, Kit.[32] Now, instead of being dull and unconvincing like them, or at least like the first two, Pinch is likable and lively. The distinction between Pinch and the other two characters cannot perhaps be determined accurately: it may be neither more nor less than the spark of genius. One can at any rate discern several elements of Pinch's character and situation which had not belonged to his predecessors.

In the first place, Tom Pinch is not perfect, not supernaturally faultless. His blindness, for instance, when John Westlock falls in love with

[32] In *BR*, *NN*, and *OCS*, respectively.

Ruth, is a comical feature and has nothing unpleasant about it, since it does not result from self-centeredness. Tom Pinch can be laughed at. John had taken Ruth's part in an argument: "However, as Tom observed, it was only in joke, and John had always been famous for being polite to ladies, even when he was quite a boy. Ruth said 'Oh, indeed!' She didn't say anything else" (chap. xxxix). And, on another occasion: "Really, John was uncommonly kind, extraordinarily kind. If he had been her father, Tom said, he could not have taken a greater interest in her" (chap. l). His innocence is delightful. Besides, the reader is grateful to Tom Pinch for being pathetic only through his fate—he is hopelessly in love with Mary Graham, who loves Martin—and never through his speeches. The sadness of his fate is not too insistently marked, and it is softened by the delight he takes in other people's happiness, and by the enjoyment he derives from playing the organ. He delivers no speeches and does not even utter remarks meant to be touching or edifying. Finally, and above all, Dickens loves Pinch wholeheartedly. In all previous cases of the kind, he had shown himself theoretically attracted to simple minds, but had been unable to make them appear lovable, because his own feelings had not been profound enough to become infectious. Here they are overflowing, but he is not intimidated. For the first time, he is found to address one of his characters frequently, and always in tender terms: "Blessings on thy simple heart, Tom Pinch, how proudly thou dost button up that scanty coat, called by a sad misnomer, for these many years, a 'great' one . . . " (chap. v).

Tom Pinch becomes for the author a traveling companion to whom he imparts his own thoughts as they go along together, and whom he occasionally cheers by a word of comfort or friendship; "The loveliest things in life, Tom, are but shadows" (chap. xii); "There are some falsehoods, Tom, on which men mount, as on bright wings, towards heaven" (chap. xiii); "God's love upon thy patience, Tom!" (chap. xxiv). That attitude even suggests to Dickens a new technical audacity, and he will inform the reader of certain circumstances while ostensibly conveying them to Tom.[33] The procedure is, of course, just as artificial and destructive of illusion as the famous, time-honored, address to the "dear reader," yet it is not quite so hackneyed, and can even find its justification

---

[33] See chap. xxxix.

in the privileged sentimental relationship that has been so forcibly established. The final paragraphs of the novel are devoted to Tom. They have a warm emotional undertone, and they poetically associate the beauty of organ music with the transparent clearness of Tom's heart, in a way which causes them to be among the finest things in Dickens' works:

> What sounds are these which fall so grandly on the ear? What darkening room is this? And that mild figure, seated at an organ, who is he? Ah, Tom, dear Tom, old friend!...in those sounds with which it is thy wont to bear the twilight company, the music of thy heart speaks out. . . . Thy life is tranquil, calm, and happy, Tom. In the soft strain which ever and again comes stealing back upon the ear, the memory of thine old love may find a voice perhaps . . . thy strain soars onward to the Future. As it resounds within thee and without, the noble music, rolling round ye both [Ruth and thee], shuts out the grosser prospect of an earthly parting, and uplifts ye both to heaven! (chap. liv).

Of the novel which thus closes in an atmosphere of solemn purity, it has been seen that the manuscript has been preserved and bears the marks of the easy inspiration often felt through the book itself. Inspiration does not preclude effort, and *Chuzzlewit*, though a more inspired novel than *Barnaby Rudge* or even than *Nickleby*, is at the same time a more painstaking and careful work. The method employed in the days of *Barnaby*, which consisted in "thinking out" or "imaging forth" a section of the book before taking pen in hand, is again used by Dickens, who writes to Forster: "I have been all day in Chuzzlewit agonies—conceiving only. I hope to bring forth to-morrow."[34] Meanwhile, the other procedure invented for *The Old Curiosity Shop*, i.e. the preparation of "mems" for the number in progress, has been improved. Only two sheets of *Chuzzlewit* "mems" have been preserved. They are those for Numbers IV (chaps. ix–x) and V (chaps. xiii–xv). It is probable, though not certain, that similar sheets were used for the other installments and became lost later. Dickens' practice on that point had not yet become systematic, as is shown by the appearance of the two specimens we possess, which are not comparable to those adopted by Dickens from *Dombey* through *Edwin*

34 Forster, *Life of Dickens*, I, 290 (Nov. 10, 1843).

Drood. The first sheet has a list of the incidents in Number IV, arranged in two chapters. Dickens had made, for instance, the following notes: "Chapter IX: Todgers's; Places about the Monument; Bird's eye view from house top; Miss Pinch; Come off the grass; Boy, Young Bailey; Todgers's drawing-room; the youngest gentleman in company."[35] Here are given pell-mell, elements that were to be more methodically sorted out later, such as hints for incidents, bits of atmosphere, tentative characters' names, and even one key phrase. In the second sheet, there is only a short list of incidents, preceded by the mention "three chapters."

But those documents possess a twofold interest. They mark one stage in Dickens' progress toward his definitive procedure. And they contain, in the summary of Chapter X, the phrase "Old Martin's plot to degrade and punish Pecksniff in the end." Thus Dickens' premeditation of a central feature of his plot is formally proved. In the novel itself, his premeditation is not quite so visible, for he has given old Martin such an efficient disguise that, without such incontrovertible proof, one might have suspected him of having altered the end of his novel—as he had done in *Nickleby*—at the last moment. It is now possible to assert that Dickens' conception of the novel as a whole was clear, at least as soon as he had completed his third number.

Chuzzlewit, then, has disconcertingly varied characteristics. The novel was in many respects more conscientiously done than the previous books, yet it had also been written with greater ease. The over-all impression is that Dickens' American vacation had been good for him. He was like a schoolboy after his holiday. He was full of fresh energy and brimful of sound resolves. He had renewed his strength and reinforced his determination to adhere to the rules of his craft. The result had been a book in which mirth and beauty predominated.

Unfortunately, circumstances were unfavorable to that book. For various reasons, mostly independent of its technical or aesthetic value, *Chuzzlewit* had met with only partial success. Yet, when R. H. Horne, in 1844, published his *New Spirit of the Age*, he gave Dickens a prominent place. Dickens was the first author to be examined in that work, and came in for seventy pages of laudatory criticism. Horne thus seemed to place Dickens as the first English writer of the day. But criticism is not

[35] Forster Collection.

always at one with the general public. Criticism, with its instinctive distrust of popular fame, had been slower to bow to Boz's triumph. When
a major critical work paid its tribute to Dickens, the general public
seemed to become reluctant. It was the end of a miracle, the miracle of
the infallibly increasing sales of all the previous works from the same
pen. The American holiday had been good for the writer, but not for his
sales. The habit of buying and reading Dickens every month had been
adopted early, and the appetite thus created had been satisfied without
interruption from 1836 through 1841. A fourteen months' silence seemed
to have killed it. *Chuzzlewit* had failed to revive the habit, and Dickens
now felt the need for a new effort. The importance assumed by that
problem in his eyes is shown by the idea that fleetingly crossed his mind.
There must have been a profound upheaval of his professional position
before he could write, in a letter to a friend: "I 'think' of leaving England
for a year, next midsummer, bag and baggage, little ones and all—then
coming out with *such* a story, Felton, all at once, no parts, sledge-hammer
blow."[36]

XVII: AFTER THE ITALIAN HOLIDAY: *Dombey and Son*

IN SPITE OF THE HOPE expressed in Dickens' letter to Professor Felton, a
good deal more than a year was to elapse between the completion of
Chuzzlewit and the appearance of the next novel. Nor was the latter to
be published "all at once." The final installment of *Chuzzlewit* had been
issued in June, 1844. *Dombey and Son* appeared in nineteen numbers,
the first number was published in October, 1846, the last was published
on April 1, 1848. That was the longest interval that had ever intervened
between two consecutive novels by Dickens.

Of course, though he had succeeded in escaping for so many months
the hard labor of the novelist's calling, he had not been able to evade the
necessity of working for a living. His family was still increasing. His
fourth son was born in October, 1845, and the fifth, the Dickenses' seventh child, eighteen months later. Dickens published three Christmas
Books during that period: *The Chimes* in 1844, *The Cricket on the
Hearth* in 1845, and *The Battle of Life* in 1846. Another Christmas Book,

[36] Jan. 2, 1844, *Letters* (MDGH), III, 61.

The Haunted Man, was begun in 1847, but it had to be given up on account of the *Dombey* strain, and its publication was postponed to the following year. To the same period belongs *Pictures From Italy* in 1846. Dickens further contributed several articles to London newspapers.

But even more than by literary labor, the period was marked by ceaseless motion, traveling, restlessness, and agitation. After settling down at Albaro, a suburb of Genoa, in July, 1844, the Dickenses moved to another house three months later. In Genoa, Dickens entered into a close friendship with Madame de la Rue, to whom he came to give hypnotic treatment for her nervous disease. In December, 1844, he took a five week trip, on his own, to read the proofs of *The Chimes* aloud to a friendly circle gathered at Forster's. Other trips took place within Italy, particularly to attend the Easter celebrations in Rome, and ascend Vesuvius. Dickens' intimacy with the la Rues was a characteristic feature of the Italian sojourn.

He came back to England in July, 1845, with his family, and organized amateur theatricals in London. At the end of the same year, he was absorbed by preparations for the launching of a radical newspaper, *The Daily News*, that he had undertaken to edit for a yearly salary of £2,000. Dickens, who had thrown himself with wholehearted energy into the venture, became disgusted with it almost as soon as it was actually in process, perhaps because of the dispiriting nightwork involved. He resigned on February 9, 1846, and Forster took his place; the first number had appeared on January 21. So as to forget that galling experience as completely as possible, Dickens felt that he must leave England once more. After failing in his attempt to secure a position as a London magistrate, he went to Lausanne with the family in May, 1846. He had intended to work there on a new novel. He stayed in Switzerland for a few months only and then moved to Paris in November, 1846. From Paris, he went to London twice—in December, 1846, to look after the new, cheap edition of his complete works, to be issued by Bradbury and Evans, who had succeeded Chapman and Hall as his publishers, and in February, 1847, to complete Number VI of *Dombey*, which had been found two pages short. Two months later, he returned to England to stay. In July, 1847, and again from April through July, 1848, he organized theatrical performances, for charitable purposes, in several provincial cities.

In December, 1848, he visited Edinburgh and Glasgow. In the course of the Scottish trip, Mrs. Dickens fell ill. Throughout this period Dickens himself often felt that his own health left much to be desired.

His first purpose, when he began to write *Dombey and Son*, was to do for pride what he had done for selfishness in *Chuzzlewit*, i.e. to illustrate the evils attacked in the book by means of various examples. The original title of the book was to be "Dealings with the Firm of Dombey and Son, Wholesale, Retail, and for Exportation." This was a far briefer title than had been given to the preceding novel. Yet Dickens himself curtailed it by leaving out the last section so that his manuscript notes all bear the form "Dealings with the Firm of Dombey and Son." This must have appealed to him because of the possible equivocation on the word "dealings." Posterity remembers only the title *Dombey and Son* or even *Dombey*, which is also the form used by Dickens in correspondence about the book.

It has been seen that after *Chuzzlewit*, as after *Rudge*, and *Nickleby*, Dickens had cherished the hope that he would not find himself compelled to write new novels ceaselessly. From 1844 through 1847, the notion of creating a periodical recurs many times in his correspondence with Forster,[1] who invariably retorts, practically, that his friend's vocation is that of novelist, and that, besides, novels are the fastest way to make money. Whenever Dickens turned from novels to periodicals, the failure of his attempts and the impossibility of running a truly popular weekly or adapting himself to its demands resulted in a return to the novel. Thus Dickens, on June 28, 1846, in Lausanne, began to write *Dombey*, unenthusiastically, but with a resolve to gain firmer control of himself. The particulars of his plans were soon expounded to Forster, in a very interesting letter, giving a clear outline of the whole story:

> I design to show Mr. D. with that one idea of the Son taking firmer and firmer possession of him, and swelling and bloating his pride to a prodigious extent. . . . But the natural affection of the boy will turn towards the despised sister. . . . When the boy is about ten years old (in the fourth number) he will be taken ill and die. . . . So

[1] Particularly in 1845, when the title "The Cricket" is mentioned to Forster.

I mean to carry the story on . . . through the decay and downfall of the house, and the bankruptcy of Dombey, and all the rest of it. Then his only staff and treasure, and his unknown good genius always, will be this rejected daughter, who will come out better than any son at last . . . .[2]

The novel was written, at Lausanne and Geneva at first, then in Paris, and later in London and Broadstairs. The first impression produced by *Dombey*, when it is reread immediately after *Chuzzlewit*, is that Dickens' manner has undergone profound changes, and even that he has solved the problem of continuity. It is clear that his artistic development has continued through the long period of quasi-silence that came to an end with the first number of *Dombey*.[3] The clearest evidence is to be found in what must be called Dickens' "new style." One of the critics who commented on the first publication of *Dombey* in volume form, in 1848, already noticed that "it is, in some respects, better written, though with more apparent labour, than any of the works that have gone before it . . . ."[4]

The very first sentence of the novel is admirably constructed. The chapter heading repeats the title of the book, or its essentials, and the elements of that first sentence are harmonized with it: "Chapter One. *Dombey and Son.* Dombey sat in the corner of the darkened room in the great armchair by the bedside, and Son lay tucked up warm in a little basket bedstead . . . ."

The other chapter headings in the book are all brief, and some are very brief. A comparison between its table of contents and that of *Chuzzlewit*—and still more that of *Pickwick*—is striking. Instead of chapter headings averaging two lines and often spreading out over four or five, are to be found headings only three of which are slightly over one line in length—and these three are for Chapters II, III and VII. For the other fifty-nine chapters, the headings are short, plain, and neat. In

[2] Forster, *Life of Dickens*, II, 20–21.

[3] Of quasi silence only, for several Christmas Books were published in the meantime. Yet, however intrinsically valuable and interesting, these small volumes do not concern the historian of the Dickensian *novel*.

[4] "Humorists. Dickens and Thackeray," *The English Review*, London, Dec., 1848, pp. 257–75; quoted in *Dickensiana*, p. 256.

the early part, five of them concern Paul Dombey, whose name they contain in the possessive case.[5] Several are alliterative: "Paul's Progress ..." (chap. v); "What the Waves Were Always Saying" (chap. xvi); "... the Midshipman Mysterious" (chap. xxiii). And many are characteristic of the "new style," a concentrated style, which abounds in contrasts and which aims at creating sensation through various devices. Such are, among others, the following: "New Faces" (chap. xxi); "Shadows of the Past and Future" (chap. xxvi); "Deeper Shadows" (chap. xxvii); "Alterations" (chap. xxviii); "Contrasts" (chap. xxxiii); "Retribution" (chap. lix); "Relenting" (chap. lxi).

But of course it is chiefly in the text of the novel itself that the new style appears. One of its main features is the growing frequency of refrains, and other effects founded on repetition, symmetry, and contrast. Throughout *Dombey* such effects are plentiful. The phrase "let him remember it in that room, years to come" is used to begin and close two solemn paragraphs of Chapter XVIII. Further on, a complete paragraph —"For Florence lived alone in the deserted house, and day succeeded day, and still she lived alone, and the cold walls looked down upon her with a vacant stare, as if they had a Gorgon-Like mind to stare her youth and beauty into stone" (chap. xxiii)—is repeated twice within three pages, with only such minor changes as the substitution of "thus" for "for," of "monotonous" for "cold," and of "intent" for "mind." Other phrases of the same kind are used several times. Chapter LIX has two of these burdens: "the house is a ruin, and the rats fly from it" and "the Capital Modern Household Furniture, etc." is, successively, "on view," "on sale," and "in course of removal."

The impressionistic nature of the device is shown by Dickens' use of it for his descriptions of fast journeys. In the chapter devoted to the flight and death of the villain Carker, a sensation of motion and speed is thus conveyed through the repetition of several more or less onomatopoeic forms. They are, first, at the moment of departure: "Halloa! Whoop! Halloa! Hi! Away at a gallop, over the black landscape, scattering the dust and dirt like spray" reappearing later as "Hallo! Hi! Away at a gallop over the black landscape; dust and dirt flying like spray, the smoking horses snorting," then a grand evocation of the traveler's visions:

[5] Chaps. v, vi, viii, xi, xii.

"It was a vision of long roads. . . . It was a fevered vision of things past and present. . . . A vision of change upon change, and still the same monotony of bells and wheels, and horses' feet, and no rest"—the end of which is repeated six times (chap. lv). The whole passage sounds extremely modern, and the narrative becomes a kind of rhythmic lament. The device is not unlike the technique used in some films. The incidents are not described by the narrator, but merely conveyed to us through the rapid succession of one character's confused perceptions.

In an earlier chapter, a railway journey had been similarly presented, with some grandiloquence, no doubt, but also with great suggestiveness: "Away, with a shriek, and a roar, and a rattle. . . . Away, and still away, onward and onward ever. . . . Away with a shriek and a roar and a rattle. . . . Away once more into the day, and through the day, with a shrill yell of exultation, roaring, rattling, tearing on . . . " (chap. xx). It may be thought that such a description bears the mark of a somewhat naïve emotion in front of the mystery of the railway. But it also provides evidence of a keen sensitiveness to the poetry of rapid motion.[6] That journey is the modern counterpart of Tom Pinch's obsolete stagecoach journey from Salisbury to London, and shows that, since his recent traveling, Dickens has endeavored to adapt himself to the surrounding world and to escape from the magic circle of his childhood remembrances.

Repetition is not the sole device in the "new style." Another more and more frequently recurring method is the transference of feelings—or, at any rate, of their expression—from persons to objects. In the very first scene, at Mrs. Dombey's death, the husband's and the physician's anxiety, their profound silence and the throbbing of their hearts, are not directly described, but suggested by "the loud ticking of Mr. Dombey's watch, and Doctor Parker Peps's watch, which seemed in the silence to be running a race. . . . The race in the ensuing pause was fierce and furious. The watches seemed to jostle, and to trip each other up." Likewise, in Chapter XXIV, the emotion of little Florence on overhearing a conversation about herself is not analyzed, but the flowers she was holding in her hand are seen to drop to the ground, one after the other. Again, when Miss Tox hears of Mr. Dombey's second marriage, only the motions of her scissors

[6] In "Mugby Junction," a Christmas story published in *All the Year Round,* there is a chapter called "The Signalman," which gives a disturbing picture of the power and mystery of railroads.

and her little watering can express her dismay (chap. xxix). The wooden statue over the door of the nautical instruments shop similarly conveys the owner's situation and feelings.

Thus is Dickens' style modified and turned from the easygoing, natural and jovial language used in *Pickwick*, to a more mature, deliberate and artistic medium, and to one that is less clear and fluent. Some passages even acquire an esoteric character through the accumulation of symbolic leitmotivs. The reader must remember precisely when and where each of the leitmotivs had been first introduced, or each of the key phrases—often to be found on the "mems"—in order to understand the later allusions fully. "Very often afterwards, in the midst of their talk, [Paul] would break off, to try to understand what it was that the waves were always saying . . . ."[7] The phrase concerns Paul's illness. Similar references are made with increasing frequency until he is about to die; he then understands what the waves had been saying. Another example of this is Captain Cuttle's "Whittingtonian hopes" about young Walter Gay, a clerk at Dombey and Son's. The phrase can be understood only in connection both with the fate of Dick Whittington, who rose from poverty to the lord mayorship of London, according to the famous ballad, and with the circumstances in which the good captain contemplates his young friend's future.

Lastly, many passages in *Dombey* are written in a seemingly inspired tone, which is at once poetic and almost disquieting because it seems to betray the author's vivid emotion and unbalanced sensibility. A foretaste of this exclamatory style had been given in his apostrophes to Tom Pinch in *Chuzzlewit*.

But the *Chuzzlewit* apostrophes had been tender; in *Dombey* they are for the most part exalted and tragic and suggest the existence in Dickens of the inner tenseness and high pressure that is confirmed by our knowledge of his unsettled life at this time. The final paragraph of almost every chapter belongs to that category. Such is the invocation to Dombey which closes with an almost Shelleyan image: "Oh! could he but have seen, or seen as others did, the slight spare boy above . . . breasting the window of his solitary cage when birds flew by, as if he would have emulated them and soared away!" (chap. xii). And such is the twofold address to Edith

[7] Chap. viii. Other allusions will be found in the title of Chap. xli—"New Voices in the Waves"—and in chap. lvii.

and Florence: "Edith Granger, any song but that! Edith Granger, you are very handsome . . . but not the air that his neglected daughter sang to his dead son! Alas, he knows it not; and if he did, what air of hers could stir him, rigid man! Sleep, lonely Florence, sleep! Peace in thy dreams, although the night has turned dark, and the clouds are gathering, and threaten to discharge themselves in hail!" (chap. xxi) in which, once more, the harmony between ominous events and the life of nature is used with striking effect. It was again Edith whom the author was apostrophizing a little later: "Oh, Edith! It were well to die, indeed, at such a time! Better and happier far, perhaps, Edith, to die so, than to live on to the end!" (chap. xxx). When the death of Mrs. Skewton—Dombey's mother-in-law—draws near, the author exclaims, in a style both esoteric and exalted: "Draw the rose-coloured curtains. There is something else upon its flight besides the wind and clouds. Draw the rose-coloured curtains close!" (chap. xli).

With *Dombey* also begins the phase of Dickens' work in which the death of the characters is to be surrounded by some original imaginative, and poetical aura. When addressing Dombey himself, Dickens stands as an inspired prophet, but his warning is of course all the more tragic because it is not in the nature of things that it should be heard: "Awake, unkind father! Awake, now, sullen man! The time is flitting by; the hour is coming with an angry tread. Awake!" And: "Awake, doomed man, while she is near! The time is flitting by; the hour is coming with an angry tread; its foot is in the house. Awake!" (chap. xliii).

Dickens has thus, from *Pickwick* to *Dombey*, traveled a long distance and achieved a profound metamorphosis of style. Yet, in spite of the presence of that new style, a good deal still links *Dombey* with the preceding books and shows it to be the work of the same hand, especially the two equally characteristic, but mutually contradictory, tendencies to humor and to pathos.

Dombey is not a purely, nor even a markedly, humorous novel. It is actually, apart from *Barnaby Rudge*, the least amusing of the books written thus far by Dickens. There is no observable trace in *Dombey* of the "rollicking facetiousness" the author had believed he was putting in the book.[8] Yet it does arouse the reader's laugh or smile more than once,

---

[8] Forster, *Life of Dickens*, I, 399.

either through the accuracy of its observation, or through the presentation of eccentric characters. Increasing eccentricity is perhaps the dominant feature in this new phase of the Dickensian comedy. Unlike the spontaneous and natural overflow of mirth in *Pickwick*, *Nickleby*, or the most uproarious pages of *Chuzzlewit*, the comic in *Dombey* concerns itself with exceptional incidents, features, or turns of speech. Even so, it achieves delightful results. The style of Susan Nipper, Florence Dombey's maid, with her fondness for negative similes, is palatable, and even faintly redolent of Wellerism: "I may not be Meethosalem, but I am not a child in arms. . . . I may not be a Indian widow, sir, and I am not and I would not so become but if I once made up my mind to burn myself alive, I'd do it!" (chap. xliv). Major Bagstock, with his trick of speaking of himself in the third person and applying to himself all kinds of endearing nicknames, is a truly Dickensian and humorous figure: "'When my friend Dombey, sir,' added the Major, 'talks to you of Major Bagstock, I must crave leave to set him and you right. He means plain Joe, sir—Joey B.—Josh Bagstock—Joseph—rough and tough old Jo, sir. At your service'" (chap. xxvi). A few other figures are just as felicitously presented. Young Toots is, like Tom Pinch, one of the truly appealing simpletons created by Dickens. The first time he meets Walter Gay after the latter has nearly got drowned in a shipwreck, he can only ask him: "How-de-do? I—I—I'm afraid you must have got very wet" (chap. l). Probably the most fascinating invention of all is Mrs. Skewton, a decrepit lady in reduced circumstances, whose affected speech, rich only in spurious and second-rate refinements, almost equals, in its truthfulness, the language spoken lower down in the social scale, by Mrs. Nickleby or Mrs. Gamp.

And the reactions of Dombey's servants, when confronted by the various events in the novel—the first Mrs. Dombey's death, Paul's death, Dombey's second marriage, his second wife's flight, and so forth—are very realistically described and form—deliberately, we shall see—a kind of comic chorus. The servants comment on the tragic incidents in a jocular or resigned tone which makes them seem less distressing, so that their interludes produce a kind of drunken-porter effect.[9]

Dickens the humorist is not, therefore, wholly absent from *Dombey*,

[9] See Chaps. iii, xviii, and lix, particularly.

but Dickens the man of sentimentality and pathos is much more prominently present. The general atmosphere of the book is in fact sentimental and pathetic. Florence Dombey, who may be regarded as the heroine, is not, in spite of her supernatural virtues and precocious perfection, a dull and impassive figure like Little Nell; yet, according to one reader's calculations, she sheds tears no less than eighty-eight times in the novel,[10] and some of her speeches sound as unnatural and melodramatic to our ears as the constant flow of her tears becomes irksome. When, as a married woman and happy mother, she comes back to her ruined, invalid father, she implores him in language that does not ring true: "Papa, dear, I am changed, I am penitent. I know my fault. I know my duty better now. Papa, don't cast me off, or I shall die!" (chap. lix). This seems to owe more to the false language of theatrical melodrama than to real life.

Nor does Florence monopolize such expressions and feelings. There is in *Dombey* a set of characters of exasperating dullness and unreality, so that the reader's heart sinks whenever they appear in the novel. John Carker is the brother of Dombey and Son's commercial manager. Because he had in his youth embezzled some money belonging to the firm, John Carker is doomed to occupy an inferior position as "Junior Clerk" in the firm—which enables Dickens to call him Carker the Junior, though he is the elder brother, a kind of effect that Dickens was inordinately fond of, but which is not inexhaustible—and to become converted to humble and penitent holiness. His sister Harriet devotes her life to him, and that is almost an additional part of his punishment, for she is utterly devoid of liveliness and spontaneity.[11] Morfin is another saintly person in the employment of Dombey and Son, and will eventually marry Harriet. Alice Marwood, formerly the mistress of Carker the Manager and later the inmate of a common prison, dies in drab repentance declaring: "Evil courses, and remorse, travel, want and weather, storm within, and storm without, have worn my life away. It will not last much longer" (chap. lviii). The reader is likely to welcome that announcement with a shout of relief, rather than subscribe to the praise of the whole episode by one of its actors who states, in language character-

[10] See "Letters to the Editor," *The Dickensian*, Oct., 1925.
[11] See the dreadfully boring scene in chap. xxxiii.

istic of the whole group's superhuman modesty: "I have no right to mar the end of a great history by any obtrusion of my weak self" (chap. lviii). George Gissing, a shrewd and generally well-disposed critic of Dickens, says of Alice Marwood that "a figure less life-like will not be found in any novel ever written."[12] He might have used similar terms about the other members of the lugubrious circle.

Two of the major characters deserve, at least in part, the same kind of criticism. Edith Granger, the widow who becomes the second Mrs. Dombey, is a cold, proud, haughty creature. The presentation of her personality is unconvincing, in spite of Dickens' feeble attempts at psychological analysis. She performs two unaccountable actions. She marries Dombey—as Mercy Pecksniff had married Jonas[13]—without loving him, without harboring any illusions as to their mutual feelings or their chances of happiness in matrimony, which are nonexistent, and, therefore, without any real motive. In fact, she marries him without any apparent motive other than the technical convenience of the union, needed by Dickens in view of the later tragedy. On the eve of the wedding, she is still analyzing her suitor's attitude with a clear-sightedness which would have caused any normal human being to beat a retreat: "You know he has bought me. . . . He has considered of his bargain . . . he thinks it will suit him, and may be had sufficiently cheap. . . . God, that I have lived for this, and that I feel it!" (chap. xxvii). After this nothing can justify her acceptance of such a repellent marriage. Her later allusions to the psychological motivation of her acts remain hazy and obscure: "I have dreamed . . . of a pride that has been galled and goaded, through many shameful years, and has never recoiled except upon itself . . . ."[14]

After a few months' unhappy wedlock, she runs away with Carker the manager, a servile, abject man, whom she hates and despises more than anybody else and whom she has selected, it would seem, for that

12 Ch. Dickens, Critical Study, 86.

13 And as, later, in HT, Louisa Gradgrind marries Bounderby.

14 Chap. xliii. Before or after her speech, the comment made by Percy Fitzgerald (*Life of Dickens*, II, 231) is unquestionably valid: "her case is altogether disposed of by the question: What or who compelled her to accept the husband who was so odious to her? Nothing—No one!" Wilkie Collins (*Pall Mall Gazette*, Jan. 20, 1890) says: "That the same man who could create Nancy [in OT] created the second Mrs. Dombey is the most incomprehensible anomaly that I know of in literature."

very reason. But she refuses to give herself to him.[15] In the French inn where she finds herself alone with him for the first time, she melodramatically threatens to kill him if he comes near her. The artificiality of that unintelligible scene is enhanced by the stupendously conventional language in which it is couched: " 'Too late!' she cried, with eyes that seemed to sparkle fire. . . . He would have sold his soul to root her, in her beauty, to the floor. . . . 'Strumpet, it's false,' cried Carker."[16] Dickens certainly intended to make Edith moving and her fate interesting to the reader, but he has signally failed to do so. Without the shadow of a convincing motive, she is no more than a cruel and perverse woman, who ruins the career of one man by marrying him without love and refusing to yield to his will, and then causes the death of another, whom she hates, by giving him the dangerous appearance of being her lover. She is above all inexplicable, because Dickens stopped short of the normal consequences of his bold original conceptions regarding her, for reasons that will be seen later.

The case of little Paul Dombey is different. That puny, sickly child, who seems to have been suggested to Dickens by the example of his nephew Harry Burnett,[17] is a fairly promising creation at the beginning of the novel. By making him precociously shrewd, the writer opened up certain comic potentialities.[18] But he lapsed all too soon into the quest for pathos, early foreshadowing his sad fate: " 'That's what I mean to do, when I—' He stopped and pondered for a moment. Mrs. Pipchin's grey eye scanned his thoughtful face. 'If I grow up,' said Paul" (chap. xiv). Then, again under the influence of his impending doom, Paul's figure becomes idealized and a saintly halo can be seen to grow around his head, while his premature death approaches. He decides to be "a gentle, useful, quiet little fellow, always striving to secure the love and attachment of the rest . . . modestly rendering . . . some little voluntary service" (chap. xv). Yet, when Paul's death itself is reached in Chapter XVI, it is written

[15] It will be seen that Jeffrey was responsible for Edith's failure to become Carker's mistress.

[16] Chap. liv. I have found no example of the obsolete and theatrical word "strumpet" being used by Dickens elsewhere.

[17] Harry was the son of Fanny, Dickens' musical sister, whom he loved tenderly, and who died of tuberculosis while *D&S* was in progress.

[18] See, in chap. xii, the conversation with Mrs. Pipchin.

in a peculiar style, not unlike that of the *Copperfield* "Retrospects," which is a sure sign of the author's vivid emotion. In spite of a cheap joke in a letter to Forster—"Paul, I shall slaughter at the end of number five"[19]— it is undeniable that when he wrote the chapter, Dickens was profoundly upset. He says in the preface: "When I am reminded by any chance of what it was that the waves were always saying, I wander in my fancy for a whole winter night about the streets of Paris—as I really did, with a heavy heart, on the night when my little friend and I parted company for ever." It should be noted that the chapter was completed on the eve of Forster's arrival in Paris, and that the expectation of two weeks' keen enjoyments must have facilitated the rise in Dickens of the suitable emotional attitude for his narrative. For, with him, vivid personal joy and vivid literary sadness had their roots in the same intense sentimental exaltation.

Dickens' emotion, as in the case of Little Nell's demise, proved infectious. Oceans of tears were shed by contemporary readers. The testimony of Thackeray, who was at the time bringing out the monthly installments of his first major work of fiction, *Vanity Fair*, is particularly striking: "There's no writing against this," he told Mark Lemon, "one hasn't an atom of a chance; it's stupendous."[20] The modern reader's emotion is not likely to be quite so vehement, for the part played by literary artifice in the episode will probably be more clearly felt, while the later exploitation of the event, and the sentimental blackmailing practiced by Florence, will be resented. Once she has married Walter Gay and brought forth a child, she goes to her father and implores him: "A boy, papa. His name is Paul. I think—I hope—he's like. . . . Dear papa, for the sake of my child, for the sake of the name we have given him, for my sake, pardon Walter . . . " (chap. lix). The place held by pathos in *Dombey* is considerable, and while it was the occasion of the author's self-satisfaction,[21] it also accounts for the less enthusiastic judgments passed by posterity.[22]

[19] Forster, *Life of Dickens*, II, 30.

[20] See Pope-Hennessy, *Ch. Dickens*, 251. Thackeray, it should be remembered, had been one of the few readers unaffected by Nell's pathos.

[21] See letter quoted by Forster (*Life of Dickens*, II, 61–62): "I have a strong belief that if any of my books are read years hence, *Dombey* will be remembered as among the best of them."

[22] Usually echoing Wilkie Collins' unindulgent opinion (*Pall Mall Gazette*, Jan. 20,

Dickens was pleased with his achievement in *Dombey*, but the un-precedented circumstances under which he had worked on that book—it was begun in Switzerland, continued in France, and completed in England—caused him to become conscious of some facts concerning his inspiration. He felt for the first time, for instance, that he could not work efficiently unless he lived in a crowded city.[23] He told Forster how stupendously difficult he found it to settle down to his work in Lausanne: "I suppose it is partly the effect of two years' ease, and partly of the ab-sence of streets and numbers of figures. I can't express how much I want these. It seems as if they supplied something to my brain, which it cannot bear, when busy, to lose ... the toil and labour of writing, day after day, without that magic lantern, is IMMENSE!"[24] A few days later, he re-verted to that point: "The absence of any accessible streets continues to worry me ... in a most singular manner. It is quite a little mental phe-nomenon. ... I don't seem able to get rid of my spectres unless I can lose them in crowds."[25] Well could he speak of a "mental phenomenon," which it is difficult to account for in a perfectly sane and balanced mind. But perhaps it was in part an illusion around which he concentrated and crystalized all the growing difficulty he found in the act of writing, be-cause he did not like to confess to himself that his inspiration had become less steady, more fitful.

Many incidents betrayed the comparative drying-up of a hitherto prodigiously fertile vein. Saddened confessions abound in the letters written to Forster at that time. It is made clear that it had become im-possible for Dickens to write rapidly: "You can hardly imagine what infinite pains I take, or what extraordinary difficulty I find in getting on FAST. Invention, thank God, seems the easiest thing in the world. ... But the difficulty of going at what I call a rapid pace, is prodigious: it is almost an impossibility."[26] The phrase about invention seems to have been introduced by Dickens in order to reassure himself. Nor does the usual verbal inflation, working both ways—infinite, extraordinary,

1890): "The latter part of Dombey no intelligent person can have read without astonish-ment at the badness of it."
    23 See Forster, *Life of Dickens*, I, 333–34.
    24 *Ibid.*, 420 (Aug. 30, 1846).
    25 *Ibid.*
    26 *Ibid.*, 419.

prodigious—leave us free to attach much literal significance to the words "the easiest thing in the world."

Later on, in Paris, the situation became worse: "Couldn't begin, in the strange place . . . sat six hours at a stretch, and wrote as many lines."[27] Because he found it just as difficult to work on his Christmas Book, *The Battle of Life*, and because Paris could hardly be regarded as having too few streets and people in it, Dickens now endeavored to convince himself that the source of his uneasiness lay in the strain of having simultaneously begun two narratives, although he had earlier written *Oliver Twist* simultaneously with *Pickwick* or *Nickleby* blithely enough, or at any rate without anything like the present despondency. The tone of his letters grew more anguished than ever:

> Up to Wednesday or Thursday last, I really contemplated at times, the total abandonment of the Christmas book this year. . . . I cancelled the beginning of a first scene—which I had never done before—[28]

> I am going to write you a most startling piece of intelligence. I fear there may be NO CHRISTMAS BOOK! . . . I have written nearly a third of it. . . . I am fearful of wearing myself out if I go on, and not being able to come back to the greater undertaking with the necessary freshness and spirit. If I had nothing but the Christmas book to do, I WOULD do it, but I get horrified and distressed beyond conception at the prospect of being jaded when I get back to the other . . . my soul sinks before the commencement of the second part. . . . I suppose it is the having been almost constantly at work in this quiet place; the dread of the *Dombey*. . . . The beginning two books together is also, no doubt, a fruitful source of the difficulty. . . . I am sick, giddy, and capriciously despondent . . . .[29]

Again, there is a good deal of verbal inflation here, but a few phrases have a new ring in them, and sound moving and significant.

In the days of *Pickwick*, Dickens had never had reason to fear that he might become worn out or jaded, and his calling had been to him

[27] *Ibid.,* 447.
[28] *Ibid.,* 421–22 (Sept. 20, 1846).
[29] *Ibid.,* 422–23 (Sept. 26, 1846).

mostly a source of joy, not of horror, distress and despondency. His present attitude is in one sense more natural and normal, but it must have been disheartening to him to feel the change. Certainly the difficult beginnings of *Chuzzlewit* had undermined his self-confidence, and the inordinate expense of creative energy, uninterrupted from 1836 through 1841, seemed to him to have squandered his faculties. The Christmas book was written in due time; yet Dickens could hardly fail to realize, however reluctantly, that neither the absence of streets and crowds nor the presence of two works in progress on his desk were at the root of the matter. It was, instead, a decrease in his powers, stupendous as they still were. When Forster advised him against postponing to Number II of *Dombey* a chapter that was too long to go into Number I, and to substitute a shorter chapter for it, he admitted: "I had been counting, alas! with a miser's greed, upon the gained ten pages."[30] Before publishing the first part of *Dombey* in October, 1846, he had written two complete installments. It was the first time he had insisted on placing himself thus ahead of the printer. His purpose had even been to have three numbers ready and to preserve his advantage all the way through. But it was soon frittered away and, from Number III on, reduced to nothing.

In the midst of such difficulties and anxieties, Dickens was not deserted by his most faithful friend and comrade. The letters of that period disclose once more Dickens' implicit reliance on Forster and his judgment. He was forever requesting his advice and taking it. For his Christmas book he left Forster free to decide on the historical background to be given it, saying: "I ease myself of it by throwing it out to you."[31] He adopted alterations suggested by his friend and wrote: "I am glad you like the alterations. I feel that they made it complete, and that it would have been incomplete without your suggestions."[32] For *Dombey* also, he was eager to have Forster's opinion about every detail of the work: "This question of [Walter] is very important. . . . Let me hear all you think about it."[33] And he trusted him about the cutting of the proofs: "I have taken out about two pages and a half,

30 *Ibid.*, II, 23 (Aug. 9, 1846).
31 *Ibid.*, I, 435 (Oct. 29, 1848).
32 *Ibid.*, 437 (Nov. 21, 1848).
33 *Ibid.*, II, 21 (July 25, 1846).

and the rest I must ask you to take out with the assurance that you will satisfy me in whatever you do."[34]

The principle of such consultations was no novelty in Dickens' career. On the contrary it has been seen that his desire to be informed of his friends' and his readers' reactions had influenced his adoption of the periodical mode of publication. The history of *Dombey* provides two striking instances of his wish to adapt himself to the reader's tastes and demands. It has been observed that Edith's conduct when she ran away with Carker and yet refused to be his mistress was incoherent and improbable. It becomes less so when one finds that the author's original purpose had been different, and that Edith had at first been meant to become Carker's mistress. But no sooner had he, in Number XIV, laid the ground for the adultery, than he received a letter from Lord Jeffrey and wrote to Forster in consequence: "Note from Jeffrey this morning [December 21, 1847] who won't believe (positively refuses) that Edith is Carker's mistress." And, at once deferring to the objection of the veteran critic, Dickens modified his plans: "What do you think," his letter to Forster went on to explain, "of a kind of inverted Maid's Tragedy, and a tremendous scene of her undeceiving Carker, and giving him to know that she never meant that." To which, in the *Life of Dickens*, Forster merely adds: "So it was done."[35] So it was done, indeed, in a way. But the scene in the inn at Dijon can hardly be called "tremendous." It is rather bombastic and incredible. Yet the point is that Dickens had not dared to disregard the opinion of one reader he respected, and had altered the purport of a significant episode in his novel, making Edith explain that "she had never meant" what Dickens had in fact meant her to mean.

In another case, a similar scruple is still more openly avowed. About Walter Gay, Florence Dombey's prospective husband, who put in an appearance as early as Number I, Dickens was writing to Forster as follows:

> About the boy . . . I think it would be a good thing to disappoint all the expectations that chapter seems to raise of his happy con-

[34] *Ibid.*, 30 (Nov., 1846). See also, *infra*, Forster's alterations in the description of Paul's christening.
[35] *Ibid.*, 34.

nection with the story and the heroine, and to show him gradually and naturally trailing away, from that love of adventure and boyish light-heartedness, into negligence, idleness, dissipation, dishonesty and ruin . . . to show how the good turns into bad, by degrees. If I kept some little notion of Florence always at the bottom of it, I think it might be made very powerful and very useful. What do you think? Do you think it may be done, without making people angry?[36]

The final phrase is of peculiar significance. Dickens was reluctant to displease his readers. And his fear—which results mainly from his need of mutual sympathy and his desire to be loved—is the key to many changes of purpose and other technical weaknesses in his fiction, judged by modern standards. In order to understand these weaknesses completely, the psychology of the Victorian public and the way in which Dickens regarded that public ought to be taken into account, for the novels were directly addressed to them in the hope of gaining their affection quite as much as their admiration.

Of the final disclosure of that kind yielded by Dickens' correspondence with Forster, it can be said that it illustrates, not merely the novelist's acceptance of his readers' desires, but the perfect coincidence of his own desires with theirs. At the end of the book, he was horrified to perceive that he had forgotten to settle the fate of no less a character than Diogenes, a dog that had been friendly to both Paul and Florence Dombey. While he was correcting the last batch of proofs, Forster received the following appeal:

> I suddenly remember that I have forgotten Diogenes. Will you put him in the last little chapter? After the word 'favourite' in reference to Miss Tox, you can add, 'except with Diogenes, who is growing old and wilful.' Or, on the last page of all, after 'and with them two children, boy and girl' (I quote from memory), you might say 'and an old dog is generally in their company,' or to that effect. Just what you think best.[37]

Forster chose the second solution (chap. lxii).

There is more information extant about Dickens' work on the com-

[36] *Ibid.*, 21.
[37] *Ibid.*, 34 (March 25, 1848).

position and writing of *Dombey* than about any preceding novel. Besides the particulars provided by the letters to Forster—themselves more numerous because the novelist was away from London at the time—nineteen sheets of memorandums have been bound together with the manuscript. Both on account of the increasing fitfulness of his inspiration and because of his growing concern with technical problems, Dickens had been led to organize his work more methodically. This is shown by his final adoption of a system of preparatory notes. Since the *Dombey* "mems" are the earliest complete set to have been preserved, they deserve close examination and afford an interesting view of the writer's creative process.

Each sheet corresponds to one monthly number and is composed of two sections. On the left-hand side is a list of notions set down in the order in which they occurred to the author's mind: new characters, psychological evolutions, proper names, incidents, significant phrases, etc. On the right-hand side, the number in the making is divided into chapters, complete with numerals and headings, and Dickens has set down the contents of each chapter in chronological order. The aspect of the "mems" suggests that Dickens would first fill up the left-hand portion, partly, it would seem, while he was still writing the preceding number, partly at a later date. He would next decide on the number of chapters in the forthcoming installment, divide his material into chapters, and then write the chapters according to the plan thus outlined. It is fairly certain that, while he was writing a part of his novel, Dickens would keep the relevant sheet of "mems" at hand and under his eyes, so that the "mems" bear the marks of his hesitations and doubts and of every stage in his creative work.

The value of such documents is revealed in the very first sheet. On the left-hand side is to be found, for instance, the phrase "boy born; to die," which confirms that Paul Dombey's death was one of the novelist's earliest ideas for the new novel. A few lines down, Mrs. Chick, Dombey's sister, is described by an admirable phrase, which does not appear in the text of the novel itself, but corresponds to her character throughout the narrative: "Mrs. Chick, common-minded family humbug." For the title of Chapter I, it will be seen that Dickens had temporarily discarded the form he finally chose—"Dombey and Son"—in favor of a longer one

—"In Which Dombey and Son Are Presented to the Reader," thus show-ing himself from the very beginning divided between his new taste for the concise and his older fondness for the explicit.

In the second sheet of "mems," Dickens is seen to give directions to himself, on the left-hand side, as though he were addressing a sub-ordinate in his capacity as editor of a periodical or a series: "Make child-ish romance of Florence being found by Walter." On the right-hand side, the summary of Chapter VI comprises a mere brief note, explan-atory of its title: "Chapter VI. Paul's Second Deprivation. That is, his nurse." The left-hand part of the third sheet is entitled: "General mems for No. 3" and contains hints concerning the creation of Mrs. Pipchin—who keeps a boardinghouse in Bath. Dickens had first written "Mrs. Roylance," which was the real name of a lady in London, in whose house he had spent a few weeks as a child, while his father was in prison, then added "house at the sea-side," and finally groped for a suitable name for her: "Mrs. Wrychin, Mrs. Alchin, Mrs. Somchin, Tipchin" before hitting on Pipchin. Two incidents are mentioned, which Dickens de-cided not to make use of in the current number: "Miss Tox's party. Her uncle the magistrate. The Major. To stand over." They have stood over so long that neither Miss Tox's party, nor her uncle, appear in the novel. Likewise: "Carker. Offices in the City. To stand over." But this time, the introduction was indeed only postponed. A key phrase rel-ative to little Paul's impressions was then written down: "As if he had taken life unfurnished, and the upholsterer were never coming" though it was not inserted into Number III.[38]

In the fourth sheet, Dickens was once more giving himself precise directions, usually about points that would demand subtle treatment, as in the following phrase: "Paul's gradually increasing coldness to his father and closer and closer inclining towards his sister." He even gave himself the curt command, "Send Walter to the West Indies." In the summary of Chapter XIV Dickens debated with himself: "Paul's illness only expressed in the child's own feelings. News of Paul's illness. No. Not otherwise described." And for the next chapter, he was asking him-self regarding Captain Cuttle: "Qy. Introduce his friend Bunsby," and energetically replying to himself: "Not yet."

[38] It was put aside, and comes in at the end of chap. xi (No. IV).

The "mems" of Number VI, which followed Paul's death, began, interestingly, with the general principle: "Great point of the number. To throw the interest at once on Florence. Not to make too much of the scene with the father, or it may be too painful." While, for the seventh number, Dickens gave himself terse advice: "Take care of the Major."

For the next number (Number VII) a certain amount of wavering is observable. This was a difficult moment in the plot. Dombey was at Leamington, courting Edith. It was necessary to impress upon the reader an idea that the courting lasted for some time, and that there was in both Dombey and Edith some psychological evolution before they thought of marriage. How could the interval be occupied? Dickens toyed with several notions which he discarded one after the other. Thus one reads on the left-hand side: "Carker going down to Leamington? No. 9—Or Mrs. Skewton in the Major's dining-room? No. 9—To Mr. Carker the Junior and his sister? Uncle Sol to die? No—Run away, to look after Walter." The last-mentioned item alone was retained for the current number, and Uncle Sol's disappearance—he is Walter Gay's uncle —was in the novel surrounded with complete mystery, to be elucidated years later, so that the unpublished phrase of the "mems" remains once more the single proof of Dickens' premeditation at that point. Other suggestions are also listed, more or less perfunctorily, but not introduced into the text: "Pipchin. Blimbers. Good Mrs. Brown. Mr. Feeder and Mr. Toots." The list sounds like a reserve battalion of characters to be kept available in case the main incidents of the number, each of which must form one chapter, proved insufficiently bulky.

For Number IX, Dickens set himself the following task: "To bring on the marriage gradually. Connect Carker with Edith *before the wedding*." And over against the summary of Chapter XXVI on the right-hand side, he wrote down and underlined the two words "very important" in front of the phrase, which he had also underlined, "First interview between Carker and Edith." The notes concerning Number X began with a question of internal economy which it is rather surprising to find Dickens raising even before the incidents had been selected: "Qy. Two chapters or three? THREE." Then came a characteristic phrase which does not belie the impression produced by the novel—

that Miss Tox's transformation is very sudden and arbitrary. At the beginning of the novel, she had been but one of the brazen-faced, consistent toadies that Dickens had often complacently depicted.[39] He now suggests: "Miss Tox to dawn as an *honest* toady, in so far as Mr. Dombey is concerned." The verb "dawn" is significant. The belated dawning of the truth about a character hitherto misunderstood—through the first half of the book—looks suspiciously like extemporization, especially as the later part ascribed to Miss Tox makes it obvious that her transformation was necessary for technical rather than psychological reasons.

"Mr. Carker the Junior and his sister" were then named again. They were the tedious pair whose dread virtues have been mentioned above. The novelist may have felt that it would have been ill-advised to introduce them into an installment already likely to be deficient in vitality. In any case, he could not please himself with the episode and postponed it for the second time—to the "Next No." Finally he gave a clear definition of the device he was using when he made the Dombey servants comment on the events: "Carry on the servants as a sort of odd chorus to the story." All three chapters of that number are summarized in detail on the right-hand side. Another conscious device is hinted at in the opening section of the "mems" for Number X:

> Mr. Carker the Manager
> &
> Mr. Carker the Junior
> with Harriet   Companion pictures.

Increased nervousness is disclosed by the sequel of those notes, which comprise many questions: "Mr. Toots and the Chicken. Qy. Good Mrs. Brown and *her daughter*. Qy. Any news of Uncle Sol. Qy. Mr. Morfin. Qy." To the second and fourth queries Dickens replied in the affirmative and each "Yes" is underlined three times—and for Mr. Morfin, he added "with a view to the future," thus giving further evidence of his firm control over the outline of the plot. On the right-hand side, he evinced once more his growing fondness for contrasts, of which there are two in that one installment: "Indication of a contrast to Mrs. Skewton and Edith." His quest for greater subtlety also led him to undertake difficult

---

[39] See the whole Kenwigs family in *NN*.

tasks. "The altered home and its expression, as it were, of Edith" at the beginning of the twelfth sheet was something that could not easily be conveyed to the average reader. Meanwhile, as he proceeded with his narrative, the novelist became more excited, and his characters more real to him. This is shown by the two following notes: "Florence's purpose. Remember her old loneliness, and observe her present state of mind"; and "Be patient with Carker. Get him on very slowly, without incident."

The next sheets contain but little fresh information about Dickens at work. They are made up mainly of incidents suggested and adopted or rejected. However, the left-hand page of Number XIII is worth quoting because it closes, a very rare occurrence, with a note concerning the following number, jotted down probably because the idea had cropped up unexpectedly and the sheet lay on the desk: "Open next No. with Carker at home." The right-hand page closed with a phrase characteristic of the circumstances under which Dickens worked: "Qy. Cousin Feenix and the Mausoleum. Yes. ROOM ENOUGH." He had conceived something that he thought valuable, but was content to give it up if it could not be introduced without modifying other parts of his narrative.

The summary of Chapter XLV (No. XIV) yields the following note: "Carker and Edith. The last view of them before the elopement. She relenting." It is through such phrases, when they are compared with the published text, that the "mems" seem to take us offstage and into the wings of the Dickensian novel. Nothing in the printed version of the chapter foreshadows the elopement of Edith with Carker, unless perhaps one perceives a subtle change in the atmosphere of their interview. But Dickens had made a note of his purpose because he wanted to make their words more solemn and, also, to avoid introducing into their conversation anything that might, in the light of later events, appear unlikely or shocking.

The fifteenth sheet comprises one mystery: Dickens has inserted into it a change of plan he had adopted while writing the chapters themselves. In principle, and no doubt in practice also, the use of the number plans was all directed toward the future, toward the making of the number in progress. It is therefore intriguing to find a note like the

following: "Mem. The Thunderbolt Chapter [XLVII] originally intended for the last of the No. and the middle chapter [XLVIII] meant
to have led up—But the Thunderbolt Chapter being written first, plan
altered to leave a pleasanter impression upon the reader." Brief and dry
as it is, that note provides ample food for thought. It shows that Dickens
had departed from his usual practice by writing the final chapter of a
number before the "middle chapter," perhaps out of impatience, perhaps because he wanted to make sure of having "elbow-room" for his
Thunderbolt, and to develop it harmoniously, without having to take
into account the printer's demands.

It is obvious that Dickens' purpose had been to write later only what
would both fill up the space left free in the number and "lead up to the
Thunderbolt." It is equally obvious that after having written the dramatic chapter, he was almost frightened by his own achievement and
the impression it was going to produce. He gave up the chapter of transition—thereby making his thunderbolt all the more violent and brutal
—but he completed the number, after disclosing the elopement and showing Dombey's dismissal of Florence, by means of a quieter chapter in
which Florence and Captain Cuttle appeared. All of which is interesting,
understandable, and coherent. What is more disconcerting is the presence of the above-quoted note in the "mems." If the memoranda were
truly what their name literally means—things, ideas and facts to be
remembered—the precaution taken here, of writing down, after the
event, one particular incident in the composition, falls outside their normal scope. But perhaps Dickens wanted to make his "mems" historical
as well as prospective and preparatory. At any rate, though Forster does
not explain how and when the thing was done, the "mems" have been
collected and bound together with the relevant manuscripts, apparently
by Dickens himself, who may have felt that he had gained a sufficient
footing in the literature of his country for even slight circumstances in
the genesis of his works to be memorable and worthy of a place in the
memoranda. Curiously enough, the "mems" were to be ignored, although
they had been advertised by Forster, for some eighty years before Dickensian criticism began to exploit them and to find in them a storehouse
of information about the development of Dickens' craftsmanship.

A choice item is a sheet mistakenly attached to the plan for Number

VI, which ought in fact to precede that for Number XVI. It is a note entitled "Florence's Age mems." When he was about to present to the reader a love scene between Florence Dombey and Walter Gay, shortly before their marriage, Dickens felt he must calculate the heroine's age—of which, in common with his readers, he had only a hazy notion—and make sure that she was not too young. He began with laying down retrospectively, the principle that in Number VI "Florence was little more than a child—not yet fourteen." Then he summed up the various periods of time that had elapsed since Number VI, and ascribed to each an approximate duration. He wrote, for instance: "After that comes their journey to Paris, and their return home, and their dinner-party . . . and Mrs. Skewton's first attack of paralysis—say, in all, a space of six months." He thus concluded: "Making Florence in No. XV nearly seventeen," after which he added a paragraph whose tone of objective observation and pleased surprise is rather amusing: "Before Mr. Carker goes down to Leamington, and there meets the Major and Mr. Dombey's intended, Uncle Sol disappears. And a year is said to have taken place between Uncle Sol's disappearance and Mrs. Skewton's first attack of paralysis, which seems to agree perfectly with this calculation."

For Number XVII, Dickens gave himself impressionistic directions as to the way in which the atmosphere of the narrative was to be treated. The number was to contain the pursuit of Carker by Dombey and Carker's death at the very moment when Dombey overtakes him. "Still carry Mr. Dombey's pursuit through," he had written on the left-hand side; and on the right-hand side, in the summary of Chapter LIII: "Pursuit ending still carried through, quick and fierce." And again, in the summary of Chapter LIV: "Pursuit still carried through, quick and fierce."

For the final double number, which must unwind every tangle and settle the fate of all the characters, the "mems" had to be particularly abundant. After the list of incidents to be included, came the question: "Qy. Order of chapters." The summary of Chapter LIX is cryptic and can be understood only through comparison with the text of the novel. Dickens must have been both weary and excited and did not take the trouble to formulate his ideas in a way that could be understood by any-one but himself: "Truth of Miss Tox. Verge of suicide. FLORENCE."

"Verge of suicide" refers, not to Miss Tox, but to the ill and ruined Dombey. Florence's name tersely refers at once to Dombey's most frequently recurring thoughts and to his daughter's final apparition. The plan of Chapter LXII was significantly modified when it came to be written, and the "mems" reveal that Dickens had originally intended to close the book with a reference to the symbolic theme connected with little Paul Dombey: "End with the sea—carrying through what the waves were always saying, and the invisible country far away." But for that conclusion he substituted, when he wrote the last pages, a more sober picture of Dombey's tenderness for his granddaughter.

The corrected proofs of *Dombey* confirm the impression created by those of the *Curiosity Shop*. *Dombey,* like the other novels published in monthly installments, had to consist of exactly thirty-two pages each month. On one occasion, the number had been underwritten, and two whole pages had to be extemporized to supply the deficiency. But on the whole, there was too much rather than too little matter in the proofs, and many cancellations had to be effected by Forster and Dickens. Unfortunately, the bound volume of corrected proofs does not seem to contain the earliest set. For a few monthly parts, like the first, two successive sets of proofs have been collected. But for most others, the paucity of corrections tends to show that the preserved set was a late one—the second or even the third set of proofs—and closer to the published text than to the manuscript version.

The early parts of *Dombey* are the most interesting to examine at proof stage. In its original form, Number I was thirty-eight instead of thirty-two pages long. It was cut down to the required size through two series of deletions effected first by Dickens, then by Forster. The magnitude of the necessary sacrifice, amounting to one-fifth of the installment, suggests in itself that valuable material must inevitably have gone by the board. In fact, many of the cancelled sentences were as felicitous as those that were preserved. Such is the case with a paragraph about Dombey's religious position:

> That hope deferred, which as the Scripture tells us (very correctly tells us, Mr. Dombey would have added in a patronising way; for his highest idea even of Scripture, if examined, would have been

found to be, that as forming part of a general whole, of which Dombey and Son formed another part, it was therefore to be commended and upheld) maketh the heart sick.[40]

The note of irreverence sounding through that paragraph may not have survived Forster's correcting, for he was uncompromising on that point. In the description of Paul Dombey's christening (chap. v), Forster cancelled a joke characteristic of Dickens' imagination, but which his friend no doubt thought both impious and macabre: "The font—a rigid marble basin which seemed to have been playing a church-yard game at cup and ball with its matter-of-fact pedestal, and to have been just that moment caught on top of it." And in the course of the same chapter several changes were made by Forster—there are references to those changes in the letters from Dickens published in the *Life*—to forestall a possible charge of irreligious spirit. When the clergyman conducts the christening service, Dickens had written "in delivering the closing exhortation," but Forster inserted "very unaffectedly and simply." A little later, Forster wrote the whole of the following paragraph, in an attempt to tone down the impression that the ceremony was being sacrilegiously and irreverently caricatured: "It might have been well for Mr. Dombey if he had thought of his own dignity a little less; and had thought of the great purpose and origin of the ceremony, in which he took so formal and so stiff a part, a little more. His arrogance contrasted strangely with its history."[41] It can thus be seen that Forster's contribution to the development of Dickens' novel was not wholly negative.

Among the mutilations undergone by the first number, a humorous phrase addressed by Mrs. Chick to her husband is also worth quoting. She was taking him to task because he hummed a tune at an unsuitable moment, and charged him with conducting himself "more like a professional singer with the hydrophobia than a man in your station of life" (chap. ii). Other cancellations, however, ought to occasion no similar regrets. For instance, there was a rather long paragraph of psychological analysis in which Dickens had attempted mercilessly to

40 Unpublished; Forster Collection.
41 Those lines are inserted in Forster's hand on the proofs. It is possible that they had been sent him by Dickens in a letter, now lost, and were merely copied out by Forster. Yet nothing in the style and tone of the sentence, or in Dickens' artistic scruples, precludes the suggestion that Forster was the author of the insert.

disclose Dombey's secret thoughts when he was engaging a wet nurse for his son. The first section was deleted by himself and the rest by Forster:

> "It would be harsh, and perhaps not altogether true, to say of him that he felt these rubs and gratings against his pride more keenly than he had felt his wife's death: but certainly they impressed that event upon him with added weight and bitterness. It was a rude shock to his sense of property in his own child, that these people— the mere dust of the earth, as he thought them—should be necessary to him . . ." (chap. ii).

A charwoman employed by the novelist's mother-in-law while young Charley Dickens was ill, once asked: "Lawk ma'am! Is the young gentleman upstairs the son of the man who put together *Dombey*?" and eventually confessed to the cause of her incredulous surprise: "Lawk ma'am! I thought that three or four men must have put together *Dombey*!"[42] The good woman no doubt meant the remark to be complimentary and to convey her admiration of a gigantic work of art. Yet her phrase might be regarded as justified in another way, for *Dombey*, like some of the preceding works, may be regarded as deficient in unity, as though the complex multitude of incidents in it had been "put together" by three or four different writers. Some weaknesses in the construction of the book lend support to such a view. Dickens, for instance, was not very fair to his reader when he quoted a newspaper report concerning Walter Gay's ship as saying, "There can be no doubt . . . that every soul on board perished" (chap. xxxii), for the young man reappeared later, sound in wind and limb. A question asked by James Carker, the manager, of his brother John, "Well, John Carker, what brings you here?" (chap. xlvi), remains unanswered to any practical purpose and thus only stresses the real cause for the visit, i.e. the author's need for such a conversation between the two brothers in order to disclose the history of their relationship. Elsewhere, when Florence finds shelter in Captain Cuttle's house, we are told that "her little stock of money amounted to but a few guineas" (chap. xlix). Yet we are likely to be surprised at the magnitude, not the smallness of the sum, considering that when

---

[42] See Forster, *Life of Dickens*, I, 454.

she came down from her room for the last time, the girl did not even intend to go out of her father's house. The reason why she had supplied herself with several guineas remains wrapped in mystery. Dickens more than once resorts to the usual secret cousinship revealed at the last minute: "Show me Mrs. Dombey" says the mother of lugubrious Alice Marwood, "and I'll show you my Alice's first cousin" (chap. lviii). As to the final chapters, they contain the traditional concatenation of grossly improbable incidents, due to the charitable purpose of rewarding the good and organizing the closing procession.[43]

Yet such details do not affect the essential aspects of the construction, which is distinguished from the preceding works by a clear progression. Dickens' fondness for intricate plots has not vanished. He even thinks them inevitable. When he expounded to Forster the outline of his narrative, he made haste to add: "So I mean to carry the story on, through all the branches and offshoots and meanderings that come up." And also: "That is what the cooks call 'the stock of the soup.' All kinds of things will be added to it, of course."[44] Such expressions as "branches," "offshoots," "meanderings," "come up," and particularly "of course," are revealing. Yet they do not mean that Dickens had failed to give serious thought to the technical problems of making novels, or to perceive the advantages of unity. In 1847, during the progress of *Dombey*, he penned a new preface for *Pickwick*, in which he made the following statement: "Experience and study afterwards taught me something, and I could perhaps wish now that these chapters were strung together on a stronger thread of general interest."

In *Dombey* itself, however, it is not a single guiding thread that is found throughout, but a close web of threads connecting the various characters and episodes together. The plot of the book is characterized by these manifold links. The different sections of the tale first seem to develop independently, and the threads which are interwoven and make up the unity of the book are only gradually disclosed. The development of that complex structure is not often interrupted by minor incidents. There is only one large-scale digression.[45]

---

[43] See chaps. lx–lxii.
[44] Forster, *Life of Dickens*, II, 20–21.
[45] The beginning of chap. xlvii.

Dickens' progress in the concrete technique of plot-making is paralleled by his increased interest in psychology and the evolution of his characters. Dombey himself is the clearest case in that respect. Forster denies that the original of Dombey, in so far as his physical appearance is concerned, was a man named Chapman, who worked for Lloyd's.[46] Such a denial is, of course, in itself suspicious, even if it does not amount to complete confirmation. Yet it seems much more likely that the novelist and his illustrator thought in fact of Samuel Carter Hall. The portrait of the latter in 1847—at the time of *Dombey*—which serves as a frontispiece to his volume of recollections, shows that he was not unlike Dombey, which is abundantly confirmed by the style and tone of his book.[47]

The character of Dombey, as depicted by Dickens, is at many points excessive—for instance, when he declares "the idea of opposition to Me is monstrous and absurd" (chap. xlii)—but it comprises an interesting psychological attempt. The early letters to Forster have shown that Dombey's final conversion did not result from improvization or from a last minute change of heart in the author, but was to be logically and naturally achieved after minute preparation. It is satisfactorily accounted for by the novelist's explanation in his 1859 preface:

> An obstinate nature exists in a perpetual struggle with itself. Mr. Dombey undergoes no violent internal change, either in this book or in life. A sense of his injustice is within him all along. The more he represses it, the more unjust he necessarily is. Internal shame and external circumstances may bring the contest to the surface in a week, or a day; but it has been a contest for years, and is only fought out then, after a long balance of victory. . . . I have not been impatient to offer this critical remark upon him, and I offer it with some confidence.

A fresh interest in the psychological development of his characters and a tightening of his structure are the two improvements Dickens could offer in *Dombey* to compensate for the comparative drying-up of his inspiration and the partial eclipse of his comic vein. The improve-

---

[46] See Forster, *Life of Dickens,* I, 311.
[47] *Retrospect.* The portrait is by Paul de la Roche.

ments are valuable in themselves. Yet, of all the works published during the first period of Dickens' career, *Dombey* is the least felicitous. There are greater differences between *Chuzzlewit* and *Dombey* than there had been between *Nickleby* and *Chuzzlewit* or even between *Pickwick* and *Nickleby*.

Leaving aside *Oliver Twist*, as a novel published in shorter and more irregular fragments, and Master Humphrey's two weekly narratives, the evolution of Dickens' technique through the first period of his career is thus clearly defined. Pickwick is a mere assemblage of thinly connected, but richly inspired, episodes. *Nickleby* is a long picaresque comedy, whose outline is now almost invisible, now drawn with a too heavy hand. *Chuzzlewit* is almost the first Dickens novel in monthly installments upon which embryonic unity is conferred by its moral theme. *Dombey*, finally, is a work constructed on the whole with skill and energy, but not upheld by a creative impulse comparable to that which had enlivened the preceding novels.

Dombey was the end of Dickens' apprenticeship, or rather journeymanship, in his craft as a periodical novelist. If he had died in 1848, it might have seemed that his years of experiment had finally exhausted the creative resources and the exuberant spontaneity which were the best part of his literary gifts, and of his originality. Yet it is clear that technical progress cannot be held responsible for *Dombey*'s comparative dullness. Dickens realized that *Nickleby* and *Pickwick* might have been better books if they had been more carefully constructed. Nor has the preponderance of psychological and moral preoccupations drained the Dickensian novel of its vitality. *Chuzzlewit* had done for selfishness what *Dombey* did for pride, and *Chuzzlewit* had been on the whole a brilliant success.

But that kind of moral fresco was not in itself a fit subject for Dickens, and, by trying to transpose into literature what Hogarth had done in the eighteenth century, what George Cruikshank was still doing in the nineteenth, by attempting to write a novel that might read like a "Proud Man's Progress," Dickens had betrayed his true vocation as a teller of tales. That is why his fine two-directional improvements—his increasing psychological and technical mastery—had failed to yield their best fruits.

But when the increased mastery is finally brought to bear on a subject that really inspires Dickens—on a truthful, moving, simple, story full of natural vividness and mirth—it contributes to making *David Copperfield* a truly great achievement.

3

AT THE TOP

XVIII: From *Dombey* to *Copperfield*

ONE SHOULD NOT UNDERESTIMATE the importance of one event which occurred between the appearance of *Dombey and Son* and *David Copperfield;* namely the growing success of William Makepeace Thackeray, who, since he had decisively asserted himself with *Vanity Fair,* from January, 1847 through July, 1848, could not but be regarded as Dickens' rival. Certainly, the figures of his monthly sales remained inferior to Dickens'. But the very similarity in the mode of publication made the rivalry more glaring, and Dickens must have known that henceforth his supremacy would no longer remain unquestioned, as it had for twelve years. He would have to compete with Thackeray for popular applause or, at least, share the applause with the newcomer. Dickens had not, of course, been the only popular novelist from 1836 through 1849. Such names as Edward George Bulwer-Lytton, William Harrison Ainsworth, and Frederick Marryat, for instance, were sufficiently well known.

But the novelty lay in the fact that there had now risen a writer who, while placing himself on the same ground as Dickens and addressing himself to the very same public, was possessed of all the advantages that Dickens might be thought deficient in, and which he had not even sought to acquire, such as a regular academic culture, a real knowledge of continental Europe and her contemporary literatures, and a varied and protracted apprenticeship in the writer's craft. In short, the problem was whether the purchasers of novels in monthly parts were ready to spend two shillings instead of one, and, if not, what proportion of them were going to desert Dickens in favor of Thackeray. Among the deserters were some choice readers, such as Mrs. Carlyle and the Brontës.

During the early years of Dickens' career, it has been seen that he read but little and did not take much interest in his rivals' successes. So that evidence of a competitive spirit is mostly to be found in Thackeray's letters, as is only normal since Dickens was several years ahead of him in the field. Thackeray was ever a generous rival, and never sparing of the public or private expression of his admiration for Dickens. Yet the rivalry became more acute with *David Copperfield* pitted against *Pendennis. Copperfield* appeared from May, 1849, through November, 1850; *Pendennis*—with a break due to the author's illness—

appeared from November, 1848, through December, 1850. The two are works of similar length and have many resemblances in theme and method. A detailed comparison is outside the scope of the present work, and an attempt to set one above the other is relatively useless literary criticism. However, it is interesting to note that the two writers must have been by then fully conscious of their relative situation. It will be remembered that Thackeray had already expressed his feeling that he was writing *Vanity Fair* "against" *Dombey*. On another occasion, he went so far as to say of Dickens: "He knows that my books are a protest against his—that if one set are true, the other must be false."[1] About *David Copperfield*, while claiming that Dickens' artistry had been improved by his own example, he was also confessing that his rival's improvement in its turn stimulated him and urged him to higher endeavor. Dickens, on his own side, though he did not scrutinize the other writer's works, cannot but have taken into account this new factor in the literary situation.

The single perceptible modification in Dickens' manner adopted under Thackeray's influence, or at any rate apparent at the time of Thackeray's early successes, is the more and more frequent assumption of a light and detached narrative tone. This had in fact begun in the Christmas books, where it was partly called forth by the often resorted to device of the humorous supernatural. But in all his novels previous to *Copperfield*, Dickens had hardly ever detached himself from his narrative to offer comments on his characters or to give general psychological observations. When he had done so, it had been in the form of tender or tragic addresses to his heroes—in *Chuzzlewit* and in *Dombey*. Thackeray's procedure, in both *Vanity Fair* and *Pendennis,* is, of course, far different and, indeed, highly idiosyncratic, turning the narrative into a kind of leisurely ramble, and constantly interrupting its course in order to enrich its substance. Thackeray ever stood as the observer and commentator of events rather than as their mere historian. Dickens will be seen to tend somewhat toward a similar attitude in the novels written between *Dombey* and the close of his career.

The publication of *Dombey* had been completed in April, 1848. Dick-

[1] Quoted by Phillips, *Dickens, Reade and Collins*, 22.

ens gave himself but a few months' rest before he went to work on the composition of *Copperfield*. In this case, a number of factors accounted for the delay. He always needed at least two or three months for investigations, gropings, and maturing, before he could create a new major work of fiction, and this period could not be described as inactive or restful. For Christmas, 1848, Dickens wrote the last of the Christmas books,[2] *The Haunted Man*. Finally, much time was claimed by his preparations for his forthcoming periodical, *Household Words*. Thus, in spite of the twelve months' interval between the completion of *Dombey* and the visible inception of *Copperfield*, the novelist's holiday in 1848 had, in fact, been limited to his summer visit to the seaside. The brevity of the interval can be regarded as the first sign of a revival of fecund inspiration, to be confirmed by the quick succession of *Copperfield* and *Bleak House*, after *Dombey*, with *Hard Times* not far behind.

The eighth child and sixth son of the Dickenses was born on January 16, 1849. His father first thought of having him christened as Oliver Goldsmith Dickens, but changed his mind and dedicated the boy to another of his great predecessors, naming him Henry Fielding Dickens. The choice of Fielding rather than Goldsmith, or Smollett, is worth mentioning, since it was made at the time when Dickens was about to begin the eighth novel of his career. One month after his eighth child's birth, indeed, in February, 1849, he was busy inventing names for the book. From Brighton, whither he had repaired for a few days, he was writing to Forster: "My mind running, like a high sea, on names; not satisfied yet, though."[3] The creative labor that was to result in the production of *David Copperfield* had begun.

XIX: ELABORATING THE NOVEL

THE QUEST FOR a suitable title had always been the earliest phase of Dickens' work on a new novel. In the case of *David Copperfield* the quest proved unusually protracted, not because of a paucity of ideas, but rather because of a plethora of possibilities and a keen desire to select

---

[2] *The Christmas Stories*, or special Christmas numbers of *Household Words* and *All the Year Round*, written in collaboration with other contributors, were to be less strenuous.
[3] Forster, *Life of Dickens*, II, 48.

the very best of them. The final solution was very slowly and gradually approached, as item after item in the title ceased to be a matter for hesitation.[1] The first title contemplated by Dickens had been "Mag's Diversions," and the hero was to have been called Thomas Mag, then David Mag. Thomas Mag was to have been an inmate "of Blunderstone House," and so was David Mag, but in a fourth version he became "David Mag of Copperfield House." Dickens must have been struck by this fortuitously happy alliance of the names David and Copperfield, since, with the very next attempt, "David Copperfield and his Great Aunt Margaret,"—Margaret doubtless being the first sketch of the immortal Miss Betsey—he made the alliance closer and henceforth stuck to it.

The stages of the quest for the name of Copperfield itself are set down on a separate manuscript sheet, and seem to have been very deliberate. There is at first a list of possible beginnings and endings: "Stone, bury, Flower, Brook, Well, Boy, Field." A second list makes tentative combinations into complete names: "Wellbury, Flowerbury, Magbury, Copperfield, Copperfield"; the immediate appeal of Copperfield to Dickens' ever alert mind and ear is shown by the striking repetition. A third list comprises further trials: "Trotfield, Trotbury, Spankle, David, Copperboy, Topflower, Copperstone." And the page closes with a revealing suggestion—"Charles Copperfield."[2] Later a series of titles is to be found in which the only variable elements are the name of the house—called, by turns, "Blunderstone House, Copperfield Cottage, Blunderstone Lodge, Blunderstone Rookery"—and the general designation of the book, for which Dickens had tried: "The Copperfield Disclosures, Records, Confessions, Survey of the World as it Rolled, The Last Living Speech and Confession of, The Last Will and Testament of, Copperfield Complete, Copperfield's Entire." Some of these memoranda may sound eccentric, yet they may have been written down rather in order to exorcise than to use them, and the list as a whole does define the main characteristics of the book he was intending to write and does bring out one essential aspect—the desire for absolute sincerity.

---

[1] The information is supplied by Forster (*Life of Dickens*, II, 77–79). A list of tentative titles is also to be found at the beginning of the MS of *DC* (Forster Collection). It will be observed that some items in the list were used for other characters in the novel (Trot, Brook, Stone).

[2] MS of *DC* (Forster Collection).

The title finally adopted, at the last minute, and in spite of Forster's and the author's avowed preference for the form "Survey of the World as it Rolled," was, of course, the more reasonable, but less sensational, "The Personal History, Adventures, Experiences and Observations of David Copperfield the Younger,"[3] four-fifths of which have long been forgotten. The reason for this final choice is given by Forster in words that emphasize the paradoxical character of Dickens' technique at that point: "His completion of the second chapter defined to himself, more clearly than before, the character of the book."[4] Thus had been demonstrated how impracticable the novelist's usual method had become. He had been unable to mold his narrative in accordance with a preconceived, arbitrarily selected title. The title, quite properly, had been compelled to adapt itself to the story it would have to define.

Thanks to the documents in the Forster Collection, the elaboration of *David Copperfield* can be followed step by step. They comprise nineteen sheets of memoranda, each divided into two sections—the complete manuscript, and the corrected proofs. A minute examination of those documents, completed by a few hints taken from Dickens' contemporary correspondence, will afford an opportunity for studying the general structure of the book and the detailed devices used in it. *David Copperfield*, more than any other Dickensian novel, deserves and repays close study.

The first number of *Copperfield* appeared on May 1, 1849, and had been written by Dickens during the month of April. As for the two preceding novels, he had found it difficult to write the beginning: "Deep despondency, as usual, in commencing, besets me,"[5] he told Forster in a letter. His despondency must have been the consequence of his inevitable anxiety, with the galling remembrance of the recent crisis, before a huge new task. And on April 19, only a few days before he completed one of the most masterly numbers of the book, one that gives an impression of splendid ease, he was again writing: "My hand is out in the matter of *Copperfield*. To-day and yesterday I have done nothing.

[3] Cf., 'The History of Pendennis, His Fortunes and Misfortunes, His Friends and His Greatest Enemy."

[4] *Life of Dickens*, II, 79.

[5] *Ibid.*, 77.

Though I know what I want to do, I am lumbering on like a stage-waggon. . . . I am quite aground . . . and the long Copperfieldian perspective lies snowy and thick this fine morning."[6]

The first number comprised the three chapters called "I am born," "I observe," and "I have a change," and included David's birth with the introduction of his widowed mother and his great-aunt Betsey Trotwood, together with Peggotty and little Dr. Chillip, then a few scenes of David's early childhood and the first appearance of Mr. Murdstone, soon followed by a suggestion that he might marry Mrs. Copperfield, and finally David's visit to the Peggotty family in Yarmouth, his baby love for Peggotty's niece Emily, and his return home to find his mother married again. The very brief working notes for that number have been reprinted by Forster in his *Life of Dickens*. One of their most interesting aspects is the quest for a suitable name for Mr. Murdstone. Dickens obviously tried to convey through his very name an idea of his hardness and cruelty: "Harden, Murdle"—a variant of which was to be used later in *Little Dorrit*—"Murden, Murdstone." Also of interest is the definition of Mrs. Copperfield's character in the summary of Chapter I: "Young mother. Tendency to weakness and vanity." This is much cruder than anything to be found in the novel, since the autobiographical form of the narrative precludes any such harsh judgment of a tenderly loved parent. Yet it will be seen later how Dickens did manage to suggest what David could not express.

The next three chapters made up Number II, written in May and published on June 1, 1849. In Chapter IV, David's new life is described, in the home now ruled by Murdstone and his sister who bully the young mother. David is caned by his stepfather, bites him, and is sent away to school at Salem House, near London. His journey from Blunderstone to Yarmouth and London, where he is taken in charge by a poor usher named Mr. Mell, fills up Chapter V. At the school, David is solitary, for the other boys have not yet come back from their summer vacation. In Chapter VI, the reader is shown the arrival of the headmaster, cruel Mr. Creakle, and the boys, one of whom, James Steerforth, has extraordinary glamor. The memoranda for that second installment are a

[6] *Ibid.*, I, 79.

good deal richer than those for the first. The contents of Chapter IV are heralded by the following notes: "Miss Murdstone—Their religion —Picture of all that and its effect on Davy's life. . . . Qy? His books and reading? His offence and confinement upstairs—*Child's remembrance of the latter*. Sent away." The italicized words—underscored by Dickens himself on his manuscript—correspond to a section of the chapter that he felt deeply about. It is in fact excellently conveyed in the novel, and the coincidence of the author's hopeful enthusiasm with successful creation is a sign of improving artistic control.

The impression of autobiographical truthfulness produced by the whole number is such that it comes almost as a surprise to find Dickens in his private notes writing of David in the third person: "Progress of his mother's weakness under the Murdstones. . . . Beats him. . . . Bites. . . ." The text of the novel suggests the more complete spiritual and sentimental identification of author with character. In the last sentence of the number (chap. vi), Dickens had to correct on the proofs a curious mistake he had made. Carried away by his love for metaphors, he had written: "There was no shadowy picture of his [Steerforth's] footsteps in the garden that I dreamed of—the garden that I picked up shells and pebbles in, with Little Emily, all night." Probably because he remembered in time that shells and pebbles are hardly to be picked up in a garden, but partly also because, on second thought, the association of Steerforth's image and Emily's appeared to him premature, he preserved only a more sober form: "the garden that I dreamed of walking in, all night."

The third installment of *David Copperfield* was written with remarkable ease. As early as June 6, 1849 (the first number was not due to appear until July 1), Dickens was writing to Forster: "Copperfield half done. I feel, thank God, quite confident in the story. I have a move in it ready for this month; another for the next; and another for the next."[7] The second move is David's exile to working life in London, and the third is his flight to Dover, but the first was Mrs. Copperfield's death at the close of Number III, about which he had warned another friend, Mark Lemon: "Get a clean pocket-handkerchief ready for the close

[7] *Ibid.*, II, 90. In the *Life* that comment is mistakenly connected with Number II.

of Copperfield No. 3, simple and quiet, but very natural and touch-ing."[8] The summary of that third installment can be given in Dickens' own words, on the left-hand side of his "mems": "Schoolmaster—Steerforth—Goes home—Mother with a baby—Comes back to school and receives news of her death—Goes home again to the funeral." The middle chapter was devoted to David's holiday. He had luckily arrived at Blunderstone in the Murdstones' absence, and had thus been enabled to spend one happy half-day in company with his mother and Peg-gotty, before the rest of his holiday began to be spoiled by irksome and monotonous constraint. For that chapter, Dickens had found it hard to please himself in the matter of a title. It was only after rejecting "I enjoy one afternoon's holiday," then "The holidays are concentrated into one afternoon," and "My holidays" that he had finally adopted "My holidays. Especially one happy afternoon."

The left-hand page of the memoranda for Number IV, written through July and published on August 1, is of pathetic brevity. In that number, after showing Murdstone's neglect of David and Peggotty's marriage to Barkis the messenger, Dickens intended to relate accurately his own childhood experiences in the blacking factory. The "mems" contain the single phrase: "What I know so well." In the number itself, after Chapter X had been devoted to preparation and transition, the narrative took David to London, where he began to work at Murdstone and Grinby's and to live with the Micawbers, whose financial difficulties provided an element of comic relief in an otherwise saddened and even tragic part of the story. At the end of the number David made up his mind to run away to his great-aunt Betsey Trotwood (chap. xi–xii). Significantly, in the section of the "mems" summing up the contents of the chapters, Dickens wrote for the first time in the first person: "Run away to Aunt Betsey." As the greater part of the number was made up of excerpts from Dickens' own autobiographical fragments, almost literally reproduced, it was written with particular ease, and the relevant passages of the manuscript have practically no erasures.

A chronological study of Dickens' literary creation in *Copperfield*

[8] *Letters* (MDGH), I, 207, June 25, 1849. In order to show that he was writing in character, i.e., as a popular journalist, Dickens signed the note "Evening Bore."

must include mention of the incidents in his private life that were contemporary with each stage of his work. It is important, for instance, to remember that Dickens spent the summer of 1849, no longer at Broadstairs according to his recent habit, but at Bonchurch on the Isle of Wight. He was at first delighted with the change and enjoyed the mildness of the climate. In August, he described his working arrangements at Bonchurch: "I have made it a rule that the Inimitable is invisible until two every day. I have not worked quickly here yet, but I don't know what I *may* do."[9] His satisfaction and optimism proved shortlived. Just as irritation and agitation had soon superseded early enthusiasm in the States, in Italy, in Switzerland and in France, the disadvantages of Bonchurch fast became monstrous and intolerable. Dickens analyzed the effect of the local climate on his health in his usual immoderate language: "Almost continual feeling of sickness. Extreme depression of mind . . . dull, stupid languor . . . incapable of reading . . . deep monotonous and constant [cough]."[10]

Fortunately, the literary labor accomplished at Bonchurch—Numbers V and VI of *Copperfield*, written in August and September, and published respectively on September 1 and October 1, 1849—bears no traces of such catastrophic influences. The chief interest of the "mems" for Number V—Chapters XIII, XIV and XV, including David's tramp to Dover, his becoming Miss Betsey's ward, and his entering Dr. Strong's school in Canterbury and the Wickfield home—lies in a few hints given by Dickens as to his general purpose in the book. In the very first lines jotted down on the left-hand side, the reader's attention is arrested by a mysterious phrase: "Chatham—Canterbury—Sunshine—Tramps—first of her?" The meaning of "her," which cannot be connected with any of the preceding items, is elucidated only a few lines down, where Dickens has written: "Introduction of the real heroine." It is interesting to find that Dickens, in those early days, was already considering Agnes Wickfield as the real heroine, and also knew at the time that there was going to be another heroine, less real in one sense, but more obviously cast for the part than Agnes. The implicit reference to Dora occurs here many chapters before the child-wife has taken shape. On the other

[9] Forster, *Life of Dickens*, II, 51.
[10] *Ibid.*, 53.

hand, even when "her" has been identified as referring to Agnes, who was in fact introduced at the end of Number V, part of the mystery remains unsolved. How was the "first of Agnes" to be shown in the course of David's journey to Dover? This we can never know. We can only surmise that, since Agnes lived in Canterbury and David walked through Canterbury on his way to Miss Betsey's, the novelist had contemplated a fortuitous encounter with Agnes, whose quiet beauty would probably have impressed the young boy, and become at once associated in his mind with the sunshiny peacefulness of the old city. Agnes might have taken pity on the miserable-looking, touching little traveler. An intimate familiarity with the novel and its genesis makes such conjectures a little more than probable; yet they must also remain a little less than certain, since Dickens finally postponed the "first of her," the earliest interview between David and Agnes, to a later part of the same installment.

The sixth number (chaps. xvi–xviii) relates David's beginnings at the school, takes us into Dr. Strong's home, where we are shown his young wife Annie, her mother Mrs. Markleham and her cousin Jack Maldon, introduces Wickfield's hideous clerk Uriah Heep and his mother, revives Mr. and Mrs. Micawber in Canterbury, and closes with a chapter called "A Retrospect," whose peculiar style will call for comment later on. Furthermore, the number sums up several years of David's school life together with his first innocent calf loves. The memoranda for that number are interesting in several ways. The material to be dealt with was more variegated than in the preceding numbers, written under the powerful and unifying influence of vivid inspiration. Dickens therefore, as he had already done for several parts of *Dombey*, asked himself many questions, one of which, together with the reply, remains obscure: "My Aunt? Qy.—No—only generally."[11] Dickens cannot have wondered merely whether he ought to mention Miss Betsey, for that he could not well avoid doing, at least, as he says, "generally." His "No" is to be accounted for only if he had some more precise purpose in view, some particular action or disclosure. It may have been something about Miss Betsey's husband, whose survival is hinted at more than once through the novel, but is made explicit only when the end of the novel is in sight and the end of his life has come. But there is too little to go on here.

11 The first person is used here again: *"My* aunt."

The aspect of the manuscript shows that Number VI made great demands on the writer's energy. At proof stage it had to be curtailed to the extent of two whole pages[12] and many deletions were made.

In the seventh number, David's schooldays come to an end. He takes leave of the Wickfields and the Strongs, and goes to London in order to choose a profession. He meets with his former schoolfellow of Salem, James Steerforth, in whose home he spends a few days—James' mother is a widow and lives with a baffling young relative called Rosa Dartle—before taking Steerforth with him to Yarmouth, when David resumes his relationships with the Peggottys (chap. xix–xxi). The summary of Chapter XIX in the memoranda has one phrase that can be understood only in connection with an unpublished fragment of the original manuscript: "Pave the way with Mr. Wickfield," Dickens told himself, and added, "Do. Agnes. Do. Mrs. Strong." In the chapter as finally published, there were but a few lines about Mr. Wickfield, and nothing that could be said to "pave the way" or hint at future developments. But a passage cancelled at proof stage justifies the phrase of the "mems":

> He talked of the time that had glided away since I first dined with him, the change that had stolen imperceptibly upon myself and Agnes. He sometimes felt that he was changed too, he said, and not for the better, as we were, but let that pass—and he drank his wine. . . . [He] said, with a melancholy kind of smile, that always became him well, that his great hope in life had been to see his daughter grow up at his side to what she now was, and yet that he could be well content to live the last five years of his life again. . . . I was glad to see that he was carried away from his wine by the current of our talk, and for the time forgot it.

The reason for such a major cancellation was not purely artistic. Certainly, Dickens selected the passage from among many others, because he thought it premature or too revealing, but it is no less certain that, had the part not been too long—there was, at the end of the set of proofs for Number VII, one page entitled "overmatter to Copperfield November Number"—he would have preserved it. Another passage of similar value

[12] The two pages are entitled "Copperfield over."

was deleted for the same reasons. About the end of the number, the scene of Steerforth winning over Mrs. Gummidge, the disconsolate and grumbling widow sheltered in Mr. Peggotty's home, which is only summed up in the published version, was described with much amusing detail.

In November, 1849, Dickens was busy writing Number VIII of *Copperfield*. A major difficulty arose. The youthful hero had left his aunt and his teachers in order to look for a profession. After the few weeks of idleness at Steerforth's and with Steerforth at Yarmouth— Chapter XXII remains focused on Yarmouth and is comprised of visits to Blunderstone, an encounter with the fallen girl, Martha Endell, and the appearance of dwarfish Miss Mowcher—the matter of the profession is still unsettled. It must now be solved. Dickens and Forster gave much thought to it, but came to a decision only at the last moment. The number was to appear on December 1, and the final choice had to be made in the second chapter of that installment. On November 15, Dickens was still undetermined and was writing to Forster: "I think it is necessary to decide against the special pleader. . . . I am not sure but that the banking house might do—I will consider it in a walk."[13] The consequences of the meditative walk were communicated to Forster two days later, in the form of a decision that claimed to be only provisionally final: "Banking business impracticable on account of the confinement: which would stop the story, I foresee. I have taken, for the present at all events, the proctor."[14] And the same letter contained a comforting assurance: "I am wonderfully in harness, and nothing galls or frets." In fact the number was completed with remarkable speed and ease. It would seem that the last two chapters—XXIII, David's return to London to meet his aunt, to be articled to Spenlow and Jorkins and to take possession of lodgings at Mrs. Crupp's; and XXIV, Steerforth's visit, and David's drunkenness and inopportune encounter with Agnes at the theatre—were written within four days. For it was on November 20, 1849, that Dickens wrote to Forster: "Copperfield done after two days' very hard work indeed; and I think a smashing number. His first dissipation I hope will be found worthy of attention, as a piece of gro-

13 Forster, *Life of Dickens*, II, 90–91.
14 *Ibid.*, II, 91.

tesque truth."[15] That the truth of the episode was guaranteed by the author's personal experiences is confirmed by a hint on the "mems": "His first time of getting tipsy. Description of it exactly." And the description was even more complete in the original version, which included, for instance, the following details, deleted at proof stage: "I was so far from wanting words, that I had only too many of them. I didn't know what to do with them. I floundered among them as if they were water which I was splashing about."

One further point in the "mems" for that number demands mention. Dickens appears to have chosen the names of the proctors to whose firm David was to be apprenticed after some trial and error: "For the proctors Aiguille and Tanguille. Tanguille and Jorker. No. Spenlow and Jorkins." It is highly disconcerting to find that such a grotesque thought had even fleetingly crossed Dickens' mind. Aiguille *or* Tanguille would have been sufficiently improbable in itself for one minor isolated English character. Duplication, symmetry, and assonance, would have made such an invention a gratuitous assault on the reader's credulity. And it can safely be inferred from the suggestion that the novelist had not yet made up his mind how he would introduce Dora into the novel. He could not have already contemplated making her the proctor's daughter. Dora Spenlow is an unobjectionable name. But, since Nicholas Nickleby was indignant at the thought that the loved one's name might be Cecilia Bobster, Dickens' favorite hero could never have fallen in love with a Dora Tanguille or—*horresco referens*—a Dora Aiguille!

The first year of *Copperfield* had closed with Number VIII. The next installment, although composed in December, 1849, was published on January 1, 1850. The memoranda for Number IX finely express the magic of Steerforth, not only in David's, but also in Dickens' eyes, since he found it necessary to caution himself: "No Steerforth this time. Keep him out." Even without Steerforth, however, Number IX was sufficiently rich in incidents, revivals, and promises. In Chapter XXV, David has a long conversation with Agnes, who warns him that he has made a dangerous friendship, then he meets Uriah Heep, more repellent than ever, and now openly declaring his love for Agnes. In Chapter XXVI,

[15] *Ibid.*

David is invited to spend one week end at Spenlow's, finds Miss Murd-stone installed as Miss Spenlow's companion, and falls hopelessly in love with the girl. In Chapter XXVIII, he meets another of his former schoolfellows at Salem House, Tommy Traddles, now a legal student and the lodger of the Micawbers.

The corrected proofs of that number contain evidence of Forster's belated revolt, on Dickens' behalf, against the printer's narrow tyranny. The three chapters were once more too long and there was a consider-able amount of "overmatter." On the first page of the proofs, Forster wrote in an imperious hand: "The overmatter must be got in somehow —by lengthening the page." It was not an unreasonable demand. There could be no justification, artistically speaking, for the hitherto accepted system of massive deletions at the last minute. The only surprising cir-cumstance is that Dickens and Forster had consented to it for fourteen years, passively, whereas the market value of Dickens' name was such that any publisher would have been only too glad to publish any work by him on any terms. His word could have been law. But his word, on that point, had not been spoken in opposition to the publisher's rigid and seemingly absurd regulations. This acceptance is accounted for by the fact that both Forster and Dickens liked regular habits, and prob-ably preferred the routine established by Chapman and Hall to the effort of adapting themselves to other methods. The monthly arrange-ments were tacitly continued under Bradbury and Evans' authority when Dickens moved from Chapman and Hall to them. The above-quoted outburst on Forster's part must have been caused by some unusual cir-cumstance. Perhaps Number IX seemed to him too exceptionally good to admit exorbitant sacrifices being made. Perhaps he was unwell or merely out of humor—his health was just as uncertain as Dickens', and his temper notoriously worse—or perhaps the time of the year, in the Christmas season, seemed unpropitious to even voluntary labor. In any case, his rebellion does not seem to have been very effective. Many cuts were made on the proofs of Number IX, and if part of the "overmatter" was indeed "got in," it cannot have amounted to much. And it should be borne in mind that no authoritarian pronouncement to the effect that the overmatter "must be" got in helped the printer solve the real tech-nical problem of packing additional type into a very close-set page.

The tenth number of a novel published in nineteen monthly parts is the center of the book. Number X of *Copperfield* does contain a decisive turn in the plot. It is made up of four chapters (chaps. xxviii–xxxi). David gives a dinner party to Traddles and the Micawbers and is visited by Steerforth's servant, Littimer, and later by Steerforth himself, who is involved in mysterious actions. David spends a day at Steerforth's, before going on to Yarmouth at the call of Peggotty, whose husband Barkis is dying. On the very day of the funeral, Steerforth elopes with Emily, and the number closes with the revelation of that dramatic event, which has been very carefully led up to and skillfully staged.

Number XI, published on March 1, was written in February, 1850. Dickens' habits were always upset in February, because of the missing two or three days in that month. On the 20th, he announced the approaching completion of his labors: "*Copperfield* runs high, and must be done to-morrow . . . some beautiful comic love, I hope, in the number."[16] The comic love in question is of course David's for Dora, of which the narrator said in a cancelled fragment of Chapter XXXIII: "For all this, I know that I was in my heart so innocent and young, so earnest, so impassioned and so true, that while I laugh, I mourn, and while I think of the discretion I have gained, I remember with a touch of sorrow what I have lost." Besides the secret betrothal of David and Dora, the number contains an attempt at exonerating Miss Mowcher from all blame, a visit paid by Mr. Peggotty to Mrs. Steerforth before he goes on an indefinite search for his niece (chap. xxxii), and a meeting with Traddles. At the end of Chapter XXXIV, David hears that his aunt is ruined and she comes to live with him in London. On the "mems," the summary of that chapter consisted of its title only, "My Aunt astonishes me," a very rare occurrence, and one that shows how vivid Dickens' sense of the contents must have been, since he needed no further help when it came to writing the chapter.

The twelfth part, written in March, and published on April 1, 1850, comprised Chapters XXXV, XXXVI and XXXVII. Its main purpose was to show the consequences of Miss Betsey's changed financial position. On talking it over with his aunt, David is led to mention his love for Dora, and Miss Betsey comments, sadly, after their talk, "Blind!

16 *Ibid.*

Blind! Blind!" a discreet, though sufficient, reference to Agnes' love for David. Betsey intuitively knows all about it, though to the reader no straightforward disclosures are made before the next to the last chapter of the novel. But one paragraph of subtle introspective analysis was cancelled at proof stage which commented—perhaps Dickens thought, too explicitly—on Miss Betsey's outcry: "Whether her tone of pity was for me, or for herself, or for anybody else, I could not decide, did not ask myself, perhaps; but I know that it made me feel uneasy afterwards, and that it sounded in my fancy like a sorrowful strain of music I had sometimes heard at a distance before that night" (chap. xxxv). Agnes and Uriah reappear in London. Dr. Strong, who had retired in Highgate, gives employment to David as his amanuensis, while Mr. Micawber becomes the clerk of Uriah Heep, who is now Mr. Wickfield's partner, in Canterbury. Finally Dora, informed by David of his reduced circumstances, shows herself unable to face the situation.

The memoranda with the help of which Dickens prepared these three chapters have a more sentimental ring and show greater psychological subtlety than had been the case before: "Progress of David to a working state, still tinged, romantically, by his youth and character and overdone. No similar progress on the part of Dora. Poor little Dora not made for the world or a working life." Again, no similar statements can be found in the text of the novel itself, though one sees here more clearly what Dickens proposed to do, and by comparing his notes with the relevant passages in the book, how successfully he achieved his purpose. The summary of the three chapters of Number XII—on the right-hand side of the "mems"—is wholly made up of key phrases, i.e. of significant and striking expressions for use in the text. It is only in moments of easy inspiration that Dickens could dispense with the intermediate stage of a list of incidents and go on directly to the coining of his key phrases. For instance, the final part of the summary of Chapter XXXVII—Dora's reactions to the announcement of David's poverty—reads: "Oh, take me to Julia Mills and go away, please!—Taking a guitar-case through the Forest of Difficulty—I used to sit thinking of it of a night sometimes, until I felt quite grey."

The chapters for the following month, April–May, 1850 (chaps. xxxviii–xl), relate how David toils at shorthand, how Mr. Spenlow discovers, thanks to Miss Murdstone, the secret correspondence between Dora and David, then dies all of a sudden, how David goes to Dover and Canterbury and has an interview with Agnes and finds that Uriah Heep is gaining stronger control over Mr. Wickfield, and finally, how on his return to London, David one evening meets Mr. Peggotty, who informs him of the disappointing results of his quest so far.

The memoranda for that number are once more couched in somewhat delicate and esoteric language: "To carry on the threat of Uriah, carefully and not obtrusively; also of David and Agnes." And once more, it is mainly through comparison with the written chapters that such phrases assume their interest and significance. In the same memoranda one notion is mentioned, in question form: "Miss Murdstone—Mr. Murdstone—Qy." And the reply is "Not yet." Dickens' urge to say something more about the interesting pair reappears, month after month, to the end. He must have contemplated some significant incident in which they might be involved, apart from the final settling of accounts.

The June installment, Number XIV, written in May, again comprises three chapters—XLI, XLII, and XLIII. In the first of these, David repairs, escorted by Traddles, to Dora's two maiden aunts, who have taken her with them after her father's death and who grant him permission to visit Dora at regular intervals. Thus the engagement now becomes officially recognized. In the second, Uriah basely draws Dr. Strong's attention to the suspicious intimacy between his young wife Annie and her cousin Jack Maldon. At the end of a painful scene, David strikes Uriah, and Dickens is so indignant himself at Uriah that he identifies himself with David on the "mems" and writes in the first person once more: "Slap Uriah's face." The third chapter, "Another Retrospect," describes, in the peculiar and felicitous style of the other "Retrospects," David and Dora's wedding.

On the preparatory notes for Number XIV, a number of interesting points can be observed. The influence of the winding-up, still remote but already looming on the horizon, makes itself felt in such phrases as: "Back to the Strong incidents and clear the way."[17] The whole sen-

---

[17] The same episode is summed up on the right-hand side in familiar style: "Uriah Heep, jealous of interlopers, works it out about the Strongs."

tence is underscored twice. Similarly, Dickens instructs himself to "clear Julia Mills off." Julia was Dora's friend and a convenient go-between in the days of secret relationships, but she has become cumbersome now that David and Dora can conduct their courtship openly.

Number XIV had proved too short on the proofs, and two paragraphs were added at the last moment, both in the first chapter (chap. xli).

On July 1, 1850, Number XV, which had been written in June, was published. It comprised three chapters.

Chapter XLIV is devoted to David's early married life, including difficulties with the servants, the first quarrel with Dora, and the dinner given to Traddles, all of which are suggested in the memoranda by the phrase: "Carry through incapacity of Dora, *but affectionate.*" The purpose of Chapter XLV was expressed as follows: "Mr. and Mrs. Strong to be adjusted." And in fact Annie Strong somewhat melodramatically explains and justifies her attitude, while charging her mother with clumsy interference. Dickens' avowed intention, as expressed in the "mems"—"Show the faults of mothers and their consequences"—must have been directed at Mrs. Hogarth. And in Chapter XLVI David, having had news of Emily through Littimer, imparts it to Mr. Peggotty and goes with him in quest of Martha, the fallen girl from Yarmouth, in the hope that she might help them find and save Emily.

The memoranda for Number XV also contain information about less obvious and more fleeting purposes at that stage—"Qy. Mr. and Miss Murdstone? *No.* Consider for next No." And further on Dickens contemplated a more detailed eventuality: "Qy. My aunt's persecutor and any indication of Mr. Murdstone in communication with her? *No.* Consider for next No." Thus he twice made use of a phrase—"Consider for next No."—which did not amount to complete rejection—marked simply by "No"—but did not mean certain postponement, expressed by "No, next No." In both cases, however, consideration was to result in final abandonment of the idea. The kind of relationship or communication Dickens had thought of establishing between Murdstone and Miss Betsey can no longer be elucidated. It does not belong to the novel proper, but it is part of the history of its birth pangs; it is part of the picture of Dickens at work on *Copperfield.*

Again in the same number, Dickens had instructed himself to "Carry Steerforth through by means of" Mrs. Steerforth and Rosa Dartle. The verb used here, "carry through," applied now to a character, now to a feeling, now to a character's "thread"—Dickens would speak of carrying through Agnes, the love of Agnes, the thread of Agnes. This word apparently had a precise meaning to him. What that meaning was, i.e. the way in which the directions were carried out, the "mems" cannot disclose. Only the text itself can do so, at least in part.

On July 7, 1850, Dickens was in high spirits and wrote to Forster: "Still undecided about Dora, but must decide to-day."[18] He needed to include a new turn in the story in the sixteenth number, on which he was beginning to work, for he was reaching the final quarter of the book. The turning point came with the reply—"Yes"—to the question: "Dora in declining health. First intimation?"

The other incidents in the number are characterized by an acceleration in the narrative tempo. The preparatory notes suggest that Dickens felt almost overwhelmed by the number of points he still had to settle before the novel was finished:

> Carry through the unravelling of Uriah Heep [underscored twice]. Carry through also the married life [double rule again]. Little Emily and Mr. Peggotty—Qy. to close the No. with her discovery? Yes [query underscored twice; reply three times].

Such of the above incidents as were used by the author, whose exaltation is marked by his multiple underscorings, were distributed among the four chapters, Chapters XLVII–L, of the number. Martha is found by David and Mr. Peggotty under romantic circumstances, and promises to help them, thus providing "Emily with the means of HER redemption," as the summary of Chapter XLVII puts it. In David's home there are increasing difficulties with servants, and Dora's health is deteriorating. Mr. Micawber comes to London, is overwhelmed and preyed

---

18 See Forster, *Life of Dickens*, II, 91, implying that the letter was written on May 7, 1850, though the question of Dora's fate could not have arisen before the beginning of July. The rest of the letter was printed by Forster in a footnote omitted from the Everyman edition of the *Life*; it ran, in French: *"La difficulté d'écrire l'anglais m'est extrêmement ennuyeuse. Ah mon Dieu! si l'on pouvait toujours écrire cette belle langue de France!"*

upon by remorse and invites his friends to Canterbury to attend the downfall of Uriah Heep. Finally, with Martha's help, Emily is found out by David and her uncle in a slumlike lodginghouse.

The state of the manuscript shows that Chapters XLVII and XLVIII demanded particularly strenuous work. And when the proofs came out, they were one whole page short. For the first time in his career, Dickens did not content himself with adding small bits of insignificant dialogue and description here and there. He availed himself of the deficiency in length to greatly modify the substance of one important incident. In the original manuscript version, Mr. Peggotty stood by David's side when Emily was discovered. He was thus made to listen passively to the violent scene in the course of which Rosa Dartle wildly insulted and attempted to strike his niece. The shocking and improbable situation is altered in the final version, in which Mr. Peggotty arrives only after Rosa has gone, so that David and Martha are the only witnesses of her savagery.

Dickens' enthusiasm and inspiration endured to the end of the novel. On August 13, 1850, he wrote to Forster about Number XVII of *Copperfield*: "Work in a very decent state of advancement. . . . I hope I shall have a splendid number. I feel the story to its minutest point."[19] Three days later a daughter was born in the Dickens home. Carried away by his enthusiasm for his novel, the father gave to the child the names of two of the female characters, Dora and Annie. The choice was a surprising one in that it omitted Agnes. It was infelicitous and astonishing—considering that Dickens was undoubtedly superstitious —in that the "mems" for the August number began with the words: "Dora to die in this number. Yes, at the end."

Yet, for the time being, the novelist was wholly absorbed in the fast-moving number—the last but two—he was now composing. In it, Mr. Peggotty relates the story of Emily's elopement and flight and announces his determination to emigrate, David goes to Yarmouth to break the news to Ham and Peggotty (chap. li), Mr. Micawber denounces Uriah's dishonesty—Dickens, ever vividly irritated by Uriah, had written in the summary of Chapter LII, "Smash Uriah Heep by means of Mr. Micawber"—and Dora dies (chap. liii). The "mems" included once

[19] Forster, *Life of Dickens*, II, 91.

more the query "Mr. and Miss Murdstone?" with the reply "Not yet," and the summary of the final chapter, which had been composed with great care: "Three times. White line between each—speaks of herself as past"; and the novelist had drawn a double rule under the words: "Present Little Dora's death through Jip's death. David sees him lie on the rug and die. Agnes comes down. All over." Although Jip is Dora's dog, the chapter is less namby-pamby than the summary suggests. It is even very moving; so much so that Dickens' sprightly tone, in his August 20 letter to Forster, sounds almost sacrilegious: "I have been very hard at work these three days, and have still Dora to kill. But with good luck I may do it to-morrow."[20] Number XVII had a whole page of overmatter at proof stage, yet no considerable deletions seem to have been made. Perhaps the printer had at long last found a way of partly and temporarily complying with Forster's injunction and "getting in" the overmatter.

Dickens' working notes for the eighteenth and penultimate number of *Copperfield* are particularly interesting and informative. The left-hand page begins with the phrase: "To finish from last No. Uriah," which is repeated on the right-hand side in the summary of Chapter LIV, as "Uriah Heep's business finished." Then comes the perennial query: "To bring up. Mr. and Miss Murdstone? *No*, last number." After which Dickens gives a definition of the forthcoming installment as "the Emigration No." and lists the characters he can dispose of by that means: Mr. Peggotty, Mrs. Gummidge, Emily, and Martha form the first group and are bracketed together. Mr. and Mrs. Micawber and their children form the second group and are similarly bracketed. "Agnes—Carry through," Dickens then added, presumably meaning that no new incident concerning Agnes should occur in that installment, but that the permanence of her presence and personality should be felt by the reader. Then came the summary of a chapter to which Dickens attached great importance, the chapter in which Ham and Steerforth, Emily's fiancé and ravisher, were to be united in tragic circumstances and finally in death:

> Ham and Steerforth. Steerforth in a sinking ship in a great storm in Yarmouth Roads—Ham goes off in a lifeboat or with a rope

[20] *Ibid.*

round his waist? through the surf. Both bodies washed ashore together? No—A mighty wind.

In that first sketch of the narrative can be observed the artist's decisions in the making on two significant points. Dickens had added, "To
remember, the last parting—'He was lying easily with his head upon
his arm.'" The phrase referring to David's last vision of Steerforth before the elopement is repeated in the summary of Chapter LV, on the
right-hand side of the "mems," in slightly modified and completed form:
"I saw him lying with his head upon his arm, as I had often seen him
lie at school." Slight as it is, the modification is significant and illustrates
Dickens' desire to achieve greater unity of atmosphere and tone in his
novel. For he has finally preferred to connect the sight of Steerforth in
death, not with the period immediately before the elopement, but with
David's remembrance of his school days. The general notes on the left-
hand side close with two lines, each of which is twice underscored:
"Close with David's going on a tour abroad (lapse between this number and the next)."

On the right-hand side, when it comes to arranging the distribution
of the incidents between the various chapters, there is an amusing note:
After the words "Mr. Micawber arrested" in the summary of Chapter
LIV, Dickens added and underscored twice the phrase "over and over
again." He thus showed himself aware of the comic value that lay in
the repetition of such an incident. And in the summary of the next chapter, one passage makes Dickens come to life by disclosing the way in
which he made use of the very recent past, in the form of fortuitous
observations, to enrich his work in progress. Chapter LV is the "Tempest" chapter. Dickens wrote: "The wind, the spray. He coming to the
sea. The town. Flying sand, seaweed and flakes off ocean." The last
three words were underscored twice and followed by the explanatory
note: "Scene seen here at Broadstairs last night. Flying in blotches."
Under the heading "Chapter LVI," Dickens wrote "two chapters here,"
and the number did close with two separate scenes, the announcement
to Mrs. Steerforth of her son's death (chap. lvi) and the departure of
the emigrants' ship (chap. lvii). The corrected proofs contained several
considerable inserts—all in Chapter LVII—for the number had been

underwritten by one whole page. Yet it had been written with exceptional gusto and fervor, as appears from several letters to Dickens' friends. To Forster, on September 15, 1850, he said:

> I have been tremendously at work these two days; eight hours at a stretch yesterday and six hours and a half to-day, with the Ham and Steerforth chapter, which has completely knocked me over, utterly defeated me![21]

and two days later, to W. H. Wills: "I am in that tremendous paroxysm of Copperfield—having my most powerful effect in all the story on the Anvil . . . .[22]

The nineteenth and last installment of *David Copperfield* appeared on November 1, 1850. It had been written in October and was called "Nos. XIX & XX." In point of length, it was equivalent to one and one-half ordinary numbers. The author's craftsmanship in it is rather less interesting to study, not because the concatenation of events tends to become less intricate or more natural, but on the contrary, because the novelist has given himself a freer hand with conventions and licenses. There are seven chapters in the final part of *Copperfield*. David travels and gradually, under the influence of Agnes' letters, recovers an interest in life and work. He understands that he is in love with her, but believes he has no right to tell her so, after having ignored her for so many years (chap. lviii). He returns to England and sees Traddles, now married, poor and happy (chap. lix). He sees Agnes and treats her as his sister, in spite of Miss Betsey's veiled warning (chap. lx). Chapter LXI is an interlude in which David, as a famous novelist, is invited by his former schoolmaster Creakle to visit a model prison and meets among its inmates both Uriah Heep and Littimer. Chapter LXII contains David's avowal of his love for Agnes, who in her turn confesses she has always loved him. Ten years after their wedding, Agnes and David are surrounded by their children when Mr. Peggotty calls and brings them news of all the emigrant group (chap. lxiii). The final chapter, called "A Last Retrospect," is an emotional vision of the lapse of time and of David's matrimonial happiness with Agnes. In the course of the num-

---

[21] Forster. The paragraph is omitted from the Everyman edition of the *Life of Dickens*. In the Tauchnitz edition: IV, 279.

[22] *Dickens as Editor*, 41.

ber, many minor characters have come in for a parting word or a reference to their fate.

A few sentences from a letter written by Dickens to Forster on October 21, 1850, form the fittest conclusion to the study of the novel's chronological development:

> I am within three pages of the shore; and strangely divided as usual in such cases, between sorrow and joy. Oh, my dear Forster, if I were to say half of what Copperfield makes me feel to-night, how strangely, even to you, I should be turned inside out! I seem to be sending some part of myself into the shadowy world.[23]

When the general composition of *David Copperfield* is compared to that of the preceding novels by Dickens it will be seen that, together with a good deal of unquestionable technical progress, there are traces of the old weaknesses. Coincidence, for instance, is still unscrupulously exploited. A list of only the major coincidences in *Copperfield* is impressive. In Chapter XVII, David is having tea with the Heeps in Canterbury, when Mr. Micawber happens to pass by and see him, because the street door is open at that time.[24] The first time David returns to London as a young man, he puts up by chance in the hotel where Steerforth, whom he has not heard of since the days at Salem House, happens to be staying (chap. xix). The first time Miss Betsey comes to London, she meets her husband on the streets (chap. xxiii). When David, after a chance encounter with Agnes at the theatre, is invited to dinner by the Waterbrooks with whom Agnes is staying, he meets his other Salem House companion, Traddles, at the dinner party. And Dickens-David brazenly insists on the fortuitousness of the meeting: " 'It's a curious coincidence,' said I. 'It is really,' returned my host, 'quite a coincidence that Traddles should be here at all: as Traddles was only invited this morning ...' " (chap. xxv).

There are more coincidences. At Mr. Spenlow's, Dora's companion happens to be Miss Murdstone, David's stepfather's sister (chap. xxvi).

---

[23] Forster, *Life of Dickens*, II, 98.

[24] The second quarter of the novel has hardly begun when Dickens already thinks it necessary to recall characters he had temporarily dismissed. Mr. Micawber exclaims: "Copperfield! Is it possible!" One is tempted to retort: "No, but it is extremely entertaining!"

Traddles, when David calls on him about the same time, happens to be living with the Micawbers, thus fortuitously revived for the second time (chap. xxvii). Peggotty comes to Mr. Spenlow's office about her husband's will on the very day when Mr. Murdstone in his turn reappears and is getting a marriage license (chap. xxxiii). Betsey Trotwood and David are ruined, but David's former master, Dr. Strong, chooses that very moment to settle down in a London suburb, and happens to be in need of a young secretary (chap. xxxv). Uriah Heep engages a clerk and most improbably selects the most indiscreet man known to the reader of *Copperfield,* namely, Mr. Micawber (chap. xxxvi). Mr. Spenlow pays a high price for having created inconvenience by discovering the secret correspondence between David and Dora: he dies within twenty-four hours (chap. xxxviii). Rosa Dartle finds Emily in London miraculously, a few seconds before David and Martha come to her, and Rosa goes away a few seconds before Mr. Peggotty arrives in his turn (chap. l). On the day when a terrible storm breaks out in Yarmouth Roads, David has just arrived from London, and Steerforth's yacht is blown in just in time to allow for the most dramatic encounter (chap. lv). When David comes back to London after three years' absence, he puts up at a hotel and meets by chance Dr. Chillip, formerly of Blunderstone, who has moved to another part of England, but happens to be again Mr. Murdstone's neighbor there (chap. lix). In the model prison of Chapter LXI, the first of the two star prisoners is Uriah Heep, and on seeing the second, David significantly declares: "I had been so much astonished already, that I only felt a kind of resigned wonder when Mr. Littimer walked forth, reading a good book!" He then hears that Littimer's arrest had been due to another coincidence, a fortuitous encounter with Miss Mowcher.

Perhaps that massive use of coincidence was a natural consequence of the kind of book Dickens was writing. Since *David Copperfield* was to be the story of a lifetime, it was practically inevitable that some of the characters should temporarily disappear to return later in the novel, for otherwise the list of secondary figures might have become tiresomely and confusingly long. Besides, there are at least a few coincidences in every average human life, and there was no reason why David's should form an exception to the rule. Finally, whenever Mr. Micawber enters the procedure is justified by the gusto with which his successive reappearances are presented after each temporary eclipse.

Besides these coincidences, which were at any rate deliberately introduced, there are in *David Copperfield* a number of inconsistencies and little mistakes which Dickens would have avoided but for the fragmentary form of his labors over a period of nineteen months. They are of a trifling character, though a more conscientious artist would certainly have eliminated most of them from the later editions. David, for instance, seems to have only a hazy idea of the date of his birth. He tells us at first that he was born in March (chap. i). Later he says of one of his birthdays: "How well I recollect the kind of day it was! . . . I see the hoar frost . . . the breath of the boys wreathing and smoking in the raw cold as they blow upon their fingers and tap their feet upon the floor" (chap. ix). And later, speaking of "one hot evening," he adds "it may have been my birthday" (chap. xi). It is difficult besides to see how a whole year may have elapsed between the last two incidents. The chronology of events in *Copperfield* is far from clear.

Similarly, Miss Betsey's house in Dover is at first "sold . . . to good advantage"(chap. xliii), but the advantage must have been quite sensationally good, for Miss Betsey can soon return to her house without having to repurchase it (chap. lv). A minor mystery is contained in the phrase: "The two forefingers of his [Heep's] skeleton right hand" (chap. xvii). Finally, there is considerable uncertainty about the distance between Blunderstone and Yarmouth. It takes almost a whole day to get from one place to the other in Barkis' carriage (chap. iii), but later David can walk from Yarmouth to Blunderstone in the morning, spend a whole day there, and walk back to Yarmouth in time for dinner (chap. xxii). Meanwhile Barkis' arrangements have been wrapped in deepening mystery. He lives in Yarmouth and spends every evening and night there (chap. x). Yet he invariably leaves Blunderstone early in the morning (chaps. iii, v, x). In fact he is never seen to go from Yarmouth to Blunderstone.

Of course, there is in all that no more than a little occasional remissness, which does not seriously affect the reader's impression of Dickens' growing technical mastery. There is evidence that he has accustomed himself to the size of his canvas and moves with greater ease and certainty in many directions. This is particularly obvious where the naming of characters is concerned. There had been awkwardness and hesitation in *Pickwick* and *Nickleby*, whether the characters were anonymous or not. In *Copperfield*, Dickens' invention of names has become almost invariably masterly. One name only is reminiscent of the former jocular tendency. A maidservant engaged by David and Dora was called "Paragon. Her nature was represented to us, when we engaged her, as being feebly expressed in her name" (chap. xliv). But her case is isolated. For his other characters, whether principal or secondary, Dickens has coined felicitous names, like Murdstone, Quinion, and Passnidge, in Chapter II, Waterbrook and Gulpidge in Chapter XXV;[25] Tiffey, Spenlow's old clerk and reminiscent of Anthony Chuzzlewit's old clerk Chuffey; Mrs. Kidgerbury the charwoman; and the parties in Traddles' first case, Jipes and Wigzell.

An interesting innovation is introduced into the designation of the characters in *Copperfield*. It is the frequent use of different names or different forms of one name, applied to the same character by various members of his or her circle, a device which emphasizes the differences in the nature of the relationships involved. Miss Betsey is the most systematic coiner of idiosyncratic variants of people's names. Her arbitrariness is always one of her most striking and diverting features, and she takes obvious delight in imperiously modifying the name of almost every person who comes into contact with her. In this aspect, she is like Dickens himself in private life, and for the same reason, for she is keenly alive to the subtle relationship between sounds and ideas or feelings. Of Mr. Murdstone she says, "A Murderer—or a man with a name like it," and of Peggotty she says, "That woman with the Pagan name" (chap. xiii). Miss Murdstone becomes to her: "That murdering woman of a sister, on whom I think no pain or penalty would have induced my aunt to bestow any Christian or Proper Name, or any other designation."[26] Later, Miss Betsey alone calls Peggotty "Barkis," because, she claims, "It sounds less as if you wanted a missionary" (chap. xxxiv). Dr. Strong's

[25] With names like Gulpidge, Passnidge, and Gummidge, the "-idge" ending tends to supplant the old favorites "-kle" and "-dle."

[26] Chap. lix. When that phrase had first been used, however, in chap xxiii, Miss Murdstone had been called, not a "murdering woman of a sister," but a "murdering sister of a woman . . . . This had been, ever since, the only name my aunt knew for Miss Murdstone."

mother-in-law is one Mrs. Markleham, but the pupils in his school nickname her "The Old Soldier." Miss Betsey does not content herself with that and must make the designation twice as esoteric by turning it into "our military friend" (chap. xlv). For Dora she coins charming little names in Chinese style: "Little One, Blossom, Little Blossom" (chap. xlviii).

Yet the most subtle effects achieved by Dickens through the procedure of modified names concern the hero of the book, David himself. Practically every character has his or her own way of addressing him. Mr. Murdstone alone calls him "David." Traddles and Micawber alone normally call him "Copperfield." There are many variants of the two names. David is "Davy" to his mother, "Master Davy" to Peggotty, "Mas'r Davy" or "Mas'r Davy bor'" to Mr. Peggotty and Ham.[27] He is "Master Copperfield" to Uriah, "Mister Copperfield" to Mrs. Micawber, and even "Mister Copperfull" to Mrs. Crupp—"Firstly, no doubt, because it was not my name, and secondly, I am inclined to think, in some indistinct association with a washing-day" (chap. xxxvi). Quinion, Mr. Murdstone's friend, nicknames David "Brooks." There is still more arbitrariness in the names chosen by the people closest to David. Miss Betsey christens him "Trotwood"—and he is called thus by the Wickfields and Mr. Dick—which she at once shortens to "Trot." Steerforth makes a bold use of the name "Daisy," and Dora coins the charming word "Doady," "which was a corruption of David" (chap. xli).

Finally, the case of Agnes Wickfield's name is interesting. Several critics seem to have paid scant attention to her last name. Admittedly, she is mostly called Agnes, but her father is always called Mr. Wickfield. Yet, in criticism about *Copperfield,* one comes across forms like Wickford,[28] Wakefield,[29] and Wickham.[30] The writers who committed such mistakes must have failed to notice the curious fact that David Copper*field* marries Agnes Wick*field* and that the beginning of her last

---

[27] To the end of the novel. See chap. lxiii, " 'Mas'r Davy,' said he. And the old name in the old tone fell so naturally on my ear."

[28] *The Dickensian,* Oct., 1917, p. 277.

[29] Stephen Leacock, "Fiction and Reality. A Study of the Art of Charles Dickens," *Essays and Literary Studies* (London, 1916), 171.

[30] Gissing, *Ch. Dickens, Critical Study,* 49; Marzials, *Life of Dickens* (London, 1887), 112. A similar mistake is made by G. A. Sala, (*Charles Dickens* [London, 1870]) who calls Creakle, *Crinkle.*

name is identical with the end of *Pickwick*, a name of crucial importance to Dickens' career and containing most of his favorite letters—"i," "w," and "k." Without insisting on the additional assonance between *Wick*-field and *Dick*ens, but taking into account the fact that Dickens was deeply surprised and moved to find that he had unwittingly given to David his own initials in reverse, it seems that there is a close network of subconscious links between the three names David Copperfield, Charles Dickens, and Agnes Wickfield.

Generally speaking, the choice of names in *David Copperfield* does not, as in the preceding books, distract the reader's attention, but contributes both firmly and subtly to creating the unity of the novel.

Similar subtlety appears in the composition of *Copperfield*, which is harmoniously organized and makes use of a number of separate themes before creating and constantly reinforcing the connections between them. Since *Copperfield* extends over a considerable number of years, the treatment of time and the variations in the tempo of the narrative assume particular importance and reveal Dickens' growing interest in the technical problems of the novel. The concept of time is in fact introduced into the story with great adroitness. One typical sentence will illustrate this point:

> The rooks were sailing about the cathedral towers; and the towers themselves overlooking many a long unaltered mile of the rich country and its pleasant streams, were cutting the bright morning air, as if there were no such thing as change on earth (chap. lii).

This conveys David's impressions on finding himself once more at Canterbury in the house where he had spent the happiest years of his childhood. The simultaneous reference to the notions of change and permanence often imparts to his recurring visits to Canterbury, as is the case here, the value of a pause in the evolution of things and people, a pause devoted to meditation and the re-examination of events and alterations.

A similar attempt is made in the four admirable "Retrospect" chapters.[31] They are admirable in every respect, but particularly in the high

---

[31] Chap. xviii, "A Retrospect"; chaps. xliii and liii, "Another Retrospect"; chap. lxiv, "A Last Retrospect."

quality of the style and in the clever use made of them for the general construction of the novel. The "Retrospects" also interrupt the continuous progress of the narrative, and both accelerate and slow it down. They accelerate it in that they contain a summary of several years or at least months—David's schooldays are wholly contained within the first, the period preceding and comprising David's first marriage within the second, Dora's decline and death within the third, David's and Agnes' married happiness within the last—yet it is no paradox to say that at the same time those chapters slow down the rhythm of the story, thanks to their contemplative character. The reader, as he comes to them, feels as though he were emerging from the turmoil of active life and entering an area of comparative peace where all that takes place goes on within hearts and souls. That characteristic of the "Retrospects" is expressed at the beginning of each of them:

> My school days! The silent gliding on of my existence—the unseen, unfelt progress of my life—from childhood up to youth! Let me think, as I look back upon that flowing water, now a dry channel overgrown with leaves, whether there are any marks along its course, by which I can now remember how it ran (chap. xviii).

> Once again, let me pause upon a memorable period of my life. Let me stand aside, to see the phantoms of those days go by me, accompanying the shadow of myself, in dim procession (chap. xliii).

> I must pause yet once again (chap. liii).

> And now my written story ends. I look back, once more—for the last time—before I close these leaves. I see myself, with Agnes at my side, journeying along the roads of life . . . (chap. lxiv).

The use of the word "pause" in two of those texts and of the phrase "look back" in the other two, shows that they are unquestionably to be understood as moments when there is a contemplative arrest of time.

Another procedure is used by Dickens in order to emphasize the continued progress of time. Every significant event in *Copperfield* is foreshadowed by a multiplicity of warnings and signs, which make it cast its shadow backward as well as forward. For instance, the death of Mrs. Copperfield-Murdstone is heralded in several ways, through hints concerning her frailty and her pining away under the Murdstones' tyranny, and also by a few more explicit sentences. Relating the one happy afternoon of his holidays, David says: "We were very happy; and that evening, as the last of its race, and destined evermore to close that volume of my life, will never pass out of my memory" (chap. viii). At the end of the same chapter, he again suggests the same notion, after having called forth in moving terms the last vision he had of his mother before returning to the school: "So I lost her. So I saw her afterwards, in my sleep at school—a silent presence near my bed—looking at me with the same intent face—holding up her baby in her arms."

The case of little Emily and Steerforth presents a more striking example still, for their fate is hinted at from the very beginning of the novel, with occasional reminders later on. While describing the first walk taken by the child David with Emily, the narrator says: "There has been a time since . . . when I have asked myself the question, would it have been better for little Emily to have had the waters close above her head that morning in my sight; and when I have answered Yes, it would have been" (chap. iii). Dickens adds, "This may be premature. I have set it down too soon, perhaps. But let it stand." Yet the corrected proofs show that the passage did not result from some irresistible impulse of the author's, soon to be almost deplored. For the whole passage, remorse and all, was inserted by Dickens while correcting the first set of proofs. It is therefore a very deliberate effect, achieved in order to lay the ground, long in advance, for the character's future. Preparatory hints of this kind become increasingly numerous as the elopement draws nearer. Steerforth invites David to visit him in his home shortly before that event and asks: "who knows when we may meet again, else?" (chap. xxviii). And in fact they will meet no more on this earth. David accepts the invitation and relates a few incidents: "One other little circumstance . . . I must not omit . . . for I had reason to remember it thereafter, when all the irremediable past was rendered plain" (chap. xxix).

At the close of the visit, Steerforth appeals to his friend solemnly: "Think of me at my best, if ever circumstances should separate us!" And when Steerforth has gone to sleep, David gazes on his peaceful form:

The time came in its season, and that was very soon, when I almost wondered that nothing troubled his repose, as I looked at him. But he slept . . . and thus, in this silent hour, I left him.—Never more, Oh God forgive you, Steerforth! to touch that passive hand in love and friendship. Never, never more!

As soon as he has arrived in Yarmouth, David notices that Emily, though betrothed to Ham, "seemed to cling closer to her uncle, even to the avoidance of her chosen husband" (chap. xxx). As soon as the elopement has taken place, Dickens begins to make preparations for the last act in the same drama, the simultaneous death of Ham and Steerforth. On the beach, David observes Ham's glance and tone: "The remembrance of this . . . haunted me at intervals, even until the inexorable end came at its appointed time" (chap. xxxii).

This device of giving advance signs of tragic events is due in great part to the nature of the book. In an autobiography written and organized late in life, the narrator cannot help mingling with the remotest events the remembrance of their more recent consequences. The element of mutability in human life is thus present in *Copperfield* and contributes to the harmony of the book. And the element of permanence throughout all change is expressed in the recurrence of a number of objects or sensations, as of a series of landmarks with which the reader feels himself becoming pleasantly familiar. Such are Peggotty's sewing materials and her crocodile book, which embodies and symbolizes the continuity of love through the turmoil of changing situations.[32] Such are the rooks and the towers of the cathedral at Canterbury.

Such is, above all, the pervading presence and soothing influence of Agnes through the greater part of the book, testifying to the care and skill with which the composition associates, just as does living thought, past, future, and the twofold present of the event related and the moment when it is being related. The first appearance of Agnes becomes the occasion for writing such sentences as:

> I see her, with her modest, orderly, placid manner, and I hear her beautiful calm voice, as I write these words. The influence for all

[32] See particularly chaps. li and lxiv.

good, which she came to exercise over me at a later time, begins already to descend upon my breast (chap. xvi).

The adverb "already" refers to the period when David saw Agnes, but the present in "I see her" refers to the time when David is telling his story. Similarly, long before the end of the book, David will say, "My narrative proceeds to Agnes, with a thankful love" (chap. xlii). This is a fine definition of the harmonious, unified composition of *Copperfield*, and accounts for the outstanding success of Dickens' craftsmanship in that book.

XX: AUTOBIOGRAPHICAL REALITY AND INVENTION IN *David Copperfield*

THE READER'S FIRST IMPRESSION of *David Copperfield* is one of profound truthfulness. It had not been achieved to the same extent in Dickens' previous novels. Admittedly, he had already given evidence of his psychological insight and of his ability to depict the concrete world realistically. But in *David Copperfield*, there is more than that. Owing in part to the autobiographical form, Dickens is felt to be offering not merely the outcome of his external observation, however acute, he is also giving something of himself and of his own life.

Such a sensation has been systematically sought after, through the recurring use of striking phrases to emphasize the vividness and permanence of Dickens' visions. Yet these phrases have a tone of sincerity and conviction about them. In the chapter describing David's first walk with Emily on the beach at Yarmouth, one reads: "The incident is so impressed on my remembrance, that if I were a draughtsman I could draw its form here, I daresay, accurately as it was that day . . ." (chap. iii). When Mr. Mell takes David on a visit to his pauper mother, the narrator gradually leaves the past tense to adopt the present, in an impressionistic succession of brief sentences, and achieves similar results (chap. v). Further on are found exclamatory sentences like "How vividly I call to mind the damp about the house . . ." (chap. v), or "How well I recollect our sitting there, talking in whispers . . ." (chap. vi). Mr. Peggotty's visit to Salem House is also rendered vividly present to the reader: "He stands before me again. . . . Good Heaven, how it all comes back to me this long time afterwards!" (chap. vii). Of his mother's funeral David says, "If the funeral had been yesterday, I could not recollect it better" (chap. ix). And of the warehouse in which he is doomed to labor: "Its decaying floors and staircase . . . are things, not of many years ago in my mind, but of the present instant . . ." (chap. xi).

In the course of the same episode, the use of the present tense once more conveys an impression of truthfulness: "I see myself emerging one evening from some of these arches. . . . Here we stand, all three, before me now" (chap. xi). The tramps met by David on the Dover Road have inspired him with "a dread that is yet quite fresh in my mind" (chap. xiii). When Steerforth has eloped with Emily, Ham's attitude is described with striking force:

> The face he turned up to the troubled sky, the quivering of his clasped hands, the agony of his figure, remain associated with that lonely waste, in my remembrance, to this hour. It is always night there, and he is the only object in the scene (chap. xxxi).

A few days later, Mr. Peggotty goes on his long and uncertain search and takes leave of David who writes: "I cannot leave him, even now, without remembering with a pang, at once his modest fortitude and his great sorrow" (chap. xxxii). When Annie Strong is about to exculpate herself in her husband's eyes, the narrator again makes use of a striking phrase: "The gentleness of the Doctor's manner and surprise . . . I see and hear, rather than remember, as I write about it" (chap. xlv). And of the tempest that is about to take both Ham's and Steerforth's lives, he says likewise: "As plainly as I behold what happens I will try to write it down; I do not recall it, but see it done; for it happens again before me" (chap. lv).

It is interesting to observe that, through this procedure, Dickens imparts remarkable convincingness to many scenes, some of which were taken out of his own experience, while others were purely imaginary. In *Copperfield* the intermingling of truth and fiction is very close and skillful. "I really think I have done it ingeniously," Dickens wrote to Forster, from Broadstairs, on July 10, 1849, of the introduction into the novel of the autobiographical fragment his friend had already read,

"And with a very complicated interweaving of fact and fiction. Vous verrez."[1] It would be futile to attempt to distinguish, from their degree of verisimilitude or convincingness, which episodes of *Copperfield* were borrowed from the author's life. The outstanding measure of inspiration due to the use of several significant and genuine incidents seems to have spread over the rest of the book and imparted to it the same hue of unmitigated truth. External biographical knowledge alone, then, can enable one to determine the relative parts played by memory and imagination.

Three major episodes played a decisive part in both the writer's, and his hero's, career. James Lamert's blacking factory becomes Murdstone and Grinby's warehouse in the novel. Dickens' youthful attachment to Maria Beadnell provided him with the original of Dora and other valuable material for the episode. Furthermore, Dickens, like David, taught himself shorthand and later became a successful novelist. There are a number of significant differences between Dickens' experience and David's, however. Dickens entered Doctors' Commons as a stenographer, whereas David was already there, and about to become a full-fledged proctor, when he had to take up shorthand because his aunt was ruined. So Dickens' experiences as a stenographer have really supplied him with two distinct veins of information for use in his novel. The slow and arduous apprenticeship to the art of shorthand writing is movingly depicted in *Copperfield*. However, the criticism of Doctors' Commons, of its illogicality, defects, corruption, dangers and scandals, is no doubt perfectly competent and intrinsically interesting, but somewhat digressive and even intrusive.[2] Factual autobiography is of slighter value than sentimental autobiography.

Besides the three major themes that have just been quoted, *Copperfield* borrows many additional elements from reality, and they are more or less successfully connected with the general outline of the narrative. A fairly well-known, but characteristic case is Miss Mowcher's. Miss Mowcher is the dwarf whom Steerforth employs in Yarmouth. She is officially supposed to be a hairdresser and manicurist, but the tone of her speech tends to show that she is in fact chiefly preparing to play the

---

[1] See Forster, *Life of Dickens*, II, 48.
[2] See particularly chaps. xxii, xxvi, xxxiii, and xxxix.

dishonorable part of a go-between for Steerforth and Emily. She is made unpleasant at first sight, not merely through her vulgarity (of which Dickens may not have been conscious), but also through her aggressive and slightly perverse volubility.

It happened that Miss Mowcher's external appearance and precise gestures had been copied by Dickens from a living original. He had not imagined the woman might recognize herself in the picture and feel hurt at seeing her deformity and other physical characteristics associated with a hateful personality playing a hateful part in the novel. Yet that was exactly what happened, and, on December 28, 1849, Dickens wrote to Forster: "I have had the queerest adventure this morning, the receipt of the enclosed from Miss Mowcher! It is serio-comic, but there is no doubt one is wrong in being tempted to such a use of power." The biographer relates the sequel of the story. Dickens wrote to the original of Miss Mowcher, a Mrs. Seymour Hill, that:

> He was grieved and surprised beyond measure. That he had not intended her altogether. . . . That he felt nevertheless he had done her wrong, and would now do anything to repair it. That he had intended to employ the character in an unpleasant way, but he would, whatever the risk or inconvenience, change it all, so that nothing but an agreeable impression should be left. . . .

It was impossible to achieve that result or, by that means, any result except glaring improbability and incoherence. Yet Dickens sincerely made the attempt, and Forster's narrative is concluded by a phrase which superbly characterizes the weakest aspect of Dickens' technique: "The thirty-second chapter went far to undo what the twenty-second had done."[3] It did go far, but of course it could not go far enough, in the sense that it could not cancel a word of what had already been published. Dickens could only, and did, add favorable explanations of suspicious appearances and emphatic moral comments. He lapsed into pathos. His painstaking demonstration of the innocence of a character he had meant to be guilty is unconvincing. David sees Miss Mowcher again after the elopement and tells her: " 'I am surprised . . . to see you

---

[3] Forster, *Life of Dickens*, II, 99. See also Edgar Johnson, *Ch. Dickens: Tragedy & Triumph*, II, 674–75. The name of the unfortunate woman, Mrs. Seymour Hill, was first given by Edwin Pugh (*The Dickens Originals* [London, 1912], 295).

so distressed and serious!' . . . 'Yes, it's always so!' she said. 'They are all surprised, these inconsiderate young people, fairly and full-grown, to see any natural feeling in a little thing like me!' " (chap. xxxii).

Dickens cries *peccavi* with a loud voice. He heaps up touching details: a father, a brother, a sister, all dwarfs, all invalids, all fed by good little Mowcher. And when this proliferation of dwarfs can be supposed to have duly mollified the reader's sensitive heart, Dickens lets out his explanation. Wicked Steerforth and his footman Littimer had deceived the innocent dwarf and induced her to believe that, not Steerforth, but David, was in love with Emily. Conscientiously, Dickens ransacked Chapter XXII to unearth details that might lend color to such an impudent misrepresentation of what had really happened: "I saw Steerforth soothe and please you by his praise of her! [Miss Mowcher says] you were the first to mention her name. You owned to an old admiration for her . . ." (chap. xxxii). But no one is likely to be taken in by this flow of circumstantial evidence unless he has forgotten all about the early scene, in the course of which, far from owning to an old admiration for Emily, David had attempted to cut short an equivocal conversation about her by making a serious and dignified speech: "She is as virtuous as she is pretty. She is engaged to be married to a most worthy and deserving man in her own station of life. I esteem her for her good sense, as much as I admire her for her good looks"(chap. xxii).

There is no need to expatiate on such painful results of Dickens' belatedly praiseworthy purpose. He has emptied to the dregs the cup of penance and voluntary humiliation, accepting and enlarging upon Mrs. Hill's lesson:

> "You know you wouldn't mistrust me, if I was a full-sized woman." I felt that there was much truth in this; and I felt rather ashamed of myself. "You are a young man," she said, nodding. "Take a word of advice, even from three foot nothing. Try not to associate bodily defects with mental, my good friend, except for a solid reason" (chap. xxxii).

That little misadventure is astounding for two reasons. On one hand, Dickens' blindness to the possible consequences of his copying from life was a curious phenomenon. On the other hand, once he had realized he had put himself in the wrong by what he euphemistically called his "use of power," he disregarded just as blithely the rules of art and the readers' right to be presented with a coherent narrative.

His use of personal experiences was not invariably quite so questionable as in the Mowcher-Hill affair. An example of the way in which such elements could be incorporated into the narrative is provided by Chapter LXI, called "I am Shown Two Interesting Penitents" and relating a visit paid by David and Traddles to a model prison run on the separate confinement principle. That chapter came out in the final number on November 1, 1850. In his newly-launched weekly, *Household Words,* Dickens had published on April 27, 1850, an article called "Pet Prisoners" describing the Pentonville Prison, of which the fictional prison is closely reminiscent. In 1847, Dickens had already become acquainted in Glasgow with that system, which had seemed to him "absurd and hideous."[4] Yet the criticism in the book concerns the Pentonville experience rather than the Glasgow one, as is shown by the use in the "mems" for that installment of the phrase "Pet Prisoning," a phrase not repeated in the text. The significant fact is the arbitrariness with which the theme was forced into the novel. If Dickens, in 1850, had taken an active interest in fire brigade stations or lunatic asylums, David might have found Littimer and Heep in another kind of establishment. So, once more facts whose appearance in the novel is not justified by any inner necessity are less convincing and sound less truthful than some imaginary circumstances. Although Dickens' own first visit to Yarmouth had been paid in January, 1849, the whole Yarmouth episode is much more successful than the prison scenes, and much more successfully integrated into David's childhood than are the prison scenes into his later life.

But, of course, emotions and feelings are of greater value to autobiographical literature than are concrete facts. The latter inevitably belong to one man's personal and limited experience, and, however cleverly and sincerely depicted, they cannot arouse the same universal echo as the

---

[4] See Forster, *Life of Dickens* (Tauchnitz edition, IV, 164): "Tremendous distress at Glasgow, and a truly damnable jail, exhibiting the separate system in a most absurd and hideous form." The footnote containing the above fragment from a letter of Dec. 30, 1847, is omitted from the Everyman edition of the *Life.* See, also, Collins, *Dickens and Crime.*

evocation—even in fictitious scenery—of the emotions common to all men.

That is why the first chapters of *David Copperfield,* concerning the hero's early childhood, have always been regarded as the most admirable and outstanding section of the book. They are so full of simple, fresh, direct observations that no reader can fail to find in the child David some part of himself. Such are the famous sentences of Chapter II: "The first objects that assume a distinct presence before me, as I look far back into the blank of my infancy, are my mother . . . and Peggotty . . . ." Then come the first vivid emotions, like the boy's departure for Yarmouth: "The day soon came for our going. It was such an early day that it came soon even to me, who was in a fever of expectation, and half-afraid that an earthquake or a fiery mountain, or some other great convulsion of nature, might interpose to stop the expedition" (chap. ii). This is followed by the arrival in Yarmouth and the reflections it elicits from David: "I could not help wondering, if the world were really as round as my geography book said, how any part of it came to be so flat. But I reflected that Yarmouth might be situated at one of the poles, which would account for it" (chap. iii). Next he describes his desolation on returning to Blunderstone, finding his mother married again, and being exiled to a new, grim bedroom:

> I thought of the oddest things. Of the shape of the room, of the cracks in the ceiling, of the paper on the wall, of the flaws in the window-glass making ripples and dimples on the prospect. . . . I was crying all the time, but, except that I was conscious of being cold and dejected, I am sure I never thought why I cried (chap. iv).

Finally we come to the approach of the first holiday, when David has become a schoolboy:

> I well remember . . . how the distant idea of the holidays, after seeming for an immense time to be a stationary speck, began to come towards us, and to grow and grow. How, from counting months, we came to weeks and then to days. . . . How the breaking-up day changed its place fast, at last, from the week after next to next week, this week, the day after to-morrow, to-morrow, to-day,

to-night—when I was inside the Yarmouth mail and going home (chap. vii).

It would be difficult to convey a more striking impression of sincerity. George Orwell, on reading *David Copperfield* for the first time when he was nine, found "the mental atmosphere of the opening chapters . . . so immediately intelligible . . . that I vaguely imagined they had been written by a child."[5] Yet, he goes on to explain, those chapters lose none of their charm to the adult who reads them again later, for Dickens "has been able to stand both inside and outside the child's world."

That double position of the narrator posed a delicate problem. The scenes and the conversations reported by David are supposed to have been observed by a child and usually have been preserved in his memory only in the imperfect form of the childish perception of them. Yet, many of those scenes have to suggest to the adult reader far more than David could see in them at the time. To satisfy this twofold need, Dickens has recourse to certain devices. In the first place, he lays down two rules which condition the verisimilitude of the narrative: "If it should appear from anything I may set down in this narrative that I was a child of close observation, or that as a man I have a strong memory of my childhood, I undoubtedly lay claim to both of these characteristics" (chap. ii). He further specifies that, in some cases, the events reported have been in part reconstructed with the help not of memory only, but also of the more enlightened judgment of the mature man: "My later understanding comes, I am sensible, to my aid here" (chap. ii). For even an exceptionally observant child like David could not but miss many things: "I could observe, in little pieces, as it were; but as to making a net of a number of these pieces and catching anybody in it, that was, as yet, beyond me" (chap. ii). In spite of this confession, the unfailing accuracy of his memory might still have appeared exaggerated. Therefore, David increases the verisimilitude through a few signs of hesitation and uncertainty:

> It seems to me, at this distance of time, as if it were the next day when Peggotty broached the striking and adventurous proposition

[5] "Ch. Dickens," *Critical Essays*, 17.

I am about to mention; but it was probably about two months afterwards (chap. ii).

I am not certain whether I found out then, or afterwards, that . . .
[Mr. Murdstone] had some share in, or some annual charge upon
the profits of a wine-merchant's house in London . . . but I may mention it in this place, whether or no (chap. iv).

I think it occurred to me that I had already begun [life on my
own account] in my poor way—but it occurs to me now, whether
or no (chap. x).

Thus does the inaccuracy of a few particulars contribute to enhancing
the general impression of absolute truthfulness.

Dickens has been charged with having sinned against verisimilitude
when he has David report conversations that take place out of his presence and even before his birth. Such criticism, made, among others, by
Gissing, is unfair. It could be applied only to the scene in the first chapter, with Miss Betsey and Mrs. Copperfield at first, and later with Dr.
Chillip. But in that chapter, Dickens has taken great care to mention
David's sources of information precisely, in phrases like "my poor dear
mother used to say," "so, my mother suspected at least," or "as he told
my mother afterwards."

Finally, the child's memories and the adult's reflections are confronted
more than once. This device was inevitable, since two periods of time
are constantly intermingling and interacting in the narrator's mind—
the time about which and the time at which he writes. Dickens achieves
this very skillfully: "I knew [the compliments of Murdstone's friends]
pleased her. I knew it quite as well as I know it now" (chap. ii). While
describing Mr. Murdstone's face as seen by the child David, the narrator
pauses to insert a vindictive apostrophe all his own: "The rich white,
and black, and brown of his complexion—confound his complexion and
his memory!—made me think him, in spite of my misgivings, a very
handsome man" (chap. ii). Later he will say: "I knew as well that he
could mould [my mother's] pliant nature into any form he chose, as
I know, now, that he did it" (chap. iv).

The same method of confronting childish memory and adult judgment is again observable in other sections of the novel. David relates the happenings in the Salem House dormitory and says: "A certain mysterious feeling . . . steals over me again . . ." (chap. vi). And, writing about Annie Strong: "Distinctly as I recollect her look, I cannot say of what it was expressive. I cannot even say of what it is expressive now, rising again before my older judgment" (chap. xvi). Again, David has fallen in love with Miss Larkins and strolls near her house in the night, "wondering which is Miss Larkins's chamber (and pitching, I dare say now, on Mr. Larkins's instead)" (chap. xviii).

Yet all the skill and all the devices in the world cannot efface the impression of improbability created by the famous scene at Lowestoft, in which Mr. Murdstone and his friends laugh at David before his face and nickname him "Brooks of Sheffield" without his perceiving anything. Yet even that slight departure from truthfulness is easily forgotten and forgiven on account of the delightfully humorous effects derived from it:

> I was quite relieved to find that it was only Brooks of Sheffield; for, at first, I really thought it was I. . . . When the wine came, he made me have a little, with a biscuit, and, before I drank it, stand up and say, "Confusion to Brooks of Sheffield!" The toast was received with . . . such hearty laughter that it made me laugh too; at which they laughed the more. In short, we quite enjoyed ourselves (chap. ii).

Partly on account of the devices used by Dickens, partly also in spite of them, *David Copperfield* impresses upon the reader the author's obsessive and poignant nostalgia for childhood. This was no new thing in Dickens' fiction, but it is most movingly conveyed in the sentences following every episode of innocent childish happiness: "I wish I had died. I wish I had died then, with that feeling in my heart! I should have been more fit for heaven than I ever have been since" (chap. viii). Again, in Chapter X is to be found the description of an ideal world, similar to that imagined in childhood, and the freshness of Dickens' own magical vision of the childish universe accounts for the success of the attempt made in *David Copperfield* to picture the child's soul from inside:

What happiness (I thought) if [Emily and I] were married, and were going away anywhere to live among the trees and in the fields, never growing older, never growing wiser, children ever, rambling hand in hand through sunshine and among flowery meadows, laying down our heads on moss at night, in a sweet sleep of purity and peace, and buried by the birds when we were dead! (chap. x).

Generation after generation of Dickensian critics have put forward the view that David Copperfield is a dim, vague, uninteresting, and slightly incoherent figure. Stephen Leacock even contends that "there is, so to speak, no such person, David is merely the looking-glass in which we see the other characters, the voice through which they speak."[6] That view is not borne out by a close examination of David's personality, which emerges with sufficient clarity from such an examination and is then seen to coincide at many points with that of Charles Dickens. Psychological autobiography even plays such a considerable part in *Copperfield* that Dickens might also have called the book "The Growth of a Novelist's Mind" in emulation of Wordsworth's subtitle for *The Prelude*. Detailed comparison between David and Charles Dickens is required in order to discover what devices and methods have been used to achieve identification as well as, sometimes, distinction.

The first self-portrait of David as a child might have been Dickens' at the corresponding age: "A child of excellent abilities, and with strong powers of observation, quick, eager, delicate, and soon hurt bodily or mentally" (chap. xi). But after that early period, through which the qualities and features listed by David-Dickens are indeed the most striking, one of the most forcible impressions created by the fictional character is one of pronounced self-centeredness. Admittedly the use of the autobiographical form can account for, excuse, and even necessitate the narrator's concentration on his own person. Yet in David's case, it is not merely a matter of point of view. There are also a number of circumstances—and they are not the least reminiscent of Dickens—in which other people are ignored or ill-treated, not by David the narrator, but by David the actor with the unmitigated approval of David-Dickens the narrator. Brief reference will suffice for phrases like "if ever child

[6] *Charles Dickens. His Life and Work* (London, 1933), 121.

were stricken with sincere grief, I was" (chap. ix), or for the description of David's sufferings at Murdstone and Grinby's. In such cases, indeed, if the hero seems to be placed by himself at the center and on the summit of the universe, it is for stylistic rather than moral or psychological reasons. Dickens is much given to the use of excessive and superlative expressions.

More significant is David's attitude at the time of Barkis' death. David knows that his friend the carrier is lying; so, he says, "I . . . directed my steps thither, with a solemn feeling, which made Mr. Barkis quite a new and different creature" (chap. xxx). This is a fine example of David's egocentric tendency. Mr. Barkis becomes a different creature to him, not because Mr. Barkis is about to die, but because of the feeling aroused in David by the old man's approaching death. Besides, the context shows that the feeling is not so much one of pity or sadness as a kind of wondering and flattered interest in his own part in the event. Likewise, the chapter following Steerforth's elopement with Emily, an event that has plunged two families into deep grief, presents David's reactions in significant order: "The more I pitied myself, or pitied others, the more I sought for consolation in the image of Dora" (chap. xxxiii). Instead of deploring his own responsibility in the drama—he had introduced Steerforth at Yarmouth and remained blind, in spite of some clear warnings, to the dangers for his friends of an unscrupulous and dissolute man like Steerforth—instead of first of all pitying the distress of victims much more cruelly hurt than himself, David begins with self-pity.

Still more serious is the attitude of David as a young husband, for David is as ill-equipped for the part as Dickens later proved to be. Dora is ill, almost dying, when David, twice in one week, yields to friendly solicitations and to curiosity and deserts her. Once, without a word to Dora, he goes to London in order to see Emily when Martha summons him. He also goes to Canterbury with his aunt in order to be present at Micawber's exposure of Heep and to disguise from Dora the seriousness of her state of health: "We agreed . . . that we would both go, and that Dora was a little Impostor, who feigned to be rather unwell, because she liked to be petted" (chap. lii). Poor little dying Impostor!

This other consequence of Copperfield's self-centeredness, his blindness to the feelings and sufferings of other people, is also a feature he shares with his creator. The case of Miss Mowcher and Mrs. Hill was undoubtedly not the single example of Dickens' attitude. Absorbed in the interest he took in the manifestations of his own sensitiveness, he forgot to take that of his closest friends and relatives into consideration and remained unaware of the wounds he could inflict upon them. His immoderate worship, a year after his marriage, of the memory of Mary Hogarth, his affectionate attitude toward his other sister-in-law, Georgina, and the disgust he never wished to dissemble whenever a new birth became probable or certain in the family must have profoundly pained Kate Dickens for years before their marriage was finally broken.

Dickens also accepted, without any apparent qualms of remorse, Georgina's celibacy, sacrifice, and devotion to himself and his children. All that was done for him he regarded as normal, and David resembles him in that respect, either because Dickens made his character purposely like himself or because he liked to exploit the technical convenience of the hero's blindness. Agnes loves David, but David will know nothing of her love until the end of the story. Meanwhile he keeps trampling the heart of the girl he calls his sister and wounding her with his cruel questions. When they have been discussing David's early skin-deep loves, he says:

> "Times are altering now and I suppose I shall be in a terrible state of earnestness one day or other. My wonder is, that you are not in earnest yourself, by this time, Agnes." Agnes laughed again, and shook her head. "Oh, I know you are not! said I "because if you had been you would have told me, or at least," for I saw a faint blush on her face, "you would have let me find it out for myself!" (chap. xix).

Blindness could hardly be more complete. It is again a lack of perceptive interest in other people's feelings which prevents David from comprehending the many hints of Steerforth's purposes which enlighten the reader. His friend announces to him that he has just bought a boat:

> "She's the Stormy Petrel now. What does Mr. Peggotty care for Stormy Petrels! I'll have her christened again!"
> "By what name?" I asked. "The Little Emily." As he had continued

to look steadily at me, I took it as a reminder that he objected to be extolled for his consideration, I could not help showing in my face how much it pleased me, but I said little, and he resumed his usual smile, and seemed relieved" (chap. xxii).

And when it comes to analyzing his own feelings toward Agnes, David, while recognizing her powerful and mysterious appeal to him, evinces the same lack of clear-sightedness. It is, he says, "as if, in love, joy, sorrow, or disappointment, in all emotions, my heart turned naturally there, and found its refuge and best friend" (chap. xxxiv). But the love mentioned in that sentence is love for Dora. Upon Agnes he can still bestow only his truest friendship. A little later, in the midst of his trials, he meets Agnes and tells her: " 'An influence comes over me in that short interval that alters me, oh, how much for the better! What is it? What is your secret, Agnes?' Her head was bent down, looking at the fire" (chap. xxxix). But he still fails to guess her secret and in the course of the same conversation calls her once more "my adopted sister" (chap. xxxix). Dora is more open-eyed; on hearing there is no blood relationship between Agnes and David, she says to her intended husband: "I wonder why you ever fell in love with me?" (chap. xlii). Betsey Trotwood is still more clear-sighted. In fact, David alone is blind, and David is very much like Dickens.

David's own feelings, on which his whole attention is centered, are characterized by exceptional and highly Dickensian intensity. The energy with which he undertakes the study of stenography is an interesting example and the comment—unusually moderate—he writes about it has unmistakable introspective and autobiographical value: "I did not allow my resolution, with respect to the Parliamentary debates, to cool. It was one of the irons I began to heat immediately, and one of the irons I kept hot, and hammered at, with a perseverance I may honestly admire" (chap xxxviii). The intensity of David's, as of Dickens', feelings, can result in positive hardness. His hatred, in particular, is of most unChristian vivacity and pertinacity. When he has struck Uriah Heep's face, David says: "I heard that he went to a dentist's in London on the Monday morning, and had a tooth out. I hope it was a double one" (chap. xlii). Already, as a boy, he had bitten the hand of his stepfather who was caning him. The first time he saw Mr. Murdstone again after the incident, he relates: "I could not restrain my eye from resting for an instant on a red spot upon [his hand]" (chap. viii).

The antipathy between Mr. Murdstone and David is mutual and unbounded. Yet there is a likeness between them which is all the more interesting as the author seems to have neither desired nor perceived it. David's hostility to Mr. Murdstone originates in great part in the latter's attempt to form Mrs. Copperfield's character once he has married her— a cruel attempt to which David is referring when he says: "I was still held to be necessary to my poor mother's training, and, as one of her trials, could not be suffered to absent myself" (chap. viii). And Miss Betsey gives a more picturesque description when she tells Murdstone: "And when you had made sure of the poor little fool . . . you must begin to train her, must you? begin to break her; like a poor caged bird, and wear her deluded life away, in teaching her to sing *your* notes?" (chap. xiv). Yet, after his own marriage, David experiences a disappointment not unlike Murdstone's at his young wife's childishness, frailty and inefficiency, and he is momentarily tempted to adopt a similar attitude: "What other course was left to take? To form her mind? This was a common phrase of words, which had a fair and promising sound, and I resolved to form Dora's mind" (chap. xlviii).

In fact, the education of David at the hands of the relative he loves and reveres more than any other, Betsey Trotwood, is wholly dominated, like the Murdstone ideal, by the notion of firmness. David scathingly denounces the Murdstones' firmness:

> Firmness . . . was the great quality on which both Mr. and Miss Murdstone took their stand. . . . The creed . . . was this: Mr. Murdstone was firm; nobody in his world was to be so firm as Mr. Murdstone; nobody else in his world was to be firm at all, for everybody was to be bent to his firmness . . . . My mother . . . might be firm, and must be; but only in bearing their firmness, and firmly believing there was no other firmness upon earth" (chap. iv).

Yet after that denunciation David hears and approvingly retails to the reader the moral rule of life propounded by Miss Betsey and, behind her back, no doubt, by Dickens himself:

> What I want you to be, Trot . . . is, a firm fellow, with a will of
> your own. With resolution . . . with determination. With character,
> Trot—with strength of character that is not to be influenced, except
> on good reason, by anybody, or by anything. That's what I want
> you to be (chap. xix).

The only item in that definition that is not in strict conformity with
the Murdstone code is the restrictive phrase "except on good reason,"
which is so very vague that it leaves a wide field open to personal interpretation and can by no means act as a safeguard against the temptations
of a tyrannous temperament.

David's description of Dr. Strong is in striking contrast with the
ideal outlined above: "It was very pleasant to see the Doctor with his
pretty young wife. He had a fatherly, benignant way of showing his
fondness for her which seemed in itself to express a good man" (chap.
xvi). Finally David and Dickens pronounce themselves in favor of both
firmness and mildness. The two qualities are not irreconcilable and an
examination of the most characteristic scenes involving the Murdstones
casts some light on the apparent contradiction. A fair example of the
Murdstone attitudes arousing David's hatred is provided by the following conversation about the boy's education:

> "I think, Clara," said Mr. Murdstone, in a low, grave voice, "that
> there may be better and more dispassionate judges of such a question
> than you." "Edward," replied my mother, timidly, "you are a far
> better judge of all questions than I pretend to be. Both you and
> Jane are. I only said . . . ." "You only said something weak and in-
> considerate," he replied. "Try not to do it again, my dear Clara, and
> keep a watch over yourself." My mother's lips moved, as if she an-
> swered, "Yes, my dear Edward," but she said nothing aloud (chap.
> viii).

As for Jane Murdstone, it is on the occasion of her sister-in-law's funeral
that she comes out in the most revealing light:

> Miss Murdstone . . . asked me, in an iron whisper, if I had been
> measured for my mourning. I said "Yes." "And your shirts," said
> Miss Murdstone; "have you brought 'em home?" "Yes, ma'am. I

have brought home all my clothes." This was all the consolation that
her firmness administered to me. . . . She was particularly proud of
her turn for business; and she showed it now in reducing everything to pen and ink, and being moved by nothing (chap. ix).

Thus, what David reproaches the Murdstones with is not firmness.
Betsey is firm, David himself is—often—firm, as Dickens was firm to
the point of hardening himself in some of his attitudes. His criticism is
aimed at cruelty, at the lack of tenderness or of mere sensitiveness.

The hero's own sensitiveness is, like Dickens', remarkably vivid. On
more than one occasion, it even appears to be almost feminine in its
nature and in its expressions. The femininity of the hero is indeed strikingly, though in all probability unconsciously, harped upon. In Chapter
I, Betsey Trotwood asserts that the forthcoming child is going to be
a girl and expresses intense disgust at the birth of a boy. Later she will
use as an example for her nephew to follow a mythical sister, Betsey
Trotwood Copperfield, who, apart from the slight disadvantage of never
having been actually born, had every perfection and enjoyed her aunt's
and godmother's preference. The invention of that unreal creature—
not unlike Mrs. Harris in that respect—is mainly intended to produce
comic effects, but it also incidentally steeps David, from the beginning,
in a feminine atmosphere. This is confirmed by another, less noticeable
episode. In the dormitory where Steerforth is about to go to sleep for
the first time near his young schoolfellow, he asks the latter a significant
question:

> "You haven't got a sister, have you?" said Steerforth, yawning.
> "No," I answered. "That's a pity," said Steerforth. "If you had had
> one, I should think she would have been a pretty, timid, little, bright-
> eyed sort of girl. I should have liked to know her. Good-night, young
> Copperfield." "Good-night, sir," I replied (chap. vi).

Thus, twice a purely imaginary sister, who is something like the embodiment of the feminine side of David's personality, and of Dickens',
is described by two distinct and unrelated characters.

Through the rest of the novel it is mainly in connection with Steerforth's friendship that David's feminine sensitiveness and sentimentality

are expressed. Dickens cannot be held to have intended to hint at the existence of unnatural feelings—not to speak of intercourse—between David and Steerforth. What he was interested in, what he consequently made interesting, was the psychological study of a friendship so vivid and intense, and experienced by such a sensitive person, that many of its incidental expressions and manifestations resemble those of love. David is moved by his friend's physique and even by his clothes: "When Steerforth, in white trousers, carried [Miss Creakle's]parasol for her, I felt proud to know him" (chap. vii). He was to preserve through life a poignant remembrance of that affection: "I admired and loved him, and his approval was return enough. It was so precious to me, that I look back on these trifles now with an aching heart" (chap. vii). When Steerforth insults Mr. Mell, the poor Salem House usher, and has him dismissed, a curious scene takes place, in the course of which the boy is seen in a hateful light, as a selfish, conceited, cruel, caddish being. But Dickens' art consists in conveying that impression to us while Steerforth is described in glowing terms by his worshipper David. The obvious inference is that Steerforth's defects are effaced in David's eyes by his friend's seductiveness, and the only argument the younger boy can put forward in defense of Steerforth is the worthless argument of love. At the very moment when Steerforth is about to crush Mr. Mell under his unjustifiable malevolence, David says: "I could not help thinking, even in that interval, I remember, what a noble fellow he was in appearance, and how homely and plain Mr. Mell looked opposed to him" (chap. vii).

When David is returning to his mother for the holidays, the thought that he will find her with Murdstone elicits from him the feeling: "On the road—I am not sure I was glad to be there—not sure but that I would rather have remained away, and forgotten [the happy past] in Steerforth's company" (chap. viii). In the course of his terrible journey from London to Dover, while spending a night in the open air, close to the wall of the school, David suddenly wakes up: "I . . . found myself sitting upright, with Steerforth's name upon my lips, looking wildly at the stars . . ." (chap. xii). When they meet again several years later, David sheds tears of joy and Steerforth affectionately nicknames him *Daisy,* then treats him as a sort of plaything (chaps. xix–xx), at which

David is "glowing with pleasure" (chap. xx). "I joyfully believed that he treated me in life unlike any other friend he had. I believed that I was nearer to his heart than any other friend, and my own heart warmed with attachment to him" (chap. xxi). And indeed the tone in which Steerforth talks to him has something exceptional about it: "I am never contented, except with your freshness, my gentle Daisy" (chap. xxii). The last words spoken by David to Steerforth on this earth are still brimful with warm affection: " 'You have no best to me, Steerforth,' said I, 'and no worst. You are always equally loved, and cherished in my heart' " (chap. xxix). Every expression of David's feelings for Steerforth reveals in the hero, as in the author of *Copperfield,* a unique gift of friendship and an extraordinary vividness of emotion.

Copperfield can thus be seen clearly as a study in psychological autobiography, in which Dickens has not spared himself, since, together with many amiable or even admirable qualities, he has also imparted to his hero and representative many weaknesses painted equally from the living model. Yet, in spite of the regard for truth with which Dickens has endeavored to depict the least flattering aspects of his hero, he seems frequently to feel the urge to justify, or at least excuse, such weaknesses by generalizing them: "What is natural in me, is natural in many other men" (chap. xxxii), David writes, for instance, before mentioning his unimpaired affection for Steerforth after the elopement with Emily. There are other little defensive assaults against mankind:

> I suppose that when I saw Dora in the garden and pretended not to see her, and rode past the house pretending to be anxiously looking for it, I committed two small fooleries which other young gentlemen in my circumstances might have committed—because they came so very natural to me (chap. xxxiii).

He is distressed by Miss Betsey's loss of her fortune, but there is something clearly defensive in his insistence on the non-selfish motives of his feelings: "I was roused from my amazement, and concern for her—I am sure, for her—by her falling on my neck" (chap. xxiv). Similarly, after confessing to the jealousy aroused in him by Mr. Spenlow's death and its absorbing effect on Dora, David demonstrates that his conscience is not clear: "In the trouble of this state of mind—not exclusively my own, I hope, but known to other people . . ." (chap. xxxviii). And when he has occasion to pass an over-all judgment on his own personality, he tries once more to lose himself in the anonymous crowd of humanity: "I write the truth, whatever contradictions and inconsistencies there were within me, as there are within so many of us . . . I knew nothing of . . ." (chap. xxxix).

It will be observed that all of the above examples belong to the same section (chaps. xxxii–xxxix) of the novel, that is, to a single period of David's life—the troubled time during which he shows himself in the least pleasing light. It is as though Dickens had so closely associated himself with David that he was ashamed of appearing to the reader in such an unflattering aspect and attempted to extenuate the impression produced.

Of course it was only as David Copperfield, in an ingenious disguise, that Dickens appeared in the book. But as early as 1850, part of the truth was guessed by more than one reader, and the *Fraser's Magazine* reviewer, for instance, wrote as follows:

> We have several reasons for suspecting that, here and there, under the name of David Copperfield, we have been favoured with passages from the personal history, adventures and experiences of Charles Dickens. Indeed, this conclusion is in a manner forced upon us by the peculiar professions selected for the ideal character, who is first a newspaper reporter and then a famous novelist. There is, moreover, an air of reality pervading the whole book to a degree never attained in any of his previous books.[7]

That critic's insight was not emulated by some members of the Dickens circle, who failed to suspect the amount of autobiography in *Copperfield*. The novelist's second son, Sir Henry F. Dickens, confesses in his *Memories* that in 1869,

> I had not the faintest idea that he had gone through those terrible days, when, as quite a child, he tied up bottles of blacking for a small pittance. I knew, in a general sort of way, that David Copperfield

---

[7] Dec., 1850, pp. 689–710; quoted in *Dickensiana,* 105.

to a certain extent portrayed some of his own life; but it never entered my mind that he had gone through this pitiable struggle until Forster's Life was published.[8]

His testimony is revealing of the reticent atmosphere in Dickens' home and of the sincere disgust with which the novelist regarded his childish experiences. In order to relieve himself of them, he had found it easier to give a public, but indirect, confession, than to impart the whole truth directly to his wife and children.

A number of additional documents confirm Dickens' intense emotional involvement in the creation of *Copperfield*. They are the various prefaces he wrote for the successive editions of the novel and the few letters in which he had occasion to mention it. To Mrs. Watson he wrote on September 16, 1850, while he was composing the beginning of the last number, that in order to take up his private correspondence he had had first of all to emerge from *Copperfield* "into a condition of temporary and partial consciousness" and went on to describe the effect the book was having on himself:

> There are some things in the next "Copperfield" that I think better than any that have gone before. After I have been believing such things with all my heart and soul, two results always ensue: first, I can't write plainly to the eye, secondly, I can't write sensibly to the mind.[9]

And to the generality of his readers he made, in the brief 1850 preface, similar disclosures:

> I do not find it easy to get sufficiently far away from this book, in the first sensation of having finished it, to refer to it with the composure, which this formal heading would seem to require . . . all that I could say of the story, to any purpose, I have endeavoured to say in it. . . . It would concern the reader little, perhaps, to know . . . how an author feels as if he were dismissing some portion of himself into the shadowy world, when a crowd of the creatures of his brain are going from him for ever. Yet I have nothing else to tell. . . . No

[8] *Memories of My Father*, London, 1932.
[9] *Letters* (MDGH), I, 226–27.

one can believe this Narrative in the reading, more than I have believed it in the writing.

Finally, when the *Charles Dickens Edition* of his complete works was published in 1867, he had the original preface reprinted and merely added to it a few words: "The foregoing remarks are what I originally wrote under the head of Preface to the Personal History of David Copperfield. I have nothing to add to them at this time."

Keen as were Dickens' interest in and love for the character on whom he had bestowed such a considerable part of his inner self, there is no absolute coincidence between the two. John Forster, who has often been regarded as his friend's impudent hagiographer and systematic whitewasher, stresses with moderate severity one essential difference: "It would be the greatest mistake to suppose that the youth [Dickens], who then received his first harsh schooling in life, came out of it as little harmed or hardened as David did."[10] Forster must have carefully weighed his words, for he never wished to bear severely on the memory of the friend he had not ceased to respect and to love faithfully. His few reservations must be trusted implicitly, because they were reluctant admissions and Forster was in a position to find out just how much Dickens, unlike David, had been harmed and hardened by his early trials. So there is one more aspect of psychological autobiography in *Copperfield*. It does not merely describe or relate what Dickens had actually been or done, it also reveals, involuntarily perhaps, what he wished he had been or done instead.

There is, therefore, side by side with a great deal of confession, some transposition of events and tendencies. The use of emigration on such a large scale in *Copperfield* is not simply due to technical convenience. It also expresses an aspect of Dickens' personality. The technical advantages—for emigration enables the novelist to dispose of troublesome characters as efficiently and less saddeningly than death—had already been exploited in *Pickwick*, where its victims had been Jingle and his servant and the two medical students. In *Copperfield*, the procedure has been considerably enlarged and improved. Julia Mills and her father are the first to go: "Mr. Mills . . . had brought his conduct to a climax

[10] Forster, *Life of Dickens*, II, 105

by taking it into his head that he would go to India" (chap. xli). But it is mostly with the massive departure for Australia of the Peggottys, reinforced by all the Micawbers, then by Mrs. Gummidge, and finally by Martha Endell, that the British Empire comes into its own as the safest storage place for used-up characters. It will be revealed later that Mr. Mell has also found a refuge in Australia, which, in his case, is fairyland as well as storage place, since he has miraculously acquired a doctorate and become headmaster of a school which, with miraculous forgetfulness of the injustice and humiliation he has endured, he calls "Colonial Salem House" (chap. lxiii).

A significant speech of Miss Betsey's shows the link between emigration and psychological autobiography in *Copperfield*. Dickens' constant attitude in private life is known to have consisted in similarly sending away any member of the family whose presence he did not wish for. All his sons had either to emigrate or find distant employment. As early as 1851, he sent two of his sons to study in Germany, one in Leipzig and the other in Hamburg. No doubt, whenever he was led to make such decisions, Dickens succeeded in convincing himself that they were in conformity not only with his children's "best interest," but also with their desires and tastes. He was like Miss Betsey who, after unequivocally suggesting that Mr. Micawber go away—"Mr. Micawber, I wonder you have never turned your thoughts to emigration" —replies a few moments later to Mrs. Micawber's question with superb assurance: " 'There is but one question, my dear ma'am, I could wish to ask. . . . The climate, I believe, is healthy.' 'Finest in the world' " (chap. lii). Her assurance and her enthusiasm are those of people who have never been, and are determined never to go, to the countries in question. They reassure and comfort themselves in that way. Another illustration of the same attitude had been provided earlier in the novel when Jack Maldon, Annie Strong's cousin, was about to leave for India. In the course of the conversation about his prospects, all those who stayed back had succeeded in persuading themselves that the young man's fate was enviable: "I recollect that it was settled by general consent that India was quite a misrepresented country, and had nothing objectionable in it, but a tiger or two, and a little heat in the warm part of the day" (chap. xvi). Leipzig and Hamburg, and Australia and

India, must have been discussed in similar terms by Dickens with his sons.

The author's parents and his relationship with them have been more subtly transposed in *David Copperfield*. David has no parents in the book, after Mrs. Copperfield's death in Chapter IX. Yet, although Mr. and Mrs. John Dickens did not become Mr. and Mrs. Copperfield, some of their traits were introduced into the narrative in various ways. Their outward aspects were embodied in Mr. and Mrs. Micawber, who are among the most successful figures in the book. Mr. Micawber in particular enjoys the critics' and readers' unanimous affection. Thackeray called him "the accomplished, the Epicurean, the dirty, the delightful Micawber,"[11] and George Gissing takes off his hat to the same character, in a felicitous phrase: "To speak severely of Mr. Micawber is beyond the power of the most conscientious critic, whether in life or art."[12] Yet our present concern is not with moral or even aesthetic judgments on the Micawbers, but with the amount of autobiographical revelation and transposition their portraits may contain. The most interesting aspect of the situation from that point of view is the division of the part played by Dickens' parents in reality among several fictional characters. Mrs. Copperfield stands for sentimental, uncritical, not to say unintelligent, love and tenderness. Mr. Murdstone embodies the cruelty of the decision which sentences the young boy to a life of degrading labor. As to the Micawbers, they have inherited the essential part, two picturesque and appealing personalities in spite of serious deficiencies. Miss Betsey, who fulfills with greater efficiency and intelligence than anybody else the function of parent to David, whose guide, adviser, protector, and comforter she is, represents what Dickens understandably wished he had had. The fact that there had been no Betsey Trotwood in Dickens' real life no doubt accounts for the radical difference pointed out by Forster between Dickens and David. Betsey Trotwood embodies the novelist's notion of what a parent must be in order to be at the same time, and in the fullest acceptation of the term, an educator.

Micawber has an intrinsic interest, somewhat like Mrs. Gamp's, for his appeal is rather mysterious. The existence of a few characters like Mr. Micawber and Mrs. Gamp, whose charm is irresistible, has prob-

11 *The Works of Thackeray*, XXXV, 372.
12 *Ch. Dickens, Critical Study*, 100.

ably done more than any other element to make Dickens' work immortal. But the nature of the creative process involved is infinitely elusive. Some devices are so obvious that they cannot cast much light on the result, for other writers could have used, or have used, the same devices with different results. And the rest can hardly be defined. In Micawber's case, however, there is at least one element that is sufficiently concrete and original to be commented on. Mr. Micawber's language is highly idiosyncratic. The few letters by John Dickens that have been preserved and his son's passing allusions—"as my father would say"—show that Mr. Micawber's speech had its source in the living model. An inordinate fondness for Latin words of legal origin and for pedantic circumlocutions is the most obvious characteristic. When he enters Traddles' room and finds a stranger there, Micawber apologizes as follows: "I was not aware that there was any individual, alien to this tenement, in your sanctum." Then, on being questioned about his health and the health of his wife and family, he replies: "I am in *statu quo.* . . . Mrs. Micawber . . . is also, thank God, *in statu quo.* . . . [The children] are likewise in the enjoyment of salubrity" (chap. xxvii). The last phrase is said to have been one of John Dickens' favorite expressions. When Mr. Micawber is pressed for details about his wife's chronic condition, he says: "Mrs. Micawber is in a state of health which renders it not wholly improbable than an addition may be ultimately made to those pledges of affection which—in short, to the infantine group . . ." (chap. xxvii). He almost invariably loses himself amid the complexities of his circumlocutions and has both to cut them short and to translate them back into understandable English. When he has had to evade his creditors' watchfulness through a twofold subterfuge, he refers to it grandiloquently: "I have been under the necessity of assuming a garb from which my natural instincts recoil—I allude to spectacles—and possessing myself of a cognomen to which I can establish no legitimate pretensions" (chap. xxxvi). Besides his display of verbal difficulties, Dickens has reinforced Micawber's comic power by making him display his financial difficulties in a way which associates the humor of repetition—of phrases and situations—and the humor of contrast—between his brilliant economic principles and his lamentable practice.

Finally, there is one more device that can be defined with precision.

It consists in ascribing to Mr. and Mrs. Micawber ever renewed and grandiose plans for the future, even when present circumstances are at their most sordid and unpromising. One of the best illustrations is the passage in which Mr. Micawber explains how he will organize his life once the famous advertisement penned by his wife has yielded its fruits. In the announcement, it is his intention to "describe himself plainly as so and so, with such and such qualifications, and to put it thus: 'Now employ me, on remunerative terms, and address post-paid to W.M., Post-Office, Camden Town.'" And when affluence has been secured:

> There would probably be an interval, he explained, in which he should content himself with the upper part of a house . . . say in Piccadilly—which would be a cheerful situation for Mrs. Micawber; and where, by throwing out a bow-window, or carrying up the roof another story, or making some alteration of that sort, they might live, comfortably and reputably, for a few years (chap. xxviii).

Not all that Dickens has written about the Micawbers is in the best of taste. Mrs. Micawber does not enjoy his respect even in her emotions, and whereas each of David's childish tears is felt to be venerable and sacred, Mrs. Micawber's grief for her parents' death is not to be taken seriously:

> "My mama departed this life," said Mrs. Micawber, "before Mr. Micawber's difficulties commenced, or at least before they became pressing. My papa lived to bail Mr. Micawber several times, and then expired, regretted by a numerous circle." Mrs. Micawber shook her head and dropped a pious tear upon the twin who happened to be in hand (chap. xii).

Certainly the association here established between Mrs. Micawber's conventional sorrow and two of her comic mechanisms—reference to financial difficulties and presence of one twin at her breast—precludes compassion and calls for an attitude of amusement. In any case, there can be no doubt that Dickens sincerely loved the Micawbers. The only pathetic episode in which Micawber takes part is quite moving. He cannot bear to remain the unwilling accomplice of Heep's dishonesty and to such moral agony he prefers the mirthful poverty of yore: " 'It is my fate,' said Mr. Micawber, unfeignedly sobbing, but doing even that, with a shadow of the old expression of doing something genteel; 'it is my fate, gentlemen, that the finer feelings of our nature have become reproaches to me . . .'" (chap. xlix). And the clown's struggle against his overwhelming sorrow is described with understanding and insight, due in great part to the author's filial love. John Dickens had not been the exact counterpart of Wilkins Micawber. The novelist's father, for instance, had learned shorthand before his son did so, an achievement of which the character in *Copperfield* would not have been capable. And Dickens' epitaph for his father, in which he called him "a zealous, useful, cheerful spirit."[13] shows that a purely Micawberish view of John Dickens would not be justified. Yet many of the qualities which gained Charles Dickens' love for both of them, and the love of generation after generation of readers for the fictional person, had indeed been among the characteristics of the living original.

One more character can cast some light upon the ways of psychological autobiography in *David Copperfield*. Betsey Trotwood has sometimes been regarded as the real heroine of the novel. She is at any rate its most powerful creation and she embodies, better than David does, an interesting aspect of David's personality and aspirations. She is all that the novelist loved most: superficially eccentric and arbitrary, but at bottom generous and sensitive.

In the course of her long and glorious career is revealed an extraordinarily vigorous personality, which obviously enthralls Dickens and has captivated all his readers since. In the very first chapter, before David's birth, she asserts herself authoritatively and erroneously:

> "I have no doubt it will be a girl. I have a presentiment that it must be a girl. Now, child, from the moment of the birth of this girl—" "Perhaps boy," my mother took the liberty of putting in. "I tell you I have a presentiment that it must be a girl," returned Miss Betsey. "Don't contradict. From the moment of this girl's birth, child, I intend to be her friend . . . ."

Later, she takes up Mr. Dick's defense with lovable bad faith, which

---

13 Forster, *Life of Dickens*, II, 92.

can only originate in her generous affection. After summing up Dick's sister's life in very general terms—"She did what they all do—took a husband. And he did what they all do—made her wretched."—she comes to the ticklish point, which is Mr. Dick's tendency to refer to King Charles' head: "That's his allegorical way of expressing it. He connects his illness with great disturbance and agitation, naturally, and that's the figure, or the simile, or whatever it's called, which he chooses to use, and why shouldn't he, if he thinks proper!" In her defense of Dick she also makes use of an argument which can probably be regarded as the masterpiece of arbitrariness: "If he likes to fly a kite, what of that! Franklin used to fly a kite. He was a Quaker or something of that sort, if I am not mistaken. And a Quaker flying a kite is a much more ridiculous object than anybody else" (chap. xiv).

Miss Betsey is characterized by the remarkable brusqueness of her manners, which imparts to her every speech and step the charm of the unexpected. One morning, after a few weeks' peaceful life at Dover, she suddenly asks David: " 'Should you like to go to school at Canterbury?' I replied that I should like it very much, it being so near her. 'Good,' said my aunt. 'Should you like to go to-morrow?' " (chap xv). When she goes to London in order to help her nephew with his choice of a profession, she expresses systematic distrust of the food presented to her, acting by a peremptory principle:

> "I hope the steak may be beef, but I don't believe it. Nothing's genuine in the place in my opinion, but the dirt." "Don't you think the fowl may have come out of the country, aunt?" I hinted. "Certainly not." returned my aunt. "It would be no pleasure to a London tradesman to sell anything which was what he pretended it was" (chap. xxiii).

Among many other examples which might be given of Miss Betsey's original firmness of thought which makes her style vigorously idiosyncratic, one more will suffice. It has reference to one of her most powerful antipathies, her dislike of Uriah Heep, who has been unfortunate enough to indulge before her in a few contortions:

> "Don't be galvanic, sir." "I ask your pardon, Miss Trotwood,"

returned Uriah; "I am aware you're nervous." "Go along with you, sir!" said my aunt, anything but appeased. "Don't presume to say so! I'm nothing of the sort. If you're an eel, sir, conduct yourself like one. If you're a man, control your limbs, sir! Good God!" said my aunt with great indignation, "I am not going to be serpentined and corkscrewed out of my senses!" (chap. xxxv).

The presence of Betsey Trotwood in *David Copperfield* is the supreme achievement of Dickens' art in his autobiographical novel. Miss Betsey is an entirely imaginary creation, yet she is fully as convincing, as lively, and as real as the characters painted from identifiable originals. The high degree of veracity achieved by the novelist in that book, thanks to the use of many psychological facts, spreads over the imaginary section of the work. That superior truthfulness secures the unity and the permanence of the whole book.

XXI: Dickens' Language and Style in *David Copperfield*

Dickens' most inspired and spontaneous, and his most careful and elaborate, novel is probably *David Copperfield*. It is, therefore, particularly well adapted to a study of the author's language and style. The pages, paragraphs, sentences, and even words of that book illustrate how fifteen years of literary life and success have perfected the wonderful instrument which nature and the accidents of an eventful formative period had placed at the writer's disposal.

Dickens' use of language in *Copperfield* is characterized above all by the frequent recurrence of a number of words each of which corresponds to some aspect of his personality. In the first place, there are three adjectives whose significant repetition emphasizes the author's sentimentality: "little," "own," and "old." "Little" is constantly used by Dickens where another author might have used "small." His preference for this word, which has, according to the *Oxford Dictionary*, "emotional implications not given by small," reveals his personal emotional approach to situations in a way that makes "little" the most characteristic word in the whole Dickensian vocabulary. In a series of fourteen chapters—Chapters IX–XXIII—without taking into account the many occasions when Emily is called "Little Em'ly," this favorite adjective occurs 186 times.[1] Its sentimental value is easily perceived. Within a single page of Chapter IX, while David is in the shop of Mr. Omer, the Yarmouth undertaker, shortly before Mrs. Copperfield's burial, a moment when the atmosphere is supremely emotional, the word "little" is used five times. David asks: "Do you know how my little brother is, sir?" Then, on hearing that the child is in his mother's arms, in other words, dead, he exclaims: "Oh, poor little fellow!" All so far is quite normal and in strict accordance with the traditional distinction between "little" and "small." Yet emotion soon extends from persons to things and David speaks of the "little room" in which he finds himself, of the "little trip" which Minnie plans to take with her young man on the occasion of the funeral, and even of the "little nails" —they are coffin nails, of course—which the workman keeps in his mouth.

The frequent recurrence of "own" has a slightly different connotation. It is particularly striking in the Murdstone and Grinby episode, a passage of intense self-pity. In the same group of fourteen chapters as above there are eighty-five "owns." Most of them are applied by David to himself, often quite appropriately, but sometimes unnecessarily. Let us look at three examples from one page of Chapter X: "A solitary condition . . . apart from the society of all other boys of my own age, apart from all companionship but my own spiritless thoughts," and "A little small light-haired wife, whom I can just remember connecting in my own thoughts with a pale tortoise-shell cat." The first two are legitimate, as their function is clearly to oppose David's solitude to the normal outside world, but the third could have been dispensed with. There is even something morbid in David's way of emphasizing the privacy of his thinking.

"Own" is occasionally employed by other characters, such as Mr. Murdstone, who is of course not sentimental, but who is intensely proud, with similar results: "I have my own opinion . . . founded . . . in part on my knowledge of my own means and resources. . . . I place this boy under the eye of a friend of my own, in a respectable business," he tells Miss Betsey, who then retorts: "About the respectable business

[1] Most of the figures mentioned in the following paragraphs concern that section of the novel.

. . . if he had been your own boy, you would have put him to it, just the same, I suppose!" And Miss Murdstone cuts in with: "If he had been my brother's own boy . . . his character, I trust, would have been altogether different" (chap. xiv).

A complete examination of Dickens' sentimental vocabulary in *Copperfield* ought to deal with the emotional use of "poor" and "miserable," but they are not of comparable importance to the third favorite—"old." In Chapters XI–XXI, "old" occurs ninety-seven times. Dickens' liking for that adjective is striking and he almost invariably uses it in the emotional sense of "familiar" rather than in the primary sense of "not young." This is not surprising in a novel written under the influence of sincere and vivid emotion and in which sentimental complacency in the contemplation of the past imparts to whatever belongs to former days—to the time "of old,"—an irresistible charm. There are numerous examples of this attitude in *Copperfield*. Speaking to David of his young, dead mother, Peggotty says: "The last time that I saw her like her own old self was the night when you came home, my dear . . ." (chap. ix). Here the combination of the two keywords "own" and "old" is the sure sign of an emotional crisis, like the combination of "old" and "little" in a tender description of Little Em'ly: "She sat, at this time, and all the evening, on the old locker, in her old little corner by the fire" (chap. xxi). At the end of the novel, when David, now a widower, sees Agnes again in her home after three years' separation, she tells him: "Here are the old books, Trotwood, and the old music" to which he replies: "Even the old flowers are here . . . or the old kinds" (chap. lx). Dickens' fondness for the word is such that even when he uses it in its primary sense, he cannot help presenting it in an amiable light. David, for instance, is immediately under the spell of Mr. Wickfield's home, where everything is old: "the quaint little panes of glass and quainter little windows . . . as old as the hills"; "the tall old chimneypiece"; "a wonderful old staircase"; "old oak seats"; "all old nooks and corners"; "a glorious old room" (chap. xv).

Besides his sentimental tendency, many other aspects of Dickens' character are illuminated by the study of his vocabulary. His natural intensity is clearly revealed by words like "quite," "great," "indeed," by the phrase "a good"—or "a great"—"deal," and by the presence of numerous superlatives and other forms of reinforcement. "Quite" appears eighty-nine times in Chapters IX–XXI, and that adverb is called upon to intensify a wide variety of adjectives throughout the narrative. Its frequency is strikingly great in the Yarmouth scenes, which shows its implicit connection with his sentimental vocabulary. It is first found in Chapter III—"I Have a Change" on David's first visit to Mr. Peggotty's—and in that single chapter occur the following expressions: "I was quite tired"; "the counterpane made my eyes quite ache"; "you're quite a sailor"; "I felt it difficult to picture him quite at his ease"; "I hardly know enough of the race . . . to be quite certain"; "I am sure I loved that baby quite as truly, quite as tenderly"; "I did not quite understand"; " 'Peggotty!' said I, quite frightened"; "I knew quite well that he was looking at us both." Within eight chapters—XIV–XXII—are to be found thirty uses of "indeed," most frequently in the characters' speeches. Uriah Heep, in his constant fawning and in his desire to be persuasive, is a great wielder of "indeed." The slightly childish "a good deal" and "a good many" for "much" or "many" also crop up often. Finally, in the intensifying vocabulary, the first place is occupied by "great," which appears as the counterpart of "little." The difference between "great" and "big" or "large" is said, by the *Oxford Dictionary* again, to be that "great" is employed "usually with implied surprise, contempt, indignation, etc." so that Dickens' preference once more goes to the more sentimental English word. In Chapters XI–XXI, "great" occurs eighty-five times.

Intensity is expressed in other ways also. The superlative recurs so often in *David Copperfield* that there can hardly be a single emotion not experienced by the hero in its supreme degree, or a single kind of sight not seen by him in its most representative form. In the quotations that follow, it will often be observed that the superlative is itself reinforced and intensified by "ever" or "never." Of the old clothes dealer in Chatham, David says: "There never was such another drunken madman in this line of business" (chap. xiii), and to him the laid up Barkis "looked the queerest object I ever beheld" (chap. xxi); yet when Miss Mowcher appeared, "I never did in my days behold anything like Miss Mowcher" (chap. xxii). "In my days" does not add perceptibly to the meaning and is only a way of reinforcing and intensifying the expression.

David meets with a fierce-looking milkman: "As to his dealing in the mild article of milk . . . there never was a greater anomaly" (chap. xxvii). Of Mrs. Crupp he tells us: "I never was so much afraid of anyone" (chap. xxviii). Miss Dartle's song is "the most unearthly I have ever heard in my life, or can imagine" (chap. xxix), in which "in my life"— like "in my days" of the previous quotation—and perhaps "or can imagine" add very little to the sense of an expression which really means: Miss Dartle's song was very unearthly. Of Miss Betsey, her nephew writes, "I believe there never was anybody with such an imperturbable countenance when she chose" (chap. xxxv); of Mr. Micawber: "I never saw a man so thoroughly enjoy himself . . . as Mr. Micawber did that afternoon" (chap. xxviii); and of Mr. Micawber's culinary masterpiece, one page later, "There never was a greater success." When Agnes and Dora become acquainted: "I never was so happy. I never was so pleased as when I saw those two sit down together" (chap. xlii). Within a single page of the melodramatic scene on the bank of the Thames with Martha Endell occur two superlative notes: "I have never known what despair was, except in the tone of those words. . . . I never saw, in any painting or reality, horror and compassion so impressively blended" (chap. xlvii), and again after the departure of the emigrants' ship: "A sight at once so beautiful, so mournful and so hopeful . . . I never saw" (chap. lvii). David makes the acquaintance of young Mrs. Traddles and concludes: "A more cheerful, amiable, honest, happy, bright-looking bride, I believe . . . the world never saw" (chap. lix).

When they are thus accumulated, such vigorous expressions destroy one another's effect. When the characters' whole emotional life goes on in the superlative degree, there occurs a downward leveling of all emotion. The author's fondness for strong expressions is shown explicitly in a fragment of conversation between the hero and Littimer, who says:

"Mr. Steerforth will be glad to hear how you have rested, sir."
"Thank you," said I, "very well indeed. Is Mr. Steerforth quite well?"
"Thank you, sir, Mr. Steerforth is tolerably well." Another of his characteristics. No use of superlatives. A cool calm medium always (chap. xxi).

It will be observed that the contrast between David-Dickens' warm words ("very well indeed," "quite well") and the servant's prudent coolness ("tolerably well") does not seem sufficiently clear to the author. He must emphasize the point: "No use of superlatives." Mildness of speech is a serious, unforgivable offense. It is hardly an exaggeration to say that the absence of superlatives, the cold, calculating reticence, and the lack of impulse and passion already betray the criminal in Littimer and foreshadow his later imprisonment. Dickens will not have "a cool calm medium," or certainly not "always."

Now and then, however, Dickens would realize the potential danger in his excessive fondness for intense and energetic expressions and use such terms as "almost," "nearly," and "hardly ever," (instead of "never") in order to tone down the effect of being too categorical in his assertions. The use of extenuating phrases even becomes a secondary, though perceptible, characteristic of his style. Within a few pages, in Chapters X and XI, an imposing series can be found: "so squeezed that I could hardly bear it"; "until the breath was nearly wedged out of me"; "he ... almost choked her"; "[Steerforth] will give you almost as many men as you like at draughts, and beat you easily"; "I have almost lost the capacity of being much surprised by anything"; "I hardly ever ... saw both the twins detached from Mrs. Micawber at the same time."

Still, Dickens' tendency to use and even abuse reinforcing adverbs is very pronounced—they will often miss their aim when they are applied to terms intrinsically energetic. The tendency is perceptible in Dickens' letters, always written in a highly tense style, and also in *Copperfield,* especially, it would seem, when his self-control is relaxed and he lapses into his most spontaneous, least elaborate modes of expression. Words like "heart-broken," "dejected," "angelic," "luxurious," "wretched and miserable," "atrocious," "worn out," "dreadful," "assuredly," "terror," "elated," "amazing," and "appalling," are undoubtedly among the most energetic in the English language. For this reason, any attempt at further intensifying them can only detract from their vigor, since it amounts to treating them like ordinary adjectives and disguising their distinctive force. Yet that is just what Dickens does when he writes: "quite heart-broken," "greatly dejected"; "perfectly angelic"; "a very luxurious state of mind"; "a very wretched and miserable condition"; "a most atrocious criminal"; "quite worn out"; "the most dreadful manner"; "perfectly miserable"; "most assuredly"; "infinite terror"; "greatly elated"; "most amazing"; "most appalling."[2]

Another kind of leveling can be achieved through a less close juxtaposition. For instance, when the adverbs "exquisitely," "utterly," and "perfectly" are all three used in one and the same paragraph (chap. xi), or within a few lines of each other, one finds the following expressions: "in a most distrustful manner"; "such extreme joy," "a very unmelodious laugh"; and "a most delicious meal" (chap. v), an impression of uniformity is created, instead of the impression of high relief that Dickens was aiming at in each case.

The remarkable and sustained vigor of expression in Dickens' style is accompanied by a curious hesitancy which nothing in his character seems to suggest, but which is revealed by the recurrence of the phrases "a kind of" or "a sort of." Dickens' thinking and creative vision were vague or blurred very little, yet the text of *Copperfield* leaves no doubt about the existence of the opposite tendency. In Chapters IX–XXI, the two phrases are employed no fewer than seventy-seven times. This may result from an attempt at compensating for the excessive trenchancy to be found more often. Or it may be due to the author's desire to produce, by dint of apparent scrupulousness, a greater sense of truth, again in connection with the autobiographical character of the work. But, as the frequency of such forms is hardly less in Dickens' other novels, it is more probable that the main cause for this phenomenon lies in Dickens' liking for approximate illustration and simile. Dickens was aware that the proliferation of "a sort of" or "a kind of" was mainly characteristic of unintellectual and uncultivated persons. His awareness is shown by the implicit criticism contained in the awkward speech of men like Mr. Omer—"By that sort of thing we very often lose a little mint of money" (chap. ix)—or the coachman who takes David from Canterbury to London. Yet David's own frequent use of these phrases is not of decidedly higher quality. Almost invariably, "sort of" or "kind of" could be cancelled without suppressing anything except an element of un-

---

[2] Chaps. ii, iii, iv, v, x, xiv, xxii, lv. In *SB* were already to be found the forms "the most hopeless extreme" ("Scenes," chap. xi); "perfectly astonishing" ("Scenes," chap. ix); "most striking" ("Scenes," chap. i); "a perfectly wild state" ("Tales," Bk. I, chap. ii); "most inimitably" ("Tales" chap. xi); and, as in the famous letter about *OT*, "indispensably necessary" ("Tales," chap. xii).

profitable inaccuracy: "it made no sort of difference in her"; "he carried a jaunty sort of a stick"; "he was a sort of town traveller"; "a sort of grass-grown battery"; "in a sort of tune"; "with every sort of expression but wonder"; "with a strange kind of watery brightness."[3]

To bring to a close the list of the external, though significant aspects of Dickens' language in *Copperfield*, a word should be said of the stage directions with which the speeches of the characters are interspersed. It will be observed that he usually designates the author of each speech with great care. It is very seldom that a phrase, however brief, and even when it occurs unequivocally in dialogue, is mentioned without some specific reference to its origin. Almost invariably, there is at least a "said he" after the speech. Nor is there much variety in that respect. Sometimes, in the longer speeches, a second "said he" or an "added he" is inserted at or near the end, but the predominance of "said" over all the other verbs that can be similarly used is overwhelming. In Chapters XVI–XVIII, for instance, are to be found the following verbs: "asked" ten times and "inquired" twice, but "said" is often used after an interrogation in the sense of "asked"; "returned" twenty-one times; "answered" four times; "replied" six times; "retorted" three times; "exclaimed" three times; "observed" twice; "interposed" once; "pursued" and "repeated" three times each; "continued" and "hinted" once each; while "said" occurs ninety-three times. Only nineteen speeches are given without any verb. These rarely exceed a word or two—"Shall I?" "Certainly," "Yes, sir"—and when they occur in rapid conversation, they can be completed by a genuine stage direction without a verb, for instance, "with astonishment." Finally, within speeches already introduced by "he said" are to be found one "he added" and eleven repetitions of "he said."

The clear predominance of "said" shows that Dickens does not take much interest in this particular aspect of the presentation of dialogue. He is often bordering on theatrical writing, in which information of this kind has no place, while the suggestion of gestures and emotions plays a great part. This is precisely what happens in *Copperfield*. One can take a conversation from that novel almost at random, and the results will always be the same. For example in the case of the brief interview

[3] Chaps. x, xi, xiii.

between David and Steerforth in a London hotel (chap. xix), there are many stage directions:

> I looked at him . . . but I saw no recognition in his face. . . . I grasped him by both hands, and could not let them go. . . . shaking my hands heartily. . . . I brushed away the tears. . . . I made a clumsy laugh of it, and we sat down together, side by side. . . . clapping me on the shoulder. . . . He laughed as he ran his hand through the clustering curls of his hair, and said gaily. . . . Steerforth laughed heartily . . . clapping me on the shoulder again . . . "Holloa, you, sir!" this was addressed to the waiter who had been very attentive to our recognition at a distance, and now came forward deferentially. . . . the waiter with an apologetic air. . . . the waiter, still apologetically.

Every detail is described and the reader can visualize the scene as though he were seeing it performed in a theatre. The amount of attention bestowed by Dickens on gestures and attitudes is almost greater than his interest in the words spoken by the characters. His passionate attraction to the stage and the influence it had on his fictional art are made perceptible in such passages, which also confirm the somewhat visual and external rather than analytical nature of his approach to psychology and characterization.

Dickens' style in the days of *Copperfield* is much more distinctly his own than it had been at the time of *Sketches by Boz*. The words, phrases, and devices studied in the foregoing paragraphs ought to make a page by Dickens easily identifiable. And the habits concerned are, by the time of *Copperfield,* so ingrained that, with minor variations, they endure to the end of his career.

In spite of the recurrence of a number of words and phrases, Dickens' style in *Copperfield* is, of course, by no means uniform or monotonous. There is, on the contrary, considerable variety, if only because the novelist has created one specific idiom for each character according to his or her age, personality, social position, and training. This partly accounts for Dickens' comparative lack of interest in the explicit identification of the speakers taking part in a conversation. Each is unequivocally identified by his manner of speaking. In addition to their individual peculiarities, the members of the Yarmouth group are characterized by their use of the local dialect. The name of David's native village is derived from Blunderstone, a real place in Suffolk.[4] There are many Suffolk characters in the novel. Some are of trifling importance, like the anonymous coachmen, waiters, and fishermen. But the whole Peggotty circle also belongs to that group and their language is transcribed by Dickens with great care. Ham and his uncle and their friend Mrs. Gummidge have the most colorful dialect. They not only use peculiar pronunciations for current words—"fortnut" for "fortnight" (chap. iii); "wureds" or "wurems" for "words"[5] or "worms"; "a bahd's neezing" for "a bird's nesting" (chap. li); "somewheers" for "somewhere" (chap. xl); "keinder" for "kind of" (chap. xl); etc.—but also special words or phrases which Dickens sometimes sees fit to elucidate by means of a translation into ordinary parlance. Mr. Peggotty speaks of a "bacheldore" instead of "bachelor" (chap. iii). He says, threateningly, that he will be "gormed" if anybody refers to his generosity (chap. iii). The only explanation of that enigmatic word supplied by the author is not very encouraging: "It appeared, in answer to my enquiries, that nobody had the least idea of the etymology of this terrible verb passive to be gormed; but that they all regarded it as constituting a most solemn imprecation." One of Dickens' biographers suggests a possible origin: "'Gorm' was the name of the Scandinavian Cerberus—the dog of Hell."[6] It is again Mr. Peggotty who says: "We have had a mort of talk" (chap. xxxii); Mrs. Gummidge takes "to wimicking; . . . to find a Beein fur her wheer she can fisherate for herself" (chap. li); "I had my thowts o' coming to make inquiration for you, sir, to-night" (chap. xl). "Wimicking" is explained in the text as "our old county word for crying," and after "fisherate for herself" Dickens had added, "A beein signifies, in that dialect, a home, and to fisherate is to provide."

Since Dickens knew little of the area in which these episodes take place, having only spent a few days in Suffolk when he first visited it in January, 1849, his accurate knowledge of its dialect might be thought surprising. But the way in which he acquired such knowledge has been elucidated by an article in the *Times Literary Supplement,* whose

[4] See Wright, *Life of Ch. Dickens,* 205.
[5] Their pronunciation of this word is not always thus represented (in chap. l, Mr. Peggotty says "words.").
[6] Wright, *Life of Ch. Dickens,* 205.

author shows that Dickens derived the bulk of his East Anglian vocabulary and syntax from Major Edward Moor's book, *Suffolk Words and Phrases* (1823). Though he can bring forward no formal proof in support of his assertions—for, as he says himself, "The book is not recorded among those that were in [Dickens'] library, and [he] nowhere makes any reference to it."[7]—the author of the article places them beyond doubt. For instance, the word "beein" was explained by Moor as follows: "A home—a place to be in—if I could but git a beein I can fisherate for myself." Moor does not account for the mysterious verb "gorm" and merely lists a series of similar imprecations: "goles," "gooh," "gorns." "Wimicking" seems to have been inaccurately copied by Dickens from Moor's book, which gives the word as "winnicking." Similarly "to arrize," used in that form by Mr. Peggotty (chap. xlvi), is only to be found in Moor as "to awize." When he corrected the proofs, Dickens did alter "rr" to "w," but his correction was disregarded by the printer and has never been introduced since. In spite of such minor mishaps, the discovery of Dickens' source shows the instinctive skill with which he had selected a few elements out of Major Moor's book to impart to his characters' speech a local flavor.

Dickens' personality manifests itself through the style of *David Copperfield*. A typical expression of his personality is what may be called the "Dickensian detail." The acuteness of his observation of details is made evident by the frequent appearance, within a commonplace sentence, of a seemingly insignificant or superfluous word or detail, which nobody else would have thought of. Such notes are made inimitable through their very gratuitousness and increase the impression of life and truth produced by the descriptions to be found in *Copperfield*. One example is provided by the sentence in which David manages to combine a sentimental with a physical impression while describing Peggotty's embrace. Instead of writing, like everybody else, "She squeezed (or pressed) me to her heart (or bosom)," "the inimitable Boz" writes: "She squeezed me to her stays" (chap. v). Equally characteristic are the following examples:

---

[7] "David Copperfield and Dialect," From a Correspondent, *Times Lit. Sup.*, April 30, 1949, 288. The "correspondent" was Dr. K. J. Fielding.

An allusion was made by Mr. Peggotty over his pipe to the loss I had sustained (chap. x).

I have known [Mrs. Micawber] to be thrown into fainting fits by the king's taxes at three o'clock, and to eat lamb-chops breaded and drink warm ale (paid for with two tea-spoons that had gone to the pawnbroker's) at four (chap. xi).

In the second instance cited, all the factual information conveyed would have been neatly expressed by something like: "I have known her to be thrown into fainting fits by taxes at three and to make a hearty meal at four." The sentence is thus almost entirely made up of Dickensian details: "king's," "lamb," "warm," "two," "tea"; yet the most characteristic word undoubtedly is "breaded." Behind the old clothes dealer's shop in Chatham, David sees "a prospect of more stinging nettles and a lame donkey" (chap. xii); Mr. Dick, when watching the schoolboys' games, is seen clapping, not his hands, but "his worsted gloves in rapture" (chap. xvii); when Dora has fainted, "I ravaged Miss Mills's work-box for a smelling-bottle and in my agony of mind applied an ivory needle-case instead . . ." (chap. xxxviii). "Lame," "worsted," and "ivory" are again good examples of the pervasive Dickensian detail, which does much to create the originality of his style.

The language and style employed by Dickens in *Copperfield* are certainly not beyond criticism or reproach. In the first place, there is occasionally too great an accumulation of clauses, allusions, and factual notations within one sentence. These often result in disjointed, involved, and interminable sentences in which the clarity is seriously impaired. Some paragraphs are composed of a single sentence, consisting of a number of short, linked fragments:

We were sitting as before one evening (when my mother was out as before) in company with the stocking and the yard-measure, and the bit of wax, and the box with St. Paul's on the lid, and the crocodile book, when Peggotty, after looking at me several times, and opening her mouth as if she were going to speak, without doing it—which I thought was merely gaping, or I should have been rather alarmed—said coaxingly . . . (chap. ii).

346

(In the latter part of this quotation the verb "said," in particular, is remote from the subject "Peggotty.") Often excessive complexity makes the construction of a sentence somewhat unclear, or even indistinct to the point of being faulty:

> I set down this remembrance here, because it is an instance to myself of the manner in which I fitted all my old books to my altered life and made stories for myself out of the streets, and out of men and women, and how some main points in the character I shall unconsciously develop, I suppose, in writing my life, were gradually forming all this while (chap. xi).

The "how" with which the second part of the sentence opens results from carelessness, for it is only approximately equivalent to "the manner in which." It would have been better to read here "and in which some main points," or if "how" had to be used at all, "and of how some main points" or even "and an example of how," which would have done away with all ambiguity.

Faulty or at least loose syntax appears in David's words to Steerforth: "I understood him [Littimer] that you were at Oxford" (chap. xxviii). And Dickens' vocabulary, whose perfect Englishness and admirable wealth have often been praised, is itself sometimes rendered unsatisfactory, either through inaccuracy, or through illegitimate coinages. In Chapter VII, David speaks of the "fleshy cuts" inflicted on the unfortunate pupils by Mr. Creakle's cane. He means, and this is readily understood, strokes that cut into and hurt their flesh, but the word "fleshy" does not seem to have been used elsewhere in that sense. In Chapter VIII, he employs an adjective, "mumbly," that does not exist at all. Again, the meaning is clear enough, and it might be urged in defense of Dickens that the word ought to have existed. In Chapter X, "grope" appears as a noun, contrary to usage. In Chapter XVIII, the adjective "seedy" applied to biscuits is supposed to mean "containing seeds," like "seed-cakes," but there is no precedent. In Chapter XXIII, apparently on the analogy of "time-honoured" and "long-forgotten," Dickens coins the form "time-forgotten." In Chapter XXXIX, instead of the modern word "broker-age," Dickens uses the older form "brokery," which, according to the *New English Dictionary*, has not been current since 1641. "Hearth-

347

broomy" (chap. xli) and "immesh" (chap. lii) seem to be unjustified coinages.

Finally, there are also, in *Copperfield*, a number of involuntary repetitions of words and phrases. Admittedly, the device of repetition is usually deliberate, and even characteristic of Dickens' style. In the first chapter, for instance, there can be no doubt that a literary and psychological effect has been aimed at by that means. Miss Betsey is described "Sitting with the skirt of her dress tucked up, her hands folded on one knee, and her feet upon the fender, frowning at the fire"; and the description is repeated *verbatim* two pages later. Dickens does not content himself with then writing; "[Miss Betsey] sat down as before." Instead, he repeats every detail: "With her feet on the fender, the skirt of her dress tucked up and her hands folded on one knee." Mrs. Copperfield's conversation with Miss Betsey is several times interrupted by the younger woman's emotion, the circumstance being recorded each time in almost invariable terms. Thus one reads, within a few lines: "My mother broke down again here, and could get no further. . . . my mother [cried] in another burst of distress and breaking down again. . . . my mother [resumed] in another burst, and breaking down again . . . ." When Dr. Chillip is left alone with the formidable Miss Betsey, the same concatenation of incidents—a conversational attempt that causes Miss Betsey to unstop one of her ears, the doctor's fright, silence, the doctor's contemplation of Miss Betsey and Miss Betsey's contemplation of the fire, a brief visit of the doctor to his patient on being summoned by Peggotty, his return, etc.—is repeated twice within one page. In all those cases, the effect aimed at by the novelist is the same. He wishes above all to create an impression of familiarity and amusement.

But the constant appeal to such procedures in the book does not account for accidental repetitions like: "On another occasion . . . this same dear baby . . . was the innocent occasion of Miss Murdstone's going into a passion" (chap. vii) or "[Mr. Dick] was deeply interested in all our sports. . . . How often have I seen him . . . looking on with a face of unutterable interest . . ." (chap. xvii). There are other examples, all of which prove that Dickens occasionally worked too fast and did not reread with sufficient care what he had written.

A few illegitimate or hazardous coinages, and a few minor infelicities do not seriously detract from the general conclusion that *Copperfield* evinces mature and masterly stylistic art. Among the most striking, characteristic features of that art are to be found Dickens' images, which are of a high quality. Some are remarkable through their suggestiveness and terseness:

> The green baize on the top of the writing-table had lost all its colour, and was as withered and pale as an old pauper (chap. xxiii); [Mr. Spenlow] was obliged, when he glanced at some papers on his desk, after sitting down in his chair, to move his whole body, from the bottom of his spine, like Punch . . . .

The latter note is repeated twice in the stage directions for the ensuing speech, in increasingly esoteric terms: "With another inclination of his body. Punch again" and "Punch again" (chap. xxiii). Jip, Dora's dog, "growled within himself like a little double-bass," then "made a comfortable noise in answer, like a tea-kettle, when it sings" (chap. xxvi); Mrs. Micawber's voice when she sings is "a small, thin, flat voice, which I remember to have considered, when I first knew her, the very table-beer of acoustics" (chap. xviii).

Another group of images are less precise but more poetic. Mr. Spenlow "sat erect in Court among his papers, like a little lighthouse in a sea of stationery," while his colleagues are called "frozen-out old gardeners in the flower-beds of the heart."[8]

It is noticeable that the most vivid emotions and feelings are those that inspire Dickens with the greatest wealth of images. Thus his hatred of Uriah Heep leads him to overwhelm that character with a long series of unfavorable comparisons. Uriah is likened, for instance, to an evil spirit—an interesting kind of simile, in which a fictional creature is called upon to illuminate and illustrate the real—"I saw Uriah watch [Agnes] while she greeted us and he reminded me of an ugly and rebellious genie watching a good spirit" (chap. lii), then to a fish: "Uriah,

---

[8] Chap. xxxiii. Cf., *The Speeches of Charles Dickens*, ed. K. J. Fielding (Oxford, 1960), 134, June 9, 1851, at the Gardeners' Benevolent Institution: "a species of frozen-out old gardeners whom no thaw can ever penetrate [*hear, and laughter*]."

writhing himself into the silence like a conger eel" (chap. xlii), or again to an ape: "Looking as like a malevolent baboon, I thought, as anything human could look" (chap. xxxix).

Sometimes there will be an accumulation of images within a limited space. In the description of Mr. Creakle's afternoon class, David makes use of three revealing similes in the course of one short paragraph: "A buzz and hum go up round me, as if the boys were so many blue-bottles. . . . my head is as heavy as so much lead. . . . I sit . . . blinking at [Mr. Creakle] like a young owl" (chap. vii). And the description of the other schoolmaster, Dr. Strong, also comprises three comparisons, one of which leads to a fourth, so that the beginning of the paragraph concerning him is most characteristic:

> Doctor Strong looked almost as rusty . . . *as* the tall iron rails and gates outside the house; and almost as stiff and heavy *as* the great stone urns that flanked them, and were set up, on the top of the red-brick wall, at regular distances all round the court, *like* sublimated skittles, for time to play at. He was in his library . . . with . . . his shoes yawning *like* two caverns on the hearth-rug (chap. xvi, italics mine).

The mechanism that results in such a cascade of comparisons is here clearly to be seen. The author has at first looked for illustrations expressing the character's two main aspects, and found them in the school's rails and urns. But, once he has lapsed into description of the urns themselves, another illustrative simile is called into play. Later, the mere mention of the Doctor's shoes assumes the force of a precise vision and the vision demands another image. It should be added that at the beginning of the next sentence—still within the same paragraph—David mentions the Doctor's "lustreless eye, which reminded me of a long-forgotten blind old horse, who . . ." which is an improvement on the usual "as" or "like" employed to introduce the additional simile. Nor is such a proliferation of metaphors exceptional in *Copperfield*.

Among the metaphors most readily employed by Dickens, there is one special class which, like all the author's essential characteristics, is widely represented in *Copperfield*. That is what one might call the metaphor of negative intensification, an incongruous comparison meant to reinforce the weight of a negative phrase. Thus, Miss Murdstone's irony in her conversation with Miss Betsey "no more affected my aunt than it discomposed the cannon I had slept by at Chatham" (chap. xiv). It is a kind of *reductio ad absurdum*. A humorous example—of course the device is in its very nature humorous since it is founded on unexpected parallels—is supplied by the commentary on a question a coachman asks of young David: "'Shooting, sir?' said the coachman. He knew as well as I did that it was just as likely, at that time of year, I was going down there whaling; but I felt complimented too" (chap. xix). When he is learning stenography, David has reached the first stage at which he can take down a speech. He says that he would then have felt:

> Quite triumphant if I had had the least idea what my notes were about. But, as to reading them after I had got them, I might as well have copied the Chinese inscriptions on an immense collection of tea-chests, or the golden characters, in all the great red and green bottles in the chemists' shops (chap. xxxviii).

When he implores Ham not to undertake the impossible rescue of the man drowning in the stormy sea, David is compelled to conclude: "Against such determination as that of the calmly desperate man. . . . I might as hopefully have entreated the wind" (chap. lv).

The value of Dickens' style in *Copperfield* does not lie in superficial and external traits and devices of the kind analyzed in the foregoing pages. Therefore, although the general quality of the style is much less easily defined or even described, an attempt must now be made to show the author's stylistic progress since *Pickwick* and even since *Chuzzlewit* or *Dombey*.

The main point about that progress is that Dickens' style has become more sober. There is, of course, a good deal of truth in the traditional view that his style is diffuse, occasionally ornate or even grandiloquent. Yet, in the best pages of *Copperfield,* Dickens has successfully resisted his natural tendency to overemphasis and his permanent temptation of cumulative effects and exalted writing. There are many sentences which cannot but be regarded as genuinely sober. When David is about to leave his mother and go to Salem House, he tells us: "I tried to eat my parting breakfast, but my tears dropped upon my bread and butter, and trickled into my tea. I saw my mother look at me sometimes, and then glance at the watchful Miss Murdstone, and then look down, or look away" (chap. iv). Fastidious readers might think the two details illustrating the former sentence are not in the best of taste. But the latter is unobjectionable, has not one word too many or too few: it is perfect and perfectly sober. Nothing could more efficiently express Mrs. Copperfield's emotions, tenderness, fear, and submissiveness, than is done by that brief sentence. The announcement of Mrs. Copperfield's death to David and the relation of the funeral itself (chap. ix) are also overwhelmingly truthful and moving, owing to the simplicity of the style—a simplicity which is decidedly a novelty in Dickensian fiction.

Two other phrases will show more clearly how Dickens has achieved sobriety of style. On returning from his honeymoon trip, David defines the beginning of his married life in profound terms: "No one to please but one another—one another to please, for life" (chap. xliv). And of Mr. Peggotty he notes "that hushed concentration of his faculties which would have made his figure solitary in a multitude" (chap. xlvi). While he had been accustomed to use excessive expressions, more vigorous and intense than the objects they were meant to define, and thus surround the objects with wide circles of words that gave them a deformed and grotesque outline, Dickens is now doing the reverse. He is now drawing a tenuous line around the center of the object described and thus delicately suggesting its possible reverberations in many directions at once. This is more than a conversion from overstatement to understatement, from hyperbole to litotes. There is an intuitive discovery of the strength that belongs to restraint, of the rich and subtle resonance that can be achieved through incomplete though precise expression, of the perils of perpetual paroxysms.

Similar progress appears in the relation of Dora's death, as compared to the death of Paul Dombey and of Nell in the *Curiosity Shop.* The death of Barkis the messenger, which occurs a few chapters before Dora's in *Copperfield,* stands halfway between the old manner and the new. The narration of this event involves the use of mechanical devices, and sustained and iterative metaphors, but the emotion is already more natural and less systematically looked for (chap. xxx, "A Loss"). But

Dora's death rises to greater heights of sober narrative art. The whole of the relevant chapter (chap. liii) remains one of Dickens' most moving achievements, even in the eyes of readers and critics who tend to look down upon the Nell and Paul episodes, and even when one has read *David Copperfield* a score of times.[9] Dickens' success at this point can only be accounted for by the masterly husbanding of the stylistic and dramatic effects. David is not present at the death of his child-wife and does not hear her last words himself. He stays downstairs, alone with Dora's pet dog, Jip, also aged, ailing, and dying. No one announces Dora's death in words. David is musing alone: "As I look out on the night, my tears fall fast, and my undisciplined heart is chastened heavily —heavily." Then he sees Agnes come down. She has just left Dora's bedroom to come to him, and it is on Agnes' face and in her attitude that he reads the news:

> That face, so full of pity and of grief, that rain of tears, that awful mute appeal to me, that solemn hand upraised towards Heaven. "Agnes?" It is over. Darkness comes before my eyes, and, for a time all things are blotted out of my remembrance.

The fact that so few words should be spoken in the course of that closing scene, that there should not even be a closing scene, properly speaking, is a sure sign of Dickens' progress toward sober simplicity.

Finally, *Copperfield* contains illustrations of another stylistic tendency that had already been observable in *Chuzzlewit* and *Dombey,* the tendency to write in what sounds like an inspired tone. Such "inspired" passages are understandably more numerous in a work influenced by a powerful autobiographical urge, and the effect of exceptional inspiration on Dickens' style can be more clearly perceived here than elsewhere.

The most characteristic passages are those in which a kind of magic seems to operate and to modify the narrative rhythm and the lapse of time. Thus, in the description of David's early childhood, scene succeeds scene as in a kind of theatre of memory and the appearance of

[9] See the Copperfield Centenary issue of *The Dickensian,* and especially Bernard Darwin's excellent article (June, 1949, p. 139–41).

each new vision is ushered in by a transition belonging to that kind of inspired tone: "A great wind rises, and the summer is gone in a moment. We are playing in the winter twilight, dancing about the parlour" (chap. ii). The words are simple, the psychological phenomenon referred to is a familiar one, yet the impression produced is peculiar—it is as though a magic wand had suddenly touched the landscape or the scenery. Similarly, when David attempts to sum up in a few lines the slow end of a long term at Salem House, the skillful arrangement of the sentences, combining symmetry and rapid accumulation, conveys both the monotony of the schoolboy's daily life in the past and the swift procession of images in the memory of the man calling them up. The intermingling of the two types of duration is perceptible throughout the paragraph:

> The rest of the half-year is a jumble in my recollection of the daily strife and struggle of our lives; of the waning summer and the changing season; of the frosty mornings when we were rung out of bed, and the cold, cold smell of the dark nights when we were rung into bed again . . . (chap. viii).

And of course the four "Retrospects" afford remarkable examples of similar devices. The writer gives up the continuous narrative he has adopted for several hundred pages and substitutes for it a kind of visionary and poetical tone, a broken, though not inharmonious style, which is not unlike the later achievements in the discontinuous style of James Joyce or Virginia Woolf. At any rate, the juxtaposition of a multiplicity of brief notations does produce a powerful effect—it does put across a complete, coherent, convincing vision.

Dickens' language and style already possessed wealth and flexibility long before the days of *Copperfield*. The innovations and improvements introduced into that book have unquestionably made of it, whatever one may think of the construction and of the psychology, one of the masterpieces of English narrative prose.

XXII: *David Copperfield* AND THE PROGRESS OF DICKENS' ART

THE SUPERIORITY OF *David Copperfield* over Dickens' earlier novels is manifest in other directions besides its composition, its general truthfulness, and its language and style.

It has been seen that Dickens wrote *Copperfield* with greater ease than any previous work. Forster, who was the close witness and collaborator of its creation, has fully confirmed in advance the modern reader's impression in that respect:

> Once fairly in it the story bore him irresistibly along; certainly with less trouble to himself in the composition, beyond that ardent sympathy with the creatures of his fancy, which always made so absolutely real to him their sufferings or sorrows; and was probably never less harassed by interruption or breaks in his invention.[1]

This is an excellent description of the outward signs of felicitous and facile inspiration. The same friendly critic also points to the peculiar merits of the book produced under such favorable circumstances:

> He has nowhere given such variety of play to his invention, and the book is unapproached among his writings for its completeness of effect and uniform pleasantness of tone. . . . even the method of his narrative is more simple here than it generally is in his books. His imaginative growths have less luxuriance of underwood, and the crowds of external images always rising so vividly before him are more within control.[2]

Dickens himself no doubt experienced similar feelings, for he wrote to his friend in July, 1850, "I hope myself that some heretofore deficient qualities are there."[3]

In addition to the "heretofore deficient qualities" already described in the preceding chapters, Dickens' new audacities, his treatment of comedy and pathos, of psychology and morals, all tend to show the progress of Dickens' art in *Copperfield*.

One of the limitations, if not of the weaknesses, of his art as a novelist, had always been the reticence in his references to sexual problems, especially outside marriage. The reticence has, of course, not completely

---

[1] Forster, *Life of Dickens*, II, 90.
[2] *Ibid.*, 105–106.
[3] *Ibid.*, 98.

vanished and it is still enfeebling, obscuring and diluting the few audacities in which he now indulges. Yet the audacities are there. By daring
to show, within one novel, a prostitute (Martha Endell), a kept mistress (Little Emily), and such a remarkable case as Rosa Dartle's, Dickens was at least evincing a degree of curiosity and an exploratory spirit
to which he had not accustomed his early readers. A close examination
of Rosa Dartle's character and career will sufficiently illustrate his progress in that particular direction.

Living with James and his mother in the Steerforths' home is a
strange creature, a poor relation, confidante and lady-companion all in
one, who is an original figure and the occasion of searching psychological analysis. At first sight the quaint humors and intense passions of
Rosa Dartle might seem to be accounted for by her one-sided love for
Steerforth. On closer examination, however, it will be seen that Dickens
certainly meant her to have been the mistress—the first one—of his
youthful Don Juan, later rejected by him and henceforth repressing her
love, which thus turns to hatred. In one episode in particular, Dickens
has described one of those uncompleted actions in which modern psychology has enabled us to see the unconscious external manifestations
of such repressions. Dickens would probably have resented the use of
the word repression, but he had unquestionably sensed the reality which
the word depicts:

> She stood beside [the harp] for a little while, in a curious way,
> going through the motion of playing it with her right hand but not
> sounding it. At length she sat down, and drew it to her with one
> sudden action, and played and sang (chap. xxix).

No modern novelist would disclaim or could surpass such a description,
and none could depict Rosa's jealousy of Emily more accurately than
Dickens does:

> I would have her whipped! . . . I would have her branded on
> the face, dressed in rags, and cast out into the streets to starve. If I
> had the power to sit in judgment on her, I would see it done. See
> it done? I would do it! I detest her. . . . If I could hunt her to her
> grave, I would . . . (chap. xxxii).

The nature of Rosa's passion and the cause of her repression are only gradually disclosed, by Steerforth at first, who replies to David's innocent queries: "And I have no doubt she loves you like a brother?" . . . "Humph! . . . Some brothers are not loved overmuch; and some love—but help yourself, Copperfield! We'll drink the daisies of the field in compliment to you!" (chap. xx). The unfinished sentence is of course supposed to mean something like "some love is not brotherly," or "some love in an unbrotherly manner." The hint is slight but sure. Another time, Steerforth invites David to visit his home again: " 'I want you to stand between Rosa Dartle and me, and keep us asunder.' 'Would you love each other too much, without me?' 'Yes, or hate,' laughed Steerforth; 'no matter which. Come! Say the next day!' " (chap. xxviii). Steerforth is aware that when discussing the feelings that subsist between Rosa Dartle and himself he is on dangerous ground. So he prefers to cut the conversation short with a joke. Yet the avowal of the past tenderness is to be made later on by Rosa herself, indirectly to Emily, of whom she asks the question, "What is there in common between *us*, do you think?" (chap. l) then directly to Mrs. Steerforth after the tragic storm: "When he was freshest and truest, he loved *me*. Yes, he did! Many a time, when you were put off with a slight word, he has taken Me to his heart!" (chap. lvi). And her passionate outburst rises to the following statement, which transfigures her and makes her ferocious hatred almost sublime: "If I had been his wife, I could have been the slave of his caprices for a word of love a year."

In Rosa Dartle's case, at any rate, although the psychological reality Dickens ventured to describe was still veiled by a respectable curtain of vagueness, he had made a bolder move than in any of his previous novels and could almost be regarded as a precursor of later developments in fiction. The very desire for such a venture was a sign of his evolution. The direction in which he was moving is reflected in some of the private notes made in his "Memoranda Book."[4] He listed in it a number of ideas he had for possible treatment in his fiction. He had contemplated presenting a prostitute's dream of being respected by one young man, and also a father attracted to his son's wife. Needless

---

[4] Quoted by Mrs. J. Comyns Carr in her *Reminiscences* (London, 1925), 288–89.

to say, these ideas did not in fact find their way into his novels. But they were, nonetheless, a significant novelty in his career.

If the portraits of Annie Strong, Martha Endell, and Little Emily are less successful than Rosa's, it is only in part on account of the prudence which is still restraining Dickens' audacities. The other source of their comparative failure lies in the dreadful pathos which had already weakened so many pages of the *Curiosity Shop* and *Dombey*, for instance. In *Copperfield*, the pathos is more skillfully kept within bounds and more successfully compensated for by the overwhelming wealth of comic elements. Dickens' liking for tearful sentimentality remains, however, perceptible in more than one place, and *Copperfield* even affords an opportunity of more accurately describing the forms of Dickensian pathos.

Among the most characteristic is the "stellar" form of pathos: the use and abuse of the vaguely poetical undertone that is currently attached to stars and moon in order to move and melt the reader. A well-known "Reprinted Piece" called "A Child's Dream of a Star" supplies the most perfect specimen of Dickens' stellar pathos. And in *Copperfield*, young David, who has lately become an orphan, spends one night in Yarmouth and records:

> I still sat looking at the moonlight in the water, as if I could hope to read my fortune in it, as in a bright book; or to see my mother with her child, coming from Heaven, along that shining path, to look upon me as she had looked when I last saw her sweet face (chap. xiii).

The reader gets full measure here: "moonlight," "bright," "with her child," "from Heaven," and "shining path." Dickens has not been sparing of the words and objects that could arouse emotion. As to Mr. Dick's words, coming as they do from a permanently childish mind, the most simple-minded of all the book's simpletons, they do not ring any truer when he says of Dr. Strong: "I have sent his name up, on a scrap of paper, to the kite, along the string, when it has been in the sky, among the larks. The kite has been glad to receive it, sir, and the sky has been brighter with it" (chap. xlv).

Yet the most dreadful specimens of Dickens' sentimental style in

Copperfield are to be found in Emily's letters to her family after her elopement.[5] Her letters are disheartening, both because of their unreality and because of the contrast between Emily's action and the feelings she expresses. When we read such sentences as "I am too wicked to write about myself. Oh, take comfort in thinking that I am so bad" (chap. xxxi), we are tempted to pity Steerforth, who had never bargained for such lugubrious company. Dickens has lacked the supreme audacity of bestowing on Emily the courage and conviction that might have sustained her in her adventure. The Victorian sinner was not even entitled, officially at least, to fleeting joy; he was not allowed to lose for a moment his moral sense. He often passed judgment on himself with so much lucidity that his sinful acts became incomprehensible. Thus Emily is involved in a turmoil of exasperating contradictions and feeble tearfulness, without a flash of passion or pleasure. Verisimilitude and art are sacrificed, in her case, ruthlessly, and it is far from certain that morality derives any benefit from the sacrifice.

Emily's letters are excellent specimens of the Dickensian pathos in its purest state and reveal its mechanical devices to have been mostly exclamations preceded by "Oh!" and insistent repetition. Thus Emily writes:

> Oh, if you knew how my heart is torn. . . . oh, for mercy's sake, tell uncle that I never loved him half so dear as now. Oh, don't remember how affectionate and kind you have all been to me. . . . Oh, what will you feel when you see this writing and know it comes from my wicked hand. . . . Oh, my heart is breaking. . . . Oh, listen to my agony. . . . oh, what can I write. . . .

There are fourteen exclamation points in her three letters. Nor is the use of repetition less evident:

> When I leave my dear home—my dear home—oh, my dear home! . . . try, try,—not for my sake, but for uncle's goodness, try to let your heart soften to me, only for a little, little time. Try, pray do, to relent. . . . praying you not to be as hard with me as I deserve— as I well, well know I deserve . . . uncle, never, never to be seen in this world by my eyes again! . . . my poor, poor prayer, etc.

5 Mainly the letters appearing in chaps xxxi and xl, and to a lesser extent the brief note to Ham in chap. lv.

It should be added, in justice to Dickens, that he did not coin this exasperating idiom himself. In *The Uncommercial Traveller* he quotes a real letter sent by a bereaved mother to a clergyman, and the final sentences of the letter are wholly worthy of Emily's style: "Oh, it was indeed an eternal farewell, I do not apologise for thus writing to you, for oh, my heart is so very sorrowful."[6] Nor do Emily and Dickens apologize to us. Dickens must in fact have been quite pleased with himself for making her write as she did, so edifyingly.

It is not, therefore, in the Life and Letters of Emily that the proof of Dickens' progress will be found, but rather in the fact that the pathos in *Copperfield* is restricted almost exclusively to those fortunately rather short texts, while excellent and varied comedy spreads over the whole book. To take only one example of the comic in *Copperfield,* the case of Mrs. Crupp, David's landlady in London, deserves a detailed examination.

Mrs. Crupp seems to have been unduly neglected by the critics who have devoted their attention to *David Copperfield*. Yet she may be regarded, not only as a worthy successor to Mrs. Gamp and a forerunner of the admirable Mrs. Lirriper of the *Christmas Stories,*[7] but also as an original creation in her own right. She reveals her comic potentialities from her very first interview with Miss Betsey:

> "What's become of [the last occupant]?" asked my aunt. Mrs. Crupp was taken with a troublesome cough, in the midst of which she articulated with much difficulty "He was took ill here, ma'am, and—ugh! ugh! ugh! dear me!—and he died" (chap. xxiii).

Then, once David has become her lodger, fresh details keep being added to the glorious portrait:

> It was a wonderfully fine thing to let myself in and out . . . and to ring Mrs. Crupp up, gasping, from the depths of the earth, when I wanted her—and when she was disposed to come (chap. xxiv).

> I made discoveries: first, that Mrs. Crupp was a martyr to a curious disorder called "the spazzums," which was generally accom-

6 *UT,* chap. ii.
7 *CS,* "Mrs. Lirriper's Lodgings" (1863), and "Mrs. Lirriper's Legacy" (1864).

panied with inflammation of the nose. . . . secondly, that something peculiar in the temperature of my pantry, made the brandy-bottles burst (chap. xxvi).

Equally fine are David's conversations with her, particularly when he has fallen in love with Dora and when Mrs. Crupp, having guessed what was the matter with him, suggests an adequate remedy: "If you was to take to skittles" (chap. xxvi). Another brilliant performance is Mrs. Crupp's management of David's dinner party to Steerforth and his friends with the kind of help she enlists (chap. xxviii). Finally, there is a memorable phrase that must be quoted because it reveals at once Dickens' talent for humorously depicting a whole character through a few gestures and his masterly use of the flexibility of the English language (needless to say, the sentence is enchanting to everybody except the translators of *David Copperfield* into a foreign language):

> Mrs. Crupp, who had been incessantly smiling to express sweet temper, and incessantly holding her head on one side, to express a general feebleness of constitution, and incessantly rubbing her hands to express a desire to be of service to all deserving objects, gradually smiled herself, one-sided herself, and rubbed herself out of the room (chap. xxxiv).

There are, of course, in the comedy of *Copperfield* many more subtle and delicate elements, yet they need not be insisted on now, since there was but little room for progress in that direction for Dickens. But his progress is marked once more in the felicitous alliance of successful comedy and searching psychology. In *Pickwick* and *Nickleby,* the psychology had been simplified and schematized and eclipsed by broad comedy. In *Dombey*, the psychological analysis, though not invariably successful, had been on the whole more serious, but with damaging effects to Dickens' sense of humor. In *Copperfield*, for the first time, uproarious humor and serious psychology seem to go hand in hand.

To take only one example once more, it can be shown that *Copperfield* contains several illustrations, almost Proust-like in their perceptiveness, of the part played by unconscious sensory association in our psychological life. The link between a specific place, object, or sensation and a specific circumstance, emotion, or person is often referred to in *David Copperfield*. Some colored pictures that the child David had seen at Mr. Peggotty's house are said to be "such as I have never seen since in the hands of pedlars without seeing the whole interior of Peggotty's brother's house again, at one view" (chap. iii). In the same chapter, that psychological phenomenon is more explicitly analyzed:

> I don't know why one slight set of impressions should be more particularly associated with a place than another, though I believe this obtains with most people, in reference especially to the associations of their childhood. I never read the name, or hear the name of Yarmouth, but I am reminded of a certain Sunday morning on the beach, the bells ringing for church, etc.

In order to show that this is not an isolated and as it were accidental flash of insight, other examples must be given. They will show that Dickens was fully conscious of the value of his little psychological discovery and made systematic use of it:

> I sat looking at the parcels, packages and books, and inhaling the smell of stables (ever since associated with that morning) . . . (chap. v).

> [In Peggotty's house] I must have been most impressed by a certain old bureau . . . within which was a large quarto edition of Foxe's Book of Martyrs. . . . the Martyrs and Peggotty's house have been inseparable in my mind ever since, and are now (chap. x).

> I seemed to be sustained and led on by my fanciful picture of my mother in her youth. . . . I have associated it, ever since, with the sunny street of Canterbury (chap. xii).

> In my childhood, I had seen a stained glass window in a church. . . . When I saw [Agnes] turn round, in the grave light of the old staircase . . . I thought of that window, and I associated something of its tranquil brightness with Agnes Wickfield ever afterwards (chap. xv).

> [At Dr. Strong's] two great aloes, in tubs . . . the broad hard

leaves of which plant . . . have ever since, by association, been sym-bolical to me of silence and retirement (chap. xvi).

Lastly, after stressing the fact that all of the above examples comprise the words "associate" or "association" and "ever after" or "ever after-wards," the most famous as well as the most graceful illustration must now be given. It refers to Dora making her dog Jip smell some flowers:

> The scent of geranium-leaf, at this day strikes me with a half-comical, half-serious wonder as to what change has come over me in a moment; and then I see a straw hat and blue ribbons and a quan-tity of curls, and a little black dog being held up, in two slender arms, against a bank of blossoms and bright leaves (chap. xxvi).

This final example is more perfect than any of the others, being un-burdened by any explanatory comment—even the word "association" is not mentioned: the mere juxtaposition of the olfactory sensation and the remembrance suffices to suggest the psychological phenomenon. With that phenomenon and the details of its mechanism, Dickens could hope he had by that time sufficiently familiarized his readers.

Dickens' progress in psychology is to be felt also in his treatment of such important themes as friendship—David and Steerforth, David and Traddles—and love. As far as love is concerned, *David Copperfield* is a truly original work. Certainly, the childish love of David and Emily, David's youthful infatuations in Canterbury, and even his courtship of Dora, graceful and sometimes poetical as they are, are slight things and of little significance. Certainly also, the idyl of David and Agnes, grave and pure and beautiful as it is, is not out of the ordinary. Yet the book does contain valuable insights into the psychology of love and marriage. Nearly every Dickensian novel—and one might say nearly every novel—is a love story ending in marriage. Such is the case of *Pickwick, Nickleby, Chuzzlewit, Dombey, Bleak House, Little Dorrit,* and *Our Mutual Friend. Hard Times* does present the story of two unfortunate marriages, but it is very sketchily done. In *Copperfield,* on the contrary, one finds detailed scenes of conjugal life. The book is, among Dickens' works, *the* novel of married life. When Percy Fitz-gerald received from Dickens a copy of *David Copperfield* as a wedding gift, it was a significant and thoughtful present. For the exploration of conjugal psychology undertaken in the novel is courageous and searching and discloses facts which are not usually expounded to a prospective couple, who are left to learn for themselves. The exploration is contained in two chapters of great value: "Our Housekeeping" (chap. xliv) and "Domestic" (chap. xlviii).[8]

In his analysis David begins with laying down a principle which shows the author's desire for sincerity and his reaction against conventional sentimentality: "All the romance of our engagement put away upon a shelf, to rust" (chap. xliv). A few pages further on, he confesses that the ideal, uniform, cloudless, insipid happiness of the fairy tales has nothing in common with his own experiences: "I leaned my head upon my hand, and felt more sorry and downcast . . . than I could have supposed possible so soon after the fulfilment of my brightest hopes" (chap. xliv). His aunt, in a dignified little speech, then gives him valuable advice:

> These are early days, Trot . . . and Rome was not built in a day, nor in a year. . . . It will be your duty, and it will be your pleasure too . . . to estimate [Dora] . . . by the qualities she has, and not by the qualities she may not have. The latter you must develop in her, if you can. And if you cannot, child, you must just accustom yourself to do without 'em . . . your future is between you two. No one can assist you; you are to work it out for yourselves. This is marriage, Trot . . . (chap. xliv).

Dickens has traveled a long way since the threadbare jokes of the *Sketches* and the conventionally idyllic notions expressed in the traditional happy endings of most of his earlier novels. In the same chapter David solemnly asserts his sincerity: "I search my breast, and I commit its secrets, if I know them, to this paper. . . . I write the exact truth. It would avail me nothing to extenuate it now." He then describes the uncertainties and difficulties he is faced with and the resolves he has to

---

[8] The close link between the two chapters is curiously stressed by the fact that George Gissing mixed them up. Gissing, by no means a superficial reader of *DC*, refers (in *Ch. Dickens, Critical Study*, 181) to "the chapter entitled 'Our domestic life.'" There is no such chapter, but Gissing's enthusiastic description of it is true of either chap. xliv or chap. xlviii.

take in order to safeguard and consolidate the happiness of his young home. Later, in Chapter XLVIII, again analyzing the atmosphere of that home, he observes that its happiness is still far from perfect and carefully distinguishes those things, apart from the problems inherent in the human predicament, responsible for this state of affairs. He comes to the conclusion that, by dint of accepting many little secret and mute sacrifices, of accepting them out of love and therefore joyfully, he can enjoy the noble happiness of making Dora perfectly happy, and that this is the only thing that counts: "This was the discipline to which I tried to bring my heart when I began to think. It made my second year much happier than the first; and, what was better still, made Dora's life all sunshine." This is not only a judicious and moving analysis, but also a valuable lesson, given discreetly enough, without the slow tirades and the ponderous overstressing of the moral comments in *Chuzzlewit* or *Dombey*.

The lesson in conjugal love given here by David is only part of the "message" to be found in the book. Another, and perhaps the essential, message lies in *Copperfield*'s insistence on the value of perseverance. This is taught with more conviction and out of more genuine experience than marital indulgence, which, it is obvious, Dickens had never been particularly successful in teaching himself. The advocacy of steadfast hard work is presented at the beginning of Chapter XLII where, after the hero has confessed all his weaknesses he says, in a well-known passage of which it will suffice to quote only the basic statement, "There is no substitute for thorough-going, ardent, and sincere earnestness." The same lesson is still more eloquently conveyed through David's example, from the moment his aunt is ruined, through his patient and courageous conquest, first of a livelihood, then of affluence, Dora's hand, married happiness, fame, and glory. To that story Dickens has successfully imparted a unity of tone which holds the book together and turns its central part into a real "Novelist's Progress." And David's progress is sufficiently strong in psychological and narrative interest to make the embedded moral fable acceptable, and even artistically great.

No literary work could have been more closely associated with its author's life than *David Copperfield* with the life of Dickens. Further painful connections were to be established after the completion of the book. The child who had been born in August, 1850, had been christened Dora Annie Dickens. It is rather curious that her father should not rather have chosen to call her Dora Agnes, since he was himself so obviously impressed by Agnes' goodness, whereas Annie—Dr. Strong's wife—was of merely episodic interest. Catherine Dickens, or Georgina, whose opinions must by then have begun to count in the family councils, may have objected. Conjecture in any case is irrelevant, and Annie was only the child's middle name, her first name being meant to connect her with David's delightful child-wife.

Five days after Dora Annie Dickens' birth, the novelist was writing a letter and, when he had to use the name Dora, he felt it necessary to specify that he meant the fictional character: "Even now, I am uncertain of my movements, for, after another-splitting day, I have still Dora to kill—I mean the Copperfield's Dora, and cannot make certain how long it will take to do."[9] Dickens may have sorrowfully remembered his little joke a few months later when, two weeks after his father's death, he heard from Forster at the close of a General Theatrical Fund dinner the news that the baby had died. Dora Annie had been frail from the first, but he had left her in normal health a few hours before the dinner and she had died very suddenly on the evening of April 14, 1851. The literary history of the Victorian era affords few situations more pathetic than John Forster's on that occasion. He had been informed of the little girl's death and knew that he must impart it to his friend as soon as possible. And he heard him deliver a speech in which Dickens said, among other things: "How often it is with all of us, that in our several spheres we have to do violence to our feelings, and to hide our hearts in carrying on this fight of life, if we would bravely discharge in it our duties and responsibilities."[10] The novelist, whose keen sensitiveness to coincidence is well known, must have been painfully struck by that blow of fate and must have regretted giving to his child the name of the "Little Blossom" in the novel. Of both real and fictional characters, indeed, David's words about Dora could be used: "When my aunt had left her with a parting

[9] Aug. 21, 1850, *Mr. and Mrs. Charles Dickens: His Letters to Her,* ed. Walter Dexter (London, 1935), 143.

[10] See Forster, *Life of Dickens,* II, 94, and *Speeches* (London, n.d.), 130. In the *Speeches,* ed. Fielding, 122, a different text is given.

cry of Good-night, 'Little Blossom!' I sat down at my desk alone, and cried to think, Oh what a fatal name it was, and how the blossom withered in its bloom upon the tree!" (chap. xlviii).

Besides the accidental link between the writer's private life and his work, *David Copperfield* exerted considerable influence over his career. The book met with remarkable success financially, literarily, and personally. Financially, because, after very uncertain beginnings, it sold well. Literarily, because professional critics and cultivated readers recognized, as they must, the high qualities of the book. Personally, because Dickens enjoyed the satisfaction of realizing the progress he had made and the great intrinsic value of his novel. In every direction, then, his admirable effort met with its just reward.

But this does not mean that the publication of *Copperfield* stands at the beginning of a peaceful and happy period in his life and career. On the contrary, never had Dickens been further from the enjoyment of repose, balance, and tranquility. As soon as the final number of *Copperfield* was completed, he rushed headlong into amateur theatricals, first in the residence of his friends the Watsons, at Rockingham Castle, then in conjunction with his brother writers and other artists in the service of the Guild of Literature and Art. They acted in *Not so Bad as we Seem*, a play by Bulwer-Lytton. Dickens seemed to find it increasingly difficult to stay in one place for any length of time. In June, 1851, he paid a flying visit to Paris with his friend Daniel Maclise. Meanwhile, all the beneficent influences, all the stabilizing elements still at work in his life, seemed to be losing their hold on him. He cared less and less for his still increasing family. At the birth of another child—to whom both Lytton and Forster stood godfathers—in 1851, he expressed dissatisfaction and almost disgust: "I don't congratulate you on the Baby, because I can't bear to be congratulated on mine."[11] he wrote to Mark Lemon. On the other hand, the friendship that had had, and could still occasionally have, the happiest influence over him, that of his wise, prudent, restraining literary adviser, began to lie heavy on him. During the performances of *Not so Bad as we Seem,* he fell in with a younger man, William Wilkie Collins, whose companionship in pleasure he came to prefer to Forster's, though he could never rely on Collins in literary

[11] See Pope-Hennessy, *Ch. Dickens*, 301.

matters to the same extent. The dwindling of the truer friend's role in his life was to become more marked in 1854, when Forster at long last married—a publisher's widow, to make matters worse, for he thus seemed to be stepping into the enemy's camp—and could no longer be at the beck and call of the imperious novelist.

To give a clearer idea of the almost pathological degree of restlessness reached by Dickens in 1851, a significant fragment of a letter written in September of that year, just one year after the end of *Copperfield*, must be quoted. Even today, it has a tragic ring:

> I very nearly packed up a portmanteau and went away, the day before yesterday, into the mountains of Switzerland, alone! Still the victim of an intolerable restlessness, I shouldn't be at all surprised if I wrote to you one of these mornings from under Mont Blanc. I sit down between whiles to think of a new story, and, as it begins to grow, such a torment of a desire to be anywhere but where I am; and to be going I don't know where, I don't know why; takes hold of me, that it is like being *driven away*.[12]

His restlessness was such and took such a hold over him at that time that *Copperfield* must be regarded, not only as in many ways the summit of his novelist's career, but also as the end of it. Of course, he was still to write several great novels. But after *Copperfield*, Dickens, eaten up by a need for intense and varied activity and eager to disguise from himself the powerful urge that was carrying him away—"I don't know where, I don't know why"—could no longer be exclusively a novelist. *Household Words*, his personal periodical, had begun to appear. It was to be succeeded in 1859 by *All the Year Round*, but that was a change in title only. The facts of the case remained the same to the end of his life. As the editor, chief owner, publisher, and frequent contributor to a weekly journal, Dickens would henceforth be absorbed by many tasks, such as writing his own articles, touching up those of his contributors, conducting a huge correspondence, and arranging for special Christmas numbers. When he began to give public readings a few years later, a highly profitable but entirely exhausting occupation, there were even

12 See Forster, *Life of Dickens*, (Tauchnitz edition), IV, 220 (omitted from Everyman edition).

less time and energy left for the writing of novels, especially of the leisurely monthly type. Of the last seven Dickensian novels, only three followed the favorite pattern. In short, after *Copperfield*, novel-writing ceased to be the single focal point of Dickens' life.

When it is said that with *Copperfield*, Dickens had reached the summit of his progress as a novelist, this does not mean that he declined as an artist in the last two decades of his life. What is meant is that the line of his progress, which had been steadily continuous, now became less perceptible and more broken. His later novels correspond to various attempts at renewal of his inspiration. Several of these were brilliantly successful. But the student of Dickens' later career, seems almost to be concerned with a different writer from the author of *Pickwick*, and may find it more difficult to follow the winding course of his later career.

4

RENEWALS

XXIII: The Final Years of Dickens' Life

1. Bleak House *to* Edwin Drood (1850–70)

WHEN THE PUBLICATION of *David Copperfield* was completed, Dickens still had twenty years of literary life and labor before him. The final phase of his career was to be longer than the first and to comprise practically as many novels. Yet we have just seen in what sense it belongs less clearly to the history of the Dickensian novel. Without yielding to the temptation of the Dickensian critic to emulate G. K. Chesterton's paradoxical pronouncements, it might be seriously contended that Dickens' post–1850 novels[1] were no longer Dickensian novels to the same extent as his pre-*Copperfield* production had been. It appears, therefore, desirable to depart from the strictly chronological approach adopted in the foregoing chapters. After a brief survey of the chief events in Dickens' life between 1850 and 1870, the three most Dickensian novels of the final period will be studied together. Then the most characteristic attempts made by Dickens in new directions will be examined in one chapter, before separate chapters are devoted to *Great Expectations* and *Edwin Drood*.

2. *A Chronological Survey*

Dickens died at the age of fifty-eight. It is therefore impossible to speak of his old age. Yet, although he was only thirty-eight when *Copperfield* was completed, his body and his mind had already been somewhat impaired or at least wearied by the colossal tasks he had ceaselessly imposed upon himself.

Besides the inception of *Household Words*, which meant that he was to be the editor of a weekly periodical almost without interruption for the last twenty years of his life, his passionate interest in the theater also became more and more absorbing about the same time, as is shown by his correspondence and other biographical evidence. Wherever he happened to be, whether in London or in English provincial cities, whether in Italy, or in Paris, or even in such a small and unpromising place as Boulogne-sur-Mer, he would rush to the nearest playhouse as

---

[1] *BH, HT, LD, T2C, GE, OMF, ED.*

often as he could. He also showed himself immensely eager to act in amateur theatricals, of which he liked to be stage manager as well as principal performer.

As regards his home life, it was in 1850 that he attracted general attention for the first time to the unusual composition of his family circle by having his friend, the artist Augustus Egg, paint a charming portrait of "my little housekeeper, Miss Hogarth."

Although he had become acquainted with Wilkie Collins in the spring of 1851 and had been at once greatly attracted to him, to the detriment of the older intimacy with John Forster, it was with a friend of longer standing and a member of the Forster circle, Daniel Maclise the painter, that he visited Paris briefly in June of the same year. That summer, Mrs. Dickens made a modest literary début by publishing a book prosaically called *What Shall We Have for Dinner?* which she signed Lady Maria Clutterbuck, and which was no more than a collection of the menus served at Tavistock House. It was both the beginning and the end of Lady Maria's literary career. At the end of November, the Dickenses had settled down in London once more, at Tavistock House, and Dickens began to write *Bleak House,* the first monthly installment of which was published on March 1, 1852.

Twelve days later, on the thirteenth of March, the Dickenses' seventh son and last child was born. Within fifteen years, Kate Dickens had thus borne ten children and had four miscarriages in addition. The whole family spent the summer of 1852—July through October—in Dover, but before they returned to London the Dickenses had paid a visit to Boulogne and decided on spending the next summer there. At the close of 1852, Dickens made a fresh agreement with Bradbury and Evans for the publication of his various works.

Early in January, 1853, he went to Birmingham to receive marks of honor and admiration. He was so pleased with his warm reception that he volunteered to come back in December and give two public readings of his *Christmas Carol* for the benefit of institutions of popular culture. The year 1853 also saw the appearance of the *Child's History of England,* whose brief chapters—first published in *Household Words* —were dictated by Dickens to Georgina Hogarth. He sent his eldest son Charley to study in Leipzig and thus inaugurated the long sequence of energetic steps that eventually removed all his sons from the paternal home. In the spring he stayed briefly in Brighton, but it was in Boulogne that he spent the bulk of his vacation that year. The Dickenses arrived in France on June 13. They were visited by Wilkie Collins. *Bleak House* was completed in August, 1853, and the Dickenses left France at the end of September. In October, Dickens went on another trip, with Augustus Egg and Wilkie Collins, whom he took to Italy. At the close of that year, as at its beginning, Dickens found himself in Birmingham, where he was giving the two readings he had promised (December 27 and 29).

In January, 1854, Dickens and Mark Lemon took an active part in theatricals nominally run by their children at Tavistock House. Then, once he had made a choice of title and theme for his next work of fiction, *Hard Times*, he went to Preston in order to see something of an industrial city during a strike. In May, his letters to Forster showed that he found it increasingly difficult to turn down the offers he kept receiving for paid readings until 1858, when he determined to do public readings for profit. In the course of the summer of 1854, which he spent in Boulogne once more, Dickens was still restless and occasionally depressed. On his return to London, he was faced by the reappearance of Dora's original, the erstwhile delightful Maria Beadnell, now Mrs. Winter. Her letters at first moved him deeply and aroused undefined hopes in him. But as soon as he saw her again in the flesh—of which there was plenty, for a Dora who imprudently omits dying young tends to grow stout while remaining silly—emotion and hope yielded to disappointment, then to amusement, and finally to boredom. Maria Beadnell had sat to Dickens for Dora's portrait. Mrs. Winter unwittingly sat for Flora Finching in *Little Dorrit*. For the Christmas number of *Household Words*, Dickens wrote three chapters of *The Seven Poor Travellers* while enlisting the help of several contributors for the remaining chapters.

In 1855, his restlessness broke out in new directions. In February, he spent a fortnight in Paris with Wilkie Collins. On June 27, with his new friend Alfred Layard, M.P., Dickens addressed a political meeting at Drury Lane, in favor of administrative reform. As a help to literary creation, which came to him less spontaneously now, Dickens began to jot down in a private book possible episodes, characters, titles, and names for use in future novels.[2] That he made frequent use of the lists thus made up, is shown by the works written between 1855 and the end of his career. The summer of 1855 was devoted to the preparation of theatrical performances to be given at Tavistock House with the help of Wilkie Collins. It was in the feverish atmosphere of these preparations and performances that the novelist began work on *Little Dorrit*. In October, he took the chair at a dinner in honor of Thackeray who was going to lecture in the United States. In November, the whole family moved to Paris where they were to reside, in the Champs-Elysées, until April, 1856. On December 1, the first installment of *Dorrit* was published and for the Christmas number of *Household Words*, Dickens again wrote three chapters of a series collected under the title of *The Holly-Tree Inn*. Before the year was out, Dickens had entered negotiations with a contributor to his periodical, Eliza Lynn, from whom he wanted to purchase a house which was located in the vicinity of Rochester and which he had coveted since the days of his childhood. It was the house called Gadshill—or, as Dickens preferred to write it, Gad's Hill—Place.

Early in the next year, Dickens was conducting another kind of negotiation, in Paris, with the firm of Louis Hachette, who undertook to bring out an authorized French edition of Dickens' works. In April, 1856, Dickens was invited by Hachette to have lunch with his French translators and did not find them a particularly inspiring lot.[3] A good deal of his time in Paris was taken up by parties, at which he enjoyed at least the pleasure of rubbing shoulders with the greatest French writers. Equally time-consuming were the protracted sittings with the brothers Marius and Ary Scheffer, who were both painting portraits of him. In May, the Dickenses returned to England, but had to spend a few weeks in Dover until the Hogarths (Mrs. Dickens' parents) had vacated Tavistock House. In June, they crossed the Channel once more

[2] Excerpts from that notebook are quoted by Forster; others by Mrs. James Comyns Carr, *Reminiscences,* 280–95. The two accounts are sometimes conflicting, but the book itself is now in the Berg Collection of the New York Public Library.

[3] See F. Delattre, *Dickens et la France* (Paris, 1927), 47–53. Some correspondence, as yet unpublished, is in the archives of Librairie Hachette.

to stay in Boulogne through September; they were again visited by Wilkie Collins. They left Boulogne earlier than they had planned on account of a diphtheria epidemic. Back in London, Collins, who had made himself more and more indispensable, was appointed assistant editor of *Household Words*. The theatrical season at Tavistock House was particularly dazzling at Christmas, 1856, and even lasted until January 20, 1857. The greatest hit was made with Collins' play *The Frozen Deep,* acted by Dickens and the author in fraternal intimacy.

Turning Gadshill into a habitable place was a costly process, which began in February, 1857. It caused Dickens to turn his thoughts more and more seriously in the direction of the paid readings which, he believed, would easily enable him to earn as much as he was paying for the new house. In April, 1857, he completed *Dorrit* at Gadshill. About the same time he confided to Forster for the first time the failure of his marriage. The failure had become obvious after twenty years of incompatibility. In the summer, Douglas Jerrold's death and his widow's presumably difficult financial position, provided Dickens with a pretext for launching a fresh series of charitable theatrical performances and public readings. He rushed eagerly into the enterprise. It threw him once more into intimacy with Collins, and it was in the course of conversation with the latter that he first conceived the notion of the *Tale of Two Cities*. But there were other consequences. In order to perform in real provincial theaters, it became necessary to employ professional actresses for the parts held at Tavistock House by Georgina and the Dickens girls. Thus Dickens became acquainted with Mrs. Ternan and her two daughters. He was strongly attracted to one of them, Ellen, and it is rather more than probable that Catherine's jealous outbursts and Charles' resentment of her jealousy sealed the doom of the Dickens ménage.[4] The novelist's frequent absence from home was by no means conducive to smoothing over such difficulties. Yet, at the end of August, 1857, Dickens was already off once more for a prolonged trip with

[4] The evidence concerning Dickens' relations with Miss Ternan is limited and appeared belatedly. Canon Benham confided in Thomas Wright, who published his book in 1935. Dickens' second daughter, Kate Collins-Perugini, confided in Gladys Storey, who published her account in 1939. See Ada B. Nisbet, *Dickens and Ellen Ternan* (Berkeley, 1952), and, for the opposite view, see Edward Wagenknecht, *Dickens and the Scandalmongers.*

Collins.[5] They related their adventures in *The Lazy Tour of Two Idle Apprentices,* which they wrote and published jointly.

Early in 1858, a trifling circumstance made a series of profound changes in Dickens' life and career inevitable. His popularity as a speaker had increased and many associations kept asking him to take the chair at their meetings and public dinners. In 1858 alone, he delivered over ten speeches. On February 9, in particular, he spoke in favor of the London Children's Hospital. The sensational success of his excellent speech and his own sincere interest in the welfare of children caused him to promise that he would give a public reading for their benefit two months later.

On that decision being announced, several speculators put increased pressure on him and urged him to give readings for his own benefit. Dickens' last objections collapsed, and he gave in, much against Forster's advice, for Forster never allowed himself to be convinced that his friend's performances could be reconciled with a serious artist's dignity. In his eyes, since Dickens did not lecture, but read, and used all the actor's resources in his readings, he would be compromising his social position by doing so and identifying himself with mere actors, for profit. The actor did not occupy a highly respected position in Victorian society. The objection, nowadays, cannot be sustained on such grounds, since great actors are regarded and honored as respectable artists. One can only—and most fruitlessly, of course—deplore that Dickens should have been prevented by his public readings from writing more novels and also that he should have so recklessly impaired his health and shortened his life for the sake of huge earnings. Yet, if he deliberately chose to give intense, but ephemeral, delight to his contemporary audiences instead of working for future generations of readers, it must be admitted that his motives were by no means entirely sordid and selfish. His decision was also in great part due to his desire to be frequently away from his

---

[5] On the nature of such outings, Dickens' letters jocularly cast some light. He writes to Régnier (*Letters,* MDGH, I, 384) that he is coming to Paris with Collins "to throw myself *en garçon* on the festive *diableries de Paris,*" and in 1854 was already offering Collins an opportunity of spending a few days alone with him in London "in a career of amiable dissipation and unbounded licence . . . . If you will come and breakfast with me about midnight—anywhere—any day—and go to bed no more until we fly to these pastoral retreats, I shall be delighted to have so vicious an associate." This is probably no more than the language of a schoolboy, but one who is in great need of his vacation.

henceforth impossible home and to his avowed need for more direct and comforting contact with his admirers than his printed works could procure him.[6]

On April 15, Dickens gave the reading he had promised for the Children's Hospital, and on April 29, the first reading for his own benefit. Among the arguments the novelist had employed to convince Forster—for although he was carried away by an irresistible impulse and resolved not to take his friend's restraining advice, he still tried to gain the latter's approval—the need for constant change and novelty had occupied a prominent place, because nothing short of that could enable him to bear the irremediable collapse of his understanding with his wife. Forster had overruled that argument like all the others, foreseeing that permanent irregularity of life, far from giving Dickens peace and fostering in him the virtue of patience, would be more likely to preclude any hope of reconciliation. Forster was proved right in the event.

The first of many public readings had been given on April 29, 1858. It was in May that the husband and wife began to lead separate lives. Mrs. Dickens settled down in Gloucester Crescent with her eldest son, while the rest of the family remained at Gadshill with the indispensable Georgina. The public were informed of these circumstances by a note which Dickens himself had printed in *Household Words* as well as in every periodical which agreed to publish it. He took offense at the men who, like Mark Lemon and Bradbury and Evans, refused to insert his note in the periodicals they were responsible for. He considered that such people were in fact taking Catherine's side in the quarrel. A few weeks later, an American newspaper printed another, more intimate and detailed document which Dickens had drafted for Albert Smith, the manager of his readings. Smith was supposed to show it to people who were spreading rumors likely to harm Dickens' reputation. Rumors there were, of course, though they tended to involve Georgina Hogarth rather than Ellen Ternan. Albert Smith may well

[6] A curious passage in *UT* (chap. xi) casts some light on that particular aspect of the problem. Dickens is supposedly writing as one of the gypsies doing wickerwork in the open air: "When we sat down with our backs against the barn or the public-house, and began to mend, what a sense of popularity would grow upon us, when all the children came to look at us, and the tailor, and the general dealer, and the farmer. . . . what encouragement would be on us to plait and weave! No one looks at us as we plait and weave these words."

have been within his rights when he communicated Dickens' written explanations to an American journalist, but the novelist always referred to the incident as the "violated letter." It certainly does not redound to his credit, for in the letter he appears as a hard, cruel, malicious man. In the eyes of those who believe in the later revelations about Ellen Ternan, he even seems to have behaved as a somewhat Pecksniffian character.

In spite of his domestic disaster, Dickens went on working hard. In the spring and summer of 1858, he superintended the publication of the first collected edition of his works. Then, from August through November, he was mostly busy touring the provinces with his public readings.

Early in 1859, Dickens gave up his London House—it was sold in 1860—to settle down at Gadshill permanently. As his relationship with Bradbury and Evans had become unfriendly, he withdrew from *Household Words,* which could obviously not survive his departure, and founded a new periodical to be issued, like all his future works, by Chapman and Hall once more. For the new weekly magazine's name, Dickens' first notion was *Household Harmony.* He had to give in, very reluctantly because he did not see the point, to Forster's objection that that title might be misinterpreted as an infelicitous allusion to the recent developments in his home. He then decided to call his magazine *All the Year Round* and, to launch it the more successfully, to publish *A Tale of Two Cities* in it in weekly fragments. The first number appeared on April 30, 1859. In 1859 also, Dickens wrote for the *New York Ledger* a short story entitled "Hunted Down," for which he received £1,000.

In 1860, he began to publish in *All the Year Round* the short articles, sketches and essays later to be collected as *The Uncommercial Traveller.* His daughter Kate married Collins' brother. His own brother, Alfred Dickens, died on July 29. In 1861, Dickens spent a week at Bulwer-Lytton's in Knebworth and gave six readings in London which brought him in £500. *Great Expectations* was written in great part during that year and was completed before the summer. In November, 1861, Charley Dickens, the eldest son, married the daughter of Evans the publisher. Dickens never sufficiently relented from his hostility to his daughter-in-law's father to visit the young couple in their home. A new reading tour began in October, 1861, and lasted until the end of January, 1862. It was followed by shorter series of readings now and then in the next twelve months. In November, 1862, Dickens even toyed with the idea of going to Australia on a highly profitable tour of readings. For the Christmas number of *All the Year Round*, he wrote four chapters of "Somebody's Luggage." In 1863, he gave a few readings in Paris, lost his mother in September, went to Thackeray's funeral, and wrote two chapters of one of the best among the Christmas stories, "Mrs. Lirriper's Lodgings." His son Walter died in February, 1864. Dickens took an active interest in the London undertakings of the actor-manager Charles Fechter. On May 1, 1864, appeared the first installment of *Our Mutual Friend*. At the end of the year, John Leech's death was another of the bereavements now saddening Dickens' life. Yet the Christmas number of *All the Year Round,* "Mrs. Lirriper's Legacy," was a worthy sequel to the 1863 performance.

In February, 1865, Dickens fell seriously ill. His health had not been good for several years and the strain of the public readings had further impaired it. Dickens disguised from Forster a state of things he was confessing to other correspondents. Already in 1858, he told his daughter Mary: "I am writing in a very poor condition; I have a bad cold all over me, pains in my back, and a very uncomfortable throat."[7] Twelve days before, he had been writing to Forster, "The fatigue . . . hardly tells upon me at all." But there were soon more alarming difficulties which, in spite of temporary or superficial improvement, steadily became worse until the end in 1870. In 1865, some ill-defined disease in the left foot caused him excruciating pain and made him limp to the end of his days. He tried the effect of a short vacation in France, possibly with Ellen Ternan.[8] He had two female companions with him

---

[7] Oct. 22, *Letters* (MDGH), II, 78.

[8] Gladys Storey gives it as a proved fact. But until further evidence turns up, one cannot be too assertive. With or without Ellen, however, Dickens' brief trips to France had become for him a frequent and valued diversion. In 1864 (Oct. 25, Letters [MDGH], II, 222) he wrote to M. de Cerjat: "My being on the Dover line, and my being very fond of France, occasions me to cross the Channel perpetually. Whenever I feel that I have worked too much, or am on the eve of overdoing it, and want a change, away I go by the mail-train, and turn up in Paris or anywhere else that suits my humour, next morning. So I come back as fresh as a daisy, and preserve as ruddy a face as though I never leant over a sheet of paper."

when he returned to England on June 9, and the three of them miraculously survived the railway disaster at Staplehurst in which they were involved. Dickens, on the spur of the moment, behaved with admirable courage and energy and did not spare himself in his attention to the injured and dying passengers, but his nerves had been badly shaken and he never recovered from the shock. Traveling became even more of an ordeal to him than it had been before and there could be no public readings without a great deal of traveling by railroad. His last completed novel was finished in November, 1865. And for the Christmas number of *All the Year Round,* he wrote "Doctor Marigold's Prescriptions."

The final years in Dickens' life were a painful sequence of illnesses, about the seriousness of which he would have liked to deceive himself, of reading tours which exhausted him because he would never consent to husband his forces, and of deaths among his relatives and intimate friends. The outstanding event of that final period was an American tour—November, 1867, through May, 1868—which raised to the sum of £40,000 the amount of his earnings from the readings alone. His only literary productions after 1865 were two short stories, the lugubrious "George Silverman's Explanation" (1868) and the surprisingly fresh "Holiday Romance" (1868), and the first six monthly numbers of the uncompleted *Mystery of Edwin Drood* (January through June, 1870). On March 15, 1870, Dickens gave his last public reading, at the close of a farewell series of twelve performances.

The ensuing weeks formed a comparatively happy and peaceful time. He was ailing and worked hard, yet he was honored on all sides, surrounded by love and tenderness and still possessed of incomparable resources for literary and other activities. Whoever feels he has a debt of affection and gratitude to Dickens loves to think of those final weeks, and particularly to call up the last day he spent at his desk, amidst the sunshine and foliage that surrounded the window of the Swiss chalet that had been sent to him at Gadshill as a gift from Charles Fechter. It is pleasant to reread some of the very last sentences he wrote before he sank into unconsciousness forever:

A brilliant morning shines on the old city. Its antiquities and ruins are surpassingly beautiful, with a lusty ivy gleaming in the sun, and the rich trees waving in the balmy air. Changes of glorious light from moving boughs, songs of birds, scents from gardens, woods, and fields—or rather, from the one great garden of the whole cultivated island in its yielding time—penetrate into the Cathedral, subdue its earthy odour, and preach the Resurrection and the Life.[9]

When one thinks of the other deaths Dickens could have died, mangled in the Staplehurst accident, or collapsing in the midst of his reading of Sikes' murder—it endangered his life more than any other, yet he was fascinated by it and would read it three times out of four in the last series—it is a comfort and almost a happiness in the grief of such a premature and irreparable loss to find that he died at home and at work, content to do his work and to know that he could still do it supremely well. Of Dickens' death on June 9, 1870, can be said what was said by Carlyle in a fine commentary on Goethe's death:

A beautiful death, like that of the soldier found faithful at his post, and in the cold hand his arms still grasped. . . . Beautiful; what we might call a Classic Sacred-death; if it were not rather an Elijah-translation—in a chariot, not of fire and terror, but of hope and soft vernal sunbeams.[10]

XXIV: The Last Three Dickensian Novels

The last three novels published by Dickens in the Pickwickian form of the nineteen monthly numbers are *Bleak House, Little Dorrit,* and *Our Mutual Friend.* These three works are therefore studied here in a single chapter, although they were published at long intervals, with other novels between them. They possess the same kind of interest for a study of Dickens' technique and its evolution, for, taken together, they constitute one significant phase. The form of the monthly installments is most characteristically Dickensian. It had been born incidentally through *Pickwick*'s success and had gradually been carried to a high

[9] *ED*, chap. xxiii.
[10] *Essays on Goethe* (London, n.d.), 177.

point of artistry in *Copperfield*. Its later developments disclose some new tendencies of Dickens' art, and they can be surveyed in detail, since the "mems" of all three and the corrected proofs of two of them have been preserved.

1. *Three Sensational Plots*

The most obvious new tendency is a quest for sensational incidents in order to secure the progress of the plot. T. S. Eliot saw in that development the clearest sign of Wilkie Collins' influence on Dickens.[1] But his argument has been convincingly refuted by K. J. Fielding, who has shown that, while Dickens liked Collins as a friend, he did not think highly of him as an artist and was often irritated by his systematic sensationalism.[2] Yet even the sketchiest outline of the plots of *Bleak House*, *Little Dorrit*, and *Our Mutual Friend* points to Dickens' own increased and pronounced addiction to the sensational.

The plots of Dickens' early novels had been by no means simple, even without taking into account the rather exceptional case of *Oliver Twist*. There had often been violent incidents in them—Tigg's murder in *Chuzzlewit*, the riots in *Rudge*, Carker's death in *Dombey*, the spectacular and fateful tempest in *Copperfield*. But there had hardly ever been more than one such incident per novel, and it had never been of central or essential importance to the narrative as a whole. The three long books of the final period are, on the contrary, built around some brutal events, generally both obscure and tragic.

Bleak House, which appeared between March 1, 1852, and September 1, 1853, was written first at Tavistock House and later at Boulogne. It comprises sixty-seven chapters, which form two groups of comparable bulk: thirty-two chapters are autobiographical in form and the other thirty-five are of impersonal narrative. *Bleak House*, *Copperfield's* immediate successor in the chronology of the Dickensian novel, thus stands halfway between continuous autobiography (as in *Copperfield*) and the complete return to the impersonal narrative form found in *Hard Times*, *Dorrit*, and the other novels of the final phase. The

---

[1] See "Wilkie Collins and Dickens," 1927, reprinted in *Selected Essays* (London, 1932), 408–18.
[2] See *Ch. Dickens*, 128.

alternation between the two forms, which in itself makes *Bleak House* strikingly original in its construction, is not uniform. Sometimes the shift in method occurs after only one chapter, sometimes after as many as five.[3]

Bleak House also occupies an intermediate position in other respects. The novel at first appears to have two distinct plots. One is in keeping with the great Dickensian tradition and presents John Jarndyce, a generous and slightly eccentric character, with his young relatives Richard Carstone and Ada Clare, involved like himself in an interminable Chancery suit about a disputed inheritance. Jarndyce receives into his home his ward, Esther Summerson, the narrator of the novel's autobiographical sections. These characters are technically akin to the members of the Pickwick Club: they go about from city to city and keep meeting other eccentrics, such as the philanthropic ladies, Mrs. Jellyby and Mrs. Pardiggle; Mr. Turveydrop, the professor of deportment; or Mr. Jarndyce's two friends, Harold Skimpole the whimsical and Boythorn the boisterous.

A further link between the first plot of *Bleak House* and that of *Pickwick* lies in the resources for ever fresh starts provided by the character of Richard Carstone. He is an unstable young man in quest of a career. He takes up in turns the magistracy, medicine, and the army and each time follows the same evolution from initial enthusiasm to resignation, and then disgust. By adhering to that line, Dickens might have turned *Bleak House* into a work resembling *Nickleby*. He needed only to add to the number of Jarndyce's picturesque friends and to the careers attempted by Richard. But *Bleak House* contains, together with the Dickensian plot that has just been described, a dark and close-knit plot, itself temporarily subdivided between the aristocratic circle of Sir Leicester Dedlock and the lower class group of Cursitor Street and Tom-All-Alone's, one of whom, Hawdon, dies at the very beginning of the story. In this part of the story nothing is left to chance and nothing lends itself to fanciful developments; all is mysterious, gloomy, and strictly ordered.

---

[3] *BH* is made up as follows (A=autobiography; N=narrative; the figures show the number of consecutive chapters of one kind): 2 N, 4 A, 1 N, 2 A, 3 N, 3 A, 1 N, 2 A, 4 N, 2 A, 5 N, 2 A, 3 N, 4 A, 4 N, 3 A, 4 N, 3 A, 4 N, 1 A, 1 N, 4 A, 1 N, 2 A, 1 N, 1 A.

The two plots meet one-third of the way through (chap. xviii), when Esther is shown to be the illegitimate daughter whom Lady Dedlock had had by Captain Hawdon before her marriage. In the remaining sections of the tale, the dramatic interest lies mainly in the independent efforts made by several characters who have contacts with both plots, to discover facts already known to the reader. These characters, Tulking-horn, the clerk Guppy, and Inspector Bucket, have the same purpose but are actuated by different motives. The end of the story is steeped in the atmosphere of detective fiction and no longer has anything what-ever in common with *Pickwick* or *Nickleby*. There are, of course, within the thousand pages of the book, many scenes belonging to Dick-ens' older manner, interludes and a winding-up of the traditional type, with an elaborate and explicit dismissal of each character. Yet such elements have become almost negligible in *Bleak House,* where they are overshadowed by the importance of the sensational incidents.

Forster declares that the book is "in the very important particular of construction, perhaps the best thing done by Dickens."[4] Gissing nearly agrees with him, although he finds in the construction of *Bleak House* as much artifice as art proper: "It is constructed only too well . . . . It is a puzzle, yet ingeniously simple; the parts fitting together very neatly indeed. So neatly, that poor untidy life disclaims all connection with those doings."[5]

In fact, any attempt to draw up a list of the incidents through which the progress of the plot is secured shows them to be mostly unnatural. To quote only the main ones: Hawdon dies suddenly—of poverty, or boredom, or some still less defined cause—at the very beginning of the book. Another tenant of the same house, the old dealer in secondhand goods, Krook, who was supposed to hold documents related to Haw-don's identity, dies on the very day when he was to deliver the docu-ments. The cause of *his* decease is well known; it is, in fact, only too well known, since he dies of spontaneous combustion, while his papers are burnt just as spontaneously or, at any rate, just as opportunely as their owner. Lady Dedlock's mystery involves and destroys other victims. Tulkinghorn possesses himself of her secret, but is not allowed to

---

[4] *Life of Dickens,* II, 114.
[5] *Ch. Dickens, Critical Study,* 50.

enjoy it for long. No sooner has he threatened Lady Dedlock with exposure than he is murdered by a Frenchwoman, presumably yielding to the impulsive vindictiveness of her nation. The next victim of the fatal mystery is no other than Lady Dedlock herself, who, desperately alarmed by Tulkinghorn's suspicions, takes flight and after a breathless pursuit is found dead, of exhaustion, cold, grief, and anxiety, on the grave of her former lover. It is their illegitimate daughter who finds her. The gloomy and dramatic section of *Bleak House* would thus seem to have supplied enough corpses to appease the anger of the gods. But it is not so.

The satirical plot also describes the destruction of several characters. The various Chancery suits and the general deficiencies of society cause the deaths of Gridley, Jo, the street sweeper, and Richard Carstone. The last does not survive the complete collapse of his hopes when he finds that the Jarndyce *v.* Jarndyce case cannot go on, not because a decision has been reached, but because the costs have eaten up the whole of the disputed fortune. Such are the chief elements of the plot in *Bleak House*. They are combined with other ingredients, such as a love story and a good deal of social criticism, yet the construction is on the whole sensational. No doubt the narrative is thus more closely knit and more properly dramatic than in Dickens' earlier novels. But the kind of drama to be found in it is somewhat akin to melodrama.

Forster finds in the plot of *Little Dorrit* "a want of ease and coherence . . . and of a central interest in the plan . . . . The agencies that bring about its catastrophe, too, are less agreeable even than in *Bleak House*."[6] Few readers will agree that anything could be less agreeable than a case of spontaneous combustion, owing to which two persons are informed of their neighbor's death by seeing a black oily deposit—the residue of the combustion—appear on their window sill . But most readers will recognize the prominent and perhaps excessive place held by sensational elements once more in the composition of *Little Dorrit*.

That novel, whose publication began on December 1, 1855, and was completed on June 1, 1857, is divided into two books, comprising respectively thirty-six and thirty-three chapters. The chapters are often perceptibly shorter than in *Bleak House*, since of the nineteen monthly

[6] *Life of Dickens*, II, 184.

numbers only eight adhered to the traditional division into three chapters, while nine numbers had four chapters and two numbers had five chapters. The early part of the novel was written in Paris. Perhaps that is why the first character to appear is a Frenchman, who is incidentally a murderer and who, throughout the story, plays the part of the mysterious villain under three different names, Rigaud, Lagnier, and Blandois.

But the core of the book concerns the adventures of the Dorrit family. William Dorrit is a widower and has lived in a debtors' prison for twenty years. He has three children, the youngest of whom, Amy the "little Dorrit" of the title, was born in the prison. The rather vapid and not very youthful hero of the novel, Arthur Clennam, takes an interest in Amy Dorrit who does some sewing for his mother, the crippled Mrs. Clennam. That lady lives as a recluse in an old house with her former servant and present partner, the shady and brutal Flintwinch, yet she does not neglect her interests, although Arthur ignores them. The gloomy house is overshadowed by a mystery, and in it unaccountable noises are heard and secret councils are held.

The first unexpected event is the sudden enrichment of the Dorrits, owing to an inheritance whose origin is left unspecified. The Dorrits move immediately from the prison into high life, traveling about and making friends. They become acquainted with, among others, a Mr. Merdle, a renowned financier. The elder Dorrit girl marries Merdle's stepson. Then, no less suddenly, William Dorrit and his brother die, Merdle kills himself, and his transactions turn disastrous. Arthur Clennam, who had invested his own money and that of his partner, the inventor Doyce, in Merdle's business, is imprisoned for debt in his turn. The Dorrits are ruined once more. The only obstacle to Arthur's marrying Amy Dorrit, now that they can live in idyllic misery, an unfailing source of happiness, is the mystery of the Clennam house. Opportunely, Mrs. Clennam finds herself strong enough to leave the house, for the first time in many years, in order to visit her son in prison, just as the ancient building is about to collapse of its own accord under the weight of its advanced age, burying the French traitor and perhaps also the infamous Flintwinch.

Everything is made easy then, for Arthur was not really the son of that unamiable woman, so that his birth, even if illegitimate once again, is untainted by the shady doings of the Clennam family. A fantastic will restores Arthur's self-respect. Meanwhile, Doyce, the partner, is thriving, so that Arthur can leave the prison and rush straight into the nearest church with Little Dorrit. Here again it is seen that the timely occurrence of sensational incidents almost entirely accounts for the plot's development, while psychological evolution plays a much more restricted part than in *Copperfield*. Again, there are in the narrative a crowd of secondary characters and a large number of minor events, but they do not modify the general outline given above. The fact that it is not necessary to mention them for the outline to be coherent shows that the plot is not absolutely rigorous and has even preserved at some points a certain Dickensian freedom.

There is a gap or almost ten years between *Little Dorrit* and *Our Mutual Friend*. Yet the last novel completed by Dickens is much more closely akin to *Bleak House* and *Dorrit* than to its immediate predecessors in the chronology of Dickens' career, *A Tale of Two Cities* and *Great Expectations*. *Our Mutual Friend* appeared from May 1, 1864, to November 1, 1865. Its nineteen monthly numbers—seven of four chapters, eleven of the traditional three-chapter type, and the final number in six chapters—are divided into four books and comprise, like *Bleak House*, sixty-seven chapters in all. The book gives evidence of a new attempt at originality, mostly directed at the construction of the plot. In fact, despite the presence of one or two interludes—such as Bella Wilfer's escapade at Greenwich with her father—the narrative technique employed in *Our Mutual Friend* is unusual.

The novel begins at the moment when John Harmon's corpse is fished out of the Thames. John was a rich heir, whom his miserly grandfather's eccentric will would have compelled to marry Bella Wilfer in order to enjoy his inheritance, Bella Wilfer having been selected on account of her notoriously disagreeable character. The Boffin couple, two old people who had been the grandfather's servants, come into the inheritance after John's death. They are surrounded by a number of eccentrics—Silas Wegg, the one-legged, illiterate public reader, and his friend Venus, taxidermist and articulator of skeletons; a pauper woman, Betty Higden, whose great-grandson Johnny is about to be adopted by the Boffins as a substitute for John Harmon, when he is suddenly taken ill and dies; the Wilfer family and particularly the girl Bella, whom the Boffins take to live with them. The Boffins also employ as their secretary a mysterious young man, who calls himself John Rokesmith, but whose real name is John Harmon. His would-be murderers had not quite so completely drowned him as they had hoped, and there had been a slight mistake in the identification of the corpse found at the beginning.

John Harmon falls in love with Bella, who rejects him as not rich enough to please her taste in his Rokesmith disguise. Meanwhile, Hexam, who had pulled the corpse from the Thames, has been charged by a colleague with having murdered Harmon and is found dead under his own boat. A schoolmaster falls in love with Hexam's daughter Lizzie and tells her of his love so passionately and violently that she vanishes. Hexam's colleague, Riderhood, is in his turn fished out of the Thames. He is believed dead, but after protracted efforts is restored to life and leaves London. Betty Higden dies in the country, assisted at the end by Lizzie Hexam. Boffin becomes a miser, and insults and turns out Rokesmith. Bella is made indignant, leaves the Boffins, and marries Rokesmith, who does not disclose his identity to her.

The schoolmaster finds he has a gentlemanly rival for Lizzie Hexam's affection and duly tries to murder his rival. Lizzie, a worthy daughter of her father, fishes the gentleman out of the river just in time. On hearing that his rival is not dead and is marrying the girl, the schoolmaster has a fit of hysteria.

There are scenes just as violent and tragic among the other groups of characters. One swindler thrashes another. The drunkard father of Lizzie's crippled friend dies suddenly. Finally, the schoolmaster and Riderhood, who had been pulled from the Thames earlier, die together in the course of a quarrel, and the Thames has to receive two more corpses.

However, everything is finally arranged satisfactorily. It is revealed that Boffin's miserliness had been a gigantic hoax meant chiefly to convert Bella to a less interested view of life and love, and incidentally to encourage one-legged Silas Wegg in his ridiculous plot to capture the Harmon fortune. Two more wills are literally unearthed, so that, after many vicissitudes, the good are rewarded, the mediocre turn good, and the bad are all dead or exiled.

The plethora of corpses, wills, and plots does not mean that *Our Mutual Friend* is devoid of humor or of the freshness of observation and verve which had been the chief attraction of Dickens' previous works. *Our Mutual Friend* is rich in picturesque figures and admirable scenes. But, whether Collins' influence had anything to do with it or whether it resulted from Dickens' own inevitable evolution, a freer play than ever before is given to Dickens' liking for melodrama and to the morbid tendencies that had always existed in him but had been checked or kept within reasonable limits owing to Forster's advice. The change is not a complete one. There has been no sudden springing-up of new tendencies, no total suppression of the older characteristics. But the proportion of the various ingredients in Dickens' literary personality has been altered. Dickens had for many years become increasingly preoccupied with problems of construction. In *Our Mutual Friend* he has achieved unquestionable coherence, but it has been achieved at the cost of a perilous departure from naturalness and verisimilitude. This is a characteristic which *Bleak House, Dorrit,* and *Our Mutual Friend* have in common, but it has become more pronounced in the last novel.

2. *Essential Themes and Episodes in the Last Three Dickensian Novels*

One of the most striking characteristics of the final period is the growing intrusiveness of the novelist's didactic purposes. It will be seen to have been particularly damaging in *A Tale of Two Cities* and even more so in *Hard Times.* Again, didacticism was by no means a new attitude in Dickens' fiction. In *Chuzzlewit* and *Dombey,* he had already set out with a clear purpose and with a general moral argument directed against selfishness in one case, against pride in the other. In *Copperfield* he had passingly satirized Doctors' Commons. But not since *Oliver Twist* and *Nickleby* had he placed a significant English institution at the center of his fiction. This is what he did again with the Court of Chancery and English justice in general in *Bleak House,* and with the whole system of government in *Little Dorrit.* In *Our*

Mutual Friend, he was too busy unraveling the complex threads of his plot to launch a similar large-scale attack, yet he shot a few arrows at Parliament and also attempted to rehabilitate the Jews, whom he had reason to think his portrait of Fagin in *Oliver Twist* had offended. In each case Dickens' thesis is presented both implicitly and explicitly.

Dickens must have come across the Court of Chancery in his youth, as a shorthand writer and journalist. In *Pickwick*, he had already referred to the scandalous slowness of its proceedings and to the acceptance of that state of things as normal by English lawyers in general.[7] In 1844, a disagreeable personal experience had drawn his attention to the defects of that same court. He had brought suit against several persons who had pirated his works and had gained theoretical satisfaction, but he had failed to have the costs paid by the offenders. In 1850 again, he had written a scathing article for *Household Words* about "The Martyrs of Chancery." However his most energetic criticism is to be found in *Bleak House*. The following sentences contain an adequate summary of his grievances against the Court of Chancery:

> Complaints had been made of the Court of Chancery; of its dilatory proceedings; of the enormous expense which it entailed on its suitors . . . . It was beyond a doubt . . . the greatest grievance of the nation . . . It was confidently asserted by persons of great weight that there were depending in that court 23,000 causes, some of which had been going on for five, ten, twenty and thirty years! that there had been spent therein thousands of pounds, to the ruin, nay, utter undoing, of many families! . . . that what was ordered in it one day was contradicted the next, so that in some causes there had been 500 orders or more; and that, at last, when the purses of clients began to be emptied, and their spirits a little cooled, then, by a reference to some gentleman in the country, the cause came to be suddenly ended! In one word, that the Court of Chancery was no better than "a mystery of wickedness and a standing cheat."

These energetic lines are not by Dickens, though they coincide at some points with the letter and at all points with the spirit of his own onslaught. They may indeed have been one of his sources of information,

[7] See *PP*, chap. xxxi.

for they are by John Forster and refer to the "Little Parliament" debate in the seventeenth century.[8]

The sequel of Forster's narrative is interesting and significant. The suppression of that undesirable court had been passed, but there had arisen difficulties as to the practical details of the suppression, so that four successive schemes had been rejected and the House had been dissolved before a final decision could be made. Two centuries later, when Dickens in his turn attacked the same institution, the position had undergone but little change, though more than he implies in *Bleak House*. An expert on British judicial history, Sir William Holdsworth, considers that the novelist's criticism was valid at the time of the action of *Bleak House*—which he takes to be about 1827—but was no longer justified in 1850.[9] Certainly not everything had been reformed, but some of the most scandalous excesses had vanished in the course of the slow evolution, though without disarming the popular hostility they had created. On the other hand, no one denies that the Court of Chancery in the early 1850's was still a deplorable institution and that Dickens' satire was still justified in its spirit if not in its details.

Even some of the details are supported by historical evidence, and part of the author's preface is devoted to enumerating them in reply to some criticisms made in reviews of *Bleak House*. Also, the case of Gridley, "the man from Shropshire," reproduces the circumstances of the real and indeed notorious "Jennings case."[10] Dickens had undoubtedly examined the relevant documentation with great care before he placed the Court of Chancery at the center of *Bleak House*, for that is the position he did give it. From the very first chapter, with its superb description of a sitting—"The Lord High-Chancellor . . . with a foggy glory round his head, softly fenced in with crimson cloth and curtains," etc.—to the scene in which the case comes to an end, to the immense delight of the lawyers and Richard Carstone's fatal despair (chap. lxv), the shadow of "Jarndyce *v.* Jarndyce" lies heavy over the book and penetrates its very substance. With occasional ponderousness (espe-

---

[8] "Cromwell," *Statesmen of the Commonwealth*, (1839), VII, ii, 204–205. Forster's account is a summary of the document entitled "The Exact Relation."

[9] See *Charles Dickens as a Legal Historian* (London, 1928), 79–80. Also, Trevor Blount, "Chancery in *Bleak House*," *Dickensian*, 1966, pp. 47–52, 106–10.

[10] See Pope-Hennessy, *Ch. Dickens*, 295.

cially in Chapter LV), but usually with great gusto, Dickens has launched a large-scale attack against that iniquitous, obsolete, and ruinous court. He may have feared he had even gone too far, since one of the most trenchant passages remained unpublished, having been cancelled at proof stage. In that passage Esther Summerson related how she had warned Richard, entreating him "not to put any trust in Chancery, which no one trusted, and which was held in universal dread, contempt and horror; I entreated him to regard it as something so flagrant and bad, that nothing short of a miracle could bring any good out of it to any one."[11] Forster must have advised against such phrases, for he considered that "this book has suffered by the very completeness with which its Chancery moral is worked out. The didactic here . . . is of sterner stuff, too little relieved, and all-pervading."[12]

The satire in *Dorrit* is at once more comprehensive, more ambitious, and more good-humored than his onslaught against the Court of Chancery. This is all the more striking as the over-all atmosphere of *Dorrit* is considerably gloomier and less bright than that of *Bleak House*. But the satirical section of *Dorrit*, in which Dickens criticizes the famous "Circumlocution Office" and analyzes with great verve the whole science of government (Chapter X, "How not to do it"), results from a vivid feeling in him, and his indignation for once produces artistic effects. It is needless to expatiate on those supremely well-known passages which have made the Circumlocution Office a familiar phrase in daily speech.

In *Our Mutual Friend*, together with a great deal of social criticism of the diffuse and symbolic kind, Dickens has a specific argument to defend once more. It is not central to the story, but it is very clearly expounded. Dickens' purpose in that respect is defined by Forster as follows: "The benevolent old Jew whom he makes the unconscious agent of a rascal, was meant to wipe out a reproach against his Jew in *Oliver Twist* as bringing dislike upon the religion and race he belonged to."[13] Forster further states that, two years before the publication of *Our Mutual Friend*, Dickens had heard that complaint made by a

---

[11] Forster Collection, "The Corrected Proofs of Bleak House," chap. xxiii.
[12] *Life of Dickens*, II, 115.
[13] *Ibid.*, 291. Forster is inaccurate. Riah may be unwilling, but is not unconscious.

"Jewish lady" with whom he was on friendly terms. Yet, apart from a trite allusion made by Mr. Micawber in *Copperfield* (chap. liv) and a coarse caricature of the Jewish accent in *Great Expectations* (chap. xx), it is impossible to find in his works a single unfavorable comment on the Jewish race, still less on the Jewish faith. On the contrary, in the *Child's History*, Dickens had shown his indignation at the persecutions undergone by the Jews at the hands of "numbers of savage persons calling themselves Christians"[14] In his *American Notes* he had protested with similar vigor against slavery, another form of racial injustice, and more generally against the oppression of colored people. It was in *Oliver Twist* alone, then, that Dickens might be held to have sinned against the chosen people. Even in *Oliver*, it should be observed that Fagin was the only Jew in the gang—apart from an insignificant waiter of whom the reader gets only a passing glimpse—while all the others, Sikes, Monks, Charley Bates, Dawkins, and Claypole, were non-Jewish; thus Dickens' youthful production could by no means be regarded as aimed at the Jewish nation as a whole.

Yet the novelist, who had been chastened by his experiences in the cases of Miss Mowcher (in *Copperfield*) and Skimpole (in *Bleak House*, to be discussed later) was all too ready to admit that there were grounds for the friendly woman's reproach, all too eager to repair the damage he might have done. As usual in such cases, he gives the reader full measure. He has his Jewish character, Riah, make a little speech defining and condemning the offense committed in *Oliver Twist*:

> In bending my neck to the yoke I was willing to wear, I bent the unwilling necks of the whole Jewish people . . . . Men find the bad among us easily enough—among what people are the bad not easily found?—but they take the worst of us as samples of the best. . . . doing what I was content to do here . . . I could not choose but compromise the Jews of all conditions and countries . . . (Bk. IV, chap. ix).

If Dickens had, in *Oliver Twist*, compromised the Jews "of all conditions and countries," he was out to redeem himself by means of a tribute just as all-embracing as his implicit criticism had been.

14 *CHE*, chap. xiii. See also, chap. xvi.

There are other Jews in *Our Mutual Friend* besides noble-hearted Riah. Lizzie Hexam speaks of the people who have sheltered her in the country: " 'The gentleman certainly is a Jew,' said Lizzie, 'and the lady, his wife, is a Jewess, and I was first brought to their notice by a Jew. But I think there cannot be kinder people in the world!' " (Bk. III, chap. ix). The "but" at the beginning of the last sentence might seem to imply that Lizzie and Dickens share—or have shared—the common prejudiced view, and this may not have soothed the Jewish woman's feelings, though the general purpose is sufficiently clear and favorable. Dickens may have grown weary at times of the effort he had made to idealize the whole race he feared he had offended. In any case, it is difficult to determine whether, in the conversation between Riah and the dolls' dressmaker Jenny Wren, the author is not sympathizing with the young woman as well as, for other reasons, with the old man. Riah has been holding forth for some time in a solemn, moralizing tone. When he says, "Jenny dear . . . it is the custom of our people to help," Jenny grows impatient—as Dickens was perhaps growing impatient at having so laboriously advocated a generous but vague cause—and interrupts him, exclaiming, "Oh! Bother your people!" (Bk. IV, chap. ix).

In all three cases (Chancery, Circumlocution, and the Jewish people), it is clear that in the final phase of his career Dickens had become more aggressive and even more openly ready than before to use his fiction as a weapon in the service of non-fictional purposes.

3. *Verbal and Stylistic Effects*

The distinction between innovations and permanent elements is less clear cut in Dickens' style than in other fields, for his style had already undergone a profound and subtle evolution all through the earlier phase of his career.

He is still attaching great importance to the titles of his novels. *Bleak House* is a quaint title. Few English writers would have regarded "bleak" as possessing connotations of comfort and heartiness. In the *Oxford Dictionary*, the word is defined as meaning "wanting colour, bare, exposed, windswept, chilly, dreary." Curiously, in *Copperfield*, Mr. Peggotty had already been exclaiming, "A'most as bleak to-night as heart could wish!" (chap. li), thus connecting the notion of bleakness with the same kind of sentimental atmosphere associated with it by John Jarndyce and his cousins. The final title was adopted only after protracted hesitation. There are two pages of possible titles in the manuscript, most of which contain the name Tom-All-Alone's, which does play a part in the novel (that is where Jo the street sweeper lives), but not a part of sufficient importance to justify its appearance in the title. It is thus obvious that Dickens had at first contemplated giving that name to John Jarndyce's house. Among the author's rejected ideas are the titles "Tom All-Alone's," "The Ruined House," "The Solitary House"; the words "building," "factory," and "mill"; and such clauses as "that never knew happiness," "that was always shut up," "where the grass grew," and "where the wind howled." Further on, the form "the ruined house" recurs with increasing frequency, while the clause "that got into Chancery and never got out" gradually comes to supplant all the others. In his third attempt Dickens had contemplated a possibility which he had discarded and resumed only at the end of his quest, "Bleak House Academy," followed by the words "and the East Wind." So the title finally chosen, "Bleak House Academy and the East Wind. How They Got into Chancery and Never Got Out" resulted from protracted reflection and owed much to its various stages. The first two numbers still bore in Dickens' manuscript notes the title "Bleak House and the East Wind," but the only title that saw the light of print was the one by which the novel is now known, *Bleak House*.[15]

The case of *Our Mutual Friend* is exactly opposite. Instead of first conceiving a number of general ideas about a possible plot, Dickens chose the title *Our Mutual Friend* as early as 1861. Between 1861 and 1865, his notions about the contents of the novel varied several times. This may account for the fact that the title seems after all ill adapted to the book, although it is feebly justified by a short passage (Bk. I, chap. ix) in which Mr. Boffin says "I may call him Our Mutual Friend." In both cases, and also for *Dorrit*, whose title is somewhat more natural and easy, the author's quest had been for a clear and striking form combined with harmonious sounds.

The same kind of quest still marks the choice of characters' names. Dickens evolved in the direction of increased eccentricity, both in private

15 Forster Collection, "The Original MS of *BH*."

life and in his literary production. In 1853, Dickens decided to simplify the familiar nickname of one of his sons; thus Plornishghenter was substituted for Plornishmaroontigoonter.[16] A further abbreviated form of the same name was later to be used in *Dorrit*, for Mr. and Mrs. Plornish, while Dickens' son came to be called Plorn. It is thus seen that, for Dickens, the man's and the author's inspiration is one and the same, so that the verbal fantasies in which he indulges with his fictional characters should not be thought surprising. Of course, no novelist can content himself with names like Smith, Morris, and Watson for his characters, and some creative imagination must be employed in coining names for them. But few writers have devoted so much ingenuity or attached so much importance to names as did Dickens.

Even without taking into account a few merely jocular names with a more or less allegorical connotation—Blaze and Sparkle's are jewelers, Sheen and Gloss's are mercers[17]—as well as the series of politicians— Boodle, Coodle, Doodle, and so forth, inevitably leading to Noodle— the three novels under consideration contain an imposing list of significant or evocative names. Jarndyce is obviously modeled on jaundice and Dedlock on deadlock. Tulkinghorn is meant to suggest talking horn— he was called Talkinghorn on the manuscript and the early proofs. Jobling—a name that had already been used in *Chuzzlewit*—Dingo, Bucket, Chadband, Turveydrop, and Squod are all eccentric names more or less transparently alluding to various psychological or professional characteristics. Perhaps the most felicitous coinage is the name of Vholes, since the spelling, if not the pronunciation, of his name is irresistibly reminiscent of "ghoul" and thus calls forth his voracious character. So much for *Bleak House*. Nor is there any dearth of eccentricity in *Dorrit*. Reference is made to one Captain Maroon. The head of the Circumlocution Office is called Tite (tight) Barnacle, with clear allegorical intent. Flintwinch is connected by his name with both hardness or heartlessness (flint) and with tightness (winch), with perhaps an additional connotation of mystery (through the resemblance between winch and witch). Sparkler is ironically the name of a dullard. Pancks and Affery (the first name of a woman who is forever afraid) are baroque inventions. Mr. Meagles

---

[16] *Life of Dickens*, II, 129.
[17] *BH*, chap. lviii.

is extravagant enough to give his young maidservant the name of Tatty-coram. Finally, considering Dickens' familiarity with the French language in those days, there can be no doubt of his intentions when he gave the morally despicable financier the name Merdle (*merde*, excrement).

In *Dorrit's* case, it can be seen from some unpublished fragments of both manuscript and corrected proofs that Dickens' search for originality was conscious and systematic and that, in the last resort, he would rely on his instinctive feeling for adequate sounds. Flintwinch's name, for instance, was adopted only after the rejection of Casby—to be used later for another character in the same novel—Crag, Casblack, Casbeach, and Flintwich, while his first name was changed from Matthew to Jeremiah and his wife's, Affery, had earlier been Jessie.[18] The heroine is called Amy Dorrit, but only after Dickens had toyed with Clara (both David's mother and Peggotty in *Copperfield* had been Claras), Fanny (her elder sister's first name), and Ellen. Pancks had first been called Panx, Gowan had been Gowran, and Rugg is an extenuated form of the earlier infelicitous Bugg.

The same characteristics are again found in *Our Mutual Friend*. Fledgeby is the name of a callow young man, a social fledgling; Veneering has only the thinnest and most superficial coating of brilliancy; and Podsnap's name conveys the stiffness of his deportment and the brusqueness of his speech. Venus is a particularly odd invention.

Nor is the eccentricity of the names he has chosen enough to satisfy Dickens. The new tendency in his last completed novel is to the coining of nicknames whose origin is sometimes indeterminate, but which he manipulates with evident relish. Hexam is nicknamed Gaffer and his rival Roger Riderhood is called Rogue Riderhood. The latter's ugly daughter is called Pleasant Riderhood. Jenny Wren is not the dolls' dressmaker's real name. Sloppy is also a mere nickname. Reginald Wilfer comes to be called Rumty and Miss Potterson is called Miss Abbey. The same process applies to names of places. The reader is told that old Harmon's house had been nicknamed Harmony Jail, of course without the slightest idea of harmony attaching to it (Bk. I, chap. v). Dickens plays with names in various ways. Rogue Riderhood addresses Light-

---

18 Forster Collection, MS of *LD*, "mems," No. I.

wood as "Governor," Wrayburn as "T'other Governor," and Bradley Headstone as "T'other t'other Governor," then as "T'otherest Governor" or "T'otherest."[19] Wrayburn mentions his father only as "M.R.F.": "My respected father—let me shorten the dutiful tautology by substituting in future M.R.F., which sounds military, and rather like the Duke of Wellington" (Bk. I, chap. xii).

All these eccentricities are enjoyed at least by the author, who bestows upon all his characters, from top to bottom of the social scale, a liking for verbal amusements which is in fact the original hallmark of his own temperament. The variations of his sensitiveness to sounds can be followed from novel to novel, for there are pairs or trios of cognate names in each book to show which are for the time being the author's favorite sounds. In *Bleak House*, there are Bucket and Bagnet on the one hand, Guppy, Guster, and Gusher on the other. In *Dorrit*, Meagles and Merdle, and also Flintwinch and Finching, to which ought to be added the early version of Mrs. Bangham's name on the manuscript, where she was called Mrs. Flinx, a name itself resembling Pancks, or Panx, besides.

Examination of the manuscripts shows that Dickens did not devote the whole of his energy in writing and revising to such second- or third-rate inventions as have just been mentioned. He was chiefly occupied with securing for each novel a unity of tone and atmosphere, and his concern in that respect is apparent from the memoranda and the corrected proofs as well as from the text proper. Great care is taken to achieve the effects of contrast and symmetry.

Bleak House is a book in which many macabre or morbid details strike the reader. Yet it is clear that at proof stage Dickens had made considerable effort to keep the macabre tendency within reasonable limits and had cancelled many revealing passages. Generally, Dickens' stylistic work shows that he was becoming less and less inclined to let himself go. He made use of more conscious and elaborate devices in writing, and those devices have often been referred to, disparagingly, as "mannerisms"; yet they can also be regarded as evidences, always interesting and often felicitous, of his stylistic art.

In *Bleak House*, for instance, the murder of Mr. Tulkinghorn by the

---

[19] See, e.g., Bk. III, chap. xi. In *Dickens: The Dreamer's Stance* (Cornell U.P., 1965), 223, Taylor Stoehr provides a most ingenious commentary on that strange superlative.

Frenchwoman Hortense is narrated in a very original manner. The whole tale is composed of interrogative sentences, and yet Dickens manages to convey with great delicacy and efficiency the contrast between the brutal event and the profound peace of night (chap. xlviii).

Another example is provided by Dickens' creation of a kind of Anglo-French speech, almost entirely composed of English words interspersed with an occasional *Monsieur, Mademoiselle,* or *merci,* easily identified by the least erudite of his readers, and an effective use of French syntax. The Anglo-French speech is used either by foreign characters speaking English, a legitimate procedure of the realistic novel (employed with good effect by Thackeray for Alcide Mirobolant in *Pendennis*), or for dialogues taking place in foreign countries among foreign speakers. The unwonted phrases and the few genuinely foreign terms do create in the English-speaking reader the feel of a language that is not his own though he understands it perfectly. Dickens has unquestionably succeeded in his attempt.

The evolution of Dickens' style as a whole has not been invariably felicitous. The use of loose or even faulty turns of phrase became somewhat more frequent by the end of his career. In *Our Mutual Friend,* for instance, he liked to write things like "Wegg was a knotty man, and a close-grained" (Bk. I, chap. v), "A modest little cottage, but a bright and a fresh" (Bk. IV, chap. iv), or "He lived in the Albany, did Fledgeby" (Bk. II, chap. v). On the other hand, his writing has lost a great deal of the freshness and brilliancy that had characterized his early works. In other words, he has developed increasingly complex devices and has come to exert greater control, but there is less and less danger of a spontaneous and excessive overflow of imagination. One is almost reminded in some respects of the poet Roy Campbell's lines about certain novelists:

> *You praise the firm restraint with which they write.*
> *I'm with you there, of course:*
> *They use the snaffle and the curb all right.*
> *But where's the bloody horse?*[20]

For this reason it would be both difficult and superfluous to analyze the Dickensian comedy in these three novels, for it does not occupy a

[20] Quoted by Rayner Heppenstall, *Four Absentees* (London, 1960), 148.

prominent place. It has not vanished, but it is eclipsed by the melodramatic elements and by a marked return to pathos. The three novels are characterized by care and labor rather than inspiration. Since he has achieved greater control and mastery of his medium in them, they afford an opportunity of perceiving his deliberate conception of the art of writing.

Dickens has by now become a firm believer in the value of allegory. Together with, and later instead of, the picturesque images of former days (these images are now sometimes included under the term grotesque)—at one point imparting life to inanimate objects, at another immobilizing the characters in grotesque attitudes—he now uses large visions in which he neglects the particular to concentrate on the general. Images of the old type can still be found here and there, for a sense of the picturesque was too deeply rooted in Dickens' instinct for him to resist the temptation to describe, for instance, the mediocre goods displayed at a fair in anthropomorphic terms:

> Some despairing gingerbread that had been vainly trying to dispose of itself all over the country, and had cast a quantity of dust upon its head in its mortification, again appealed to the public from an infirm booth. So did a heap of nuts, long, long exiled from Barcelona, and yet speaking English so indifferently as to call fourteen of themselves a pint.[21]

Had Dickens become unable ever to write like that, not much would have remained of his charm as a writer. But the allegorical images are already being multiplied in *Bleak House*. Having imparted allegorical suggestiveness to the ceiling of Tulkinghorn's rooms, the novelist thereafter contents himself with esoteric allusions to it, and with phrases like "Allegory looks pretty cool in Lincoln's Inn Fields" (chap. xii). The same device, applied to a clock at the time of Tulkinghorn's death, yields dramatic effects: "If it said now, 'Don't go home!' What a famous clock hereafter, if it said to-night, of all the nights that it has counted off, to this old man, of all the young and old men who have ever stood before it, 'Don't go home!' " (chap. xlviii).

---

[21] *OMF*, Bk. IV, chap. vi. See the article "L'Expression dans *Our Mutual Friend: Manière ou maniérisme?*" in *Etudes Anglaises*, 1957, X–1.

In *Dorrit*, a sequence of extremely short headings carries on an implicit allegory by introducing the last four chapters in the style of an auctioneer knocking down one lot: "Closed," "Going," "Going!" and "Gone" (Bk. II, chaps. xxxi–xxxiv). In *Our Mutual Friend*, as in *Dorrit*, several characters are depersonalized and, under an allegorical name, stand for a whole class or section of society. Merdle's guests are called "Bar, Bishop, Treasury, Bench, Physician," and at Veneering's dinner party are to be met "a Member, an Engineer, a Payer-off of the National Debt, a Poem on Shakespeare, a Grievance and a Public Office" (Bk. I, chap. ii). In neither case are the guests' real names given. Dickens does not need the names. The guests are not living characters, but merely types and allegories.

Even before his artistic ambition rose above the descriptions, narratives of events, and dialogues, at which he excelled, Dickens had often written passages so seemingly inspired as to deserve the term poetical. His quest for poetical effects, by becoming more systematic, had by now altered his stylistic character. There are many fine fragments, for instance, in *Bleak House*; one of the best and most famous is the description of the fog: "Fog everywhere. Fog up the river, where it flows among green aits and meadows; fog down the river . . ." (chap. i). Here the symmetry of the clauses and their lack of articulateness emphasize the exaltation of the tone. Or one might instance the invocation to night that begins with the words, "Come night, come darkness, for you cannot come too soon, or stay too long, by such a place as this! Come, straggling lights in the windows of the ugly houses . . ." (chap. xi). Equally noteworthy is the passage in *Dorrit* when Clennam realizes that Pet Meagles' heart will never be his. That evening, Dickens tells us, "He softly opened his window, and looked out upon the serene river. Year after year so much allowance for the drifting of the ferry-boat, so many miles an hour the flowing of the stream, here the rushes, there the lilies, nothing uncertain, or unquiet" (Bk. I, chap. xvi). It is interesting to turn to the relevant part of the manuscript, where the sentence had been sketched out in the memoranda and had been carefully revised, showing that Dickens had directed considerable attention to it. It also shows that the earliest form was the more solemn: "So flows the quiet river—so many miles an hour the set of the current—here the lilies, there the rushes—nothing distracted, nothing put out—on, on, to the Eternal seas."[22] It can be observed that in the final phase of Dickens' life the objects that suggest his poetical flights are almost always connected with water—the rain, the sea, and the river being the main themes of his semipoetical passages.

Yet it is in *Our Mutual Friend* that Dickens most clearly rises to lyricism, so far as lyricism implies a writer's participation in the emotion he is endeavoring to arouse in his reader. No other word, in any case, could describe the astonishing passage that begins with a rendering of Lizzie Hexam's thoughts on the night of her father's death:

> Father, was that you calling me! Father! I thought I heard you call me twice before! Words never to be answered, those, upon the earthside of the grave. The wind sweeps jeeringly over Father, whips him with the frayed ends of his dress and his jagged hair, tries to turn him where he lies stark on his back, and force his face towards the rising sun, that he may be shamed the more . . ." (Bk. I, chap. xiv).

The whole paragraph rests on the association of the notion of death, of feelings ascribed to the elements released, and of human thoughts and fears. It acts as a kind of interlude or chorus—the chorus comprising one character with the author and the readers communing in the same anxiety—and as a pause at a dramatic point in the narrative.

It is again with Lizzie Hexam that Dickens identifies himself, and it is again on the occasion of a man being drowned that he shifts to the first person, without any transition or inverted commas, when the girl catches sight of Wrayburn's body in the water:

> Following the current with her eyes, she saw a bloody face turned up towards the moon, and drifting away. Now, merciful Heaven be thanked for that old time, and grant, O Blessed Lord, that through thy wonderful workings it may turn to good at last! To whomsoever the drifting face belongs, be it man's or woman's, help my humble hands, Lord God, to raise it from Death and restore it to some one to whom it must be dear! (Bk. IV, chap. vi).

The author's invocation, in close association with his character, here

[22] Forster Collection, "mems" of *LD*, No. V.

assumes the form of entreaty and prayer. There is one more case in *Our Mutual Friend*, and again it occurs under macabre circumstances—when Riderhood's body has been taken out of the Thames and slow efforts are being made to bring it back to life. The labor of describing the efforts seems to have impressed Dickens with the sensation that he had himself witnessed them or even taken part in them, for he writes, for instance, of "this flabby lump of mortality that we work so hard at with such patient perseverance" (Bk. III, chap. iii). On three distinct occasions, then, the novelist has identified himself with the emotional life of one character or group of characters, and, in order to convey their emotion to the reader, he has first made it his own. Such an attitude goes beyond a mere stylistic device, but the artistic intent embodied in it has, inevitably, profound influence on the style. Even when the stylistic tendencies appearing in the last three Dickensian novels are no more than further developments of earlier characteristics, it is clear that Dickens has become more of a writer, more of a fastidious stylist than he had been in the days of facile inspiration.

4. *The Characters: Protagonists and Others*

It is almost inevitable that there should be a difference between Dickens' treatment of his chief characters and his attitude toward the secondary characters, even if the difference does not quite result in his having three-dimensional *v.* two-dimensional, or "flat" *v.* "round" characters. The kind and the degree of psychological and artistic interest cannot be the same for a figure occupying a central position throughout a story and one of merely occasional or episodic value.

Among the secondary characters in the last three Dickensian novels, several are reminiscent of the earlier periods of Dickens' career and many are drawn with a sure hand. The Bagnet family in *Bleak House* is a pleasant and amiable group. In *Bleak House*, also, Dickens has depicted a household after his own heart—a house whose inmates are mostly generous and all eccentric. There dwells Miss Flite, a Chancery victim mentally unhinged by its treatment of her. There dwells Krook, dealer in secondhand clothes and nondescript goods, drunkard, and eccentric to the point of dying the oddest of deaths, through spontaneous combustion.[23]

[23] See *BH*, e.g., chap. xiv.

Among the other successfully delineated characters in *Bleak House,* many critics have been reluctant to include the street sweeper Jo. Yet Dickens has certainly taken much interest in him and has treated him with a mixture of subtle humor and deep pathos, while embodying in him his own perception of the extent of destitution, an extent which many privileged people are unable to conceive. The report of Jo's questioning by the coroner is a fine example: "Name, Jo. Nothing else that he knows on. Don't know that everybody else has two names. Never heerd of sich a think. Don't know that Jo is short for a longer name. Thinks it long enough for *him. He* don't find no fault with it . . ." (chap. xi). There is in such passages a great deal of truth and naturalness. When Dickens aimed at showing the extremity of human misery and moral indigence, he adopted a semi-indefinite style which shows his emotional identification with the life of the most rudimentary being:

> It must be a strange state to be like Jo! To shuffle through the streets, unfamiliar with the shapes, and in utter darkness as to the meaning, of those symbols, so abundant over the shops, and at the corners of streets . . . . To be hustled, and jostled, and moved on . . . . Not merely to be told that I am scarely human . . . but to feel it of my own knowledge all my life! (chap. xvi).

> [Jo's own speech is admirably rendered; he mentions some money he has received], "A sov'ring as was give me by a lady in a wale as seds he wos a servant and as come to my crossin one night and asked to be showed this 'ere 'ouse and the 'ouse wot him as you giv the writin to died at, and the berrin-ground wot he's berried in. She ses to me she ses 'are you the boy at the Inkwich?' she ses. I ses 'yes' I ses . . ." (chap. xix).

The dim vision of reality apprehended by Jo's clouded intelligence is shown in such phrases as, "I went and giv' a illness to the lady as wos and yit as warn't the t'other lady . . ." (chap. xlvii). Jo has something in common with Sam Weller and with Paul Dombey. He is akin to Pip in *Great Expectations* and to Boots in the Christmas story called "The Holly-Tree Inn." But above all he is, and remains until his death, described with a kind of solemn discretion—"The light is come upon the dark benighted way. Dead!" (chap. xlvii)—an original and inspired creation.

There are many other episodic figures in the last novels which adhere to the great Dickensian tradition and are sometimes brilliantly entertaining. Such are Guppy and Bucket in *Bleak House,* Flora Finching in *Dorrit,* and Lady Tippins in *Our Mutual Friend.* Guppy is the young clerk of the lawyer Kenge. His marriage proposal to Esther Summerson is couched in delightfully unexpected language: "My mother has a little property, which takes the form of a life annuity . . . . She is eminently calculated for a mother-in-law" (chap. ix). Flora Finching had been a youthful flame of Arthur Clennam's. When he sees her again, she has become an abundantly mature widow, but is still coquettish and amorous. In her case, based, as has been seen, on Dickens' meeting with Mrs. Winter—*née* Maria Beadnell, the original of *Copperfield's* Dora— he has obviously sinned against delicacy and expressed his childish disappointment at finding that the lovely girl he had been madly in love with had become, twenty years later, stout and elderly. But Flora's language is as irresistibly droll as Mrs. Nickleby's had been, and Dickens realized how successful he had been.[24] He wrote to Forster, "There are some things in Flora in No. 7 that seem to me to be extraordinarily droll . . . ."[25] Lady Tippins plays, in the conversations of *Our Mutual Friend,*[26] a part analogous to Flora's in *Dorrit* and equally amusing. Bucket, the detective in *Bleak House,*[27] is precise, methodical, smiling, ingenious, efficient, and subtle. He can be regarded as a worthy successor of Poe's Dupin and a forerunner of Sherlock Holmes and the long line of great fictional detectives, so that Dickens has sometimes been called the father of modern detective fiction, "and a parent how much more lively and entertaining than his children."[28]

Not all the secondary characters in the three novels are of such high quality. Among the least satisfactory are the caricatures of Leigh Hunt and Walter Savage Landor as Harold Skimpole and Laurence Boythorn in *Bleak House.* The two cases have often been discussed. There

---

[24] See, e.g., *LD,* Bk. I, chap. xxiii.
[25] *Life of Dickens,* II, 183 (April 7, 1857).
[26] See Bk. II, chap. xvi.
[27] See chap. liii.
[28] Osbert Sitwell, *Charles Dickens* (London, 1932), 15.

is a difference between the two, for the caricature of Landor is not malicious. Forster thinks it is accurate and harmless, and even refers to Dickens' portrait in his own biography of Landor. So does Malcolm Elwin in a more recent life of Landor.[29] Landor himself does not seem to have relished the portrait; however, he never published his reactions, although he allegedly confided in Mrs. Lynn-Linton, not a particularly trustworthy witness. The impression of an impartial reader acquainted with Landor's character is that, in Boythorn's portrait, Dickens has introduced nothing either unpleasant or amiable that was not part of Landor's real personality. But Landor was so exceptional a figure that the very faithfulness of the portrait accounts for the lack of ease and verisimilitude in the Boythorn scenes of *Bleak House*.

Dickens' and Hunt's attitudes in the Skimpole affair have been minutely described and analyzed in Louis Landré's study of Leigh Hunt,[30] from which it is apparent that Dickens knew he had seriously harmed Hunt and been unfair to him, even though the portrait was in the main accurate. Throughout that painful episode, Dickens acted hypocritically, not to say perfidiously. In his autobiography, published for the first time in 1850, shortly before *Bleak House*, Leigh Hunt had paid a loyal tribute to Dickens, calling him "my admirable friend Dickens."[31] In *Bleak House*, Skimpole is presented as a character whose seductiveness, laboriously stressed by the narrator, is purely superficial, while his faults are serious and evident. Phrases like "There was a perfect charm in him. All he said was so free from effort and spontaneous, and was said with such a captivating gaiety, that it was fascinating to hear him talk" (chap. vi), or "the engaging frankness with which he made [a] declaration" (chap. xliii), are alarming rather than reassuring when they are applied to a person intended to play a villainous part in the novel. Dickens' real purpose is far from clear. When he sincerely wishes to make the reader share his own conviction that a character possesses "a perfect charm" and is "engaging," "fascinating," and "captivating," he does not say so, but shows it convincingly. But what can be observed of Skimpole's character is almost entirely un-

29 See Malcolm Elwin, *Savage Landor* (London, 1931), xvii.
30 *Leigh Hunt* (2 vols., Paris, 1936), I, 269–74.
31 *The Autobiography of Leigh Hunt* (2 vols., London, 1903), I, 75; II, 229.

pleasant. He has a kind of pseudopoetical simplicity, resulting from his determination to ignore the difficulties of life, as when he speaks of his butcher: "My butcher says to me, he wants that little bill. It's a part of the unconscious pleasant poetry of the man's nature, that he always calls it a 'little' bill—to make the payment appear easy to both of us ..." (chap. xv).

But Skimpole's merits—if merits they are—are only skin deep and cannot eradicate from the reader's memory the remembrance of the day when he consents to be paid for delivering into the hands of detective Bucket the boy Jo, who is ill with smallpox. Skimpole's airy explanations cannot alter the nature of the case:

> "Observe the case, my dear Miss Summerson. Here is a boy received into the house and put to bed, in a state that I strongly object to. The boy being in bed, a man arrives—like the house that Jack built. Here is the man who demands the boy who is received into the house and put to bed in a state that I strongly object to. Here is a bank-note produced by the man .... Here is the Skimpole who accepts the bank-note ..." (chap. lxi).

Such verbal virtuosity will hardly convince the reader that Skimpole is honest and does not know the value of money much better than he claims when his debts are at stake. Nor does it convince us of Dickens' own good faith, since he has deliberately painted an unpleasant character with a friend's features. It has been alleged in his defense that "Dickens and his friends had been sorely tried by Hunt's difficulties and not the least by his airy, pleasant indifference to the idea of obligation."[32] But that might have justified private remonstrances, not an indirect and public form of revenge. Dickens did make an attempt at proof stage to extenuate the harm he was doing. He wrote to Forster, in reply to the protest of that more faithful friend of Hunt: "I have no right to give Hunt pain, and I am so bent upon *not* doing it that I wish you would look at all the proof once more and indicate any particular place in which you feel it particularly like, whereupon I will alter that place."[33] As a result, Skimpole's first name was changed—on the proofs

[32] Fitzgerald, *Life of Dickens,* II, 117.
[33] March 18, 1852. See *Life of Dickens,* II, 101. Forster himself declares he was

of Chapter V in the second number, *Leonard* is systematically crossed out and replaced by Harold—and three fragments were cancelled. One was characteristic of the man's spuriously disinterested attitude: "I can't regret being the child I am, when I am blessed with such a power of appreciating the practical wisdom our common mother teaches to some favoured creatures."[34] Unfortunately, another of the cancelled passages, which may have been "particularly like," happens to be the most attractive description of Skimpole and concerns the single circumstance in which Esther—through whose eyes so much of *Bleak House* is seen—feels the charm of his personality:

> He kissed my hand with quite a child's gallantry, and replied with such fervour and earnestness, and was so familiarly eloquent upon youth and grace, and loveliness, and upon their influences expanding like circles in the water, or sounds in the air, that I could have listened for an hour.[35]

Even if the resemblance was too great in those lines and the rest of that cancelled fragment, it is a pity that they were not left to subsist, so that the brighter side of the truth might have been added to the least pleasant aspects of the caricature.

Within a year of the above-quoted letter to Forster, Dickens was writing to Mrs. Richard Watson:

> Skimpole. I must not forget Skimpole . . . . I suppose he is the most exact portrait that was ever painted in words! . . . the likeness is astonishing. I don't think it could possibly be more like himself . . . . There is not an atom of exaggeration or suppression. It is an absolute reproduction of a real man.[36]

The triumphant tone of these remarks forces upon the critic the conclusion that Dickens deserved Forster's posthumous indictment:

---

seventeen when he "derived from Hunt the tastes which have been the solace of all subsequent years" (*ibid.*, Tauchnitz edition, V, 21, footnote omitted from Everyman edition).

[34] Forster Collection, corrected proofs of *BH*, chap. v.

[35] *Ibid.*, chap. vi.

[36] Quoted by Luther A. Brewer, *Leigh Hunt and Charles Dickens. The Skimpole Caricature*, privately prtd. (Cedar Rapids, Iowa, 1930), 11 (Dickens' letter is dated Sept. 25, 1853).

The pleasant, sparkling, airy talk, which could not be mistaken, identified with odious qualities a friend only known to the writer by attractive ones; and for this there was no excuse . . . nothing was possible to Dickens but what amounted to a friendly evasion of the points really at issue.[37]

The whole episode forms one of the least pleasing incidents in Dickens' career, but it is not without its significance.

Other minor characters in the last three long novels justify other criticisms. Mrs. Jellyby and Mrs. Pardiggle in *Bleak House* illustrate one of Dickens' pet theories—that spectacular philanthropy is radically different from true charity. In an unpublished passage, indulgent John Jarndyce himself was advocating the author's thesis on that point by saying:

"Excellent people! Do a deal of good, and mean to do a good deal more. But they want one pattern out of all the varieties of looms, they *must* be in extremes, they will knock in tin tacks with a sledge hammer, they make such a bustle and noise, and they are so counfoundedly indefatigable!"[38]

It has been contended that both Mrs. Pardiggle and Mrs. Jellyby were partial portraits of another contemporary writer, Harriet Martineau, but, in spite of her later hostility to Dickens when she thought that in *Hard Times* he was slandering the enlightened mill-owners of England, there is very little likelihood that she was aimed at in *Bleak House.* The trouble with the two worthy ladies is that they are too visibly the embodiment of an idea to be lively and entertaining figures.

Likewise, in *Dorrit,* the pseudopatriarch Casby, who dissembles under a venerable countenance and a kindly demeanor the sordid soul of a voracious and ruthless landlord, is but a mediocre demonstration of a familiar truth. The machinery contrived by Dickens to show the reader that appearances are not to be trusted, that men are not what they seem, is out of all proportion to the value of such a discovery. The author's indignation against Casby is also highly disconcerting. He

---

[37] *Life of Dickens,* II, 101–102. Hunt is known to have been grieved by the caricature and to have reproached Dickens with it. See "Wilkie Collins about Charles Dickens," in *Pall Mall Gazette,* Jan. 20, 1890.

[38] Forster Collection, corrected proofs of *BH,* chap. viii.

cannot refrain from insulting his character—he calls him "the blundering old booby" (Bk. I, chap. xxxii). Nor can he refrain from wreaking childish vengeance on him—Casby must have his hoary mane cut off publicly at the end of a protracted session of denunciation of what had long since been abundantly obvious.

In *Dorrit* is also to be found Mrs. General, a professional lady companion for genteel people, whom Dickens treats, at the end of the novel, with the same kind of gratuitous malice. In spite of the phrase which has immortalized her—"The word Papa . . . gives a pretty form to the lips. Papa, potatoes, poultry, prunes and prism, are all very good words for the lips; especially prunes and prism . . ." (Bk. II, chap. v)—she is mostly artificial and uninteresting. The heroine's uncle, Frederick Dorrit, is similarly wanting in animation and naturalness. His personality is all too easily summed up: "He never, on any occasion, had any other part in what was going on than the part written out for the clarionet; in private life, where there was no part for the clarionet, he had no part at all" (Bk. I, chap. xx).

Other minor characters are, on the contrary, rather too clearly defined, but through one or two features only, which seem to make up the whole of their personality. Thus Jenny Wren, the dolls' dressmaker in *Our Mutual Friend*, tirelessly repeats, "I know your [or "their"] tricks and manners!" and the author appears to believe that her repetition of the phrase can divert the reader and can suffice to make the character live forever. Nor is the reader's embarrassment relieved when Dickens later attempts to bestow on Jenny the melting influence of a poetical soul, when he has her explain:

> "As I sit at work, I smell miles of flowers. I smell roses till I think I see the rose-leaves lying in heaps, bushels on the floor. I smell fallen leaves till I put down my hand—so—and expect to make them rustle. I smell . . . all sorts of flowers that I never was among" (Bk. II, chap. ii).

Such language, which bears no resemblance to realistic psychology, and even deliberately departs from realism, may have touched the sentimental Victorian public. The modern reader is more likely to resent the moral blackmail to which he is submitted in such episodes.

But it was with the Smallweeds in *Bleak House* that the damage done to the Dickensian novel by caricatural psychology had become most apparent. The Smallweed family comprises two young people, brother and sister, and their grandparents (for, of course, like the heroine Esther and her two fellow-wards, Ada and Richard, the young Smallweeds are orphans). The grandmother's character is the most lugubrious example, throughout Dickens' work, of the perverse pleasure he could derive from presenting feeble automata and cheap puppets. Grandmother Smallweed is a helpless dotard. Whenever she emerges from her silence, it is to repeat incoherent sentences made up almost entirely of figures and sums, whereupon her husband coarsely insults her and silences her by throwing a cushion at her. The incident is repeated several times, whenever Mr. and Mrs. Smallweed are seen together. The mechanical nature of the proceedings is emphasized more than once; Mr. Smallweed is described as "having run down, he lapses into grinning silence," then as having "run down again" (chap. xxxix). As for his wife, she begins to speak when something "touches a spring in Grandmother Smallweed" (chap. xxi), while in another part of the manuscript Dickens had written: "Mrs. Smallweed, *as if she were a mechanical figure, and some spring in her had been touched* [italics mine] instantly begins to shake her head."[39] An artist of Dickens' caliber cannot be charged with ingenuousness or inexperience. It is clear that such devices are deliberate and result from one aspect of his artistic theory. Difficult as one finds it to share his amusement, his own amusement is real and sincere and he has wished and hoped to communicate it to us. Yet, even if there had been in the presentation of the Smallweeds no exaggeration or unlikelihood, it would still have been far from amusing, for it is a picture of the extremity of human decrepitude, something never amusing to contemplate.

The more uneven inspiration, the increasing tendency to caricature, and especially the more sombre tone apparent in the portraits of the minor characters are equally pronounced where the protagonists are concerned. Dickens' presentation of heroes such as Nicholas Nickleby or Martin Chuzzlewit had admittedly been lacking in profundity. But those young people had been carried along by a fervor, a spirit, a gusto

[39] Corrected proofs, chap. xxxiii. The italicized clause has alone been cancelled.

that infected the books in which they played their parts. David Copperfield was both ardent and profound. The vitality of these characters has
deserted the heroes and heroines of *Bleak House, Little Dorrit,* and
Our Mutual Friend. And the directions in which Dickens now carries
his psychological exploration are so abnormal that one hesitates to
assert that the comparative lack of exuberant creative energy is compensated for by added psychological depth.

Esther Summerson, the heroine and part-narrator of *Bleak House,*
is by no means a satisfactory creation. Dickens had been able to make
himself identical with the narrator-hero of *Copperfield,* and, since the
incidents of David's life were in great part like those of his own past,
he had generally lived, thought, and felt in close communion with the
character who was telling the story. *Bleak House* is in many respects
a more ambitious, more ingenious, and even, in some ways, a more
talented performance than *Copperfield,* but, in spite of all his energetic
endeavors, Dickens has been unable either to identify himself successfully with a modest, innocent girl, or to prevent her from speaking and
writing in his own style. What was acceptable in Copperfield's case,
since David achieved immediate success as a novelist, is not justifiable
in Esther. Once more, the case is stated clearly enough by John Forster,
who comments:

> To represent a story-teller as giving the most surprising vivid-
> ness to manners, motives and characters of which we are to believe
> her, all the time, as artlessly ignorant as she is also entirely un-
> conscious of the good qualities in herself she is naively revealing
> in the story, was a difficult enterprise, full of hazard in any case,
> not worth success, and certainly not successful.[40]

The lack of success in the creation of Esther can be seen from her treatment by critics ever since. George Gissing dismisses her with a brutal
phrase: "Esther Summerson cannot count, she has no existence."[41] Yet
the clearest expression of the feeling aroused in many readers by poor
Esther was coined, as early as 1853, by a reviewer of *Bleak House*: "Such
a girl . . . certainly would not bore one with her goodness till the wicked

[40] *Life of Dickens,* II, 113–14.
[41] In *Ch. Dickens, Critical Study.*

wish arises that she would either do something 'spicy' or confine herself to superintending the jam-pots at Bleak House . . . ."[42]

And indeed it would be a sheer waste of time to attempt a psychological portrait of such an insignificant personality. The first feature
she defines and flaunts is her own modesty, but a modest person's proclamation of her modesty can hardly have a true ring, and Esther soon
becomes exasperating. Her very first words are to tell the reader, "I
have a great deal of difficulty in beginning to write my portion of these
pages, for I know I am not clever, and I always knew that" (chap.
iii). When the same assertion has been repeated many times through
thirty chapters, the reader is sickened and runs the risk of overlooking
the many sterling and brilliant merits of a book which has almost as
many good things in it as any other Dickens novel, with the exceptions
of *Copperfield, Great Expectations,* and possibly *Martin Chuzzlewit.*

It might be thought that Dickens' comparative failure with Esther
resulted from the extraordinary technical acrobatics to which he doomed
himself, and through which he doomed her, when he determined to
alternate between first person and third person narrative chapters in
Bleak House. Yet when in *Dorrit* he returned to a more classical narrative procedure, the heroine was found to suffer from similar disabil-
ities. Dickens consistently failed to create artistically satisfactory heroines,
because he wished them to be possessed of every moral perfection. A
comparison with George Eliot is illuminating on this point. Her Maggie
Tulliver and, to a lesser extent, her Dorothea Brooke are in love with
moral grandeur but can only aim at it from a distance and wage an
unceasing battle against the weaknesses of their temperaments. The
beauty of their struggle is more likely to make virtue attractive than is
the dull perfection of Little Dorrit. Amy Dorrit has no inner battle. Her
life is neither happy nor easy; quite the contrary, the author more or
less consciously counts on the reader's pity to make him accept the unlikely uniformity of aspiration in the girl. Doubt is unknown to her.
She knows what her duty is and no obstacle, no pressure, can deflect
her from trying to do it. She is saintly, but she is not human and lifelike.

Little Dorrit is dull, because she always studiously refrains from

---

[42] "Dickens's *Bleak House*" by G. Brimley, *The Spectator*, Sept. 24, 1853, p. 923–25,
quoted in *Dickensiana,* 266.

expressing personal opinions. This does not mean that her brain does not function. Rather her mind like those of the other pure and simple-hearted characters in Dickens, can concoct the most elaborate reasonings. Dickens tells us why she did not wish Clennam to see her shoes: "Little Dorrit was not ashamed of her poor shoes. He knew her story, and it was not that. Little Dorrit had a misgiving that he might blame her father if he saw them," etc. (Bk. I, chap. xiv). Her peculiar complexity often appears in her speech and sometimes makes it painfully absurd, as in the question she asks Clennam (in which the two fragments are separated by three lines of comments on her attitude and feelings): "Before I say anything else . . . may I tell you something, sir?" (Bk. I, chap. xiv). In the course of the same conversation, she overwhelms Clennam with her conjectural thanks for an act of anonymous generosity and lapses into tearful eloquence and pathos: "And if I knew him, and I might, I would go down on my knees to him, and take his hand and kiss it, and ask him not to draw it away, but to leave it—oh, to leave it for a moment—and let my thankful tears fall on it, for I have no other thanks to give him!"

The girl's actions, also meant to be touching, are sometimes as delirious as her speech. When she has had to spend a night outside the prison in which her father is resting, Amy "went to the closed gate, and peeped through into the courtyard. 'I hope he is sound asleep,' said Little Dorrit, kissing one of the bars, 'and does not miss me'" (Bk. I, chap. xiv). Her filial devotion is peculiar, gloomy, and melodramatic. But the prison is a capital element in the sentimental atmosphere in which Dickens has chosen to place Little Dorrit, and the contrast between the closed and dilapidated state of the jail and the girl's fresh youthfulness was meant to be the emotional theme of the novel. However, the freshness is not there. So Little Dorrit is neither more truthful nor more lively than her immediate predecessor, Esther Summerson. At that point in his career, Dickens seemed particularly unable to draw satisfactory portraits of women. His own love for his wife, which may never have been passionate, had died out. And in *Copperfield*, he has already embodied in the character of Agnes his heart's aspiration toward the dream figure of the perfect woman.

Nor are the heroes of the novels much more felicitously presented than their uninspiring helpmates. *Bleak House* has in fact no hero, properly speaking. Allan Woodcourt, the young physician who eventually marries Esther, is not often seen in the novel and his character is a mere sketch. He simply happens to be the young man of the novel. Dickens' obvious intention was to have the reader consider John Jarndyce as the major male figure in the book. John Jarndyce, generous and sensitive as he is, is clearly different from the impetuous young men Dickens had portrayed before. He is the same age as the author, at least forty, and he is at the same time the author's mouthpiece and a projection of the author's opinion about himself. Dickens saw himself as very much like that somewhat whimsical and arbitrary, but tolerant, hospitable, and essentially kind man. The final scene in which Jarndyce gives up Esther's hand in order to allow her to marry Woodcourt and expounds to her the reasons for his attitude (chap. lxiv) is characteristic. Its sentimental complexity makes the scene feeble and unconvincing. As in *Humphrey's Clock*, it is thus seen that a Dickens deprived of his angularity, idealized, and altogether devoted to benevolence and self-denial, a Dickens who lacked his impulsiveness, self-centeredness, and sense of humor, would have been but a pale and unattractive person.

And yet John Jarndyce is, thanks to his whimsicality, superior to his immediate successor Arthur Clennam, whose virtues are ill-defined or nonexistent. Clennam is again a mature, almost an elderly man, who is unexpectedly called upon to play the part of the hero in *Little Dorrit* and to marry Amy. He has an imperturbable seriousness and dignity. The reader never laughs or smiles at him or because of him.

The hero of *Our Mutual Friend*—variously called John Harmon, Julius Handford, John Rokesmith, etc.—belongs to a different class. He is not a very young man, but he is certainly not over thirty at the beginning of the novel. He is much more lively and appealing than Jarndyce, Woodcourt, or Clennam. But his personality is steeped in such mystery during a critical phase of the story, in which he assumes four distinct aliases, that the reader cannot keep a very clear vision of him. Of the other young man in *Our Mutual Friend*, Eugene Wrayburn, there have been diverging opinions. Dickens seems to have intended to make him the occasion of a novel experiment—a portrait of a human being in whom good and bad elements were closely intermingled. At the beginning of the story, Eugene is a careless and idle young man, who has never done anything useful and who is greatly disillusioned. His single merit is that he can hold his own in worldly conversation. Dickens has obviously intended him to be possessed of a certain mental and social distinction. However the intention has not been successfully carried out, for in many of Wrayburn's remarks, instead of the easy superiority and lightness of tone that Dickens has tried to convey, one notices unpleasant vulgarity. This is unquestionably the case when Eugene, in order to dismiss Riah, the largehearted Jew, tells him, "If Mr. Aaron . . . will be good enough to relinquish his charge to me, he will be quite free for any engagement he may have at the Synagogue" (Bk. II, chap. xv). His indelicate and unimaginative reference to Riah's religion is not even amusing. Yet in the end, Eugene undergoes cathartic experiences and is regenerated through the purity of his love for Lizzie and through the ordeal of mortal danger. Consequently, he remains with the reader as a clearer and more interesting figure than many of the characters created by Dickens in those days.

In the persons of John Harmon and Eugene Wrayburn, *Our Mutual Friend* possesses two heroes. The latter marries Lizzie Hexam and the former Bella Wilfer, for the role of heroine is also distributed between two characters. But while Lizzie Hexam resembles Esther in her cold faultlessness, and Amy Dorrit in her tendency to poeticize the humble realities in whose midst she lives, Bella Wilfer is a creation of the very first order. In contrast to the gallery of artificial characters in these three novels, now stilted, now hysterical, one comes across her with a shock of surprise. For Bella is at first a real girl, then a real young woman— lively, changeable, emotional, coquettish, impulsive, and passionate and, by turns, haughty, selfish, self denying, generous, and loving. The reader almost feels that something must have happened to Dickens. Many Dickensians see in his portraiture of Bella Wilfer the clearest evidence that he had entered on an intimate relationship with Ellen Ternan. Out of the ten first Dickensian novels, very few youthful women characters emerge. Two or three alone come to life: Dora in *Copperfield*, Ruth Pinch in *Chuzzlewit*, and perhaps Dolly Varden in *Barnaby Rudge*. Now, in *Our Mutual Friend*, the author appears to have been rejuvenated. The male characters themselves, unsatisfactory as they are in many respects, have little in common with the steady and mature lovers, the fatherly husbands of *Bleak House* and *Dorrit*. Dickens has ceased to regard himself as belonging to that category. The father of ten children, who had accustomed himself in his fifties to play with women the part of an experienced friend or a kindly uncle, finds, after he has dismissed his wife, a new youthfulness of the heart in a body impaired by age and illness. This is the main reason why the probable intrigue of Dickens with a young actress is an event in literary history. Even if his love remained platonic, Bella Wilfer is there to show that, between the writing of *Little Dorrit* and *Our Mutual Friend*, the novelist had had frequent contacts with, and a tender feeling for, a much younger woman than Kate or Georgina Hogarth.

Bella is indeed portrayed much more forcefully and colorfully than any of her immediate predecessors in Dickens' work. On one occasion only does she yield to the fatal weakness that makes so many Dickensian heroines lapse into melodramatic verbosity. That is when Mr. Boffin turns out John Rokesmith and she exclaims, "Oh! Make me poor again, Somebody, I beg and pray, or my heart will break if this goes on!" (Bk. III, chap. xv), and she goes on in the same tone for a short while. But on the whole, by alternately repelling and touching the reader, she comes alive in his eyes. She is the occasion of slight poetical touches, often pleasant and successful. When she is about to board a train with Rokesmith, a graceful image is at once coined: "The railway, at this point, knowingly shutting a green eye, and opening a red one, they had to run for it" (Bk. III, chap. ix). In the course of the young man's conversation with her, a crowd of details makes it obvious that Dickens had at any rate attentively watched a pretty girl's face at the time. Bella apologizes "in a pretty shy way" and not with the tremulous gravity of Amy Dorrit or Esther Summerson. One of the most charming notes concerning Bella is the following: " 'Now that you *can* begin, sir,' returned Bella, as if she italicised the word by putting one of her dimples under it, 'what were you going to say?' " (Bk. III, chap. ix). It does not take many such paragraphs to raise Bella above the rest of Dickens' contemporary characterizations.

In addition to the results embodied in the individual characters, Dickens' psychology also appears to have been directed into new channels and to have become more ambitiously exploratory. In *Dorrit*, for instance, there is the curious figure of Miss Wade, a mysterious, contemptuous, and hateful woman, who has very little to do with the story and finds herself there mainly, it would seem, as a sort of a case study. In fact a separate chapter has to be devoted to her and written in the first person in order to show the purpose and the scope which the author wishes to give to her portrait.[43] Part of the letter he wrote to Forster in reply to his criticism regarding that point is vividly interesting, for we have few documents expressing so directly and precisely the novelist's intention on one particular point:

> It is sometimes really impossible to present, in a full book, the idea it contains (which yet it may be on all accounts desirable to present), without supposing the reader to be possessed of almost as much romantic allowance as would put him on a level with the writer. In Miss Wade I had an idea, which I thought a new one, of making the introduced story so fit into surroundings impossible of separation from the main story, as to make the blood of the book circulate through both.[44]

Judging by the reactions of most readers and many—but not all—critics, it is probable that Dickens has failed in that attempt. Miss Wade's character is farfetched and unconvincing, and it is only moderately interesting. Furthermore, the "introduced story" is not noticeably superior to the "inserted tales" in *Pickwick*, at least in so far as its artistic value is concerned. Yet the very nature of the attempt is remarkable, as is the fact that the introduced story contains no comic or dramatic incidents. There are few examples, in Dickens' work, of a story based wholly on psychological actions and reactions. Further proof of Dickens' broader scope is provided by the appearance, in *Bleak House*, and especially in *Dorrit*, of foreigners, and also, in *Bleak House*, of aristocrats, who are no longer mere caricatures. Dickens has achieved considerable progress since the time when the typical foreigner was for him *Pickwick*'s Count Smorltork. However, he has not yet become very profound in his exploration of the French or Italian national characteristics. Mlle

---

[43] Bk. II, chap. xxi, "The History of a Self-Tormentor."
[44] *Life of Dickens*, II, 184–85.

Hortense, the irascible lady's maid in *Bleak House*; Rigaud, the professional villain; and his involuntary companion, the unfortunate little Italian Cavaletto, have not broken away from the conventions of melodrama. Yet there is an element of sympathy in Dickens' attitude. He is less insular than some of his contemporaries, and does not, for instance, share the prejudices of the inhabitants of Bleeding Heart Yard (in *Dorrit*) for whom "it was a sort of Divine visitation upon a foreigner that he was not an Englishman" (Bk. I, chap. xxv), which is also the doctrine of the ineffable Mr. Podsnap in *Our Mutual Friend*.

Similarly, the attempt to depict real aristocracy in the final phase of his career reflects a significant change in Dickens' attitude since the days of Sir Mulberry Hawk and Lord Frederick Verisopht in *Nickleby*. Dickens' most sincere and searching study of aristocratic persons is to be found in *Bleak House*, in the portraits of Sir Leicester and Lady Dedlock. Of course, Dickens has not dismissed at one blow all his anti-aristocratic prejudices, and he still shows himself on the whole severe in his judgment of his baronet. The novelty of his attitude consists in his no longer regarding as incompatible the nobility of the heart and that of the blood, high social position and exalted feelings. The noblemen in *Nickleby* talked and behaved at best like parvenus, whereas Sir Leicester truly possesses innate distinction. On the day of his trial, when he learns that his wife has concealed from him a fault that dishonors him, the deep virtues that had lain dormant behind his haughtiness come to light. He then tells his cousin Volumnia:

> "I am on unaltered terms with Lady Dedlock . . . . I assert no cause whatever of complaint against her. . . . I have ever had the strongest affection for her, and . . . I retain it undiminished . . . . [and Dickens comments] His noble earnestness, his fidelity, his gallant shielding of her, his generous conquest of his own wrong and his own pride for her sake, are simply honourable, manly, and true" (chap. lviii).

Yet the author feels called upon to add, as a conclusion, a profession of his democratic faith, in case he could be suspected of having presented an aristocrat in a too favorable light: "Nothing less worthy can be seen through the lustre of such qualities in the commonest mechanic, nothing less worthy can be seen in the best-born gentleman. In such a light, both aspire alike, both rise alike, both children of the dust shine equally." The psychological study of Lady Dedlock is more interesting than that of her husband. She belongs to the aristocracy only through her marriage, but she is intellectually superior to Sir Leicester and all his relatives. So it is she who raises the tone of the aristocratic circle of which she has become a member: "In this society, and where not, my Lady Dedlock reigns supreme. . . . her influence in Sir Leicester's house, however haughty and indifferent her manner, is greatly to improve it and refine it . . ." (chap. xxviii). A striking aspect of her character is her contempt for her husband. When he reads to her, "My Lady . . . after a languid effort to listen, or rather a languid resignation of herself to a show of listening, becomes distraught" (chap. xxix). And it is curious to observe that the scarcely repentant sinner's contempt is depicted by Dickens with sympathy. The fault committed by Lady Dedlock before her marriage was not a whit less serious than Emily's offense in *Copperfield*, but its remoteness in time and Lady Dedlock's haughty dignity cause it to be more easily forgotten than the fault of the timid Yarmouth girl. Dickens never seems to deny his sympathy for an intelligent woman who despises her husband, like Edith Dombey, or Louisa Gradgrind-Bounderby in *Hard Times*. This may have resulted from some artistic transposition of his own feeling toward Kate Dickens, still repressed in the days of *Bleak House*, and even of *Hard Times*. In any case, Lady Dedlock embodies the novelist's aspiration to broader and deeper psychological studies than he had contented himself with formerly.

Another illustration of Dickens' psychological probings is to be found in the case of Bradley Headstone, the schoolmaster in *Our Mutual Friend*, whom jealousy turns into a criminal and who is the occasion of one of Dickens' most original psychological and moral remarks: "If great criminals told the truth . . . they would very rarely tell of their struggles against the crime. Their struggles are towards it" (Bk. III, chap. xi). And the concrete traces left by Dickens' labor confirm his desire to depict increasingly complex and delicate feelings and emotions. The following phrases, from the "mems" of *Dorrit*, significantly define his purpose: [No. VI, chap. xix] "Condense, if possible, the whole fatherly character . . ."; [No. VIII] "Clennam on the summer evening—scene with Pet, delicately showing that the father and mother have been for him, and that they all know of his affection. VERY DELICATE"; [No. X] "Clennam has already pledged himself to Pet to use his influence with her father towards elevating her husband in his good opinion. Observe this always;"[45] [No. XII] "Lead very carefully on . . . . Anatomize Gowan, and see what breeds about his heart"; [No. XIV] "Delicately trace out the process of Fanny's engagement to Sparkler: showing how it came about, and how such a mind in such a person, naturally worked that way"; [No. XVI] "THE HISTORY OF A SELF-TORMENTOR. From her own point of view. Dissect it; [No. XIX] Very quiet conclusion."[46] Words like "anatomize" and "dissect" are striking innovations in the style of the "mems" and the frequency of the adverb "delicately" is hardly less remarkable.

Perhaps my comments on the characters of *Bleak House, Little Dorrit,* and *Our Mutual Friend* in the foregoing pages will seem unduly harsh. I should therefore like to record here my conviction that these three novels are still eminently worth reading. It so happens that they do not contain a single figure ranking with Pickwick and his friends, with Mrs. Nickleby or Mrs. Gamp or nearly all the major characters of *Copperfield*, from the point of view of the entertainment they provide. But they contain abundant evidence of a remarkable and largely successful renewal of Dickens' interests.

5. *The Writer at Work*

As in the case of *Copperfield*, it is possible to see the writer at work on his last three great novels by examining the manuscripts, the corrected proofs, and the letters quoted in Forster's biography. The genesis of *Dorrit*, for instance, can be followed in detail. That novel, according to Forster, developed from a tenuous starting-point, "The notion he had of a leading man for a story who should bring about all the mischief in it, lay it all on Providence, and say at every fresh calamity, 'Well, it's a mercy, however, nobody was to blame, you know!' "[47] And in fact, the

---

[45] The sentence (through "opinion") is underscored once by Dickens and the word "observe" three times.

[46] Forster Collection, MS of *LD.*

[47] See Forster, *Life of Dickens,* II, 179.

book was originally meant to be called *Nobody's Fault*. The notion became diluted among several characters: Henry Gowan, Rigaud, and Clennam himself, to whom the word "Nobody" clearly refers in such chapter headings as "Nobody's Weakness" (Bk. I, chap. xvi), "Nobody's Rival" (Bk. I, chap. xviii), and "Nobody's State of Mind" (Bk. I, chap. xxvi).

Other elements of the story are outlined in various notes made by Dickens in his *Memoranda Book*, to which the plot of *Our Mutual Friend* also owes much. On the other hand, in letters to Forster, Dickens had written: "I think a man, young and perhaps eccentric, feigning to be dead, and *being* dead to all intents and purposes external to himself, and for years retaining the singular view of life and character so imparted, would be a good leading incident for a story,"[48] clearly a sketch of the character of John Harmon-Rokesmith. "A poor impostor of a man, marrying a woman for her money; she marrying *him* for *his* money; after marriage, both finding out their mistake, and entering into a league and covenant against folks in general";[49] this was done with the Lammles, who play a secondary part in the plot. "Some Perfectly New People . . . everything new about them. If they presented a father and mother, it seemed as if THEY must be brand new, like the furniture and the carriages—shining with varnish and just home from the manufacturers."[50] The last notion might have seemed a little thin, unlikely to lend itself to broad developments and profound analysis. Yet the characters created in accordance with that sketch, the Veneerings, are treated artistically and successfully. In the first paragraph mentioning them, Dickens made use of almost the same words as are in his letter to Forster: "Mr. and Mrs. Veneering were brand new people . . . if they had set up a great-grandfather, he would have come home in matting from the Pantechnicon . . . French-polished to the crown of his head" (Bk. I, chap. ii).

Yet the remote origins of the novels remain a little indistinct. It is only when Dickens is composing the first number that his general plan takes shape. The "mems" for Number I of *Dorrit* supply an interesting

---

[48] *Ibid.*, 291. Forster gives no precise date for that letter or the next two, merely stating that they were written between 1861 and 1864.
[49] *Ibid.*
[50] *Ibid.*

example of the way in which Dickens' mind would function at that critical moment of literary creation. The left-hand side of the sheet reads:

Waiting-room? *No.* Office? *No.* French town? *Yes.*—Man from China? *Yes.* Prison? *Yes.* Quarantine? *Yes.* Family and two daughters? *No.*—Working jeweller and *his* daughters? *No.* People to meet and part as travellers do and the future connexion between them in the story not be now shown to the reader, but to be worked out as in life. TRY THIS UNCERTAINTY AND THIS NOT-PUTTING OF THEM TOGETHER as a new means of interest. Indicate and carry through this intention.[51]

For such a sifting process to be successfully carried out, after a series of questionings and eliminations, the novelist must already have had in mind at that moment a fairly detailed conception of his story. But no general plan of the whole novel, in Dickens' handwriting, if such a plan ever existed, has been preserved for *Dorrit* or for any other book.

By the fifties and sixties, literary labor had become more painful to Dickens, and, for each of the three long novels of the period, he recorded his difficulties. While writing *Bleak House,* he complained of his "inability to grind sparks out of his dull blade."[52] The beginnings of *Dorrit* were particularly troublesome. The author was a prey to restlessness from the very first number: "The story is breaking out all round me, and I am going off down the railroad to humour it,"[53] and a little later he wrote, "I am in the second number, and last night and this morning had half a mind to begin it again and work in what I have done afterwards."[54] Nor did he find it much easier to work on the third number: "I am just now getting to work on No. 3: sometimes enthusiastic, more often dull enough. There is an enormous outlay in the Father of the Marshalsea chapter in the way of getting a great lot of matter into a small space."[55] In fact, his difficulties kept increasing until he neared the end of the book.

[51] Reproduced in facsimile in *Life of Dickens* (II, 180–81) and not restored to the MS of *LD* in the Forster Collection.

[52] *Life of Dickens,* II, 123.

[53] *Ibid.,* 179.

[54] *Ibid.,* 182. Dickens' anxiety was due to the opening scene, in which he was not sure it was a good thing to have shown his characters already acquainted with one another.

[55] *Ibid.* No date is given by Forster for these letters.

Our Mutual Friend was the occasion of still more pressing anxiety. The worry caused by his readings and his failing health made him write: "Whether, with all this fluctuating distress in my mind, I could force an original book out of it, is another question."[56] Yet he was full of hope when the time came to launch into his new enterprise: "I am full of notions for the new twenty numbers. When I can clear the Christmas stone out of the road, I think I can dash into it on the grand journey."[57] A year earlier, he had confessed to Forster: "Alas! I have hit upon nothing for a story. Again and again I have tried."[58] That crisis had been surmounted, but it had taught him something, and, at the end of the year 1863, he was formulating his prudent resolve: "I am exceedingly anxious to begin my book. I am determined not to begin to publish with less than five numbers done . . . . If I don't strike while the iron (meaning myself) is hot, I shall drift off again, and have to go through all this uneasiness once more."[59] During the writing and publication, his anxiety became more acute: "If I were to lose one page of the five numbers I have proposed to myself to be ready by the publication day, I should feel that I have fallen short. I have grown hard to satisfy, and write very slowly";[60] "Although I have not been wanting in industry, I have been wanting in invention, and have fallen back with the book";[61] "I have not done my number. . . . yesterday and the day before I could do nothing; seemed for the time to have quite lost the power; and am only by slow degrees getting back into the track to-day";[62] "Alas! for the two numbers you write of! There is only one in existence; I have but just begun the other."[63] The new demands Dickens was trying to impose upon himself by attempting to begin publication with five numbers ready did not make his task any easier. On the contrary, he had fallen into the habit of being stimulated in his creative effort only by immediate urgency. The lack of immediate urgency, for which he would have liked to substitute the moral com-

[56] *Ibid.*, II, 244.
[57] *Ibid.*, 292 (Aug. 30, 1863).
[58] *Ibid.* (April, 1862).
[59] *Ibid.*
[60] *Ibid.*, 292–93 (March 29, 1864).
[61] *Ibid.*, 293 (July 29, 1864).
[62] *Ibid.*, Fall, 1864.
[63] *Ibid.*, 294 (July, 1865).

fort of a fragile reserve of copy, resulted in depriving him of one of the most efficient goads to his inventive energy.

He soon felt that the conditions under which he was practicing his art had changed. While proofreading the preface to *Bleak House*, he deleted the little phrase he had mechanically written, in remembrance of the days of facile and happy inspiration: "My labour of love is, so far, ended."[64] No doubt, he no longer felt he could call his work as a novelist a "labor of love." In his difficulties, the "mems" remained helpful. Those of the last three Dickensian novels are similar in general appearance to those of *Dombey* or *Copperfield*. They preserve the division of the materials between the left-hand side devoted to lists, written *currente calamo*, of characters, incidents, and phrases for possible use in the number, and the right-hand side where the same materials are divided and organized into separate chapters. But there are signs of an evolution in Dickens' use of the "mems." Their main purpose is still to serve the original prospective or "planning" function. But the tendency, faintly discernible in the *Dombey* "mems," to make them serve, in addition, a retrospective or "recording" function, and thereby help Dickens' failing memory, and more imperfect grasp of his story as a whole, has become more clearly observable. The fact that Dickens sometimes employs black ink instead of blue ink makes it possible in some cases to determine the order in which particular jottings had been made. Ernest Boll's study of the manuscript of *Our Mutual Friend* is a useful pioneer work in that respect.[65]

Not all such details are interesting, of course. But a few significant instances can be given here. In Number VI of *Bleak House*, it is clear that Dickens had first written the general summary on the left-hand side and the numbers of the three chapters on the right-hand side. The summaries and headings of Chapters XVIII and XIX, which are alone written in black ink, appear to have been added later. Other "mems" confirm that such was often Dickens' practice. For *Dorrit*, there is the following passage, in which my capitals represent Dickens' black ink, my lower case letters his blue ink:

---

[64] Forster Collection, corrected proofs of *BH*.
[65] "The Plotting of *Our Mutual Friend*," *Modern Philology*, XLII, 2, (Nov., 1944), 96–122, an article introducing the "mems" of *OMF*.

Charging everything on Providence?*NO*—Miss Wade. Her sur-
roundings and antecedents? *NO*—The Meagleses? *NO*—Bleeding
Heart Yard? and the Plasterer? YES—Clennam's old sweetheart.
YES FLORA. FLORA CASBY. More of his character? YES. How
he stands towards Dorrit? HARDLY? FAINT INDICATIONS.
—Lagnier?—*NO*—The Theatre? *NO*.[66]

Here, with the single exception of the question concerning Lagnier (or
Rigaud or Blandois), which Dickens has felt he could solve by an immediate negative, all his queries remained momentarily unanswered. All
the right-hand side summaries of chapters are written in the same black
ink as the replies to queries on the left-hand side. Later on in the same
novel (No. XVIII), over against the suggestion, "The Merdle image
smashed," Dickens notes "DONE LAST No.," thus pointing to the
fact that the "mems" for that installment had been at least begun before
the preceding one had been completely written. Similar discoveries can
be made by studying the appearance of the chapter headings, in the
preparatory stage, in the manuscript of the story itself, or a proof stage.
When the headings were missing from the "mems," they have been
copied into it later, and thus "recorded."

One significant aspect in the evolution of the "mems," through the
final phase of Dickens' career, is a change in the comparative importance
of the two sides of each sheet. At the beginning of *Bleak House*, there
is very little on the right-hand side. In the second and third numbers,
it bears no more than the numbers and headings of the relevant chapters. But when Dickens is being carried away by inspiration and the
strong interest he takes in his story, the jottings on the left-hand side
have become an almost superfluous intermediate stage, and in Number
XIII, for instance, every query is followed by a triumphant "yes" energetically underscored twice or three times: "Krook's cat. Yes.—The
Smallweeds, in connection with the Court. Yes.—Sir Leicester Dedlock? and the Cousins? Yes.—Lady Dedlock? Yes.—Finds that Mr.
Tulkinghorn has discovered her secret? Yes—Their interview at night,
at Chesney Wold? Yes." It is only at the end of the list that Dickens
experiences his single hesitancy: "Wind up with Esther's narrative?

[66] Left-hand side of "mems" for No. IV.

No. Frenchwoman. Lay that ground."[67] It is therefore not surprising to find Dickens, when he knows precisely where he wishes to go, doing entirely without the left-hand part of his notes and going to work at once on the chronological summary of the chapters in his number. He has done so in Number VIII of *Bleak House* (Chaps. XXIII–XXV) and, apart from a few words here and there, in most of the numbers of *Our Mutual Friend*.

The nature of the hints Dickens gives himself on his preparatory sheets evolves in the same direction as his general method of work. His tendency is toward more and more detailed summaries of the various chapters. He goes on advising himself in general terms, sometimes delicately enough:

> Mr. Tulkinghorn and Lady Dedlock. Each watching the other. Open that interest and leave them so [*Bleak House, No. IV*]. Get all the affairs square and the Boffins square. Clear the ground, behind and before . . . . Kill Gaffer retributively . . . . Bring on Eugene. IMPLY some change between him and Lizzie. Don't show them together. . . . wind up the book as skillfully as I can . . . . Work up to Bella's account of the change in Mr. Boffin—broken to the reader through her . . . . Lay the ground very carefully all through.[68]

Phrases like "work up to," "work through," "carry through," and "lay the ground" are of striking frequency. Moral and psychological purposes are also defined in the "mems," not without subtlety:

> Esther's love must be kept in view, to make the coming trial the greater, and the victory the more meritorious; Begin grim shadow on [Tulkinghorn]; pursuit interest sustained throughout [Nos. X, XIII, XVIII].

> [Bella] says she is mercenary and why. But indicate better qualities. Interest the reader in her; More books, and the misers, and about hidden Wills—Relieve by making Wegg as comic as possible.[69]

[67] Forster Collection, MS of *BH*. The first four "Yeses" have two underscorings; the last two have four.

[68] See "The Plotting of *OMF*," MP, XLII, 2 (Nov., 1944), "mems" for Nos. II, IV, V, XI.

[69] *Ibid.*, "mems" for Nos. VIII and XII.

One of the incidental points of interest in the "mems" lies in Dickens' frank use of technical terms which may sound coarse, as compared with the tone adopted in the narrative. When he is making ready for one of his famous final scenes of retribution and distribution, Dickens almost cynically defines the task lying before him: "Take up the characters to be disposed of,"[70] or draws up a list of all the minor figures—without omitting even such a vague person as the anonymous "debilitated cousin"—and ticks off those he has taken care of,[71] or again he expresses himself brutally and writes, "Charley not wanted any more. Hints out his own future career." Thus Dickens sets himself, methodically, to unravel his many threads, and, for instance, to "unwind Venus and Wegg."[72] The most astonishing discrepancy between the tone of the "mems" and that of the narrative concerns the moving scene of Jo's death in *Bleak House*, heralded in the summary of Number XV by a phrase of laconic ruthlessness: "Jo? Yes. Kill him," with three satisfied underscorings of the murderous program thus outlined.

Finally, for both *Dorrit* and *Our Mutual Friend*, Dickens' working notes contain pages of recapitulation. In such sensational stories, the author needs to get a clearer view of the details he had sometimes lavishly introduced without elucidating them. Two sheets of the *Dorrit* notes are entitled, "For Nos. XIX and XX. Mems for working the story round," and each is divided into two columns, one called "Retrospective," the other "Prospective." A similar document, in the "mems" for Number X of *Our Mutual Friend,* is called simply, "Position of Affairs at the end of the second book." In both cases it can be seen that Dickens paid a high price for any lack of foresight in planning his stories ahead, for the adaptation of the end to the beginning demanded an enormous outlay of ingenuity.

Valuable as they were, the "mems" could not solve all the problems or alleviate all the difficulties Dickens was now faced with in literary creation. Forster quotes a letter of July, 1855, in which the novelist wrote to him: "Fancy! Fancy my having underwritten No. 16 by two and a half

---

[70] Forster Collection, MS of *LD*, Nos. XIX and XX.

[71] Forster Collection, MS of *BH*, Nos. XIX and XX.

[72] "The Plotting of *OMF*," *MP*, XLII, 2 (Nov., 1944), "mems" for Nos. XVII and XIX–XX.

pages—a thing which I have not done since Pickwick!"[73] The biographer's comment on that statement, in one of his final chapters, is as revealing as the novelist's own astonishment. Forster writes:

> Not the least remarkable feature in all his manuscripts is the accuracy with which the portions of each representing the several numbers are exactly adjusted to the space the printer had to fill. Whether without erasure, or so interlined as to be illegible, nothing is wanting, and there is nothing in excess.[74]

It is somewhat difficult to conceive why Forster thought fit to record such a manifest untruth. He knew better and he had more than once let his readers into the secret. He knew better because he had read all Dickens' novels in proof sheets. He had himself altered and shortened many installments. And he had described how, on one occasion, Dickens had had to travel all the way from Paris to London to eke out a number of *Dombey* that was two pages short. The truth is that, while writing *Bleak House*, Dickens as usual did his best to supply the required number of pages and lines, but did not always succeed. The second installment had thirty-three pages instead of thirty-two. The fourth was half a page short. The ninth had fifty-nine lines of "matter over the two sheets." The tenth was completed by a manuscript addition extemporized at the last moment on the proofs. The sixteenth, which was two pages short, also received three manuscript inserts at proof stage. The case of the thirteenth number is rather peculiar. The last page of Chapter XL had a blank space of approximately two-fifths of its height. Dickens first thought of inserting an additional paragraph at the top of the page. He began to write it in the blank space and drew an arrow to show where the new paragraph ought to come in. But he got no farther than the first word—"Lady"—before he changed his mind, crossed out the "lady" and the arrow, and wrote instead: "Printer. Manage to bring this down, as I would rather not write more in. It can be easily done by bringing the previous chapter over a little. C.D."

Dorrit affords another illustration of Dickens' struggles to fit his

[73] *Life of Dickens*, II, 294
[74] *Ibid.*, 367.

material into the required pattern. It has been pointed out above that the division of his novels into books was a late development in his work. The documents in the Forster Collection do not preclude the conclusion that the innovation was in part due to his desire to gain space. The installments of *Little Dorrit* average fifty pages of ordinary print. Three of them are perceptibly shorter, and two of those three are numbers I and XI, placed at the beginning of Book I and Book II respectively. These are about three pages shorter than the others. That much can be found out by merely looking at any edition of the novel. The suspicion thus aroused is transformed into an absolute certainty on examination of the manuscript and proofs. On the one hand, Dickens' now constant preoccupation with the space to be filled is betrayed, as in *Bleak House,* by such injunctions as, "Printer. Please so to arrange the matter as to bring it down a little more on this page. C.D."[75] On the other hand, he had inserted on his manuscript, at the beginning of Book II ("Book Two. Riches") the explicit note, "Printer. What would otherwise be the first two pages of this number are to be set apart for this title." Dividing a novel into two books meant for Dickens having four fewer pages to write. The facts, therefore, belie the quiet assurance and infallible accuracy that Forster ascribes to Dickens as regards "the habit he most prized."[76] Certainly Forster lied with the best intentions, but that he did lie on that point there can be no reasonable doubt.

On the whole, Dickens felt a growing need for planning ahead. Yet the development of his narratives is never strictly and irrevocably organized in advance. It was while writing the third number of *Dorrit,* for instance, that he wrote to Forster, "I am not resolved, but I have a great idea of overwhelming that family with wealth."[77] His confession, that he is "not resolved," when the public have already begun to read the book and when his indecision concerns such a major element in the story, is disconcerting. "Riches" was to be the title of the second book, and, if the Dorrits had not become rich, the novel would have been entirely different. Dickens' uncertainty at that point is more reminiscent of *Pickwick*—"Where shall we go next?"—or of *Chuzzlewit* and

[75] Forster Collection, corrected proofs of *LD,* Bk. II, chap. xi. The blank space is about two-thirds of the page.
[76] *Life of Dickens,* II, 370.
[77] *Ibid.,* II, 182.

the suddenness of Martin's departure for America, than of *Dombey* or *Copperfield*. The working notes of the three novels under consideration contain other examples of similarly incomplete mental preparation (what Dickens, in the days of *Barnaby Rudge*, had prettily called "imaging forth"). They are suggestions momentarily contemplated, but not carried into effect. In *Dorrit*, besides the above-mentioned uncertainty of the first magnitude, Dickens had thought of incidents like "Miss Wade in the prison? Not yet" (No. IV) (in spite of the "not yet," Miss Wade in fact never visits the prison) or "Letter from Mrs. Gowan to her daughter-in-law" (No. XIII). This is a tantalizing allusion, for such a letter could not have failed to be considerably more diverting than angelic Amy's epistles to Arthur of the sorrowful countenance.

Our Mutual Friend is under stricter control than *Dorrit*. Its "mems" show with what seriousness Dickens had attached himself to working out the details of the plot. In the first installment, he had told himself to "work in two witnesses by name. For end of story. Ship's steward. Potterson. Job Potterson. Passenger, Jacob Kibble." This program had been carried out very discreetly, so that the reader, who could not guess, and who was of course not told that the two names were there "for the end of the story," was not much enlightened when the names recurred later on. Dickens himself had not lost sight of them and had even been tempted to refer to them passingly about the middle of the story, [78] but he had in fact not done so. Another hint as to the long-distance preparation in *Our Mutual Friend* is in the "mems" of Number IX: "Secretary disguised. Work on to prepossessing the reader with the fact that he is John Harmon" (summary of Bk. II, chap. xii). Again, in Number XVI, while discussing the plotting of Venus and Wegg against Boffin, he bears in mind the end of that part of the story and notes, "Lead on to 'Check-mate' chapter in No. XIX" (summary of Bk. IV, chap. iii).

The *Dorrit* "mems" point to the fact that Dickens had similarly made an effort to have a sketch of the whole story constantly present to his mind. The final collapse of the Clennam dwelling, sapped and eaten out by pests and decay, is referred to more than once in the author's notes, long before the end of the story. The point is all the more inter-

[78] "The Plotting of *OMF*," *MP*, XLII, 2 (Nov., 1944), "mems" for No. IX, "The Fellowship Porters. Miss Potterson and her brother (from p. 23)."

esting as Dickens was accused by some contemporary reviewers of having introduced the episode at the last moment, in order to infuse a topical appeal into an installment published shortly after several houses had collapsed in Camden Town. It is in the summary of Chapter XV (Bk. I, No. V) that Dickens notes, "Begin (with a view to Rigaud catastrophe) the mysterious sounds in the old house," and he returns to this in the summary of Chapter XXIII (Bk. II, No. XII): "Pave the way . . . with the noises—to impress them again, for their connection, from the first, with the catastrophe there," and again in Number XVIII, where he has the circled reminder, "Prepare finally for the last scene at the old house." Similar preparation precedes other important incidents in the same novel: (1) Pancks' disclosures leading to a reversal of the Dorrits' situation—"Pave the way for his discovery and the end of Book First [No. VII]; Carry through . . . . Family spirit, working up to what they are likely to be in a higher station . . . . Pancks, immensely excited—strong preparation for the end of the book [No. IX]." (2) Mr. Merdle's fraudulent bankruptcy—

> The physician and Mr. Merdle's mysterious complaint (to wit: Fraud and Forgery, bye and bye) . . . [No. VI]; Pave the way for a change in Mr. Merdle's manner [No. X]; Pave the way—with the first stone—to Mr. Merdle's ruining everybody [No. X]; Pave the Merdle way; Pave on the Merdle way; Work distantly up to Mr. Merdle [No. XII].

(3) And the final love scene of Arthur and Amy—"*Prepare for the time to come*, in that room, long afterwards" (No. IX). The hints given by the "mems" as to the later course of events can also, as a rule, be found in the text of the relevant chapters, but only in a veiled and discreet form. The "mems" alone disclose the author's purpose at a specific point and at a specific time. Some of the intentions outlined in the working notes have not been carried over into the manuscript, and still fewer into the printed text. Even when Dickens wished to let the reader dimly foresee the solution of some riddle or the outcome of some inner debate, he occasionally feared excessive explicitness and, on second thought, had cancelled at proof stage a reference that appeared to him too clear or

premature. That is one of the reasons why the corrected proofs are worth examining.

Dickens' belated prudence is apparent on several occasions in the proofs of *Bleak House*. Unquestionably, he was more than once afraid of having said too much about Esther's parentage. He cancelled, for instance, a sentence describing Guppy looking at her "in a manner that reminded me, I well remembered afterwards, of a person studying a likeness in a picture" (chap. ix). A little further on, he cancelled a fragment of a conversation between Lady Dedlock and John Jarndyce which, if it had remained, might have made the situation more complex in the end by giving to Jarndyce too precise a knowledge of Esther's origin (chap. xviii).

In *Dorrit*, it was mostly about the Clennam dwelling that the novelist feared he had gone too far. He deleted from the corrected proofs several passages concerning the extremely decayed state of the old building:

> So disused was the spot, and so long was it since it had known repair, that the whole concern seemed to be resolving itself into the city mud and dust . . . . The outer surface of the bricks turned to powder under the hands; the painted wood peeled off in layers . . . . What manner of worms were underneath it, Heaven knows; but those that occasionally died upon the surface were as black as the twigs, and as brittle, and assumed their forms, and crumbled like them, and cast their undistinguishable mites of rottenness into the general bank (Bk. I, chap. xv).

This description might well have been premature if Dickens had wished the reader to be taken by surprise when the house crumbles down at the end, but, from every other point of view, it would have been worthy of inclusion as a brilliant and characteristic specimen of Dickens' style.

His increasing, though still intermittent, endeavor to shape out in detail and in advance the future events of his novels was not due mainly to a deterioration or dispersal of his creative faculty but to the fact that the plots themselves were structures of growing complexity. In particular, it has been seen that Dickens had deliberately woven multiple links between the characters or groups of characters. These links are different from the gross coincidences of his early stories. He had not given up his liking for miraculous encounters, and in *Bleak House,* for instance, chance is extraordinarily obstinate in bringing together Esther and Allan Woodcourt, first when the young physician comes back to England (chap. xlv), and then in London, in the street, in a little frequented district (chap. lix). But the novelty consists in having real and permanent contact between apparently remote human beings. Such relationships are only gradually disclosed, even when they have been foreseen and prepared for from the very beginning. In *Bleak House,* the interweaving of the threads linking the various characters together is particularly striking, as can be shown from a few examples. Allan Woodcourt is at first the assistant of Dr. Badger (chap. xiv)—with whom Richard Carstone will try his hand at the medical profession—before he is called upon to play a prominent part in the novel. Poor Jo is in touch with Hawdon, the Snagsbys, Lady Dedlock, and the Jarndyce circle. Hortense, Lady Dedlock's former maid, becomes Inspector Bucket's lodger (chap. liv). The Dedlocks' housekeeper, Mrs. Rouncewell, identifies her long-lost son in the person of the ex-soldier George, who had himself known the mysterious Captain Hawdon. Krook is the elder Smallweed's brother-in-law. One and the same little girl, Charley, becomes the servant, first of the Smallweeds and later of Esther.

The philosophy behind this practice is formulated by Dickens more clearly than ever at the time of the last three great novels. His favorite metaphor of the threads spun by life between human beings becomes almost obsessive, and, in his technical directions to himself, he makes frequent use of the vocabulary of weaving. "Gather up the ironmaster and Rosa," he writes (No. XV) or "Throw the interest back to the first chapter. Run the two ends of the book together" (No. XVI), or again, and still more clearly, "Gather up Boffin threads."[79] The same notion is conveyed in the text of *Dorrit,* where the poetical style shows Dickens' acute sense of the moving mystery which surrounds the secret relationship between people who believe themselves strangers to one another:

> And thus ever, by day and night, under the sun and under the stars, climbing the dusty hills, and toiling along the weary plains,

[79] *Ibid.,* "mems" for No. X, II–XIV.

journeying by land and journeying by sea, coming and going so strangely, to meet and to act, and re-act on one another, move all we restless travellers through the pilgrimage of life (Bk. I, chap. iii).

The image of the novelist as a weaver is most strikingly expressed in the "Postcript in Lieu of Preface" with which *Our Mutual Friend* closes:

> It would be very unreasonable to expect that many readers, pursuing a story from month to month through nineteen months, will, until they have it before them complete, perceive the relations of its finer threads to the whole pattern which is always before the eyes of the story-weaver at his loom.

When there are too many threads and they get mixed up, the story-weaver who is thus found to have overtaxed his ingenuity can no longer take refuge in noble, imaginative language. Hence the little note that had to be inserted in Number XVI of *Dorrit,* because of the triple identity of Rigaud-Lagnier-Blandois, not yet overtly declared to be a single character:

> By an oversight of the author's, which he did not observe until it was too late for correction in the first impression of the Number for last month (No. XV) the name RIGAUD is used in the seventeenth chapter instead of BLANDOIS. The personage in the story who assumed the latter name is habitually known to the author by the former, as his real one; hence the mistake. It is set right, if the reader will have the goodness to substitute the word BLANDOIS for RIGAUD in that chapter, when it occurs.[80]

Dickens, as is well known, was not fond of pleading guilty, and the tone of his rectification is not precisely apologetic and not at all pleasant. He is no longer, as in the days of *Pickwick,* amused by his own mistakes. He cannot regard them as amiable weaknesses, he is disturbed by them, refuses to consider them as serious and would like to believe that they can be easily explained away and even justified.

Even the most careful planning ahead and the most elaborate memoranda could not solve all the technical difficulties raised by such large-

---

[80] Forster Collection, corrected proofs of *LD,* "inserted slip."

scale novels as *Bleak House, Little Dorrit,* and *Our Mutual Friend.*
Dickens therefore had recourse to some devices that seem rather feeble
and youthful in an experienced novelist. This is the case of the occasional
personification of the story to account for a shifting of the narrator's
point of view. This occurs in *Dorrit*: "Arthur Clennam rose hastily and
saw her standing at the door. This history must sometimes see with
Little Dorrit's eyes, and shall begin that course by seeing him.—Little
Dorrit looked into a dim room . . ." (Bk. I, chap. xiv). It occurs twice
in *Our Mutual Friend*:

> Riah went into the fog, and was lost to the eyes of St. Mary Axe.
> But the eyes of this history can follow him westward . . . (Bk. III,
> chap. i).

> That Pa's daughter should be so contemptuous of Pa's lodger was
> odd; but there were odder anomalies than that in the mind of the
> spoilt girl . . . . Be it this history's part, however, to leave them to
> unravel themselves (Bk. II, chap. viii).

In addition to such worn-out devices and the reserve of names,
themes, characters, and incidents in his *Memoranda Book,* from which
he now borrowed freely, Dickens would also make use of little details
observed in real life. In his working notes for *Dorrit,* he has recorded
suggestions (1) for use in the portrait of Amy's uncle—"Ruined
brother (The clarionet-player I saw at the Ambigu in Paris)" (No.
XI); (2) for a scene at an inn—"Describe small auberge of Mutsort
[?]" (No. III); (3) for Nandy, William Dorrit's protégé—to be drawn
after "old men in the Marylebone workhouse" (No. IX); and (4) a
scene taking place in Venice—"Remember the Bank of Venice" (No.
XII). *Our Mutual Friend* supplies a similar example on a larger scale.
The story has been told by Forster. Dickens had had to postpone to a
later number a chapter that had proved too long for immediate inclusion
and was looking for a shorter substitute chapter. His friend Marcus
Stone happened to call and had just seen a quaint shop. Dickens at once
went out with him, had a look at the shop, took to the idea, and created
the character of Mr. Venus with his strange trade.[81] The "mems" bear the
mark of the incident, for the summary of the substitute chapter (Bk. I,

[81] *Life of Dickens,* II, 292.

chap. vii) is wholly made up of the words, "Picture of the queer St. Giles's business with Imaginary man."[82]

Finally, the corrected proofs of the last novels show that Dickens had not desisted from his habit of taking an interest in even the slightest details of his style. Thus, in *Bleak House* (chap. xxiii), the adverb "indeed" was first deleted from the proofs, then on second thought restored. Forster still played his part as proofreader and still played it in the same spirit of balance and moderation, toning down whatever seemed to him excessive and deleting whatever he thought superfluous. The whole of Number V of *Bleak House* bears corrections in Forster's handwriting. There have been, therefore, no major changes in Dickens' practice in that field.

At every major point, Dickens seems to have moved in the direction of more laborious endeavor and less spontaneous inspiration. There has been a kind of drying up of the personal and literary faculties that had made the earlier part of his career so splendidly easy. His private correspondence in the middle sixties yields a similar impression. In reply to his wife's good wishes for his second trip to America, Dickens wrote the following note on November 5, 1867, when they had been living apart for nearly ten years:

> My Dear Catherine,
>
> I am glad to receive your letter, and to accept and reciprocate your good wishes. Severely hard work lies before me; but that is not a new thing in my life, and I am content to go my way and do it.
>
> Affectionately yours.
> Charles Dickens.[83]

Admittedly, no intimate jocularity was to be expected under the circumstances. Dickens had, in fact, nothing to say to Catherine, no wish to say anything to her. Yet it is difficult to believe that he could have penned such a dry and austere note in his earlier years. It is of almost funereal sadness and conveys a sense of the irrevocability of the past and of age.

[82] "The Plotting of *OMF*," *MP*, XLII, 2 (Nov., 1944).
[83] See Dexter, *Mr. and Mrs. Charles Dickens: Letters.*

Returning for a moment to the above-mentioned "clarionet-player" at the Ambigu, it would be tempting to connect the extreme sentimental poverty of the note to Mrs. Dickens with the need for a fleeting, but real, vision of an old man before Dickens could create a fictional character. But in fact, the "clarionet-player" points to the inevitable limitations of a purely technical study of a writer like Dickens. Such a study can show that his work had become harder for him and at what points and in what ways the difficulty was experienced and overcome. What it leaves out, however, is probably the essential part of Dickens' creative work. And probably that essential part had remained unimpaired. Thousands of men and women must have looked at the "clarionet-player" at the Ambigu. One man alone saw him and immortalized him.

Dickens' unique power of transmutation had become more fitful, but it still worked. *Bleak House, Little Dorrit,* and *Our Mutual Friend* may be inferior to *Copperfield* in many technical respects, but they are three of the major works of English fiction all the same.

XXV: Two Interludes: Social and Historical Novels

1. *The Two Least Dickensian of Dickens' Novels*

Two NOVELS MUST BE EXAMINED apart from the rest of Dickens' work—*Hard Times* and *A Tale of Two Cities.* They are by far his shortest novels. While the monthly novels average a thousand pages each, the two narratives in *Master Humphrey's Clock* nearly seven hundred pages, and even Dickens' other two short novels—*Oliver Twist* and *Great Expectations*—go beyond the five-hundred-page limit, the *Tale* is barely above four hundred and *Hard Times* barely above three hundred pages long.

Part of the difficulty that may account for such unusual brevity lies in the author's return to the weekly form of serialization. The experience of *Humphrey* had been unfortunate; it had made Dickens suffer and he had claimed that he was relinquishing the weekly fragments with relief. Yet it has been seen that by launching *Household Words* and later *All the Year Round,* Dickens had increased both his income and his influence over the reading public, but at the same time had restricted his own freedom. When the sales of the periodical went down, its popularity had to be restored by the publication of a novel from the editor's own hand. And when a novel was published under such circumstances, he obviously had to write it week by week.

The return to methods and constraints that he disliked did not go without difficulties and sufferings. As the weekly fragments were shorter than those in *Humphrey's Clock*, Dickens complained in letters to Forster that he lacked "elbow-room" and was up against what he called "crushing" difficulties.[1] He did not specify what those difficulties were; therefore, his comments remain, like the rest of his pronouncements about his own art, tantalizing to the critic. To Mrs. Watson he wrote that "the compression and close condensation necessary for that disjointed form of publication gave me perpetual trouble."[2] His disclosures concerning the *Tale* are hardly more detailed; "The small portions thereof drive me frantic,"[3] he told Forster on July 9, 1858. Yet he gives very characteristically sentimental reasons for his determination to publish the *Tale* simultaneously as a weekly serial and in monthly numbers. The monthly installments will appear, he writes, "in the green cover, with the two illustrations, at the old shilling. This . . . will give me my old standing with my old public."[4] The repeated use of "old"—particularly striking in the case of "the old shilling," and one wonders why he did not think of mentioning even the old illustrations—shows his emotional mood. He has a nostalgia for the form of publication that had ushered in all his major triumphs.

The two manuscripts in the Forster Collection bear witness to the intense effort to which Dickens submitted himself in order to achieve the indispensable condensation required by such short fragments. The manuscript of the *Tale* is particularly full of erasures and insertions. Dickens' handwriting is irregular and becomes more and more minute toward the end of each chapter, as though he was unconsciously hoping to get more material within the space at his disposal. The "mems" for *A Tale of Two Cities* have not been preserved.[5] But those for *Hard*

---

[1] *Life of Dickens*, II, 120. The phrases are applied to *HT*.

[2] November 1, 1854, *Letters* (MDGH), I, 371.

[3] *Life of Dickens*, II, 281.

[4] *Ibid.*

[5] They may have existed in the usual form, but in that case they must have been destroyed or mislaid. Several pages of the MS are missing and the novelist has recorded

Times are available and are on the whole similar to the preparatory notes for the novels studied in the preceding chapters. The chief revelation they provide is a curious confirmation of Dickens' nostalgia for the monthly form. The first page of the notes begins as follows:

> Friday, January 20th, 1854. Mems: Quantity. One sheet (sixteen pages) of Bleak House, will make ten pages and a quarter of Household Words. Fifteen pages of my writing will make a sheet of Bleak House [a line or two more than a page].[6]—A page and a half of my writing will make a page of Household Words.—The quantity of the story to be published weekly, being about five pages of Household Words, will require about seven pages and a half.

It was normal that Dickens should base his calculations of length on *Bleak House*, the last monthly novel he had completed. But the next remark is more striking: "Mem: write and calculate the story in the old monthly numbers."[7] And in fact he did adopt the strange twofold division into monthly installments, which remained entirely imaginary— since *Hard Times* was never published in that form—and into weekly numbers. He was thus enabled to preserve the traditional aspect of his manuscripts, and merely added here and there a rule and the words "Weekly No." so and so. He carried his scrupulous regard for his own conventions to the point of conceiving a double final number, corresponding to the usual "Nos. XIX and XX," but here less ambitiously called "Nos. V and VI." Then, since the usual double final number contained as a rule some seventy-five pages instead of fifty, he instructed himself to enlarge the contents of the four real weekly fragments that were to make up the fictitious number: "Weekly Nos. to be enlarged to ten of my sides each—about." Such a device shows that Dickens, while suffering from having to write in the weekly form, endeavored to acquire at least the illusion of monthly numbers and thereby to make inspiration easier.

(Bk. III, chap. i, pp. 8–14) "These pages of the ms became mislaid during its publication, and I could not afterwards find them." This is a unique incident, and it reveals the disadvantage of a change in the writer's settled habits.

[6] The words between square brackets have been deleted.

[7] Forster Collection. The sentimental use of "old" is again striking. The "mems" for

The chapters of the two novels are also noticeably shorter than in the more normal Dickensian ones. *Hard Times* has thirty-seven chapters in its 313 pages, or an average of 8½ pages per chapter. The average length is slightly higher—9½—in the *Tale*, which has forty-five chapters in 431 pages. The longest chapter is 17 pages long in the *Tale* (Bk. I, chap. i), 14½ pages long in *Hard Times* (Bk. I, chap. v). The shortest is 4 pages long in the *Tale* (Bk. III, chap. x) and 1 page only in *Hard Times* (Bk. I, chap. i). All the above figures (average, maximum, and minimum length of chapters) are considerably lower than in the case of the more traditional Dickensian novels.

In addition to such external features as the length of their chapters and their mode of publication, the two novels under consideration possess significant points of resemblance. Both belong to the phase of Dickens' career when Wilkie Collins was taking a larger place in his professional and personal life and while Thomas Carlyle was influencing his thinking and his ambitions. Collins' name appears in the first sentence of Dickens' preface to the *Tale*: "When I was acting, with my children and friends, in Mr. WILKIE COLLINS's drama of The Frozen Deep, I first conceived the main idea of this story."

Carlyle's influence is of greater importance still and links *Hard Times* and the *Tale of Two Cities* together more powerfully than any other factor. It is proclaimed in the dedication of *Hard Times*, "Inscribed to Thomas Carlyle," and in the tribute paid at the close of the preface to the *Tale*, "No one can add anything to the philosophy of Mr. CARLYLE's wonderful book."[8] But it is most significantly to be detected in Dickens' desire to write more seriously and to exert greater moral and, above all, social action than in any of his previous works. Thus did *Hard Times* turn out to be almost exclusively a novel with a social thesis, while the *Tale*, though it is mainly a historical novel, also presents social views with great vigor. Carlyle's influence, therefore, must not be lost sight of, nor its effect on Dickens' art overlooked.

HT are reprinted in *HT*, ed. G. H. Ford and S. Monod, New York, 1966 (Norton Critical Editions).

[8] According to Fields (*Yesterdays with Authors,* 238) Carlyle's *French Revolution* was for Dickens "the book of all others which he read perpetually and of which he never tired— a book for inexhaustibleness to be placed before every other book." In 1850, Dickens had already described himself to Forster as "reading that wonderful book, the French Revolution, again, for the 500th time. . . ." In *UT*, chap. xxxvi, he quotes *Sartor Resartus*.

2. Dickens as Social Novelist

The story told in *Hard Times* can be very briefly summarized. Two sets of characters are presented in clear-cut opposition. There are, on the one hand, the masters, Gradgrind, theoretician, economist, and Member of Parliament, whose eyes are to be opened at the end of the novel when the failure of his "system" is made apparent by the misfortunes and mistakes of his children, and Bounderby, millowner, self-made man, hard, vulgar, and narrow-minded, who will turn out to have been a moral impostor. And there are, on the other hand, the workers, among whom the conspicuous figures are Stephen Blackpool, a saint and a martyr, and his friend Rachael.

Hard Times presents two theses. One is clear enough and has to do with the divorce laws. Through the agency of Blackpool, whose wife is a drunkard and almost completely brutish, Dickens voices his indignation at the costliness of divorce, which remains a privilege of the rich. He may have been thinking already, in 1854, of the possible collapse of his own home life, and he may have wished publicly to assert his position in favor of the easier dissolution of all unhappy marriages. Yet the case of Blackpool and his wife is so different from that of Charles and Catherine Dickens that the link is by no means certain.

The second social purpose of *Hard Times* is less easily defined. It seems to be concerned with a radical criticism of the very structure of society, that is, according to Dickens, of the oppression of the poor and of the workers by the rich. But the novelist's attitude is partly obscured by his wish to attack, simultaneously, a particular school of economic thinkers, so that his conclusions in that direction remain indistinct. Besides, other elements interfere with the clarity and pungency with which his social ideas are expressed in *Hard Times*.

The sincerity of Dickens' social feeling is not to be called in doubt. Few men have been so vividly struck as he was by the sufferings of the poor, by the unfairness of fate, and by the frequent cruelty of privileged people. Some of his statements on these points are quite clear. In *Hard Times*, Stephen Blackpool delivers a speech which has little profundity, but is inspired by sincere emotion:

"Deed we are in a muddle, sir. Look around town—so rich as

'tis—and see the numbers o' people as has been broughten into bein heer, fur to weave, an to card, an to piece out a livin', aw the same one way, somehows, twixt their cradles and their graves. Look how we live, an wheer we live, an in what numbers, an by what chances, and wi' what sameness; and look how the mills is awlus a goin, and how they never works us no nigher to any dis'ant object—ceptin awlus, Death. Look how you considers of us, an writes of us, and talks of us, an goes up wi' yor deputations to Secretaries o' State 'bout us, and how you are awlus right, and how we are awlus wrong, and never had'n no reason in us sin ever we were born. Look how this ha growen, sir, bigger an bigger, broader an broader, harder an harder, fro year to year, fro generation unto generation. Who can look on 't, sir, and fairly tell a man 'tis not a muddle?" (Bk. II, chap. v).

Even in the curtailed form in which it is given here, the speech sounds lengthy. But it contains the most complete definition ever given by Dickens of what, according to him, lies at the root of social evil in general.

It should be observed also that the Lancashire dialect used by the character has a twofold effect. In the author's view, it stresses the speaker's simplicity and, as an indirect implication, his sincerity and virtuousness, and thus makes his words more genuine and weighty. But in fact, it also creates a certain distance between the man who is speaking and the author, who does not assume the whole responsibility for his protest. What David Copperfield had been saying about Parliament in intensely and brilliantly Dickensian style had belonged to the author as well as to the character. Blackpool, on the other hand, is a deserving worker, but he has an ignorant mind and a muddled brain, so that Dickens does not take him so unreservedly as his mouthpiece. In any case, the most striking characteristic of Blackpool's speech, when he sums up the social purpose of the novel, is the extreme vagueness of the reproaches he is voicing. The two notions on which he lays stress, the confused state of the system (or "muddle") and the monotony of the workers' lives ("aw the same one way . . . sameness . . . .") can only be regarded nowadays as secondary aspects of the social problem. George Orwell was justified in writing that the whole message of Dickens in *Hard Times* "is one that at first sight looks like an enormous platitude: If men would behave decently the world would be decent."[9]

It is rather remarkable that the most vigorous paragraph of social criticism ever written by Dickens should have remained unpublished. It is to be found among some passages deleted from the corrected proofs of the *Curiosity Shop*. In a long, significant fragment, Dickens commented scathingly on the living conditions of urban laborers in unwholesome surroundings,

> in places where, let men disguise as they please, no human beings can be clean or good, or sober or contented—where no child can be born but it is infected and tainted from the hour it draws its miserable breath and never has its chance of worth or happiness—in such noisome streets they, the tens of thousands, live and die, and give birth to others, tens of thousands more, who live and die again, never growing better, but slowly and surely worse . . . .[10]

We shall never know why Dickens discarded that passage, whether the deletion was due solely to technical reasons, or whether Forster, liberal-minded but ever prudent and moderate, was responsible for it. Yet it is clear that Dickens, at least in the early years of his career, was capable of giving free vent to his indignation and of expressing himself vigorously and efficiently against some specific injustice that had drawn his attention. But there was a considerable gap between such isolated outbursts and the ability to forge a coherent theory in order to solve the problems of society. The gap has not been bridged in *Hard Times*, in spite of Dickens' resolve to strike a heavy blow.

When it is applied to specific points, Dickens' criticism sometimes hits the target, but does so at the expense of his over-all purpose. The workers' fate is not inevitably to be improved by attacks against certain economic theories. Such is, however, Dickens' oblique method when he criticizes, without naming them, the utilitarians. The best parts of *Hard Times* devoted to that theme are well known. The opening words of the book are a parody of their doctrine: "Now, what I want is, Facts . . . .

---

[9] "Ch. Dickens," *Critical Essays*, 10. Orwell admitted later that the message "is not such a platitude as it seems," p. 22.

[10] Corrected proofs for *OCS*, Forster Collection. The passage had been intended for chap. xliv.

Facts alone are wanted in life . . . ." The portrait of Thomas Gradgrind is no less characteristic: "Thomas Gradgrind, sir. A man of realities. A man of facts and calculations . . . " (Bk. I, chap. ii). A little later, a quasi-religious reverence for facts is discreetly hinted at through the adaptation of a familiar ejaculation: "Not that they knew . . . anything about an Ogre. Fact forbid!" (Bk. I, chap. iii).

Finally, one cannot ignore the conversation between Mr. Gradgrind and his young daughter Louisa, when the decision is made to have her marry fifty-year-old Bounderby. The arguments put forward by Mr. Gradgrind to convince his daughter and his deliberately dismissing from the debate any sentimental consideration, seem representative of a mind dried up by its habitual worship of a systematic theory. The scene, in spite of its tendency to lapse into caricature, is one of the most successful in the book. To prove to his daughter that she need not take into account the disparity in years between Mr. Bounderby and herself, Mr. Gradgrind tells her:

> "Now, what are the Facts of this case? . . . In considering this question, it is not unimportant to take into account the statistics of marriage, so far as they have yet been obtained, in England and Wales. I find, on reference to the figures, that a large proportion of these marriages are contracted between parties of very unequal ages . . . . It is remarkable as showing the wide prevalence of this law, that among the natives of the British possessions in India, also in a considerable part of China, and among the Calmucks of Tartary, the best means of computation yet furnished us by travellers, yield similar results. The disparity I have mentioned, therefore, almost ceases to be disparity and (virtually) all but disappears" (Bk. I, chap. xv).

Love, on the other hand, he declares to be in this context irrelevant and calls it a "misplaced expression."

Dickens seems to have harbored great distrust and dislike of all makers of statistics. His feeling is conveyed by a few sentences deleted from the corrected proofs:

> It may be one of the difficulties of casting up and ticking off human figures by the hundred thousand, that they have their indi-

vidual varieties of affections and passions, which are of so perverse a nature, that they will not come, under any rule, into the account.[11]

Dickens' manuscript notes cast some additional light on his intentions in the criticism of economic theories. In the summary of Chapter IV, Mr. Bounderby is called "the bully of humility," a phrase that is not used in the text itself. The doctrine expounded by Gradgrind is defined in the summary of Chapter II merely as "Marlborough House doctrine," and the part to be played by James Harthouse—he is to court Louisa after her marriage—is twice stressed in significant terms. The first sheet of "mems" already mentions "the man who, by being utterly sensual and careless, comes to very much the same thing in the end as the Gradgrind school," and the fourth takes up the same comparison in greater detail: "To shew Louisa, how alike in their creeds, her father and Harthouse are?—How the two heartless things come to the same in the end?—Yes—Do it almost imperceptibly."[12] Dickens' teaching at that point is thus sufficiently clear and presented in an original manner. The use of the epithet "heartless" in the last quoted fragment is revealing. The sentimental aspect of social and economic questions is still the most immediate one for Dickens. His sensibility is more awakened than his thought, and he wishes to appeal to the reader's sensibility rather than to his intelligence.

In any case, the appeal is doomed to remain of questionable efficiency for lack of a precise ideal in favor of which it might have been launched. The positive side of Dickens' social criticism is nonexistent and his thinking far from coherent. This deficiency is most glaring in the chapters devoted to "trade-union" agitation in Coketown. Dickens is known to have repaired to Preston in order to witness the effect of a prolonged strike and to be in touch with the workers' association. His letters and the *Household Words* articles on the subject do not show that he was unfavorably impressed in Preston by clumsy or dishonest popular orators. It is probably, therefore, on account of his unfortunate youthful experiences in the House of Commons and his subsequent lifelong contempt for all political bodies that he instinctively distrusted the in-

[11] Forster Collection, chaps. i–ix. All the cancelled passages of *HT* are reprinted in the Ford-Monod edition of that novel.
[12] MS of *HT*, Forster Collection.

cipient workers' unions and presented the Coketown "agitators" in a very ugly light. Dickens' attitude can hardly be regarded as surprising. Twelve years later, George Eliot, in *Felix Holt* and in her essays, was to give similar impressions and to preach similar doctrines, though she was undoubtedly a more advanced social writer and thinker than Dickens. But the attitude of Stephen Blackpool, an ardent believer in the workers' cause, yet preferring to be ostracized by his companions and dismissed by his employer rather than join an association whose purposes he approves of, is never satisfactorily accounted for. To Dickens himself, it was enough of a reason that he had "passed a promess" to Rachael to "let such things be." The promise is itself obscured by some inadvertent deletions at proof stage. But even if the cancelled passages had been left to subsist, Stephen's attitude would have been incompletely justified. His attitude is one of the mainsprings of the action, so that a considerable part of the book is unconvincing. Dickens' dislike of the workers' unions seriously impairs the defense of the workers he had intended to effect in his book.

The effectiveness and the convincingness of his arguments are further weakened by another circumstance. It has already been observed more than once that the very poor and the very unhappy, when he presents them in his novels, paralyze Dickens and deprive him of his comic power. He is held back by a mixture of sincere pity and self-consciousness. He will not have the reader laugh at them and therefore bestows on them none of those amiable eccentricities and harmless foibles which render his lower middle class people so attractive, so that his noble-hearted, humble figures, possessed of astonishing virtues, are completely devoid of charm and almost devoid of life. The author's purpose was to have them arouse admiration, but the modern reader tends to find them unspeakably tedious. The deficiency is nowhere so apparent as in *Hard Times*, where the two major victims are Stephen Blackpool and Rachael. About them, the novelist had harbored singular illusions. "I have done what I hope is a good thing with Stephen, taking his story as a whole,"[13] he wrote to Forster. Perhaps he had done a good thing in the sense of a well meant and virtuous attempt, but not in the sense of a successful artistic creation.

[13] *Life of Dickens* (Tauchnitz edition), V, 63 (July 14, 1854), footnote omitted from Everyman's Library edition.

In his preparatory notes for the final number, he referred to Stephen's death as "the great effect" and enthusiastically underscored these words twice. Yet all the scenes in which Stephen and Rachael take part are sad and dull. They invariably speak in the tone of virtuous people who are all too conscious of their virtue. When Bounderby asks Stephen whether the presence of Mrs. Sparsit is not an impediment to the confidences he is preparing to make: " 'Sir, I hope I never had nowt to say, not fitten for a born lady to year, sin' I were born mysen',' was the reply, accompanied by a slight flush" (Bk. I, chap. xi). Such unalloyed holiness deserves the highest admiration, but it cannot make of the man who practices and flaunts it either an entertaining companion or an attractive fictional character. A little later the same Stephen tells his friend that she is an angel, to which she retorts: "I am, as I have told thee, Stephen, thy poor friend. Angels are not like me. Between them, and a poor woman fu' of faults, there is a deep gulf set. My little sister is among them, but she is changed" (Bk. I, chap. xiii). The little dead sister embarrasses the reader who has been guiltily deploring that Rachael was not just a little more "fu' of faults." Dickens reveals none of her faults, for he believes her to have none, so that her very modesty is but one more perfection. But the reader is hindered from complaining of Rachael's lugubrious perfection when Dickens uses his favorite form of sentimental blackmailing and forcibly refers to a child's death.

Stephen's own death is a characteristic example of the stellar pathos to which Dickens remains addicted. A star shines over the last hours of Stephen's life: "It ha' shined upon me . . . . It ha' shined into my mind. I ha' lookn at 't an thowt o' thee, Rachael, till the muddle in my mind have cleared awa, above a bit, I hope" (Bk. III, chap. vi). And the same theme is relentlessly harped upon by narrator and character alike to the end of that slow chapter.

Stephen's faulty grammar is another form of sentimental blackmailing, for the reader cannot refuse to be moved by such ignorance or to see in it the incontrovertible evidence of Stephen's purity of mind. The temporary eclipse of Dickens' comic vein is shown in the fact that Stephen's tone is identical with Uriah Heep's, which David had found intolerable to the point of striking Uriah's cheek, an unequivocal sign of his disapproval. Stephen was certainly meant to please and did please readers a century ago, but the type of the saintly worker, which owed so much to piety and so little to realistic observation, has had its day. Rather than the enthusiastic praise of a nineteenth century critic like Walter Crotch[14] or the narrator's admiring commentaries, the modern reader is likely to echo the words spoken by James Harthouse, Louisa's lover: "An infinitely dreary person he appeared to me to be. Lengthy and prosy in the extreme. It was knowing to hold forth, in the humble-virtue school of eloquence, but I assure you that I thought at the time 'My good fellow, you are overdoing this!' " (Bk. II, chap. x). Were not Harthouse a contemptible person, it would be pleasant to fancy that there was a twinkle of amused sympathy in Dickens' eye while he wrote these words. Yet the most adequate comment on the social significance of Stephen's portrait is to be found in a critical essay by a Frenchman who exclaimed: "What an abyss there is between Stephen's resignation and the malignant tirades which the socialist novelists of France present in their fiction!"[15] The abyss is there, undoubtedly, but it is neither more nor less than the abyss which lies between reality and a certain ideal, between men as they often are and men as, according to Dickens, they ought to be.

Finally, hampered by his distrust of all associations and paralyzed by the unreal pathetic tone he thought it right to adopt, Dickens did not succeed in putting forward a clear, coherent, persuasive thesis. His attitude can be defined as a kind of sentimental socialism. He was conscious of the existence of a problem, but it was one that acted on his emotions rather than on his intelligence, and thus the solutions he contemplated were all of the benevolent, patronizing kind. His idea seems to have been the substitution of Cheerybles for all the Bounderbys of the world. He placed his trust in the kindness of enlightened employers to secure for the worker the decent life to which he had a right, though he did not in fact enjoy it, as Dickens well knew. For he had written in *Hard Times*, "I entertain a weak idea that the English people are as hard-worked as any people upon whom the sun shines" (Bk. I, chap. x). It was a good thing to have that "weak idea" more widely spread and perhaps in the

---

14 See W. Walter Crotch, *The Soul of Dickens* (London, 1916), chap. i.
15 André Joubert, *Charles Dickens, sa vie et ses oeuvres* (Paris, 1872), 16.

end generally accepted, but Dickens did very little to show the way toward a better state of things.

3. Dickens as Historical Novelist: A Tale of Two Cities

When Dickens decided to make *A Tale of Two Cities* the second historical or half-historical novel in his career, he had two main purposes in mind. He wished on the one hand, to present to his public and impress on them his own ideas and views about the French Revolution. On the other hand, he wished to link within one narrative Paris and London, the two cities that by then had become almost equally dear to him. The opportunity to practice his technical abilities is obvious in the statement of his purposes. The historical novel was to be a novel with a thesis once more, while the alternation or overlapping of two separate sets of scenes was to demand close-knit and ingenious construction.

As will be seen later on, the second purpose is by no means achieved, in the sense that Dickens' *Tale* does not concern the two cities to the same extent. And the historical value of the novel lies mostly, as in *Barnaby Rudge* and the best pages of the *Child's History*, in Dickens' special talent for conveying the emotions and evolutions of crowds and mobs. However, his own temperament was not adapted to a true historian's part. In the *Child's History*, he had indulged in moral judgments on historical personages and in sentimental partiality. His dislikes and contempt—notably for the Catholics—were obviously violent and arbitrary. Such serious deficiencies were partly counteracted by Dickens' admiration for generous actions, sacrifices, and martyrdom, and by his humor and his gifts as a storyteller, which were applied to anecdotes and minor incidents as well as to the description of grand mob scenes. The same defects and the same virtues are apparent in the *Tale*, where the fall of the Bastille, for instance, is told in an impressionistic style, through the juxtaposition of brief notes: "Cannon, muskets, fire and smoke; but still the deep ditch, the massive stone walls, and the eight great towers. Slight displacements of the raging sea, made by the falling wounded . . . " (Bk. II, chap. xxi). The description of the Carmagnole is no less remarkable: "There could not be fewer than five hundred people, and they were dancing like five thousand demons . . . " (Bk. III, chap. v). A dozen such powerful passages contribute to the creation of both atmosphere and emotion, but they cannot entirely efface the defects of the book as a historical novel.

These defects are serious. Two circumstances make the author's situation more complex and his purpose correspondingly less clear. The social aspects assume, in his eyes, greater importance than historical problems, so that he takes sides energetically. And the personal interest attached to all the events he is describing results in the loss of a proper distance between himself and those events. In two ways, therefore, Dickens is too committed to act as a real historian.

It has been seen above that in the first sentence of his preface to the *Tale*, Dickens mentioned a performance of Wilkie Collins' *The Frozen Deep* as the immediate source of the impulse that led him to write the book. The idea that was suggested to him by *The Frozen Deep* must have been Sidney Carton's sacrifice of his life in favor of his happier rival. But the confession or proclamation made in the preface at the same time accounts, in the eyes of whoever knows the state of prolonged exaltation induced in Dickens by all his theatrical efforts, for the atmosphere in which he must have worked on the *Tale* and for the vivid emotion aroused in him by that book.

The author's intense emotional involvement in the events of the story is clearly asserted in the sequel to the preface: "Throughout its execution, it has had complete possession of me; I have so far verified and suffered what is done and suffered in these pages, as that I have certainly done and suffered it all myself." The assertion cannot be detached from the theatrical context. The words used by Dickens might be those of an actor trying to explain how he had endeavored to identify himself with the character he was embodying. And Dickens adds, "A strong desire was upon me then to embody it in my own person; and I traced out in my fancy the state of mind of which it would necessitate the presentation to an observant spectator, with particular care and interest." He is thus seen to have been working for an imaginary spectator rather than for the usual reading public. The consequences of such an attitude are apparent from many parts of the narrative itself. At one dramatic point in the story, he writes in the first person plural, "Our four horses are taken out . . . " (Bk. III, chap. xiii), and goes on in a lyrical style that shows how inseparable are his and his characters' emotions.

453

The student who remembers Dickens' interest in names, sounds, and initials cannot fail to be struck by the fact that Charles Darnay has the author's first name and the initial of his last name. No other figure in Dickens is so closely linked, in that way, with the novelist himself. There are also significant psychological resemblances between the two. Darnay is already a husband and a father when he yields to the attraction of personal adventure and deserts his wife and child, without letting them know that he is rushing to Paris among all the perils of the Revolution. The only valid explanation provided by the author for such a step is the one that also accounts for many circumstances in his own private life, like the American, Italian, Swiss, and French journeys; the theatricals; and the public readings: "Like the mariner in the old story, the winds and streams had driven him within the influence of the Loadstone Rock, and it was drawing him to itself, and he must go" (Bk. II, chap. xxiv). The magnetic appeal, all the more powerful because it is unaccountable and can therefore be defeated by no reasonable argument, was only too well known to Dickens, who wrote to his daughter, on the eve of his second American tour: "I begin to feel myself drawn towards America, as Darnay, in the Tale of Two Cities was attracted to the Loadstone Rock."[16]

Dickens' emotional state and theatrical attitude were incompatible with the historian's objectivity. But he did not lay claim to objectivity; the French Revolution was, for him, more than a mere opportunity for historical narrative. It also gave him a chance to support a social thesis, again inspired by Carlyle. The end of the preface lays stress on that aspect of the novelist's purpose: "It has been one of my hopes to add something to the popular and picturesque means of understanding that terrible time, though no one can hope to add anything to the philosophy of Mr. CARLYLE's wonderful book." The warning could hardly have been clearer. History is not there as a mere décor. Dickens aims at giving us the means for understanding it better, and he is not afraid of claiming his philosophical ambition. Under such circumstances, it is no surprise to find that he is frequently led into exaggeration in support of his very simple theory that, however hateful the excesses of the Revolution may have been, they were explained and even excused by the cruelty of the

[16] See *Letters* (MDGH), II, 299.

French aristocrats. A characteristic example is provided by the conversation between Charles Darnay and his uncle. The uncle is the embodiment of a ruthless and impenitent class, and he is made to utter speeches of the most improbable cynicism:

France in all such things is changed for the worse. Our not remote ancestors held the right of life and death over the surrounding vulgar. From this room, many such dogs have been taken out to be hanged . . . . Repression is the only lasting philosophy. The dark deference of fear and slavery . . . will keep the dogs obedient to the whip . . . (Bk. II, chap. ix).

Such phrases may have been spoken in real life, but only in extreme and isolated cases, not, as Dickens would have his reader believe, in the daily small talk of the aristocracy.

The novelist's thesis, as he has pointed out himself, is wholly contained in Carlyle's book, *The French Revolution*. Many passages show the close parallelism between Dickens' novel and Carlyle's study. The central historical and social theme of the *Tale*, the idea that under the old regime there existed a sharp contrast between the nobles and the people and that the contrast in itself called for the revenge of the people, is clearly expounded in *The French Revolution*.[17] Dickens' reference to an uprising in 1773, in consequence of which was erected "a new gallows forty feet high"[18] is borrowed from Carlyle, to whom his story of the taking of the Bastille also owes much.[19] Perhaps the staccato rhythm of that narrative is due to the same influence, though in that case the disciple must be admitted to have surpassed his master, for Carlyle was a better teacher of thinking than of writing. The complete list of the incidents which are to be found in both books is of course much longer, but it is of slight interest here, since Dickens never denied, but constantly advertised, his indebtedness to Carlyle.

Yet, together with many passages or episodes inspired by Carlyle, there are cases in which it is Dickens' own indignation that bursts forth, somewhat incongruously. When he describes a crowd watching a pris-

[17] Cf. Carlyle, *The French Revolution* (London, n.d.), I, 11–12, and *T2C*, Bk. I, chap. i.
[18] Carlyle, *French Revolution*, I, 30.
[19] *Ibid.*, 273, and *T2C*, Bk. II, chap. xxi.

oner, he comments: "Whatever the gloss the various spectators put upon the interest, according to their several arts and powers of self-deceit, the interest was, at the root of it, Ogreish" (Bk. II, chap. ii). Both the neologism and the capitalization emphasize the author's intrusion into his novel and his remoteness from the true historian's dignity and detachment. One contemporary critic took him to task, not without reason, from his systematic belittling of the inhabitants of the two cities in the past: "No popularity can disguise the fact that this is the very lowest of low styles of art . . . . The childish delight with which Mr. Dickens acts Jack Horner, and says, 'What a good boy I am, in comparison with my ancestors!' is thoroughly contemptible . . . ."[20] "The very lowest" and "thoroughly contemptible" are unduly harsh phrases, but it is true that Dickens, who was unquestionably a very great novelist, was neither a great social writer nor a great historian. He was too sentimental and too passionate to play successfully either of the two roles he had chosen to assume. *A Tale of Two Cities* no more achieves its essential purpose than does *Hard Times*. The latter is not a convincing plea for social justice; the former is not a trustworthy picture of the French Revolution. Yet, even more than *Hard Times,* the *Tale* is a book that possesses brilliant literary merits. Dickens even tended to regard it as his masterpiece.[21] The two books must now be examined, not as what they attempted and failed to be, but as what they are, not as theses, but as novels.

4. The Evolution of Dickens' Art in Hard Times
and A Tale of Two Cities

Dickens had become famous, almost overnight, because of his humor. In *Pickwick* he had begun to shine as a humorist beore he had become a novelist. In *Copperfield* also, the comic parts had been of paramount importance and value. If Dickens' career had closed with the two works studied in the present chapter, one would be forced to conclude that his priceless gifts as a humorist had suddenly declined and all but disappeared.

The survival of the Dickensian humor in *Hard Times* is thin and

[20] *Saturday Review,* Dec. 17, 1859, quoted in *Dickensiana,* 284.
[21] See William Winter, *Old Friends* (N.Y., 1909), 183, and Letter to Régnier, Oct. 15, 1859, *Letters* (MDGH), II, 102: "I hope it is the best story I have written."

feeble. It is mostly applied to the character of Mrs. Gradgrind, herself a pale and lifeless figure endowed with very few amusing traits. She is described as muddle-headed and therefore ill adapted to live in a house devoted to science and reason. Her mental confusion is such that she gives her children the not particularly probable order: " 'Go and be some-thingological directly.' Mrs. Gradgrind was not a scientific character, and generally dismissed her children to their studies with this general injunction to choose their pursuit" (Bk. I, chap. iv). There is, in fact, more than mental confusion in Mrs. Gradgrind; there is downright foolishness, which yields some amusing effects, though they are often ponderously overemphasized, as on the day when Mr. Bounderby tells her about his destitute childhood: " 'I was so ragged and dirty that you wouldn't have touched me with a pair of tongs.' Mrs. Gradgrind faintly looked at the tongs, as the most appropriate thing her imbecillity could think of doing" (Bk. I, chap. iv). Yet, when she is told of the engage-ment of her daughter Louisa to Bounderby, her reaction offers such a contrast between the trifling details she at once thinks of and the magni-tude of the event, her reaction is so incongruous and futile, that she fleetingly reminds the reader of Mrs. Nickleby's humorous greatness: "I must give you a kiss of congratulation, Louisa; but don't touch my right shoulder, for there's something running down it all day long. And now you see . . . I shall be worrying myself morning, noon, and night, what I am to call him" (Bk. I, chap. iv).

There are all too few such mildly sparkling moments. Mrs. Grad-grind is so colorless that the words, "Good gracious me!" are thought. In *Pickwick* he had begun to shine as a humorist before he had become a too vigorous for her. On the corrected proofs they are deleted and re-placed by a commonplace "Oh!"[22] When she is about to die, she seems to have exhausted her thin comic vein and can only repeat her little mannerisms once more, so that her last appearance is a somewhat pitiful performance (Bk. II, chap. ix). Apart from Mrs. Gradgrind, the only other traces of humor in *Hard Times* consist in a few isolated observa-tions. Mr. Sleary, the circus master, is made elaborately picturesque, but he is not convincing enough to be really funny.

The *Tale* is even more destitute than *Hard Times* in this respect. One

[22] See corrected proofs of *HT*, Forster Collection (chaps. i–xv).

scene is entirely successful. It is the first of Charles Darnay's three trials in London. Part of the cross-examination of a false witness by the prisoner's counsel can testify to the quality of the passage (the witness in question is a professional spy):

> Had he ever been a spy himself? No, he scorned the base insinuation. What did he live upon? His property. Where was his property? He didn't precisely remember where it was. What was it? No business of anybody's. Had he inherited it? Yes, he had. From whom? Distant relation. Very distant? Rather. Ever been in prison? Certainly not. Never in a debtors' prison? Didn't see what that had to do with it . . . (Bk. II, chap. iii).

In the same way that Mrs. Gradgrind was entertaining mostly when she recalled Mrs. Nickleby, Darnay's trial is amusing only in proportion as it bears a faint resemblance to the great trial in *Pickwick*.

In both novels there still occur a few genuinely Dickensian expressions. For instance, while describing the inside of a fine old house, the novelist writes, "A Cupid . . . was still to be seen on the ceiling, in the coolest linen" (Bk. III, chap. ii), and that ingenious reference to nakedness sounds like an echo of the past greatness of Dickens' verbal humor.

The opposite tendency, the often deplored Dickensian pathos, has, on the contrary, been reinforced. In *Hard Times*, Stephen and Rachael have appeared as dreadful examples. The *Tale* is too often both pathetic and melodramatic. There are moments of real emotion and beauty, such as the death of Sidney Carton (Bk. III, chap. xv), but there are unbearably unreal dialogues. When Mr. Lorry reveals her parentage to Lucie Manette, he has to tell her, "No, don't kneel! In Heaven's name, why should you kneel to me!" and hear the reply, "For the truth. O dear, good, compassionate sir, for the truth!" (Bk. I, chap. iv). In the same early chapter, the same young person utters other incredible speeches. To her father, the old doctor just released from the Bastille, she says: "All that I may tell you, here and now, is that I pray to you to touch me and bless me. Kiss me; kiss me! O my dear, my dear!" Then she addresses the two witnesses of the scene, a wine-merchant and a bank-clerk: "Weep for her [my mother] . . . and for me! I feel his sacred tears upon my face, and his sobs strike against my heart. O see! Thank God for us, thank God!"

Lucie's emotion is no doubt highly creditable, but it is not credibly expressed. Such scenes—which cannot be quoted in their entirety—do not deserve the same kind of immortality as is enjoyed by nearly the whole of *Pickwick* or *Copperfield*. The language of many of the characters becomes ponderous. Sidney Carton declares his love to Lucie in a speech so reticent and involved that it can move no reader of today:

> "If it had been possible, Miss Manette, that you could have returned the love of the man you see before you—self-flung away, wasted, drunken creature of misuse as you know him to be—he would have been conscious, this day and hour, in spite of his happiness, that he would bring you to misery . . . . I know very well that you can have no tenderness for me; I ask for none; I am even thankful that it cannot be" (Bk. II, chap. xiii).

His words are more of a declamation than a declaration. Yet the acme of melodrama is reached only in the narrative which Doctor Manette is supposed to have written in his cell with a view to bringing down the revenge of heaven and earth on a cruel, aristocratic family. In that stupendous piece of prose, he mentions the case of a man whom that family had compelled to drag a cart, like a horse, "taken out of harness one day at noon, to feed—if he could find food—he sobbed twelve times, one for every stroke of the bell, and died on her bosom" (Bk. III, chap. x). That such a nicely timed winding-up should occur on the very cheapest of stages is only too probable. But it is difficult to believe, as Dickens would have us believe, that the Bastille prisoner used his own blood mixed with soot to record such stupid details. Shocked by that outrageous melodramatic bad taste, the reader is tempted to emulate Lady Macbeth and exclaim, "Who would have thought the old man to have had so much blood in him," and to have turned it to such a use.

While there is an increase in excessive sentimentality and melodrama, Dickens' style is also more and more shot through with the little verbal tricks that are often termed his mannerisms. One should be chary of using the word mannerism too casually, but there are unquestionable mannerisms in the *Tale* and they run counter to the natural flow of Dickens' style. The light-handed use of an Anglo-French form of speech in *Bleak House* or *Dorrit* has been described as successful. The same device is used in the *Tale* on a larger scale. That is, from one point of view, normal, since many scenes take place in Paris among French people. The Anglo-French speech can foster in the English reader the illusion of a foreign language which remains intelligible to him. In a number of cases, the effect sought is achieved: "Live the Bastille prisoner" (Bk. III, chap. ii); "I salute you, citizeness" (Bk. III, chap. v); "Good-day, citizeness" (Bk. III, chap. v). One might also instance Madame Defarge's insults: "Woman imbecile, and pig-like!" (Bk. II, chap. xiv), or the brief conversation with a civil servant " 'Behold your papers, Jarvis Lorry, countersigned!' 'One can depart, citizen?' 'One can depart. Forward, my postilions! A good journey!' " (Bk. III, chap. xiii). Yet that kind of effect is too artificial not to pall through repetition.

The Anglo-French language in the *Tale* thus becomes wearisome. It is also objectionable for another reason. If it were what it implicitly claims to be, the literal translation of current French phrases into English, it ought to be possible to translate the phrases back into French without difficulty, but this is not the case. Not only is the tone of many of the Anglo-French expressions much more solemn than that of the corresponding French idioms, but it is often difficult to find the precise phrases Dickens had in mind. "A good journey" in the last quoted example is an anglicized version of "Bon voyage." "Take you my knitting" (Bk. III, chap. xiv), which Madame Defarge uses while addressing a fellow-*tricoteuse,* is even a totally unjustified German construction. "The Bridge of the Pont-Neuf" (Bk. III, chap. viii) is unnecessarily and improbably redundant. In short, the Anglo-French language should have been used more sparingly in the *Tale,* both because the point of satiety might have been avoided and because the author would not then have gone beyond the bounds of his knowledge of French. In fact, the text of the novel confirms what is shown by Dickens' letters written in French: they are easy and often elegant, but they abound in minor inaccuracies.[23]

Dickens' use of English in the two novels under consideration is extremely careful and controlled. The two manuscripts and the cor-

---

[23] He thanks Louis Hachette, for instance, for "l'honneur très flattante" done to him (unpublished; Librairie Hachette archives).

rected proofs of *Hard Times* give evidence of serious and even ambitious stylistic labor. Where the style seems to be loose or relaxed, it is in general purposely so because Dickens is aiming at some impressionistic effect. This is by no means a novelty in his work. But Dickens' practice of the disintegrated sentence has become increasingly frequent and masterly. An adequate illustration is provided by a short paragraph from *Hard Times* conveying, like similar passages in *Dombey,* the rhythm of railroad traveling:

> The seizure of the station with a fit of trembling gradually deepening to a complaint of the heart, announced the train. Fire and steam, and smoke, and red light; a hiss, a crash, a bell and a shriek; Louisa put into one carriage, Mrs. Sparsit put into another: the little station a desert speck in the thunderstorm (Bk. II, chap. xi).

But the most striking aspect of Dickens' style in *Hard Times* and *A Tale of Two Cities,* and the most likely to justify the charge of mannerism, is the overwhelming frequency, the systematic and even labored adoption of the effects of repetition. Dickens' attitude already becomes clear at the beginning of *Hard Times,* as a brief sample from a typical paragraph will show: "The speaker's square forefinger emphasized his observations by underscoring every sentence with a line on the schoolmaster's sleeve. The emphasis was helped by the speaker's square wall of a forehead . . . . The emphasis was helped by the speaker's voice . . ." (Bk. I, chap. ii). In the same chapter, the word "fact," which is the leitmotiv of the novel, is repeated eleven times within seven lines.

The stylistic use of repetition reaches its climax in the *Tale.* The first paragraph in that novel opens with a long series of symmetrical and contrasted expressions: "It was the best of times, it was the worst of times; it was the age of wisdom, it was the age of foolishness; it was the age of belief, it was the epoch of incredulity . . . ." Later, the word "hunger" is used in eight consecutive sentences (Bk. I, chap. v) and the word "death" eight times in as many lines (Bk. II, chap. i). The contemptuous reference to the monarch as "our serene, illustrious, excellent, and so forth" is reproduced four times within one paragraph (Bk. II, chap. ii). And the description of the noise made by the audience at Darnay's English trial—"A buzz arose in the court as if a cloud of

great blue-flies were swarming about the prisoner" (Bk. II, chap. iii)—
occurs five times in one chapter. There are less flagrant, though similarly
characteristic examples of insistent word repetition, as in the sentence,
"He emerged into the heavy mist of the heavy streets with a heavier
heart" (Bk. II, chap. xxiv).

The use, and perhaps even abuse, of repetition, is thus the most significant phenomenon in the evolution of Dickens' style during that
period. Repetition can, of course, serve various purposes. It can be the-
matic or it can be musical. Dickens shows in *Hard Times*, that he was
conscious of the analogy between his novel and the musician's work—
"Let us strike the keynote again before pursuing the tune" (Bk. I,
chap. viii). Perhaps his musical ambition accounts for his frequent use
of assonance and alliteration. He had been taken to task for often writing blank verse in his prose, especially in *The Old Curiosity Shop*.
Against the tendency to blank verse, his interest in impressionistic effects
was an efficient defense. But Dickens, like most of the major Victorian
novelists, still indulged persistently in alliteration. A characteristic example can be found in the *Tale*: " 'Here they come, fast, fierce and furious!'
It was the rush and roar of rain that he typified . . ." (Bk. II, chap. iv).

Finally, in his considerable effort to make his style more artistic, to
conform to what he believed should be the practice of a professional
man of letters, Dickens makes a broader use of the symbols and allegories that had long been dear to him. In *Hard Times*, he early substitutes for objects the symbolic designations he has chosen to represent
them by, for example, "The Fairy Palaces burst into illumination . . .
and all the melancholy mad elephants, polished and oiled up for the
day's monotony, were at their heavy exercise again" (Bk. I, chap. xi).
If he wishes to understand such a description, the reader must remember—he is helped by several repetitions—that the "Fairy Palaces" are
the textile mills and the "melancholy mad elephants" the pistons of
the machinery.

In another passage in the same novel, the reader witnesses the birth
of an allegory which is to be used through several chapters. Harthouse
is courting Louisa and they are watched by Mrs. Sparsit, Bounderby's
housekeeper:

Now, Mrs. Sparsit was not a poetical woman; but she took an idea, in the nature of an allegorical fancy, into her head. Much watching of Louisa . . . must have given her as it were a lift, in the way of inspiration. She erected in her mind a mighty Staircase, with a dark pit of shame and ruin at the bottom; and down those stairs, from day to day, and hour to hour, she saw Louisa coming (Bk. II, chap. x).

That Mrs. Sparsit is "not a poetical woman" has very little importance, for the author's imagination is sufficiently rich to fill the minds of all his characters with allegories. Also in *Hard Times,* there is the allegorical treatment of the lapse of Time as "The Great Manufacturer," and the headings of the three books into which the novel is subdivided—"Book I: Sowing; Book II: Reaping; Book III: Garnering" are allegorical.

Dickens' work on the proofs of *Hard Times* reveals his new stylistic tendencies, or at least reveals the development of some features of his style at the expense of others. He deliberately cancels whatever might have recalled the gusto of his former days. From the description of a gentleman who has come to visit the Coketown school, he cuts out every picturesque and amiable detail. Thus the sentence, "The third gentleman now stepped forth. A bustling pleasant little gentleman he was, a mighty man . . . ," becomes "The Third gentleman now stepped forth. A mighty man . . . ." And in what follows, Dickens has deleted "here he complacently smiled again" and the comments "cheerfully," "with three brisk little claps of his hands," and "with a blithe sententiousness peculiar to him" (Bk. I, chap. ii). The text may not be improved by these changes, but they give evidence of the novelist's desire to bridle his fancy, which would have been out of keeping in such a context. Not all the changes introduced at proof stage are of the same kind. To his description of Mrs. Sparsit, Dickens unquestionably adds a picturesque note when he replaces "a stately resignation" by "a sort of social widowhood" (Bk. I, chap. vii).

As for the titles of the novels, a patient quest and prolonged hesitation are not an innovation in Dickens' work. Yet the story Forster told of how the title *Hard Times* was selected is interesting.[24] Dickens had sub-

[24] See *Life of Dickens,* II, 119–20.

mitted to his friend a list of fourteen possible titles for the projected novel, telling him that three of them—he did not specify which—were his own favorites and asking him to choose three in his turn. Number six alone chanced to be approved by both friends, and thus *Hard Times* came to be adopted through a kind of critical lottery. The manuscript itself shows that Dickens had contemplated more than fourteen possible titles. The complete list on the sheet dated January 20, 1854, runs as follows:

Stubborn things / Fact / Thomas Gradgrind's facts[25] / Hard-headed Gradgrind / The Grindstone / Hard heads and soft hearts / The Time grinders / Mr. Gradgrind's grindstone / *The Family Grindstone / *Hard Times / The *universal general grindstone / Hard Times / Heads and tales / Two and two are four / Prove it! / Black and white / According to Cocker / Prove it! / Stubborn things / *Facts are stubborn things / Mr. Gradgrind's *grindstone facts / The *John *Thomas *Thomas *Thomas *Mr. Gradgrind's grindstone / Hard Times / Two and two are four / *Calculations / *According to Cocker / *Damaging Facts / Something tangible / Our hard-headed friend / Rust and Dust / *The real *times *days / *There is no / *No such thing sir / *Extremes meet / *Unknown quantities / Simple arithmetic / A *mere matter of calculation / A mere question of figures.

A close scrutiny of that list, in which the same words or ideas recur several times, suggests that Dickens needed to familiarize himself with a title before he could adopt it. There are many suggestions on the list; yet it does not leave an impression of ease and wealth of inspiration, for many of Dickens' ideas were impracticable, not to say feeble.

No similar document exists for the *Tale*. There is in fact a list of forty-two titles in the manuscript book kept by Dickens about 1854, and the list is headed: "How as to a story in two periods—with a lapse of time between, like a French drama. Titles for such a notion."[26] This fits in well enough with the outline of *A Tale of Two Cities*, but that particular title is not included. Some of the suggestions listed served for

25 With two variants, John and *George instead of Thomas. The headings or words preceded by an asterisk are those deleted by Dickens himself from his list.

26 See Ley's annotated edition of Forster's *Life of Dickens* (London, 1928) or Mrs. Comyns Carr's *Reminiscences*.

other works: "Somebody's Luggage" and "No Thoroughfare" for short stories; "The Grindstone" and perhaps "Dust" for ideas embodied in *Hard Times*; "The Cinder Heap," "Rokesmith's Forge," and "Our Mutual Friend" for the novel which bears the last name, while the idea of the forge seems to have been transferred to *Great Expectations*.

It has been seen that the choice of a title was for Dickens, curiously enough, a preliminary step to be taken before he could construct his novel. To the construction proper of *Hard Times* and *A Tale of Two Cities* he devoted considerable care. The plot of *Hard Times* has been summarized above. That of the *Tale* can be expounded in a few sentences. Dr. Manette, after being a prisoner in the Bastille for eighteen years, is released in 1775 and goes to London to live with his daughter Lucie. Five years later another London Frenchman, who calls himself Charles Darnay but who in reality belongs to an aristocratic family he disapproves of and has disassociated himself from, marries Lucie. Another suitor of Lucie's has been the dissolute barrister Sidney Carton, who strangely resembles Darnay. Darnay's true identity is steeped in mystery, which torments the old doctor. At the outbreak of the French Revolution, Darnay is drawn to Paris by the appeal of a former servant of his family who is in great danger. Darnay is arrested. His wife, daughter, and father-in-law endeavor to save his life. However, he is sentenced to death because of an incriminating document penned by Dr. Manette, while in the Bastille, denouncing the guilt of the Saint-Evrémonde family, to which Darnay belongs. He is saved only through Carton's sacrifice, for Carton takes advantage of his resemblance to Darnay to take his place on the scaffold.

The general impression produced by the construction of the novel is the very opposite of that indicated by the critic of the *Saturday Review* on January 17, 1859:

> The broken-backed way in which the story maunders along from 1775 to 1792, and back again to 1760 or thereabouts, is an excellent instance of the complete disregard of the rules of literary composition which have marked the whole of Mr. Dickens's career as an author . . .[27]

[27] Quoted in *Dickensiana*, 282.

On the contrary the *Tale* is almost a model of firm, symmetrical construction, based on a physical resemblance that is called into play twice, at the beginning and at the end of the book, to save the hero's life. Several mysteries which had puzzled the reader from the early chapters are gradually elucidated. Unquestionably, every detail has been conceived and presented with a view to the whole, and there has been an amount of premeditation never before achieved by Dickens.

The title itself suggests that the author's wish had been to write a novel in two distinct parts; or rather a book which might, without losing its unity, be as it were astride two countries. Of course, the wish has not been fulfilled nor the title justified. There are altogether forty-five chapters. Two are general and concerned with a parallel picture of events in the two countries. Sixteen chapters are located in London and three in other English cities, while eighteen are located in Paris and six in other parts of France. A fair balance is thus preserved, in the book as a whole, between France and England. But it should be observed that all the English chapters are to be found in Books I and II, while the majority of the French chapters make up by themselves the whole of Book III. The *Tale*, therefore, cannot be said to closely unite and associate the two cities. It merely relates the story of an Anglo-French family, a story which is set first in England, and later in France.

The comparative novelty of its method does not prevent the author from relying on some devices he has long cherished. The novelty is only comparative in the sense that the alternation between the two cities resembles the alternation between the English and American scenes in *Chuzzlewit* or the alternation between the third- and first-person narratives in *Bleak House*. Coincidences have preserved all of their past importance. The Defarges, revolutionary publicans, and their friends, like the country road mender, continuously reappear and finally leave the reader under the impression that they were by themselves the masterminds of the rising revolution.[28] In order to expose and intimidate the spy Barsad, who alone can allow for the final rescue through substitution, the streets of Paris are suddenly peopled—in 1792—with all the English characters of the novel, and we thus meet Lucie's governess, Miss Pross, who very opportunely turns out to be Barsad's sister;

[28] See, e.g., chaps. ii–xv.

Jerry Cruncher, the messenger of Tellson's Bank; and Sidney Carton, whose arrival remains unexplained.

To the convenient and excessive use of coincidence must be added a development of the cheapest conventional devices to be found in serial fiction, because of the influence both of Dickens' growing love of the sensational and of his close linking of the novel and the stage. Phrases calculated to capture the interest of the reader at little imaginative expense abound, especially at the end of a chapter, as in the following: "Who could that be with Mr. Lorry—the owner of the riding-coat upon the chair—who must not be seen? From whom newly arrived, did he come out, agitated and surprised . . ." (Bk. III, chap. v). There are also many dramatic situations, elaborately staged and emphasized, like the reading of the document penned by the Bastille prisoner: "In the dead silence and stillness—the prisoner under trial looking lovingly at his wife, his wife only looking from him to look with solicitude at the reader . . ." (Bk. III, chap. ix). And of course the incriminating document itself, telling how a physician had been secretly carried to an unknown place to tend nameless wounded people and was punished by a *lettre de cachet* for having shown virtuous curiosity, belongs to the paraphernalia of the most conventional kind of fiction, in addition to its being written with the prisoner's blood (Bk. III, chap. x).

Finally, the composition of the novel reflects, mostly in the chapter headings which convey the author's purpose in that respect, some of the mannerisms of his style, such as his quest for symbols, allegories, contrasts, and *double-entendre*'s. In the *Tale,* there are headings like "A Hand at Cards" and "The Game Made" (Bk. II, chaps. viii, ix), ushering in a form of metaphorical expression which will be adopted in the character's conversations, or more general terms which, through one of their meanings, are accurately applicable to specific situations, like "A Knock at the Door" (Bk. III, chap. vii), "The Night Shadows" (Bk. I, chap. iii), and "In Secret" (Bk. III, chap. i), with its double reference to general secrecy and to secret confinement. There are similar cases in *Hard Times*: "Murdering the Innocents" (Bk. I, chap. ii), "A Loophole" (Bk. I, chap. iii), "The Whelp" (Bk. II, chap. iii), etc. It is in the *Tale,* however, that the technique is used with the greatest ingenuity, as is shown by the encroaching of one chapter on the next and the progression through verbal association at the beginning of the novel. The first chapter closes with the words, "Thus did the year one thousand seven hundred and seventy-five conduct . . . the creatures of this chronicle . . . along the roads that lay before them." Then Chapter II ("The Mail") begins: "It was the Dover Road that lay, on a Friday night late in November, before the first of the persons with whom this history has business. The Dover road lay, as to him, beyond the Dover mail, as it lumbered up Shooter's Hill. He walked uphill . . . ." And there are in the same book several sequences of chapter headings showing the author's interest in effects of symmetry, contrast, and repetition. Four successive chapters are called "Two Promises," "A Companion Picture," "The Fellow of Delicacy," and "The Fellow of No Delicacy" (Bk. II, chaps. x–xiii), and four others are titled "Knitting," "Still Knitting," "One Night," and "Nine Days" (Bk. II, chaps. xv–xviii).

John Forster, when he ventured to criticize several details in the construction of *A Tale of Two Cities*, elicited from Dickens pointed replies. They show, on the one hand, that the novelist had a clearer view than ever of the composition of his work and was less inclined to yield to the impulses of inspiration, and, on the other, that he was increasingly impatient of even the friendliest criticism. He defined his essential purpose in the *Tale* as follows:

> Nothing but the interest of the subject, and the pleasure of striving with the form of treatment—nothing in the way of mere money, I mean—could else repay the time and trouble of incessant condensation. But I set myself the little task of making a *picturesque* story, rising in every chapter, with the characters true to nature, but whom the story should express more than they should express themselves in dialogue. I mean in other words that I fancied a story of incident might be written . . . pounding the characters in its own mortar, and beating their interest out of them.

Such an attempt seems to run counter to the natural bent of the author's genius. On a more specific point, the somewhat accidental death of Madame Defarge, the revolutionist killed by the old English governess, Miss Pross, who is covering her master and mistress's flight, Dickens replies to Forster's reproach:

I am not clear, and I never have been clear, respecting the canon of fiction which forbids the interposition of accident in such a case as Madame Defarge's death. Where the accident is inseparable from the passion and action of the character; when it is strictly consistent with the entire design, and arises out of some culminating proceeding on the part of the individual, which the whole story has led up to; it seems to me to become, as it were, an act of divine justice. And when I use Miss Pross . . . I have the positive intention . . . of opposing that mean death . . . to the dignity of Carton's. Wrong or right, this was all design, and seemed to me to be in the fitness of things.[29]

More and more forethought, more and more subtlety—these are the qualities Dickens' pleading is meant to assert. His forethought is not yet complete. Perhaps it cannot be for any writer, and perhaps it is not even desirable that it should be. It is only on account of the fragmentary method of publication adopted by Dickens that one may deplore his not having determined in advance the outline of events in his stories. In that respect, the two novels under consideration in the present chapter are less imperfect than others. The only significant change introduced while Dickens was at work on one of them is the subdivision of *Hard Times* into three books. The novel was published in twenty-one weekly portions, and it was only after the fifteenth had been written that Dickens made a note on his "mems": "Republish in three books? 1. Sowing. 2. Reaping 3. Garnering."[30] But formal perfection has little to do with the average reader's enjoyment. In his letter to Forster, Dickens had hit upon the real problem when he wrote, "I have never been clear, respecting the canon of fiction which forbids the interposition of accident . . . ." The truth is, of course, that there are no canons of fiction. The novelist's single duty is to convince or delight his reader. Observance of certain laws may help him achieve that result but they cannot guarantee success. In *Hard Times* and *A Tale of Two Cities*, Dickens had more conscientiously than formerly adhered to the supposed canons of fiction. They certainly did not raise the two books above the rest of his work.

29 *Life of Dickens*, II, 281, 282.
30 Original MS of *HT*, Forster Collection.

5. Half-Success or Failure?

A Tale of Two Cities has, to be sure, some admirers. It even happens to be the favorite Dickens novel of a number of readers who are not particularly fond of Dickens. It is sometimes well liked by Frenchmen who are not attracted to English literature and culture, and whose minds are more disconcerted by the humor of *Pickwick*, and the Pickwickian side of the major novels, than by the sensational incidents and plot of the *Tale*. Forster praises the book for one valid reason: "Its distinctive merit is . . . as a specimen of Dickens's imaginative story-telling."[31] Though that is indeed a merit, it is not specifically Dickensian, nor is it powerfully attractive.

Hard Times has some important advocates, but, in general, it has fared no better than the *Tale*. The admiration of Ruskin and Taine has been expressed in well-known sentences and is not unreserved. George Bernard Shaw thought highly of *Hard Times*, and F. R. Leavis, sees in it Dickens' only "serious" or "adult" work.[32] But both Shaw and Leavis base their appreciation of *Hard Times* partly on qualities which are much more obvious in Dickens' other novels. A number of critics have expressed great disappointment.[33] Macaulay wrote in his diary, "I read Dickens's *Hard Times*. One excessively touching, heart-breaking passage, and the rest sullen socialism."[34] Gissing calls *Hard Times* "a book quite unworthy of" Dickens.[35] John Middleton Murry refers to the time "when we are incapable of rejecting anything to which Dickens put his hand (unless it is 'Hard Times'),"[36] and F. G. Kitton, the author of *Dickensiana*, does not even regard *Hard Times* as worthy of inclusion among Dickens' novels.[37]

Of this unfavorable response some explanations have been provided in the foregoing pages. But the most glaring fact, the essential difference from the other novels, lies in the necessity in which Dickens had found himself, for both *Hard Times* and the *Tale*, of looking for inspiration

[31] *Life of Dickens,* II, 283.
[32] *The Great Tradition* (London, 1948).
[33] See Forster, *Life of Dickens,* II, 120.
[34] August 12, 1854, quoted in *Dickensiana,* 424.
[35] *Ch. Dickens, Critical Study,* 18.
[36] "Charles Dickens," *Critical Essays,* 431.
[37] *HT* is included among the *Minor Writings of C.D.* (London, 1900), 28.

beyond the field of his daily experience, enlarged by the natural play of his imagination. In order to write *Hard Times*, he had had to visit Preston and get in touch, superficially, of course, with the working class of which he was totally ignorant. In order to write *A Tale of Two Cities*, he had had to read many historical works. In spite of G. K. Chesterton's assertion that "Thomas Carlyle had read a great deal about the French Revolution. Dickens had read nothing at all, except Carlyle,"[38] Carlyle is known to have sent Dickens, at his request, hundreds of books[39] and Dickens asserted in his preface: "Whenever any reference (however slight) is made here to the condition of the French people before or during the Revolution, it is truly made, on the faith of trustworthy witnesses." Moreover, he is known to have quoted his sources; in letters to Forster he mentions Mercier's *Tableau de Paris*, Rousseau, and the tax-tables.[40] But bookish contact with the history of a foreign nation is no closer than the contact established between the casual observer of a strike and the soul of an industrial city. Dickens is as ill at ease in the description of the French aristocracy or the French popular classes as in his attempt to make a small group of English workers come to life in his reader's eyes. In both cases, he gets out of his depth. The severe phrase of *Blackwood's Edinburgh Magazine* concerning *Hard Times* is equally true of *A Tale of Two Cities*: "The book is more palpably a *made* book than any of the many manufactured articles we have lately seen."[41] The deficiency in the two books is also defined adequately by the French critic Louis Cazamian when he speaks of "the lack of true intimacy between the author and his subject."[42]

XXVI: BACK TO THE AUTOBIOGRAPHICAL FORM

AFTER BRINGING OUT in quick succession *David Copperfield* and *Bleak House*, Dickens did not use the autobiographical form in his major fiction for several years. Nevertheless, throughout the final period of his career, that form played a growing part in his minor works, such

---

[38] *Appreciations*, 193.
[39] See Fields, *Yesterdays With Authors*, 238.
[40] See *Life of Dickens*, II, 282.
[41] April, 1855, 451–56. Quoted in *Dickensiana*, 112.
[42] *Le Roman social en Angleterre* (Paris, 1904), 312.

as his Christmas tales, his articles, and his short stories. It is to be found, for instance, in *The Holly-Tree Inn*—"In Three Branches; First Branch: Myself"—in "George Silverman's Explanation," in "Somebody's Luggage" (both for the central narrative and for one of the inserted tales), in "Doctor Marigold's Prescriptions" (again both for the central story and for the inserted tale, "A Trial for Murder"), in "Mugby Junction" (and the two inserted tales "The Signalman" and "The Boy at Mugby"), in "A Fly-Leaf in a Life," "Hunted Down," the two "Lirriper" stories, and "The Ghost of Art." In most of these cases, the supposed narrator is a mediocre or vulgar character, whose personality it amuses Dickens to assume. He can thus at once express his own views under a disguise, compose works that will be adapted to public readings without modification, and indulge in a style of writing in which he excels—the imitation of the way humble people speak and think.

Ten years after *Copperfield*, Dickens made up his mind to once more employ the autobiographical form in a full-length story. *Great Expectations* was the result, and that novel occupies, in the final phase of his career, a position similar to that held by *Copperfield* in his work as a whole.

The treatment of autobiography is, of course, not the same in *Great Expectations* as it had been in *Copperfield*, the earlier novel being autobiographical in matter as well as manner. *Great Expectations* does not concern the events of the author's life, though it contains elements of psychological and moral introspection.

The evolution of *Great Expectations* began early in 1860. The stages of its development are traced in Forster's *Life of Dickens*, where he claims that he was responsible for suggesting to Dickens, that, instead of frittering away his talent among a multitude of minor narratives, "he should let himself loose upon some single humorous conception, in the vein of his youthful achievements in that way."[1] After some time, the novelist replied:

> From a little piece I have been writing . . . such a very fine, new and grotesque idea has opened upon me, that I begin to doubt whether I had not better cancel the little paper, and reserve the notion for

[1] *Life of Dickens*, II, 284.

a new book. . . . it so opens out before *me* that I can see the whole of a serial revolving on it, in the most singular and comic manner.[2]

According to Forster, the idea Dickens was alluding to in that letter was the relationship between Pip, the young narrator-hero of *Great Expectations*, and the convict Magwitch. His first scheme, then, had been to write a short story on that theme. On second thought, he contemplated a novel in twenty monthly numbers. But the sales of *All the Year Round* happened to be going down at the time, in consequence of Charles Lever's failure to keep up the subscribers' interest in his current serial. Dickens thus had to alter his plans once more and adopt the method of the weekly fragments. The total length of the projected book was also to be reduced by half. The letter in which he communicated the change to Forster refers very openly, and not too pleasantly, to the part played by financial preoccupations in his artistic creation: "The sacrifice of *Great Expectations* is really and truly made for myself. The property of *All the Year Round* is far too valuable, in every way, to be much endangered."[3]

The first portion was published on December 1, 1860, and publication went on through September, 1861. Of course, Dickens complained bitterly, as usual, of the difficulties due to the weekly form of serialization: "As to the planning out from week to week, nobody can imagine what the difficulty is, without trying. But, as in all such cases, when it is overcome, the pleasure is proportionate."[4] The reduction of the book to half the size of a monthly novel can similarly be regarded as a source of "proportionate pleasure" to the reader.

Although *Great Expectations* is one of Dickens' best-known works, a summary of its plot is required to show how the story is articulated. Young Philip Pirrip, nicknamed Pip, lives with his sister, Mrs. Gargery, whose husband, Joe, is a blacksmith. One day, Pip encounters in the churchyard a man who terrifies him into providing food stolen from Mrs. Gargery's pantry and a file stolen from Joe's workshop. The man turns out to be an escaped convict, who is soon recaptured, together with another, with whom he seems to be bound by mysterious links

[2] *Ibid.*
[3] *Ibid.*, 284–85 (October 4, 1860).
[4] *Ibid.*, 288–89.

and vivid hatred. Pip's childhood passes in the village, diversified only by two circumstances. One is the series of visits he pays to Miss Havisham, an eccentric old lady in the neighboring city. At Miss Havisham's he meets Estella, a beautiful but haughty little girl. The other noteworthy event is the appearance in the village of an anonymous man who gives a present to Pip and exhibits a file in a mysterious manner. Pip becomes his brother-in-law's apprentice. Mrs. Gargery is brutally assaulted and, though she is left alive, she loses all her mental and bodily powers, so that Biddy, a girl from the village, has to come and live with the Gargerys. Pip is divided between Biddy's presence and the remembrance of Estella, who has gone abroad. This first stage comes to an end on the day when the lawyer Jaggers—who is also Miss Havisham's lawyer—comes and tells Pip that an anonymous benefactor is making his fortune, so that he now has "great expectations."

The second stage is located mostly in London, where Pip is being educated, becoming a spendthrift, and making friends with Herbert Pocket, a relative of Miss Havisham's and the son of Pip's tutor. Pip falls in with Estella again and finds her as cold as ever, but more and more attractive. The London scenes are interrupted by Pip's visit to his native village, to attend his sister's funeral. This period comes to an end on the day when Pip's real benefactor turns up in London. The benefactor is not Miss Havisham, but Abel Magwitch, the former convict who has become a prosperous farmer in Australia and who endangers his life by revisiting England in order to see the young man whom his gratitude has turned into a gentleman.

The third stage is overshadowed by Pip's disappointment. He believes he can accept no benefit from Magwitch, but feels impelled to protect him. Many revelations are made in quick succession. Magwitch's implacable enemy (the other escaped convict of the beginning) is one Compeyson, the man who had deserted Miss Havisham on the day appointed for their marriage and who thus caused her eccentricities. Estella is the daughter of Magwitch and a female criminal now in the employment of Jaggers. As Compeyson is pursuing Magwitch, it becomes necessary to smuggle him out of the country. An attempt is made, but fails, and Compeyson is killed while having Magwitch arrested once more. Magwitch himself has been seriously injured and dies shortly after hearing himself sentenced to death. Meanwhile, Estella has married a rich, young aristocrat who is also a stupid bully. When Pip emerges from a protracted illness and is ready to content himself with marrying Biddy, she has already become Joe's wife. Pip can only join his friend Herbert in Egypt, where he has acquired a position, thanks to Pip's money, a substantial portion of which had been transferred to Herbert before the benefactor's identity had been disclosed.

The mainsprings of the plot are, therefore, the convict's gratitude to the boy who had aided him, and the confusion created in Pip's mind, and fostered by Dickens in the reader's, by Miss Havisham and Magwitch happening to employ the same lawyer. What the reader is asked to admit is not inconsiderable, but there is no absolute unlikelihood in the novel, which is very solidly built.

Dickens made a serious attempt to keep within the limits of verisimilitude, and even of truthfulness, at a number of points. The scenes connected with the attempt to get Magwitch abroad at the end of the book had been, Forster tells us, the occasion of careful study on the author's part: "To make himself sure of the actual course of a boat in such circumstances, and what possible incidents the adventure might have, Dickens hired a steamer for the day from Blackwall to Southend."[5] The novelist's own working notes include, together with various calculations relative to the age of the characters in the final episode, a table of the tides at the time of the attempt.[6] Part of the section concerning the age of the characters can be given here:

> Magwitch tells his story in the Temple, when Pip is 23. Magwitch is then about 60. Say Pip was about 7 at the opening of the story, Magwitch's escape would then be about 16 years ago. If Magwitch says he first knew Compey about 20 years ago, that would leave about 4 years for his knowledge of Compey and the whole association with him up to the time of the escape. That would also make him about 40 when he knew Compey, and Compey was younger than he.[7]

---

[5] *Ibid.*, II, 287.

[6] "Mems" attached to MS of *GE* (Wisbech Museum). Printed by John Butt in *The Dickensian*, March, 1949, 78–80.

[7] Compey was the provisional name, when the notes were written, of the character called Compeyson in the novel.

The use of conditional forms and phrases like, "Say Pip was about 7 ...," suggests that even in such a firmly conceived and constructed novel as *Great Expectations,* Dickens had left the details of chronology unsettled almost to the last moment.

The composition of the book calls for one more remark. The last two pages are an appendix, or an additional episode, which has been omitted from the above synopsis, because it had no place in the author's original plans. The letter in which the change was announced to Forster is worth quoting, as an example of the conditions under which Dickens accepted, and even chose to do his work—submitting himself to the influence of his public and his friends. The end of *Great Expectations,* as Dickens had conceived it and as it has been described above, would have made that novel the only one in Dickens' whole work that did not possess the traditional happy ending. Now, shortly before the publication of the last number, he wrote to Forster:

> You will be surprised to hear that I have changed the end of *Great Expectations,* from and after Pip's return to Joe's . . . . Bulwer, who has been, as I think you know, extraordinarily taken by the book, so strongly urged it upon me, after reading the proofs, and supported his view with such good reasons, that I resolved to make the change. You shall have it when you come back to town. I have put in as pretty a little piece of writing as I could, and have no doubt the story will be more acceptable through the alteration.[8]

The "pretty little piece of writing" is a page in which Pip, eight years after Joe's marriage, meets widowed Estella and glimpses a prospect of happiness with her. The most astonishing characteristic of the incident is the part played in it by Bulwer. It is difficult to understand nowadays why Dickens attached any importance to an opinion expressed by a facile writer who was devoid of genius. Perhaps both Forster and Dickens, as self-made men, were impressed by Bulwer's rank and wealth. As for the result of Bulwer's advice, it has often been treated contemptuously by critics. Gissing writes: "Is there not much pathos in the story of Pip's foolishness? It would be more manifest if

[8] *Life of Dickens,* II, 289.

we could forget Bulwer's imbecile suggestion, and restore the author's original close of the story."[9] In practice, any modern editor of *Great Expectations* will feel that he must reprint both endings of the story. And perhaps the critic who can forget that Bulwer originated the change and remember that Dickens wholeheartedly accepted it and truly made it his own, will come to see that, while the unhappy ending reinforced the irony of the title by disappointing all the great expectations, the happy one has its own adequacy as well as its own poetry, since it substitutes for the ruined "great" expectations the fulfillment of a slighter and more natural hope. In short, perhaps the novel is not, as Dickens believed, made "more acceptable through the alteration," but it is acceptable and admirable either way.

The external organization of *Great Expectations* calls for little comment. Like Dickens' other "weekly" novels, it is brief and is composed of brief chapters. It has fifty-nine chapters to its 525 pages, or an average of 9 to 10 pages per chapter. The chapters have no headings, only numbers, and the novel is not divided into books, although it has three distinct parts or "stages," clearly marked by the phrases (in the text itself): "This is the end of the first stage of Pip's Expectations" (chap. xix), "This is the end of the second stage . . ." (chap. xxxix). Two of the chapters (chap vi, xiv) are of unusual brevity, being only two pages long. The longest chapter (chap. xix) runs to sixteen pages. There are no systematic "mems"; however, there are 3 pages of fragmentary notes concerning mainly the end of the story.

Both Dickens' usual deficiencies and his new artistry can be recognized in the composition of *Great Expectations*. The use of coincidence is again often excessive. It would seem, for instance, that there can be in the whole of England only three convicts: Magwitch, Compeyson, and Magwitch's mysterious messenger. So, when Pip, as a young man, returns to his native village by mail coach, he happens, by mere chance, to have a convict among his fellow-travelers, and that convict is no other than the man who had taken to him Magwitch's gift and shown the revealing file (chap. xxviii). A number of other coincidences have been made apparent in the synopsis of the novel, the least colossal of

[9] *Ch. Dickens, Critical Study,* 171.

which are not those involved in Estella's genealogy. Yet the only coincidence that plays a major part in the plot (Jaggers' twofold position) is justified, in Dickens' name, by Miss Havisham:

> "Mr. Jaggers . . . had nothing to do with it and knew nothing of it. His being my lawyer, and his being the lawyer of your patron, is a coincidence. He holds the same relation towards numbers of people, and it might easily arise. Be that as it may, it did arise, and was not brought about by anyone" (chap. xliv).

In *Great Expectations*, and existing side by side with devices familiar to the readers of *Nickleby* and *Chuzzlewit*, are more subtle effects, which Dickens has sought after and achieved. For instance, he has overcome the difficult art of transition and the remote preparation for later developments. Thus Pip passes smoothly enough from the narrative of one particular visit to Miss Havisham on to the general description of a whole series of similar visits: "I insensibly fall into a general mention of these journeys as numerous . . ." (chap. xii). In this way he also stresses the seemingly accidental association in his mind between Estella's person and the atmosphere of prisons, to extenuate in advance the shock of the final revelations about the girl's identity.

The atmosphere of the novel is surprisingly fresh in spite of a certain gravity of tone and purpose. Its freshness, considering the time when it was written, the place it occupies in Dickens' career, and the relative tenseness and dryness of *Hard Times, Little Dorrit,* and *A Tale of Two Cities* is particularly striking. Of the efforts required by its composition and of the difficulties encountered on the way, nothing can be perceived by the reader.

There is a marked renewal of Dickens' comic vein. "You will not have to complain," he wrote to Forster in a letter referring to the first chapter, "of the want of humour as in the *Tale of Two Cities*. I made the opening, I hope, in its general effect, exceedingly droll."[10] And the author's enthusiasm has been abundantly matched by his critics, for comedy is a delightful feature in *Great Expectations*. Of course, pathos and tears are not absent, and Dickens goes on believing in the moral value of tears. He writes, "Heaven knows we need never be ashamed of our tears,

[10] *Life of Dickens,* II, 285.

for they are rain upon the blinding dust of earth, overlying our hard hearts" (chap. xix). As for the comic elements, they are not invariably of the highest quality. The reader still comes across a number of puns or half-puns supposedly due to the ignorance of some of the characters: "purple leptic fit" for "apopleptic fit" (chap. vii), "coddleshell" for "codicil" (chap. lvii). The representation of unusual pronunciation is sometimes unduly exploited for comic, or at least picturesque, effects— it is difficult to see in what way the spelling "hart" can reveal an inaccurate or unusual pronunciation of the word "heart" by Joe (e.g., chap. xiii).

Some of the themes treated in the comic episodes had also been long familiar to the readers of Dickens' earlier fiction. But the power of his comic imagination is all the more triumphantly demonstrated, for he shows himself still able to derive inexhaustible effects from the inadequacy of domestic servants or incompetent actors. The whole character of the page nicknamed "The Avenger" is a brilliant example of the former kind; this is also illustrated by

> an inflammatory old female, assisted by an animated rag-bag whom she called her niece . . . . They had both weak eyes, which I had long attributed to their chronically looking in at keyholes, and they were always at hand when not wanted; indeed that was their only reliable quality besides larceny (chap. xl).

On the other hand, the chapter describing Mr. Wopsle in the part of Hamlet (chap. xlvii) is one of the most memorable in Dickens' works. But what is more characteristic of his humor in *Great Expectations,* and what raises it to the same heights as in *Copperfield,* is mostly the delicacy of a number of remarks and the close alliance between humor and melancholy, or even downright sadness. Dickens, who in the days of *Pickwick* and its unreserved jollities, had ignored the borderland between laughter and tears, now moves in it with masterly ease: " 'Biddy!' I exclaimed, in amazement, 'Why, you are crying!' 'No, I am not,' said Biddy, looking up and laughing. 'What put that in your head?' What could have put it in my head but the glistening of a tear as it dropped on her work?" (chap. xvii).

Of the same nature, though in a different tone, are the observations

479

concerning Pip's childhood. Pip's ignorance and innocence and his wonder in front of the unaccountable strangeness of life and society, arouse in the reader a mixed feeling of amusement and compassionate emotion. His convict has threatened him, in case the boy betrayed him, with the visitation of a certain young man who eats up little boys' livers. Pip believes he sees the young man in question: " 'It's the young man!' I thought, feeling my heart shoot as I identified him. I dare say I should have felt a pain in my liver, too, if I had known where it was" (chap. iii). And when his sister educates him, she says, for instance, "Ask no questions, and you'll be told no lies." Pip comments, "It was not very polite to herself, I thought, to imply that I should be told lies by her, even if I did ask questions. But she was never polite, unless there was company" (chap. ii). One day, Miss Havisham, the most mysterious and disquieting of human beings, tells Pip, "with some displeasure: 'You are growing tàll, Pip!' I thought it best to hint, through the medium of a meditative look, that this might be occasioned by circumstances over which I had no control" (chap. xii). The same lady is the heroine of one of the most strikingly humorous scenes in the book when, while playing with Pip, she learns from him a blacksmith's song. The recluse in her wedding dress singing "Old Clem" is a choice example of the humor of incongruity.

Together with the burlesque drama of Pip's misunderstood childhood, the book offers a picture of another drama, closely allied to the first—the drama of Joe Gargery's protracted and even eternal childishness. Like Mr. Dick in *Copperfield*, and like many other simple-minded men in Dickens' fiction, Joe has preserved in his grownup's body a child's generous heart and an infantile brain. The child Pip is for him an ideal playfellow. But when Pip becomes a man, poor Joe, who remains just as childish as ever, is outdistanced, dismayed, and left alone. Dickens has succeeded both in making the reader aware of Joe's sincere and pitiable desolation, and in conveying the drollery of the paradoxical situation thus created.

The reader who is aware of the troubled state of Dickens' private life at the time of *Great Expectations* is likely to be surprised, not only by the relaxed atmosphere created in that novel, owing to the wealth of comic scenes, but also by the simple and wholesome morality that pervades it. The moral import of the novel is adequately expressed by Joe Gargery, whose secondary, but not unimportant, function is to voice the author's message. His advice to the child or the adolescent Pip, made all the more acceptable by his picturesque speech, is based on common sense and straightforwardness: "Lookee here, Pip, at what is said to you by a true friend. Which this to you the true friend say. If you can't get to be oncommon through going straight, you'll never get to do it through going crooked . . ." (chap. ix). Pip knows that Joe is right and that his brother-in-law's friendship is his most valuable resource. The most significant moral theme of the novel may well be Pip's inward struggle, when he is caught between his love for Joe and his yearning to rise into a social sphere to which Joe will never have access. The analysis of Pip's feelings when Joe is about to visit him in London is, if not penetratingly original, at any rate lucid and vigorous:

Not with pleasure, though I was bound to him by so many ties, no, with considerable disturbance, some mortification, and a keen sense of incongruity. If I could have kept him away by paying money, I certainly would have paid money. My greatest reassurance was, that he . . . would not fall in Bentley Drummle's way [Drummle is Estella's future husband and a thoroughly contemptible being]. . . . I had the sharpest sensitiveness as to his being seen by Drummle, whom I held in contempt. So, throughout life, our worst weaknesses and meannesses are usually committed for the sake of the people we most despise (chap. xxvii).

The attempt at generalization in the last sentence ("our worst weaknesses and meannesses"), with its enlargement of the first person from the singular into the plural, is reminiscent both of George Eliot's constant practice and of Dickens' own occasional attitude in *Copperfield*. It is thus seen that psychological, and above all moral, autobiography plays a considerable part in *Great Expectations*. On a similar occasion, when Pip has succeeded in persuading himself that there were many valid reasons that made an encounter with Joe undesirable, he concludes:

All other swindlers upon earth are nothing to the self-swindlers, and with such pretences did I cheat myself. Surely a curious thing

.... An obliging stranger, under pretence of compactly folding up my banknotes for security's sake, abstracts the notes, and gives me nutshells; but what is his sleight of hand to mine, when I fold up my own nutshells and pass them on myself as notes! (chap. xxviii).

There is no mistaking the sedate, sterling quality of the moral reflection behind such phrases.

In spite of the many considerable merits that have just been listed, *Great Expectations* certainly has its weaker sides. Estella's character is unnatural and almost monstrous. She cannot be regarded as the heroine of the novel, for, as has sometimes been pointed out, *Great Expectations,* not unlike Thackeray's *Vanity Fair,* concerns itself with the weaknesses and pettinesses of mankind and can have no real hero or heroine, but she is the central female figure in the book. Some of her speeches are indeed strikingly improbable, as when she says:

"It seems that there are sentiments, fancies—I don't know how to call them—which I am not able to comprehend. When you say you love me, I know what you mean, as a form of words, but nothing more. You address nothing in my breast, you touch nothing there. I don't care for what you say at all" (chap. xliv).

The other major female character in the book, Biddy, forms a drastic contrast with Estella, but she is hardly more appealing at first sight. She has sometimes been numbered among the failures of Dickens' characterizations in that book. She belongs to the same category as Agnes Wickfield, although Biddy is less radiant. What she has in common with Agnes is her improbable and irksome perfection, her tendency to teach and preach morality—to stress, for Pip's benefit, that "pride is not all of one kind" (chap. xix) or to accept Pip's unfair reproaches with ostentatious and exasperating resignation, as when she says, "Say so over and over again, if you have the heart to think so" (chap. xix). Yet, on rereading the novel many times, the real beauty of Biddy's character will become clearer. She can be taxed only with being infallibly right. This may be an artistic weakness; it is not a moral one. Her moral significance comes from the partly autobiographical nature of the book. When he is publicly confessing his faults, Dickens uses Biddy, masochistically, for explicit reproof, as well as for the implicit lesson of a permanent contrast.

The attack launched by Pip against his uncle, Pumblechook, the conceited grocer, is no less ponderous than the demonstration of Biddy's somewhat dull perfection. After his mean blustering has been decisively exposed in the early chapters, it is difficult to see why other offensives are pursued against him to the end of the novel. Dickens may have had in mind a specific person, some member of his circle of intimates. In any case, he is unable to present Pumblechook without weighing him down with superfluous insults.

Another difficulty of Dickens' characterization in *Great Expectations* is the excessive place held by eccentricity. The eccentricity of Magwitch, who is a rough and uneducated person, is not unacceptable. It is made up mostly of ignorance and superstition, and it increases the dreadful picturesqueness of his figure, as when he swears his interlocutors to secrecy on "a greasy little clasped black Testament out of his pocket," which he carries for that purpose and never reads (chap. xl), or when he evinces his "extraordinary belief in the virtues of 'shorts' as a disguise" (chap. xl). His eccentricity, therefore, enhances the impression created by his remarkable, convincing speech (e.g., chap. xlii). Orlick's eccentricity—Orlick is a laborer employed by Joe Gargery, and the secret but ruthless foe of the whole family—is again acceptable because it is mainly verbal and belongs to a recognized type in Dickens' fiction:

> "Well then," said he, "I'm jiggered if I don't see you home!" This penalty of being jiggered was a favourite supposititious case of his. He attached no definite meaning to the word that I am aware of, but used it, like his own pretended Christian name, to affront mankind ....[11]

Other forms of eccentricity are to be found in the lawyer Jaggers, whose calculating coldness gives him a curious appearance and an extraordinarily abrupt mode of speech, but these features can be accepted as an extreme case of occupational absorption, Jaggers being not merely a lawyer, but *the* lawyer. The reader finds it harder not to rebel against

---

[11] Chap. xvii; see chap. xv, "He pretended that his Christian name was Dolge—a clear impossibility."

the macabre imagination which gave birth to Miss Havisham's character. The lady lives alone, in the dark and in her wedding dress, and with the table still laid for the wedding banquet. She has been living thus ever since her fiancé deserted her on their intended wedding day. Miss Havisham brings up young Estella by her side with the sole purpose of teaching her to hate men and to make them suffer. Or one may rebel against the unbridled fancy that creates Wemmick's (Wemmick is Jaggers' head-clerk) house, a miniature castle complete with cannon, moat, and drawbridge; an aged and deaf father; and the lady Wemmick is doomed to marry under stupendous circumstances: " 'Halloa!' said Wemmick. 'Here's Miss Skiffins. Let's have a wedding.' "[12]

Finally, in the Pocket family, if young Herbert chiefly displays amiable and charming whimsicality, his parents are downright caricatures.[13] The household looks like a lunatic asylum, and the father, Mathew Pocket, has one fantastic habit, described for the first time in the following lines and repeated again and again whenever he puts in an appearance:

> To my unutterable amazement, I now, for the first time, saw Mr. Pocket relieve his mind by going through a performance that struck me as very extraordinary, but which made no impression on anybody else, and with which I soon became as familiar as the rest. He laid down the carving-knife and fork—being engaged in carving at the moment—put his two hands into his disturbed hair, and appeared to make an extraordinary effort to lift himself up by it. When he had done this, and had not lifted himself up at all, he went on quietly with what he was about (chap. xxiii).

Again the only possible motive for including such a piece of shocking improbability in a realistic novel was Dickens' having met in real life a person behaving as extravagantly as Mathew Pocket does here. But that does not detract from the sheer improbability. Nor does it produce any artistic effect or yield much amusement. Dickens probably never

---

[12] Chap. lv. In a review of the original French edition of the present book by Pansy Pakenham (*The Dickensian*, March, 1954), I was taken to task for showing insufficient familiarity with English life and habits, to the point of boggling "at certain characters, Wemmick, for instance, who will seem natural enough to native readers" (p. 67).

[13] See in chap. xxii Herbert's reasons for deciding to call Pip, Handel.

went quite so far elsewhere in the direction of gratuitous and unattractive unlikelihood. With the exception of *Bleak House, Great Expectations* has the largest gallery of eccentrics in all Dickens' novels.

What distinguishes *Great Expectations,* more than anything else, from the other works of the same period,[14] is the development of what has already been called Dickens' "new style." The new style had come into existence many years before, in the days of *Dombey* and *Copperfield,* but it had not yet found its highest expression. It is interesting, from that point of view, to reread *Martin Chuzzlewit*—one of the most satisfactory books of the first period—immediately after reading *Great Expectations.* The experiment is likely to leave one under the impression of going down immensely, as though there had been what Gerard Manly Hopkins, in one of his "terrible sonnets," calls "cliffs of fall." The unsophisticated comedy of *Chuzzlewit* appears coarse and vulgar, overloaded, and almost untidy; and the contrast shows that the later work has a more delicate flavor, a tone of restraint, soberness, and subtlety. The proofs of *Great Expectations,* or at any rate, the fragments preserved in the Forster Collection, have very few corrections. Unless they are a late set, this suggests that Dickens' inspiration had never been so certain, that he had never before controlled his art more masterfully.

A French critic very unfairly complained of the absence in Dickens' whole work of *"un récit contenu et impassible, une scène où l'écrivain ait l'art supérieur de laisser porter de leur poids propre les événements et les idées qu'il exprime et retrace."*[15] The French critic's view was shared by some of his British contemporaries, but what he asserts cannot be found in Dickens' work is, in fact, just what one finds in *Great Expectations.* And a great part of the superior value of that book is due to its *"récit contenu et impassible."*

A few short quotations may sufficiently illustrate the point. Pip is about to leave his village:

> I had told Joe that I wished to walk away all alone. I am afraid—sore afraid—that this purpose originated in my sense of the contrast there would be between me and Joe if we went to the coach together. I had pretended with myself that there was nothing of this taint in

14 *LD, T2C, OMF.*
15 Hennequin, *Ecrivains Francisés,* 10.

the arrangement; but when I went up to my little room on this last time, I felt compelled to admit that it might be done so, and had an impulse to go down again and entreat Joe to walk with me in the morning. I did not (chap. xix).

The reader is certainly not, as Hennequin claims he always is by Dickens, *"poussé du coude"* (nudged). On the contrary, the neat and spare conclusion of the paragraph—"I did not"—suggests the sincerity of Pip's confession and self-examination. A little earlier, Pip was already writing:

"Whatever I acquired, I tried to impart to Joe. This statement sounds so well, that I cannot in my conscience let it pass unexplained. I wanted to make Joe less ignorant and common, that he might be worthier of my society, and less open to Estella's reproach" (chap. xv).

The moving scene in the course of which Magwitch reveals to Pip whence his money has come is pervaded by a kind of dramatic tenseness which comes once more from simple seriousness—from the lack of any grandiloquence. The critical point of that scene is the simple question asked by the convict, " 'May I make so bold,' he said then, with a smile that was like a frown, and with a frown that was like a smile, 'as ask *how* you have done so well, since you and me was out on them shivering marshes?' " (chap. xxxix). Pip reads his doom both in the words spoken and in the man's facial expression, analyzed with unusual subtlety.

A more vivid sense of the variety of shades of feeling and a clearer consciousness of more complex psychological phenomena characterize many passages in *Great Expectations*. After Magwitch's disclosures, Pip writes: "With these fears upon me, I began either to imagine or recall, that I had had mysterious warnings of this man's approach . . ." (chap. xxxix); and instead of relating some crude premonitory dream, he describes a variety of real or imaginary presages. The contradictory effect produced upon him by Estella's presence is twice mentioned in lucid terms:

The room was all in all to me, Estella being in it. I thought that with her I could have been happy there for life (I was not at all happy there at the time, observe, and I knew it well) (chap. xxxiii).

I never had one hour's happiness in her society, and yet my mind, all round the four-and-twenty hours was harping on the happiness of having her with me unto death (chap. xxxviii).

As in *Copperfield*, there are also in *Great Expectations* some Proust-like observations on time (chap. xxii), and on the association between specific sensations and specific memories.

The unusually high quality of Dickens' art is shown, finally, by the fact that two of the episodes that might have lent themselves to melodramatic treatment assume genuine tragic value. Melodrama is to be found in at least one scene, when Orlick has Pip at his mercy and tortures him (chap. liii). But the attempt at getting Magwitch out of England and its interruption by the police are dealt with soberly. And so is Magwitch's trial. Together with thirty-one other prisoners of both sexes, he is sentenced to death. The atmosphere of the court is solemn. The final section of that admirable scene, which is devoid both of facile tearfulness and of verbal ingenuity, is a fine sample of Dickens' new style almost at its best:

> The sun was striking in at the great windows of the court, through the glittering drops of rain upon the glass, and it made a broad shaft of light between the two-and-thirty and the judge, linking both together . . . . Rising for a moment, a distinct speck of face in this way of light, the prisoner said, "My Lord, I have received my sentence of death from the Almighty, but I bow to yours," and sat down again . . . (chap. lvi).

In 1883, Robert Louis Stevenson had been rereading *Great Expectations* twice in order to turn it into a play. He wrote to his father Thomas Stevenson,

> The play, in its rough outline, I now see; and it is extraordinary how much of Dickens had to be discarded as inhuman, impossible and ineffective: all that really remains is the loan of a file . . . and the fact of the convict-father's return and disclosure of himself to the son whom he has made rich. Everything else has to be thrown aside. . . . it was curious how Dickens had to be rolled away; he had made

his story turn . . . not on a good human basis, such as I recognised. . . .[16]

Stevenson's tone here, in its brutal severity, reminds one of John Dryden's attitude to the plays of Shakespeare when he was hoping to improve them and to make them fitter for performance on the stage. *Great Expectations* was perhaps unfit for the stage, but surely that was not due to its lack of a "good human basis," but rather to its wealth as a novel of a kind that Stevenson, among others, could never have successfully emulated.

XXVII: THE UNFINISHED FUGUE, OR *The Mystery of Edwin Drood*

A CERTAIN TYPE OF Dickensian construction has sometimes been termed symphonic. The unfinished *Mystery of Edwin Drood*, however, is rather reminiscent of a fugue. The complex and yet harmonious structure of that work rests on a few themes separately introduced and later to be taken up or mingled at regular intervals. In *Edwin Drood*, music plays a more prominent part (in and around the Cloisterham Cathedral) than in any other of Dickens' novels. For its first installment the author had instructed himself on his "mems" to "touch the keynote."[1]

The first idea of the new novel was conceived by Dickens some time in July, 1869. He had published no full-length work since the completion, in 1865, of *Our Mutual Friend*. He now wrote to Forster:

> What should you think of a story beginning in this way?—Two people, boy and girl, or very young, going apart from one another, pledged to be married after many years—at the end of the book. The interest to arise out of the tracing of their separate ways, and the impossibility of telling what will be done with that impending fate.[2]

On August 6, he announced to his friend that he had given up the original idea—but the plot of *Edwin Drood* has preserved something of it all the same. He wrote, "I laid aside the fancy I told you of, and

---

[16] *The Letters of R. L. Stevenson to His Family and Friends,* ed. Sidney Colvin (London, 1899), I, 262 (March 17, 1883).
[1] See MS of *ED* in Forster Collection.
[2] *Life of Dickens,* II, 365.

have a very curious and new idea for my new story. Not a communicable idea (or the interest of the book would be gone), but a very strong one, though difficult to work."[3] The incommunicable idea was in fact never to be communicated, except in the form of a few fragmentary confidences. In spite of hosts of ingenious inferences, it can be regarded as having largely remained the novelist's own secret and as having been buried with him in his grave. Its conception had, however, served as the basis for a contract between Dickens and Chapman and Hall. The work was to be published in monthly numbers of the usual size. Two clauses in the contract were unprecedented and showed how much justified alarm the novelist's health was already inspiring at the time. There were to be, not the usual twenty, but only twelve parts—or rather, taking into account the final double number, eleven instead of nineteen —and the possibility of the author's decease in the course of publication was explicitly foreseen and provided for.

His death occurred on June 9, 1870, when only four installments had appeared, and two more had been written, one of which was not complete. The portion written by Dickens is, of course, the only source of interest, although there have been any number of continuations by other pens. Dickens' *Mystery of Edwin Drood* comprises twenty-three chapters, or about three hundred pages. The shortest chapter is, as in some other cases during that period, the first one, which has but four pages. Through the rest of the book, the chapters are of fairly regular length, varying only between twelve and eighteen pages. It is rather curious to find that the two longest chapters—of about twenty-two pages each—were the last two Dickens wrote, just before he died.

The plot of the novel revolves around the disappearance of Edwin Drood, the nephew of John Jasper, a musician attached to Cloisterham Cathedral. In accordance with the dying wishes of both their fathers, young Edwin, an orphan, had been from childhood intended to marry charming little Rosa Bud, a boarder at a local school. Edwin disappears on Christmas Eve. Jasper, who is hopelessly in love with Rosa but intensely disliked by her, gradually comes to be suspected of having done away with his nephew. After the reader's suspicions have been thus awakened, they are seen to be shared by Rosa's guardian, Mr.

[3] *Ibid.*, 366.

Grewgious, by Canon Crisparkle, and then by one Mr. Datchery, an idler who has only recently come to live in Cloisterham. But Jasper manages to deflect the suspicions of the authorities and of the public toward another orphan, Neville Landless, Crisparkle's pupil, a quick-tempered boy who had already quarreled violently with Edwin. The pen fell from Dickens' hand at the moment when, thanks to an old woman from London who knew a great deal about Jasper's addiction to opium, Datchery's enquiry was taking a great stride forward.

No summary of the plot can give any idea of the high quality of the fragment that has survived. The only justification for the existence of the spawning "Drood literature" that will be alluded to later on lies in the feeling of painful frustration with which one closes the book, so full of promise and of achievement. Unfortunately, the Drood literature is largely unconcerned with the literary merits of the book itself.

The characters that Dickens had had time to introduce were a singularly attractive group. Crisparkle, the generous and athletic canon, is the most pleasant clergyman, and one of the pleasantest men, ever created by Dickens. Edwin's young fiancée, Rosa Bud, nicknamed Rosebud so easily and, indeed, obviously that it sounds as though her names had been chosen with a view to the nickname, is so delightful that she defeats Gissing's bitter misogyny. "At first we have misgivings," he writes, for he had feared she might be one of those women "whose reason for not knowing her own mind was probably the old one—that she had no mind to know,"[4] but the sequel of his discussion shows that, in common with every other reader, he has succumbed to Rosa's appeal. As to the central figure, Jasper the artist and opium addict, he is frighteningly earnest in his pursuit of Rosa's love, and he is depicted with great imaginative power. He is a most sinister being, at times almost diabolical—he has probably murdered his own nephew—but he is not unconvincing, and he has some human and moving reactions.

Another reason for deploring that *Edwin Drood* remained unfinished is that it not only contained superb specimens of Dickens' successful characterization, but that it had not one tedious figure, a much rarer achievement with Dickens. As the story seems to have been firmly conceived, constructed, and carried out as far as it went, *Edwin Drood*

[4] *Ch. Dickens, Critical Study*, 152.

is eminently tantalizing. The book creates in the reader an appetite that will never be satisfied.

One of the most obvious characteristics of the fragment, and one that Dickens had obviously taken particular pains over, is the quality of the composition. Curiously, the novelist had grown nervous and anxious as to the success of his effort in that direction. He experienced, Forster reports, "a fear that he might have plunged too soon into the incidents leading on to the catastrophe, such as the Datchery assumption in the fifth number . . . ."[5] The immediate occasion of Dickens' anxiety was the fact that the first two installments, composed in advance, had proved too short by twelve pages. He had then had to transfer one chapter from Number II back to Number I and to rework Number II entirely. Other evidence of his unusual nervousness and real difficulties is to be found in the few pages of corrected proofs that have been preserved. Comparing such pages with the corresponding parts of the published text shows that the deletions proposed at proof stage have not been made, because there was no overmatter in the manuscript. There is no reason to regret that such passages were in fact preserved, for some of them are among the best pages of the book.[6]

The memoranda provide confirmation of Dickens' comparative scarcity of inspiration. He seems to have used too soon the incidents he had been counting on to keep the plot going to the end. On the notes for Number III, there is the entry, "Rosa's guardian? Done in No. II," and on the notes for Number V: "Edwin and Rosa for the last time? Done already—Kinfrederel—Edwin disappears—The mystery: Done already."[7] Such details are revealing. Dickens had prepared in advance all his memoranda sheets for the whole story. The *Drood* manuscript contains the last five, bearing in Dickens' handwriting the general title of the novel and the numbers VII, VIII, IX, X, XI and XII (XI and XII were a single number). But the five sheets are blank. The writer had no doubt, at the close of his career, made his first attempt to conceive in advance, not only the outline of a plot, but also the distribution of its incidents among the various installments. His attempt had failed. As he had long

---

[5] *Life of Dickens*, II, 370.

[6] See, e.g., chap. xviii, the conversation between Datchery and the Mayor about justice.

[7] MS of *ED* (Forster Collection). "Kinfrederel" is Deputy's version of the word "cathedral."

accustomed himself to extemporizing the details, he had been unable to move within a rigid frame, and his plans had been upset as early as the second installment.

Yet the care with which he worked at his last novel is unquestionable. The first two chapters, in particular, are splendidly contrived. Chapter I begins with a series of questions: "An ancient English Cathedral Tower? How can the ancient English cathedral tower be here? The well-known massive grey square tower of its old cathedral? How can it be here!" Gradually, the opium addict's misty vision is dispelled. He becomes conscious of the place where he is, a dingy room with a slightly mysterious atmosphere.[8] He goes out, and the chapter closes with another evocation, which takes up the words of the opening paragraph, but in a more literal sense: "That same afternoon, the massive grey square tower of an old cathedral rises before the sight of a jaded traveller." The traveler steps into the cathedral and puts on his robe, "and then the intoned words 'WHEN THE WICKED MAN . . .' rise among groins and arches and beams of roofs, awakening muttered thunder." There is no more to it, but the reader has thus been made acquainted, within a few neat pages, with Jasper's double life as a sublime singer and as the frequenter of a shady opium den. The second chapter completes the indispensable introduction in a natural and attractive manner.

The esoteric hints of the "mems" are acted on with consummate skill. They are, in the first installment, the musical metaphor quoted above, "Touch the keynote," and the following definition of the atmosphere to be created: "Cathedral town running throughout." Then comes, in the preparatory sheet for Number II, an important note: "Jasper lays his ground."[9] All the corresponding effects are achieved in the text without the reader becoming aware of any particular effort on the author's part. Each character is described at his or her first appearance and several of the portraits in *Edwin Drood* are among the best ever penned by Dickens. The private notes are more vigorous than the published text as regards the Mayor of Cloisterham, Mr. Sapsea, who appears in the

---

[8] Fields (*Yesterdays With Authors*, 202) relates the visit he paid in Dickens' company to a "horrid opium-den" and says the visit provided all the details for that description.

[9] MS of *ED* (Forster Collection). The two phrases are underscored twice.

"mems" as the "Old Tory jackass" and the "solemn donkey." But the printed description of Durdles, the mason and gravedigger, is a masterpiece, of which the opening lines will give a faint idea:

> Durdles is a stonemason, chiefly in the gravestone, tomb and monument way, and wholly of their colour from head to foot. No man is better known in Cloisterham. He is the chartered libertine of the place. Fame trumpets him as a wonderful workman, which, for aught that anybody knows, he may be (as he never works); and a wonderful sot—which everybody knows he is (chap. iv).

The final lines of each chapter preserve the solemn tone common at the close of Dickensian chapters since the days of *Chuzzlewit* and *Dombey*. The device has even become more systematic. The end of the chapter tends to have a symbolic and mysterious value. A characteristic example is provided by the conversation between Jasper and Mr. Grewgious at the end of Chapter IX, when they have been discussing Edwin's engagement to Rosa:

> "That is my understanding," said Mr. Grewgious, as they shook hands to part, "God bless them both!" "God save them both!" cried Jasper. "I said, bless them," remarked the former, looking back over his shoulder. "I said, save them," returned the latter, "is there any difference?"

Such a device, which raises the tone of the narrative or the dialogue and stresses the structural unity of the chapter, is not without some analogy with the rhymed couplet heralding the end of a scene in Elizabethan drama.

The degree of technical mastery achieved by Dickens in *Edwin Drood* is perhaps best illustrated by the decisive fourteenth chapter, which closes with Edwin's disappearance. The future victim, murderer, and suspect are to have dinner together at Jasper's. The very title of the chapter, borrowed with a slight adaptation from the first line of *Macbeth*, seems to invite comparison with Shakespeare.[10] The chapter itself relates how the hours preceding the dinner were spent by each of the three men. For each of them, Neville, then Edwin, then Jasper, the

[10] It is called "When Shall These Three Meet Again?"

little narrative closes with the identical phrase—"and so *he* goes up the postern stair." The reader does not attend the dinner. He only sees, from the outside, a light shining, while a storm breaks out, in harmony with the violence of the events then happening, and the chapter comes to an end when, next morning, Jasper comes, wild-looking and disturbed, to ask of Mr. Crisparkle the question, "Where is my nephew?" It is clear at that point that the question asked in the title of the chapter, "When Shall These Three Meet Again?" is to be answered by the simple word, "Never."

In the very last page written by Dickens is to be found definite proof of the progress of his art. Jasper is singing in the cathedral, unaware of being watched by the ominous old woman in whose den he habitually smokes opium on his visits to London. The boy, Deputy, is watching the old woman and the singer alternately. And the mysterious Datchery, from within a stall, watches all three by turns (chap. xxiii). That threefold secret watch, which the author's minute preparations have made entirely acceptable, shows with what ease Dickens, at the close of his career, could handle even the most complex situations.

The very nature of the subject chosen for *Edwin Drood*, and of the effects sought, accounts for his use of many devices akin to those of the stage once more. Dickens again often adopts a style close to that of stage directions, one of the few signs of weariness to be detected in the book.[11] Also, there are, in *Edwin Drood*, a number of gestures and attitudes which the reader must remember once they are described, for they will be referred to later, but not repeated. During the lively conversation which opposes Edwin and Neville in Jasper's presence, the latter's attitude is at first described in detail: "Mr. Jasper looks quickly to his nephew for his rejoinder. Mr. Jasper looks quickly to the other for his retort . . . ." But almost at once Dickens seems to find such minute description tedious and substitutes for it a general comment: "Mr. Jasper's play of eyes between the two holds good throughout the dialogue, to the end" (chap. viii). Likewise, on the first occasion when Jasper and Edwin are shown together, the novelist states: "Once for

---

[11] They are far from justifying Wilkie Collins' unaccountable severity when he called *ED*, "Dickens's last laboured effort, the melancholy work of a worn-out brain," *Pall Mall Gazette*, Jan. 20, 1890.

all, a look of intentness and intensity—a look of hungry, exacting, watchful, and yet devoted affection—is always, now and ever afterwards, on
the Jasper face, whenever the Jasper face is addressed in this direction . . ." (chap. ii).

Such devices undoubtedly detract from the naturalness of the narrative. But they cannot prevent the reader from identifying the author
of *Edwin Drood* with the traditional Dickens, or with the Dickens of
Great Expectations. Both his usual power and charm, and his usual
weaknesses are evidenced. As in *Great Expectations*, his weaknesses are
mostly those of a few minor unlikelihoods and exaggerations. The
names of some characters, for instance, are improbable, for the author
has invented them with a view to his own enjoyment, for instance, the
name of the aggressive philanthropist—Honeythunder—or the baroque
though evocative surname—Mr. Grewgious. Such deviations from realism are trifling, harmless, and customary. Some episodes are more objectionable, for they make too great demands on our credulity, like
the scene during which modest Mr. Crisparkle manages to deliver a
long and severe tirade without being interrupted by the explosive
Honeythunder. Dickens undoubtedly enjoys Honeythunder's discom-
fiture, but he does not succeed in making it probable (chap. xvii). The
song invented by the boy, Deputy, to escort home Durdles, whom he
is pelting with little stones (chap. v) is made up of mysterious words—
which Dickens terms "mystic"—and Durdles himself, who had been
defined as a "wonderful sot" suddenly proves capable of extemporizing
in verse (chap. xviii). Both Deputy's song and Durdles' quatrain are
entertaining, but they are out of place in a novel with any claim to
realism.

The acme of that kind of unlikelihood—but also one of the summits
of Dickens' humorous invention—is reached with Mr. Sapsea's epitaph
for his wife's grave. Omitting only the typographical variations and
embellishments, the epitaph reads:

> Ethelinda, reverential wife of Mr. Thomas Sapsea, auctioneer,
> valuer, estate agent, etc., of this city. Whose knowledge of the world,
> though somewhat extensive, never brought him acquainted with a
> spirit more capable of looking up to him. Stranger, pause, and ask

thyself the question, canst thou do likewise. If not, with a blush retire (chap. iv).

At the end of his life, Dickens seems occasionally to have lost all sense of the limitations of art, when it aims at picturing reality. Mrs. Sapsea's epitaph is, in that respect, reminiscent of Mathew Pocket's insane gesture in *Great Expectations*.

As in *Great Expectations* also, some of the author's intentions are heavily overstressed. He could have dispensed, for instance, with pointing out that the indignation aroused in Crisparkle by Honeythunder is a "just indignation" (chap. xvii). Nor does it become a novelist to lose his self-control in front of his own creatures to the point of writing: "'*I* remember!' replies the auctioneer. And the solemn idiot really believes that he does remember" (chap. xii).

The style of the novel is not beyond criticism either. British critics have complained of Dickens' increasingly frequent use of "that . . . that . . ." instead of the received forms "so . . . that . . ." or "such . . . that . . . ." In *Edwin Drood*, Dickens writes of Honeythunder, "His philanthropy was of that gunpowderous sort that the difference between it and animosity was hard to determine" (chap. vi). Of the former sailor Tartar's apartment, he says, "The floors were scrubbed to that extent that you might have supposed . . ." (chap. xxii), and of the quarrel between Neville and Edwin, "This insulting allusion . . . infuriates Neville to that violent degree that he flings the dregs of his wine at Edwin Drood" (chap. viii). More regrettably, this same dubious construction is again selected for the lesson of English grammar given by the dean of the cathedral to his sexton. Thus the lesson is made most obscure, and in the end the pupil speaks more correctly than his master (chap. ii).

One incoherent image can be laid to Dickens' charge in the following sentence from *Edwin Drood*, "This was said with a mysterious wink; or what would have been a wink, if, in Mr. Grewgious' hands, it could have been quick enough" (chap. xi). Of course, intentional incoherence with a humorous purpose is not to be ruled out in this case. Similarly, the appearance in two distinct places of almost identical phrases may be due to some specific intention as well as to remissness.

In any case, we find in Chapter V the statement: " 'Yer lie, I did,' says Deputy, in his only form of polite contradiction," and in Chapter XII, " 'Yer lie, I didn't,' replies Deputy, in his one form of polite contradiction." Dickens may have thought the irony too palatable to be used only once. He is not averse to repetition, and Mr. Grewgious' allusions to his "angularity" recur so often that they lose a great deal of their initial appeal (see chaps. ix, xi, etc.). On the other hand, it must be admitted that the device of the identifying verbal mannerisms of the characters, so frequent and so tedious in the days of *Nickleby* and even at the end of *Copperfield,* has been almost given up in *Edwin Drood.*

One major characteristic of Dickens' language has been preserved. He has remained keenly alive to the intrinsic appeal of sounds. Hence we find a number of effects which have something in common both with poetical alliteration and assonance, and with ordinary puns. In one of the above quotations occur the words, "a look of intentness and intensity," in which the use of the two cognates is probably due to their mutual attraction through sound. In other cases the effect is more far-fetched and doubtful—"Certain devoted orphans had been glutted with plum-buns and plump bumptiousness" (chap. vi), or "the blunderbusses of blunder-headedness" (chap. xvi). Dickens' sensitiveness to sounds is also reflected in his patient and minute quest for his protagonists' names. Edwin Drood was chosen only after James, Gilbert, Alfred, Edwyn, Oswald, Arthur, and Edgar and Wakefield, Brood, Brude, and Drude had been rejected. Neville and his sister Helena—earlier called Olympia—were first intended to be called Heyridge or Heyford, until the final inspiration arose, probably from the subconscious part of Dickens' mind, and they became Neville and Helena Landless.[12] Whatever the exact part may have been that Ellen Lawless Ternan played in Dickens' life, the similarity with Helena Landless is striking. The most unsatisfactory name in the book, Honeythunder, is an improvement on the early suggestion—Honeyblest. On the contrary, the sexton's name became less jocular when Tope was substituted for Peptune.

Naturally the discussion of a few details of Dickens' language and style in *Edwin Drood,* while it helps build up a picture of the last stage in the artist's evolution, leaves the essential quality of the book un-

12 Details from the MS of *ED.*

touched. That essential quality is almost indefinable, but it is vividly borne in upon the reader in any descriptive paragraph.[13] The style possesses remarkable fluency in description and firmness in the narrative and dramatic parts. The whole has unquestionable beauty, the result of a highly advanced artistry.

The originality of *Edwin Drood* lies in its successfully conveyed atmosphere, or rather in the skillful association and intermingling of two atmospheres. There is the quiet old city living in the shadow of its cathedral, a city which is readily identified with Rochester, where Dickens had lived as a child, close to Gadshill where he wrote *Edwin Drood* and where he was soon to die. Rochester had been the starting point of the Pickwickian odyssey and thus of Dickens' triumphant career. It is found again at the very end of that career. But its peace is now disturbed by the other atmosphere of the book—the atmosphere created by the dark and even sinister personality and actions of Jasper. There is close interaction between the two, for, while Jasper's presence and misdeeds darken the very air of the city,[14] the ancient and majestic background of the drama tends to restore the reader's peace of mind and leave him free to enjoy the beauty of the writing.

The harmony thus preserved, the softening down of the horror in the mystery, create a significant difference between *Edwin Drood* and *A Tale of Two Cities*, in which there had been more sustained tension. Another difference lies in the presence of many comic passages. Dickens gave free vent to his comic vein in *Drood* and produced many effects of the first order, which do much for the reader's pleasure and relaxation.

So the book has merits which might have raised it at least to the level of *Great Expectations*, in spite of the gruesomeness of the central notion. Yet no one can tell what the end of the story would have been if Dickens had completed it. There are two reasons for deploring its unfinished state: first, the reader feels frustrated, and, second, later writers have possessed themselves of the mystery and worked on it in a spirit and in a way which have, for many years, obscured the great value of the book, even in the eyes of some competent Dickens critics.

13 A fine example is the first description of Cloisterham (chap. iii).

14 See the storm that breaks out during the crime, (chap. xiv) and the other storm that Jasper's threats to Rosa almost seem to let loose (chap. xix).

Between criticism and *Edwin Drood* there stands, like a spiked wall, the body of books and articles called the "Drood literature," the literature devoted to the mystery of Edwin Drood, not to *The Mystery of Edwin Drood*.

Some of the earliest contributions to that body were, in chronological order: *Clues to Dickens's Mystery of Edwin Drood*, by J. Cuming Walters (London, Heywood, 1905); *Keys to the Drood Mystery*, by Edwin Charles—a predestined or a made-up name—(Birmingham, Skimpin, 1908); *About Edwin Drood*, by H. J. (Cambridge University Press, 1911); *The Complete Mystery of Edwin Drood. The History, Continuations and Solutions (1870-1912)*, by J. Cuming Walters again— who won for himself the title of "Writer on *Edwin Drood*"—(London, Chapman & Hall, 1912); *The Mystery in the Drood Family*, by Montagu Saunders (Cambridge University Press, 1914). To this list one must add several continuations of the story and many articles in *The Dickensian*, some of them by J. Cuming Walters, before and after he turned to spiritualism for the solution. The spawn of *Drood* literature grew less overwhelming after World War I, but as recently as 1965, a notable addition was made to it when *The Drood Case* was published by Felix Aylmer, and in 1966, with the appearance of an article by D. M. Bilham in *The Dickensian* (Autumn Number) called *"Edwin Drood* —To Resolve a Mystery."

Most of the *Drood* books are alarmingly serious in tone. Their authors often seem to forget that they are dealing with a novel, with imaginary characters, and with one of the greatest humorists of all time. There is not a single smile from beginning to end of Montagu Saunders' long study, and Edwin Charles' book opens with the lugubrious assertion that, in *Edwin Drood* "the story itself reeks of the charnel-house and the tomb."[15]

The books concern themselves mainly with two problems: Who is Datchery? Is Edwin really dead? Both questions are idle. Even if, as the most eminent Droodists believe, the answer were implicitly contained in, and could be logically inferred from, the text as it stands and the meagre documents that add anything to it, it is by no means certain that Dickens would not have introduced significant modifications at the

[15] *Keys to the Drood Mystery*, 2.

last moment and departed from any intentions he had had before June, 1870. The creation of any Dickensian novel is continuous and unpredictable until the publication of the final installment.

In addition, the data of the two problems provide no decisive elements. Datchery, according to some, might be Helena Landless in disguise (J. C. Walters' theory); according to others, he is Bazzard, Mr. Grewgious' clerk (Edwin Charles' theory).[16] But it is difficult to choose from the often brilliant demonstrations in support of the rival theories. They are equally attractive, but they tend to slur over equally troublesome difficulties and unlikelihoods. And they seem to have been adopted because of preconceived preferences which signally fail to carry conviction with their opponents.

As to the notion of Edwin's possible survival, it can be supported by some of the titles Dickens had contemplated and jotted down at the beginning of his manuscript: "The Loss of James Wakefield" (and five other titles containing the ambiguous word "loss"); "James's Disappearance"; "Flight and Pursuit"; "The Flight of Edwin Drood"; "Edwin Drood in Hiding"; "The Disappearance of Edwin Drood"; "Dead or Alive?" Like the title finally chosen, all of the above alternatives leave open the possibility of Edwin's survival, and some of them—"Flight," "in Hiding"—even suggest a form of disappearance other than death. As regards the use of the word "disappearance," one may add to the list a fragment from a letter written by Dickens on September 2, 1869, to Robert Lytton, who had sent him for *All the Year Round* a narrative called *John Acland*: "I think your title open to . . . objection, and therefore propose to substitute: THE DISAPPEARANCE OF JOHN ACLAND; this will leave the reader in doubt whether he really *was* murdered, until the end."[17] Such arguments are potent and would be almost decisive if it had not been proved that the title of a Dickens novel was often selected before the story was thought out in every detail. And

---

[16] Believers in Edwin's survival take Datchery to be the supposed victim himself. Another candidate is Tartar, the friend and neighbor of the Landlesses.

[17] *Letters* (MDGH), III, 285. The argument has never, as far as I know, been used in *Drood* studies, though the relationship between *ED* and *John Acland* is mentioned by Aurelia Brooks Harlan in *Owen Meredith, A Critical Biography of Robert, 1st Earl of Lytton* (London and N.Y., 1946).

there are arguments pointing to the contrary position also. There are, for instance, Dickens' confidences to Forster:

> The story . . . was to be that of the murder of a nephew by his uncle . . . . Discovery by the murderer of the utter needlessness of the murder for its object was to follow hard upon commission of the deed; but all discovery of the murderer was to be baffled till the close, when, by means of a gold ring which had resisted the corrosive effect of the lime into which he had thrown the body, not only the person murdered was to be identified, but the locality of the crime and the person who committed it. So much was told me before any of the book was written.[18]

Clear as they are, these hints are not to be accepted as final proof of Edwin's death for three reasons. Forster's memory cannot be trusted implicitly; he is often at fault about the details of the facts he is relating, and he has been found guilty of tampering even with the letters he was quoting; besides, he may have mixed up his remembrance of direct oral confidences with his knowledge of the book as published. Then, no one can be sure that Dickens had been sincere with him when expounding to him by word of mouth a notion of which he had written earlier—that it was "not a communicable idea (or the interest of the book would be gone)." Finally, even if Dickens' confidences were sincerely made and accurately remembered, the fact that they were received "before any of the book was written" deprives them, for the reason given above, of any conclusive value.

Dickens' "mems" provide more solid support to the theory of a real murder of Edwin. In the summary of Chapter II occurs the entry. "Uncle and nephew. Murder very far off," and in the summary of Chapter XII: "Lay the ground for the manner of the murder to come out at last."[19] There remains, however, the possibility that Dickens, who jotted down such notes in great haste and for his own use exclusively, was using the word "murder" in the not unexampled broader sense of "attempted murder," while he had in mind the impression he wanted to create in

[18] *Life of Dickens*, II, 366.
[19] MS of *ED*.

the reader, at least temporarily, of a murder pure and simple. The illustration on the cover of the original monthly parts has been made much of by some Drood experts, but it is too obscure to be very helpful and in fact it has served the purposes of both camps. Perhaps after all one may rejoice to think that the mystery of Edwin Drood is thus meant to remain the most perfect mystery in literature, in that it will be mysterious for ever.

Dickens died at work, like Thackeray seven years before him. Both of them left a promising work of fiction unfinished. Thinking of the two great contemporaries and rivals, Percy Fitzgerald aptly wrote that one sentence from *Edwin Drood* (chap. xii) could be applied to both: "The two journeymen have left their two great saws sticking in their blocks of stone . . . ."[20]

XXVIII: Conclusion

No ATTEMPT HAS BEEN MADE in this book to evaluate Dickens' personality or even his stature as a novelist. What has been attempted is a history of his art—a study of its evolution.

Inevitably, however, I have come to hold certain views about Dickens both as a man and as a writer. But they are of only the slightest possible interest to a study of this kind. Besides, they have fluctuated again and again. But over one point I have not varied, and I should not have undertaken the labor of translating and revising my early book for the present American edition if I had ceased to believe that Dickens is one of the major figures of English literature. The conviction of his greatness I acquired as a boy. It has been reinforced by close study of his works over a quarter of a century.

I do not claim to have totally achieved even the limited and technical purpose of my study. Much remains to be done. But there are so many Dickens students at work—mostly in Great Britain and the United States, but also in other countries such as France and Russia[1]—that much is being done even now and more will be done soon. What seems to me to be most urgently required is critical editions of all the Dickens

20 *Life of Dickens*, II, 317.
1 The Dickens Bibliography compiled by I. Katarsky and published in Moscow in 1962 lists 2,256 Russian Dickensiana up to 1960.

novels, as well as detailed histories of his style, of his characterization, of his thinking, etc.

Through an examination of Dickens' work at close quarters, such as has been attempted in this book, he appears to have been an artist from the beginning to the end of his career. At first he wrote more impulsively than systematically. But he became steadily more conscious of his power and his purpose. From *Pickwick* to *Edwin Drood,* his evolution was characterized by a decrease of the part played by the spontaneous elements of literary creation. *The Old Curiosity Shop, Dombey and Son, Hard Times,* and *Our Mutual Friend* are significant stages in a decline of Dickens' humor, at least of his humor for humor's sake. The decline never resulted in complete disappearance. No book by Dickens is totally empty of humorous phrases, scenes, and characters. *Edwin Drood* is certainly a less comic and, above all, a less merry book than *Pickwick,* but the figures of Crisparkle and Durdles are not inferior to those of Jingle or Winkle or Wardle. And if there is no second Sam Weller, Mrs. Nickleby, or Mrs. Gamp in *Our Mutual Friend,* it is simply because there could not be a second example anywhere of characters that were essentially unique.

Conversely, the part played by the more conscious and deliberate elements in Dickens' novels steadily increased, particularly in the field of composition. The plot of *Pickwick* meanders freely. Those of *Nickleby* and *Chuzzlewit* are better organized, but still comprise a fair amount of extemporization and arbitrariness. In *Dombey* and *Copperfield,* the outline of the story had been determined from the outset, and only minor departures from it occurred on the way. With *Bleak House, Dorrit,* and *Our Mutual Friend,* Dickens had achieved a degree of detailed preparation of his stories which was not surpassed by even his most scrupulous contemporaries. Yet, the fragmentary mode of publication he adhered to still created obstacles to harmonious composition, in spite of his clearly marked and constant progress.

At many points, the documents preserved in the Forster Collection provide evidence of Dickens' earnest, conscientious, even anxious work, and particularly of his passionate, lifelong interest in language and style, an interest abundantly reflected in the evolution of his own handling of written English. Whatever admixture of vulgarity may shock the reader of the *Sketches*, whatever facile use of the bombastic or mock-heroic tone subsists in *Pickwick* or *Oliver Twist* have practically vanished from his later books. In *Copperfield*, in *Great Expectations*, and in the beginning of *Edwin Drood*, Dickens achieves true soberness of tone. It is only natural that such progress should have been accomplished only through trial and error, and among the errors must probably be ranked the mannerisms so perceptible in *Dorrit* and *A Tale of Two Cities*. But Dickens' faults, if faults they are are, were not due to a lack of passionate interest in the concrete problems of the writer's art.

That, at any rate, is how, at the close of this study, I have come to regard the evolution and the dominant characteristics of Dickens as an artist. My views have sometimes been criticized or corrected in the past. I am quite ready and shall even be sincerely delighted to be set right again in the future by Dickensian scholars who, because they embrace a less immense field, may well achieve a truer and clearer perception of many of its aspects.